Of an Alien Homecoming

SUNY series in Contemporary Continental Philosophy
———————
Dennis J. Schmidt, editor

Of an Alien Homecoming
Reading Heidegger's "Hölderlin"

CHARLES BAMBACH

Published by State University of New York Press, Albany

© 2022 State University of New York

All rights reserved

Printed in the United States of America

No part of this book may be used or reproduced in any manner without written permission. No part of this book may be stored in a retrieval system or transmitted in any form or by any means including electronic, electrostatic, magnetic tape, mechanical, photocopying, recording, or otherwise without the prior permission in writing of the publisher.

For information, contact State University of New York Press, Albany, NY
www.sunypress.edu

Library of Congress Cataloging-in-Publication Data

Name: Bambach, Charles, author.
Title: Of an alien homecoming : reading Heidegger's "Hölderlin" / Charles Bambach.
Description: Albany : State University of New York Press, [2022] | Series: SUNY series in Contemporary Continental Philosophy | Includes bibliographical references and index.
Identifiers: ISBN 9781438488134 (hardcover : alk. paper) | ISBN 9781438488141 (ebook) | ISBN 9781438488127 (pbk. : alk. paper)
Further information is available at the Library of Congress.

10 9 8 7 6 5 4 3 2 1

For Hannah . . . für alles

Is there now, in these times, still something like a "home," a dwelling, an abode? No, there are "dwelling machines," urban clusters, in short: an industrialized product, but no longer a home.

—Martin Heidegger
Four Seminars: 74

Contents

Abbreviations	xi
Acknowledgments	xvii
Preface	xix

Introduction   1
    I.   Hölderlin as a "Transition"   1
    II. Philosophical "Andenken": Hölderlin as the
        Voice of the Other Beginning   9
    III. Who is Heidegger's Hölderlin?   13
    IV. Language, "Ethos," and the Ethicality of Being   18

1 Hölderlin's Hymns "Germania" and "The Rhine"   33
    I.   "Hölderlin" and the Great War   33
    II. Norbert von Hellingrath and the Hölderlin Myth   42
    III. Heidegger and the "Secret" Germania   49
    IV. Hölderlin without History   61
    V. "The Rhine": Heidegger and Originary Springing
        Forth   65
    VI. "Physis" as "Poiesis": Beyng as Poetic Event   69
    VII. The Mystery of "das Reinentsprungene" and the
        Vocation of the Poet   75
    VIII. The Beyng of the Demigods   80

2 Heidegger's "Remembrance" Lectures   93
    I.   Hölderlin and "The National"   93
    II. A Metapolitics of the *Volk*   102

	III.	Staging the "Remembrance" Lectures: The Vestibule 110
	IV.	The Greeting of the Wind 116
	V.	Jews, Greeks, and the Occlusion of the First Beginning 125
	VI.	The Time of the Festival and the Graeco-German Beginning 136
	VII.	Festival, Equinoctial Time, and the Balance of Equilibrium 145
	VIII.	Heidegger's Destinal Politics of a German National Mission 153
	IX.	The Passage to the Foreign and the Journey Homeward 161

3 Heidegger's "Ister" Lectures: Ethical Dwelling in the (Foreign) Homeland 177
    I. "Hölderlin" as the Name for an Other Beginning of Thinking 177
    II. Dwelling in the Intimacy of Truth: Oppositional Harmony and the Böhlendorff Logic 182
    III. Translation and the Uncanny Essence of Human Being 185
    IV. Tragedy and the Definition of the Human Being as a "Katastrophe" 190
    V. The Language of Contradiction: Oxymoron and Tragic Manifestation 193
    VI. Poet and River as Demi-Gods 198
    VII. "At home is spirit not at the beginning" 199
    VIII. Of Time and the River: Naming, Reversal, and Historical Dwelling 204
    IX. German Hospitality? 224

4 Historical Interlude: Heidegger in 1945–1946 227
    I. Heidegger's "Kahlschlag": The Poverty of Thinking 227
    II. Heidegger's Revenge: War-Guilt, Retribution, and the Politics of *Ressentiment* 234
    III. Hölderlin, the West, and Destiny 252

5 Heidegger in Dialogue with Hölderlin: "The Western Conversation" 263

I.	Heidegger's "Conversation" with Hölderlin	263
II.	The *Schwung* from the First to the Other Beginning	266
III.	The Opening of "The Western Conversation"	272
IV.	The Ister as Fateful Site of an Ordeal	277
V.	Hölderlin, Destiny, and the German Bequest	279
VI.	Poetic Geography and Destinal History: The *German* Danube	294
VII.	The Bread and Wine Fragment and German Destiny	298

Postscript	313
Notes	329
Bibliography	357
Index	373

Abbreviations

Note: Unless otherwise indicated, all translations from the German are my own.

SS   Spring Semester
WS   Winter Semester

Heidegger

BFL   *Bremen and Freiburg Lectures*. Trans. Andrew Mitchell. Bloomington: Indiana University Press, 2012.

BN I   *Ponderings II–VI: Black Notebooks, 1931–1938*. Trans. Richard Rojcewicz. Bloomington: Indiana University Press, 2016.

BN III   *Ponderings XII–XV: Black Notebooks, 1939–1941*. Trans. Richard Rojcewicz. Bloomington: Indiana University Press, 2017.

BT   *Being and Time*. Trans. Dennis Schmidt. Albany, NY: SUNY Press, 2010.

BW   *Basic Writings*. Ed. David F. Krell. New York: Harper & Row, 1977.

CP   *Contributions to Philosophy*. Trans. Richard Rojcewicz and Daniela Vallega-Neu. Bloomington: Indiana University Press, 2012.

E   *The Event*. Trans. Richard Rojcewicz. Bloomington: Indiana University Press, 2013.

EdP	"Europa und die deutsche Philosophie." In *Europa und die Philosophie*. Ed. Hans-Helmuth Gander. Frankfurt: Klostermann, 1993.
EHP	*Elucidations of Hölderlin's Poetry*. Trans. Keith Hoeller. New York: Humanity Books, 2000.
EM	*Einführung in die Metaphysik*. Tübingen: Niemeyer, 1953.
FS	*Four Seminars*. Trans. Andrew Mitchell and Francóis Raffoul. Bloomington: Indiana University Press, 2003.
G	*Gelassenheit*. Pfullingen: Neske, 1988.
GA	*Gesamtausgabe*. Frankfurt: Klostermann, 1975 ff.
GA 2	*Sein und Zeit*. Ed. Friedrich-Wilhelm von Herrmann. Frankfurt: Klostermann, 1977.
GA 4	*Erläuterungen zu Hölderlins Dichtung*. Ed. Friedrich-Wilhelm von Herrmann. Frankfurt: Klostermann, 1981.
GA 5	*Holzwege*. Ed. Friedrich-Wilhelm von Herrmann. Frankfurt: Klostermann, 1977.
GA 7	*Vorträge und Aufsätze*. Ed. Friedrich-Wilhelm von Herrmann. Frankfurt: Klostermann, 2000.
GA 9	*Wegmarken*. Ed. Friedrich-Wilhelm von Herrmann. Frankfurt: Klostermann, 2004.
GA 10	*Der Satz vom Grund*. Ed. Petra Jaeger. Frankfurt: Klostermann, 1997.
GA 11	*Identität und Differenz*. Ed. Friedrich-Wilhelm von Herrmann. Frankfurt: Klostermann, 2006.
GA 12	*Unterwegs zur Sprache*. Ed. Friedrich-Wilhelm von Herrmann. Frankfurt: Klostermann, 1985.
GA 13	*Aus der Erfahrung des Denkens*. Ed. Hermann Heidegger. Frankfurt: Klostermann, 2002.
GA 15	*Seminare*. Ed. Curd Ochwadt. Frankfurt: Klostermann, 1986.
GA 16	*Reden und andere Zeugnisse eines Lebensweges*. Ed. Hermann Heidegger. Frankfurt: Klostermann, 2000.
GA 35	*Der Anfang der abendländischen Philosophie*. Ed. Peter Trawny. Frankfurt: Klostermann, 2012.

GA 36/37 *Sein und Wahrheit.* Ed. Hartmut Tietjen. Frankfurt: Klostermann, 2001.

GA 38 *Über Logik als die Frage nach dem Wesen der Sprache.* Ed. Günter Seubold. Frankfurt: Klostermann, 1998.

GA 39 *Hölderlins Hymne "Germanien" und "Der Rhein."* Ed. Susanne Ziegler. Frankfurt: Klostermann, 1989.

GA 40 *Einführung in die Metaphysik.* Ed. Petra Jaeger. Frankfurt: Klostermann, 1983.

GA 46 *Zur Auslegung von Nietzsches II. Unzeitgemässer Betrachtung "Vom Nutzen und Nachteil der Historie für das Leben."* Ed. Hans-Joachim Friedrich. Frankfurt: Klostermann, 2003.

GA 50 *Nietzsches Metaphysik.* Ed. Petra Jaeger. Frankfurt: Klostermann, 1990.

GA 51 *Grundbegriffe.* Ed. Petra Jaeger. Frankfurt: Klostermann, 1991.

GA 52 *Hölderlins Hymne "Andenken."* Ed. Curd Ochwadt. Frankfurt: Klostermann, 1992.

GA 53 *Hölderlins Hymne "Der Ister."* Ed. Walter Biemel. Frankfurt: Klostermann, 1993.

GA 54 *Parmenides.* WS 1942/43. Ed. Manfred Frings. 1992.

GA 55 *Heraklit. I. Der Anfang des abendländischen Denkens; II. Logik. Heraklits Lehre des Logos.* Ed. Manfred S. Frings. Frankfurt: Klostermann, 1994.

GA 65 *Beiträge zur Philosophie.* Ed. Friedrich-Wilhelm von Herrmann. Frankfurt: Klostermann, 1989.

GA 66 *Besinnung.* Ed. Friedrich-Wilhelm von Herrmann. Frankfurt: Klostermann, 1997.

GA 69 *Die Geschichte des Seyns.* Ed. Peter Trawny. Frankfurt: Klostermann, 1998.

GA 70 *Über den Anfang.* Ed. Paola-Ludovika Coriando. Frankfurt: Klostermann, 2005.

GA 71 *Das Ereignis.* Ed. Friedrich-Wilhelm von Herrmann. Frankfurt: Klostermann, 2009.

GA 73	*Zum Ereignis-Denken.* Ed. Peter Trawny. Frankfurt: Klostermann, 2013.
GA 75	*Zu Hölderlin-Griechenlandreisen.* Ed. Curd Ochwadt. Frankfurt: Klostermann, 2000.
GA 76	*Leitgedanken zur Entstehung der Metaphysik, der neuzeitlichen Wissenschaft, und der modernen Technik.* Ed. Claudius Strube. Frankfurt: Klostermann, 2009.
GA 77	*Feldweg-Gespräche.* Ed. Ingrid Schüssler. Frankfurt: Klostermann, 1995.
GA 79	*Bremen und Freiburger Vorträge.* Ed. Petra Jaeger. Frankfurt: Klostermann, 1994.
GA 81	*Gedachtes.* Ed. Paola-Ludovika Coriando. Frankfurt: Klostermann, 2007.
GA 94	*Überlegungen, II–VI (Schwarze Hefte, 1931–1938).* Ed. Peter Trawny. Frankfurt: Klostermann, 2014.
GA 95	*Überlegungen, VII–XI (Schwarze Hefte, 1938/1939).* Ed. Peter Trawny. Frankfurt: Klostermann, 2014.
GA 96	*Überlegungen, XII–XV (Schwarze Hefte, 1939–1941).* Ed. Peter Trawny. Frankfurt: Klostermann, 2014.
GA 97	*Anmerkungen I–V (Schwarze Hefte, 1942–1948).* Ed. Peter Trawny. Frankfurt: Klostermann, 2015.
GA 98	*Anmerkungen VI–IX (Schwarze Hefte, 1948/49–1951).* Ed. Peter Trawny. Frankfurt: Klostermann, 2018.
HAS	*Heidegger und der Antisemitismus. Mit Briefen von Martin und Frtiz Heidegger.* Freiburg: Herder, 2016.
HBB	*Martin Heidegger-Elisabeth Blochmann Briefwechsel, 1918–1969.* Ed. Joachim Storck. Marbach: Deutsche Schillergesellschaft, 1990.
HCW	*The Heidegger Controversy.* Ed. Richard Wolin. New York: Columbia University Press, 1991.
HGR	*Hölderlin's Hymns "Germania" and "The Rhine."* Trans. William McNeill and Julia Davis. Bloomington: Indiana University Press, 1996.
HHI	*Hölderlin's Hymn "The Ister."* Trans. William McNeill and Julia Ireland. Bloomington: Indiana University Press, 2014.

HJB	*Martin Heidegger/Karl Jaspers Briefwechsel.* Frankfurt: Klostermann, 1990.
HIB	*Martin Heidegger/Imma von Bodmershof Briefwechsel.* Stuttgart: Klett-Cotta, 2000.
HKB	*Martin Heidegger/Kurt Bauch Briefwechsel, 1932–1975.* Freiburg: Alber, 2010.
HR	*The Heidegger Reader.* Ed. Günter Figal. Bloomington: Indiana University Press, 2009.
IM	*Introduction to Metaphysics.* Trans. Gregory Fried and Richard Polt. New Haven, CT: Yale University Press, 2000.
MLS	*"Mein liebes Seelchen!": Briefe Martin Heideggers an seine Frau Elfride, 1915–1970.* Ed. Gertrud Heidegger. Munich: Deutsche Verlags-Anstalt, 2005.
OWL	*On the Way to Language.* Trans. Peter Hertz. New York: Harper & Row, 1982.
P	*Parmenides.* Trans. Andre Schuwer and Richard Rojcewicz. Bloomington: Indiana University Press, 1992.
PLT	*Poetry, Language, Thought.* Trans. Albert Hofstadter. New York: Harper and Row, 1971.
PM	*Pathmarks.* Ed. William McNeill. Cambridge: Cambridge University Press, 1998.
PR	*The Principle of Reason.* Trans. Reginald Lilly. Bloomington: Indiana University Press, 1991.
SZ	*Sein und Zeit.* Tübingen: Niemeyer, 1976.

Hölderlin

BL	Böhlendorff Letter. Trans. Dennis Schmidt. *On Germans and Other Greeks.* Bloomington: Indiana University Press, 2001, 165–167.
DE	*Death of Empedocles.* Trans. David Farrell Krell. Albany, NY: SUNY Press, 2008.
DKV	Deutscher Klassiker Verlag Ausgabe. Ed. Jochen Schmidt. In *Sämtliche Werke und Briefe in drei Bänden.* Frankfurt: Deutscher Klassiker Verlag, 2004.

ELT	*Hölderlin: Essays and Letters on Theory*. Ed. Thomas Pfau. Albany, NY: SUNY Press, 1988.
E&L	*Essays and Letters*. Ed. Jeremy Adler and Charlie Louth. Harmondsworth: Penguin, 2009.
H	*Hyperion*. Trans. Ross Benjamin. Brooklyn: Archipelago Books, 2008.
SA	*Grosse Stuttgarter Ausgabe. Sämtliche Werke*. Ed. Friedrich Beissner. 8 Vols. Stuttgart: Kohlhammer, 1943–1985.
SPF	*Selected Poems and Fragments*. Trans. Michael Hamburger. Harmondsworth: Penguin, 1998.

Hellingrath

HV	*Hölderlin-Vermächtnis*. Munich: Bruckmann, 1944.

Acknowledgments

Philosophy takes place in language, in its exchanges, gestures, appropriations, and contentions, which is to say it takes place in a world of discourse shared with others. Books get written in isolation, yet they are profoundly marked by the voices of others who, even in their absence, make themselves heard. Over the last years of a worldwide pandemic, that absence has left its own mark. As I think back on the people who have made this project possible, I simply wish to acknowledge the power of these voices through a word of thanks.

I begin on a note of absence—and of thoughts of remembrance: for my brother John, his son Louis, and for Elisa McCauley and Joe Odermatt. Your lives have been an inspiration to me.

At my home institution, the University of Texas-Dallas, I want to thank Dean Nils Roemer for granting me SFDA leave and for his strong support of my scholarship. I am also grateful to my friends at UTD, Peter Park and Michael Wilson, as well as to Réne and Martine Prieto.

In Dallas, I want to express my appreciation for members of the DASEIN seminar who have made our monthly meetings a special event—Robert Wood, Cynthia Nielsen, Mark Curtis-Thames, Parker McDill, Gary Brown, Andy Amato, Rod Stewart, Aaron Claussen, Amanda Dunbar, Fatemeh Tashakori, and Farshad Sadri. A debt of gratitude goes to Heather Almanza for her technical support. I also want to send special thanks to three friends who have made Dallas a place where philosophy lives—Dale Wilkerson, Kate Davies, and John Loscerbo. Moreover, I want to thank my dear friends Rod Coltman and Candace Uhlmeyer for hosting our yearly Heidegger Symposium in McKinney. This yearly symposium has been a source of real inspiration because of the spirited contributions of Sean Kirkland, Jennifer Gaffney, Jim Risser, John Sallis, Andrew Mitchell, and Dan Dahlstrom. A special thanks to Will McNeill,

Krzysztof Ziarek, and Ian Moore for being at the center of it all and to Ted George for his generous friendship and collaboration.

At SUNY Press, I would like to thank Michael Rinella for taking on this project and for his help in ushering it along. More especially, I want to thank the editor of this series, Denny Schmidt, who has always encouraged me to write on Hölderlin and whose own work on philosophy and poetry has been a genuine inspiration. I wish also to extend my appreciation to Holger Zaborowski for his friendship and philosophical support.

In Germany, I want to thank Günter Figal and Antonia Egel for their collegial generosity in hosting several conferences at the Freiburg Institute for Advanced Studies, where I was able to deliver papers that helped develop the themes of this book. I also want to extend warm appreciation to my friends in Tübingen, where a good portion of this book was written. At the Philosophisches Seminar, I owe a debt of gratitude to Dietmar Koch for inviting me to participate in his Leserkreis. I also want to acknowledge the help of Michael Franz of the Hölderlin Gesellschaft for sponsoring me and for our Hölderlin-Gespräche. For making me feel welcomed during sabbaticals and summer stays, I have been helped by Christian Backer, Tina Schwarz, Ekki Kirsch, Joe Lawrence, Penny Pinson, Margarete Kolmar, Friederike Scholvin, and especially Horst Fromm für sein Entgegenkommen. I would also like to thank my two favorite Buchhändler, Norbert Schüler of Bader Antiquariat and Wolfgang Zwierzynski, whose Quichotte shop provides a special place for lovers of books. Most of all, I want to thank my dear friends Karin Bukenberger and Rolf Maier, who have made Tübingen a second home for me and my family. Es lebe die Freundschaft.

A last thank you to my New York family—my sister Linda and her husband Mario Ascrizzi, my sister-in-law Jane, as well as my nieces and nephews for so generously hosting us during our frequent visits. I also want to thank Joe McClain and Pat Diffley for our lifelong friendship. More than all of this, I want to thank my wife Lucy McCauley, whose work as a writer and documentary filmmaker has been an inspiration to me. Many thanks to her and my indomitable daughter Hannah for helping me get through one extremely difficult year of the pandemic. So much of this book owes its energy to your love and support.

Preface

> Hölderlin is . . . the beginning of the deepest convulsion of Western metaphysics——that is, of the West's history of being.
>
> —Martin Heidegger, *Gesamtausgabe*[1]

> The movement toward the future is a return toward the arche-origin. That is to say, toward the homeland.
>
> —Jacques Derrida, *Geschlecht III*[2]

Heidegger's "Hölderlin"

It is with the movement of return that philosophy always already begins. We find the echoes of such a movement in Anaximander's originary recursions of being in accordance with the homeward journey of time. We likewise can identify such an arc of return in Heraclitus's reflections on the palintropic play of the *aion* that unfolds like a child, returning its draughts to the boardgame of human existence.[3] Such a principle of return as the *arche* of all things finds its classic expression in Plato's *The Republic*, which, paradigmatically, begins in/as a return from the world of the dead, a *nekyeia* to the Peiraeus—the land beyond the river—that ends in Er's return back from across the Lethe.[4] In this way, the philosopher's return to the cave, like Odysseus's return to Ithaca, will be grasped as a homecoming from out of the exile of wandering, a homecoming to the soul's proper place within the order of being. At the very end of *The Republic*, as Socrates concludes his recollection of the long *katabasis* to Hades, he tells Glaucon that the mythos narrated by him, like Er's own mythos, has been saved and not lost. And then he reveals to Glaucon the very sense of the mythos that *The Republic* has told: "If we believe it, it will save us, too" (*Republic* 621C). This Greek notion of return will help to form the very basis of the philosophical quest itself as a salvation narrative spun around the soul's journey, away from its home and then back again.

In deep and striking ways, this philosophical *nostos* will come to understand itself in conversation with the great homecoming narratives of Homer, Pindar, and the Greek tragedians, who spun their tales of heroes longing for a return home from the battles of Troy. As in Homer's *Odyssey*, whose prologue references *nostos* five times in its opening twenty lines, the theme of poetic homecoming emerges as essential—not only to the stories of the ancient Greeks but also to the very practice and tradition of poetic art. In this way, Greek poetry comes to shape itself not only as a tradition dedicated to the narration of homecoming but, more essentially, it understands its own poetic art in a recursive sense whereby the poetic telling of the homecoming becomes itself a way of coming home. In his Fourth Pythian Ode (vv. 32, 196), Pindar sings of favorable homecoming (*nostos*) for sailors at sea, for athletes gone to compete in the games, for Jason and the Argonauts. In the process of narrating these stories, we find Pindar crafting a larger design, however: that it is only through our own poetic telling that this homecoming comes to pass. It is this Greek discourse of return, understood as a *nostos*, a homecoming, that will shape Heidegger's own relation to Hölderlin.

Hölderlin's late hymns, the ones that Heidegger turns to in his lecture courses from WS 1934/35 to his last course dedicated to Hölderlin in SS 1942, all traffic in the myth of homecoming that Hölderlin inherited from the Greeks. Moreover, in both his epistolary novel *Hyperion* and in his translations of Pindar's epinician odes, Hölderlin becomes possessed by the double movement of spirit's journey outward from its home (*Ausflug*) and its journey of return (*Rückkehr*). It is this topos of homecoming that will come to serve Heidegger as a way of understanding the rhythms, oscillations, and reversals that mark not only German history but the history and unfolding of Germany's relation to the ancient Greeks. In 1943, in his essay on Hölderlin's elegy "Homecoming," Heidegger writes: "The poet's vocation (*Beruf*) is homecoming" (EHP: 32–33, 47/GA 4: 13–14, 28). Moreover, he explains, "What constitutes the homecoming is that the countrymen must first become at home in the still withheld essence of their homeland." That is, the homeland is not something that is present there for the sojourner on his return home. As Heidegger puts it, "The one returning home has not yet reached his homeland simply by arriving there." Rather, the homeland is still withheld; it is not a factical entity waiting there to be possessed. Understanding homecoming in this way is to see it as marked by temporal and spatial absence. This is the lesson of the Greeks. As Michael Theunissen expresses it in his reading of Pindar's Fourth Pythian Ode, "In a certain sense—the journey of return is not a repetition or recurrence" (*Die Rückkehr ist keine Wiederkehr*).[5]

The act of undertaking a journey immediately transforms the homeland from being a stable site of residence and belonging to its becoming a strange and foreign land that appears to the returning sojourner as "alien." As Hyperion writes to his friend Bellarmine after his tumultous travels to and from Hellas:

> But it is no longer the world as it was to which I return. I am a stranger (*Fremdling*), like the unburied dead when they come up from the Acheron and were I even on my native (*heimatlichen*) island, in the gardens of my youth that are barred to me by my father, Ach! Still, still, would I be like a stranger on the earth and no god would any longer bind me to what is past. (DKV II: 165)

Seizing upon this Hölderlinian image of a homecoming marked by strangeness and the encounter with something foreign, Heidegger takes it up as a way to model his own sense of what it means to be German. But the promise of a German future for Heidegger does not lie in a self-focused scrutiny of Germanity. On the contrary, it needs to unfold as a journey outward from the native sphere of Germanity into a confrontation (*Auseinandersetzung*) with the ancient Greeks. Such a journey begins, however, with the poetry of Hölderlin. It is in the poetic word of Hölderlin that Heidegger finds the essential movement of German history, which he reads capaciously as the decisive turning point within the history of the West. Much depends, however, on the way we approach the poet's words. Heidegger's essential confrontation with Hölderlin does not, however, take place within a vacuum. It belongs, in the most intimate sense, to the political history of Germany in the first half of the twentieth century—its loss in the First World War; its failed political attempt at a socialist republic during the economic crises between 1923 and 1932; its moment of hoped-for national renewal in the Hitler revolution; its devastating loss in the Second World War; and the traumatic experiences in Germany after the *Stunde Null* of 1945. By the time he celebrated his sixtieth birthday in 1949, Heidegger had witnessed five regime changes in Germany: from an empire (1871–1918) to a socialist republic (1919–1932), from a fascist dictatorship (1933–1945) through a foreign occupation (1945–1949) to the founding of the Federal Republic (1949). Through all this change, "Hölderlin" accompanied him along the way, and it is in Hölderlin's name that Heidegger preserves his dream of an authentic Germany, a "secret Germany" that lives far beyond all the political failures and miscalculations of the actual German regimes that shaped his life. Heidegger was hardly alone among the Germans in ascribing to Hölderlin the role of founder, prophet, savior, and hero.[6] Hölderlin's legacy was taken up with enthusiasm in the early years of the twentieth century by the Stefan George Circle, especially by the editor of the first genuinely critical edition of the poet's work, Norbert von Hellingrath. Heidegger's *Hölderlinbild* was deeply shaped by the influence of Hellingrath, and it is in his memory that Heidegger carries out the work of "unfolding" (*auseinanderlegen*) that legacy (GA 4: 48).

But why Hölderlin? Among all the many voices of other German and Greek poets, thinkers, tragedians, and prophets, why Hölderlin? What is it in Hölderlin's work that leads Heidegger to call him a "destiny"? And in what sense can Hölderlin be a destiny? In what follows, I want to take up these questions by looking at some of the most important texts in Heidegger's lifelong conversation with Hölderlin, including the three lecture courses from the *Collected Works*—*Hölderlin's Hymns "Germania" and the "Rhine"* (GA 39), *Hölderlin's Hymn "Remembrance"* (GA 52), and *Hölderlin's Hymn "The Ister"* (GA 53)—as well as the dialogue "The Western Conversation" (GA 75) from the *Nachlass*. There is no single book in English that deals with these crucial texts or with Heidegger's longstanding engagement with Hölderlin.[7] Perhaps the task is too daunting because to engage Heidegger's Hölderlin is to travel the path from the time of the "Kehre" in Heidegger's thought in the early 1930s until the very end of his writing in the 1970s. Five volumes of Heidegger's *Collected Works* are devoted to Hölderlin (among his published works and manuscripts only Nietzsche receives more attention).[8] Several others (GA 5, GA 8, GA 9, GA 16, GA 80) can only be read in conjunction with Heidegger's engagement with Hölderlin. Moreover, I would argue that crucial texts from the 1930s such as "The Origin of the Work of Art" (1935), *Introduction to Metaphysics* (1935), *Contributions to Philosophy* (1936–1938), and *Mindfulness* (1938–1940) can hardly be understood without direct reference to Hölderlin.⁹ No matter how we interpret these various texts, however, the presence of Hölderlin within Heidegger's thinking remains decisive. Heidegger's turn toward language, art, and poetizing (and with this his critique of scientific thinking and technicity) happens as a way of thinking through the role of Hölderlin in the epoch of homelessness and the abandonment of the gods. Moreover, Heidegger's whole postwar language of *Gelassenheit*, poetic dwelling, measure-taking, nearness, sojourn, remembrance, the holy, and the fourfold bears a direct relation to the language of Hölderlin's poetry and to the way Heidegger reads it in the age of the gods who have fled. One could make a strong case that Hölderlin stands as the decisive figure within Heidegger's corpus, the one whose influence extends longest and whose status as a "destiny" remains secure through all the political-historical changes that Heidegger experiences in his enthusiastic embrace and subsequent disenchantment with National Socialism, his postwar banishment from the university, and his re-emergence during the 1950s as the leading thinker in the Western world. Through all these various stages and *Inszenierungen* on Heidegger's thought path, Hölderlin remains *the* poet who poetizes the possibility of finding our lost home amidst the homelessness brought about in the epoch of technological thinking.

In the chapters that follow I focus on the crucial years of Heidegger's thoughtpath—from the failure of the rectorate in 1934 through the National Socialist years, on to the period of his breakdown, decline, and rebirth, as it were. During this fifteen-year period, one of the most turbulent in all of German history, Heidegger's thought will dramatically shift its focus.¹⁰ Here Heidegger will rethink this historical emergency of 1933–1948 by conceiving it not merely as a manifestation of Germany's urgent plight within contemporary Europe but, rather, in terms of an overarching history of beyng that he confects during this time.¹¹ As the poet of/for this time of destitution, Hölderlin comes to stand for Heidegger as the one undefiled figure whose voice cries out in the wilderness of modern nihilism to prepare for what is coming. There is much about Hölderlin's work that appeals to Heidegger: his paratactic style that undermines the rationalistic metaphysics of modernity, his ethical attunement to dwelling in the age of the world's night, his grasp of the poetic character of art, his hymnal songs that call for a new language and a renewed relation to the natural world. Ultimately, however, what matters for Heidegger is Hölderlin's status as the herald of a future Germany, one whose authentic identity remains concealed to all but the few who know how to attend to the poet's call. It is this commitment to Germany's future—and its sense of a national mission to save the West from the nihilism of the world's night—that will fundamentally shape Heidegger's whole approach to the poet. Heidegger was hardly the first to co-opt Hölderlin's poetry for the sake of the German national mission, but the way he was able to conscript Hölderlin's unique language for his own philosophical vision of German exceptionalism has been unparalleled in the history of the Hölderlin reception. Reading Hölderlin has constituted a German national vocation over the last century and more. Figures such as Dilthey, Nietzsche, Rilke, Stefan George, Georg Trakl, Walter Benjamin, Brecht, Adorno, and Paul Celan have all been deeply struck by the influence of Hölderlin. And yet within this catalog of distinguished and devoted Hölderlin readers, nowhere does the sheer influence of the poet's work stand as powerfully as in Heidegger's. Besides the five volumes in the *Gesamtausgabe* devoted exclusively to Hölderlin (GA 4, GA 39, GA 52, GA 53, GA 75), several other volumes (including the *Black Notebooks*) also deal with Hölderlin, his language, and his influence.[12] As we will see, Heidegger's readings of the poet and his poetry are fraught with all manner of tendentious "elucidations" that not infrequently reduce the poet to Heidegger's own stratagems and designs. Many of these ways of approaching Hölderlin will be marked by his human—all too human—affinities to the rural roots of his Swabian homeland and to the political-racial perceptions that he learned there at the end of the nineteenth century. These rural values emerge at a time before Heidegger learned how to think philosophically—and yet they remained with him throughout his life as he rose to become one of the leading philosophical voices of the twentieth century. This is not, I believe, a mere piece of Heidegger's cultural baggage; it is something to notice and pay attention to. We cannot simply read Heidegger's work on Hölderlin as a philosophical "encounter" with the poet—or his poetry—since so much of the tenor and direction of his interpretive enterprise rests upon nonphilosophical assumptions that implicitly betray the task of thinking that Heidegger sets for himself.

Clearly, Heidegger's work on Hölderlin makes philosophical demands on its readers, demands that separate such work from the usual standards of philological "explanation" and the "historiographically correct" accounting of the work (GA 39: 1; GA 52: 3–4). What Heidegger aims at instead is to "disclose the truth of history," and to do so in a way that exposes both us and Hölderlin's own work to the dangers posed by historical engagement. Heidegger was ever aware of the precariousness of his Hölderlin readings, yet he determined nonetheless to offer a different kind of measure by which to approach the work of the poet. Succeeding generations of philologists have not always been well disposed to such readings. Jochen Schmidt, one of the leading Hölderlin scholars of the last half-century, dismisses Heidegger's work as being distinguished by what he calls its "ideological" preconceptions nurtured on his rightwing commitment to the George Circle and later to National Socialism. Schmidt views Heidegger's work as complicit in the whole political project of expropriating and usurping the poet's work. As Schmidt sees it, Heidegger's co-optation of Hölderlin is less a misunderstanding of the poet than a full-scale reduction of his work to Heidegger's own "fundamentalist" reading.[13] There are so many ways to criticize Heidegger's approach from the point of Hölderlin-scholarship; these include his virtual inattention to the theoretical writings, the early work, *Hyperion*, *The Death of Empedocles*, or to his various poetic forms—the ode, the elegy—and why these shifts in poetic form matter so much to the development of Hölderlin's poetic idiom. Heidegger's whole approach to the work of Hölderlin is to remove it from its historical context and thereby open the text "itself" to a form of philosophical colonization, to borrow a pervasive metaphor from Heidegger's reading of the "Bread and Wine" Strophe IX revision.[14] It is through this act of dehistoricizing the poet's work—from the effects of German Idealism, from French revolutionary influences and the work of Rousseau, from the political milieu of republican friends such as Isaak von Sinclair—that Heidegger is able to perform his own singular reading of the poet in terms of a mythos of German national destiny. This mythos takes on a new form after the end of the political revolution of 1933–1934—that is, after the failure of Heidegger's ambitious program for revolutionizing the German university.[15] Now he attempts what he terms a "metapolitical" form of philosophical-poetic revolution that seeks to transform the German *Volk* into a sense of readiness for what is to come (GA 94: 115–116, 124). But that too soon fades after 1934, even as the dream of "a secret spiritual Germany" nurtured on the vision of Hellingrath and the George Circle lives on (GA 94: 155). This dream will take different forms over the course of this fifteen-year focus on the work of Hölderlin (1934–1948), but it will always express Heidegger's eschatological-soteriological hopes for the saving power of Hölderlin to rescue Germany from its suffering and humiliation.[16] Even in the early postwar years, as Heidegger seizes upon Hölderlin's mytheme of "poverty" (*Armut*) to express the reigning mood of desolation and destruction afflicting the homeland, Heidegger still cleaves to his Hölderlinian hope of poetic-philosophical "revolution." In one of his notebooks, he writes: "We are nearing the moment of the world-historical trial of the Germans" (GA 97: 19). Worrying that the Germans themselves are hindering their own prospects for "awakening the contemporary forces" of revolutionary potential that still persist through the debris, Heidegger speaks to the prospect of authentic "revolution," which he interprets "literally as the revolutionary return of essence back to what is inceptive."

It is this movement of return, nurtured on the themes of home-coming, *Heimkunft*, *Heimkehr*, that will characterize Heidegger's entire approach to Hölderlin—and to Hölderlin's role as the mediator between Hellas and Hesperia, antiquity and modernity, the ancient Greeks and the modern Germans. In this way, Hölderlin's poetic word serves as "the transition from the first to the other beginning" since Hölderlin's hymnal poetizing cannot be considered "art" in the sense of an "aesthetics" modeled on the metaphysics of modernity. On the contrary, this poetic word "has left metaphysics behind" as it "prepares the other beginning of the history of beyng" (GA 70: 150, 167). Yet within the guild of Hölderlin scholars, such an approach was understood as a violation of philological scholarship and the rigors of textual interpretation. As early as 1942, Max Kommerell writes to Heidegger that his insistence that "Hölderlin is a fate" lays bare a rhetoric that qualifies less as "scholarship" than as "a new esoteric."[17] Such an approach moves dangerously away from the canons of philological rigor into a kind of "Hölderlin violence" that verges on being "a sublime form of suicide." In the years that followed, a succession of Germanists would proffer their own critiques, many focused on Heidegger's attempt to commandeer Hölderlin for his own philosophical mission of *Heimatpolitik*. During the 1960s, Robert Minder and Theodor Adorno each delivered blistering critiques to the Hölderlin Gesellschaft on Heidegger's Hölderlin contributions. Minder attacked Heidegger for trafficking in the same political gutter inhabited by other National Socialist philosophers, such as Alfred Baeumler and Kurt Hildebrandt, who had co-opted Hölderlin for their own vision of a brown revolution. Like Heidegger, Baeumler would assert that "Hölderlin's path is the fateful path of German spirit that, sojourning to Hellas, find its way back home to Germania."[18] Moreover, he too would argue that "Hölderlin offers a decision that points into the distant future." Minder also was insistent on reading Heidegger's Hölderlin contributions within the National Socialist Hölderlin reception and documenting their "fateful submission to the Führer."[19] What struck Minder as reprehensible in Heidegger's whole approach to the poet was his impulse to sequester Hölderlin in an encapsulated and secretive "Hölderlin-Kult" of initiates. Adorno would likewise come to regard Heidegger's "Hölderlin" (and indeed his entire philosophy) "as fascistic to its innermost core."[20]

Beyond this political critique, other scholars have pointed to Heidegger's narrow vision of Hölderlin as a writer and thinker. As part of this pattern, they have seen his writings as egregious attempts to import his own thoughts into Hölderlin's verses in a kind of "Hinein-Interpretieren" and/or as a form of "Hölderlin-theology."[21] Jochen Schmidt speaks of Heidegger's "hubris," but his was hardly a singular voice.[22] Habermas notes that Heidegger's whole rhetorical style is infused with an autocratic, perlocutionary effect that demands "obedience" and that brings its listeners into an intimate bond with "pseudo-sacral powers."[23] Given this long lineage of scholarly philosophical critique, it would be foolhardy to write a book on Heidegger's Hölderlin lectures without recognizing their rebarbative character. As Peter Trawny notes, there is something "fatal" about Heidegger's decision to harness his interpretation of Hölderlin to National Socialism.[24] With the publication of the *Black Notebooks* we see how Heidegger was not insensitive to these mounting critiques. He was so angry at the Hölderlin Gesellschaft for inviting both Adorno and Minder to speak that he sent a curt, one-sentence letter to the Society announcing: "I declare herewith my resignation from the Hölderlin Society."[25] In conjunction with these attacks on his Hölderlin essays, he later writes: "The present age no longer has the ability to hear the voice of Hölderlin." Heidegger never changed his critical assessment of the contemporary world and its ability to hear Hölderlin's word. Only a few months before he died, he writes to Norbert von Hellingrath's erstwhile fiancée, Imma von Bodmershof, that "Norbert's Fourth Volume always lies near."[26] He goes on to cite the opening lines from Hölderlin's "Die Titanen" (v. 1–3) and laments, "And who today still hears these lines amidst the din of the mass media and its clamoring demand that everything—even poetizing and thinking—be made serviceable to praxis" (HIB: 143–144). The lines from Hölderlin read as follows:

> But it is not yet
> Time. They are still
> Untethered. What is divine does not strike those who do not
>   take part. (DKV I: 390)

Even as he confronts his own death, Heidegger is concerned about "what Hölderlin has to say to today's world." As he writes to Imma, "This is the care (*Sorge*) of my thinking: . . . whether the call of the divinity of the most distant god still strikes and awakens those who will take part" in the coming feast. This was always Heidegger's concern with Hölderlin, to find "the right time, the *kairos*" for the return of the gods. Homecoming proves to be a necessary precursor to such a time—and the work of such homecoming involves exposing oneself to the power of the gods in withstanding the uncertainty/ambiguity of dwelling at the liminal threshold between night/day even as one risks being overpowered by its force (GA 39: 223–224, 232). This is what Heidegger means when he writes that "the poet's vocation is homecoming, by which the homeland is first prepared as the land of nearness to the origin" (EHP: 47/GA 4: 28). It is as the preservation of the meaning and faith in this mission that Heidegger's "Hölderlin" takes form. This homeward journey to our proper dwelling place is no simple *Heimkehr*, *nostos*, or return. It involves, rather, a critical passage *through* the foreign, the strange, the alien, and the other that tears us from our domestic settlements in a *Riss* (rip, tear) that renders us as foreign to ourselves. It is this double movement of the *Riss* as the riven, that which rends and tears us spatially/temporally that makes such a journey possible.

It is this essential *Riss* that tears Semele from Zeus, mortals from gods, even as it "tears (*herausreisst*) human beings out of the habitual middle of their lives" (GA 53: 32). Moreover, it is this concern with tearing (*reissen*) that underlies Hölderlin's river hymns and helps to account for Heidegger's sustained preoccupation with rivers. Rivers tear apart the land, transporting streams across landscapes and leaving them riven. Such a rift rives or splits apart the terrain as it heads from its source to its mouth. In this rich etymological field of signifiers, rivers take on the sense of that which tears apart and separates while also fulfilling the law of homecoming and return.

For Hölderlin, rivers become a way of tracing the course of human history as a journey outward from the source on the way toward its end. For him, as for Heidegger, they come to stand for the effusive unfolding of poetic creativity. In this way, they engage both the native sphere of the homeland and the journey through the foreign that defines the poetic task of homecoming. As Heidegger puts it in the Ister lectures: "The journey outward (*Ausfahrt*) is not merely a leaving something behind; it is already the first—and in this sense—decisive act of a return (*Rückkehr*) to the homeland (*Heimat*)" (GA 53: 166). In this critical tension between *Ausfahrt* and *Rückkehr*, Heidegger finds what he calls "the law of history" that defines the possibility of poetic dwelling for human beings upon the earth. What this "law" demands is that the human being must journey outward into the alien so as to return home to confront the alien element within the native homeland. Such a law holds not only for the German *Volk* as it confronts its own historical vocation but also holds for the act of translation that encounters a foreign language so as to confront the alien idiom within one's native tongue. This same law holds for "rivers which, in their journeying, bring about a becoming homely (*Heimischwerden*) in being unhomely (*Unheimischsein*)" (GA 53: 184). For Heidegger, the task set for the German people is to enact this poetic truth of what I will call "an alien homecoming" to the native and proper out of the encounter with the foreign. This poetic truth, bequeathed to Heidegger from Hölderlin's Böhlendorff letter—"That the historicity of history has its essence in a return to what is proper, a return that can only take place as a journey outward into what is foreign (*als Ausfahrt in das Fremde*)" (EHP: 118/GA 4: 95)—will come to frame the way he will read Hölderlin as the voice shaping German history, which means—its future.

Such a truth proves precarious in Heidegger's hands, even fatal. In his takeover of Hölderlin's myth of Germania, Heidegger announces the coming of a historico-destinal politics of the *Volk* that opens onto the preparation for an other beginning. But it also emphasizes the historical exceptionalism of the Germans in a way that gets tied to a discourse of racialist exclusion and condemnation. On Heidegger's telling of this myth, "the Jews" become not merely a synecdoche for "the foreign" but are seen as complicit *agents provocateurs* in "the overpowering of life by machination" (GA 96: 56).

With the publication of the *Black Notebooks*, we see how intimately Hölderlin is enmeshed in Heidegger's political ruminations from 1933 to 1948. At the same time, I also believe that given our awareness of Heidegger's deadly political uses/misuses of Hölderlin and the way he was made to serve Heidegger's own visions of Germany's national mission, it is an excellent time to rethink their meaning. In this book, I offer close readings of Heidegger's four major Hölderlin texts (GA 39, GA 52, GA 53, GA 75) and seek to situate them within Heidegger's own thought path. At the same time, I also believe we need to read these texts with an eye toward the historical situation within Germany and within Heidegger's own work that he is reacting to. Against Heidegger's tendentious program of taking Hölderlin out of his own historical context and reading him in terms of a mythic national renewal, I want to resituate these texts within the turbulent years between 1934 and 1948 while not reducing them to a merely historicist reading.

A *last note to readers*: the subtitle of this book is partly in quotation marks to indicate a complex relationship of one author to another. This relationship is certainly not one that can be taken for granted. As the discourse of postmodern literary criticism has indicated, the use of quotation marks offers an interwoven, citational form of duplication and duplicity. In pointing to a citation, what is "original" is made nonoriginal in and through the very act of its being cited. In his essay "Interpreting Signatures," Derrida asks this telling question: "Now what happens when a proper name is put between quotation marks?"[27] In *Disseminations*, Derrida points to the problematic use of what he calls the "double mark," which he sees as seizing and entangling its object in a binary opposition:

> This structure itself is worked in turn: the rule according to which every concept necessarily receives two similar marks—a repetition without identity—one mark inside and the other outside the deconstructed system, should give rise to a double reading and a double writing.[28]

For Derrida, situating a name under quotation marks serves as a way to strategically displace or place under suspicion the very name that is cited. Beyond this, quotation marks "serve as a sufficient precaution" for a reader attuned to the default of a guiding name or concept. We can find the same kind of careful relation to the quotation mark in Derrida's essay "Shibboleth" that focuses on the poetry of Paul Celan. Celan deftly uses quotation marks to set off names and themes from their traditional meaning. For him, these marks indicate a strangeness, foreignness, or alterity in whatever is cited such that, by being cited, it immediately becomes other. In his study of Celan's poetic citation,

Arno Barnert argues that there is something *unheimlich* in the citation itself that marks the very boundary of difference.[29] As Barnert sees it, citation offers the "perception that between the native and the foreign there emerges an unbridgeable realm . . . an abyss that the quotation marks seek to mark." As Celan himself puts it in one of his notebooks, "Truth is revolutionary. I believe that. But when I hear it cited, it becomes something that I sneeze at."[30]

Certainly we can understand placing Hölderlin's name within quotation marks as a way to incite suspicion. Indeed Heidegger's use/misuse of the poet invites such a reading. Again, in "Of Spirit," Derrida writes: "It's the law of quotation marks. Two by two they stand guard: at the frontier or before the door, assigned to the threshold in any case, and these places are always dramatic. The apparatus lends itself to theatricalization."[31] He then adds: "I recall that in German 'quotation mark' is *Anführungsstriche* or *Anführungszeichen*. *Anführen*, to conduct, to take the head, but also to dupe, to make fun of or brainwash somebody." Whether we believe that Heidegger is duping us in his Hölderlin readings or not, what we cannot miss is his dramatic staging of the Hölderlin lectures for his understanding of Germany's place within the history of beyng.

But there is more to Heidegger's relationship to Hölderlin than one of mere political co-optation or deployment. In his Remembrance lectures, Heidegger tells his students, "This lecture course does not pursue any literary-historiographical aims. It therefore also renounces any claim to make us aware of the 'historiographically correct' 'Hölderlin.'" Here we see Heidegger himself placing the poet under the double quotation marks. In doing so, Heidegger shows that he is self-critically aware that the figure of Hölderlin lends itself to every manner of literary-historiographical-political-cultural appropriation and that there can be no "'correct' Hölderlin" (HHR: 3–4/GA 52: 4). What Heidegger sets out to do, he claims, "is solely to think what Hölderlin has poetized, and in thinking it, to come to know it." Within the opening pages of the Remembrance lectures Heidegger repeats this claim six times.

But even more than this, Heidegger's Hölderlin becomes the name of an unexpressed possibility for language—one whereby thinking can emerge only out of an intimate dialogue with poetizing. If Heidegger sometimes forgets his own insight into the revolutionary power of Hölderlin's poetic language and deploys it instead for his own destinal vision of German national renewal, then we need to take him to task. Paul de Man once remarked that there was something deeply troubling about Heidegger's reading of the poet: "It is the fact that Hölderlin says exactly the opposite of what Heidegger makes him say."[32] And while de Man's remark may be hyperbolic and deeply tendentious, it also demands an attentiveness to Heidegger's overall strategy and design. Without dismissing the relevance and/or timeliness of de Man's critique, there is, I will argue, something incredibly powerful about Heidegger's writings on Hölderlin, something that cannot be reduced to Heidegger's own political-nationalistic misuse of the poet. Heidegger's student Hans-Georg Gadamer understood something about this genuinely positive dimension of Hölderlin within his teacher's work. As Gadamer put it:

> A renewed encounter with Friedrich Hölderlin enabled him to make an authentic breakthrough to his own language. . . . This was a daring turn that opened new ways within Heidegger's thinking. Hölderlin loosened Heidegger's tongue for his own thinking.[33]

Nonetheless, Gadamer also understood that there was a violence in Heidegger's own approach to Hölderlin:

> [Heidegger's] Hölderlin interpretations indirectly attest that his thinking was in search of a language that would allow for new insights. These explications of Hölderlin's difficult poems and verses were a kind of identification. It would be a wretched undertaking to account for the violence that allowed such identification. Such an account could only yield what we who have followed Heidegger's thinking already know—that Heidegger only found resonance with those whose work proved accommodating to his own, that he was able to hear only that which promised an answer to his own questions.

Gadamer goes on to claim that "it seems to me that no encounter with Hölderlin since Hellingrath's compares to Heidegger's in intensity and therewith in disclosive power—despite all of its distortions and disfigurings."

While not unmindful of all the devastating revelations in the *Black Notebooks* about Jews, Nazism, the rectorate, and the postwar cover-up, even at this late date, I concur with Gadamer's assessment. Heidegger's "Hölderlin" is still worth pursuing—even as we must always remember the meaning of the double quotation marks.

Introduction

Hölderlin is a beginning.

—Martin Heidegger, *Überlegungen*, VII–XI[34]

I. Hölderlin as a "Transition"

Few themes resonate as powerfully on Heidegger's long and winding thoughtpath as those connected to homeland, *Heimat*, homecoming, and *Heimkehr*. There are, of course, many dimensions to this preoccupation with home in Heidegger's work. In his writings from the 1930s we can find a strong political emphasis on themes connected to rootedness, the homeland, the *Volk*, the German nation, and the earth. In the years after the Second World War we can notice the preeminence of the native region as a way to withstand the calculative thinking that pervades the atomic age and its technological dominion. During the 1960s, the theme of the homeland runs through virtually all of Heidegger's occasional speeches in Messkirch and southern Germany that speak to the effect of homelessness upon the fate and destiny of the human being. In the *Spiegel* interview, Heidegger stresses that "everything essential and great has arisen solely from the fact that humans had a home and were rooted in a tradition" (HR: 325/GA 16: 670). In all of these different iterations and reflections on the home and on the alien effects of uprooting, the one voice that resonates most powerfully is that of the Swabian poet Friedrich Hölderlin. Hölderlin's writing will have an enormous influence on Heidegger as he comes to approach questions about art, the earth, language, time, technology, and the sacred. In so many of his excursions into new realms that emerge in his thinking—the dialogue between thinking and poetry, the meaning of the fourfold, the claim of language as it relates to nearness, dwelling, measure, and the appropriating event—the figure of Hölderlin looms large. More than this, the very structure and trajectory of Heidegger's whole sketch of a history of beyng belongs, I will argue, to Hölderlin's poetic understanding of history as one marked by the departure and hoped for return of the gods.

Hölderlin, in this sense, stands not as a historical figure who belongs to a specific era of German history or intellectual life; on the contrary, he stands for Heidegger as the name of a myth, thought as a possibility and hope for a German future. What this myth of "Hölderlin" countenances is a decision about the future of the West, a future whose very possibility rests upon the Germans resolutely giving heed to Hölderlin's call for authentic homecoming. Yet even as Heidegger will take up his dialogue with Hölderlin, he will renounce any attempt to situate his reading of the poet in a traditional literary or historical way. Rather, he states, "we renounce the claim to uncover the historically correct Hölderlin" in favor of a beyng-historical reading of the poet (GA 52: 4). This version of Hölderlin envisions him as proposing a conflictually intimate (*innig*) relation to the earth that is "no longer metaphysical" (GA 52: 99).[35] Through his poetizing, Heidegger will claim, Hölderlin is able to provide the hints and intimations of "slow footbridges" (*langsamen Stegen*) that afford an opening to a "transition" (*Übergang*) between the time of the gods' departure and the time of their coming (GA 52: 94–96). This poetic transition in a time of need offers to Heidegger a way of thinking through the nihilistic plight of Western humanity announced in Nietzsche's proclamation of the death of God. In this way, Hölderlin becomes for Heidegger the poet blessed with "knowing about the realm of decision between the godforsakenness of beings . . . and the grounding of a godhood of the gods" (GA 75: 7). What this decision involves is, however, less a "moral-anthropological" or "existentiell" choice than it is an originary de-scission (*Ent-scheidung*) that cuts off and scissions the connexus between human beings and gods through an appropriating event that reconfigures history (CP: 69, 81, 179/GA: 65, 87, 103, 227). For Heidegger, this decision essentially occurs "as the erupting fissure of beyng itself," something that needs to "to be grasped beyng-historically, not *morally-anthropologically*." To enter into the time-space of this decision, Heidegger insists, demands a "leap" or *Sprung* "into the belonging to beyng in the full essential occurrence of beyng as event."

It is only through this leap—a leap reserved "*For the few—For the rare*"—that there can be anything like a "first penetration into the domain of the *history of being*." But before this leap can happen, Heidegger avows, there must occur a preparation and "preparedness for the transition from the end of the first beginning and into the other beginning." Moreover, for both this preparation and transition there needs to occur a revolutionary turn or *Kehre* in the human being's relation to language, one whereby language is understood not as a tool for communication or control but as "that appropriating event (*Ereignis*) that disposes over (*ver-fügt* . . . *über*) the highest possibility of human being" (HR: 121/GA 4: 38). And it is in this breach between the thoughtless application of language to effect mastery over the world of beings *and* that "domain in which poetry unfolds its power" that Hölderlin stands before us as the poet "of" decision—in a double sense (GA 39: 213–214). That is, not only does Hölderlin's poetic word prepare a historical decision for the Germans but this word is itself the expression of a de-scission or *Riss* that emerges from beyng itself and that stands as the beyng-historical expression of a profound conflict at the heart of beyng.

What this decision entails is something that Hölderlin's poetic word prepares us for, a preparation that stands before the German *Volk* as its ownmost mission, task, and vocation. And for Heidegger it is Hölderlin who, as "poet of poets, poet of the Germans," stands as that essential figure whose historical destiny is "to become a power in the history of our Volk." Here, Heidegger speaks of Hölderlin as the poet who stands as "the founder of beyng"—or more specifically, "the founder of German beyng because he has projected such beyng the farthest . . . out ahead into the most distant future" (HGR: 194–195, 201/GA 39: 214, 220). To grasp Hölderlin's place within the German future becomes for Heidegger one of the decisive tasks of his beyng-historical thinking. Taking up such a task and embracing it as the highest vocation of the Germans becomes for Heidegger an expression of "'politics' in the highest and authentic sense"—what Heidegger in his *Black Notebooks* would term "metapolitics" (GA 39: 214; GA 94: 115–116, 124). There, Heidegger writes:

> *The end of "philosophy."*—We must bring it to an end and thereby prepare what is wholly other—metapolitics.

What emerges out of this "metapolitics 'of' the German Volk" is a deeply political appropriation of Hölderlin's poetry for a nonmetaphysical *mythos* of an other beginning of/in history. Within such a history, Heidegger positions the Germans as the saviors of the West. As he puts forward this metapolitical vision it is the German *Volk* that stands out as playing a singular and exceptional role in preparing "the transformation of beyng," one in which "only the German can say and poetize being in a new, originary way" (GA 95: 18; GA 94: 27, 95). Throughout his career Heidegger will repeat his messianic-nationalist claims that it is "the Germans alone" who await the task of "accepting the distant injunction of the beginning," one bequeathed to them by the ancient Greeks.

Authorized by Hölderlin's poetic word to offer a nonmetaphysical pathway out of the first Greek beginning, Heidegger turns to the German future to think through what he initially termed "the complete otherness of the second beginning" (BN I: 243/GA 94: 333). During the early 1930s Heidegger would refer multiple times to this possibility of "a second beginning" of thinking, one that he understood as pure possibility, a beginning whose very inception eludes the historicizing proclivities of modern scientific-technological thinking (BN I: 153–156, 171, 173, 175–176, 178, 243/GA 94: 209–213, 234, 236, 239, 241, 244). This possibility, as Heidegger thinks it, cannot be historically calculated in terms of a "utopian" future. Even less can it take the shape of a political program of reform. At root, the other beginning endures as a revolutionary hope for what exceeds human capability, a hope whose coming cannot be engineered or calculated in advance. The time of the other beginning, rather, comes to us as revolutionary and transformative; it is marked by suddenness and by the abrupt scission and tear that Hölderlin himself characterizes as "die reissende Zeit," "the time that tears."[36] For Hölderlin it is this kairological time of revolution and transformation that bespeaks the time of the gods' coming.

What Heidegger draws from this Hölderlinian encounter with the time of the gods' coming is a powerful sense of Germany's destinal mission to save the West by coming into its proper sense of national identity, an identity characterized by an alien homecoming. Such a homecoming, Heidegger contends, can happen only through a poetic-philosophical dialogue with the ancient Greeks. Only by journeying outward from the German *Heimat* into the strange otherness of the Greek beginning, a journeying prefigured in Hölderlin's famous Böhlendorff letter, can the German *Volk* come into its ownmost and proper sense of its authentic identity (E&L: 207/DKV III: 459–462). For Heidegger this journey outward from the home into the foreign occurs as a way "to learn from the foreign for the sake of what is one's own" (HHI: 132–133/GA 53: 165–166). Such a journey "names the law of being un-homely as a law of becoming homely." This vision of what I will call "an alien homecoming" constitutes a "law of history" for Heidegger, one that appears as "the essential law of Western and German humankind" (HHI: 137/GA 53: 170). It is this theme of an alien homecoming to Hölderlin's poetic hymns that will constitute the focus of this book. In chapter 1 I will provide the background necessary to understand the historical-philosophical situation of Heidegger's "Hölderlin" by going back to the influence of Norbert von Hellingrath, the George circle, and the legend of a "secret Germany." I will then situate Heidegger's reading of *Hölderlin's Hymns "Germania" and "The Rhine"* by positioning it against the failure of Heidegger's Rectorial Address and how in these hymns Heidegger finds a "metapolitical" form of an authentic apolitical politics of the homeland. In chapter 2, I take up this theme of an alien homecoming by offering a reading of Heidegger's WS 1941–1942 lecture course *Hölderlin's Hymn "Remembrance."* There I explore how, in his reading of the poem "Andenken," Heidegger reflects on Hölderlin's journey to Bordeaux from Swabia against the logic of the Böhlendorff letter and its law of history as a journeying into the foreign as a return marked by an alien homecoming. While exploring Hölderlin's sojourn in southern France, one that he understands as a kind of journeying to the ancient Greeks, Heidegger underlines the significance of "the experience of the foreign" as what remains essential to any proper homecoming. Homecoming here is always understood as a homecoming to what is one's own; but, at the same time, it also involves a homecoming that is foreign to one's own—since, Heidegger contends, at the heart of the homely lies something un-homely, uncanny, strange, and alien. It is in this sense that I speak of Heidegger's Hölderlin lectures as an "alien homecoming" since, according to this peculiar logic, the proper comes to itself only in its coming into the foreign. Chapter 3 offers a reading of Heidegger's SS 1942 lecture course *Hölderlin's Hymn "The Ister"* and continues with the theme of an alien homecoming to highlight the war years. Chapter 4 suggests a historical bridge to understand and properly situate Heidegger's dialogue, "The Western Conversation" (1946–48), the focus of chapter 5. These two chapters present a view into the postwar changes within Heidegger's earlier *Hölderlinbild*. Here, Heidegger's own Swabian heritage comes to play an inordinate role in the way he conceives of this postwar German situation.

 This turn to Hölderlin is not to be understood, however, as a nostalgic return to a simpler time of unity and un-alienated oneness. On the contrary, what Heidegger learns from Hölderlin is the profound experience of separation, scission, and alienation that lies at the heart of all homecoming. Heidegger locates the source of such a scission in

Sophocles's choral ode from *Antigone* where he finds a reenactment of the tragic law of all alien homecoming—namely, that only by becoming homely within our home can we ever come to a proper sense of how it is utterly pervaded by the un-homely. As he reflects on Sophocles's chiastic pairings of *hypsipolis/apolis: pantoporos/aporos*, Heidegger claims that it is only by being alienated from the hearth of the home that we become homely in being un-homely. It is this *deinos* character of our being that pervades the human sojourn upon the earth as one marked by an alien homecoming. That is, in its dwelling at home in the hearth of its own settlement, the human being is simultaneously marked by an uncanny, strange, and unsettling force that renders it alien to itself, unhomely in its home. As Heidegger puts it in the Ister lectures: "The human being in its own essence is a *katastrophe*—a reversal that turns it away from its own essence" (HHI: 77/GA 53: 94).

Heidegger will undertake this journey of alien homecoming through his conversations with pre-Socratic philosophers (Anaximander, Heraclitus, Parmenides) and archaic poets (Pindar and Sophocles). Yet part of this conversation will also be mediated in and through Heidegger's dialogue with the poetic hymns of Hölderlin, whose own vision of the Greek dawn pervades Heidegger's work—especially during the 1930s and '40s. We shall see in what follows how Heidegger, in the midst of the National Socialist Hölderlin-mania of the 1930s, carves out his own singular relation to the poet, a relation that is curiously bifurcated and chiastic. On the one hand, Heidegger will distance himself from the crude political uses of Hölderlin's poetic word carried out by National Socialist partisans such as Kurt Hildebrandt, Willi Könitzer, and the contributors of politically aligned journals such as *Nationalsozialistische Monatshefte* and the *Völkischer Beobachter*.[37] In response to these crudely constructed appeals to "Hölderlin's poetry as one of the most precious avowals of the racially- and blood-bound bequest of the German soul," Heidegger will write in the *Black Notebooks*: "Hölderlin— . . . It would be better if for the next hundred years we still did not utter that name or allow it in our newspapers" (GA 94: 265). And yet, on the other hand, Heidegger will conscript "Hölderlin" in the service of his own *Heimat*-bound vision of authentic National Socialism, purged of its own machinational designs and brutal political calculus. This Hölderlinian dream of German national self-renewal and transformation will grow out of Heidegger's reaction to the devastating defeat of the First World War and the humiliation inflicted on the German *Volk* by the revanche-inspired Treaty of Versailles (GA 96: 40; GA 94: 148).

As Heidegger sees it, in our way of taking up Hölderlin's poetic word, we are faced with a decision about the future of being. On the one hand, we find the human being positioned between commemorating the first beginning and preparing for an other beginning. At the same time, we humans have lost the very thread that might help us to bind ourselves back to the event of beyng that gives itself over to us even as it withdraws into concealment.

If we are to be capable of ever corresponding to the event of beyng (in the sense of *Ent-sprechen*), Heidegger avows, then the path to such correspondence must lead to a genuine encounter and confrontation with Hölderlin. It is this encounter that marks one of the most decisive struggles in Heidegger's entire corpus. From the time of the rectorate up through the 1960s, Hölderlin will remain for Heidegger an essential conversation partner, the poet whose very name bespeaks the plight of humanity in the godforsaken world of technological machination and positionality. In this sounding of Hölderlin's poetic word, Heidegger seeks to locate a site for thinking the one thing necessary: the decision about the flight and arrival of the gods.

But it would be foolhardy to misread what Heidegger says about Hölderlin: he is not and can never become the "savior" of the German *Volk*. Such grandiose hopes serve only as a palpable example of the bankruptcy within contemporary German thinking. On the contrary, Hölderlin—or, more properly, the late hymns of Hölderlin—offer(s) an *Übergang* or transition for the German *Volk* between their historical *Untergang* or decline and their futural *Aufgang* or ascent (GA: 71, 271–272). Hölderlin's works do not and cannot of themselves save. Rather, they prepare a pathway from out of the darkness of the world's night in that they genuinely encounter the gods' failure to arrive—*der Fehl Gottes* (GA 5: 269; SPF: 82–83). Moreover, they help those who hear their word by attuning them to the profound loss and devastation of such a destitute time—its abyssal *Abgrund*—by initiating a mood of sacred mourning (*heilige Trauer*). This sacred mourning comes to us not merely as sadness at the loss and departure of the old gods; on the contrary, "it is nothing less than the sole possible, resolute readiness for awaiting the divine. . . . That the gods have fled does not mean that divinity has banished from the Dasein of human beings. Here it means that such divinity precisely prevails, yet as something no longer fulfilled, as becoming dark and overcast, yet still powerful" (GA 39: 95). Here, sacred mourning is understood less as an affective-psychological state than as what needs "to be thought in a more inceptual way as an attunement through which the silent voice of the [poetic] word attunes the essence of the human being in its relation to being" (GA 54: 157). This focus on the inceptual force of sacred mourning will constitute one of the essential themes of chapter 1 focused on *Hölderlin's Hymns "Germania" and "The Rhine."*

In a profound and essential sense, then, sacred mourning is far more than a subjective response to a condition of loss; it emerges, rather, as a preparatory attunement for a transition to an other beginning for thinking. By granting access to what has vanished from the earth, sacred mourning attunes us to the temporal happening of *remembrance* or *Andenken*: "not a mere making-present (*Vergegenwärtigung*) of something past (*Vergangenen*)" but a "commemorative thinking (*Andenken*) of what has been (*das Gewesene*) as the not yet unfolded" of a futural coming (GA 4: 16, 100). Remembrance, in this sense, thinks futurally from out of that which has been—but not in any traditional philosophical or scientific way. Rather, remembrance comes to us as a decision concerning the absconding and arrival of the gods. But again, this decision is not a moral-anthropological one. It manifests itself not in any straightforward "historiological" way (*historisch*) but emerges out of the scission of gods/humans within the history of beyng (*Seynsgeschichte*), one that lets the appropriative event come into play. And since beyng eventuates as withdrawal, concealment, refusal, restraint, and mystery, it is hardly surprising that the thinking and commemoration of what is coming must forego the metaphysics of presence to attune itself to the absencing/absconding of the gods. Within the history of beyng, this departure of the gods properly occurs as a decision "of" being and it is in response to such a decision that Heidegger's reading of Hölderlin's poetic word will unfold.

In the early years of National Socialist rule, Heidegger believed in the proximate possibility of a revolution in German Dasein that would help to usher in "the empowerment of being" (GA 94: 36, 37, 43, 45, 62). This empowerment would entail not the mere empowerment of beings or of individual subjects, but of being itself (GA 94: 57, 45, 40). That meant above all that philosophy could not initiate this revolution, nor could it steer it onto an originary path for the *Volk*. All philosophy could do is to *prepare* the way for such a revolution through incessant questioning. The Greeks were the first to engage in "the relentless questioning struggle concerning the essence and being of beings." This beginning by the Greeks "still is," Heidegger insists; "it brought about a wholly new attunement in whose resonance we still stand" (GA 36/37:

8). As Heidegger conceives it, this Greek beginning fell into oblivion starting with the work of Plato and Aristotle. Over the course of two millennia and more, the history of this oblivion has only intensified, culminating in the machinational dominion over beings set into place by the early modern philosophical revolution in science. What emerges from this bleak antimodern diagnosis of modernity's spiritual bankruptcy is nothing less than a vision of a new German task and vocation: to recommence what the Greeks once commenced in the first beginning. Such a task, Heidegger insists, constitutes "the innermost and utmost charge of the Germans" (GA 94: 66).

This dream of German greatness, nourished on the energy of the political revolution of 1933, would founder, however, on the failure of the movement itself and on Heidegger's disastrous experiment as rector of Freiburg University. The miscarriage of the National Socialist revolution, its failure to confront the unbridled dominion of planetary technology by authentically rooting the *Volk* in the homeland, leads Heidegger to seek a purer form of revolutionary, national transformation that he finds in the poetic language of Hölderlin. It was in Hölderlin alone that Heidegger uncovered an essential turn back into the inceptual, a turn that would keep the promise of the futural revolutionary power of the Germans. Yet one of the lessons that Heidegger learned from the failures of the National Socialist experiment was that it would take time to prepare the way for a genuine revolution. Even after the trauma of the German defeat and his denazification tribunal, Heidegger would still cling to Hölderlin—but now with the awareness that it would require an immense amount of work to begin to genuinely hear his word. Writing in January 1946, Heidegger confesses:

> I have the feeling that a hundred years of concealment are still needed until one has an inkling of what awaits us in Hölderlin's poetry. (GA 97: 70)

II. Philosophical "Andenken": Hölderlin as the Voice of the Other Beginning

What endures during the period of Heidegger's Hölderlin writings that constitute the focus of this book (1934–1948) is a fundamental question: can a space be opened for inceptual thinking? Moreover, can Hölderlin's poetry help us to open such a space? Throughout all the changes of Heidegger's complex and labyrinthine *Denkweg*, through the political disappointments, the *Auseinandersetzung* with planetary technology, the thinking of the history of beyng, the reflections on art and poetry, Hölderlin remains *the* voice that Heidegger hears as he attempts to reflect on the authentic task and mission of the German *Volk*. As Heidegger continually emphasizes, Hölderlin's poetic word "prepares the other beginning of the history of beyng" (GA 70:167). Moreover, considered in its beyng-historical sense, Hölderlin's word provides nothing less than "a *transition* from the first beginning into the other beginning," a transition from the destitution of a world in which the gods have fled into a world that prepares itself for their return (GA 70: 167). And in this delicate and difficult relation between the first beginning and the other beginning, Hölderlin teaches the Germans to ready themselves for this leap by preparing the *Anlauf* (running start) through an attuned form of *Andenken* (remembrance). In this way *Andenken* becomes essential for Heidegger as a form of *commemorative thinking of* a beginning whose inception is still to come, a beginning that remains as a beginning only in its coming. As Heidegger puts it, "such *Andenken* springs forth from out of a dialogue of thinking with poetizing," a dialogue whose very meaning lies in granting a site for humans to dwell in a poetic relation to the earth.

In his own inimitable way, Hölderlin concerned himself with the fate of language in an epoch where the gods had fled. Reflecting on the beyng-historical significance of this plight, Heidegger comes to think it precisely through Hölderlin's topoi of "homecoming" and "poetic dwelling"—of the human being's "Aufenthalt" or sojourn upon the earth ("Der Rhein," vv. 127–129). It is by confronting "the bounds / Which God at birth assigned / To him for his term and site" (Der Rhein, vv. 127–129) that the human being comes to its own proper *ethos* or sense of dwelling/abiding the destinal dispensation granted to it by history (SPF: 202–203). Yet the bounds of human life are not the only bounds within which Dasein finds itself. On the contrary, there are epochal lines of partition granted by the history of beyng that shape the destiny of those, like Heidegger, who understand history in terms of homecoming and the advent of the gods. These lines of partition fall outside the sphere of philosophical engagement; their power derives from a *mythos* about the history of beyng shaped by Hölderlin's own *mythos* concerning the departure and the arrival of the gods. Heidegger's elegiac lament—"we come too late for the gods and too early for being"—echoes throughout his work as a way of characterizing this epochal transition "between the times" (GA 97: 54–55; GA 13: 76). And only insofar as the human being addresses the gods' departure in the spirit of sacred mourning, and only to the extent that it prepares itself for the return of the gods in a comportment (*Verhalten*) of reserve and restraint (*Verhaltenheit*), will the opening for the other beginning properly occur (*sich ereignen*). But again, the path to such an opening cannot be engineered, nor is it a matter of sheer waiting. Letting the opening appear will properly occur only insofar as human beings are appropriated to the event of such an opening, an e-vent that comes as a *remembrance*. Here *Andenken* does not *re*present something past as what lies behind the poet in the realm of memory or reminiscence. Rather, it stands before him as both a task and "decision concerning the essence and vocation of the Germans and therewith the destiny of the West" (GA 95: 18).

The poetic power of *Andenken* lies in enacting a living relation between past and future as well as between what is local and native *and* what is strange and foreign. For Heidegger, this poetic sense of *Andenken* provides a way of thinking (*denken*) *toward* (*an*) this dynamic movement between past and future, future and past, that is never uni-directional but always a back-and-forth oscillation between what has been and what is coming. The encounter with Hölderlin comes to constitute a deeply mindful reflection on the history of thinking understood against and in terms of the history of beyng. Because the Germans have not yet been able to embrace Hölderlin as "*the* poet of poets," they have been unable to connect with their futural task and calling. Moreover, if the Germans fail to heed this calling, Heidegger concludes, then their own failure would constitute not merely a national fate but would encompass the fate of the entire Occident. In this way, Heidegger goes back and forth between offering his devastating critique of modern machinational existence and holding out hope for the coming to self-awareness of the German *Volk* that will "save the West." As he puts it in his Heraclitus lectures of SS 1943:

> The greatest and the authentic trial of the Germans is at hand, that trial . . . whether they, the Germans, are in accord with the truth of beyng, whether beyond their readiness to die they are strong enough to save what is inceptual in its inconspicuous flourishing against the small-mindedness of the modern world. (GA 55: 181)

And yet, as ever in Heidegger's reflections about the fate of the modern world, it is "the Germans and only the Germans who can save the West" (GA 55: 108). During the war years it is this commission, granted to the Germans from out of the history of beyng, that animates Heidegger's own ingrained sense of a national supremacy marked by the Germans' status as a chosen people.

> We have a task. Only the question remains whether we ourselves are capable of *being* this task. Every German man has died in vain if we are not engaged hourly in saving a beginning for the German essence beyond the now utter and final self-devastation of the whole of modern humanity. (GA 96: 256)

As Heidegger confronts the devastation and destructiveness of technological modernity in all its depredatory forms, he returns to this theme of German preeminence and singularity, since it is "only the Germans who can poetize and say being in a new originary way" (GA 94: 27). As Heidegger lays out his reading of the history of beyng, the special German role within this history gets conjoined with the voice of Hölderlin. Here the name of "Hölderlin" predominates as synonymous with "the preparation of the inceptuality of the other beginning" (GA 70: 156, 167). Heidegger goes on to ask, "why is it that Hölderlin's word still has not been experienced and still yet has not been known as the voice of beyng?" This way of posing the question forcefully attests to Heidegger's own claim that his way of engaging the work of Hölderlin does not take the form of an "interpretation." Rather, he understands it as an "Aus-ein-ander-setzung" or confrontational setting-asunder that does not spring forth from his own reflections, but from what he terms "the voice of beyng" (GA 71: 337). In this affirmation that Heidegger's engagement with Hölderlin is one that proceeds from a "hearkening" to the voice of beyng, we find ourselves in the perilous waters of what Max Kommerell has called Heidegger's "Hölderlin violence."[38] If this violence were merely circumscribed within the realm of Hölderlin philology or philosophical-poetical criticism, we might be able to overlook Heidegger's tendentious reading of the poet. But Heidegger's uninterrupted conjoining of Hölderlin's work with German destiny and the future of the Fatherland extends beyond the realm of "critical" interpretation to Heidegger's own ex cathedra pronouncements that emerge from his communion with "the voice of beyng." All of these tendentious dispositions come together to render Heidegger's Hölderlin writings highly controversial, precarious, and even perhaps unsparingly "fatal."

What ultimately confronts us, then, in Heidegger's alien homecoming to Hölderlin is a crisscrossed testament to the oppositional force and contentious strife that Heraclitus identifies at the heart of being, a chiasm redolent of the Greek tragedians. There we can locate a difficult legacy of contradiction and paradox—of a deeply ethical thinker who abandons the tradition of ethics for his own *metapolitical* reading of a German *Heilsgeschichte*—a destinal history of beyng with the Germans as the only people capable of "saving the West" (GA 55: 108; EdP: 40). It is as a chiasm between an ethical attunement to the hiddenness of being *and* an overreaching errancy marked by arrogation and arrogance that Heidegger's thinking comes to us. In the Hölderlin lectures we find the difficulties of this crisscross as what marks and shapes the very movement and energy involved in thinking the authentic vocation of the German *Volk* as it comes to terms with the legacy of the first Greek beginning. Moreover, it is this chiastic structure that will mark Heidegger's Hölderlin lectures as a doubled form of an alien homecoming: both to the privileged vocation of the Germans in a *Sonderweg* version of *Seynsgeschichte* and to a poetic form of dwelling that holds forth the hope of a recovery/*Verwindung* from the machinational destiny of Western metaphysics and technology. We will need to remain attentive to the crisscrossing patterns of each of these initiatives as we trace the paradoxes that come to shape Heidegger's alien homecoming to, through, and with the poetic voice of Hölderlin. For what Heidegger's engagement with Hölderlin offers is nothing less than the brutal contradictions of his own National Socialist metapolitics of "poetic dwelling." Yet, given all of these chiastic crossings and double movements, we are pressed to ask: who *is* Heidegger's Hölderlin?

III. Who Is Heidegger's Hölderlin?

To follow all the twists, turns, bends, detours, and dramatic divagations along the path of Heidegger's life journey with Hölderlin would require the skills of a master navigator schooled in the practice of philosophical reflection and poetic imagination, as well as in the subtle arts of theatrical self-staging and -presentation.[39] Heidegger did not simply read

Hölderlin and offer commentary on his work. He needed Hölderlin as the "mouthpiece" (*Sprachrohr*) for a new and radical form of thinking, a poetic-philosophical attempt to open up a language that would be able to "turn back," "get over," or "recover from" (*verwinden*) the language of Western metaphysics.[40] Reinhard Mehring goes so far as to claim that in 1934 Heidegger donned a "Hölderlin mask that required the grand staging of regularly scheduled lectures."[41] Yet no matter how cynically or innocently we read Heidegger's Hölderlin reception, it is hard to separate the idiosyncratically political use of Hölderlin from the various attempts at Heideggerian self-staging. As Mehring sees it, Heidegger's own language becomes "rhapsodic" in its engagement with the texts of Hölderlin taking on the character of a poetic-thinkerly song announcing the dawn of a new age. But whether we read Heidegger's distinctive voice throughout his Hölderlin lectures naïvely, critically, reverently, or condescendingly, it is difficult not to notice its singular character. Heidegger does not simply "comment" on Hölderlin's poems, as if he were engaged in the academic work of interpretation, exegesis, or critique. There is a unique style and tone to the lectures that emerges out of Hölderlin's own distinctive language and yet is unmistakably Heideggerian. Anyone who has heard the disc recordings of his Hölderlin readings can attest to the inimitable timbre, resonance, and inflection of Heidegger's voice with its dramatic, if not prophetic, tone quality.[42] Heidegger enters into the world of the poet in hallowed tones, opening himself and his listeners to a fundamental attunement that does not follow the lines of calculative reckoning but beckons us to the hidden possibility of poetic dwelling. Throughout the Hölderlin lectures, this form of dwelling will take different shapes. During the mid-1930s it will take the form of a radically German *Kampfgemeinschaft* or "community of struggle" in battle with the forces of Western enlightenment rationality; by the postwar period, however, Heidegger will have shifted ground and will come to speak of a non-nationalistic form of Hölderlinian dwelling as "a destinal belongingness to other peoples" (PM: 257/GA 4: 337–338).

Yet throughout all of the political shifts—from his early enthusiasm for the National Socialist revolution (1933) through his despair in 1945–1946 on to his postwar revival and triumph in the 1950s–1960s—the role of Hölderlin in his thinking will remain essential. Heidegger expressed the fundamental tenets of this Hölderlinian faith in one of his entries from *Contributions to Philosophy*:

The historical destiny of philosophy culminates in the knowledge of the necessity [*Notwendigkeit*] of making Hölderlin's word be heard. The ability to hear corresponds to an ability to say, which speaks out of the question-worthiness of beyng. For this is the least that must be accomplished in preparing a space for the word. (If everything were not perverted into a "scholarly contribution" marked by a "literary-historical" approach, then one would have to say that a preparation for thinking must be created in order to interpret Hölderlin. To "interpret" here does not mean making "understandable"; instead it means to ground the projection of the truth of his poetry in the meditation and attunement in which futural Dasein sways.) (CP: 334 /GA 65: 422)

Heidegger continues to deny that his way of engaging Hölderlin takes the form of an "interpretation." Rather, he understands it as an "*Auseinander-setzung*" or "confrontation" with Hölderlin that does not spring forth from his own reflections, but from "the voice of beyng":

for this thinking about Hölderlin is a kind of "setting-asunder" (*Auseinander-setzung*), which is, however, again taken in a beyng-historical sense and not as a wrangling about what is and is not correct. This is a "setting-asunder" of historical necessities in their historicity; in this sense, it is not a "thetically imposed" arrangement (*veranstaltete"Setzung"*) from us but, rather, an obedient listening to the voice of beyng. (GA 71: 336–337)

But how are we, as obedient listeners, to find our proper relation to "the voice of beyng"? And who might be able to discern whether the echoes that we hear in Hölderlin's words stem from our own historical position or from that of beyng itself? Heidegger's posture of prophetic intimacy with the word of Hölderlin made some of his listeners extremely uneasy already in the 1930s. Among fellow National Socialists, the critique of Heidegger's "Hölderlin and the Essence of Poetry" (1936) was immediate. In 1937, Dr. Willi Könitzer published a "response" to Heidegger's essay in *Wille und Macht*, "the leading Organ of National Socialist Youth" edited by the NS Minister of Youth Affairs, Baldur von Schirach. Könitzer, who praises Hölderlin as "the German poet whose work was just as much a deed as the sacrificial deed of [World War I] heroes whose spirit he celebrates in song," finds Heidegger's rendering of Hölderlin troublesome. Könitzer charges that "Herr Professor Heidegger wants to interpret Hölderlin's poetic work and the essence of poetry on the basis of five arbitrarily chosen words, which do not interpret the work of the poet in the spirit of devoting himself to that work. Rather, he employs the means of a language that, in its essence, is wholly foreign to us and he does so with the methods of a philosophical orientation for which at the very least we can find no trace in Hölderlin."[43] Könitzer then attacks Heidegger for being too attached to his own *Weltanschauung* and its goals. Against Heidegger's vision, he claims, "We want to view Hölderlin in light of *the experience of a whole Volk*, not in the obscure gloom of the academy's departmental clubs. The poet who stands close to the Volk (not = popular!) belongs to the Volk (not = masses!), and whoever seeks to serve him, opens the path to understanding him." For orthodox National Socialists such as Könitzer, Heidegger's own cryptic language threatened to bury the *völkish* pronouncements of Hölderlin under the mantle of academic hermeticism.[44]

But even serious Hölderlin specialists such as Max Kommerell had problems with Heidegger's highly individual approach to Hölderlin's texts, finding in it an "interpretative violence" that went far beyond anything authorized by the profession of literary scholarship.[45] In a letter to Heidegger from July of 1942, Kommerell offers his thoughts on Heidegger's essay "Hölderlin's Hymn: As on a Holiday" (1941), claiming that he "does not understand the basic premise of [Heidegger's] essay." He sees immediately that what Heidegger offers here is not in any traditional sense an "interpretation" but rather a "document of [his] encounter" with Hölderlin. What emerges from this encounter, Kommerell suggests, is that Heidegger "authorizes" a "turn in/of destiny" whereby, as he tells Heidegger, "the destiny that is Hölderlin reveals itself as that destiny for which you stand." Here Kommerell penetrates to the core of Heidegger's *Hölderlinbild* in that he questions the very basis of Heidegger's approach, asking him on whose authority does he make claims that burst forth as ex cathedra pronouncements, pronouncements which, like Hölderlin's own oracular utterances, appear to resemble the entreaties of a prophet: "Where is the transition point where your own philosophy flows into Hölderlin and where, in such a decisive way, from out of your description of the human situation, does it become a metaphysical pronouncement marked by an absolutely final certainty?" Kommerell recognizes the brilliance of Heidegger's approach and the singular significance of his thinkerly contributions, yet he remains troubled by Heidegger's assumption of a prophetic role that seems to him ill-suited to the time. As he closes his letter to Heidegger, Kommerell comes to his final observation: "After so much candor, let me risk one last thing: Your essay could be—I do not say it is—it could very well be a disaster!?"

Kommerell's insights remain striking even after the long trail of commentary on Heidegger's work. He recognizes the abiding tension in Heidegger's Hölderlin essays between their interpretive violence and their philosophical profundity, a tension that shapes so much of Heidegger's work on the poet and that we will have to explore in the coming chapters. But Kommerell also discerns another crucial feature of Heidegger's approach—namely, how Hölderlin's prophetic voice in the poems will be transformed and metamorphosed into Heidegger's own form of philosophical prophecy bound up with the power of myth and the call of the gods, forces that decidedly fall outside the realm of both literary-historical scholarship and academic philosophy. Hans-Georg Gadamer touches on such a reading in his remark that "it was Hölderlin who first loosened Heidegger's tongue" (FS: 51/GA 15: 351).[46] Through Hölderlin, Heidegger opened himself to the powerful insight that "language is the supreme event of human existence" (EHP: 58/GA 4: 40). Moreover, he came to see language as the domain in which we stand nearest to the mystery of being, hearkening to its hidden resonances in a way that we are brought into being's sway, appropriated to its own way of holding us in its playful, yet dangerous, way of manifesting. In fundamental Hölderlinian words—earth, homeland, the holy, beyng, the gods, dwelling, destiny, conversation, danger, event, destitution, nearness, flight, measure, the open, beginning, sign, coming, transition, turning—Heidegger unearths a nonmetaphysical possibility for doing philosophy in an originary, poetic way. Authorized by Hölderlin as it were, Heidegger now finds a new voice that abandons the academic jargon of *Being and Time* for a new thinkerly means of expression that seeks "a genuine revolution in our relation to language" (GA 40: 57). What begins to emerge in his first Hölderlin lectures and talks comes to fruition in the still private manuscripts *Beiträge zur Philosophie* and *Besinnung* that offer a new way of speaking, one highly influenced by a Hölderlinian inflection.

In these years during the mid-1930s Heidegger attempts to achieve something that, analogously, Nietzsche ventured in *Thus Spoke Zarathustra*:

a prophetic voice that seeks to deconstruct the authority of all other prophets by authorizing its own form of "saying" (*Sage*). If Zarathustra becomes a "Wahrsager" ("prophet" or, more literally, "truth-teller") for a distinctive and new kind of truth, then we can also say that Heidegger, in attuning himself to the language of Hölderlin's late hymns, likewise becomes a "Wahrsager" authorized by Hölderlin's own voice.[47] Kommerell recognizes this profound transformation in Heidegger's language, one that involves Heidegger in an "event of appropriation" (*Ereignis*) whereby "Hölderlin became [for Heidegger] an inescapable destiny."[48] In the years just after he finishes his cycle of university lectures on the poet, Heidegger attempts to write in a wholly new idiom: the dialogue form. In 1946/1948 he composes "Das abendländische Gespräch"—a lengthy conversation between an "old man" and a "young man" about the meaning of Hölderlin for the contemporary situation in postwar Europe. As the young man puts it, "in the poetry of Hölderlin the possibility of another appearance of beyng awaits us, a possibility that can not be accomplished through willing," but only through a releasement toward our destiny, a *Gelassenheit* that honors the mystery of beyng's way of withdrawal, concealment, withholding, and dispossession (GA 75: 81). This comportment of honoring the mystery of things that we do not understand abides as Heidegger's Hölderlinian release toward the "destiny of beyng" (GA 75: 82). Many see in this Heideggerian comportment a kind of hermetic mysticism or authoritarian arrogance that cloaks itself in a language of destinal inevitability, one that relieves Heidegger of any political responsibility for the notorious "error" of his National Socialist affiliation. And yet we can also find here a new kind of ethical thinking, a poetic *ethos* of dwelling authentically upon the earth that calls us to our originary home in being, an *ethos* marked by a deep responsibility to being's own way of self-disclosure in/as concealment.

IV. Language, "Ethos," and the Ethicality of Being

Before we take up this question of poetic dwelling, however, we will need to address these underlying tensions in Heidegger's appropriation of Hölderlin. Heidegger himself understands this appropriation as Hölderlin's word calling to him in a "primordial calling that is itself called by that which is coming (*das Kommende*)" (EHP: 98/GA 4: 77). There are deeply ethical moments in Heidegger where we are confronted by the uncanny polarities of human being, those irreconcilable tensions that render us as beings in kinship with both gods and beasts. Heidegger's interpretation of Sophocles's *Antigone* chorus—in both *Introduction to Metaphysics* (1935) and *Hölderlin's Hymn "The Ister"* (1942)—attempts to explore these polarities in terms of the uncanny (*un-heim-liche*) violence at the heart of human attempts to find a home (*Heimat*) within being. What emerges from Heidegger's reflections on Antigone's fate is a deep distrust of any "ethical" pronouncements about human comportment. What Heidegger unearths here is a deeply metaphysical impulse to erect rules, principles, and directives that set "standards" (*Maßstäbe*) for human behavior that will be binding in advance. These kinds of calculative measures wind up detaching human beings from their specific historical ground, uprooting them from the earth and rendering them as useful pieces that fit within the system of the *Gestell*, a "positionality" that positions whatever is present.[49] From his earliest lectures in Freiburg, Heidegger understood ethics in an Aristotelian sense as intimately bound up with what Aristotle termed "rhetoric." Rhetoric in this sense involves becoming attuned to the unique, ever-changing temporal contexts/moods that shape our understanding of language in its practical, concrete situatedness in the world. Rhetoric speaks to these moods, highlighting their kairological significance and rooting speech in the habits, familiar practices and ways of dwelling that constitute our world. Here Heidegger comes to understand language as intimately bound up with our *ethos*, our habitual haunts (*ethea*) and ways of abiding in the abode granted to us in our dwelling. For him, language is the genuine abode (*ethos*) of human beings, the place where we belong and that we share with other beings. Language forms our very sense of community and of our belonging to a specific people in a historical epoch, situating us in terms of that people's historical destiny.[50]

Since so much depends upon how we engage language and since, in the present epoch our language has been threatened by the very technicity that weaves all beings into instrumental units comprising a great web of cybernetic information, Heidegger deems it essential that we rethink our relation to language. But, as Heidegger reminds us, "we are not yet underway to [language]. We must first turn back to that place where we already properly abide (*eigentlich aufhalten*)" (GA 12: 179). But we can only come to such a place if we can "find in the proximity of poetic experience with the word a possibility for a *thinking* experience with language," since it is precisely this proximity "that everywhere pervades our sojourn (*Aufenthalt*) upon this earth" (GA 12: 177–178). What matters above all to Heidegger here is that we become attuned to the language of the poet and let it appropriate us to our authentic belongingness to being where we come to experience language as our proper home, "the house of being" (PM: 239, 274/GA 9: 313, 361). Poetry, especially the poetry of Hölderlin who poetizes the essence of poetry as the poet's highest vocation, can help "human beings find the way to their abode (*Aufenthalt*) in the truth of being." As such an abode, poetic dwelling takes the form of an *ethos* where we are held open (*aufhalten*) to the withholding (*vor-enthalten*) event of being. Language, as our proper *ethos*, becomes a deeply ethical concern for Heidegger especially as a way of measuring our responsibility for being and for recognizing the claim (*Anspruch*) that language (*Sprache*) makes upon us. But despite its ubiquitous presence in our lives as a means of communication, and as an instrument for speech that makes things accessible to us, "language still denies us its essence" (PM: 243/GA 9: 318). As Hyperion puts it in a letter to Diotima:

> Men chatter like birds . . . but believe me, and consider that
> I say to you from the depths of my soul: Language is a great
> superfluity. (H: 159/DKV II: 131–132)

But language's proper essence (*Wesen*), the way that it prevails essentially (*west*), occurs as a "saying" (*Sagen*) that relinquishes (*ent-sagen*) its propriety into that which is improper. If we were to say this in German, we might say something like this: "Die Sprache west nicht einfach als ein Sagen, sondern als ein Ent-Sagen (language essentially occurs not simply as a 'say-ing,' but as the withholding/renunciation of say-ing)." This movement of withdrawal, concealment, withholding, and recession belongs to language as that which is most proper to it, that which is its own. Poetry, as the primordial form of language, that which makes language possible, does not deny this concealment or simply try to "overcome" it by transforming concealment into revelation (GA 4: 43). Rather, poetry discloses this concealment *as* concealment, or that which ever recedes from human machination and control, the hidden dimension of the earth that makes the artwork possible in the world of human dwelling.

In our quotidian exchanges with language, what takes precedence are topics of immediate interest, daily occurrences, questions, and concerns.

But "in everyday speech what does *not* come to language is language itself; rather, it holds itself back" (OWL: 59/GA 12: 151). Poetry opens language to this hidden dimension of its self-withholding, a dimension that expresses the very play of truth as *a-letheia*, the struggle/strife of unhiddenness and hiddenness. Here, poetic truth will be understood as "ethical" in a new and radical sense that breaks with the metaphysical discipline of ethics. If traditional ethics begins with the subject as the autonomous self who, of its own volitional power, renders judgments and decisions, Heidegger's *ethos* presupposes our historical belongingness to a world that is not of our own making, a world in which we already find ourselves as thrown entities and not as masters of our domain. This is what Heidegger in *Being and Time* termed our attunement/disposition (*Befindlichkeit*) and thrownness (*Geworfenheit*) (BT: 130–145/SZ: 134–149). *Ethos* here will be understood as our abode, our sojourn upon the earth (*Aufenthalt*), that is not a permanent character trait that belongs to us but much more a movement within which we find ourselves belonging to a destiny that Hölderlin termed "the bounds which God at birth assigned to [us] for [our] term and site" (SPF: 202–203). *Ethos*, then, as our proper abode, is language. Language is the proper place, *Ort*, or abode where being dwells, its "house," as Heidegger so famously put it in "The Letter on Humanism" (PM: 219/GA 9: 313). This means nothing less than that being itself (although, of course, there is no subjective genre here) is deeply ethical—but in a different sense than that in traditional metaphysics. I follow Jean-Luc Nancy here in taking Heidegger's thinking as "a fundamental ethics"—that is, a thinking that attempts to think not an ethics for the human being but the very ethicality of being.[51] Here being is understood not as a substance but as an *event*, understood etymologically from its Latin roots in *venir*, as a "coming" whose advent always exceeds the possibility of arrival. Being's coming always comes even after if "arrives"; this arrival shows the promise of such coming more than it does the completion of a process whose coming is somehow "fulfilled."

In thinking the ethicality of being, however, Heidegger also rethinks traditional ethics' way of interpreting the human being. Dasein's conduct (*Verhalten*) is here understood as "the bringing into play of being."[52] In this play, to which Dasein is appropriated (*ereignet*), being grants Dasein an abode, an *Aufenthalt*, an *ethos*. But this *ethos*, as gift, happens as the bringing into play of being's own *ethos*; its own way of sojourning within the time-space-play of being as event, of manifesting itself as the unity of *ethos-physis*. Going back to the early pre-Socratics, being was understood as the unity of *physis-logos-ethos* where each word was grasped as another name for the self-generating gatheredness and play of all that is, its own way of dwelling or finding its proper haunts (*ethea*) within the world of human beings. *Ethos* and *physis* in this sense belong together as a *logos*—that is, being as self-generating coming to presence (*physis*) dwells amidst human beings (*ethos*) both in and as a gathering of all beings (*logos*) into the play of giving (that is, as Anaximander reminds us, likewise a taking-away or withdrawal). If we wish to understand what Heidegger means by *ethos*, we will need to place it against this much larger sphere of pre-Socratic reflection where *ethos-physis-logos* all become synonymous for what, in the language of metaphysics, is called "being." *Ethos* as a form of poetic dwelling, an abiding in the abode granted to us as our proper sojourn upon the earth, belongs within—and is an attunement toward—the *ethos* of beyng that "properly occurs" (*sich ereignet*) in the event of beyng (*Ereignis*). This event of appropriation can only appropriate us, however, when we are open to its claim—which is why the poetry of Hölderlin plays such a decisive role in the way that Heidegger thinks the *ethos* of beyng.

When, recalling Hölderlin, Heidegger writes that "poetically the human being dwells upon the earth," he addresses this question of the ethicality of being (PLT: 213–229/GA 7: 191–208). Already in his 1936 essay "Hölderlin and the Essence of Poetry," Heidegger would claim: "Human Dasein is in its ground 'poetic' . . . it is not something earned, but is rather a gift" (EHP: 60/GA 4: 42). Poetry brings to language this gift of dwelling, letting us enter into this *ethos* that is being's own way of appropriating us. *Ethos*, as *Aufenthalt*, means here "dwelling in the midst of beings" (GA 55: 349). Yet how do we become open to this ethicality of being? By dwelling poetically, by letting being's own *poiesis* claim us, by letting ourselves be open to this claim (*Anspruch*) that sounds in poetic language (*Sprache*). This opening of ourselves, Heidegger insists, does not involve philosophical skill or professorial devotion to the bends and turns of poetic diction. It involves, rather, a comportment (*Haltung*) that, as sojourn (*Aufenthalt*), is attuned to being's own way of holding itself in reserve (*aufbehalten*), of withholding itself (*ent-halten*) and maintaining itself in what is withheld (*Vorenthalt*). Such a *Haltung* demands *Verhaltenheit* (restraint) on the part of human beings who wish to abide (*sich aufhalten*) in the event of being as poetic dwelling. Heidegger touches on this in his comment on Heraclitus's *daimon* in "The Letter on Humanism" where he writes that "the abode (*Aufenthalt*) of the human being contains (*enthält*) and preserves the advent of what belongs to the human being in its essence" (PM: 269/GA 9: 354). Poetic dwelling brings us into nearness with the gods. But, as Heidegger understands it, the gods do not dwell in an empyrean sphere on Mt. Olympus. They abide, they hold themselves up (*sich aufhalten*), in the simple, everyday occurrences of our lives, such as warming ourselves by a stove on a cold winter's day. Yet in these familiar places of dwelling there occurs too that which is unfamiliar. The story of Heraclitus's stove reminds us that even in the most perfunctory happenings there too "the gods come to presence." There in our accustomed haunts, hidden in the ligatures of the familiar, we can follow the traces of being's way of holding us within our dwelling, the *ethos* granted to us by being.

Dasein is called to correspond to being, to heed the call that being makes to it, to respond to this call as the call to dwell poetically, that is, to dwell in correspondence with being's own poietic way of manifesting. Even though "we seldom heed the call (*Zuspruch*) of being, the correspondence to the being of beings does, to be sure, continually remain our abode (*Aufenthalt*)" (GA 11: 20). As Heidegger comes to experience the limitations of his own earlier attempts to think being in a nonmetaphysical language, he turns to the poetic word of Hölderlin:

> Hölderlin's poetry is for us a destiny. It waits for the day when mortals will correspond to it. Correspondence leads to the path of entry into the nearness of the gods who have fled: in the region of their flight, a flight that spares us. (EHP: 224/GA 4: 195)

The authentic dwelling to which Hölderlin's poetizing calls us is an *ethos* that corresponds to the ethicality of being, of being's own way of appropriating us in the great "Weltspiel" ("world-play" or "play of the world") that happens in the "mirror-play of the fourfold of heaven and earth, mortals and divinities" (GA 12: 202; GA 11:121). To dwell poetically in this Heideggerian sense means to let the play of being as *Ereignis* appropriate us to the interplay of the fourfold that "properly occurs" (*ereignet sich*) in letting ourselves correspond to being's *ethos*. Heeding the poetic word, listening to (*hören auf*) its claim upon us, we are claimed by the appeal of language in a way that prepares us to belong to (*gehören*) the holy dimension of *physis* that speaks in the poet's word. Poetry here will be understood as the play of language—which, in turn,

Heidegger interprets as the concealing play of being—the bringing into play of being's *ethos*, of poetizing being as *ethos*. This *ethos* claims Dasein as the place for its sojourn, yet only when we are poetically attuned to this sojourn, to being's own way of bringing us into the interplay of the fourfold, do we dwell poetically upon this earth.

Heidegger's Hölderlin writings attempt this radical rethinking of ethics as a nonanthropological event rather than as a specific philosophical discipline dealing with rules of behavior to be applied to human subjects. If ethics belongs to being as its most proper way of coming-to-be, then reflection on ethics moves outside the sphere of an egological enclosure to embrace the open expanse of being as an "ethical" event that appropriates us to its playful dynamic. In this way ethics is much like language—it is not "something that we have, as it were, in the same way that an automobile has its horn.—It is not we who have language; rather, language has us" (GA 39: 23). Here we might say that Hölderlin's poetry performs an "awakening" to the "all-creative" manifestation of being as nature. In his hymn "As on a holiday," Hölderlin expresses this task of corresponding to being as the vocation of the poet. Nature is "omnipresent," Hölderlin intimates; it is ever on the way to its coming (SPF: 172–174). Heidegger will draw on this Hölderlinian insight and claim that nature's "coming is the presencing of this omnipresence and so it is the essence of the 'omnipresent'" Only insofar as there are those who have intimations are there those who belong to nature and correspond to it. Those who co-respond to the wonderfully omnipresent, to the powerful, the divinely beautiful, are 'the poets'" (EHP: 78/GA 4: 55). What Heidegger will find here is a way of poetizing that does not fit within the preordained categories of "logic"-"physics"-"ethics" that have dominated the language of Western metaphysics. Rather, such poetizing offers a nonmetaphysical thinking of these categories so that logic can be thought back to its original ground as *logos* (the self-gathering gatheredness of being); physics can be deconstructed back to pre-Socratic *physis* (the self-generating process of coming-to-presence and withdrawal that happens as the event of being) and ethics can be imagined as that which belongs to being as its *ethos*, its way of abiding or dwelling in the abode that is language. Hölderlin becomes so crucial to Heidegger's thinking about ethics here because he offers him a way to move out of the realm of subjectivity to think ethics as that which has us. Again, Heidegger expresses something of this in his very first Hölderlin lectures where he begins to grapple with a new language of being as event and of poetry as a way of properly opening ourselves toward this event. On the contrary, our proper way of dwelling upon the earth has nothing to do with any kind of human achievement. Our proper way of beyng is "poetic"—whereby we need to understand the poetic not as a mode of literary refinement or as a belletristic sensibility; rather, as Heidegger puts it, "the poetic . . . is an exposure to beyng and as such exposure is the fundamental occurrence of the historical Dasein of the human being" (GA 39: 36).

But there is an even more essential dimension of poetic dwelling at stake in Heidegger's notion of *ethos*: *ethos* as a way of our dwelling poetically that co-responds to the *ethos* of being that is itself a *poiesis*, in the sense of an originary making of the world. Heidegger at times clandestinely alludes to this broadly imagined vision of being's *poiesis* whereby being poetizes/founds all that is as a barely heard "world-poem" (*Welt-Gedicht*) that only the poet hears. Writing to Hannah Arendt in 1950, Heidegger gives voice to this hidden, poetic dimension of being by posing a fundamental question:

| And who corresponds | *Und wer entspricht* |
| to the poem that is the world? | *das Welt-Gedicht?* |

(GA 81: 274)

Beyond this, Heidegger asks, "Whose ear is awake for this poem?" (GA 81: 275). In the age of the *Gestell*, such hearing is rendered well-nigh impossible by the constant clamor and tumult of the world-machine that produces information and minute-to-minute newsflashes. But Heraclitus in Fragment B52 had understood *physis* as a "Welt-Spiel" (the play of the world), a game in which the human being was a co-player in the "play of the world" (GA 46: 203). Moreover, Hölderlin had taken up this Heraclitean image and rendered it as a poietic form of play, a poem of being as it were in the fullness of its unfolding. What the early Greeks had experienced in the rhythmic, countervailing currents of *physis'* mode of revelation/concealment, Hölderlin had imagined for a futural Germany. This is why Heidegger could designate him "the poet of the other beginning" (GA 70: 160). Hölderlin was alone among poets in his ethical attunement to a Heraclitean *ethos* of dwelling in nearness to the gods. But he also understood that the possibility of such dwelling had been altered by the flight of the gods from the earth and the reign of human faithlessness in the age of the world's night. This Hölderlinian scheme of the history of the West as a journey from daylight (poetic dwelling in nearness to the gods) to night (falling away from our belonging to the earth) that awaits a turning toward the rebirth of a new day of the gods' return will ultimately provide Heidegger with the outlines for his own sketch of the history of being.

Heidegger follows Hölderlin in envisioning (and calling for) a radical turn within human history. In this way, his thinking appears revolutionary. Yet Hölderlin was deeply skeptical about the power of human beings to initiate this change of their own power and volition. As he conceived it, only *physis* itself could bring about such change, for—as he put it in "As on a holiday"—*physis* is older than the ages / And higher than the gods of Orient and Occident" (SPF: 172–175). No calculative planning or cybernetic innovation could engineer this revolutionary turn within human history. Heidegger follows Hölderlin here as well in claiming that "the human being is not the master of beings. The human being is the shepherd of being" (PM: 260–261/GA 9: 342). This means that we need to rethink our role as Cartesian subjects armed with the instruments of *techne*, who strive to become "masters and possessors of nature."[53] As Heidegger so famously put it in his "Spiegel Interview": "Only a god can still save us" (HCW: 107/GA 16: 671–672). Such a claim is double-edged: on the one hand, we are powerless; on the other, we need to acknowledge this powerlessness and turn our attention to the task at hand of preparing for the futural arrival of such a god. Facing this perplexity, Heidegger acknowledged that "we cannot bring forth [a god] through our thinking; we can at most awaken the readiness of expectation." The task of thinking in the time "between the times" of the gods' withdrawal and their coming again involves nothing less than "the construction of the most proximate foyers in whose spatial structure the word of Hölderlin can be heard" (CP: 333/GA 65: 421). Hölderlin's poetic word "calls out in the turning of time," turning us toward our proper task of making ready for a new advent by "preparing a sojourn (*Aufenthalt*) in nearness to the gods" (EHP: 226, 224/GA 4: 195, 197).

Everything depends upon this alone: that in hearkening to the words of the poet we come to find a dwelling place, an abode or *ethos* that co-responds to the *ethos* of being. This is Heidegger's radical, revolutionary insight: that ethics, as it is currently constituted, is metaphysically bankrupt and that what is called for is a new *ethos* of the ethical rooted not in human values and measurements, but in the more originary *ethos* of poetic dwelling in the nearness of being. Here Hölderlin's poetry comes to exceed its standing as a work of "literature" and becomes an originary *poiesis* of being's own poetic self-manifestation. For what comes to be in Hölderlin's poetry, claims Heidegger, "is learning to become at home in nearness to the origin." Here Hölderlin's *poiesis* does not merely bring us into dwelling in nearness to being; rather, it *is* this dwelling itself. That is, as a form of *poiesis* it is the *poiesis* of being as the event of appropriation whereby, in hearkening to its call, we come to our proper home in being via the poet's word

What follows in the next several chapters is an attempt to think through this extraordinary Heideggerian reflection on Hölderlin's poetry as a *poiesis* of being rather than as a contribution to literary criticism or even as a "philosophical" interpretation of poetry. Heidegger sought more than a dialogue between poetry and philosophy. He attempted to help bring about a radical revolution of/within German Dasein as a way of helping to initiate another, more primordial revolution or "turning" within the history of being. During the euphoric months of early 1933 Heidegger set to work to bring this dream into line with the political revolution of National Socialism. But as he soon came to realize, despite this *Gleichschaltung*, the time was not yet ripe enough for a profound revolution of the *Volk*.[54] In the wake of his overwhelming disappointment at failing to guide the revolution, he turned to Hölderlin. At the same time, however, several other NS-inspired philosophers, philologists, and cultural theorists were also recruiting Hölderlin as the prophet of the "genuine" National Socialist Revolution.[55] Heidegger was especially attuned to this timely, all too timely, cultural interest in Hölderlin and wanted desperately to distinguish his own thinkerly encounter with the poet from the reigning interest of the day. In his notebooks he addresses this situation and attempts to underline the uniqueness of his own approach.

> Yes, one can even lament that here, in the thoughtful confrontation with Hölderlin's poetry, that this poetry is misused and made to fit the aims of "a particular philosophy." These laments may even be within their rights. Apart from this, there nonetheless exists the possibility of a questioning that has nothing to do with either the historiographical interpretation of this poetry or with the kind of "philosophy" carried on today but, rather, has its source in beyng itself and its history—and has its own necessity. In view of this necessity

there are no other "considerations." Here an epoch can either be in default of everything or it can reconcile itself to an originary obedience. To this obedience everything is exclusively a plight. (E: 292/GA 71: 337)

Heidegger admits in another one of his notebooks that perhaps his interpretation of Hölderlin is "wholly mistaken" and that he is constantly aware that his readings have "no presumption of absolute correctness" (GA 70: 158). What matters is not in any sense a historiographical-philological attempt to get Hölderlin "right" (whatever that could mean). Rather, everything depends on preparing us for the readiness necessary to enter into the play of being, to let being appropriate us to its playful event so that we might begin to co-respond to it and come to a form of poetic dwelling upon the earth that is open to the poietic dimension of being. Hence, Heidegger proclaims, it is necessary to ready ourselves for "the obedience of a hearkening to the voice of beyng" (GA 71: 337).

Clearly, to engage Heidegger on the work of Hölderlin is to come to terms with the palimpsest of a *Rezeptionsgeschichte* that is fraught with both risk and peril. I want to trace the lineaments of such a reception in Heidegger's relation to Hellingrath and to Heidegger's own National Socialist contemporaries and to situate his Hölderlin lectures in their specific historical context. I do so not out of any "historicist" impulse on my own part, but precisely because I believe that one of the most essential features of Heidegger's *Hölderlinbild* is its impulse to de-historicize Hölderlin and read him without his attendant historical context. Here, Heidegger reads Hölderlin apart from his belonging to the philosophical world of German idealism; he refuses to acknowledge the influence of Rousseau and of French Enlightenment culture. Moreover, Heidegger ignores (and suppresses) Hölderlin's embrace of the French revolutionary ideas of liberté-égalité-fraternité that stand so dramatically at odds with the German political revolution of 1933. Beyond this, his privileging of the late hymns at the expense of the elegies, early poems, and *Hyperion*; his inattention to metric structure and poetic form; his arbitrariness in deciding what is "essential" to the poet's work; and his ex cathedra pronouncements that emerge from his communion with "the voice of beyng"—all these tendentious dispositions come together to render Heidegger's Hölderlin writings highly controversial, perhaps untenable, and even "dangerous."[56] One cannot ignore this fundamentally precarious element in Heidegger's Hölderlin or attempt to justify it in the name of

Heidegger's unique contribution. As Max Kommerell so trenchantly put it, when one reads Heidegger, one is confronted by "the frightfulness of [his] interpretive violence."[57]

And yet, despite the persuasiveness of all these charges against Heidegger, there is an undeniable force and power in these writings that point to something essential that can hardly be approached through the traditional readings of philological scholarship. What is at stake in these writings is the promulgation of a new *mythos*, a revolutionary call to experience "a real revolution in our relationship to language" (IM: 56/GA 40: 57). What Heidegger calls for, following the tradition of the George Circle with its embrace of the *poeta vates* (the poet as prophet), is to once again imagine the possibility of abiding poetically in being, of finding our home upon the earth in an epoch of homelessness and deracination. What is at stake here for Heidegger is nothing less than the fate of the earth and of the human being's place upon the earth, configured within the fourfold gathering that is our destiny—and to which we are called. I read this to mean a fundamental revolution in ethics and the call to a new *ethos* that is more originary than the old metaphysical ethics that emerges out of the isolated human subject who thinks in values, judgments, and worldviews. Such an *ethos*, Heidegger holds, is the very expression of being itself, its way of coming to be, its *poiesis*. In this essential attunement to the ethicality of being, one prepared by the poetic word of Hölderlin, Heidegger challenges us to rethink the fundamental meaning of our existence in accord with the play of the world. Such a challenge is essential. It places us in danger. It involves the risk of shipwreck and failure. Indeed one might venture to say that perhaps Heidegger's work cannot be genuinely understood without this existential risk of failure as the condition of its possibility. As Heidegger himself put it, "He who thinks greatly, must err greatly" (GA 13: 81, 254).

For those who attempt to navigate the difficult terrain of Heidegger's "Hölderlin," it becomes necessary to attend to this danger and to this errancy. In the teeth of such danger, however, a danger to which Heidegger both leads and which he embraces, we might even begin to let this danger take us in its grasp in order to attune us to its power—the power that the poet calls "the saving power" (*das Rettende*) (SPF: 230–231). For at their most essential core, Heidegger's Hölderlin encounters take the form of a salvific promise to rescue us from the dangers of our own epoch, the age of the world wars, the threat of atomic destruction, and the danger of all dangers: our entrapment in the *Gestell* of instrumental thinking whereby we fail to recognize this danger at all.[58] Within such a danger we fall victim to the self-medicating myth of cheerful complacency and the willful self-knowledge that we are already too worldly-wise to fall victim to any possible myth about danger. Heidegger's Hölderlin speaks to us from out of the wilderness of desolation (*Verwüstung*) and destruction, calling out in the darkness of the world's night like a modern John the Baptist, proclaiming the coming of the god for which we must prepare ourselves. This is "the one thing necessary" ("das Eine was Not tut").[59] As Heidegger undergoes his own metamorphosis from an academic philosopher who writes about "a poet in a destitute time" to a Zarathustran prophet who understands himself as "a thinker in a destitute time," he calls upon us to undergo our own transformation and to respond to the call from being that he hears. As he expresses it in his very first lecture course on the poet, "The fundamental attunement must first of all be awakened. For this battle to transform the attunements that still dominate and perpetuate themselves at any given time, the first-born must be sacrificed. They are the poets who, in their saying, think in advance of their time and tell of the futural beyng of a people in their history; in so doing, they go unheard, by necessity" (GA 39: 146).

As we begin to concentrate our attention on the dangerous and errant path staked out in Heidegger's Hölderlin texts, we will need to be open to this call of awakening, this Pauline exhortation to attune ourselves to the event of the god's coming. Without this kind of readiness and preparation, their *kerygma* will likewise fall upon deaf ears. At the same time, however, it would be foolhardy to read these texts without the keen awareness of a profound default in their way and manner of performance. As we shall see, there is an unsettling political legacy at the core of these texts that Heidegger will cover over and elide in his postwar efforts at rehabilitating his legacy in the wake of the de-Nazification committee's charges at Freiburg University in 1945. Part of the difficulty, then, in coming to terms with Heidegger's Hölderlin will be to think through the essential tensions and contradictions that emerge in Heidegger's call for authentic existence and in the inauthentic re-interpretation of his own work that takes place just after the war and into the 1950s. As Maurice Blanchot so poignantly put it, "Nazism and Heidegger, this is a wound to thinking itself in which each of us is profoundly wounded."[60] In coming to terms with Heidegger's Hölderlin we risk opening that wound again, a wound whose depth ruptures all of us who engage Heidegger's willful use of Hölderlin for his own revolutionary concerns. How to balance these concerns with our own? How to appropriate the thinkerly force of Heidegger's writings without remaining blind to their own philosophical blindness? How to read Heidegger's "Hölderlin" in Heidegger's own spirit without succumbing to its own dangerous allurements?—these are the questions that will preoccupy us as we endeavor to engage Heidegger's own *Auseinandersetzung* with Hölderlin.

1

Hölderlin's Hymns "Germania" and "The Rhine"

The uniqueness of Hölderlin in the history of beyng must be established . . .

—Martin Heidegger, *Contributions to Philosophy*[1]

O eternal secret (*Geheimnis*), what we are
And what we seek, we cannot find; and what
We find, that we are not—yet what is
The hour?

—Friedrich Hölderlin, *The Death of Empedocles*[2]

I. "Hölderlin" and the Great War

The lectures that Heidegger delivers in the winter semester of 1934–1935 mark an important turning point in his path of thinking. From the very first day of the winter semester, Heidegger attempts something daring, radical, and new: a philosophical reading of Hölderlin that understands language as an originary event that opens up being while simultaneously preserving its fundamental concealedness. In these lectures, the very name "Hölderlin" comes to function as the name of a way to understand history eschatologically as a history of beyng marked by two crucial events: the departure and the return of the gods from the earth. Within this broadly conceived history of being, Heidegger understands his own age—and his own work—as a transition (*Übergang*) from out of decline (*Untergang*). "Hölderlin," then, comes to function as the name for a "turning" or *Kehre*—both within the history of beyng and within Heidegger's way of understanding the vocation of philosophy within the destiny of the West. In *Contributions to Philosophy*, that work attuned to the meaning of such a turning, Heidegger designates Hölderlin as the poet who announces the possibility of a turning, the poet who serves as the voice of a tectonic shift in the history of the earth as the place where human beings can dwell poetically. He stands as the prophetic voice between the *first* beginning of Greek philosophy and the *other* beginning of a futural German awakening that holds forth the promise of the return of the gods to the earth. As Heidegger puts it:

> Hölderlin is in an exceptional sense the poet—that is, founder—of German beyng, because he has projected such beyng the farthest. That is, he has projected it out ahead into the most distant future. He was able to open up this supremely futural expanse because he brought forth the key from his experience of the most profound need of the withdrawal and approach of the gods. (HGR: 201/GA 39: 220)

But what could Heidegger possibly mean here—that Hölderlin is the "founder" (*Stifter*) of German beyng? And why does Heidegger designate "the Germans" as the only ones who are capable of "subduing the danger of the darkening of the world" and of "saving the West" (IM: 52/GA 40: 53; EdP: 40)? These are questions whose answers remain philosophically elusive—and yet, I think, to understand these questions as genuine questions and not simply as the arbitrary utterance of a singularly willful German ideologue, we will need to situate them against the reigning *Hölderlinbild* of the early twentieth century and the role this played among literary critics, poets, social theorists, and philosophers. Hence, before I turn to discussing Heidegger's lecture course titled Hölderlin's Hymns "Germania" and "The Rhine," I want to look at the way Hölderlin was employed by prominent thinkers and writers to form a generational idea of German identity. Against this background, which will constitute the first three sections of this chapter, I will then turn to Heidegger's own singular reading of Hölderlin both for his history of beyng and for his understanding of German national destiny.

"Hölderlin" comes to serve Heidegger as the name for his own innermost hopes concerning German's futural possibilities. Its power as a name allows him to move beyond the narrow confines of "university" philosophy and penetrate to the core of a secret history of beyng borne by a primordial kinship between the archaic Greeks and the futural Germans. This myth of German destiny, marked by a belief in Germany's special role and elect status among nations and peoples, will define Hölderlin's standing for Heidegger as "the poet of poets," "the poet of the Germans," "the poet who first poetizes the Germans" (HGR: 201/GA 39: 220). This crucial role that Hölderlin plays within Heidegger's own thinking will, of course, be decisive for the way he understands Germany's own status within Europe during the 1930s and beyond. But it will also come to shape the way Heidegger thinks about language—especially the way he frames the conversation between poetry and philosophy as that which is essential to any possible "thinking" of being. As John Llewelyn has put it, for Heidegger, "the thinking of being cannot come to pass without primordial poetry. Being's thinking is poietic."[3]

As we come to think about Heidegger's relation to Hölderlin, I believe it is important that we understand how Hölderlin's poetry opens up for Heidegger this poietic dimension of being. As Heidegger emphasizes, "thinking is a co-poetizing"; it brings us into the heart of being's poietic character and lets us enter into the event of appropriation that occurs in a language attuned to being's simultaneous revelation and/as concealment (GA 52: 55). What is required to read Hölderlin, Heidegger believes, is a *"thoughtful* encounter with the *revelation of beyng,"* one that rethinks philosophy's traditional understanding of language as subject-predicate assertions organized in formal logical claims. Such traditional logic "rashly flattens and alienates and misconstrues the essence of language" and reduces it to a mere expression of the human subject (LQ: 141/GA 38: 169). In this way, language circumscribes the domain of beings without thinking in an originary way about being. But "this claim (*Anspruch*) needs to be more originarily conceived and relentlessly renewed from out of the originary conception of the essence of language (*Sprache*)." And this, Heidegger claims, is the task of the poet: to bring a people into an originary relation to its own language as a way of opening it up to the very ground of its historical Dasein. Yet oftentimes the poet's word falls upon deaf ears in an epoch where language is conceived instrumentally as a tool for communication, planning, and calculation. Hence, one of the aims of Heidegger's "Germania" lectures is to awaken a readiness amongst the German people for a proper hearing of Hölderlin's poetic word. During the 1930s Heidegger would try to awaken this readiness by thinking anew philosophy's own historical vocation in relation to Hölderlin.

At the heart of Hölderlin's originary relation to language as poetic word is the hope for a futural home for the Germans amidst the storms and ravages of their historical experience. This is one of Heidegger's lifelong preoccupations, the hope for a home amidst the homelessness of modern existence. In a lecture from 1950, Heidegger writes: "To reflect on language means: to come to the speaking of language in such a way that it properly occurs (*sich ereignet*) as that which grants an abode (*Aufenthalt*) for the being of mortals" (PLT: 192/GA 12: 11). During the 1930s Heidegger would understand this abode as the "fatherland" and as the political destiny of a *Volk* whose futural hopes lay in "the spiritual-historical conquest of the Great War" (GA 16: 284). In so many ways the Great War would become the spiritual center of Heidegger's Hölderlin interpretation since it came to form the historical co-ordinates according to which Heidegger would organize his understanding of German history as a "mission" (*Sendung*) to save the West from the devastation (*Verwüstung*) and world-darkening (*Weltverdüsterung*) brought on by the totalization of modernity (GA 39: 41, 131, 175, 263; GA 40: 48, 53). In the forces unleashed by the Great War Heidegger detected "the increased rending of the *Volk* into classes and parties through the disintegration of everything spiritual, through the falsification of all standards of measure, through the heightened rootlessness and aimlessness of the state" (GA 16: 300). What comes to pass out of this rootlessness is a crisis of nihilism that afflicts the West at its very foundation. It is in terms of this crisis that Hölderlin will appear to Heidegger as the singular voice of German healing and deliverance.

What Hölderlin's word promises is a pathway from out of the human destruction and spiritual desolation of the Great War, this "frightful occurrence" whose repercussions still remain hidden to us, Heidegger claims. In May of 1934 just months before he begins his Hölderlin lectures, Heidegger reflects on the death of those soldiers who lost their lives in battle for the fatherland. In a speech honoring the war dead from his gymnasium in Konstanz, Heidegger takes up the theme of their sacrifice not as a memorial recollection (*Gedächtnis*) but as a remembrance (*Andenken*) whose genuine meaning proves to be futural (GA 16: 280; GA 39: 3).

> The Great War is only now coming upon us. The awakening of our dead, the two million casualties from out of the endless graves that, like a secret wreath, stretches around the borders of Germany and of German Austria, this awakening is only now beginning.
> The Great War is only today becoming for us Germans—and for us first among all peoples—a *historical* reality of our *Dasein*, for history is not what has been (*das Gewesene*), nor what is present (*das Gegenwärtige*). Rather, history is the futural (*das Zukünftige*) and our mandate for the futural. (GA 16: 280)

Out of the ashes of the Great War and the failure of the Weimar Republic, Heidegger sees the possibility of the German *Volk* awakening to a sense of its own "mandate for the futural." Through the "spiritual conquest and creative metamorphosis of the Great War," the *Volk* might be made whole—but only if it comes to embrace "the destiny of the German *Volk*" that constitutes its ownmost vocation and task (GA 16: 300). Such a destiny and its history "remain a *secret*," however (GA 16: 248). Moreover, we can only "grasp this secret as a secret in that we . . . decide either *for* or *against* it." Heidegger announces to his listeners that "we stand in the middle of this decision" and the possibility of coming to terms with its spiritual-historical meaning lies in "the awakening and prevailing of the will of the *Volk* to its ownmost mission" (GA 16: 231).

In Heidegger's "spiritualization" of the meaning and mission of the Great War, Hölderlin comes to play a decisive role. But it is also crucial to understand that Heidegger's "Hölderlin" is essentially a creation of the Great War and owes much to the "Hölderlin Renaissance" that emerges in the work of Norbert von Hellingrath and the members of the George Circle in the years around 1914. That is, Hölderlin is not a poet whom Heidegger randomly chooses to provide a way of explaining the German experience in the Great War and the years of struggle thereafter. Rather, Heidegger's *Hölderlinbild* emerges out of the myth of national destiny that takes hold in the cultural debates during World War I about Germany's *Sonderweg* or "special path" that grants to the Germans alone a spiritual mission to save the West. In his winter semester (WS) 1934–1935 lectures on "Germania," Heidegger focuses on "this unique, singular destiny" and "the singular uniqueness of our world-historical situation" as well as on "how Hölderlin's poetizing as a whole will come to word and to work in the accomplishing of our historical vocation" (GA 39: 184–186). Within this vast, overarching vision of Germany's vocation, mission, and *Sonderweg*, Hölderlin—or, rather, the "Hölderlin-mythos"—will come to play a double role. In one version, with his myth about the departure of the gods, Hölderlin will provide Heidegger with the co-ordinates for a philosophy of history that will turn the "decline of the West" (Spengler) and "the declining Fatherland" into a discourse about a coming god and the hope of rescue and salvation. In another telling, Hölderlin's poetic attunement to the untapped possibilities of language will offer a way out of the cul-de-sac of metaphysical thinking that has defined the West since the philosophical ascendency of Plato and Aristotle. In both these ways—in providing a new beginning in *history* and in *thinking*—Hölderlin comes to be thought of as *the* poet of revolution who, as the "poet in a destitute time," alerts the *Volk* to "the great turnings of time" even as he serves as "the herald of the overcoming of all metaphysics" (GA 39: 106; GA 52: 143).

In this sense Hölderlin becomes for Heidegger "the" poet—the one who poetizes the essence of poetry in a way that transforms the very possibilities of language itself and, in so doing, offers us a glimpse into "an other beginning" for thinking. The meaning of this Hölderlin myth is always futural, always to come. Only if Hölderlin's poetry becomes our vocation, Heidegger warrants, can we open up to our proper history, can we become who we truly are. But who is the "we"? And how does Hölderlin's poetry help in the determination of this proper identity? For the Heidegger of the 1930s, this "we" is thought of as <u>the</u> *Volk*, the historical community that emerges out of the possibilities afforded by language. The isolated, Cartesian self—that staple of social contract theory—appears to Heidegger as a diseased form of "addictive egocentrism" (*Ichsucht*) that inevitably brings with it a sense of "self-forlornness" (*Selbstverlorenheit*) (LQ: 52/GA 38: 45–57). Yet the National Socialist revolution offers an alternative to the failure of the isolated bourgeois subject formed by the consumerist ethos of the marketplace. For Heidegger, the question "Who are we?" has a clear "answer: the Volk" (GA 38: 59). However, the *Volk* does not emerge wholly formed out of the cocoon of history; it arises out of a shared "exposure" (*Ausgesetztheit*) to beings that happens only in language. As Heidegger puts it in the "Germania" lectures: "Poetizing is the originary language of a *Volk*. Within such language there occurs a being exposed to beings as they thereby open themselves up. As the accomplishment of such exposure, the human being is historical" (GA 39: 74, 77). By entering into dialogue with Hölderlin's poetic language, "we"—as the *Volk*—"enter into the originary historicity of our historical Dasein" and come to knowledge of who we properly are.

This vision of the *Volk* as a community formed through *language* rather than "biological" kinship (Kolbenheyer), "race" (Rosenberg), or "cultural soul" (Spengler), shapes the "Germania" lectures in the spirit of Hölderlin as handed down in the work of Norbert von Hellingrath (GA 39: 26–27). Hellingrath was convinced that the essence of "the nation or the ethnic community (*Stammesgemeinschaft*)" lay neither in biological ancestry nor the political character of the state but in language. In Hellingrath's words, "language is the soul of the *Volk*, the limit of the *Volk*, the core of the *Volk*."[4] Growing out of his earliest encounter with Hölderlin as a Gymnasium student in 1908 and with Hellingrath as a Freiburg student in WS 1911–1912, Heidegger slowly comes to grasp poetic language as a hidden bequest granted the German *Volk* to find its path out of the impoverished tradition of metaphysical thinking that has dominated the West for more than two millennia. Coming out of the desolation and failure of the Great War, Hellingrath's Hölderlin comes to signify the possibility of an "other" Germany, one whose essence lies not in the past, but in a still unthought future that calls the *Volk* to its vocation. Hellingrath's dream of an other Germany, born from out of his frustration and disillusionment with the realities of the existing German state, would become a rallying cry for disaffected poets and thinkers of the war generation. Georg Simmel, who received a signed copy of Hellingrath's Hölderlin edition, expressed this same conviction in 1917 that "the Germany in which we became who we are has foundered like a dream that is no more and that no matter how present events turn out, we will experience our future on the ground and soil of an other Germany."[5]

Both in his disillusionment with what he perceives as the barrenness and spiritual exhaustion of Weimar culture from 1918–1933 and in his renewed hope for a spiritual revolution of the *Volk* in 1933 and after, Heidegger takes up this idea of a "poetic bequest" granted to the Germans by Hölderlin. Drawing on Hellingrath's conviction that "the poet is a seer who peers beyond his time, proclaims the future and . . . out of the night [of the departed gods] prepares a new arrival of the gods on earth,"

Heidegger positions Hölderlin as "the poet of futural German beyng" (GA 39: 220). What Hölderlin offers Heidegger, then, is a poetic vision of the future that offers a genuine revolution in our relation to language, one that offers "the possibility of another way of beyng to show itself" (GA 75: 81). I think that here we are confronted by the unresolved tensions and aporias within Heidegger's thinking about Hölderlin and within his thinking as a whole, tensions that will concern us as we try to read the Hölderlin lectures as texts that constitute the very heart of Heidegger's thinking. This means that we cannot simply dismiss his foray into National Socialist politics as a brief "mistake" confined to the years 1933–1934 or that we can somehow reject this disturbing feature of Heidegger's biography and go right ahead with a "philosophical" reading of his own writings on Hölderlin. We shall need to address this troubling aspect of his *Hölderlinbild* and locate it squarely within the political context of his time. That means that we also need to realize that we cannot easily separate Heidegger's political commitments from his attempted Hölderlinian revolution of language. There is a deeply political strain that runs through all three of the Hölderlin lecture courses from WS 1934–1935 (GA 39), WS 1941–1942 (GA 52), and spring semester (SS) 1942 (GA 53)—as well as in his "Western Conversation" of 1946–1948 (GA 75: 57–196)—although the "political" character of these texts will shift significantly in response to Germany's own dramatic political (and military) fortunes. Heidegger himself acknowledges this explicitly political function of Hölderlin's writing in his very first Hölderlin lecture course where he speaks of "the historical decision" that confronts "us" when we take up Hölderlin's work. This decision concerns our readiness to imagine a revolution in thinking spurred by the poetic song of "the poet of the Germans." As Heidegger puts it:

> Because Hölderlin is this concealed and perplexing figure—the poet of poets as the poet of the Germans—he has not yet become a force in the history of our Volk. Because he is not yet such a force, he must become one. To participate in this process is "politics" in the highest and authentic sense, so much so that whoever accomplishes something here has no need to talk about the "political." (GA 39: 214)

Yet as entangled as Heidegger's "Hölderlin" project was in the political situation of the National Socialist revolution, we cannot simply reduce it to this.⁶ Clearly, there were many points of intersection in the National Socialist craze for Hölderlin and Heidegger's own idiosyncratic reading of the poet.⁷ In the work of National Socialist philosophers such as Kurt Hildebrandt, Alfred Baeumler, Ernst Krieck and compliant philologists like Ernst Müller, Paul Böckmann, and Friedrich Beissner, we find many of the same thematic concerns as in Heidegger: the vision of Hölderlin as the poet of the fatherland; the emphasis on "poetic vocation," "the German mission," and Germany's elect status among nations; the interpretation of "Germania" as a mandate for German self-assertion; the reading of the myth of the gods' departure as a call for German rebirth; a reading of German destiny in terms of the *Volk*, and others.⁸ One sees this in its crudest form in a recruitment poster for the Hitler Youth group that features an Aryan-looking young boy in a para-military uniform earnestly looking out at an undefined horizon with the inscription: "Das kommende Deutschland" ("The Coming Germany").⁹ Still, Heidegger's "political" interpretation of Hölderlin was hardly in line with such lockstep Nazi philosophers as Kurt Hildebrandt, who maintained that in his "Rhine" hymn "Hölderlin created an Aryan vision of Christ" and in "The Migration" he presaged the historical movement of the Germans, this "white race" to which was vouchsafed "our world-historical *Lebensraum*."¹⁰ Nonetheless, Heidegger's path of thinking intersected in significant and unsettling ways with the legacy of National Socialism and his Hölderlin lectures offer no exception to this. These thematic concerns—the staging of German national destiny in terms of its purported 'elect' status among peoples, the repeated emphasis on the German "mission" to save the West—cannot, especially given the historical catastrophe of the Nazi regime, simply be read as the expression of a hypertrophied patriotism or the misguided political sorties of a fundamentally unpolitical academic. To write about Heidegger's "Hölderlin," then, demands that we confront these vexing questions. At the same time, I do not wish to reduce Heidegger's Hölderlin writings to his National Socialist commitments. But let me be clear: Heidegger's whole association with the vision and political program of National Socialism constitutes a profound "wound to thinking," as Blanchot expressed it, and to understand these writings we need to attend to that wound. To read Heidegger's Hölderlin is to confront the enigma and mystery of this whole encounter, its daring attempt to proffer a new and radically different form of poetic thinking that might offer a way out of the impasse of metaphysics. Yet reading Heidegger's Hölderlin also involves us in the ruinous project of German nationalist destiny, a destiny marked by a tragic blindness that extends into Heidegger's fateful meeting with Paul Celan in 1967.[11]

How to weigh and balance those countervailing strains in such a way that we can understand how they belong together in a deep and fundamental sense? How to read Heidegger's Hölderlin as the profound contribution to thought that it is while simultaneously acknowledging its grave flaws politically, philologically, historically? This is part of the task that I hope to address in the chapters that follow. To understand Heidegger's one-sided embrace of Hölderlin as "the" poet, that singular voice capable of preparing the way to an "other" beginning of thinking, we need to address in greater depth the emergence of the whole Hölderlin myth in the work of Norbert von Hellingrath. Hellingrath's "discovery" of the late hymns of Hölderlin—especially in conjunction with the myth of national destiny that grows out of the generation of the Great War—will decisively shape Heidegger's whole approach to the poet and will endure down to his very last days.[12] The role that "Norbert's Hölderlin" plays in Heidegger's formulation of his own Hölderlin myth can hardly be overestimated (HIB: 133).

II. Norbert Von Hellingrath and the Hölderlin Myth

The work of Hölderlin as an important contribution within German literature goes back to the first collected edition of his poems in 1826 by Ludwig Uhland and Gustav Schwab. Other editions followed in 1846 by Christoph Schwab, in 1884 by Karl Köstlin, and in 1896 by Berthold Litzmann.[13] During the course of the nineteenth century, Hölderlin's importance was recognized by such imposing figures as Nietzsche, Dilthey, and Theodor Fontane, yet still he remained a second-tier author in German letters. During the first years of the twentieth century, however, three new editions were launched: Wilhelm Böhm's *Complete Works* begun in 1905, Marie Joachim-Dege's *Collected Works* of 1908, and a "historical-critical" edition of several volumes edited by the Tübingen philologist Franz Zinkernagel. It was within this context that Hellingrath's philological labors revolutionized Hölderlin scholarship in a resolute way. Some of these early Hölderlin editions elided some of the poems written after the onset of Hölderlin's "madness," especially the period after 1806, though for some even earlier. But Hellingrath challenged this accepted practice and, through his archival researches at the Königliche Landesbibliothek in Stuttgart, he uncovered hitherto unknown texts including several of Hölderlin's late hymns as well as his translations of Pindar. Hellingrath wrote his dissertation on the Pindar translations and considered them essential to understanding Hölderlin's maturation as a poet, especially in his use of Pindaric forms such as "hard jointure" (*harmonia austera*).[14] On the basis of this intense engagement with Hölderlin's texts, Hellingrath decided to produce a much more informed historical-critical edition than any that had appeared.

Hellingrath instinctively understood that Hölderlin's Pindar translations were far more than an adaption of a Greek poetic style. Rather, what Hölderlin tried to bring to light through his poetic labors was an experience of communion with the gods that he believed permeated Pindar's epinician odes. In the Pindaric understanding of human beings as those ephemeral creatures "exposed" (or in Hölderlin's terms, "ausgesetzt") to chance, luck, coincidence and the shifting favor of the gods, Hölderlin uncovered a tragic vision of human fate whose meaning could only be gained by entering into a community of fellowship with the gods, with nature, and with other human beings (DKV II: 768).[15] Here Hellingrath read Hölderlin as *the* poet whose poetic task consisted in the invocation of just such a community—even where, and precisely because, it did not yet exist. In the deficit of this hope, Hellingrath uncovered a Hölderlin who could not be approached philologically, but who demanded an aesthetic-religious "devotion" to "the sacred stature of the poet" (HV: 245). Despite his rigorous training as a philologist, Hellingrath believed that a scholarly approach to Hölderlin was incapable of penetrating to the hidden core of his poetic vision. As he wrote to his dissertation advisor, Friedrich von der Leyen, in 1910: "I don't know what to do with the notion that scholarship (*Wissenschaft*) stands as superior to, or of equal rank with, religion . . . In the face of the burning questions of this living time one cannot be a mere historian" (HV: 226). He then confesses that "all the deeper forces within me and really all of my interest in . . . the Greeks and Hölderlin . . . has something religious about it." Like Friedrich Gundolf and Stefan George, Hellingrath too would see Hölderlin as the "seer-poet" and "the herald of a new god," the figure who would serve as the prophet of a coming revolution of spirit whose genuine power lay in the concealed potency and depth of the German language.[16]

All that Hölderlin had achieved in the realm of language, however, had been misinterpreted by the philologists since they viewed his poetic style—especially its strange and incongruous Pindaric enjambments, paratactic constructions, chiasms, and hard jointure—as the signs of an impending madness and the products of a diseased imagination. As a result, some of the late hymns in the period after 1802 were left out of some Hölderlin editions. Contributing to, and reinforcing, this image of poetic madness was a 1909 study by the psychiatrist Wilhelm Lange, *Hölderlin: Eine Pathographie*, that dismissed the late work as showing signs of "catatonic babbling" in which Hölderlin's "surroundings appeared strange to him and pushed him into an uncanny, unintelligible remoteness."[17] But Hellingrath responded to these claims by insisting on the poetic genius and radicality of the late poems inspired by Hölderlin's long apprenticeship in translating Pindar. Lange's reduction of Hölderlin's poetic accomplishment to a form of "psychic abnormality" did not take account of the work, but only the life. These difficult, jarring, and sometimes incomprehensible poems did not present "the first symptoms of madness"; they constituted, rather, "the first performance of a new art form and what appears to the psychiatrist as merely catatonic babbling, we see as the ultimate maturation and divine elevation of the poet . . . One cannot separate them and declare: here is madness and here is art. No, art is madness—and madness, art" (HV: 245). In forging an intimate connection between Hölderlin's life and his work—and by insisting that we honor the work as the product of an original and enigmatic confrontation with the unorthodox style of Pindar—Hellingrath succeeded in radicalizing the effect of Hölderlin's poetry and helping to make it essential to modern Germany's sense of its own contested identity. His effect on the young generation of aesthetes, philosophers, cultural theorists, writers, and thinking during the Great War and after, was so dramatic, it has led some scholars to describe this generation as having been "Hellingrathized" and filled with a "Hellingrath-enraptured" enthusiasm for a new vision of Germany.[18]

What mattered most to Hellingrath was that the Germans come to understand themselves as a special, elected *Volk* whose genuine identity had remained hidden to them. Only by attending to the secret, concealed essence of the German language that came to expression in its poets, could the Germans fulfill their innermost responsibility to *be* German. Here Hellingrath subscribed to Stefan George's credo of a "Priesterdichtung" whereby the poet came to serve as a priestly voice who attempted a communion with the gods on behalf of the *Volk*. As Friedrich Wolters, a devoted member of the George Circle put it: the poet, "as friend of the fatherland, seeks to found a new community of free and lofty human beings, among whom the poet is king."[19] Exemplary of such poetic kingship, Wolters professes, is Hölderlin, who is distinguished by his "singularity within German letters as a whole." As the poet who first called forth the German *Volk* to its authentic home in language, Hölderlin stood as "the most German of poets" (HV: 125). Yet Hellingrath stressed that Hölderlin was "only a herald, not—even in his most secret (*geheimsten*) thoughts—the one who brought fulfillment; hence, Hölderlin stands as an unknown, concealed figure within his *Volk*" (HV: 139). In his poem "Hölderlin," Stefan George poetizes this fate in terms of the "secret" that is Hölderlin's poetic work:

> The sibylline book long hidden in a reliquary because no one could read it, is now conveyed to the people at large and to the astonished glance there now opens an unknown world of the secret (*Geheimnis*) and of prophecy.[20]

Inspired by George's vision of the poet's priestly office within the community of the *Volk*, Hellingrath held that "the authentic secret (*Geheimnis*) of Hölderlin's language ... is that it is not filled with a yearning for the divine but is, rather, filled with the feeling of divine presence." In this way "The poet is the voice of god ... The poet is a *seer* who gazes beyond his own time and prophesies the future" (HV: 132, 135). Within Hölderlin's hands the poem becomes a kind of temple, the sacred precinct within which the last traces of the gods might appear. Yet in beckoning the gods to come, in giving voice to their historical departure, the poet frames a language that both speaks to and from the present. The gods are not hereby made "available" to mortals; on the contrary, the poet reminds us of our powerlessness to engineer their return. It is this myth of the poet's annunciation of "the return of the gods" that will prove so fateful in Heidegger's own engagement with Hellingrath. If in the years of the rectorate Heidegger will call for the self-assertion of the German *Volk*, in his turn to Hölderlin we can detect a more restrained and tempered response, one marked by a discourse about "mindfulness" (*Besinnung*) and the openness of "waiting" that helps attune us to "destiny" (*Geschick*) and the coming of the gods. Here the gods come to function as names for the temporality of historical remembrance and awaiting. For Heidegger—as for Hellingrath—only by understanding Hölderlin as a poet who comes to us from the future, and not from out of the past, can we even begin to grasp what is at stake in the poetry. Hence, Heidegger can write that "the time of poetic vocation" shapes the poet in such a way that "he must *think of* what has been (*das Gewesene andenken*) and *of* what is coming, if not to *think of* what has been *as* what is coming" (EHP: 123/GA 4: 99).

For Hellingrath, "the authentic *Vermächtnis* (bequest)" of Hölderlin to the German *Volk* is this sense of a futural coming to greatness that awaits them. This *Vermächtnis*, however, has been shrouded, hidden as if in a reliquary, since the very words of the poet were not available to read, buried in an archive amidst the unread manuscripts of the "mad" Hölderlin. In these late hymns, which Hellingrath describes as "the heart, core, and summit of Hölderlin's work," the poet gives voice to a language that is not so much his own "but wholly as if it were spoken from 'the noble spirit of the fatherland,' much like the Jewish prophets understood their words as spoken by the Lord" (HV: 104). It is this hidden, prophetic idiom of the seer-poet that characterizes Hellingrath's Hölderlin as the "unknown, hidden herald within the Volk" (HV: 139). Such a language remains cryptically buried in hints, signs, whispers, and intimations since

> . . . in hints (*Winke*) from
> Time immemorial the gods have spoken. (SPF: 50–51)

What emerges from out of this concealed, enshrouded discourse of "hints" is a vision of what Karl Wolfskehl, the George disciple, termed "the secret Germany" (*das geheime Deutschland*)—not the failed, institutional-political Reich of Bismarck and the Kaisers, but a Germany of poets, thinkers, artists, and visionaries hinted at by earlier writers, but ultimately transfigured in the poetry of Stefan George. Only in this concealed kingdom of George's poetic language did Wolfskehl find the traces of this hoped-for Germany: "For what today, as a kind of half-dream, is beginning to stir beneath the desolate, scabrous veneer—the *secret Germany*—is the only Germany that lives in this age; here, only here has it come to language. . . . The conviction that this secret Germany has not wasted away . . . , that it seeks to come to light, this gives us a profound faith in the future . . . where perhaps for the last time these depths yearn to reveal themselves."[21] Wolfskehl's friend, von Hellingrath, then transformed this myth of a secret Germany by tracing it back to the work of Hölderlin. For Hellingrath, Hölderlin comes to function as the voice of Germany's futural mission to rouse the West from its cultural slumbers, summoning it to become an authentic community of aesthetes-philosophers who find their voice in the ancient Greeks. It is this special, inner bond between the two languages that Hölderlin had uncovered in his translations of Pindar and Sophocles that Hellingrath identifies as the afflatus for the hope of a future Germania that owes its birth to Hölderlin's "dream of Hellas" (HV: 104–105, 125). Moreover, Hellingrath insists it is this "dream of Hellas" that has become "the special privilege of the Germans," because in it Hölderlin was able to find a language capable of invoking once again the old Greek gods. In this way Hölderlin "exalts Athens' past as a German future." Hence, Hellingrath contends, "Hölderlin's turn to the fatherland is only the direct consequence of his Greek being."

In an era torn by the violence and traumatic loss of the Great War and the collapse of the old Kaiserreich, Hellingrath's myth of a secret Germany would come to establish a poetic vision of German history in terms of "destiny," "mission," "the coming of the gods," and "the originary kinship between Greeks and Germans"—themes that would be taken up forcefully by Heidegger in his own Hölderlin lectures. Generationally, this involved a transition from the ideal of a Goethean "optimistic-ironic-impartial" temperament to a Hölderlinian "pessimistic-active-tragic" one, as Carl Schmitt described it.[22] As Hellingrath put it:

> I call us "the *Volk* of Hölderlin" because it is of the very essence of the Germans that their innermost, fervid core (which lies infinitely deep beneath the veneer of its dross-covered crust) can only come to light in a *secret* Germany. This innermost core expresses itself through human beings who, at the very least, must be long dead before they are recognized and find a response; and works that will always impart their secret only to the very few, saying nothing to most, and wholly inaccessible to non-Germans. Indeed, this is true because this secret Germany is so certain of its inner value . . . That it makes no effort to be heard or seen . . . Hölderlin is the greatest example of this hidden fire, of this secret Reich, of the still unrecognized coming into being of the divine burning core. (HV: 120–121)

Just as Hölderlin remains hidden amongst his *Volk* during this turbulent epoch, his voice not yet having found its proper hearing, so too Hellingrath insists, this secret Germany remains buried beneath the crude surface of the institutional-political Reich and republic, waiting to emerge at its proper time. The signs of this coming are all around us, Hellingrath insists, but they remain hidden and unread:

> All the divine signs speak to us and now comes the ancient, eternally young messenger of the highest: the eagle. He seeks the genius of Germania . . . and brings to the maiden the divine message: because she has remained imperturbable in the storms of time and has only dreamed of the highest hopefully, the heavenly ones have recognized her as the chosen one who, before all others, will experience her return in the West. The message uttered, the messenger now recounts how, in her childhood, he had brought her a gift—language—in which she could express the fullness of her heart. Now, however, she should awaken to regard the portent and to pronounce the secret (*Geheimnis*)—time wishes it. It is allowed to clearly speak it—though only in poetic words which are not surrendered to the uninitiated. (HV: 146–147)

In the language of Hölderlin's poem "Germania," this secret is spoken out—but only in a concealed poetic language for initiates. The declaration of this secret involves a curious and deeply complex relation to language, one that Hellingrath affirms and that Heidegger will follow, a path already marked out by Hölderlin himself. In "Germania," the poet declares:

> And name what you see before you
> No longer may the unspoken
> Remain a secret (*Geheimnis*)
> Though long it has been veiled; . . .
> Yet unspoken also, just as you found it,
> Innocent maiden, must it remain. (SPF: 194–195)

What Hölderlin reveals here is that the secret does not reveal itself in a revelation that can be known; rather, the secret reveals that it is ever concealed and cannot be easily accessed or understood. The secret is revealed *as* a secret whose meaning can neither be spoken aloud nor communicated. It remains shrouded in concealment, pointing to a time ahead that is so futural, so distant, that it awaits those who are coming, who alone can grasp its meaning. Hellingrath announces this secret as the very core of Hölderlin's work since it intimates the futural coming of a *Volk* whose possibility exists in the present only under the rubric of a "secret" Germany. This possibility is then enunciated by George in his poem "The Secret Germany," as that which will emerge from out of the "decline" and the "kingdom of death" that reigns in contemporary Germany, hidden to all but the initiates since "no one was prepared for this great event."[23] Here George gives poetic expression to Hellingrath's own myth of Hölderlin as the poet of the secret that awaits the German *Volk*:

> Only what is cloaked in sheltering sleep
> Where none yet detects it
> Long in the deepest hollow
> Of the consecrated earth it still rests—
> A Wonder, undecipherable in this day,
> Becomes the destiny of the day that is coming. ("Geheimes Deutschland," vv. 97–102)

The destiny of the day that is coming, George intimates, is to bring forth from out of the desolate and barren wasteland of the Great War and the German defeat, "another" Germany whose birthright was granted to them by Hölderlin, "the one who rejuvenates language and therewith rejuvenates the soul . . . of the coming German future."[24] In this secret promise and concealed faith attested to by both George and Hellingrath, Heidegger uncovers the poet who holds the key to Germany's most fragile hope, "Hölderlin . . . the poet of the coming historical time . . . The question is solely this: Whether we remain indifferent to the time that is continually and genuinely the coming time—or—whether we learn to be attentive and from this attentiveness uncover an originary remembrance of that which merits our reflection" (GA 75: 42).

III. Heidegger and the "Secret" Germania

As he begins his reading of "Germania" in WS 1934–1935, Heidegger will turn to the question of the secret—and the proper form of language for endowing it. In the very first hour of the course he cites a fragment from Hölderlin that frames his whole engagement with the text:

> Concerning what is Highest, I will be silent.
> Forbidden fruit, like the laurel, is, however,
> Above all the fatherland. Such, however, each
> Shall taste last. (SPF: 286–287/GA 39: 4)

And then Heidegger offers this commentary:

> The fatherland, our fatherland Germania—most forbidden, withdrawn from the haste of everyday life and the bustle of activity. The highest, and therefore the most difficult, that which comes last, because fundamentally first—the origin withheld in silence. This also tells us what our beginning with "Germania" does not mean. It is not our intention to offer something useful or practicable for the needs of the day . . . or to bring Hölderlin into line with the times (*Zeitgemässheit*). We have no desire to bring Hölderlin into line with our times. On the contrary: we wish to bring ourselves, and those who are to come, under the measure (*Maß*) of the poet. (HGR: 4/GA 39: 4)

With a voice whose authority is authorized from "a necessity of thought" rather than from any prevailing worldview or political doctrine, Heidegger proceeds to establish his voice as one in dialogue with Hölderlin about the proper place of Germany within the philosophical history of the West. Hölderlin alone can offer hints as to the hidden meaning of this history, Heidegger proclaims, but only if we remove ourselves from the reigning philosophemes of our day and withdraw from the haste of everyday life. The time of the fatherland is concealed from us; it does not follow the calculations and historical reckonings of the day. Moreover, "We do not know our proper historical time. The world-hour of our Volk is concealed from us" (GA 39: 50). This is so because an understanding of the time of the *Volk* requires that the poet be "transported beyond his own time and its calculable 'today' . . . into a free space" even as, on the other hand "he must alienate himself in turn from those to whom he belongs in his lifetime." To be able to utter the secret that lies at the heart of the fatherland, the poet must withdraw from the present so that he can, like the eagle-messenger in "Germania," survey the broad horizon that is the landscape of German destiny. And it is here in this tradition of a secret language of withheld silence that Heidegger will find both the inspiration for his own voice in the lectures—and—come to see a path out of the cul-de-sac that confronted him in the failure of his rectorate and his dampened political hopes. For in this rhetorical figure of the poet cut off from his own time and misunderstood by his contemporaries, Heidegger identified a viable strategy for pursuing his thwarted hopes for a German revolution—but now in a concealed way and one no longer in service to the political machinations of a party program that Heidegger had acceded to in his public speeches of 1933–1934.

This identification with Hölderlin as the voice of German destiny will determine Heidegger's own self-identification with the poet in profound and important ways. Heidegger will go to extreme lengths to craft his own myth of the fateful necessity of his encounter with Hölderlin. In a letter to Rudolf Stadelmann that connects his own philosophical work on the "Ister" hymn with the poetic saying of Hölderlin, Heidegger writes:

> Perhaps Hölderlin, the poet, must become the determining destiny for an encounter (*Auseinandersetzung*) with a thinker [Heidegger], whose grandfather, according to documented records, was born *in ovili*, in the sheepfold of a dairy farm that lay in the upper Danube valley near (*nah*) the shore of a stream under a cliff—at the very same time as the coming into being of the 'Ister' hymn and the poem 'Remembrance.' The hidden history of saying (*die verborgene Geschichte des Sagens*) knows no accidents. All is destiny. (GA 16: 370)

This intense autobiographical link with Hölderlin is hardly a passing reference. Rather, in the figure of Hölderlin as the mythic "founder of German beyng," Heidegger encounters the possibility for empowering his own vision of a German future—but now in the shadows, as it were, in a concealed, secretive discourse for those ready to hear the prophetic word. Here too Heidegger follows a path already taken by Hellingrath, George, and Max Kommerell, of the "poet as Führer."[25] Precisely at the time that Heidegger loses his position as rector and his confidence in his ability to forge a poetic-philosophical revolution, he turns to Hölderlin's poem "Germania" for a new possibility of empowerment. Hölderlin's poetic fate becomes, then, a model for Heidegger's own present predicament as the unheeded philosophical Führer of the German revolution.

Both Hölderlin and Heidegger see themselves as figures who live at the end of a tradition, what Hölderlin called *"this decline or transition of the fatherland*" (E&L: 271/DKV II: 446). What stands before us, each claims, is the possibility of founding a new history, of another beginning that might recover "the dream of Hellas" that animated the Greek world (HV: 104, 125). Both Hölderlin and Heidegger envision such a dream as the recovery of the hidden possibilities of that which has been (*das Gewesene*) that might then open up futurally for us (*das Zukünftige*) if we are but ready for these possibilities. Yet this vision of hopefulness is also tinged with a deep pathos for the tragic. For a generation that had experienced the wreckage and devastation of the war, Hölderlin's verses came to take on a prophetic quality, one tied to the tragic fate of German soldiers, like Norbert von Hellingrath, who were killed at the front. In this way, Hellingrath's "soldier's death" comes to function as a poetic-political myth of sacrifice for the futural Germania that awaits the Germans. Heidegger would, of course, transform Hellingrath's sacrificial death into a cipher for his own tragic interpretation of a secret Germany.[26] In the "Germania" lectures he writes that we need to first awaken the fundamental attunement to poetic language that will bring about a revolution of historical Dasein. Yet, he observes, "for this battle to transform the attunements that still dominate and perpetrate themselves at any given time, the first-born must be sacrificed" (HGR: 128/GA 39: 146). In this line of first-born sacrifices that include both Hölderlin and Hellingrath, Heidegger sees himself.

In a letter to Max Kommerell from 1942, Heidegger claims that "I *can* not at all identify myself with Hölderlin."[27] And yet, of course, Heidegger identifies himself all too forcefully with Hölderlin—and with Hölderlin's tragic hero Empedocles, who suffers a "sacrificial death" for his *Volk* so that they might emerge from their moribund condition of being a "fatherland in decline" (DE: 153/DKV II: 446). Hölderlin had clearly identified himself with his tragic hero and perceived Empedocles's fateful suffering as a portent of his own poetic sacrifice for the fatherland. We can detect such sentiments in a letter he wrote to his friend Casimir Böhlendorff explaining his decision to leave Germany for a position in Bordeaux:

> And so, fare well, my cherished friend, until later. I am now full of parting. I have not wept for a long time. But it cost me bitter tears when I decided to leave my fatherland, perhaps forever. For what do I have in the world that is dearer to me? But they have no use for me.[28] (E&L: 209/DKV: 462)

In April of 1934 as he abandoned his position as rector at Freiburg, Heidegger came to see himself in terms similar to those of Hölderlin when he made his decision to "leave my fatherland." Heidegger understood himself to be at a crossroads in his life. As a way of making the transition from failed rector to herald of a secret Germany, he decided to take up the mantle of Hölderlin and enter into a more profound conversation with his poetic language. This decision was to have longstanding consequences for Heidegger's work, shaping his new philosophical direction, helping him to find a new voice for engaging the topic of beyng as event that would come to language in his *Contributions to Philosophy*.

Hölderlin had committed himself to preparing the path for a "future revolution in ways of thinking and in seeing things" for which he was prepared to sacrifice himself, in the manner of Empedocles' bold sacrifice at Mount Aetna (E&L: 84/DKV III: 252). As Heidegger attempts his own philosophical-poetic revolution in WS 1934–1935, this "second, more profound" revolution that will move far beyond the mere "political" revolution of 1933, he will seize upon this notion of sacrifice as an essential readiness to expose oneself to the danger of revolutionary upheaval (HBB: 60; GA 39: 73). Both Empedocles and Hölderlin sacrificed themselves for their *Volk* and became exemplary figures in what Heidegger terms "the struggle for the essence of poetizing" (HGR: 234/GA 39: 258). What is at stake in this struggle is the attempt at a breakthrough toward the origin, toward what Hölderlin in "The Rhine" names "Reinentsprungenes" ("that which has purely sprung forth") (SPF: 198). Empedocles, in his tragic struggle to found a new beginning, stands as a figure of sacrifice. In his lectures Heidegger situates Hölderlin's Empedocles as just such a "founder of beyng":

> We must from the outset include in the sphere of this struggle those poetic attempts in which Hölderlin seeks to poetize the poet and thinker in the figure of "Empedocles," in order to establish a new commencement (*neuen Anfang*) for the poetizing of our Volk. The poetizing of *Empedocles* has indeed remained a fragment, yet we always forget that what the poetizing of *Empedocles* sought to accomplish is configured to supreme purity in such poetic works as "Germania" and "The Rhine." (HGR: 234/GA 39: 258–259)

In this identification of the tragic sphere of *Empedocles* with the topos of "Germania," Heidegger touches upon his own situation in WS 1934–1935—namely, that of the misunderstood "founder of beyng," rebuffed by the *Volk*, preparing himself for sacrifice to its highest possibilities.

Within this play of thematic concerns Heidegger reflects on Hölderlin's poem "Voice of the Volk" and remarks: "'to found' means to project in advance for the first time—and in its essence—that which is not yet" (HGR: 195/GA 39: 214). It means for the founder to project this founding into language and "to place it as a *myth* (*Sage*) into the Dasein of a Volk and thus to bring this Dasein to stand for the first time, to ground it." Yet this mythic character of language proves difficult for the *Volk* since the mystery that is "das Reinentspungene" must be sheltered and kept secret. Heidegger acknowledges this and in his lectures refrains from providing "straightforward comprehensibility." As Heidegger emphasizes, "our task is to pursue the poetizing itself as a scarcely being allowed to unveil the secret (*Geheimnis*) of what has purely sprung forth" (HGR: 234, 27/GA 39: 259, 250–251). This is "*the* poetic mandate (*Auftrag*) purely and simply, the only one"—the barely being allowed to unveil the secret. That is also the mandate of Heidegger's lecture course, to draw upon "the essence of the originarily founding, poetic language" so that in conversation with it, philosophy itself might be transformed. Only in this way can philosophy hope to approach the "secret" that is the fatherland, this "forbidden fruit" that "each shall taste last" (HGR: 109/GA 39: 120; SPF: 286–287).

This secret character of the fatherland is not, however, merely political, nationalistic, cultural, or aesthetic; it is the secret of being itself. Everything that has originary power, everything that springs forth purely from the "conflictual intimacy" (*Innigkeit*) of the "harmoniously opposed" (*Harmonischentgegengesetzte*), bears within itself "the concealing preservation of authentic being" (HGR: 106–107/GA 39: 117, 119). What Heidegger understands as beyng, this Heraclitean world-play of harmonious opposition, manifests itself as the intimate tension between veiling and unveiling, between concealment and revelation whereby neither falls to the other in a struggle that leads to "overcoming." Rather, it is this opposition itself in its mysterious enigma that preserves and shelters the secret *as* secret without revealing it, since revelation on its own merely drains the secret of its power. Hölderlin's greatness as "the poet of the Germans" and "the founder of German beyng" lies in his ability "to leave the unsayable unsaid and to do so in and through its saying"

(GA 39: 220, 119). In this he comes to express the deepest insight into the essence of truth as a "secret" (*Geheimnis*) that loves to hide itself: "The holding sway of things strives in itself toward self-concealment" (Heraclitus B123; GA 29/30: 41). As "the highest figure of truth," the secret keeps its concealing power concealed, since *physis* loves to hide its hiding. Heidegger understands his task, then, as the preservation of this secret that lies buried in the image of the secret Germany, that figure embodied in Hölderlin's "Germania" who seeks to prepare the *Volk* for the return of the gods to the earth. As "the priestess . . . quietest daughter of God . . . the child who divined a better destiny," Germania needs to be strong so that she might "bear a burdensome good fortune" that the fates have assigned to her (SPF: 192–193). This intimacy between the poet's nomination of Germania as the name for "the historical beyng of the *Volk*, the fatherland [. . .] sealed in a secret" *and* Heidegger's own thinkerly attempt to give voice to "a new fundamental experience of beyng" will shape the contours of the WS 1934–1935 course (HGR: 109, 179/GA 39: 121, 196).

Yet the way Heidegger will conjoin these themes remains highly idiosyncratic—if not tendentious. Following Hellingrath's own singular interpretation of Hölderlin as the poet of the German future, Heidegger rejects out of hand any and all attempts "to bring Hölderlin into line with the times" (HGR: 4/GA 39: 4). Rather, as Heidegger puts it, Hölderlin must remain "untimely" (*unzeitgemäß*). If other Hölderlin interpreters were attempting to make Hölderlin the prophet of a National Socialist revolution in the present, Heidegger would reject these initiatives as the crudest forms of misappropriation that violated the purity of the poetic word. In November of 1934, during the same period as his first Hölderlin lecture, Heidegger emphasized that "philosophy is essentially untimely because it belongs to those few things whose *fate* it remains never to be able—and never to be permitted—to find resonance in the quotidian affairs of our times. Hence, philosophy is also not a form of knowledge that, in a flash, can be directly applied like technical, commercial, or artisanal know-how or can be reckoned at all in terms of its usefulness" (GA 16: 318). Consequently, Heidegger claims, "a silence must be maintained around [Hölderlin] for a long time to come" (GA 39: 1).

Despite all his protests against the contemporary Hölderlin industry in Germany, however—especially around the development of a National Socialist Hölderlin—Heidegger did, in some important respects, fall victim to the all-too-timely German image of Hölderlin bandied about by his contemporaries (GA 94: 363, 487). Typical of this standard German view was the work of Carl Petersen who, in a 1934 speech, "Friedrich Hölderlin: Prophet of the German Volk," claimed that through the poet's work "the awakening of the Volk has begun."[29] Following in this tradition, Heinz Otto Bürger maintained that "Hölderlin's work culminates in the proclamation of the coming day of the Germans." Nor were they alone. In a popular edition of Hölderlin's *Vaterländische Gesänge* used by the Wehrmacht troops during World War II, Ernst Müller writes of "that which is coming," "the coming renewal of the German Volk's powers," of "sacrifice," "destiny," "the kinship between Germany-Greece," even as he also points to the German "mandate," "the community of battle," and "the process of awakening and of a coming-to-truth."[30] Müller also alludes to "the secret of that which can be uttered" that Hölderlin learned from the Greeks. Moreover, Willi Könitzer writes of the Volk's "hope of its immortal future," its "sacrifice" and its "destiny": "Rich was the German Volk in destiny . . . Blessed was the German *Volk* in its coming generations."[31] Even hardcore Nazi journals such as the *Völkischer Beobachter* and the *Nationalsozialistische Monatshefte* would come to speak of "the immense significance of Hölderlin's mission," his role as "model of a coming race," and his "shaping of a coming community."[32] For this whole generation the discourse concerning Hölderlin's poetry came to be thought of in terms of "mission," "mandate," "destiny," "danger," "sacrifice," "secret," "remembrance," "rescue," and "the return of the gods." All of these deeply Hölderlinian themes, so familiar to twenty-first-century readers of Heidegger, were the common currency of the traditional Hölderlin industry between the two world wars in Germany.[33] This is not to say that Heidegger's work on Hölderlin—especially during this period—can be reduced to the common denominator of the German nationalist (and National Socialist) *Hölderlinbild*.[34] On the contrary, Heidegger's inimitable interpretive style, his distinctive thinkerly engagement with the texts of Hölderlin as a way of "saying the unsayable," as well as his singular manner of self-staging that helped him to found his own Hölderlin-Heidegger myth, clearly distinguished his work from that of his contemporaries. Heidegger's "Hölderlin" remains one of the most distinctive figures in the history of modern thinking, an avatar of beyng's own poetic unfolding as mystery and enigma, perhaps as significant for Heidegger's thinking as Kant, Plato, Nietzsche, or Aristotle for the way he rethinks the tradition from the ground up.

Still, I would argue, Heidegger's "Hölderlin" needs to be read through and against this reigning nationalist *Hölderlinbild* since so much of his thinkerly engagement with Hölderlin is shaped by his attempts to break free from the clichés of other Hölderlin commentators. There is, of course, a deeply ironic dimension here, inasmuch as, despite these attempts, he all too often falls back in line with the thematic concerns of his generation. We can see this clearly in his postwar attempts to cover over this highly tendentious *nationalist* dimension in his Hölderlin work and to now position both the poet and himself as having abandoned a *völkisch* "egoism" that is not to be thought "patriotically or nationalistically" but, rather, that understands the Germans "from a destinal belongingness to other Völker" (PM: 257/GA 9: 338). For anyone who takes the time to read through the three sets of Hölderlin lectures (GA 39, GA 52, GA 53), it becomes clear that Heidegger is deeply committed to the singular standing of the German *Volk* among other *Völker* and that, especially during the war years, he believes that *only* the Germans can save the West from destruction. This comes to be identified in his own mind with a German military victory over the two threats to the West that he sees coming from Russia and America. In a letter to Kurt Bauch from December of 1939, just months after the beginning of World War II, Heidegger rejects what he terms "a vacuous internationalism" as a future path for the German *Volk* (HKB: 62). This is all to say that the "Hölderlin" of the NS years comes to embody Heidegger's singular hopes for a National Socialist revolution in ways of thinking that transcends the petty politics of the NSDAP. In the Black Notebooks Heidegger refers to this as a "metapolitics" of the *Volk*, one that does not succumb to the wishes of party hacks (BN I: 85, 91/GA 94: 115–116, 124). By the time of his first Hölderlin lectures of WS 1934–1935, Heidegger sees the Hitler revolution of 1933 as a mere "breakthrough" (*Aufbruch*) that has, in deeply important ways, failed. The German *Volk* still stands in need of a more thorough-going, "genuine" revolution that might offer a pathway toward an "other beginning." Such a path can only be found, however, if the *Volk* can attune itself to the poetic word of Hölderlin and his mythic vision of the return of the gods to the earth.

As Heidegger puts it in 1939:

> Hölderlin's "patriotic reversal" must not be misinterpreted as something "political"—as perhaps in the sense of a last or first

goal. The fatherland and its law is merely a through-station for the essential dimensions concerning the gods. Only from such a decision can we say what is "German"; only thus does what is "German" receive its name. (GA 75: 277)

Hence, "Against the vulgar 'political' misinterpretation of Hölderlin, which is now slowly becoming a habit," Heidegger attempts what he calls "a serious-decisive knowledge of the hidden, essential dimension of the fatherland that first needs to be founded" (GA 75: 277–278). Reading Heidegger in terms of these contemporary political misinterpretations, however, we can see how Heidegger believed that *his* "Hölderlin" was the only genuine National Socialist version and that the vulgar attempts by the Nazis—evident in the founding of the Hölderlin Gesellschaft in 1943 and of *Iduna: Jahrbuch der Hölderlin-Gesellschaft* in 1944, "under the auspices of Dr. Joseph Goebbels, Reichsminister für die deutsche Kultur"—represented both a fundamental betrayal of the genuine spirit of Hölderlin and of the "inner truth and greatness" of the National Socialist revolution that Heidegger held forth as the only authentic one (IM: 213/GA 40: 208).[35]

As he begins his cycle of Hölderlin lectures in WS 1934–1935, Heidegger is mindful of how his own failure as rector falls within the larger failure of the NSDAP to seize the fire of revolution and turn it toward the preparation for an other beginning. During the first months of the so-called "German" revolution of 1933, Heidegger believed (like the early Christians) that the "coming" was imminent. Yet a year later he was able to step back from his earlier enthusiasm in a kind of "inner emigration" that was to last through the war years. Now, as Heidegger began to identify himself more intimately with the figure of Hölderlin as misunderstood poet and as mythic symbol of psychic withdrawal, he comes to see the promise of revolution as an ever-receding possibility. His earlier confidence was so compromised by political events that in the last decade of his life he could claim, in words echoing Hölderlin, that "only a god can still save us" (GA 16: 671). In a letter to Elisabeth Blochmann from 1938, he writes that "we are entering an age in which everything essential must overcome loneliness in a way that is different and harsher than usual" (HBB: 91). This turn inward is connected in Heidegger's work with the withheld promise of poetic revelation itself. In Hölderlin's Hymns "Germania" and "The Rhine," comparing *poetic* telling

(*Sagen*) with "the *thoughtful* telling of philosophy," Heidegger claims that "in a real philosophical lecture, for example, the decisive issue is not really what is said directly, but what is kept silent in this saying" (GA 39: 41). Later in his lectures, when speaking of Hölderlin's having been misunderstood, Heidegger offers another all too autobiographical hint as to his own inner emigration. "Yet the one who is poetizing, thinking, and saying . . . comprehends solitude as a metaphysical necessity. That is, he must know that in this solitude there prevails precisely the supreme intimacy of a belonging to the beyng of his own *Volk*, even though appearances may indicate merely one who stands removed and remains unheard" (HGR: 120/GA 39: 135).

This "art" of "keeping silent" in one's saying, the art taught him by Hölderlin and Hellingrath, would preoccupy Heidegger during the 1930s in his two "secret" manuscripts, *Contributions to Philosophy: Of the Event* and *Mindfulness*. Like Stefan George, whose *Stern des Bundes* "could have for years remained a 'secret book' (*geheimbuch*)," Heidegger's *Contributions* took the form of a concealed *kerygma* "for the few—for the exceptional" (GA 65: 11).[36] There Heidegger forged an essential connection between beyng's own tendency toward keeping silent *and* the poet/philosopher's corresponding art of writing in the form of a "sigetics"—from the Greek term *sigan* (keeping silent, secrecy, stillness) (GA 65: 78–79). "Keeping silent has higher laws than any form of logic," Heidegger declares, a claim that goes back to the SS 1934 lectures on logic that served as a transition to the Hölderlin lectures of the following semester. In his important work on this sigetic dimension of Heidegger's language, Peter Trawny has argued that the key to the whole of Heidegger's philosophical thinking is its *esoteric* dimension. His book, *Adyton: Heideggers esoterische Philosophie*, draws on the meaning of *adyton* as the place in a Greek temple that constitutes "the holiest of the holy."

> The *adyton* is the site of the oracle, of divine consolation. Although it is inaccessible, individuals need to enter it. Penetrating it is not easy. Yet the god needs him who "hears" him and transmits his word. His desire constitutes an "exposure" (*Aussetzung*). To obey the god is terrible.
>
> The *adyton* is, accordingly, the inaccessible site of divine healing and divine consolation, the site in which the one who is allowed entrance, the one who makes his

way forward, receives the word and the force from out of this nearness (*Nähe*). What matters is to be admitted *into* the *adyton*, to be *in* it in order to experience the origin of life and of the word.

Heidegger's philosophy is the passageway to this *adyton*, the attempt to think that which happens in it. Naturally, it doesn't concern an actual entry into the inaccessible (what would that mean?). Rather, it concerns the recognition of an unthinkable site, which we would only be able to approach (*nähern*) by virtue of this recognition. Accordingly, the experience of its nearness (*Nähe*) is not the pre-condition of the recognition; on the contrary, the recognition is the pre-condition of the site.[37]

Perhaps we can say that the core of this esoteric thinking lies in *Contributions to Philosophy*, the public title of that secret book, (*Of the Event*), whose hiddenness within parentheses indicates its inaccessibility, like that of the *adyton*. There Heidegger attests that "we can never say beyng itself directly" (GA 65: 79). Rather, beyng remains in its essential sense a "secret"—like the hidden *arche* of thinking itself whose origin once flourished in the pre-Socratics and whose futural *arche* awaits us as the "other beginning." Hölderlin's poetry offers us a language of this inaccessibility, a language deeply attuned to beyng's own secret dimension. In this sense, we need to understand Heidegger's *topos* of the secret Germany as part of a lifelong preoccupation with the *Geheimnis* (secret, mystery) as the encoded language that the poet expresses in his attempt to enter into the *adyton* that grants nearness/*Nähe* to the few and the exceptional. The discourse of the secret Germany, then, the one already prepared by Hellingrath and George, should not merely be understood as a political "phase" that Heidegger undergoes during the 1930s and then later abandons as he steps away from official National Socialism. Rather, I would argue that the secret Germany remains Heidegger's lifelong preoccupation that, in the years after 1945, retreats into the hidden temple of his Hölderlin writings since he understands that the time is not ripe for its public proclamation. Nevertheless, under the name of "Hölderlin," Heidegger attempts his longed-for revolution in language, a language that thinks back behind "logic" to the heart of beyng's poetic *logos*.

IV. Hölderlin without History

Heidegger's secret Germany, this "forbidden fruit," never finds its home within the borders of the Reich or the Federal Republic. It lives on as a *mythos* of the futural, a *mythos* of what is coming. Heidegger associates this secret Germany with the name "Hölderlin," although the historical Hölderlin held out the promise of a very different ideal of "Germania" than the one embraced by the Freiburg philosopher. For Hölderlin, "Germania" is not the equivalent of "Deutschland" since in 1801, when the poem was composed, no such entity existed.[38] Rather, Germania signifies a spiritual-cultural ideal that has no equivalent political structure. With the territorial disunion of the various German states into kingdoms, principalities, duchies, baronies, free cities, and palatinates, the German lands were no match for the superior forces led by Napoleon. But Hölderlin believed that despite this political-military inequity, the Germans still might offer Europe something that the French could not. As the Coalition Wars were brought to a close by the Peace of Lunéville in 1801, Hölderlin imagined the possibility of a new Swabian republic that might extend northward from the Swiss Alps all the way to the Swabian Alb. This republican dream of a political brotherhood of free-spirited Germans built on the French revolutionary ideals of liberté, égalité, fraternité, would guide Hölderlin's political hopes at the turn of the eighteenth century. Fueled by his millennial dream of a radical *Umkehr* or "reversal" of the violent course of European conflict, Hölderlin envisioned the onset of an epoch-altering peace that would bring with it fundamental changes at the political and individual levels. Immediately after receiving "news of the negotiated peace," Hölderlin wrote to his sister that "all will now be well with the world . . . everything seems to be leading up to an exceptional period, days of beautiful humanity, days of certain, fearless goodness and ways of thinking that are lucid and holy and exalted and simple all at once" (E&L: 193/DKV III: 444–445). In many of the poems written to celebrate this vision of peace—"Der Frieden," "Friedensfeier," "Gesang des Deutschen," "Wie wenn am Feiertage"—Hölderlin identified the fatherland with the ideal of cosmic-universal harmony associated with the muse Urania (DKV I: 226). Moreover, his vision of Germania here is hardly militaristic or even narrowly "patriotic" in any strictly "national" sense. Rather, in terms inherited from the Swabian pietism of Bengel and Oetinger, Hölderlin envisioned an "inner fatherland" and an "inwardly-turned heavenly kingdom" that emerges from a spiritual interiority that enables a glimpse of the essence of things.[39] Already during his studies at the Tübingen Stift, Hölderlin learned these rudimentary forms of a pietistic eschatology that runs through so much of his poetic verse. Hence, when, during the period of the Third Reich, Hölderlin becomes the standard-bearer for a militantly racial and chauvinistic nationalism that seeks to conquer all of Europe (and the world) in the name of German triumphalism, we are left to ponder the trail of hermeneutic violence.

At a time when Hölderlin's work was being hailed as the "Graeco-Germanic" antidote to the poisons of "Graeco-Judaic" influences within Western culture, and when Nazi propagandists like Willi Kunz were enlisting "Battle-Comrade Hyperion" to help defeat the forces of nihilism in the West, Heidegger rejected such blatant misuse of the poet for crudely instrumental purposes.[40] Yet Heidegger's *Hölderlinbild* suffered from its own lapses and profanations. Authorized by Hellingrath to prescind historical context and to approach Hölderlin as a prophet who stands alone (with the ancient Greeks) as a voice of/from an "other" temporality, Heidegger succeeded in transposing the poets' words onto a wholly different history: the history of beyng. Like Hellingrath, Heidegger approached Hölderlin's texts against the background of an eschatological vision of temporality whereby history would be read through the promise of the coming gods. This, Hellingrath affirms, is not the time of "history" (thought as historiographical chronicle), but "the destitute time" where "the old gods are dead and live on merely in saga" (HV: 146). For Hellingrath, the time of poetic chronicling, the time of "Germania," places us at "the midday point of world history, between the magnificent past and the radiant future that unfolds itself, in that time summoned by the priestly maiden Germania, where the old gods of the earth and of the aether are once again with us" (HV: 147). In this time between the times "of the gods who have fled *and* the god who is coming," "Hölderlin first determines a new time" (EHP: 64/GA 4: 47). As Heidegger puts it, in his reconfiguration of historiographical time as the salvific time of deliverance and anticipation, Hölderlin "poetically thinks through to the ground and center of being."

This time of poetic nomination is, above all, a mythic time that gives both Hellingrath and Heidegger license to de-historicize Hölderlin and to make him the voice for their own political/philosophical visions of the German future. In the process, the most fundamental words and convictions of the poet are refashioned and transformed—one might even say profaned or transmogrified—to beget a Hölderlin in line with their own interpretive aims.[41] Perhaps nowhere is this violence more pronounced than in Heidegger's characterization of Hölderlin as the poet of redemption stirred by the awareness of a German mission (*Sendung*) to save Europe and the West. This persistent vision of Hölderlin's poetry as salvific endures throughout Heidegger's life. We find echoes of it in a letter written in 1975 to Hellingrath's fiancée, Imma von Bodmershof, about Hölderlin's future role in the world. Citing the opening lines of "The Titans,"

> Not yet, however,
> Is it time. They are still
> Untethered. What is divine does not strike those who are indifferent.
>
> (SPF: 282–283)

Heidegger writes:

> What is gathered in the simplest way with these words is what Hölderlin has to say to our contemporary world civilization. But he is being falsely portrayed as a Jacobin and this kind of machination is given assent to by public opinion. One cannot experience the demonic quality of this kind of machination because one still reckons with energies that the industrial age wants to (and, presumably, must) make use of.
> Whether the summons of the "divine" that comes from the most distant god will still strike followers and awaken them? Whether poetizing and thinking will first be freed from the alien sphere of the literary and the cultural and be appropriated over to their own destined vocation?
> This is the concern (*Sorge*) of my thinking. (HIB: 143–144)

Until the very end of his life Heidegger remained preoccupied with the meaning of Hölderlin's poetry for the West and with "Norbert's mysteriously fateful, intimate connection to Hölderlin" (HIB: 133). Nonetheless, like Hellingrath, he was completely unable—or unwilling—to grasp the political realities of Hölderlin's own work. As a committed republican who embraced the deepest ideals of the French Revolution, Hölderlin believed that the German-speaking lands might unite to form a spiritual–aesthetic republic that would lead Europe to an age of international peace marked by fraternal co-operation and an all-encompassing unity of nature, human beings, and the gods (cf. "As on a holiday"). In this festal banquet celebrated "at the Evening of Time" and presided over by "the law of love," there Germania would take its proper place among the peoples and be recognized for its spiritual merits. Yet despite this lofty vision of an epoch of peace, Hölderlin was no artless *Schwärmer*. He recognized the Jacobin leaders as "violators of the *Volk*" who would be punished by "holy Nemesis" for their "vile intrigues and barbarous designs" (DKV III: 105). After the violence of the Reign of Terror, Hölderlin lost his faith in any French version of a truly spiritual revolution. In *Hyperion*, Hölderlin's hero experiences a similar disenchantment with the Greek revolutionary forces and decides to "surrender [him]self more and more to blessed nature" (H: 213/DKV II: 173). As Jochen Schmidt has argued, "France is for him the land of shipwrecked revolutionary deed, while Germany is the land of a 'revolution in ways of thinking and imagining' . . . that so radically alters all tradition such as is to be expected only from 'revolutions.'"[42]

In so many ways, then, "Germania" needs to be grasped as a poem written by Hölderlin to address the failure of the French Revolution to bring about the profound and abiding change that he had expected. Hence, its fundamental mode of attunement is marked by a "sacred mourning" that shapes its very message (SPF: 188–189). Mirroring this Hölderlinian mood of mourning is Heidegger's own "Germania" lectures that likewise reflect a profound disappointment at the failure of [the National Socialist] revolution to bring about real, essential change. Both the poem of 1801 and the commentary from 1934 are thus the product of a poetic-philosophical mourning that does not sink to despair but keeps alive the hope for a deeper revolution in the secret-sigetic language of poetic concealment and 'hinting' that the gods favor. It is against this background of a "destitute time" that yearns for communion with the gods that both Hölderlin and Heidegger will conceive of history poetically and philosophically. And yet Hölderlin's pietistic yearning for spiritual awakening and fulfillment will fundamentally differ from Heidegger's hopes for an other beginning in that it embraces a brotherly openness to other nations and peoples that seeks a universal reign of peace, not a narrowly German exceptionalism and predominance. Moreover, against the violence of the French Terror, Hölderlin imagines a Germania who is "defenseless" and unarmed (*wehrlos*), not a Germany powered by a Wehrmacht that threatens the peace and stability of Europe. In this way we can find the fundamental points of con- and di-vergence between the poet and the thinker who seek to interpret "Germania" each according to their own understanding of the secret dimension of the secret Germany. "In search of the true time for his own time," Heidegger tells us, the poet "removes himself from the time of the present day" (GA 39: 50). Following Heidegger's directive here as a way of reading his Hölderlin lectures, we can see how his interpretation of the poet constitutes Heidegger's own attempt to "remove himself" from the narrowly presentist concerns of his contemporaries.

V. "The Rhine": Heidegger and Originary Springing Forth

Despite these political distortions in the WS 1934–1935 lectures, there is much that is philosophically relevant to Heidegger's own thought path. Heidegger's "Hölderlin" comes to embody some of Heidegger's most essential thinking during the 1930s and 1940s, a thinking ever attuned to "what is coming"—a coming that is not merely an anticipation of the future but "the coming of the beginning" as "the coming to presence of all-presence itself" (EHP: 78/GA 4: 55). This thought lies at the heart of the Hölderlin lectures, an attunement that "thinks of what has been (*das Gewesene*) in thinking of what-is-coming (*das Kommende*)" (EHP: 130/GA 4: 107). Intimately connected to the thought of what is coming, however, is the thought of remembrance (*Andenken*), a thinking-of (*an-denken*) that "*commemorates and remembers* (*des Denkens an den Ursprung*) the origin" (EHP: 153/GA 4: 131). Heidegger sees Hölderlin here as the poet who founds being in language by attuning himself to the phenomenological potencies of *physis* as "an emerging and an arising, a self-opening, that simultaneously arises as it turns back toward that from which it has emerged and in this way shrouds within itself that which in each case gives presence (*Anwesung*) to what is present (*einem Anwesenden*)" (EHP: 79/GA 4:56). At root, Heidegger's Hölderlin becomes *the* poet who poetizes that the beginning of our history is still to come, that is, still coming as a kind of homecoming to our concealed origin, an origin whose potencies have hardly been able to unfold their poetic power. What the Hölderlin lectures announce is this special German commission of taking up the problem of homecoming not merely as a historical "return" to one's own history or to the Greek *arche*. Rather, this commission will be grasped as the task of preparing the future of the beginning as *An-fang*: an opening to the beginning as that which "takes us in" (in-*ceptare*) or "seizes" (*fangen*) us in its path of unfolding *at*, *by*, *on*, and *from* (*an*) its inception. In SS 1932 Heidegger explicitly conjoins this task to the beginning of the pre-Socratic thinkers Anaximander, Heraclitus, and Parmenides: "Insofar as we exist, that beginning *is always still happening*. It *is has been* (*gewesen*), but it is not past—as having been it essentially unfolds (*west*) and holds us contemporaries in its essence" (GA 35: 98). And in his Rectorial Address Heidegger announces,

> The beginning still *is*. It does not lie *behind us* as something long past, but it stands *before* us. As the greatest moment, the beginning has in advance already passed over all that is to come and thus over us as well. The beginning has invaded our future; it stands there as the distant injunction that orders us to recapture its greatness. (HR: 111/GA 16: 110)

The Hölderlin lectures announce the coming of "a new time," the time of "the new beginning" that awaits the German *Volk* (EHP: 64/GA 4: 47; HGR: 105, 110, 234/GA 39: 115, 122, 258). This new beginning (what Heidegger in *Contributions* will then term "an other beginning") offers the promise of a revolutionary *Haltung* or comportment toward beings that transports us into (*einrücken*) the Earth and out of (*entrücken*) "an attuned relation to the gods" (HGR: 123–124/GA 39: 140). Such an attunement first opens up beings in an originary way so that we find ourselves in a wholly other relation to the Earth as a homeland that opens itself to us as a dwelling place. As Heidegger explains it, "dwelling is grounded in and through poetizing; that is, it is 'poetic'" (HGR: 197–198/GA 39: 216). Yet "poetic dwelling" does not mean that our way of finding ourselves at home upon the earth depends upon our skill at reading poetic verse or in cultivating an appreciation for lyrical rhapsodies. On the contrary, poetic dwelling has less to do with poesy as poetic composition than with the originary *poietic* character of being itself as a *poiesis*—namely, as a making, creating, or pro-ducing that brings forth and "lets what is present come forth or emerge into appearance" (GA

7: 28). That is to say, poetry is less a literary account "about" the world and its unfolding than being's very self-unfolding that lets the world come to be. Poetry poetizes this originary, creative event of beyng's unfolding, what the Greeks called *physis*. Here Heidegger understands *physis* as "this whole prevailing that prevails through the human being itself, a prevailing that it does not have power over, but which precisely prevails through and around it—it, the human being, who is always already spoken out about this" (FCM: 26/GA 29/30: 39). *Physis* happens, then, as a *poietic event* that exceeds the power of the human being to grasp it, an event that disposes over the very possibility of human being *to be* in that it opens the space for us to dwell. If Aristotle in the *Nicomachean Ethics* understood *poiesis* as a form of human "making," for Heidegger it needs to be grasped as being's own mode of appearing as the letting-be that discloses and conceals, that happens *through* human beings but is not grounded in them as Cartesian subjects. Here being itself is understood as *poietic* and poetry can happen only if the poet attunes himself to being's *poietic* character. Insofar as we attune ourselves to this *poietic* character of being, we leave open the possibility of dwelling poetically upon the earth. Being itself has no pregiven meaning; it happens as an event that has the meaning of a making that happens, as Jean-Luc Nancy puts it, *ex nihilo*—singularly, depending on nothing (literally).[43]

To dwell poetically, then, needs to be understood less as an accomplishment of human beings, something that we merit through our enterprise and will, than as something that happens through beyng's own power to which we are "exposed" or *ausgesetzt*. As Heidegger puts it:

> Poetry is not to be understood . . . as a cultural achievement of the human being . . . [It is not] one of those human-made products whose production human beings have come to earn . . . All that the human being works and effects has its necessity and is "full of merit" (*Voll Verdienst*). Yet—in sharp opposition to this—none of this reaches *his dwelling upon this Earth*, his proper *Da-sein*, for such beyng is "poetic" and has nothing to do with "merit" or cultural achievement or outward manifestations of soul. "Poetic" and poetical here mean that which sustains from the ground up the configuration of the being of the human being (*Seinsgefüge des Menschen*) as a historical *Dasein* in the midst of beings as a whole. "Poetic" does not mean some kind of "façon" or mode of providing

additional embellishment for one's life, but is an exposure to beyng and as such exposure is the fundamental occurrence of the historical *Dasein* of the human being. (HGR: 33–34/ GA 39: 36)

Coming to poetry, entering into its elemental promise, is less an "appreciation" of idyllic verses that conjure images of "purling rills" than it is an *exposure* to an originary power that far exceeds our capacity to grasp it. Poetry is dangerous, "threatening," and imbued with a "rupturing force" (HGR: 198/GA 39: 217). Only because it is so dangerous does it carry with it the potential for revolutionary transformation—and only through revolution, the Heidegger of the early 1930s believes, can the human being be "transposed into a new form of being" (EHP: 92–93/ GA 4: 71). But the power of revolution can happen only when a people is attuned to the possibility of such change. Such an attunement depends, in turn, upon the exposure of a poet to the heavenly ray of light that "strikes the poet suddenly" and threatens him with annihilation (EHP: 91/GA 4: 79). Like Semele, the poet stands "bare-headed beneath God's thunderstorms." Such a figure remains unprotected and at the mercy of sudden destruction, ex-posed to the sphere of danger in being literally placed outside of—in Latin, *ex + ponere*—the familiar abode of custom, habit, and convention (SPF: 174–175). In Heidegger's reading of Hölderlin's hymn "As on a holiday . . . ," it is precisely this exposure of the poet to "the terror of the immediate" and the "extreme danger" of unmediated unity with the divine, that later allows the *Volk* "to drink heavenly fire without danger," since the danger has already been mediated for them by the poet. But again, such a mediation does not happen solely as a consequence of the poet's own initiative; first "a god must throw the kindling lightning-flash into the poet's soul" (EHP: 90/GA 4: 68). Again and again, Heidegger will stress the power of the holy to transform the earth into a proper dwelling place for human beings—but only if human beings attune themselves to the *poietic* power of the earth as *physis*. Here Heidegger alters one of the most revolutionary interpretations of the poetic that we can find: poetry as an attunement to what is coming (*das Kommende*), an attunement to the poetic word as the foundational saying of a new time, a time of the coming. As Heidegger puts it,

> In its coming, the holy . . . grounds another beginning of another history. . . . Now the poetic word is a foundational

saying . . . This word is the event of the holy (*das Ereignis des Heiligen*) . . . This word, still unheard, is preserved in the Occidental language of the Germans. (EHP: 97–98/GA 4: 76–77)

Though the German *Volk* has not yet heard this word, its concealed power still harbors the promise of its coming, the promise of an other beginning where Hölderlin's word will find its resonance. It is this hope of revolutionary upheaval that sustains the Hölderlin lectures in WS 1934–1935.

VI. *Physis* as *Poiesis*: Beyng as Poetic Event

Within the historical moment granted to him, Hölderlin "poetically thinks through to the ground and center of being" (EHP: 64/GA 4: 47). Yet his bequest to think being anew and to do so primordially has, Heidegger insists, never found its proper hearing. What Hölderlin's poetry promises is that a new age is coming, must come, can not but help come, if only we attune ourselves to the incipient power of this coming. And yet generations have passed and the force of this annunciation has not been understood or taken up by mortals. As Heidegger puts it in "Germania" lectures: "*Dasein* has become a stranger to its historical essence, its mission and its mandate. Alienated from itself, it remains without vocation, indeterminable, and hence 'without meaning.' Its vocation remains absent because the fundamental attunement of standing within (*Innestehen*) the essential conflicts is without attuning force" (HGR: 119–120/GA 39: 135). At the site of this age of estrangement, distress, and mourning, however, stands the poet, the one who is able to endure the dark night of godlessness and glimpse the distant horizon for signs of the gods' return. In this distress the poet finds signs of this return in the power of *physis* to endure upon the earth—especially in the form of rivers, those demi-gods whose movements and contours foretoken the destiny of a coming *Volk*. Hölderlin's verses bespeak the power of *physis* as the poetic bequest of the Germans. Hence, despite the trials that confront the human being in the age of the world's night, Heidegger proclaims the enduring power of this bequest and urges his listeners to take up the concealed charge that holds its futural promise. "If we comprehend this essence of poetry, that it is the founding of being in the word, then we can divine something of the truth of that verse that

Hölderlin spoke . . . full of merit, yet poetically dwells the human being upon this Earth" (EHP: 59–60/GA 4: 42). For Heidegger, the possibility of poetic dwelling depends less, however, upon our "merit' (*Verdienst*) than it does upon our attunement to being's own *poietic* power, its originary, creative fount of possibilities that emerge into appearance even as they simultaneously recede into concealment and hiddenness.

> "Dwelling poetically" means: standing in the presence of the gods and being struck by the essential nearness of things. Dasein is, in its ground, "poetic"—which means, at the same time: it is, as founded (grounded), not something earned or merited (*kein Verdienst*), but is rather a gift. (EHP: 60/GA 4: 42)

Poetic dwelling happens, then, as a happening without human cause or merit, a happening that is, as it were, gifted to us from *beyng* (though not in the sense of being as a "subject"). Poetic dwelling unfolds as a *poiesis* or bringing-forth that is, as William McNeill acknowledges, "the event of an originary *poiesis* of which we are not the origin, yet which, happening in and through us, first enables our dwelling."[44] At the heart of this gift of *poiesis* is the way that beyng originarily grants to human beings their dwelling place—the site, abode, or place for their sojourn (*Aufenthalt*) upon the earth, their *ethos*. Here *ethos* will be understood not as a human trait—"character"—but as our fundamental belonging to the order of beyng that happens as an *event* of appropriation whereby we are opened to the self-showing concealing of beyng itself as *poietic* or "that which brings forth." In his 1935 essay "The Origin of the Work of Art," Heidegger takes up the notion of *poiesis* to show how art functions as the original site for the happening of truth. In his later 1953 essay "The Question Concerning Technology," he returns to this crucial notion that "*poiesis* is bringing-forth" (GA 7: 12). But now Heidegger explicitly links the creative power of *poiesis* with *physis* itself and claims:

> Not only handicraft manufacture, not only artistic and poetical bringing into appearance and image, is a bringing-forth, *poiesis*. *Physis* also, the rising of something from out of itself, is a bringing-forth. *Physis* is indeed *poiesis* in the highest sense. (BW: 317/GA 7: 12)

In this claim that *physis* is the highest kind of *poiesis*, Heidegger intimates something that he had already hinted at in the Hölderlin lectures—namely, that "poetizing is the fundamental event of beyng as such" (HGR: 233/GA 39: 257). Moreover, "the saying of this poetizing is in itself the jubilation of beyng . . . is the reigning of beyng (*das Walten des Seyns*)" (HGR: 231–232/GA 39: 255–256). *Physis* "essentially prevails" or *west* as a *poietic* event that discloses the very conflict or "enmity" between concealment and revelation that reigns in all coming-to-presence and bringing-forth. As Heidegger would later put it in the Ister lectures, "What essentially prevails as being . . . can only be said in poetizing" (HHI: 120/GA 53: 150). This intimative relation between *physis* and/as *poiesis* would not only come to shape Heidegger's understanding of art as originary bringing-forth out of essential strife and of poetry as the founding of being in language, but it would, more essentially, serve as the very basis for his understanding of human homelessness and deracination in the epoch of the *Gestell*. His claim in the famous "Spiegel Interview"—"The reigning of the *Ge-Stell* says: the human being is beset (*gestellt*), laid claim to, and challenged by a power that manifests itself in the essence of technology" (HR: 326/GA 16: 672)—goes back to this question about how technology distorts (*verstellt*) *physis'* manner of bringing-forth by placing it under the demands of human re-presentation (*Vor-stellen*) and pro-duction (*Her-stellen*). What poetry expresses is this sense of homecoming, of dwelling within being as if it were our proper home, of understanding homecoming itself as the proper task of the poet whereby we "return into the nearness to the origin" (EHP: 42/GA 4: 23). And yet, at the same time, poetry also gives word to the uncanny (*unheimlich*) sense that even there where we are "at home," we are not-at-home at all, cut off as we are from the very sources and energies of our own being. For the later Heidegger, it is this sense of the uncanniness (*Unheimlichkeit*) of human existence that marks the very appearance of *Dasein* as tragic since "human beings themselves in their own essence are a *katastrophe*: a reversal that turns them away from their own essence" (HHI: 77/GA 53: 94).

This sense of not-being-at-home even—and precisely when—we are at home will come to mark Heidegger's own interpretation of poetic dwelling. As Heidegger grasps it, homelessness itself is not merely a form of social-economic dislocation or psychological *anomie*, but much more an ontological condition for human existence. If we can but attune ourselves to such homelessness as "the proper plight of dwelling," if we can but *think* it as what is most proper to us, then it will come to constitute nothing less than "the sole summons that *calls* mortals into their dwelling" (PLT: 161/GA 7: 163–164). One might even say that in this turn to dwelling as sojourn, abode, stay or *Aufenthalt*, Heidegger will come to find a different way of expressing what in *Being and Time* he termed "Dasein." Dasein will be thought here as the open site for the disclosedness of being, a site whose openness recedes into concealment in the very movements and orientations that Dasein initiates. In this same way, for the later Heidegger, "Everything is founded upon learning how to dwell in the speaking of language (*das Sprechen der Sprache*)" (PLT: 210/GA 12: 30). But such learning to dwell in the speaking of language can happen only insofar as we "correspond to language" (*der Sprache entspricht*). Poetic dwelling happens as a learning to respond to this call for correspondence to language as our proper home, the site for our dwelling upon the earth (PLT: 216/GA 7: 194). As Heidegger so succinctly puts it, "Poetizing is the fundamental capacity for human dwelling" (PLT: 228/GA 7: 207). It is the way that human beings can correspond to beyng inasmuch as *physis* can be understood as an originary kind of *poiesis*. Our sojourn, stay, abode upon the earth, what Heidegger terms our "Aufenthalt," is a stay, a dwelling that holds or keeps open (*aufhält*) the polemical play between concealment (*lethe*) and revelation (*a-letheia*) that reigns in the midst of being. To hold ourselves open for such play, to withhold (*vorenthalten*) or hold ourselves back from (*sich enthalten*) any kind of mastery over beings, this means for Heidegger a comportment or *Haltung* that remains "*open for the mystery*" (*die Offenheit für das Geheimnisses*) (GA 16: 528). It is Dasein's being open to the site of being's self-showing in/as concealment that forms our poetic dwelling. Heidegger understands such poetic dwelling as *Aufenthalt*, as an *ethos* "that ponders the abode of the human being," the way it abides in "being open for that which is assigned (*Zugewiesene*), in the watchfulness for what is coming" (PM: 271/GA 9: 356; EHP: 141/GA 4: 118).

Dwelling is poetic for Heidegger in that it attunes itself to beyng's own *poietic* character of bringing-forth-into-appearance. In corresponding to beyng's *poiesis*, in exposing ourselves to, and being open for, this ever-emerging event of *physis*, we abide in the *Da* of the abode. *Ethos*, in this sense, is not something isolated within the subject as something like "character"; it is, rather, the "open region" to which the human being belongs within the play of the fourfold of being. As Jean-Luc Nancy would have it, *ethos* is properly thought as "the bringing into play of being" whereby he sees "the thinking of language and poetry as a true *ethos*."[45] When we comport ourselves in such a way that we recognize the poietic character of our dwelling as a gift, then we come to dwell poetically as our proper *ethos*. In the later Heidegger, this *ethos* of dwelling comes to be thought of as a composed releasement toward things, an *ethos* of *Gelassenheit*. Yet already in the early Hölderlin lectures we can find the basis for such a thinking in Heidegger's reading of "In lovely blueness" with its vision of poetic dwelling. This early vision of poetic dwelling will come to play a crucial role in Heidegger's thinking of *ethos* and will help bring to language the insights of *Being and Time* about human responsibility toward the other. There Heidegger shows that responsibility is less a self-enclosed, egological self-responsibility than it is the very inscription of otherness in the coming to itself of the self. *Dasein* comes to itself as a response to a call, the call to-be that is not a given possession, but a charge to become responsible for one's response to this call. As a thrown being who is not the author of its own existence, *Dasein* is charged with taking responsibility for its "da," of answering to the summons of being: "to-be." But this summons is not merely a self-generated call of conscience; it is always already, as François Raffoul argues, "an essential exposure to the other."[46]

If our existence is marked above all by "care," then it is equiprimordially a care for others in that *Dasein* comes to existence in *Mitsein*, "Being-with." As Heidegger puts it, "Being with Others belongs to the Being of *Dasein*, which is an issue for *Dasein*. Thus as Being-with, *Dasein* 'is' essentially for the sake of others" (BT: 120/SZ: 123). In responding to others, in exposing ourselves to their alterity, we come to be responsible for the very emergence of being in its temporally particular situatedness. Such otherness resists our attempts at appropriation. More properly, in the event of being that is the world, we are appropriated by what is other, summoned to respond to the call that comes, unbidden, from an alterity that never lets itself be appropriated. This sense of responsibility is not limited to other human beings. In Heidegger's work this responsibility extends to all beings, or rather, to being's way of be-ing, its happening as the play/*polemos* of concealment and revelation. This means, as Raffoul expresses it, that "being displays its own ethicality" whereby ethicality is understood as "the bringing into play of being."[47] Ethicality here, in its human form, would then be something like our very relation to being, our *ethos* of poetic dwelling that "ponders the abode (*Aufenthalt*) of the human being," that familiar abode that opens itself for the presencing of the other, the unfamiliar (*des Un-geheuren*) (PM: 271/GA 9: 356). Here again *ethos* would be understood as something that belongs to being, is being's very way of being, something to which human beings might correspond if they were to heed being's call to dwell poetically upon the earth as the basis of a poetic *ethos*. *Ethos*, then, will be thought of as something like the "conduct" of being, rather than merely as human conduct. As Jean-Luc Nancy thinks it, what is at stake in Heidegger's notion of "originary ethics" is "nothing other than the end of a metaphysico-theological foundation to morality *so as to arrive at ethics as the ground of being*."[48] In this reading of originary ethics as what belongs to being and not merely to human being, we can find the traces of a Hölderlinian *ethos* of dwelling poetically as the proper way for human being to heed, attend to, honor, celebrate, and correspond to "the jubilation . . . [and] the prevailing of beyng" (HGR: 231–232/GA 39: 255–256).

At the core of this Hölderlinian *ethos* we can find an openness to the "infinite alterity of the other," a sense that, as in the Böhlendorff letter, otherness is essential to the fostering of the proper, the self, one's own.[49] For Hölderlin, this means that the other is not there for my sake but resists my attempts at appropriation. Or rather, that in my attempts to appropriate the other, the foreign, the unfamiliar, I am appropriated in ways that I cannot foresee or direct, overtaken by the alterity of the other even when I resist it. At times, Heidegger seems not to have thought through the full implications of this Hölderlinian insight, as Lévinas has often reminded us.[50] Heidegger's "Germania" lectures are replete with instances of German exceptionalism and nationalist sentiment, yet we can also find there the basis of an originary ethics of dwelling attuned to the poietic power of beyng. Indeed, as Heidegger sees it, it is Hölderlin's own poetic efforts at giving voice to this *poiesis* that constitutes an opening for the turn to an other beginning of thinking. For at the heart of Hölderlin's poetic *ethos* of dwelling lies a receptivity to the event of coming-forth that is *physis*, an event that we must prepare ourselves for—else its emergent power passes us by and remains unheeded. This Hölderlinian vision of the human being as co-participant in the festal celebration that is beyng, a celebration that happens when human beings and gods encounter one another in all their strangeness, comes together as a reciprocal belonging together in the event of appropriation. As Heidegger puts in his "Remembrance" lectures: "The event of appropriation is what is festal in the feast" (GA 52: 77). This is the sacred dimension of our belonging to beyng, of attuning ourselves to divine powers that reign over us and to which we are beholden. When, in "As on a holiday . . . ," Hölderlin writes "let the sacred be my word," he thereby acknowledges that the very possibility of poetry can only come when the poet "lets" the word come from out of the sacred gift that *physis* bequeaths to him. It is this originary *poiesis* that makes poetry, or rather poetic dwelling, possible. As Heidegger writes, "Poetry is the founding of being in the word" (EHP: 41, 38/GA 4: 42, 38). But it is also a gift that comes to us to offer "the highest possibility of human being."

VII. The Mystery of "das Reinentsprungene" and the Vocation of the Poet

Poetic dwelling claims us more than we claim it—but only if we are ready for such a claim. Our attunement to the openness of the event and our poetic/thinkerly comportment toward its coming, lets poetic dwelling come. But as Hölderlin knew, although it has always already been a possibility, we have not yet let it happen. It is to come. It can come, it will come, only if we are open to its coming. The event of appropriation as e-vent [L. *e-venire* (to come)] can only happen then, as a *poietic* event. That is, it can only come to be within the possibility of poetic dwelling as a "standing in the presence of the gods and being struck by the essential nearness of things" (EHP: 60/GA 4: 42). Semele was struck by a god and it destroyed her. Zeus's lighting flashes proved too overwhelming and came to teach mortals that approaching the divine source can be deathly dangerous. Yet the product of the intimate encounter between Zeus and Semele was a god, Dionysus, who comes to mediate this dangerous chasm between gods and morals by "bringing the trace of the flown gods down to the godless" (GA 39: 188). Dionysus mediates the destiny of mortals in his role as a demigod "who bears witness to the beyng of both" father Zeus and mother Semele, the beyng of a primordial unity marked by oppositional force. In much the same way, Heidegger tells us, this role of mediation will be taken over by the poet who likewise mediates the destiny of a *Volk*. But Heidegger goes even further. He extends his claim beyond the poet to focus on the figure of the river as a founding middle for human beings and in his WS 1934–1935 lectures he takes up an extensive analysis of Hölderlin's poem "The Rhine" as a demigod that mediates the historical essence of human dwelling upon the earth.

As Heidegger reads it, Hölderlin's "Rhine" is not simply a poem about the mythological significance of a river and its literary symbolism.

It is much more than an "image" of the river; it is, rather, a poem that poetizes the river as the place "where humans are able to dwell, there where their essence is rooted" (GA 75: 75). As Heidegger puts it in "The Rhine" lectures:

> The river is not a body of water that simply flows past the locale of human beings; rather, its flowing, as land-forming, first creates the possibility of grounding the dwellings of humans. The river is a founder and poet (*Stifter und Dichter*), not just metaphorically, but as itself. (HGR: 239/GA 39: 264)

Hölderlin himself, drawing on one of Pindar's Fragments, comes to understand the river as "stagnant water" that is formed when it presses up against the steep banks from which it receives its movement. Forced by these banks in a certain direction, "driven on by its origin," the river "violently creates paths and limits upon the originally pathless, upward-flourishing Earth" (HGR: 84/GA 39: 92; DKV II: 772–773). In conjunction with this "natural history" of the river, Hölderlin lays out a corresponding myth of human history shaped by his narrative of the flight of the gods from the earth and the mourning that their abandonment has occasioned. If, "since the flight of the gods, the Earth has been pathless," with the animating violence of the river's flow, new paths are now cut that offer direction and limits. As the poet sings his hymn in praise of the Rhine, the gods are invited back to the earth to return to "the waters of the homeland" (SPF: 188–189). Moreover, as Heidegger explains it, "through the arrival of the new gods, the entire historical, Earthly *Dasein* of the Germans is to be pointed on a new path, creating a new determinacy and orientation" (HGR: 84/GA 39: 93). In much the same way as poetry founds being in words, rivers found being as dwelling: "river and poet both belong in their essence to the founding of dwelling and of the *Dasein* of a historical *Volk*" (HGR: 234/GA 39: 259). That is, the poem does not "symbolize" the river or simply take the phenomenon of river and place it into language. Rather, the poem instantiates the river in a different register: like the river, it is open to the event of dwelling and in this way lets this openness come to be by exposing it to possibilities that spring forth from its concealed origin.

As he comes to think the essence of the river, Heidegger focuses on distinctive Hölderlinian bywords that inaugurate the fourth and tenth strophes of the "Rhine" hymn. The *gnome* that begins the fourth strophe—"Enigma is that which has purely sprung forth"—"enunciates the entire space of this poem," Heidegger claims. But how? And why does Heidegger expend so much of his energy in the "Rhine" lectures on exploring the concealed meaning of this enigma? Apart from Heidegger's own predisposition for focusing on succinct, cryptic utterances (pre-Socratic fragments, gnomic poetic verses), this spare line alludes to the hidden power of the origin, of commencement, and the way it recedes from view even as it continues to exert its ruling force over all that proceeds forth from it. "The entire course of the river itself," Heidegger tells us, "belongs to the origin" (HGR: 184/GA 39: 202). The *arche* remains enigmatic and inscrutable—and yet in it lies the destiny of all that can spring forth from its source. In attempting to think this enigmatic springing forth "with the word 'destiny' (*Schicksal*), we hit upon the fundamental word of this poem" (HGR: 157/GA 39: 172).

The destiny of the Rhine—which for Heidegger means the destiny of the German *Volk*—lies in its enigmatic origin that has gone unthought and unapprehended. The "inner will" of this poem sets as its task the poetizing of such destiny as the "determinate, governing power" that reigns over Germania. "Destiny" here does not mean, however, anything fixed, determined, or fatalistic; on the contrary, destiny remains something to be accomplished and unfolded, something that can only come to be in the most intimate dialogue with the origin. Here, Heidegger insists, Hölderlin's notion of destiny is nothing like the early Greeks' idea of *moira*, thought in Latin terms as *fatum*. Destiny is rather, something like an *Ereignis*, an appropriating event by which we come to own "that which is proper to us," that which the Böhlendorff letter terms, "das Eigene" (E&L: 208/ DKV III: 460). But as the Böhlendorff letter so powerfully shows, it is precisely that which is proper to us, that which lies proximate and near, that is most distant and difficult to appropriate. What proves to be the most difficult task of human beings is that "we must take responsibility for the being to which we are delivered over," the destiny to which we are assigned (HGR: 160/GA 39: 175). As a thrown project given over to the historicity of its individual fate, *Dasein* confronts its *responsibility to being* as "a mission or mandate . . . to take up, in the highest way, our being as something that has come over us (*Gekommenes*)." To take on such responsibility, Heidegger intimates, requires that we truly be able to "suffer" in such a way that, within such suffering, "beyng is revealed as destiny." In his ability to think the demigods, to suffer-with them (*mit-leiden*) in suffering the enigmatic burden of beyng itself as a unity that comes to be through enmity, the poet opens himself to "the attunement of holy mourning in readied distress" (HGR: 166, 169/GA 39: 182, 185). This suffering is not mere wretchedness or dejection, it needs, rather, to be understood "as a suffering [*Leiden*] that sustains [*Er-leiden*]—a suffering that accomplishes and creates." To think the demigods, then, as suffering, is less an insight into their particular character as beings caught in the middle, as it were. Rather, it means to think beyng in its enigmatic springing forth as a destiny that occasions suffering.

The poet's fundamental attunement here is a creative passion for the co-suffering of the destiny of the demigods. In this co-suffering (*Mitleid*) that is neither a feeling of "compassion" nor of "pity," the way is opened up for the poet to experience the powerful joy that prevails at the heart of beyng. At the border of "complete hopelessness and despair . . . there ensues the most profound turn-around," a *conflictual intimacy* (*Innigkeit*) between joy and sorrow that "lets spring forth and in so doing at the same time holds apart that which has sprung forth in the hostility of its essential powers" (HGR: 130, 226/GA 39: 148, 249). Here in this notion of conflictual intimacy Heidegger finds "one of Hölderlin's key words," indeed "the foundational metaphysical word" that belongs to beyng itself (GA 39: 117, 249). "Conflictual intimacy" here does not connote anything merely "subjective" or interior to the private realm of warm feelings or sentimentality. On the contrary, it serves as the name for "the supreme force of *Dasein* . . . [that] evinces itself in withstanding the most extreme conflicts of beyng from the ground up. In short: an attuned, knowing standing within and sustaining the essential conflicts of that which, in being opposed, possesses an original unity, the 'harmoniously opposed' (*das Harmonischentgegengesetzte*)" (HGR: 106/GA 39: 117; E&L: 277–298/DKV II: 527–552). In his mourning-play, "The Death of Empedocles," Hölderlin takes up Empedocles's principle of originary opposition between love and strife (*philia* and *neikos*) as the very law of tragic being that expresses the tensions of harmonious opposition within/as *physis* that come to express the deepest sense of conflictual intimacy. Moreover, in his essay "The Ground of Empedocles," Hölderlin insists that "IN THIS BIRTH OF THE GREATEST ENMITY THE GREATEST RECONCILIATION APPEARS TO BE REAL" (E&L: 262/DKV II: 430). Intimacy here comes to serve as the name of an "originary unity of the enmity of the powers of what has purely sprung forth"—yet "conflictual intimacy does not mean the coalescence and obliteration of distinctions. Conflictual intimacy names the belonging together of the foreign, the prevailing of astonishment, the claim of awe" (HGR: 227/ GA 39: 250; EHP: 225/GA 4: 196). In this originary unity there reigns the secret (*Geheimnis*) that belongs to beyng, the conflictual intimacy that "remains enigma (*Rätsel*) through and through."

What this signifies for Heidegger is a way to read "The Rhine"—as river and as poem—as a movement of opposition, a flow that confronts a counter-flow, one that connects its outward movement away from its source as a movement in tune with the concealed, enigmatic powers that lie within the source itself. The intimacy of this play between that which springs forth purely (*das Reinentsprungene*) and the source from which it flows away is—and remains—an enigma. The narrative of the poem itself both shows and enacts this contra-puntal movement of the Rhine as the destiny allotted to the Germans. As it begins its course out of the Alps as a stream, the Rhine originally flows eastward, toward Asia (which Heidegger reads as "Greece"). Yet in the midst of this push toward Greece suddenly this orientation shifts and the river confronts a pull in the opposite direction against which it ravages and rages. After a crucial struggle that threatens its very directional thrust, the Rhine succumbs to its inward pull and "suddenly breaks off toward the North, the German land" (HGR: 209/GA 39: 229). In bending to the pull of this "counter-will," the Rhine accepts its proper "vocation" and "destiny" as what is most proper to it in achieving a "conflictual intimacy" with the same counter-turning forces operating within both nature and the poet. In attuning himself to this intimative capacity of the river, the poet intimates the mystery of *physis* itself: namely, that everything that has purely sprung forth emerges in a counter-turning strife against its origin. The poet's task here becomes one of "unveiling the mystery of beyng" (HGR: 214/GA 39: 235). Yet even such unveiling does not eliminate the mystery; on the contrary, it brings us before the mystery *as* mystery, showing us how the intimacy that reigns throughout beyng as harmonious opposition "prevails in essence as mystery" (HGR: 226/ GA 39: 250).

In such conflictual intimacy Hölderlin is able to bring the river into a new relationship to human beings whereby the Rhine comes to enact the very destiny of the *Volk*—and not merely "symbolically." Here the river comes to itself as the expression of *physis*, thought as the very power of beyng itself and not merely as "nature." Nature here does not designate a field of objects (land, water, plants, animals, air, etc.) that belongs to our planet; nor is it a "resource," a commodity, an asset, or anything that "stands over against" a subject as a *Gegenstand* or ob-ject. Nature, for both Hölderlin and Heidegger, signifies the primordial, inceptive force of coming to be, arising, and springing forth that the Greeks called "physis." Yet on Heidegger's reading, "nature" in this sense comes "to be *denatured* by way of two alien powers": first, by Christianity that reduces nature to something merely "created" and second, by modern science that "dissolves nature into domains of power belonging to the mathematical ordering of world commerce, industrialization, and technology" (HGR: 178/GA 39: 195). As Heidegger claims, even though Hölderlin still thinks within the metaphysical limits of German Idealism, he poetizes beyond them toward "another metaphysics" that opens a space for "a new fundamental experience of beyng," one that draws upon the Greek experience of *physis* but ultimately seeks to inaugurate a new German experience of "that which is coming" (HGR: 179/GA 39: 196). Yet the Germans can come to such an experience only if they enter into the essence of the river that holds forth the opening to their destiny, a destiny that is marked by a "burdensome good fortune" granted to Germania (SPF: 192–193). Much as the Rhine itself confronts the difficult counter-force that thwarts its will and bends its course and direction, so too must the Germans undergo a corresponding bend in their history (the defeat in the Great War, the burden of Versailles and the political-economic catastrophe of Weimar) to properly come into their ownmost identity. Only in undergoing this resistance and its confounding burden of pain and suffering can the Germans, like the Rhine itself, come to embrace their (its) proper destiny. Such is the enigma of all that which has purely sprung forth. Yet to enter into this destiny demands of the Germans that they also embrace the essence of the river in its beyng as a demigod.

VIII. The Beyng of the Demigods

As Heidegger continues on with his lectures during WS 1934–1935, he turns to the question of poetic suffering. Learning how to suffer, to let the necessity of suffering become part of a joyful attunement to *physis'* powerful impulse to spring forth in birth, belongs to the beyng of the poet as the teacher of the *Volk*. The way in which beyng opens itself is occasioned by the pain of birth, the suffering of emergent force that opens paths and shapes destiny. Socrates, in *The Symposium* 206b–e, learns of the maieutic art of midwifery that assists in the process of birthing, an art cultivated by Hölderlin as he comes to poetize the birth of the river. Hölderlin learned from Pindar's Fragment "That Which Animates" (*Das Belebende*) to conceive of the river as a demigod and to grasp its pull and counter-pull as a path-forming, directional movement of violence that tears through the land and provides a "middle" (*Mitte*), a way to mediate the distance between mortals and gods. The demigods' essence is precisely this "oppositional harmony" between mortals and gods since they are both more than human (overhuman) while "nevertheless remaining beneath the stature of the gods: *undergods*" (HGR: 150/GA 39: 166). When the poet asks about their essence, he undertakes a profound questioning concerning the essence of humans and the essence of the gods. In this interrogation he comes to experience the breach between gods and mortals and the suffering that distinguishes the demigods as those creatures torn between two oppositional limits. Like both Christ and Empedocles, those two figures who suffered through the cleavage imposed by these limits, the poet comes to identify with the demigods as figures attuned to the deepest intimacy of enmity and strife that reigns over all. Hence, when Heidegger claims that the opening verse of Strophe X—"Demigods now I think"—"is the pivot of the entire poem," we can properly situate it against this Hölderlinian identification of the poet with the river as demigod (HGR: 249/GA 39: 275). Here we begin to understand the relation between humans and gods as one marked by a relationality that both brings together and yet separates, a relation of godforesakenness and abandonment that helps attune the poet to the possibility of an other "coming": the return of the gods to the earth. It is within this configuration that Hölderlin holds forth his vision of poetic dwelling as the gift granted mortals that allows them to attend to their task of preparing the way for the return of the holy.

The significance of the demigod for Hölderlin's understanding of the river is profound. It comes to play the same role within the river hymn as the "caesura" in Hölderlin's interpretation of Sophoclean tragedy: it functions as "the pure word," the "pivot," that serves as "the counter-turning doubling of origin" that marks the river's essence as half-human, half divine (HGR: 235/GA 39: 260). It is the word that points to the essence of the river as the place for human dwelling *and* as the movement away from the settlements of a fixed abode toward the other and toward strange possibilities of union with the gods. In sharing this bifurcated, torn, and sundered condition, the river—as demigod—carries out the tragic law of limitation and finitude that marks all of Hölderlin's tragic writings. Destiny unfolds not singly out of a pure origin—but doubly as a counter-turn against the origin that in its enmity manages to bring forth the concealed power of the origin that needs enmity in order to unfold what is most proper to it, that which it most loves. Only in being exposed to this strange and threatening other does the self truly come to its proper self. Only in being pulled by a counter-will at the outset of its journey eastward does the Rhine come to accept its proper will as the river of the Germans, the place for the unfolding of German destiny. Here, in the destiny of the demigod, Heidegger finds the heart of his early Hölderlin interpretation—that the destiny of the Germans is a divided one, a "burdensome good fortune" marked by a tragic sense of a counter-pull toward its opposite. In confronting this strangely other possibility held out to them in their history, the Germans come to find their proper essence in struggle, scission, crisis, and enmity.

Much as in "Germania," where the Germans had to truly learn their mission and mandate as the "elected" *Volk*, in "The Rhine" Hölderlin attempts to educate the *Volk* to its "historical vocation," to transform its "native endowment" through a struggle or *Kampf* to set itself at odds with itself, to learn to enter into the chiastic relation between what is one's own (*das Eigene*) and what is foreign, strange, and other (*das Fremde*). The model for Heidegger's own understanding of this chiastic relation is, of course, the letter that Hölderlin wrote to his friend Casimir Ulrich Böhlendorff on the eve of his fateful departure to Bordeaux in December of 1801. There Hölderlin spoke of the counter-turning "reversal" that is required of the Germans if they are to properly mediate the sacred "fire from heaven" sent by Zeus to mortals. Unlike Winckelmann, whose classicism aimed at an imitation of the Greeks, Hölderlin sought a "living relation and destiny" for the Germans in their appropriation of the Greek legacy. Here Greek art would be approached not as an ideal to be imitated, but as one to be challenged, reversed, and transformed. What made the Greeks great was their willingness to strive against what was native in them and to become masters of that which was foreign, strange, and alien. Their lesson to the Germans, Hölderlin proclaims, is that finding one's own, proper identity requires an *agon* with the very gifts with which one is endowed, that which is native and inborn. Only in this way can we "truly appropriate the foreign" (E&L: 207/DKV III: 460).[51] In terms of the "Rhine" hymn, that means for Heidegger that "we Germans" must come to learn how "to freely use the national," the native, and that which has come to us as our "endowment" (*das

Mitgegebene). In order to do so, however, we first need "to transform our given endowment, the 'national,' into what is given to us as a task (*das Aufgegebene*)" (HGR: 264/GA 39: 292). This is the Germans' proper "historical vocation" to become properly German by challenging themselves to become masters of that which is their opposite: the Greeks. Yet this can only happen if the Germans overcome their classicist heritage of deference to, and imitation of, the ancients and learn how to reverse the Greek achievement by becoming masters not of "the ability to grasp: 'the clarity of presentation',", but rather in "being struck [by] 'the fire from the heavens.'" What the Germans excel in, what they are given as their endowment, is precisely this ability to grasp, plan, calculate, and organize in a sober and distantiated manner. But what stands before them as their task is to expose themselves to the sacred fire of the heavens, to open themselves to the dangerous and threatening possibility that they might, like the Greeks, "come to be struck by beyng" (HGR: 265/GA 39: 292).

Hölderlin's great achievement, pace Heidegger, is to show that the possibility of experiencing Greek sacred fire can only come for the Germans in the gods' withdrawal. That is, the only proper relation (*Bezug*) of the Germans to the gods lies in the form of their withdrawal (*Entzug*) from the earth. The force of *physis* itself pulls, draws, removes (*ziehen*) the gods away from (*ent-*) the earth, as if in a draught of wind (*Zug*). Correspondingly, this force draws humans toward (*beziehen*) a space of absence as the only possible way for us to relate to the gods' overwhelming power. Semele's destruction teaches us that the sacred fire of the gods—Zeus's unmediated appearance as the god of lightning—cannot be confronted directly, but only in and through the phenomenon of withdrawal. In his translation of Pindar's 2nd Olympian Ode (vv. 39–50), Hölderlin hits upon the very boundaries of mortal-immortal relations that shape the logic of his "Rhine" hymn (DKV II: 696). There he relates the tale of Semele's destruction and Dionysus's birth that he paradigmatically expresses in his own hymn, "As on a holiday . . .":

> So once, the poets tell, when she desired to see
> The god in person, visible, did his lightning fall
> On Semele's house, and the divinely struck gave birth to
> The thunder-storm's fruit, to holy Bacchus.
>
> And hence it is that without danger now
> The sons of Earth drink heavenly fire.
> Yet, fellow poets, for us it is fitting to stand

> Bareheaded beneath God's thunder-storms,
> To grasp the Father's ray, no less, with our own two hands
> And, wrapping in song the heavenly gift,
> To offer it to the Volk. (SPF: 174–177)

In the absence of the gods we find traces of their presence; in their concealment and recession we are privy to the only form of revelation that allows us to inhabit their space of withdrawal. Poetic dwelling, as the *ethos* (*Aufenthalt*) or comportment (*Haltung*) of holding-oneself-back (*Ent-halten*) and with-holding (*Vor-enthalten*), attunes itself to this dimension of withdrawal that shatters the elaborate scaffolding of Western thinking as the metaphysics of presence. What the poet points to, rather, is the way withdrawal comes to show absence not as something "present," but as the trace of a coming that both points back to "the unprethinkable primordiality of the beginning," even as it provides the first signs of a future coming that stands before us "as a task—to be struggled for" (GA 4: 75; GA 39: 292).

What the Böhlendorff letter announces is a radically new form of poetic dwelling that sees it as *the* essential task of the Germans "to come to be struck by beyng." This stands in constant tension with the Germans' own native endowment that lies in "the ability to grasp, the preparation and planning of domains and calculating, setting in order to the point of organization" (HGR: 265/GA 39: 292). In order to come to themselves, to find their proper identity, the Germans need to reject the neo-classical project of mimesis and, rather than imitating the Greeks, seek to reverse the Greek achievement. If the Greeks' native endowment consisted in "a rousing proximity to the fire from the heavens, being struck by the violence of beyng," then their achievement lay in "harnessing the unharnessed in the struggle for the work, grasping, bringing to a stand." Conversely, if what was native to the Germans was their "ability to grasp," "their faculty for exposition," then their future task must be to cultivate an openness to being struck by beyng, a readiness to being appropriated by "heavenly fire." What matters most to Hölderlin here—and, later, to Heidegger—is this genius for mediation (*Vermittlung*), for sheltering oneself (and one's *Volk*) from the im-mediate exposure to sacred fire by learning how to come into "conflictual intimacy" (*Innigkeit*) with beyng in a kind of Heraclitean *harmonia* of oppositional elements whose very enmity is endemic to the concealed oneness of all things. As Heidegger claims in WS 1934–1935, this requires above all a "struggle" or *Kampf* for what is given to the Germans as their proper task—namely, to reverse the Greek achievement and to come to the gods not through their presence but through their absence. In embracing this struggle precisely *as a Kampf*, the Germans—as a historical *Volk*—attain "the highest":

> Our highest achievement will come about for us if we set to work the endowment of being able to grasp, in such a way that this grasping binds and determines itself and enjoins itself to the jointure of beyng (*sich fügt der Fuge des Seyns*), if our ability to grasp does not become perverted into an end in itself and merely dissipate within the exercise of our own capacity. Only that which has been struggled for and is to be attained through struggle—not that which is merely one's own—provides the guarantee and granting of the highest. Because what is given to us as endowment and task are in each case differently apportioned to the Greeks and the Germans, the Germans—precisely in what is their own—will never surpass the highest achievement of the Greeks. That is what is "paradoxical." In fighting the battle (*den Kampf kämpfen*) of the Greeks, but on the reverse front, we become not Greeks, but Germans. (HGR: 262/GA 39: 293)

Above all else for Heidegger in the winter semester of 1934–1935, the "task" of the German *Volk* lay before them: to bear the "burdensome good fortune" that Zeus's eagle has granted to Germania, the "elected one" (SPF: 192–193). To bear this difficult good fortune requires that the Germans poetically and thoughtfully "found" beyng through an originary naming that embraces the German *Volk's* mission and mandate "to be a between, a middle, out of which and in which history is grounded" (GA 39: 289). This is why Heidegger places such significance on the opening verse of Strophe X in "The Rhine," "Demigods now I think," because it points ahead to the futural task of the Germans to serve as a "middle" or mediating power between the Greek achievement in antiquity and the coming task of preparing the earth for a return of the gods. In entering upon this task and making it the very center of German self-understanding, Hölderlin finds the right note of sacred mourning in his poem "Germania," a note that serves as the fundamental attunement of his poetizing. In "The Rhine" Hölderlin prepares "the poetic thinking of the demigods" as the enigmatic event of the purely arisen from which would spring forth the destiny of the *Volk* as a destiny attuned both to the beyng of the demigods and to the beyng of the poet as the mediating force by which the *Volk* comes to enter its assigned task as the *Volk* of the middle. What the poet names here is the Earth itself, the mother of all; what he calls attention to through this naming is the way time itself gets configured as the way the Earth opens to human beings in their position of/at the middle. As Heidegger puts it: "To think demigods means: to think toward the Earth and out to the gods from out of the originary middle" (HGR: 206/GA 39: 226). This is the destiny of the Germans bequeathed to them from out of this position at the middle of time. In this middle "there resonates the 'divinity of old' (v. 100) together with that which is to come" (GA 39: 289, 293). That is, at the middle of time, between the gods who have fled and the gods who are to come, stands Germania struggling to come to terms with "the conflictual intimacy of endowment and task (*die widerstreitende Innigkeit des Mitgegebenen und Aufgegebenen*)" that marks the destiny of the *Volk*.

Here, at the beginning of his engagement with Hölderlin, Heidegger underscores what he sees as "the violence of beyng," the enmity, conflict, strife, and opposition that constitutes the *palintropos harmonia* or "counter-striving harmony" of Heraclitus's bow and lyre (GA 39: 294, 123, 125; Heraclitus B51). This "hidden harmony" (*harmonia aphanes*, B54) is less a harmony whose inner unity is concealed or covered over by conflict than it is a harmony that lies in the essence of conflict itself as the hidden, organizing force that brings things together *in* and *as* oppositional elements that belong together essentially. That is precisely why "the free use of the national," as Hölderlin puts it in the Böhlendorff letter, is so difficult—because it demands that we find our essence in a turn against what is native to us, even as we open ourselves to the power of the alien to help us become who we properly are. On this reading, *Kampf* becomes creative, "the strife of profound conflict," which—as Heraclitean *polemos* (B53)—rules over all things. As Heidegger expresses it, "If all beings thus stand in harmony, then precisely strife and battle must determine everything fundamentally" (HGR: 112/GA 39: 125).

In this early formulation of *Kampf* (*polemos*) as "the power that creates beings" and rules over and "governs beings in their essential substance," Heidegger comes to embrace a polemology of being that runs through his work of the 1930s, especially *Introduction to Metaphysics* and the four Nietzsche courses (GA 43, GA 44, GA 46, GA 47). For Heidegger, *Kampf* first creates the possibility of decision with regard to life and death" and serves as the proving ground for beings as they properly come to themselves only in and through this *Kampf* with other beings—and with themselves. Hence, as Heidegger claims, both gods and humans need one another in order to come into their essence as gods and as humans.

> Such battle (*Kampf*), however . . . is here not arbitrary discord or dissension or mere unrest, but the strife of profound conflict between the essential powers of being, such that in such battle the gods first come to appear as gods, humans as humans, over against one another and thereby in their intimate harmony (*in innigen Einklang*). There are no gods and humans in themselves, or masters and slaves in themselves who then, because they are such, enter into strife or harmony. Rather, the converse is the case: it is *Kampf* that first creates the possibility of decision with regard to life and death. (HGR: 112/GA 39: 125–126)

All being finds its measure in *Kampf*; only through the intimate opposition of contesting strife can harmony come into its proper ownness. In Heraclitus's Fragment 50—*hen panta einai* ("One is All")—Heidegger finds the wisdom of all conflict that generates harmony as its essential being. It is this intimate relation between *polemos* and *harmonia* that spurs Heidegger's own reading of Hölderlin in WS 1934–1935, as he comes to think the necessity of Hölderlin's poetry for a new flourishing of German *Dasein*.

Only by confronting what he calls "the horrors and devastation that threatens the *Dasein* of the Occident on all sides," Heidegger insists, can the German *Volk* take up its "vocation of builders building a new world." Yet learning how to properly take on this vocation necessarily involves an essential coming to terms with the essence of Hölderlin's poetry.

> We must press ahead into that domain in which Hölderlin's poetry unfolds its power, if only there to first arm ourselves to bring about a preparedness for this poetry as such—as an essential power of every great, historically spiritual world.
>
> What we have said hitherto may suffice to clarify why, in our thoughtful and philosophical endeavor to empower the power of the essence of poetry, we have chosen Hölderlin (*um*

die Ermächtigung der Macht des Wesens der Dichtung Hölderlins).
(HGR: 202/GA 39: 222)

The very turn to Hölderlin, Heidegger implies, is authorized by the need for the Germans to "arm themselves" in the struggle for their own historical existence, an existence that needs to confront the threat to Germany—and the West—that comes from the Asiatic "other."[52] Only Germany can save the West; only a *Volk* that has come to grasp the necessity of enduring the conflictual strife within the essence of truth can hope to find a path out of the nihilism reigning in the West and come to prepare a path into an other beginning for thinking.

In his reading of Hölderlin's poetry as a poetizing of Heraclitean *polemos* or *Kampf*, Heidegger finds a way of "empowering" the Germans to come to their own readiness for battle in the struggle for a new form of *Dasein*. In this struggle it is necessary for the Germans—the *Volk* of the other beginning—to come into essential conflict/confrontation (*Auseinandersetzung*) with the Greeks—the *Volk* of the first beginning—in order to prepare the Western world for its futural mission. Here, "Hölderlin too, stands under the power of Heraclitean thought. . . . The name Heraclitus is not the title of a philosophy of the Greeks that has long since run its course . . . it is the name of a primordial power of Western-Germanic historical *Dasein*, and indeed in its first confrontation with the Asiatic" (HGR: 118/GA 39: 133–134). Drawing upon the structural oppositions of "one's own" (*das Eigene*) and "the foreign" (*das Fremde*) within the Böhlendorff letter, Heidegger comes to understand that only by confronting the foreign through Heraclitean *Kampf* can the Germans hope to appropriate the proper, that which is one's own. "*Kampf* is the greatest test of all being: in it is decided whether we are slaves in our own eyes or masters"; but only if we accept this challenge to become great ourselves, that is, to expose ourselves to the great conflict that reigns through all being, can we hope to grasp "the secret, the middle of beyng" (GA 16: 283; GA 39: 285). If German Dasein is to become its own, it must "determine itself from out of the middle of beyng." Hence, it is imperative that it think Hölderlin's two poems—"Germania" and "The Rhine"—together as a way to think the mystery of this middle, the realm of the demigods, the poet, and the river conjointly. Only from out of the middle, the site of the conflict of beyng, can the path of an other beginning commence.

For the Heidegger of these early Hölderlin lectures, this path is ruled over by *Kampf*, struggle, conflict, and strife. The rhetoric of *Kampf* here, with its paramilitary allusions to "arms," "battle," "invasion" (*Einrücken*) and "weapons" (*Waffen*), forcefully positions the Germans as battle-ready for the struggle to come (GA 39: 125, 222, 289). In retrospect, this paramilitary form of philosophy appears as a kind of preparation for another kind of *Einrücken*—namely, that of the German *Wehrmacht* into Poland in 1939 or Russia in 1941. But to be fair to Heidegger we can also see this as part of his early enthusiasm for the politics of *Kampf* that informs his Rectorial Address—"All that is great stands in the Storm"—and his other political speeches of 1933–1934. By the end of the Battle of Stalingrad, Heidegger will have rethought the essence of *Kampf* so that now he can make provision for a stance of "letting happen" or releasement that allows for conflict, but not in a volitional or calculative sense as part of what he terms "machination." Nonetheless, throughout these early Hölderlin lectures we find Heidegger bending Hölderlin's own propriative embrace of peace, entente, and brotherhood toward his own more aggressive form of philosophical nationalism. We can see this most clearly expressed in the way that he reads the last lines of "Germania," where Hölderlin writes:

> And gladly, to be remembered,
> The needless dwell
> Hospitably among the needless
> At your feast days
> Germania, where you are priestess
> And defenselessly give counsel (*Und wehrlos Rath giebst*)
> Around the kings and peoples (*Völker*) (HGR: 16/GA 39: 13; SPF: 194–195)

If here Hölderlin expresses his deeply felt longing for ecumenical peace and for a brotherhood of nations committed to the principles of liberté, fraternité, égalité, Heidegger will suppress these expressions of French revolutionary consciousness in favor of a narrowly German sense of exceptionalism and nationalist fervor. Here Heidegger challenges the common understanding of "defenselessness" (*Wehrlosigkeit*) as the mere "laying down of weapons, weakness, or the avoidance of struggle." Rather, he claims,

> "Defenseless" (*wehrlos*) means that historical greatness that no longer requires defense or resistance, that is victorious (*siegt*) through *Da-Sein*, insofar as the latter brings beings to appearance as they are, through the standing-in-themselves effected through the work. It is not some counseling or offering of prescriptions that speaks in a didactic or schoolmasterish manner—but rather that most powerful and direct pointing of the ways, which brings itself about through these paths being *taken*, *Dasein* grounding itself. (HGR: 263/GA 39: 289–290)

During the time of National Socialist triumph, the works of Hölderlin were published in a variety of small, inexpensive, paperbound pocket editions that catered to young students and soldiers. There, in editions variously titled *Hölderlins Vaterländische Gesänge* ("Hölderlin's Songs of the Fatherland") or in the assorted *Feldpost* editions suitable for packing in a rucksack, poems such as "Germania," "Death For the Fatherland," "Song of the Germans," "To the Germans" and "Voice of the *Volk*" were circulated for patriotic purposes.[53] Moreover, in the self-assertion of the German *Volk*, Hölderlin came to stand as a "symbol" for "Volk, Freedom, and Fatherland." In the Tübingen Stift, site of the poet's student years, a memorial plaque was erected by the Munich sculptor Eugen Wittmann who delivered a short speech in 1933 to commemorate Hölderlin's relevance for the new German revolution:

> We need a visible symbol that elevates us all, a symbol that brings us together and through which we come to know ourselves. And this symbol is for us Hölderlin. We have once again become Germans; we are reflecting upon who we are and upon our mission—and we are honoring the great men who have sacrificed themselves in the *Kampf* for German freedom, in the *Kampf* for the German soul.[54]

By the war years the tone and tenor of this patriotic rhetoric would be transformed by the militancy of the German mission so that Hölderlin's themes of peace, brotherhood, and understanding would be wholly suppressed in favor of a bellicose poet who called the Sons of the Fatherland to a cult of sacrificial death. As part of this transformation some admirers of Hölderlin went so far as to suppress or consciously elide his texts that made reference to "peace"or—in the case of the "Germania" hymn—to attributes such as being "defenseless" (*wehrlos*). In his lecture "Fatherland," Hermann Binder cited the last two verses of "Germania"— but now changed the text by suppressing the word *wehrlos* so that the text now read: "Germania gives advice to kings and *Völker*." This was, Binder assured his listeners, part of Hölderlin's "belief in the German mission throughout the world."[55]

Against this background of egregious Nazi violation of both the texts and the spirit of Hölderlin's poetry, we can see that Heidegger's own tendentious reading of the poet retains its philosophical integrity. This is not to say that Heidegger's Hölderlin lectures of WS 1934–1935 are not partisan—or even militantly patriotic. On the contrary, I would argue that we need to recognize how deeply "political" they were—but in Heidegger's sense of his own "private National Socialism," of a kind of Hölderlin religion nourished on Heraclitus and the hope of an other beginning. So much of Heidegger's own "personal" commitment to the fledgling German revolution is at work here in the time after the failure of his rectorate year. We can detect a strong autobiographical identification with the struggles of the past to achieve national recognition and a strong sense that, like Hölderlin, Heidegger fears that "they have no use for me" (E&L: 209/DKV III: 462; GA 39: 136). If militant National Socialism is marked by "strength through joy" (*Kraft durch Freude*), then Heidegger's Freiburg National Socialism is interfused with a Hölderlinian attunement of "sacred mourning" that attunes itself to the "conflictual intimacy" (*Innigkeit*) that abides as harmonious opposition as "an attuned, knowing standing within (*Innestehen*) and carrying out (*Austragen*) the essential conflicts of that which, in being opposed, possess an originary unity" (HGR: 106/GA 39: 117). Only the poet can attain to the conflictual intimacy required to withstand the tension between oppositional elements that subsist in a concealed harmony. Only that being who can stand firm within "the middle of time" and draw upon the power of the *arche* while opening up to the possibility of an *other* arche, an other beginning, will be able to lead the Germans to a radically new understanding of *Dasein*. This power to withstand and stand within the different ecstases of time that tear apart the fabric of human existence is granted to the poet. As he is exposed to the oscillations and resonances (*Schwingungen*) of language and learns to attune himself to their temporal disjunction, the poet comes into his vocation as "the voice of the Volk"

(GA 39: 14–15; SPF: 82–85). We shall see later how the oscillations of the river (Ister) and its resonances come to offer Heidegger a way of reframing the question about the native and the foreign.

What stands before the Germans is the difficult mission of learning how "to freely use the National (*das Nationelle*), of what we are born with" (E&L: 207/DKV III: 459–460). But to do so requires that the Germans come to terms with their own destiny or *Schicksal*—"the fundamental word" of "The Rhine" hymn (vv. 11–39–122–183; GA 39: 172). What the Rhine enacts in its difficult struggle to free itself from the fetters imposed by the steep mountain side of the Alpine ranges, a redemption narrative of release and "free use" of its native properties. The river is, like the demigod, a "mediating middle" (*vermittelnde Mitte*) between humans and gods; it mediates earth and heaven, soil and sky, and from out of its divine origin as "the purely sprung forth" (v. 46), it founds cities and culture and provides the "bounds" of the human sojourn or *Aufenthalt* upon the earth (vv. 127–129; GA 39: 194). The poet's task as poet is to enter into the mediating power of this "middle," "And, wrapping in song the heavenly gift, / To offer it to the *Volk*" (SPF: 176–177).

This is the mandate that faces the Germans, as Heidegger sees it: to take up the call of the poet and "take hold of what has been given as our task" (HGR: 266/GA 39: 294). In a dramatic conclusion to his lecture course, Heidegger announces: "The hour of our history has struck." The question is whether the *Volk* will respond to this calling and take up the most difficult task of all—coming to terms with its native endowment. Finally, at the end of his last lecture Heidegger ends with a citation from Hölderlin's Böhlendorff letter:

> We learn nothing with greater difficulty than the free use of the national.

As Heidegger thinks through his own mediating role as the thinker of this mediation, he will move away from the militant rhetoric of the "Germania" and "Rhine" lectures and come to understand that the hoped-for revolution within German *Dasein* is far from being imminent. In the next set of lectures on Hölderlin from WS 1941/42, *Remembrance*, Heidegger will shift his perspective and come to a new reading of the significance of "the national" for German destiny.

2

Heidegger's "Remembrance" Lectures

Das Andenken ist das Wesen des Denkens.
—Martin Heidegger, *Zum Ereignis-Denken*[1]

I. Hölderlin and "The National"

In a famous letter from 1801 to his friend Böhlendorff, Hölderlin writes about the precarious balance between the native and the foreign that for him harbors the mystery of authentic tragic insight. Writing in response to Böhlendorff's own attempts to write a genuine "German" tragedy, Hölderlin counsels him to cultivate those gifts that are non-native to him, since it is there that the mastery of tragic art lies. Yet the native remains essential nonetheless—even if we fail to truly grasp precisely what of our native inheritance must be foresworn and what fostered. But then Hölderlin confesses to him: "Nothing is harder for us to learn than the free use of *what we are born with*"—what in German Hölderlin terms "das Nationelle" (E&L: 207–208/DKV III: 460).

What Hölderlin means here in the phrase "das Nationelle" must be carefully parsed out a bit more than in the usual translations. When he thinks "das Nationelle" he understands it in its Latin sense of *natio*, or "birth"—whence we derive the words "nativity" and "natal." But the etymological complexities of this term from the Latin extend to a range of meanings that include "the native," "the nation," even "the race."[2] We have quickly entered a world where, without being too careful or discerning, we come to identify native birth with the idea of the nation and the national. And in our all too unreflective appropriation of Hölderlin's language of *das Nationelle*, we come to identify this concept with the idea of the nation-state or the native people—in this case, Germany and the Germans.

But, of course, Hölderlin had no "modern" sense of what such a designation would entail. For him, "das Nationelle" might better be thought as those native characteristics (language, traditions, customs, tribal identifiers) that manifest themselves in the life of a people or *Volk*. Hence, we do better to think "das Nationelle" as something like "the Swabian" or the provincial world of shared linguistic-cultural practices. But it also needs to be understood in terms of the shared destiny of a *Volk*.³ As we have seen, however, the history of Hölderlin's poetic reception reveals a neglectful—if not willfully dismissive—consideration of these loosely drawn but profoundly significant distinctions. In a range of different thinkers and writers these distinctions were often collapsed in the name of a more "originary" access to Hölderlin's "genuine" poetic idiom. For example, in various texts from the George Circle—in Norbert von Hellingrath's essay "Hölderlin and the Germans," in Wilhelm Michel's emphasis on "die vaterländische Kehre" ("national reversal") in Hölderlin's late hymns, and especially in the National Socialist portrait of Hölderlin as the poet of the Fatherland—we find the development of a highly politicized *Hölderlinbild* that forms a powerful generational ideal of "Hölderlin as (Political) Educator."⁴ It is precisely against this background that Heidegger conceived his own singular and inimitable vision of Hölderlin as "the poet of poets," "the poet of the Germans," "the most German of the Germans," and "the greatest of the Germans" (GA 39: 214; GA 16: 333; GA 96: 114). In his lectures on "Hölderlin's Hymn: Remembrance," Heidegger will offer a reading of this hymn in terms of the distinction drawn in the Böhlendorff letter between the native and the foreign and will highlight this distinction as the fundament for a poetic rethinking of history in terms of "fate" (*Schicksal*), "what is fitting" (*das Schickliche*), "the holiday" (*der Feiertag*), "the festival" (*das Fest*), and the possibility of "another beginning" for German history. In all of Heidegger's remarks we find a familiar refrain: Hölderlin is the poet of an other beginning—not only for Germany, but for the entire history of the West (GA 95: 378; GA 66: 406). What is occurring contemporaneously in Germany—viz., the Second World War that will decide the future of Europe and the world in the epoch of planetary technology—has its authentic origins in the poetic verses of Hölderlin. The enigmatic design of these verses holds the key for any possible way out of the profound crisis facing us—but before we can attune ourselves to their message, we first need to undergo a profound transformation in our ways of grasping language. In the winter semester 1941–1942, precisely in that time span when the German Wehrmacht will risk everything to secure world domination, Heidegger will offer lectures on Hölderlin's poem "Remembrance" as a way of helping his listeners to hear the world-historical intimations that lay concealed within Hölderlin's poetic "word." Before such an experience would be possible, however, Heidegger claims that "we must first seek a path toward the unity proper to that which is poetized" (HHR: 24/GA 52: 29). What matters above all for Heidegger is that we genuinely grasp what is "proper" (*eigen*), what is "our ownmost" (*eigenste*), and what is authentic (*eigentlich*) to us. And yet this pathway to what is our own proves to be something difficult, something that is not immediately given to us as our possession (*Eigentum*), but which can only be appropriated (*angeeignet*) via a journey into the foreign.

The prototype for just such a journey is, of course, Hölderlin—and more specifically Hölderlin's excursion to Bordeaux in December–January, 1801–1802. In a letter written to his friend Casimir Böhlendorff just before his departure, Hölderlin juxtaposes his spatial journey across the Rhine and into Southern France with the temporal journey to ancient Greece in search of a proper poetic measure for German art. Counseling his friend Böhlendorff on the appropriate "rules" for modern German aesthetics, Hölderlin rejects the accepted "classical" approach to the Greeks proffered by Winckelmann in his "Thoughts on the Imitation of the Painting and Sculpture of the Greeks." There, Winckelmann argued that the path to greatness for Germany lay in an aesthetic mimesis that required modern German artists to imitate the Greek ideal of beauty: "the only way for us [Germans] to become great, and indeed—if this is possible—inimitable, is by imitating the ancients."[5] Since Winckelmann deemed that the very preeminence of Greek art lay in the "noble simplicity and quiet grandeur" native to the Greeks, his aesthetic call was for Germans to abandon their own native tendencies in order to take possession of the native Greek endowment bequeathed to them from their Hellenic patrimony. Yet Hölderlin finds such a measure to be rigid and calcified. For him, what matters above all in the relationship of modern German aesthetics to the ancient Greeks is that the Germans come to an understanding of what is ownmost and proper to their own aesthetic genius. This lies, pace Hölderlin, not in an imitation of the Greek ideal, but in a reversal of what mimesis takes as its ultimate aim. In the Böhlendorff letter Hölderlin explains this complex logic as follows:

> It sounds paradoxical. But I put it to you again, for you to verify and make use of as you wish: in the process of education what we are actually born with, the national (*das Nationelle*), will always become less and less of an advantage. For that reason the Greeks are not such masters of sacred pathos, because it was native to them; on the other hand they are exceptional in their faculty for exposition, from Homer onwards, because this extraordinary man had the feeling necessary to capture the Junonian sobriety of the Occident for his Apollonian realm, and so truly to appropriate the foreign.
>
> With us it is the other way round. That is also why it is so dangerous to derive our aesthetic rules from the sole source of Greek excellence. I have labored at this for a long time and know now that apart from what must be the supreme thing with the Greeks and with us, that is, living craft and proportion, we cannot properly have anything in common with them. But what is our own has to be learnt just as much as what is foreign. For this reason the Greeks are indispensable to us. Only it is precisely in what is proper to us, in the national, that we shall never match them because as I said, the free use of what is our own is hardest of all. (E&L: 207–208/DKV III: 460)

If the Germans are to forge their own proper and authentic (*eigentlich*) form of tragedy, Hölderlin claims, they cannot merely imitate the Greek tragic model. What is required of them is a delicate retrieval of Greek tragic forms by way of a reversal. This means that the Germans must, like the Greeks, reverse what is most native in them by undergoing a passage to what is foreign to them. As the masters of sacred pathos (which Hölderlin identified with "heavenly fire"), the Greeks needed to cultivate what was most contrary to them (Junonian sobriety) as a way of letting the oppositional harmony endemic to tragic presentation come to pass (*sich ereignen*). This they did by reversing their native fervor and frenzy and cultivating a "clarity of exposition" that was foreign to them, but which they were able to master precisely to the extent that they ventured outward into the realm of otherness and difference. According to this curious and intricate Böhlendorff logic, the task of the German poet becomes one of reversing the innate German talent for clarity of exposition by cultivating its opposite—namely, Greek heavenly fire or the passion-filled intensity of direct experience. Tragic art flourishes, Hölderlin wants to say, not by following one's native inclinations but by reversing them in a bold act of cultural appropriation that seeks its opposite in the foreign element. It is this inversion or turning of things "the other way round" that Hölderlin will term "the patriotic reversal" or *vaterländische Umkehr* (E&L: 207/DKV III: 460; DKV II: 919). The dynamics of this process are complex. On the one hand, we should not, Hölderlin claims, imitate the Greeks even if, on the other, they remain wholly indispensable to us. As Françoise Dastur explains it in "Hölderlin and the Orientalisation of the Greeks":

> The Greeks are, in a way, an inverted mirror image of ourselves, they do not represent something of a bygone past. For they have more opened the possibilities of life than produced works that ought to be imitated. This is why they remain an example even though it clearly appears that they cannot nor should be imitated. We must, indeed, distinguish between the model and the example, between what has to be imitated in a static sense of reproduction, and what can be followed in a dynamic and inventive way. We can learn a lesson from the failure of the Greeks, in the sense that what caused their ruination, the obsession with form, can serve for us as an example to follow which can lead us to turn our original cultural tendency towards the unlimited in the opposite direction, and direct it towards our earthly nature. We should not imitate their art and their culture, but we can nevertheless follow their example in such a way that we return to our proper nature and accede to this hyperculture which is the learning of the *free* use of what is proper to us. It is thus in their failure itself that the Greeks remain an example for us moderns.[6]

What emerges from Hölderlin's chiastic retrieval of Greek art—and its ultimate failure—is nothing less than a warning and an exhortation: a warning to avoid an excessive preoccupation with one's native gifts *and* an exhortation to learn the free use of these same native-national abilities by turning them in the opposite direction. For Hölderlin, then, the Greeks offer us an indispensable forewarning to avoid an excessive self-absorption, even as they admonish us to open ourselves to what is wholly other. We do this so that we might properly come to what already belongs to us, even as it still remains alien and unacknowledged. In what follows I would like to take up the threads of this Hölderlinian project of national self-recognition as a way of approaching Heidegger's lectures on Hölderlin's hymn "Andenken" delivered WS 1941–1942. It is during this time that the German Wehrmacht will make its bold move eastward following the entry of America into the war in December of 1941. Without attempting to offer any overly reductionist claims about the impact of Germany's immediate political-military situation on Heidegger's lectures, my reading tries to keep it in view as the background against which Heidegger lays out his thinking of "Andenken." There he offers a prophetic reading of a German future inspired by his own presumptive image of Hölderlin as "the founder of German beyng" and as "*the* poet of an other beginning of our futural history" (GA39: 220; GA 66: 426).

Conceiving the role of the poet through the mythic lens of patriotic national destiny, Norbert von Hellingrath and the George Circle had transformed Hölderlin from a provincial Swabian bard with limited regional appeal into the poet of a "Secret Germany" whose cryptic verses contained the cipher for grasping the nation's future. Heidegger was, of course, profoundly influenced by these national appeals to a futural Germany destiny, although he was hardly alone. During the National Socialist heroicization of Hölderlin, the poet become the symbol of national renewal and authentic German courage and resoluteness in the face of unyielding fate. Already in World War I those young German students called to the front had carried with them in their rucksacks the inexpensive Reclam editions of Hölderlin's poems. The myth went forth of the young German "heroes of Langemarck" (1914) marching boldly into battle singing patriotic songs, carrying the imperial flag, inspired by the verses of Hölderlin.[7] This myth was then taken up again by Nazi architects commissioned to build the Olympic Stadium for the 1936 Berlin Games. There they erected a "Langemarck Hall" that displayed soil from the battlefield of Langemarck and an inscription from Hölderlin's poem "Death for the Fatherland." Heidegger developed his own account of Hölderlinian poetic destiny out of these selfsame martial inflections from the Great War with its myths of courage, determination, grit, and personal sacrifice. For him the voice of Hölderlin would ever be conveyed through the editorial and philological labors of Norbert von Hellingrath who, Heidegger never failed to remind his audience, "died in battle as a field artillery spotter on the frontline at Verdun" (GA 52: 16, 45). Heidegger would always refer to the specific date of Hellingrath's death—December 14, 1916—in his lectures and it became a symbol for him of the same powerful national myth of German exceptionalism (*Sonderweg*) that had propelled Germany into two world wars during his lifetime.[8] The history and depth of Heidegger's attachment to German martial glory and the myth of sacrificial death in service thereto provide the situational background against which Heidegger mobilizes his own *mythos* of German national destiny. But what invites notice here is Heidegger's philosophical use and abuse of this history—and of Hölderlin's role within it—to confect a beyng-historical justification for the German war effort and its consequences for other non-German peoples.

Heidegger completes this lecture cycle in the winter of 1942 as the German *Einsatzgruppen* begin to carry out their program of elimination in the lands beyond the borders of the Reich. In the same semester that Heidegger lectures about "the deprivations of the Second World War" and of "the most proximate and most distant future of the Germans and of the West," his former student Hannah Arendt is adjusting to life across the ocean as a stateless person in New York City (GA 52: 72, 78). In 1943 in an unheralded periodical, *The Menorah Journal*, Arendt published a searing article entitled "We Refugees" that speaks to the emergence of a new class of historical beings—the homeless, stateless, banished species of exiled, expatriated outcasts who live in concentration or internment camps, fill out endless questionnaires about their former status, and stand bewildered in the face of a threatening and uncertain future. As Arendt describes it:

> Lacking the courage to fight for a change of our social and legal status, we have decided instead, so many of us, to try a change of identity.[9]

Yet, Arendt laments, "our identity is changed so frequently that nobody can find out who we actually are." She goes on to claim that "being a Jew does not give any legal status in this world;" instead it bespeaks the image of a stateless wanderer left to try to adapt in environs that are less than receptive to one's arrival and integration. In this vision of the refugee, Arendt finds the figure of a new political category that unmoors the solidity of the old nation state with its nativist metaphysics of national-racial identity. What Heidegger performs in the "Remembrance" lectures is nothing less than the consummation of just such a nativist metaphysics of the nation—but now stripped of its crude metaphysics of blood and biology and reconfigured in and through the poetic language of Hölderlin.

Writing in response to Arendt's forgotten essay, Giorgio Agamben traces the emergence of the refugee back to the Balkanization of the nation-state after the Great War and the Treaty of Versailles. Agamben follows this thread from the demographic shifts that took place following the collapse of the old Habsburg Empire in 1918 and that continued throughout the 1920s and 1930s. A new mass phenomenon emerged, Agamben shows, where "many refugees who technically were not stateless preferred to become so rather than return to their homeland."[10] At the same time, "Russian, Armenian, and Hungarian refugees were promptly denationalized by the new Soviet or Turkish governments." By 1935, "The Nuremberg laws divided German citizens into full citizens and citizens without political rights." Those left without such rights—namely refugees—wound up at the mercy of a nation-state system that proved wholly unable to protect them. Given this new situation, the refugee comes to represent (for both Agamben and Arendt) the very crisis of the idea of "man" and of the human being's status as a "citizen" within the legal order of the nation state. This resulting crisis unhinges the holy trinity of state-nation-territory that developed in the Enlightenment discourse concerning the "Declaration of the Rights of Man and of the Citizen" from 1789 where "nation-state means a state that makes nativity or birth (that is, of the bare human life) the foundation of its sovereignty." Clearly, the current European crisis of refugees from North Africa, the Middle East, and Eastern Europe shows that the modern nation-state based on place of birth as determining one's native territory and identity has been thrown into chaos and confusion. What both Arendt and Agamben come to stress is that the old model of "nation" based on birth, nativity, and political belonging no longer works as a way of thinking the status of the human being within the political order of modernity.

Following her arrest and internment in both Germany and France during the Nazi era, Arendt finds herself seeking asylum in Portugal and the United States. Here she describes herself as one exposed to "the desperate confusion of these Ulysses-wanderers" who, unlike their Greek prototype, never can go home and never appear capable of keeping their identity since it proves ever-changing within the new demands placed upon them by their desperate need to conform and fit into a new language, culture, environment, and political system. Against the metaphysics of the nation-state and its political philosophy of granting rights only to native citizens within the polity, Arendt calls for the recognition of the human being as such—that is, as a human being first, rather than as a citizen of a specific country, territory, or political region. In her essay she offers a description of herself as a Jew, one that stands in stark contrast to the view of national belonging and political identity espoused in Heidegger's "Remembrance" lectures:

> If it is true that men seldom learn from history, it is also true that they may learn from personal experiences which, as in our case, are repeated time and again. But before you cast the first stone at us, remember that being a Jew does not give any legal status in this world. If we should start telling the truth that we are nothing but Jews, it would mean that we expose ourselves to the fate of human beings who, unprotected by any specific law or political convention, are nothing but human beings. I can hardly imagine an attitude more dangerous, since we actually live in a world in which human beings as such have ceased to exist for quite a while; since society has discovered discrimination as the great social weapon by which one may kill men without any bloodshed.[11]

This account of the human being in exodus from the legal order of in- and ex-clusion dictated by the nativist national state appears to Agamben as a way of "decisively opposing the concept of nation" itself.[12] Agamben goes on to challenge the hegemony of nationalist ideology as a form of oppression and subjugation that conceives political freedom in terms of territorial boundaries and borders that reduce the human being to a mere legal-political entity. For Agamben, "it is only in a land where the spaces of states will have been perforated and topologically deformed—and the citizen will have learned to acknowledge the refugee that he himself is—that man's political survival today is imaginable." It is in terms of this question about national political community and native belonging that I would like to explore Heidegger's unremitting emphasis on "the proper," "the native," "the ownmost," and *das Eigene* (as *eigentlich* [authentic]) in his reading of Hölderlin's hymn "Remembrance."

II. A Metapolitics of the *Volk*

Heidegger renounces of course any self-conscious form of "political" philosophy in his work since such an approach already takes for granted what it deems "the political" to be and thereby covers over and forgets its essence. Consequently, he takes a different pathway into this domain by going back to the Greeks and raising the question: "What is the *polis*?"

> *Polis* is the *polos*, the pole, the place around which everything appearing to the Greeks as a being turns in a peculiar way . . . The *polis* is not the notorious "city-state" but is, rather . . . the essential abode of historical humanity. . . .
> The essence of the *polis*, i.e., the *politeia*, is not itself determined or determinable "politically." The *polis* is just as little something "political" as space is something spatial. The *polis* itself is only the pole of *pelein*, the way the Being of beings in its disclosure and concealment, disposes for itself a "where" in which the history of a human race is gathered. Because the Greeks are the utterly unpolitical people (*Volk*), unpolitical by essence, because their humanity is primordially and exclusively determined from Being itself, i.e., from *aletheia*, therefore only the Greeks could, and precisely had to, found the *polis*, found abodes for the gathering and conserving of *aletheia*. (P: 89–96/GA 54: 133–142)

What seems remarkable here is that Heidegger sets out to think the political in terms of the Greek experience of being as *aletheia* and on this basis thinks the *polis* not as political territory or in terms of any legal-juridical constitution, but simply and definitively as "the essential abode of historical humanity." This means that the human being essentially prevails (*west*) only when it abides in a *polis*: "the *polis* is the name for the site (*Stätte*), the *Da*, within which and as which *Da-sein* is as historical" (IM: 162/GA 40: 161). It is only because the human being essentially belongs to the *polis* that it can become *apolis*—that is, "without city and site, lone-some, un-canny, with no way out amidst beings as a whole, and at the same time without ordinance and limit, without structure and fittingness (*Fug*)."

When Heidegger first decided to offer public lectures on Hölderlin in WS 1934–1935, he had just stepped down from his position as rector at the University of Freiburg. After his initial enthusiastic outburst for the Hitler regime that was marked by a series of popular speeches in 1933, Heidegger began to understand the depth of his delusions about the political program of National Socialist rule. As part of this process Heidegger came to see that the National Socialist appropriation of Hölderlin for political ends was both misguided and contrary to Hölderlin's own understanding of "das Nationelle." Heidegger himself explains in the *Black Notebooks* that his original support for National Socialism dates back to "the years 1930–1934," since at that time he believed that "National Socialism held the possibility of a transition to an other beginning" (GA 95: 408). But with the onset of the Hölderlin lectures on "Germania" and "The Rhine" in WS 1934–1935, Heidegger becomes emboldened to rethink his earlier posture. Now Hölderlin, not Hitler, becomes the name of a possibility for transforming the dormant power of a *Volk* who remains slumberous, torpid, and inattentive to the great potential that lies undeveloped within it.

If National Socialism's goal was to bring a new "German" order to Europe (by addressing the oppressive revanchist politics of the Versailles Treaty and affirming an authentic politics of German national self-assertion), Heidegger's aim involved something much grander: a new concept of "the history of beyng" with the Germans at the center of a great transformation in dialogue with the first Greek beginning. But this revolutionary upheaval could happen only if the Germans would undergo a profound revolution in their relation to language. And that, in turn, could only transpire in intimate correspondence with/to Hölderlin's poetic word. In the summer of 1934, just after he had abandoned his activist role in the political revolution by resigning as rector, Heidegger begins to speak of a second, more originary revolution ushered in by a fundamental change in the German understanding of language. At the very end of his lecture course "Logic as the Question Concerning the Essence of Language," Heidegger writes:

> The essence (*Wesen*) of language essentially prevails (*west*) there where it happens as world-forming power—i.e., where it

in advance first fits and brings into jointure (*Fug*) the being of beings. Originary language is the language of poetry . . . True poetry is the language of that being that was forespoken to us already a long time ago and that we still have never caught up with. For this reason the language of the poet is never of today, but always something in the manner of having been and of the futural. The past is never contemporary. . . .

Poetry—and with it proper language—happens only there where the ruling power of being is brought into the supreme untouchability of the originary word. (LQ: 141–142/ GA 38: 170)

In Heidegger's insistence that the poet can never be "contemporary," he boldly challenges the reigning National Socialist appropriation of Hölderlin for political ends. Here he finds the use and abuse of Hölderlin on the part of academics, cultural bureaucrats, political leaders, secondary teachers, aesthetes, and other assorted party members as a testament to the crude power grab of a brown-shirted politics of will, dominion, and technical-industrial hegemony. This instrumentalization of Hölderlin's poetry for transparently political ends strikes him as a betrayal both of Hölderlin's poetry and of what Heidegger called "the inner truth and greatness" of the National Socialist movement (IM: 213/GA 40: 208). In his original lectures from SS 1935, "Introduction to Metaphysics," Heidegger contrasted this "greatness" with "those works that are now being peddled about as the philosophy of National Socialism," works that "have all been written by those fishing in these troubled waters of 'values' and 'totalities.'"[13] He later qualified his critique by adding that what truly constituted "the inner truth and greatness of this movement" was its "encounter between planetary technology and modern humanity." During the early 1930s Heidegger had great hopes that the National Socialist movement would address these two great questions: the unbridled dominion of planetary technology that was destroying the planet by uprooting modern humanity and the social-economic effects of this transformation that had set up the self-contained, striving bourgeois subject as the ideal of human measure. On both fronts Heidegger believed that National Socialism's ecological initiatives toward a greening of the fatherland, as well as its social vision of "the New Man" who was not an "individual" but a member of the *Volk*, would provide a bolster against both the devastating nihilism of capitalist international technocracy and against communist social levelling.

In Heidegger's version of what one contemporary mocked as his own private "Freiburg National Socialism," the Führer or leader would be led by that other philosophical Führer from Messkirch.[14] Here the works of Nietzsche and Hölderlin would find their historical expression in a new vision of German greatness nurtured on the self-assertion of the *Volk* within a reconstituted European order. But again, the failure of the rectorate and the world-historical push of National Socialism toward hegemony and domination led Heidegger to clearly understand Hitler's motives as part of the spreading machination brought on by the Baconian-Cartesian metaphysics of will, dominion, and sovereignty begun in the early modern era. In the *Black Notebooks* we find Heidegger offering his own sarcastic—and oftentimes bitter—observations about the everyday operations of a National Socialistic Germany whose ultimate effect reveals a betrayal of its once energetic hopes. He speaks there of "enraged grammar school teachers, unemployed technicians, and displaced members of the lower-middle class—as guardians of the 'Volk'—as those who are said to set standards" (GA 94: 187).[15] But in all this, Heidegger insists, National Socialism has taken the short view. What matters most—both to Heidegger and to Germany—is the futural power of the National Socialist revolution. In its present form as a naked gambit for profit, plunder, and factional domination, National Socialism appears to Heidegger as a vulgar initiative for personal advancement through the manipulative engineering of ideology. The miscarriage of the National Socialist revolution, its failure to truly engage the metaphysics of technological-planetary dominion, leads Heidegger to seek a purer form of revolutionary, nationalist transformation, one that he finds in the poetic language of Hölderlin.

With their own prophetic force, Hölderlin's verses foretoken the turning of a new epoch, a time of futural possibility and transfiguration where the barrenness of a godless earth begins to open itself to receive the coming gods. Heidegger's turn to Hölderlin—especially in the wake of his disillusionment with official National Socialism—avails itself of this discourse about the gods as a way of bringing to language the shattered hopes for a new instauration upon the earth. Heidegger was a revolutionary thinker in a more than political sense. Political revolution needed to be supplemented and fortified by a second, more profoundly measured, philosophical revolution whereby present historical happenings could be understood not in terms of the history of a *Volk* or of a nation, but more fundamentally, in terms of the history of beyng (HBB: 60). During the early 1930s Heidegger came to call such a discourse "Metapolitics"—namely, a politics that went beyond the focus on individual Dasein to embrace "*the Metapolitics 'of' the historical Volk*," that is, the Germans (GA 94: 124).[16] Even though Heidegger never fleshes out this idea of a metapolitics in his writing, nonetheless I would argue that it remains a powerful influence on the way he comes to interpret both the failed National Socialist revolution of 1933 as well as his own approach to Hölderlin as the poet of a deeper more fundamental "German" revolution. In the *Black Notebooks*, Heidegger writes that "philosophy" must be brought to an end so that we can "prepare the way for something wholly other—metapolitics" (GA 94: 115). In his first set of Hölderlin lectures, Heidegger speaks of "the historical vocation of Germania," which he finds laid out by Hölderlin in the Böhlendorff letter: to learn how to freely use what is given to us as our own, native possibility—namely "the National" (GA 39: 287–292). But the free use of the national can never come to fruition unless the Germans are "transported into the domain in which an actual poetry unfolds its power" (HGR: 194/GA 39: 213). And yet, Heidegger tells his listeners, Hölderlin "has still not yet become a force in the history of our *Volk*. Because he is not yet such a force, he must become one. To commit to this is 'politics' in the highest and authentic sense—so much so that whoever brings this about does not need to speak about the 'political'" (HGR: 195/GA 39: 214). Following this reading, Heidegger poses the decisive metapolitical question to the German people: "Will we once again venture the gods and along with them the truth of the *Volk*?" (GA 94: 183).

That Heidegger understood his reading of Hölderlin to be a confrontation or *Auseinandersetzung* with official National Socialism should be clear. And yet so much of Heidegger's Hölderlin interpretation was still tied to his own version of a poetic-revolutionary National Socialism of the *Volk*. Perhaps this helps explain the allergic reaction to Hölderlin in thinkers such as Derrida and Lévinas. In one of his interviews Lévinas acknowledges that "for Heidegger, Hölderlin is more important than anything else."[17] But Lévinas also confesses that "I do not look for wisdom in Hölderlin, who is foreign to me." And in Lévinas's remarks again we find a return to the question of the native and the foreign that gets at the core of Heidegger's metapolitics of German nativism.

Heidegger's Hölderlin prizes the foreign—but, as Lévinas sees it, only as a way of bringing the native *Volk* back to itself in a kind of Odyssean return to the homeland. Lévinas, of course, finds this kind of fetishizing of the homeland to be an abrogation of philosophical responsibility to the Other. Instead, he finds in Heidegger's reverie of homecoming—which he calls "the tautology of ipseity"—a reaffirmation of the self, the native, the autochthonous, and the consanguineous whereby everything that is "the *outside of me is for me*."[18] It is this deadly metaphysics of identity, Lévinas insists, that threatens the existence of the Other, a metaphysics that Heidegger reinscribes in his private notebooks where he takes up the most banal clichés about Jews as rootless merchants and bankers bent on world "domination" (GA 95: 339; GA 96: 133).[19] Hence, Heidegger can write:

> The question of the role of *world Jewry* is not a racial question, but the metaphysical question about the kind of humanity that, *without any restraints*, can take over the uprooting of all beings from being as its world-historical "task." (GA 96: 243)

As devastating as Lévinas's critique is, it comes from a thinker who is not conversant with Hölderlin and has little feel for the nationalist resonance of his work. Yet even more striking is the critique levied by Max Kommerell, a colleague and acquaintance of Heidegger. Kommerell was a member of the George Circle in his early years and at the age of twenty-six published an important book, *The Poet as Leader (Führer) in Classical German Literature* (1928), that was well received in literary criticism and admired for its bold focus on the poet's leading role in forming a genuine folk community.[20] A long, hundred-page chapter of the book was dedicated to Hölderlin and was one of the few secondary sources on the poet that Heidegger prized.[21] Later, when Kommerell became a professor at Marburg, Heidegger wrote to congratulate him.[22] When three years later Kommerell suffered an untimely death at the age of forty-two, Heidegger delivered a brief memorial on the last day of the summer semester, calling Kommerell "the only one in his field with whom from time to time I was able to have productive exchanges concerning the historical vocation of thinking and of poetizing" (GA 16: 364). In 1941, Heidegger sent Kommerell an offprint of his essay "Hölderlin's Hymn 'As When on a Holiday'" and Kommerell wrote back offering a discerning, though trenchant, critique.

Kommerell recognized immediately the force and originality of Heidegger's essay, which he (like Heidegger himself) did not think of as an "interpretation" but as an "encounter" that addressed Hölderlin as an "ineluctable fate." As Kommerell put it: "I, like all of us who wish to understand Hölderlin, have much to thank you for . . . what one needs to learn from you is that Hölderlin is a fate: not only in the sense that in him—better: in his word—fate happens . . . but also in the sense that his is a fate for those who truly encounter him. He is like Empedocles: he leaves nothing behind him that has not been transformed or transfigured."[23] Kommerell goes on to tell Heidegger that acknowledging Hölderlin as a "fate"—or even more as the fate of a movement that is tied to the hopes for a new "beginning"—is tantamount to proclaiming that only those who share in this fate can understand Hölderlin at all. This "esoteric" approach to Hölderlin that Kommerell knew all too well from his time in the George Circle, appears to him as anything but a rigorous scholarly interpretation. He writes that he fears Heidegger's whole way of reading "does violence to Hölderlin." At one point in his letter he addresses Heidegger directly and tells him he is alarmed at "the horror of your interpretive violence."

A few months later Kommerell writes to his friend Hans-Georg Gadamer about Heidegger's essay and describes it in oxymoronic terms as "a productive train-wreck."[24] He goes on to tell Gadamer that Heidegger's attempt to treat Hölderlin and his poetic work is a mere "pretext" for expressing his own philosophy. What truly transpires there is nothing short of "an act of Heideggerian self-recognition—perhaps one that is rather tragic even as it ends triumphally." Already in his letter to Heidegger, Kommerell had challenged Heidegger's myth of the tragic fate of the Hölderlin editor, von Hellingrath, and had questioned Hellingrath's supposed "selflessness." Instead Kommerell suggested that the whole George Circle's crusade to co-opt Hölderlin as the poet of a "national fate" revealed a strongly "dogmatic" impulse that he likewise identifies in Heidegger. He then asks Heidegger directly: "Does George's self-regard appear greater to you than his vocation? A self-regard that reduces Hölderlin to a mere precursor? The self-preoccupation that prevails also in your own work here and there and instead of an authorization 'risks everything through something else': 'sic volo, sic iubeo' (I will this, I command this)."[25] Here Kommerell unequivocally challenges Heidegger's own peremptory insistence on the unassailability of his own Hölderlin-interpretation, as if he alone were equal to the task of comprehending Hölderlin as *the* fate of the German *Volk*. This "Hölderlin violence," as Kommerell designates it, cannot be understood merely as a dispute between philologists and philosophers over the "proper" way of approaching Hölderlin's enigmatic poetry. Rather, I would argue, what attracts attention here is the way Heidegger comes to position his Hölderlin *Inszenierung* (self-staging, mise-en-scène) in terms of his Hellingrathian dream about opening the path to a "secret Germany," a path that could be followed only by Germans and indeed solely by those who had a presentiment of the "special path" or *Sonderweg* of German destiny.[26] This heroicization of Hölderlin, begun by Hellingrath and the George Circle, is founded upon an esoteric, cultish belief in Hölderlin as *the* poet of an exclusionary German mission to save the West. During the Great War this vision became part of a cultural battle against the encroaching Anglicization of Europe. By 1941 Heidegger had extended it to include Germany's stand against America, the Soviet Union, and other Allied nations.

With Hölderlin as his avatar, Heidegger channels the spirit of the Greeks to offer a pathway to an other beginning. If by 1941 Heidegger has given up on a National Socialist instauration of this other beginning, he still remains committed to the singularity and superiority of the German *Volk* as the chosen vessel for fulfilling Hellingrath's dream of national self-realization. But it is precisely on this question of the national and the native that we must focus more attention. As Arendt's account of the refugee amply demonstrates, Heidegger's vision of national self-assertion came at an extraordinarily high price—especially for those who had not been initiated into the cult of Hölderlin, Hellingrath, and the Secret Germany. For what such a critique powerfully shows is that Heidegger's *Hölderlinbild* goes far beyond mere national pride, cultural chauvinism, or self-willed intransigence against the reigning Hölderlin philology. What plays itself out on the stage of Heidegger's Hölderlin lectures is a national drama about the identity of a *Volk* that rejects the openness to the foreign, the strange, or the other and rigidly insists on a vision of German greatness that reinscribes the platitudes of National Socialist racial exclusion on another, if not equally disastrous, plane. To miss this dimension of Heidegger's reading of Hölderlin is to remain blind to the persistent mythos of German national dominion that pervades Heidegger's work of the Hitler era, including of course the *Black Notebooks*.[27] What Heidegger identifies in his Hölderlin lectures is nothing less than the "decision concerning the essence and vocation of the Germans and therewith the destiny of the West" (GA 95: 18) It is against this background that we now turn to a closer reading of the "Remembrance" lectures as a way of following the path of Heidegger's singular form of Hölderlinian national exceptionalism.

III. Staging the "Remembrance" Lectures: The Vestibule

Already in the WS 1934–1935 lectures on "Hölderlin's Hymns 'Germania' and 'The Rhine,' Heidegger had privileged the opening verse of the poet's hymn as harboring a hidden cipher for situating what he called "the world-hour" of the German *Volk* (GA 39: 51). Moreover, in the very first words of the "Germania" hymn, Heidegger identified "a decision about time in the sense of the originary time of the peoples." In his "Remembrance" lectures Heidegger will follow a similar path and offer his own thoughts on the poem's opening words as pointing to the concealed meaning of time as a way of thinking about the relation between poetry and history. What will be addressed in these lectures is what the poet already had poetized in the hymn of 1803: the hidden meaning of remembrance as a foretokening of what is still to come, both for a poet and for a people. Hölderlin's "Remembrance" begins with the hint of that which is to come:

The Northeasterly blows,

(Der Nordost wehet,)

And Heidegger comments:

> "The Northeasterly blows." This is neither the factual ascertaining of wind conditions, nor the description of a contingent weather situation, nor a "poetological" "framing" for subsequent "thoughts." "The Northeasterly blows": with this first line there already begins the mystery. Indeed, this line contains the mystery (*Geheimnis*) of the entire poem. This first line resonates in every line that follows. As we transition from each strophe to the next, we must hear this line. This first line attains its full resonance only in the last line. (HHR: 28/GA 52: 32)[28]

What strikes the reader of Hölderlin's poem from the very beginning is that both the time of the wind's blowing and its location remain indeterminate. As Heidegger puts it, "'The Northeasterly blows'—that is to say: the time-space (*Zeit-Raum*) of poetizing, of the poetizing that is poetized in this poem, stands open" (GA 52: 32). By "time-space" here Heidegger does not simply mean the temporal-spatial co-ordinates that structure human action according to cartographic or calendrical calculation. Rather, as Heidegger puts it in *Contributions to Philosophy*, time-space names the originary unity of timing and spatializing as the abyss that provides both unity and separation as what allows for something like time or history to happen (GA 65: 379). Moreover, time-space unfolds as the "*the site of the moment* of the event" (*Augenblicksstätte* des Ereignisses) (CP: 256/ GA 65: 323), one where a decision about the hidden history of humanity prepares itself for the "battle against destruction and uprooting" (CP: 80/ GA 65: 101). This de-cision is not a "moral-anthropological" "choice," but "an originary determination of beings as such out of the essence of beyng" (GA 65: 103, 100, 89). For Heidegger, what transpires here in and as "the temporal-spatial character of the decision as the erupting fissure of beyng itself is to be grasped being-historically" (CP: 81/GA 65: 103). And while this decision cannot be viewed as a human "choice," Heidegger does not see it as something ineluctable or peremptory. The decision, as he puts it, shows itself as an "either-or" concerning being/ nonbeing, but one in which the deciding is not left to humans. Still, we become attuned to the realm of decision not by volition and will, but by attending to the silent stillness that remains concealed in the clangorous blare of planetary technology. That is why Heidegger can make the claim that "questioning is more originary than decision" (GA 65: 102). And what more than anything else attunes a *Volk* to this decision that awaits it is poetry. The "Remembrance" lectures rehearse the preparedness of the German *Volk* for precisely this possibility of decision by questioning who they are and by assessing their readiness for letting the winds of futural destiny come to them. These winds may be unbidden, since no human initiative can guide and direct them, and yet in the *Volk*'s stance of readiness for the "Greeting" of the northeasterly wind, Heidegger uncovers a path to German self-recognition. What is at stake in these lectures is the exposure of the German nation to its own native possibilities—but now not by means of an interior monologue or self-contained examination. Rather, Heidegger is convinced that the path to self-discovery must go outward from the native into the foreign in order for the *Volk* to truly know its own identity. And the guide for this journey of self-discovery is of course that "most German of Germans," Friedrich Hölderlin (GA 16: 333). It is Hölderlin's poetry that welcomes the foreign breezes from another place—and from another time. This welcoming holds forth the possibility that the Germans might be capable of entering the time-space of questioning, a questioning that seeks to navigate the journey of the history of beyng from the first Greek beginning to that other, futural German beginning that is coming—but only if we heed the poet's word. But what is the "word"? And how are we to properly hear it amidst the clamor that has turned language itself into an instrument of human power and dominion?

This is *the* question that begins Heidegger's path into Hölderlin's poetic word in the "Remembrance" lectures. Moreover, it serves as a way to bring our established practices of investigating poetic language into question so that we might begin to hear differently. In *Contributions*, Heidegger stresses that traditional speech practices focus solely on what is present. In "the epoch of a complete lack of questioning, an epoch whose temporal span stretches beneath time backward and forward far beyond what happens today" we no longer have the ability to hear "the essential" (CP: 86/GA 65: 108). To attune ourselves to such a hearing means that we authentically understand what Heidegger expressed in his 1936 essay "Hölderlin and the Essence of Poetry": "Language is not a tool at our disposal, but rather that appropriating event that disposes of the supreme possibility of human being" (EHP: 56/GA 4: 38). Hence, as Heidegger opens his consideration of "Remembrance," he announces that the traditional historiographical and philological approaches to the poem are to be jettisoned: "Literary-historiographical research leads itself astray and, like all historiography (*Historie*), falls prey to vanity if it presumes that with this style of research it could ever disclose the truth of history (*Geschichte*)" (HHR:3/GA 52: 3). Such historiography merely "limps along behind [and] only gives rise to the vanity of a prodigious scholarship and contributes at most to confusing our sense of history." Historiography as *Historie* merely objectifies the past, encasing it in a reliquary for scholarly dissection or ceremonial observance. But Hölderlin's poetry opens the Germans to their own history as *Geschichte*—namely, as the authentic history that bespeaks the fate of gods and mortals in a relation to time that can never be grasped chronologically—as if it were something that occurred or could occur with*in* a box called "history." Rather, the poetic time of remembrance opens itself in time-space as the decision concerning the flight and the coming of the gods.

As we follow Heidegger's discussion about history here, we would do well to reflect upon Kommerell's critique of Heidegger's Hölderlin performances. Heidegger himself grants that his approach appears "arbitrary," "unusual," and "presumptuous" (GA 52: 8–9). Further, he acknowledges that there is no "proof" that Hölderlin's word indeed poetizes something inceptual. And yet, even while professing that his work merely offers "*a* path, but not 'the' path"—perhaps even a path that evades what others cling to as the proper path—Heidegger nonetheless puts forward his reading of "Remembrance" not as an interpretation, exegesis, or commentary but as a "hearkening to the voice of beyng" (GA 52: 13–14; GA 71: 337). In this hearkening he does not attempt to hear Hölderlin's own voice as a historical figure, nor does he seek to articulate Hölderlin's own vision of history. Rather, boldly and determinedly Heidegger undertakes a thinking of history in which Hölderlin's work is taken up as a way for Heidegger to lay out his own version of the history of beyng thought in terms of the first and the other beginning. To hearken to such a history, Heidegger authorizes a reading of the poet that risks what Kommerell calls "Hölderlin violence" in service to his own thinking of history. It is in this sense that Heidegger can say: "Hölderlin's poetry is a destiny [*Geschick*] for us" (GA 75: 350). It comes to pass as the "transition" or *Übergang* from the first to the other beginning (GA 70: 149). Merely reading and commenting upon the texts of Hölderlin cannot bring us into the sway of this transition. What is required is a hearkening.

> Hearing is, to be sure, not just a receiving of the word. Hearing (*Hören*) is first and foremost a hearkening (*Hörchen*). Hearkening entails putting on hold all other modes of apprehending. To hearken is to be completely alone with what is coming (*Kommendem*). Hearkening is a being gathered in the direction of a singular and readied reaching out into the domain of an arrival (*Ankunft*), a domain in which we are not yet at home (*heimisch*). Hearers must first be hearkeners, and hearkeners are those who venture and wait at the same time. We have already ventured something when we said that the poetizing word poetizes over beyond itself and the poet. This is for the time being an assertion. It entails the acknowledgement that something inceptual comes to pass (*sich ereignet*) in the word. (HHR: 10–11/GA 52: 13–14)

Only those who truly hear can hearken. And the gift of hearkening comes only to those who open themselves to the poetic word and its historical power. As Heidegger puts it, "how can one know what history is, if one doesn't know what poetry is" (GA 76: 233). The whole tradition of Hölderlin philology can never prepare us for the event of the inceptual—that is, of finding our way back to the first beginning so that we might twist ourselves free of historical metaphysics and become open for the passageway to an other beginning. Thought from out of the history of beyng, Heidegger's lectures on "Remembrance" are to be understood as a "preparation . . . in the manner of the construction of the most proximate vestibules in whose spatial jointure Hölderlin's word can be heard" (GA 65: 422). And it as a vestibule—and not as an already completed edifice or metaphysical construction—that Heidegger lays out his reading of Hölderlin's poetic word.[29] That is why Heidegger emphasizes over and over again that his "lecture course is merely a kind of indicating" or a "pointer" that seeks to "assist in making the poetic word more audible" (GA 52: 1, 10). But Heidegger is also deeply aware that his bold initiative to construct a vestibule for hearing Hölderlin's word may likely founder: "Indeed, what we are seeking borders on the impossible. Everything here can miscarry. Every pointer remains a conjecture" (HHR:10/GA 52: 13). Throughout the lecture course Heidegger will perform a dance that borders both on "the impossible" and on a kind of errancy (*Irre*) that dares to think what Hölderlin poetizes. Heidegger is willing to go against the literary establishment and the offices of Hölderlin, Inc. set up by the National Socialist appropriation of the poet for explicit political gain, because he finds a phenomenological indication in the power of errancy itself. For Heidegger, "errancy itself is the clearing (openness-truth) of beyng" and, as such, in order for it to open itself to historical truth it needs to expose itself to historical un-truth (GA 66: 259). But we would be blind were we not to also recognize how provincial and at times intractable Heidegger's readings can be. As Heidegger himself conceded, "he who thinks greatly, must err greatly," where the issue of errancy extends far beyond questions of philological correctness to include the use and abuse of Hölderlin during the era of National Socialist rule and into the postwar era.

The name "Hölderlin" came to signify for Heidegger a pathway in preparation for the turn to an other beginning. But it also intimated a pathway back to the first beginning since it was in Hölderlin alone that Heidegger uncovered an "essential turn back into the inceptual" that could keep the promise of the futural revolutionary power of the Germans. Hellingrath had pointed the way toward just a possibility, and Heidegger remained his whole life long a devoted disciple of Hellingrath's transformative nationalist vision of Hölderlin as herald of a new epoch. Yet even Hellingrath erred, and at the beginning of the "Remembrance" lectures Heidegger challenged Hellingrath's reading of the poem as belonging to "the personal lived experiences of Hölderlin the *man* (not the poet)," rather than to the hymnal songs in devotion to the fatherland (HHR: 20/GA 52: 23).[30] Hellingrath was convinced that "Remembrance" did not truly fit in with other Hölderlinian hymns since both structurally and thematically it struck him as "differentiating itself from the hymns." Hellingrath especially emphasized that "it contained nothing that immediately concerned the fatherland" but was, on the contrary, a rather direct poem that faithfully described Hölderlin's own private "memory of the landscape of Bordeaux and his friends there who dared to embark on great sea voyages as well as describing the feelings that these thoughts awakened in him." When read against the background of these biographical details, Hellingrath claimed, "the poem is so easily understood," which is why it had been left out of earlier collections of Hölderlin's poetry edited by Ludwig Uhland and Christoph Schwab.[31] Naturally, Heidegger would see this differently, since for him it expressed the very heart of the fatherland hymns, especially in its focus on the topic of the journey into the foreign as a way of appropriating what is genuinely one's own.

Still, despite Hellingrath's editorial "errors" in thinking through the significance of the "Remembrance" poem, Heidegger's whole approach to Hölderlin was profoundly shaped by Hellingrath's way of reading Hölderlin. Primary to that reading was the centrality of the two Böhlendorff letters and their conviction that the path to German self-recognition lay in a complex and, at times, inverted relation to their Greek ancestors. Indeed, as Hellingrath put it, Hölderlin's "dream of Hellas" was the basis of his turn to the fatherland.[32] Hölderlin's aim was for the Germans "to be German to the same measure that the Greeks were Greek." Rather than idealizing the Greeks as an eternal model worthy of imitation and emulation, Hölderlin believed in cultivating the free use of one's own—which involved learning from the Greeks by inverting their style through the native appropriation of the foreign. In pursuing this strategy, outlined in the Böhlendorff letter, we can understand how Hölderlin's turn to the fatherland involved a becoming intimate with the foreign "other"—namely, the ancient Greeks. As Hellingrath succinctly put it: "Hölderlin's turn to the fatherland is the direct consequence of his being Greek." In following Hellingrath's lead by privileging the Böhlendorff letter as the cipher by which to read the hymns of the fatherland, Heidegger discovered a path for rethinking the horizon of the German future. In a sense, Hellingrath's work serves as a kind of greeting into the forecourt or vestibule of Hölderlin's poetry. In the same way, Heidegger's long introduction in these lectures provide a "threshold" that functions as "the place of transition in stepping from one domain into another": from the domain of the poem as a thing present at hand to the other domain where the poem shows itself as "the word" (GA 52: 37).

IV. The Greeting of the Wind

For seasoned readers of Heidegger's work, the "Remembrance" lectures offer two surprises. First, they provide an extraordinarily long and repetitive introduction to the problem at hand: reading Hölderlin's text. That these propaedeutical remarks focus more on Heidegger and his own singular style of reading the text should not astound us. Yet what does genuinely strike us is that once Heidegger goes through this exercise of introduction, warning, and prolegomenon on the relation of poetry to thinking and of authentic language to mere scholarly exegesis, he actually does bear down and offer a remarkable line-by-line analysis of the poem.[33] Before his penetrating ruminations, however, Heidegger reinforces that his remarks are not to be taken as scholarly "research." Nor do they attempt to present a "historiographically 'correct'" portrait of the poet. Just as little do they seek to place these poems upon a Procrustean bed of National Socialist presentism where they might become "fitting for a strong race of people (*starkes Geschlecht*)" (HHR: 9/GA 52: 12). On the contrary, Heidegger's sole aim here is "to think (*denken*) that which is poetized (*gedichtet*) in Hölderlin's hymns." This does not mean, however, "transforming Hölderlin's poetry into philosophy or placing it in the service of a particular philosophy"—namely, Heidegger's. Rather, it involves "letting what is poetized in this poetry be what it, of itself, is and first will be." And it is this deeply phenomenological comportment of *letting be* that Heidegger holds as the cipher for the poem's enigmatic mystery. In truth, the very first line of the poem—"The Northeasterly blows"—offers a poetic hint for readers to simply "let the wind blow," a gesture already known to philosophers from Plato's *Republic*. There, in the middle of a heated discussion about the proper meaning of justice for the soul, Socrates tells his companion Glaucon, "But just let the wind blow; it will set the course for the argument" (*Republic*, 394d).[34]

In Heidegger's own interpretation of this poem, the gesture of letting be offers a kind of threshold between the vestibule and the main house, a way of transitioning that no longer considers the poem "as a thing present at hand, as it were" but as "the word, which *we* do not have before us, but that instead, *proceeding from itself*, is to take us up into the space of its truth" (GA 52: 37). In this sense, the poem "Remembrance" is to be understood less as what Hölderlin "intended" than as a poetic engagement with that which came to him unbidden—like the wind—and that invites him to reflect, not merely backward in the sense of "memory" (*Gedächtnis*), but forward toward what is coming. In this sense, the poem is less a documentation about what once transpired than it is the fulfillment of this transpiring itself. In other words, the poem is not an "Andenken" in the sense of a "remembrance'; it is, rather, a *Denken* "an"—or thinking "toward" what comes forth futurally from out of the encounter with such recollection. Here the very meaning of the poem reveals itself as the expression of a poetic temporality that binds "that which has been" (*das Gewesene*) to that which is coming (*das Kommende*)—not as a temporal sequence from out of the past "toward" the future, that is, as directional "progress," but as the opening to what is sent to human beings as their destiny (*Geschick*). We will need to more fully explore what Heidegger means here by "destiny," but for the moment let us return to a consideration of the peculiar poetic temporality that announces itself in this opening line of the poem. Heidegger hints at such an enigmatic relation in his claim that the poem is not the product of the individual poet's "mind"—as if it simply lay there before us as an object produced by a subject. Rather, as Heidegger stresses, "strictly speaking, the poet is himself in the first instance poetized by that which he has to poetize" (HHR: 10/GA 52: 13). In other words, the poetic word reveals itself in the very comportment of *Andenken* with which the poet turns toward that which awaits him. But again, if such awaiting is to be authentic, it cannot project its own model of presence upon the future and thereby enclose it within a horizon of futural presence. Rather, genuine "waiting is a letting come," an accepting of the enigmatic power of time as that which can never be calcified as available "presence," but always exceeds our ability to steer, direct, and command. To abide time is to let it come—unbidden: that is, to allow it to come as enigmatically and as inscrutably as the wind.

Here, unlike Hellingrath, Heidegger thinks of "Andenken" as very much belonging to Hölderlin's other poetic hymns—especially the river hymns, since they too are preoccupied with the curious connections between source and mouth, beginning and end, that mark Hölderlin's other poetic excursions into temporality. Hence, it was not by mistake that in the semester following the "Andenken" course, Heidegger would turn to a consideration of "The Ister" in the summer semester of 1942.[35] In these lectures Heidegger sheds important light on his approach to the opening stanza of "Remembrance." He notes that time is like a river—but not in the sense that it merely "flows." Rather, like the river in its journey toward the sea, it intimates what is coming (the futural), even as it always passes away into that which has been (*das Gewesene*) (GA 53: 12). Moreover, insofar as rivers always maintain a connection between source and mouth, they likewise help us to think of how to bring together the future and that which has been into the sphere of locality and wandering. In other words, they enact a living relation between past and future as well as between what is local and native *and* what is strange and foreign. For Heidegger, the poetic sense of *Andenken* provides a way of thinking *toward* (*an*) this dynamic movement between past and future, future and past, that is never unidirectional but always a back-and-forth oscillation between what has been and what is coming. On Heidegger's reading, it is this same pendulous movement that Hölderlin attempts to initiate in his opening line "the Northeasterly blows." As Heidegger puts it, "Now that we know that in 'Remembrance' the historicity of the history of the fatherland is being thought, the opening line first unveils its full truth" (HHR: 119/GA 52: 139). What this "full truth" reveals, Heidegger claims, is a "new relationship to the Greek world that is not a turn away, but a more essential turn toward the Greek world, one that presses in the direction of a more original confrontation with it, yet indeed without seeking in it the origin and ground of one's own (*des Eigenen*). The turn to the fatherland is not a flight to Christendom . . . the turn to the fatherland is not the turn to the political either" (GA 52: 141). What this turn ultimately signifies, rather, is a turn to "the holy" whereby we understand that "the holy is the ground of the fatherland and of its historical essence." Such a turn is not, however, a re-turn to something that once existed and is no longer but, rather, a turn toward a futural task that holds one in its thrall even as it resists taking definitive shape. This turn to the fatherland indeed enacts a turning to one's own, but never as a present at hand being. In this sense, the fatherland as task, rather than as possession, is, like the wind, constantly arriving, always underway, borne toward the task that ever calls to us as the way back to our own from out of the foreign. As for the fatherland, it is not something here before us, but always ahead of us. We will never be done with its coming.

Such a reading, as powerful as it is, demands of Heidegger that he turn away from Hölderlin's own historical understanding of the "national" and of the "fatherland" as part of his longed-for dream of a Swabian Republic rooted in democratic and populist ideals. In order for Heidegger to push through his own vision of a coming fatherland, he needs to radically de-historicize Hölderlin's work, something that he succeeds in doing with the help of Hellingrath and his vision of a secret Germany. We find strong indications of this tendentious practice in the way Heidegger suppresses certain essential features of Hölderlin's understanding of the foreign—the brown women, the allusions to the West Indies, to Columbus, to political revolution, and to Asia. Instead, Heidegger reduces them all to indications of Hölderlin's attachment to Greece evidenced in the Böhlendorff letter. Throughout this chapter we will have to come to terms with Heidegger's violent suppression of these traces of the Other in the name of Graeco-German affinity. But before we do so, let us return to our discussion of the greeting.

What Hölderlin undertakes in his opening verse is both an opening to the power of the wind and to the inspiration of the poet. "The Northeasterly blows. . . ." What that signifies is less a meteorological observation than a poetological invocation. Taken literally, the wind opens the poem to both poet and reader. The most difficult task of the poet is "to begin poetically with the beginning from out of the beginning" (GA 52: 191). But how is the poet to do this? It can never occur merely as the result of the poet's willful assertion as author to compose a beginning. Such a gesture of power and dominion would serve only to rupture the connection to the beginning that needs to happen via a comportment of letting be: of letting the wind of in-spiration come (literally, an in-spiriting or taking-in of *spiritus* [breath, wind] and *pneuma* [air, breath]). That which belongs to the wind is, poetologically considered, not only its atmospheric mass or volumetric concentration, but above all its "coming." The coming of the wind is, then, an event of coming, the coming of what can only come in its proper sense by virtue of its inceptual power to come as a beginning. What the opening line precisely enacts is this coming as letting come—that is, of letting the inspiriting of poetic possibility happen as event. But as ever with the wind, every coming entails a going away, a leaving, and a departure. What comes, goes and what goes, comes back again as a gesture of opening to the other that emerges unexpectedly and brings with it the possibility of finding a way to think that which has been and that which is coming. All this the poet hints at in his opening verse, even as he gestures beyond this in the following lines:

–The Northeasterly blows,	Der Nordost wehet,
Most beloved of the winds	Der liebste unter den Winden
To me, for it promises fiery spirit	Mir, weil er feurigen Geist
And good voyage to mariners.	Und gute Fahrt verheisset den Schiffern.
But go now and greet	Geh aber nun und grüsse
The beautiful Garonne,	Die schöne Garonne,
And the gardens of Bordeaux . . .	Und die Gärten von Bordeaux . . . (vv. 1–7)

As Heidegger begins his own reading of the poem, he holds that the first line "contains the mystery of the entire poem." That is, each succeeding stanza must be read against this enigmatic opening. Here no time is given indicating when the wind comes, nor are we granted any clear sign of where the poem begins. And yet Heidegger finds a clue to the meaning of the wind by reading it through Hölderlin's Böhlendorff letter: " 'The Northeasterly'—that wind is named which, in the broad regions of the Swabian homeland, sweeps and clears the sky with its biting coolness, clearing a space for the fire from the heavens, 'the sun,' a space in which its illumination and glow can unfold" (HHR: 27/GA 52: 31). The wind here, on Heidegger's reading, references the Junonian sobriety and coolness of the German-Hesperian north. In verse three, with the reference to "the fiery spirit," we are granted notice of the reversal of this cold, detached, and even-tempered sobriety in the wind's gift of favorable passage to mariners. For Heidegger, this chiastic juxtaposition of cold northerly wind and fiery southern spirit comes to reveal Hölderlin's poetic logic of difference/affinity between modern Germans and ancient Greeks. This trope of shared opposition and contrastive sameness, precisely at the intersection of antiquity/modernity and Hellas/Hesperia, will function as Heidegger's cipher for understanding the tensions and oppositions within the poem itself.

What emerges from these reflections is an understanding of the poet's task as one granted to him by the "wind"—that is, *pneuma, spiritus, Geist*. The poet can begin the poem only by virtue of the gift of in-spiration bestowed by the wind's currents. And, in turn, only by releasing himself to the in-spiriting power of the wind, can the poet, like the mariners, be favored with a "good voyage." The wind is thus "most beloved" to the poet since only through its gift may the poet commence his journey into the foreign—and it is precisely in terms of the poet's/mariners' voyage to the foreign that Heidegger's reading will proceed. Like the mariners who wait for a favorable wind to begin their voyage, the poet begins only when the winds of inspiration come to him. This comportment of the poet is "a letting oneself go and releasing oneself into being (*das Sich-ein-und-los-lassen in das Sein*)" (HHR: 36/GA 52: 41). It is as if the poet must follow the call of that which calls, even as this following "comes to pass (*sich ereignet*) outside of mechanical compulsion." This transpires, rather, "from an *open belonging to beyng* and returns back *into it*." In this sense, "the vocation of the poet" for Heidegger remains as "a belonging to what is essential," whereby the wind "carries the poet in the essential direction of what he must fulfill." And yet as Heidegger develops his reading further, he stresses the futural coming of the wind much more than its going. We should try to pay attention to this emphasis since it harbors clues to Heidegger's own metapolitical ambitions in taking up the theme of "Remembrance." What gets privileged in such a reading is Germany's Hesperian future, whose unfolding depends upon the poet's power to let the wind return from its journey. Within Heidegger's thinkerly grammar of excursion and return, this means that the unfolding of Hesperian destiny can only happen in and through a commemorative encounter with the source or *Quelle* of its greatness—and that alone is ancient Greece, understood as "Hellas." The signs and traces of this first Greek beginning lie in the "fiery spirit" of the wind (v. 3), the "silver poplars" that are native to the Southern Mediterranean lands (v. 12), the "fig tree" that is sacred to Dionysus (v. 16), "the brown women," whose bodies are kissed by the rays of the southern light (v. 18), "the fragrant cup full of dark light" that grants the gift of the Greek wine god from "the vineyard slopes" (vv. 26–27, 52), and the mariners' journey to "Indians" that brings them into contact with the heavenly fire of the

Orient in a kind of Dionysiac return to the source (vv. 49–50). All of these poignant allusions to Greek celestial fire in foreign lands come to form, for Heidegger, a Hölderlinian poetics of history whose lineaments are laid out in the Böhlendorff letter.

What this poetics of history entails is nothing less than the self-recognition of the Germans as the bearers of a "Western responsibility (*abendländische Verantwortung*)" to save the West from itself and from the ever-encroaching nihilism that threatens to extinguish any possibility of its own greatness (GA 16: 378, 452). Only by a journey back to its Greek source can the Germans prepare the transition to another beginning for thinking. It is in this sense that, for Heidegger, Hölderlin "founds the other beginning of our history poetically" (GA 75: 336). If the Germans are to come into their proper task and mission as a *Volk*, they will need to constantly pose the question: "Who are we?" (GA 38: 78, 97; GA 39: 49; GA 65: 48–54, 100). Posing such a question, as Heidegger does over and over again during the years of National Socialist rule, first requires, however, a return to the Greek source at the first beginning of "our" history. To become German in Hölderlin's sense means to acknowledge that we are the heirs of the ancient Greeks, even as it likewise requires of us an acknowledgment of our profound difference from them. And yet Heidegger's way of framing this question of affinity/alterity will prove deeply tendentious. For him the (re)turn (*Rückkehr*) to the Greeks will be laid out as a kind of German homecoming, a *Heimkehr* that reveals itself as an *Umkehr* or "reversal," the outlines of which Heidegger finds in the Böhlendorff letter.

The special task for the Germans thus becomes—in conversation with Hölderlin—to recognize their "inner affinity with the language of the Greeks" since only through such a dialogue can the Germans come into their own (*Eigenes*) (GA 16: 679). Here Heidegger understands the essence of Hölderlin's poetry as making just such an encounter possible, one that prepares for a homecoming: "But this homecoming is the future of the historical being of the German Volk" (EHP: 48/GA 4: 30). In this way, Heidegger frames the destinal mandate of the German *Volk* as a taking up again, in a reversal, the traces of the Greek beginning that hold the mystery of and for a German future. Hence, Heidegger can write: "authentic repetition/retrieval springs forth from an originary transformation" (GA 39: 243). If in WS 1934–1935 Heidegger believed that "the world-hour of our history has struck," by WS 1941–1942 he had become less enthusiastic about an immediate transformation. Instead of thinking that the hour of revolution was on the horizon, now Heidegger understood that such a project would require a long incubation period of forbearance, waiting, and preparation (GA 39: 294). Hölderlin's poetic word might offer an outline for historical retrieval and rejuvenation, but the task of enacting a genuine turn within German history would be formidable. As Heidegger continued to emphasize repeatedly: what proves most difficult, as the Böhlendorff letter made all too clear to him, was "the free use of one's own" for one's own. Such free use of one's own would inevitably involve a journey into the foreign, but such a journey would always be made on behalf of the proper, the self, the native. Or so Heidegger always maintained. That Hölderlin's own work offered a vastly different version concerning the dynamics and the purpose of such a journey was forever lost to Heidegger. We can trace this difference in the way each approaches the question of the festival.

In his interpretation of the greeting as having a special significance for understanding the fundamental dynamic of history in Hölderlin's sense, Heidegger hits upon an enduring element in relating the greeting to the festival and to the celebration as ways of grasping the delicate relations between human beings and gods. In Part Two of the "Remembrance" lectures, Heidegger turns to the meaning of "'Holidays' and 'Festivals' in Hölderlin's Poetizing." There he attempts to show how the greeting of the northeasterly wind is the poet's way of enacting a law of history—namely, that becoming at home with one's own can happen only through a chiastic encounter with the foreign. In greeting the wind, the poet lets it come into relation with what is his own, even as he opens himself to the appropriative claim that the wind makes upon him. But this greeting does not come from the poet but is, rather, the poet's own response to something that comes unbidden. In its coming, the wind not only greets, however; it also vouchsafes a radically different understanding of the time in which it comes, the time *of* its coming. We need to hear this phrase as the playing out of a double genitive whereby "the time of coming" is both a coming "of" time as well as an indication for the timeliness and temporal singularity of such coming. In this way, the greeting announces this coming of time as the time of coming. Simply put, this means that the greeting enables the poet to attune himself to a noncalendrical, incalculable sense of time as that which can only come if we are prepared for its coming in a greeting that allows this coming to come inceptually. In Heidegger's language such a greeting is nothing other than *the* event of history (*Ereignis*) that comes to pass (*ereignet sich*) in the festival, that special time of celebration that confers the greeting of the holy as the encountering of gods and mortals.

As Heidegger puts it:

> The festival is the event in which gods and humans come to encounter one another. What is festive in the festival is the ground of this event, which can be neither caused by gods nor made by humans. The festive is the inceptual event that sustains and pervasively attunes all coming to encounter one another in such encountering. (HHR: 62/GA 52: 69)

In this reciprocal encounter, the festive inceptually attunes each of those encountered to "an inceptual greeting through which humans and gods themselves first come to be greeted in advance." Heidegger goes on to connect the poetic gesture of greeting that inaugurates the "Remembrance" poem with another inceptual greeting from Hölderlin's "As when on a holiday" and reads it as the coming of "the holy" (das Heilige).

The festival as bridal festival is the event of the inceptual greeting:

> This inceptual greeting is the concealed essence of history. This inceptual greeting is *the* event, *the* beginning. We name this greeting inceptual in the sense of the coming of the holy, because it is first and only in this greeting that the encountering of humans and gods springs forth and has the ground of its source. The festival is the event of the inceptual greeting. (HHR: 62/GA 52: 70)

For Heidegger what the festival celebrates is the holy marriage between gods and humans that both interrupts the chronological time of work, routine, repetition, and custom, as well as opens up a new time in which alone the holy can appear. Hölderlin's "Remembrance" celebrates the timeliness of this time as the *kairos* moment in which we come to find ourselves at "the right time," "the fitting moment" for letting the holy come to us. It is this "now-time" of poetic invocation that Hölderlin brings to language in his gesture of greeting and welcoming the northeasterly wind. In this poetic rendering of kairological time, Heidegger opens the German *Volk* to "the time of the always already originary beginning that is still arriving."[36]

V. Jews, Greeks, and the Occlusion of the First Beginning

In an essay that he published in 1943 honoring the 100th anniversary of Hölderlin's death, Heidegger once again set forth the basic "law of historicity" that organized his reading of Hölderlin's "Remembrance" poem. There he underlines that the very act of poetizing requires of the poet an "Andenken"—a *commemorative thinking of* that thinks back toward what has been so as to prepare the coming of a futural arrival. Such thinking both commemorates the origin from which memory has sprung forth even as it celebrates the possibility of its futural arrival as that which comes forth from out of the forgotten origin. *Andenken* thus turns back toward what has been left behind as much as it turns forward in a gesture of welcoming and greeting of an other coming. For Heidegger, the poet is the one who attunes himself to this dynamic of letting pass away and letting come within the history of a *Volk*. As attuned, the poet commemorates the origin on whose basis alone the futural can emerge. In this way, both greeting and festival belong together since what the festival celebrates is the commemoration of just such a coming together of both the greeting and those who are greeted at a special moment of time—as time-ing. What transpires here is not simply a greeting of the gods by humans or of humans by the gods; what is greeted, rather, is the greeting itself that allows for the recollection of greetings that have been as well as for the possibility of future ones to come. In this sense, we need to understand Hölderlin's poem "Remembrance" not as a poem about remembrance but as the enacting of such remembrance itself. This is why a merely biographical-psychological interpretation can never suffice since it does not recognize the poem as a commemorating of commemoration, one that prepares for a festival of future commemorations of what has been.

As Heidegger reads it, this Hölderlinian enactment of commemoration itself functions as a kind of homecoming: a "return to the nearness of the origin" (EHP: 42/GA 4: 23). For Heidegger, the hidden cipher in this act of commemoration is the bond linking the modern Germans to the ancient Greeks in an essential affinity that places the Germans at a crisis moment in the history of the West. At this *kairos* moment of greeting, the Germans are offered the possibility of "saving the West" (EdP: 40). And yet, Heidegger claims, there are many in the fatherland who "are not yet ready to receive the most proper of the homeland in its very own (*das Eigenste der Heimat*)—'the German'—as their possession (*Eigentum*). For what constitutes the homecoming is that the countryman must first become at home in the still withheld essence of the homeland" (EHP: 33/GA 4: 14). In order for this to come about, the Germans need "to learn the free use of their own possibilities," which means "always simply and solely fit themselves into being open for that which is assigned to them (EHP: 141/GA 4: 118). This alone is the *unum necessarium*—"the one thing that is necessary"—for the German *Volk* which, in turn, means being open to that which comes to them from out of the hidden and concealed Greek beginning.

Commemorative thinking attunes itself to this task in that it prepares for the greeting of the Greek bequest by way of a celebration of the *hieros gamos*—the holy marriage between gods and mortals. The feast celebrates this as an authentic homecoming, one that can happen only by way of a voyage from out of the home into the foreign and then back again in a circuitous journey. But the voyage into the foreign cannot merely be understood in a recollective or commemorative way as if it were something past. Rather, the journey into the foreign carries within its preteretive meaning a trace of futural possibility. Hence, Hölderlin will write in a fragmentary draft from "Brod und Wein" that the homeland loves the colony, or, as Heidegger puts it,

> Because the homeland demands a becomely homely, yet the latter (as a coming to itself) must be a coming-home; for this reason the spirit of the homeland itself demands the foreign from out of which such a homecoming can only ever come:
> "Colony, and bold forgetting spirit loves" (DKV I: 747; HHR: 162/GA 52: 190)

Since the northeasterly wind blows for Heidegger in the direction of Germania, it signifies the sending of something assigned to the Germans from the heavenly fire of their Greek bequest. For him, it is the poet's commemorative greeting to/of such a wind that signals a readiness for the *Volk* to open themselves to this gesture of appropriation. In response to this gesture, Heidegger hopes that the Germans might be able to come into their own through what he calls "an experience of the foreign" and, more particularly, out of "the experience of the foreign fire" that serves "to ground the mortals' dwelling in the homely" (EHP: 139, 148/GA 4:

116, 126). What the experience of the foreign enables is to expose the native sons of the fatherland to the oriental fire of their Greek ancestors so that on the basis of a "thinking of what has been," they might also prepare the transition to "a thinking of what is to come" (EHP: 139/ GA 4: 117). If the Germans are able to properly meet this task (*das Aufgegebene*) of authentically appropriating what has been given to them (*das Mitgegebene*),

> then there will be a kinship with the poet. Then there will be a homecoming. But this homecoming is the future of the historical essence of the Germans. (EHP: 48/GA 4: 30)

If Heidegger emphasizes the journey of homecoming as a futural task for the Germans, then this is because it appears to him as more essential than what lies in the past. Still, the past is never simply past for Heidegger. It also lies before us as a task to unlock the hidden and untapped possibilities of what has been for the purposes of a transitional passage to what is coming. During World War II Heidegger will rethink what this journey into the foreign means in the present context of German "Western responsibility" (GA 16: 378, 452). In a letter to his friend Kurt Bauch from 1942, Heidegger writes of what he calls "the founding vocation of the Germans," by which he means a mindful reflection on the Greek mission to encounter the originary essence of truth (HKB: 85). But again, "this world-historical test for the Germans" can never be a mere imitation of the Greeks, since the Böhlendorff letter warns us that "apart from . . . living craft and proportion, we cannot properly have anything in common with them" (E&L: 207/DKV III: 460). Nonetheless, the true German mission in the war for Heidegger lies in mindfully reflecting on this ancient Greek mission, but now in its own properly German sense as what belongs to the native. And here in the "Remembrance" lectures we can find traces of this native impulse that threatens to undermine and eradicate any sense of "the foreign" except that which proves useful to the native as a way of enabling its "homecoming." We can see such a tendency in Heidegger's heroicization and glorification of the cult of the German warrior. Going back to his 1923 lecture "Wahrsein und Dasein in Aristoteles" that celebrated the autochthonous bonds of a *Volk* to its native earth, Heidegger exalted the martial courage and patriotic zeal of the German solider as part of what he proudly trumpeted as "ein hartes Geschlecht" ("a hard race").[37] Heidegger turns to these same clichés in

"Remembrance" in his valorization of the Hölderlin-editor, Norbert von Hellingrath, whom he twice mentions "fell at Verdun in the frontmost line" (GA 52: 45, 16).[38] It is Hellingrath who, in his "Preface" to the crucial fourth volume of Hölderlin's *Sämtliche Werke*, speaks of Hölderlin's "prophesying to the German Volk their elect status and imminent fulfillment."[39] Hellingrath goes so far as to speak of the "special election" of the Germans and finds in Hölderlin's late hymns "a pledge of the proclaimed preeminence" of this *Volk*. Moreover, it is also Hellingrath who maintains that "Hölderlin's turn to the fatherland is merely the direct consequence of his being Greek."

In his essay "Hölderlin and the Germans," delivered during the Great War, Hellingrath positions Hölderlin as "the mediator between the divine and the human . . . [who] after the silence of a long world-night lets the voice of the gods once again be heard."[40] For Hellingrath, it is above all else the poetry of Hölderlin that "out of this night prepares a new return of the gods upon the earth." In doing so, the poet functions as "a prophet/seer who gazes beyond his own time, proclaiming and evoking the future." On Hellingrath's reading, it is Hölderlin alone who "from out of Athens' past now extols a German future." In this myth of Germania's exalted status "as the chosen one who, before all others, prepares the gods' return in the Occident," Hellingrath provides a model for Heidegger's own use/abuse of Hölderlin as poet. It is Hellingrath who teaches Heidegger the grammar of a "secret Germany" and of Hölderlin's role as "the herald" of German "destiny" (*Geschick*) that holds forth the hope of "saving the West" (GA 55: 108). But what Hellingrath likewise communicates to Heidegger in his essay "Hölderlin und die Deutschen" is a sense of the inaccessibility of Hölderlin's poetic word to "non-Germans": "Hölderlin is simultaneously the greatest example of that hidden, concealed fire, of that secret empire, of that still, unperceived development of a divine, incandescent image at the core" of German being.[41] Hence, Hellingrath calls the Germans "the *Volk* of Hölderlin" since their authentic identity is still hidden from them, awaiting a futural understanding of what Hölderlin's poetic word could first reveal. This alone is what matters to Hölderlin—and hence any talk of his "biographical" or "cultural" significance pales in comparison to what Hellingrath understands as the hidden mission of Hölderlin's "poetic vocation"—to be the herald of "a *Secret* Germany" that is still to come.

Hellingrath delivered this lecture during World War I and self-consciously infused it with a deeply patriotic sense of a singular German mission.⁴² One of the attendees at the lecture was Rainer Maria Rilke, who praised him in the spirit of Nietzsche, as nothing less than an "educator."⁴³ In a curious blend of martial and poetic force, Hellingrath came to style himself as a kind of educator of the Germans, modeled on his own stylized reading of Hölderlin, a reading that (despite his several philological disagreements) Heidegger took up as the prototype for his own self-staging of a Hölderlinian martial poetics during the years of World War II. Heidegger was, of course, not alone in appropriating Hölderlin's late "Hymns of the Fatherland" as a model for a new muscular form of German national self-assertion. During the years of National Socialist rule Hölderlin would be conscripted into service by academics as well as politicians for fostering the German war effort on the eastern front. In one of the many popular printings sent to soldiers in Russia, styled "Hölderlin's Songs of the Fatherland" (1942), the eminent Hölderlin scholar Ernst Müller contributes to the propagandistic use of Hölderlin for bolstering the hopes of German troops. After praising Hölderlin as "the Orphic Swabian" who inspired the soldiers of the Great War in the trenches, Müller writes: "The poet cannot do enough to extol the warriorly virtues, in apportioning the immortal glory that endures beyond time and the grave."⁴⁴ In his "Introduction" to these poems, Müller goes on to explicate Hölderlin's ode "Death for the Fatherland" as "the singular expression of the highest spirit of war belonging to the ancient heroic songs of Tyrtaeus . . . pledged to the glories of sacrificial death." It is this "heroic death which alone justifies and transfigures the life of inspired young men." Müller then initiates an interpretive gesture that will be familiar to readers of Heidegger's *Andenken* lectures. Rejecting the Kantian notion of soldierly duty as a response to "the compulsory call of conscience," Müller defines "war and battle as the highest expressions of the eternal enthusiasm of passionate young men whose souls are gripped in the Dionysian state of the festival . . . inflamed with the commemoration (*Andenken*) of victory."

Müller's interpretations of Hölderlin against the demands and necessities of war were hardly exceptional. Paul Kluckhohn, head of the Hölderlin Society and co-founder of the *Hölderlin Jahrbuch*, published several letters from soldiers on the eastern front in the inaugural issue of the journal. One soldier, a sergeant writing from the field, offers to lend financial support for the newly founded "Hölderlin Gesellschaft," which he envisions as helping in the task of coming to terms with "the destinal battle of the Germans."⁴⁵ In the same vein, Kluckhohn cites several other letters from soldiers "in the field." One writes: "For 30 years Hölderlin has accompanied me. Already in the Great War he was my comrade in arms. Now he marches through Russia with me."[46] Another soldier, "an SS-Mann" writes: "As a man of the SS and a soldier, Hölderlin's poetry accompanied me through the long months of the winter campaign in Russia. . . . The experience on the eastern front and the experience with Hölderlin are the deepest impressions of the last few years for me." What shows itself in the long trail of Hölderlin veneration throughout the two world wars—from Hellingrath and "The Ideas of 1914" through Heidegger and the "revolution of 1933"—is a marked emphasis on the chosen, elected status of "Germania" to take up the "dream of Hellas" and rescue the West from the depredations of Anglo-American commercialism and the threat of a barbarian invasion from the east.

At the crude level of war propaganda, we find these sentiments expressed in the collection of Hölderlin's writings edited by Amadeus Grohmann, *Hölderlin: Heroism (A Selection for Soldiers)* who understands the poet as offering a glimpse into "the German essence" that endures through "the war-laden present."[47] Against this reception we can well understand Heidegger's reticence to make "Hölderlin 'relevant to the present' in the sense of being 'topical'" (GA 52: 12). Heidegger warns his listeners that these crude borrowings from the poet, marked by the "extravagant fervor of the fanatic," wind up "being used arbitrarily for wholly alien designs." And yet, of course, Heidegger himself is hardly immune from the human, all too human, impulse to recruit Hölderlin for the German war effort. In his lecture "Homecoming," delivered to commemorate the 100th anniversary of Hölderlin's death, Heidegger concludes his talk by coupling the work of Hölderlin with the sacrificial death of soldiers in the field. He frames this bond by posing a decisive question:

> are not the sons of the homeland who, though far distant from its soil, still gaze into the serenity of the homeland shining toward them and devote and sacrifice their lives for the still reserved discovery, are not these sons of the homeland the poet's closest kin? Their sacrifice shelters in itself the poetic summons to those dearest in the homeland, so that the reserved discovery may remain reserved. (EHP: 48/ GA 4: 29–30, trans. altered)

In Heidegger's celebration of the poet, Hölderlin assumes the figure of a sacrificial victim, the first son offered up to/for the destiny of the fatherland. In his 1943 essay "Remembrance," Heidegger writes:

> *Remembrance* is the poetic abiding in the essence of fateful (*schicklichen*) poetic activity, which, in the festive destiny (*Geschick*) of the futural history (*Geschichte*) of the Germans, festively manifests the ground of its founding. Destiny has sent (*geschickt*) the poet into the essence of this poetic activity and singled him out to be the first-born sacrifice. (EHP: 171/GA 4: 150, trans. altered)

In joining Hölderlin to the fallen soldiers in Russia, Heidegger returns to his analysis in section 74 of *Being and Time*, where destiny is understood as a co-belonging to and in a community. Fateful destiny then becomes something like an openness to the historical possibilities offered in a generational moment to members of a (national) community. By bringing to language the very question of German national identity, Hölderlin comes to function for Heidegger as the poet "of" the Germans—understood as a double genitive. Hölderlin is the expression of what it means to be German as much as his work takes as its focus this very Germanness that always already remains a question. Much as Hölderlin sacrificed himself for this very task, Heidegger seems to say, so too German soldiers, through their sacrificial deaths, help to bring the German *Volk* into a keener awareness of its destinal mission. In this way, by virtue of its poetic language as well as through its martial triumphs, the German *Volk* expresses its authentic need for self-recognition and self-assertion. As Heidegger put it in *Being and Time*: "In communication and in battle the power of destiny first becomes free" (BT: 366/GA 2: 508).

With Hölderlin resolutely acknowledged as the poet "of" the Germans, and with the Second World War understood as "the world-historical test of the Germans," Heidegger turns to the question of sacrifice (*Opfer*) as a way of placing the German military struggle at Stalingrad within "the history of beyng" (HKB: 84–85). This impulse to conjoin Hölderlin's poetic word with German military conflict—especially in the Hölderlin memorial year of 1943 that would prove so fateful for the future of the Reich—would be echoed throughout the German academic world. In a publication from 1943, F.W. Wentzlaff-Eggebert chooses as his theme "Opfer und Schicksal [Sacrifice and Fate] in Hölderlin's 'Hyperion' und 'Empedokles,'" where he writes of "the poet as the one who sacrifices himself in service to his *Volk*."[48] In his wartime tribute to the poet, Wentzlaff-Eggebert extols Hölderlin for "recognizing the necessity of sacrifice and at the same time for submitting to the harshness and severity of fate." It is by embracing "the great thought of sacrifice" and of praising "those fallen in the battle for freedom of the fatherland" that Hölderlin seizes "the force of spirit, the inner fire" that prepares "the last path to his mission." Heidegger would, of course, reject such banal attempts at reducing Hölderlin's enigmatic and perplexing language to mere political-military propaganda and sloganeering. What Heidegger attempted, as Max Kommerell so perceptively recognized, was "first and foremost not at all an interpretation, but the document of an encounter . . . which, in turn, requires an interpretation."[49] Within Heidegger's work on Hölderlin's esoteric poems, Kommerell identifies "a new esoteric" wherein Hölderlin "becomes an inexorable fate" for Heidegger himself and where Heidegger comes to don a Hölderlin-mask that emerges from "his own sense of vocation" to offer pronouncements concerning "the national fate." Kommerell goes on to characterize these efforts as belonging to the same tradition of poetic-philosophical ambition as the national initiatives of Stefan George and Norbert von Hellingrath that were likewise "exclusionary and dogmatic." Ultimately, Kommerell presses Heidegger to answer a critical question:

> Where is the transition where your own philosophy leads into Hölderlin and where, from out of a description of the human situation, does it decisively become a metaphysical declaration, one marked by an absolute and final certitude?

Heidegger never really offered an adequate answer to Kommerell's question, but in a letter he tells Kommerell: "You are right, the essay *is* a 'disaster'"—even as it offers a "project" and "this project is a thrown project; i.e., one determined by being itself."

In the very next semester, WS 1942–1943, Heidegger will once again take up the topic of "sacrifice" that shapes so much of the "Remembrance" lectures. There Heidegger writes:

> The highest form of suffering is dying one's death as a sacrifice for the preservation of the truth of being. This sacrifice is the purest experience of the voice of being. What if German

humanity is that historical humanity which, like the Greek, is called upon to poetize and think, and what if this German humanity must first perceive the voice of being! Then must not the sacrifices be as many as the causes immediately eliciting them, since the sacrifice has *in itself* an essence all its own and does not require goals and uses! Thus, what if the voice of the beginning should proclaim itself in our historical vocation? (P: 166–167/GA 54: 249–250)[50]

Given Heidegger's insight that genuine sacrifice occurs essentially as a form of hearkening to the voice of being, it is little wonder that he would juxtapose it with the highest yearning for the fatherland. In the "Remembrance" lectures, he stresses that

> What is ownmost, the fatherland, is the highest, yet for that reason, it is what is most forbidden. This is why it is found only at the end, after long searching, after much sacrifice and difficult service. (GA 52: 134)

As he laments the loss of German soldiers sacrificing their lives in battle for the fatherland, Heidegger remarks in the *Black Notebooks* that the whole question of "sacrifice" needs to be considered from a beyng-historical perspective. Against this background Heidegger comes to reflect upon the role of "world Jewry" within such a history.

When Heidegger ponders this world-historical accomplishment of world Jewry, he cannot help but express the bile that undermines any *philosophical* consideration of this question. Instead, we find Heidegger expressing what Nietzsche could only call "ressentiment" at the Jews who profit from the war, Heidegger maintains, without having to place their lives on the line in defense of the fatherland.

> World Jewry, instigated by emigrants who have been allowed out of Germany, is everywhere intangible and elusive and, as much as it develops its power, never has to take part in the actions of war, whereas the only thing left for us is to sacrifice the best blood of the very best of our own *Volk*. (GA 96: 262)

In his critique of world Jewry, Heidegger understands it as complicit in the unfolding of a machination (*Machenschaft*) that breeds "rootlessness," "the loss of history," and the inability to engage in a "decision" concerning being (GA 95: 97; GA 96: 56). It is, Heidegger claims, "through the dogged cleverness in calculating, profiteering, and indiscriminately meddling in everything that the worldlessness of Jewry is grounded" (GA 95: 97). Such machinational calculation ushers in "the *end* of the history of the great beginning of Western humanity, a beginning in which the human being was called to the guardianship of beyng, only to immediately transform this calling into the demand of representing beings in their machinational non-essence" (GA 95: 96). Considered against Heidegger's Hölderlin lectures and their notion of sacrifice for the fatherland, we can see how Heidegger positions the poet as the one who commemorates the power of the originary Greek beginning at the "world-hour of our *Volk*" (GA 16: 319; GA 39: 50). In this sense, Hölderlin comes to be understood as that poet "who still lies ahead of the Germans," the one who "has grounded the beginning of another history: that history that starts with the struggle over the decision concerning the arrival or flight of the god" (HGR: 1/GA 39: 1). Since the Jews occlude this primordial beginning through their calculative machinations, it is left to the Germans to clear a pathway that might open up the possibility of another commencement within the history of the West. Here Hölderlin serves as the poet who can help the Germans to attune themselves to this possibility and to prepare themselves for an other coming: the coming of the gods who have fled. As Heidegger puts it:

> Within the *historical*—beyng-historical—reflection that puts into question metaphysics as a whole in its essence and in its history, Hölderlin is a beginning, and that means at the same time: the silent demand of the beginning—and of the future as a beginning—thus, everything, except one who consummates and renews. (GA 95: 378)

Because the Jews stand in the way of the German mission "to hearken back to the Greek beginning," they can never enter into what Hölderlin holds forth as the futural promise of the German *Volk*—namely, "to poetize being, 'our' being in a more originary way" (GA 36/37: 89; GA 94: 27). In the *Black Notebooks* Heidegger lays out his reading of the impasses of metaphysical-technological dominion that occlude all possibilities of hearkening back to this beginning. Jewish calculation, planning, and reckoning epitomize the machinational impulses of a modernity that brings with it the legacy of rootlessness, homelessness, and "spiritual blindness" (GA 94: 248; GA 95: 97; GA 50: 127). The way out of the devastation and destructiveness of technological modernity lay for Heidegger in a radically new kind of hearing, an attunement to the voice of beyng that was not possible for Jews or indeed for any other culture, nation, or race. As Heidegger put it, "only the German can poetize and say being in a new originary way" (GA 94: 27).

This repeated emphasis on the chosen status of the German *Volk* and on the inability of other peoples and nations to properly take up the Greek endowment represents, of course, Heidegger's own ingrained sense of racial exclusion and national supremacy. But with the publication of the *Black Notebooks* we see how deeply rooted such prejudices are in Heidegger's work that we can no longer relegate them to the realm of mere cultural predispositions, personal bigotry, or insular provincialism. It is precisely this kind of thinking that betrays its own name. For here Heidegger abandons the task of thinking and falls back upon the inherited clichés of a Swabian Catholic upbringing that rejects Jews as belonging to the authentic *Volk* or as having any connection to the originary *arche* of the Occidental tradition. As nomads, wanderers, rootless and homeless beings, the Jews not only lack the autochthonic identity of an essential *Volk*—even more essentially, they embody "the principle of destruction," a principle that is not merely cultural but beyng-historical. As Heidegger frames it:

> In the time-space of the Christian Occident, i.e., of metaphysics, Judaism is the principle of destruction. . . . Hence we need to weigh what it means for a thinking (*Denken*) that thinks the concealed inceptual essence of the Occident to commemorate (*Andenken*) the first beginning of the Greeks—a beginning that remained outside of Judaism and that means outside of Christianity. (GA 97: 20)

If in earlier interpretations of Heidegger's exclusion of Jews from his philosophical corpus we could trace this back to his own provincial Black Forest-Alemannic cult of Schlageter, Hellingrath, Hebel, and Hölderlin, with passages such as these we can no longer avoid the judgment that such remarks are not the casual prejudices of "e Ma us de Rütte," but the underlying principles of a "beyng-historical racism" that serves as an organizing *topos* in the history of the West (GA 16: 641).[51] Such a *topos* helps to shape the way Heidegger conceives of *remembrance* itself. For Heidegger, Jews are essentially—which means here beyng-historically—incapable of commemorating the first beginning of Greek thinking. Since they are committed to the activities of calculating, reckoning, planning, profiteering, and dominating, Jews remain permanently "outside" of both the Greek beginning and its commemoration and futural "thinking-toward" (*Andenken*) (GA 95: 97, 339). Moreover, as Heidegger understands it, Jewish calculation militates against thinking by its very affirmation of a machinational stance toward beings. We can see this, Heidegger claims, in the Jews' determination of a *single* god, "Jehovah . . . who presumed to make himself the chosen god and not to put up with any other gods beside himself" (GA 97: 369). But, Heidegger asks, "what if the divinity of a god were to rest in the great tranquility from which he recognizes the other gods?" That is, what if this rigid insistence on the fact of a single god was itself bound up with the departure of the gods from human history, a departure that had rendered mortals as homeless beings incapable of properly dwelling upon the earth?

VI. The Time of the Festival and the Graeco-German Beginning

In the "Remembrance" lectures Heidegger never speaks of Jews directly, nor does he address the question of their role as the embodiment of "the principle of destruction" (GA 97: 20). Nonetheless, "the Jews" as *topos* inhabit the margins of the text, especially in the way Heidegger configures the relation of the native and the foreign, as well as in his treatment of the coming of the gods and the turn to the other beginning. As "the poet of the other beginning of our futural history," Hölderlin becomes a destiny for the Germans, a destiny that is at once inexorable and unrelenting (GA 66: 426). In his notes Heidegger raises the question: "Why does the choice come down to Hölderlin? Why not Goethe? . . . Why not Schiller?" and Heidegger answers:

> Is this really a case of choosing among poets? No. We can no longer choose at all,—we can, to be sure, evade Hölderlin's poetry and, as has happened over the last century, we can pass over it without notice. However, one day we must know

what it means to do this. It means that we thereby evade our own destiny. Hölderlin's poetry is a destiny for us . . . (GA 75: 350)

A Note on Hölderlin:

An intimation thereto: Hölderlin is a destiny for us. He is not something that belongs to the past. . . . There is no choice for us; Hölderlin is a *destiny* (Geschick) in our history (Geschichte). Destiny: *sent to us* (uns zugeschickt),—as we are to it. (Essential history.) We have no choice; we can evade destiny,—through letting it slip away or through oblivion. Hölderlin is futural, still to-come (zu-künftig). (GA 75: 351)

In this same set of notes written in 1945–1946, Heidegger reflects on what he calls "the fundamental experience: . . . the holy," that he thinks not in terms of happenings such as "deeds and achievements and wars and atrocities," but as "authentic destiny" (GA 75: 355). At the end of the war, in the age of the homelessness of the world's night, Heidegger still turns to Hölderlin as a way of thinking through German destiny:

The intimation of Hölderlin's poetry named destiny as something world-historical; with this destiny and through it, the Germans are able to experience their fate. The Germans: understood not as something "national," nor understood in terms of "humanity," nor as enlightened, nor considered "humanistically," rather: destinally (geschickhaft).

For *Hölderlin's poetizing, the fateful* (das Schickliche) means: to *say* the holy and indeed in abiding the *world-moment*: the evening of time; the night; the default of God.

The holy: the "element," aether, the open, the joyous, the clearing-concealing for the emerging and appearing of divinity; and this: the element of the coming of the sons of the gods—and *this* "brings" song. (GA 75: 363–364)

As Heidegger reflects back upon Hölderlin's poem "Song of the Germans," he connects it to the festival that alone can open a pathway for poetic dwelling upon the earth:

> A *preliminary consideration of* the *highest festival*, the "marriage feast" of earth and heaven, mortals and gods. *Questioning.*
>
> Song "of" the Germans. The German sings and his song says, names "the German": ready to become, to say the holy, to hear this,—at *times*. To bring it to language and to dwell therein. (GA 75: 359)

The festival becomes for Heidegger a way of expressing the relation to history that he deems essential for experiencing history (*Geschichte*) as destiny (*Geschick*). The festival (*Fest*) is understood here as a way of celebrating (*feiern*) the coming together of gods and mortals in a holy wedding (*hieros gamos*) in and through which all participants are appropriated to a festal time—the holiday (*Feiertag*)—which is not merely a cessation of work but the opening to a dispensation of the holy (*das Heilige*). This bridal festival, however, not only celebrates the union of the divine and the mortal; nor is it an occurrence that happens "within the framework and on the grounds of history." Rather, as Heidegger emphasizes, "*the festival is itself the ground and the essence of history*" (HHR: 60/GA 52: 68). But what does this mean and how is festival, which presumably happens and has already happened within history, itself the ground and the essence *of* history? It is in addressing such a question that we enter into the heart of the "Remembrance" lectures and their thinking of what it means to be German.

Understood phenomenologically, festival involves a coming together of those who greet and those who are greeted. This traditionally happens in feasts that take place in a special time—the time of the holiday—whereby what gets celebrated is the holy on the holy-day of celebration. Here the holy is less a state or condition of the gods or anything that has to do with presence. Rather, the holy marks the trace of the gods that have fled and in doing so draws attention to their absence. In this sense it has something unsettling about it since "the holy dislodges all experience from its habituation and dispossesses it of its habitat. Un-settling in this manner, the holy is the horror of the unsettling itself. Yet this horror remains concealed in the gentleness of its light embrace" (GA 4: 63). As the unsettling, the holy does not allow for easy mediation but instead remains recalcitrant to any attempt to appropriate it for human concerns. Precisely in this sense, the holy appears to us as something "un-approachable for every solitary being, whether this be a god or a human." As the un-approachable, the holy does not allow for being appropriated—and yet the holy is itself *the* event of appropriation, Heidegger tells us, since it mediates the coming-together of gods and mortals in the feast. The logic of this encounter is difficult to follow and yet crucial for Heidegger's purposes as a way to think feast, event, history, and beginning together in a poetic form of remembrance. But this thinking of remembrance demands of those who encounter it a correspondingly special experience of time—the time of the festival—that allows the holy to manifest as what first makes history at all possible. Again, the logic of this experience—and of the relation between gods and humans in the festival—is paradoxical, so if we are to grasp the sense of the holy in relation to the festival we will need to pursue Heidegger's reading here.

The festival, Heidegger insists, is never anything that can be planned, designed, or contrived by either humans or gods. As such, the festival does not take place "in" history as a historiographically recorded happening. Rather, what makes the festival happen is the festiveness that emerges in the event of appropriation granted by the holy. In the festival, humans and gods "come toward one another from afar; and this afar is in no way something that is left behind them, but is rather the space that they bring to one another in their encounter, without having found or opened that space themselves. Encountering is the reciprocal appropriation of their essence over into the essential space that first unfolds in its expansiveness and enters into its configuration" (HHR: 68/GA 52: 77). Here the festival comes to us without any prompting and prevails in its own measure, providing a sense of direction and orientation. Reckoned in a superficial way, festivals are celebrated on "holidays," days that chart the sequence of time on a calendar and organize time sequentially according to a recurring cycle of days measured chronologically and historiographically. And yet the festival defies historically calculated time by first granting to the *Volk* the very possibility and *"essence of history"* (GA 52: 68). Just so, the festival comes to us on a holiday unbidden and unplanned as a kind of greeting of time, a greeting that opens the time of the festival as an inceptual gesture that lets time appear in its authentic sense as the time of the event—*Ereignis*. In this way it appears like the northeast wind that serves as the inceptual greeting of "Remembrance." But more than this, the festival essentially grounds an "other" history, a history that thinks the futural possibilities of the German *Volk* in terms of its essential relation to the first beginning of Western history in the early Greeks. Here festival serves as a greeting whereby gods and mortals "address their essence to one another" and, in so doing, allow for a new sense of history in terms of the first and the other beginning.

> We cannot evade the manner in which Hölderlin thinks history as soon as we want to grasp the essence of the festival. This opens up for the first time our perspective on an essential connection between festival and history that underlies the poem "Remembrance" and pervasively attunes all its telling. Thinking the essence of history, however, at the same time signifies thinking that history in which this essence of history itself became manifest as a defining truth. Thinking the essence of history means thinking the Occidental in its essence, and thereby thinking it from out of its relation to the first beginning—that is, to the Greek world and to Greece. (HHR: 60–61/GA 52: 68)

If the northeast wind allots the inceptual time that lets the poem "Remembrance" begin, then we could also say that this time of inceptuality also grants and is granted by the time of the holiday ushered in by the holy. Yet, as with the wind, this holy time instantiates nothing; it points, rather, to the trace of something absent—the trace of the gods that have fled. In a time of profound destitution and deficit, "in the age of the world's night, the poet says the holy" (GA 5: 272). Insofar as the desolation of the modern age has proceeded so precipitously, the vocation of the poet has thus become one of attending to the traces of the gods' withdrawal by alerting us that "not only is the holy foundering as the trace of divinity, but even the traces of this foundering trace are all but extinguished." This is why Heidegger can write: "How can one know what *history* is, when one does not know what poetry is" (GA 76: 233). As the poet of poets, the poet of the Germans, Hölderlin teaches the *Volk* about its own history and its own identity, an identity whose proper sense lies in awaiting the coming of the gods, through whom alone the *Volk* can find its way to the proper (*das Eigene*), to what properly belongs to it but has been blocked and covered over in the age of the world's night. The pathway to this proper identity, however, lies not in what is customary or habitual; it lies rather in what is inhabitual or that which takes us out of the ordinary—like the festival. In and through the celebratory feast that brings with it the cessation of ordinary, habitual time, we begin to open a space for the event of the holy. In this way, we can understand celebration as "awaiting the authentic (*Erwartung des Eigentlichen*), preparing to appropriate what is essential (*Vorbereitung der Aneignung des Wesenhaften*), waiting for the event of appropriation (*Ereignis*) in which the essential manifests itself" (HHR: 59/GA 52: 66). In the "Remembrance" lectures Heidegger unequivocally affirms that "the event of appropriation is what is festive in the feast" (HHR: 69/GA 52: 77). That is, *as* festive it brings human beings out of their habitual slumbers and lets them encounter what is inhabitual. As the festivity that grounds the festival, the holy allows gods and humans to encounter one another in the special time of celebration. And yet given the pervasive destitution of the world's night that has brought with it an epoch of planetary homelessness, this celebratory event that brings together gods and mortals in the festival can endure only as "Andenken" or in the mode of remembrance. It is against this reading of remembrance as belonging to the time of the festival that Heidegger will emphasize the German relation to the first Greek beginning. As Heidegger stresses, it is "this essential connection between festival and history that underlies the poem 'Remembrance' and positively attunes all its telling" (HHR: 61/GA 52: 68).

What the festival lets come—again, much like the northeast wind—is the special time of the holiday that celebrates an inception whose power still endures in the festival, a power that takes the mode of remembrance. In this special time that interrupts the flow of customary life, human beings are accorded an *opening* in and of time that "sustains and pervasively attunes, and thus *lets* happen, all encountering" between mortals and gods (HHR: 68/GA 52: 77). This singular time of remembrance, the time of the festival, opens us to the appropriating event of the holy whereby we are appropriated by the "fitting" moment to enter into the poetic *now* of the festival itself and what it requires of us. For Hölderlin, the poet is called to this now-moment by an invocation that comes forth like a wind from the northeast. This moment of appropriation, the fitting moment that occurs at "the right time," "the critical time," the opportune moment that comes in a favorable season, this is what the ancient Greeks called *kairos*. In Pindar's epinician odes we find a range of references to *kairos* as "opportunity" (Pythian IV: 286; Nemean I: 18), "fitting measure" (Olympian XIII: 48), "appropriate moment" (Pythian X: 4), "due measure" (Nemean VIII: 4), "appropriateness" (Pythian VIII: 7), "proper moment" (Nemean VII: 58)—all of which express the fullness of the "timely moment."⁵² For Pindar, as for Hölderlin after him, poetic excellence, like the excellence of lovers whose hearts "do not stray from the fitting moment," lies in letting oneself be appropriated to and by the moment so that no longer does the poet speak, but the moment speaks through him (Nemean VIII: 4).

If we follow the etymological traces of *kairos* back to its Greek beginnings, we find that it emerges out of two distinct realms of experience—archery and weaving—that come together in the notion of an "opening." The first traces of this we find in Homer's *Iliad* (Bk. VIII: 325–326) in a scene where Teucer draws forth an arrow from his quiver to kill Hector—and suddenly, just as he pulls his arm back to shoot, the armor protecting his chest opens at the collarbone to reveal a fatal spot, a *kairos*, that remains unprotected. It is this mortal spot, the *kairos*, that opens to the moment of vulnerability in battle. Moreover, in this moment we become exposed to the vulnerability of life's precarious vicissitudes—namely, those openings of time that we cannot direct, control, or master. We find a similar allusion to archery and *kairos* in Sophocles's *Oedipus the King* (v. 325) when Teirisias in the first part of the play tells Oedipus that his words, though clever, "fall wide of the mark" (*pros kairon*). But Sophocles also thinks *kairos* in relation to human insight and sagacity. In the Prologue of *Ajax* (v. 120), Athena gives praise to Odysseus since he is gifted at "doing what the occasion (*ta kairia*) required." Within Greek thinking the *kairos* will also be understood as an opportune moment that requires of us great skill and perspicuity in negotiating its brevity, a brevity fraught with danger since time's favorable opening threatens to close at any given moment. This image of the brevity of time's opening finds its source in Pindar's allusion to the art and skill required of the weaver, who must cautiously attend to the brief opening in a loom between the warp and the weft through which a shuttle must pass. In carrying the image of the weaver over into the realm of speech, so too must the rhetor know the fabric of his discourse so that he might find the timely opening for interlacing his thematic threads within the larger design of his audience's concerns.⁵³ Here the *kairos* is understood as knowing the proper texture of a text and how the threads of its fabric might be expertly interwoven at the timely moment that allow for a weaving together of diverse and disparate strands into a whole design. Much as in the realm of archery, the weaver/rhetor must send the thread through the momentary opening in the yarn so that the shuttle "hits the proper mark."⁵⁴ We can find a wide range of *kair*-related words in ancient Greek that are connected to weaving: *kairoma* (web), *kairostris* (female weaver), *kairoseon* (something tightly woven), and *kairoō* (the act of fastening threads), all terms that will come to form the rhetorical space of a temporal opening in the fabric of time.

We find some analogous hints for this rhetoric of "opening" in the Latin translation of *kairos* with the term *opportunitas*—which, taken literally, indicates something like standing before, in front of (*op*) a *porta* or gate, door, opening, place of ingress.⁵⁵ In this sense, opportunity designates that moment that opens like a portal to the one attuned to its fleeting character. And yet in none of these various Greek or Latin inflections are we to understand *kairos* or *opportunitas* as something that can be guided by mere technical skill or intelligence. The *kairos* moment opens, if ever briefly, to poetic inspiration or en-spiriting that lets the moment seize the poet rather than the other way around. No application of *techne* can render a moment kairotic; the *kairos* comes upon us in its own timely fashion and often we miss it since our timing is not properly attuned to its way of manifesting. That is why the ancient Greek poets Homer, Hesiod, and Pindar often think of *kairos* in terms of "'symmetry,' 'propriety,' 'occasion,' 'due measure,' 'fitness,' 'tact,' 'decorum,' 'convenience,' 'proportion,' 'fruit,' 'profit,' and 'wise moderation.'"⁵⁶ Against all of these various inflections of *kairos* as accenting the sense of measure and proportion, we might also consider that one of the etymological sources for *kairos* goes back to the Greek verb *kerannymi*, "to mix, mingle, or temper"—in the sense of "to regulate" but also with affinities to the Latin notion of time: *tempus*.⁵⁷ In the Greek-German lexicon compiled by Franz Passow we can also find an allusion to *kerannymi* as temper in the sense of bringing forth an *Abwechselung*, "alternation/change," or an *Ausgleich*, "balance, equilibrium, or counter-balance."⁵⁸ Here *kerannymi* conveys the sense of mixing where every conjuncture/meeting of time that forms a *kairos* requires "the right mixture" for having the shuttle/arrow ready for the evanescent opening of the proper moment. Yet in all of these ways of reading *kairos* as the time that opens a space, one that places us in a certain relation to change and alterability, we need to consider how the *kairos*-moment can also displace and unsettle us from our customary habitations. It is in this sense that the *kairos*-moment of the festival presents itself to us.

For both Hölderlin and Heidegger the festival shows itself as the opening of time that claims us in its sacred celebration of/at the conjuncture between gods and mortals. As such, the festival marks the *kairos* moment wherein we are displaced by that which is "inhabitual" (*das Ungewöhnliche*), a displacement that harbors the possibility of a fundamental turn toward what is essential—namely, the inceptual. In Heidegger's words,

> The inhabitual appears. Its appearing does not require the enormous extravagance of the peculiar, or being incited by the unusualness of the latter. Celebration is now a being freed *from* what is stultified and habitual through becoming free *for* the inhabitual. The inhabitual, however, has its concealed measure in what is simple and inceptual in all beings. The inhabitual gathers itself in the fact that beings are at all and not rather nothing. (GA 52: 75)

By letting the inhabitual appear, the festival confronts the calculative-positing habits that humans fall back upon in their experience of time as mere duration and remaining. Such experience deadens humans to the revolutionary potential of time as that which can transport us into an originary experience of time—the *kairos* time of the festival. Already in his "Germania" lectures, Heidegger had stressed that "this originary time transports (*entrückt*) our *Dasein* into future (*Zukunft*) and having been (*Gewesenheit*)" (HGR: 99/GA 39: 109). That is, as a sacred mourning about the gods that have fled, this attunement to their absence at the same time provokes us into an attunement about their futural coming. Such an originary experience of time happens as a "displacement into (*Einrücken*) and a pure self-comporting within the space of a possible new encounter with the gods" (HGR: 88/GA 39: 97). It is this experience of *displacement* that essentially belongs to the festival as that opening in the fabric of time that breaks apart the merely calculative contrivance of temporal planning and allows for an abiding in the moment, "that right time" of kairotic experience (HGR: 100/GA 39: 109). The gods disdain calculative time, Heidegger tells us, since it involves compulsion and constraint. But festival time enables us to be released from such compulsion so that we might be free for what is singular, authentic, and inhabitual.

VII. Festival, Equinoctial Time, and the Balance of Equilibrium

In the "Remembrance" lectures Heidegger draws upon this notion of the inhabitual as a way of linking the kairotic time of the festival with the very shifts of *physis*' own seasonal turnings and transitions—especially in the figure of the vernal and autumnal equinox. Festivals are often instituted as a way of aligning the human time of celebration with the natural time of seasonal turnings and transitions. Within the poem "Remembrance" Hölderlin alludes to just such a temporal transfer in the third stanza when he describes the seasonal holidays:

> In March time,   Zur Märzenzeit,
> When night and day are   Wenn gleich ist Nacht und
>   equal,   Tag,

(SPF: 250–251)

Here Hölderlin refers of course to the time of the vernal equinox, which marks the date of his own birth (March 20), and yet this image brings together a remarkable range of references: from the birth of springtime, to the death of his beloved Susette Gontard, to the powerful role played by transition (*Übergang*) in the phenomena of emergence (*Aufgang*) and decline (*Untergang*). The time of the equinox marks the point in the celestial calendar when the sun crosses the celestial equator and when the length of day and night are equal. Yet in this image of "March time" we also find a poetic structure for organizing the whole of "Remembrance"—namely, the chiasm. A *chiasmus* (from the Greek *chiasma*, "crossing") is a figure of speech in which the beginning of a clause is reversed in *chiazo* or repeated in reverse order. The Greek verb *chiazein* signifies "to mark with two lines crossing like an 'x'"—hence, the Greek letter Χ—chi. The chiasm, then, is a figure of speech that joins words together by inverting them; that is, it involves a reversal of word order in two otherwise parallel constructions.[59] In Hölderlinian terms, such a chiasmus happens where "two opposites interlock and cut into each other impurely and asymmetrically"—such as night and day, land and sea, native and foreign, homeland and colony, living in solitude and communal celebration. We could extend this chiastic relation of inverted pairs to include the oblivion and forgetfulness of Bordeaux wine and the remembrance/recollection of a holiday's commemoration. Here we might even bring in the figure of Dionysus whose own mythic identity rests upon a chiastic structure of reversal in the form of his dismemberment (*sparagmos*) as the child Zagreus by the Titans followed then by his regeneration (springtime) that plays itself out in the Greek festivals of Dionysus, the Anthesteria.

The Anthesteria festivals honoring the god take place fittingly enough in springtime since "the Greeks always connected the name *Anthesteria* with 'blossoming,' in particular with the blossom of the vine."[60] As Walter Burkert explains, "the rite of the Anthesteria implies a . . . myth of the god torn apart, whose blood is represented in the sacramental drinking of the wine." The Anthesteria festival is thus marked by chiastic gestures: it celebrates the rebirth of Dionysus through the drinking of wine in honor of the god that brings its ritual participants into community even as it also laments the god's dismemberment and death in a ritual that signifies isolation and abandonment. The festival of Anthesteria, then, involves two contrasting elements: the sacred union of gods and mortals in a marriage festival (symbolized by Dionysus's partnering with Althea, the wife of Oeneus, "the wine man") *and* a festival of the dead that on the final day of the Anthesteria commemorates the souls of the departed. As the primary symbol of the Anthesteria, wine prepares the erotic union of gods and mortals in a *hieros gamos* even as it helps to usher in the drowsy shadows of oblivion to ease our pain at the loss of a beloved. In Hölderlin's allusion to "the fragrant cup / full of dark light" (vv. 26–27) we find many of these same contrastive images that both celebrate the joyful initiation of spring in the Bordeaux festival of "March time" even as they lament the loss of Hölderlin's beloved Susette Gontard.[61] Much as the Greek festival, the Bordeaux festival hails the onset of both a natural and a cultural shift in time. What will be celebrated here is the *transition* or *Übergang*, a passage or conversion between two distinct realms: the season of death (winter) and the season of rejuvenation (spring). Moreover, this transition occurs temporally at the March time—March 20, which serves as a border or threshold between the seasons—and spatially in the city of Bordeaux—which translates to the city at the water's (*eau*) edge/border (*Bord*—). Bordeaux lies at the threshold (Gk. *limen*) of land and water, a spot that marks the crossing-over of a chiasm that not only separates these two elements one from the other but also brings them together into a deeper unity precisely at the point of the crossing—the "x" or *chi* (*χ*)—where their separation occurs. Here the spatial crisscross of land and sea intersects with the temporal crisscross of the vernal equinox that in turn marks the mythic crisscross of Dionysus's own liminal status as a demi-god who celebrates life with joyous wine and suffers death through disjunction and dismemberment.

This pattern of juxtaposed oppositions that get balanced in and at the limit/border of their merging at the intersectional crisscross of a chiasm will get played out in a whole pattern of oppositions within the poem: man/woman, east/west, love/deeds, sleep/wakefulness, mariners/poets, night/day, dark/light, oaks/poplars, mill/courtyard, sea/land, festivity/mourning, among others. What is perhaps most distinctive throughout these patterns, however, is that they do not resolve themselves into a higher third element through a kind of supersession or *Aufhebung*. Like Dionysus himself, Hölderlin's poetic language contains contradictions for which there are no resolutions. The contradictory elements are not overcome by a poetic gesture but, rather, the poetic gesture bears the contradiction precisely as a contravention that supervenes any expectation of conventional agreement. What remains is borne by the poet as an abiding in what is inceptual. The poet does not seek to overcome the oppositional elements of isolation-community, joy-suffering, festivity-tragedy; he attempts, rather, to poetize this tensional conflict as an expression of being's own way of manifesting. The god Dionysus is the god of wine, joy, celebration, erotic union, musical ecstasy, transport, and rapture; but he is also the god of tragedy—not as an opposition to all these festive elements but as a way of bringing them together *in* their opposition. Dionysus is the god who is coming, *der kommende Gott*, as Hölderlin expresses it in "Bread and Wine" (v. 54):

Thence has come and pointing back there the coming god comes./

Dorther kommt und zurück deutet der kommende Gott.
(DKV I: 287)

As the god of coming, the coming god whose essence is to come, Dionysus expresses the character of all being as a Heraclitean unity-in-contradiction: "the one at variance with itself" (Fragment B51).[62] In this sense Dionysus is not a god who dwells amongst human beings "in" nature, but rather is nature itself in the sense that "each living thing is a mask of Dionysus."⁶³ In bringing together all things in terms of their opposition, and in revealing opposition itself as a primordial form of unity, Dionysus literally em-bodies (through *sparagmos* and rejuvenation) the balance and equilibrium of the festival time as a "time of transition" (*Übergangszeit*). In grasping the March time as Dionysiac festival time, the poet is able to enter into the liminality of kairotic time that looks backward as remembrance and that looks forward in preparing a futural coming. It is this experience of time as *Übergang* that Heidegger understands as both a reconciliation and an equalizing. But what does such "equalizing" or *Ausgleich* mean? For Heidegger,

> Reconciliation (*Versöhnung*) is an equalizing (*Ausgleichen*); but equalization is not simply a making equal in the manner of a leveling out of everything into an empty and undifferentiated sameness. Reconciliation is also not the suppression and elimination of strife, but rather a releasing of each of the parties in strife into the legitimacy of their own essence in each instance. True equalization places the parties in strife back into the equality of their essence. Equalization means that each is brought, in an equally inceptual manner, into the stillness of its essence and is sustained there, so that it may receive from this stillness of its essence the strength to acknowledge its counter-essence, and in such acknowledgment also first to find itself fully. Finding oneself, however, is never a stubborn insistence on oneself alone, but rather a going over from one's own to the foreign of the other and a going back from this acknowledged foreign into one's own. Equalization is going over and going back, is transition. (HHR: 76/GA 52: 86)

By understanding *Ausgleich* as *Übergang*—that is, by recognizing that the balance between opposites involves a transition that preserves each element precisely insofar as it exists oppositionally—Heidegger's "Remembrance" lectures attempt to think what Hölderlin poetizes. Hence, if the poet intimates that the March time lets night become day and again lets day become night without each abandoning its ownmost character, then Heidegger can write:

> If, in March time, night and day are equal, then this is to say that the night, which precedes the day, has become ready

to let the day and the coming of day take precedence in the transition (*Übergang*), yet without relinquishing its other aspect, that of preserving for day that which once was. The essential equalization (*Ausgleich*) between night and day does not bring about the disappearance of both, but rather brings each into its ownmost essence in each case, and brings both reciprocally into the unity of their mutual belonging.

"When night and day are equal" does not refer to some quantitatively determined, astronomical constellation, but is rather the veiling word of supreme, inceptual equalization. In night and day being equal in early spring, night is the purest transition to day, and day stands before the beginning of its ascendant rise. This equality is the summit of the pure granting of essence. This supreme equalization is the characteristic sign of the essence of the festival, of the event of the encountering of gods and humans. (HHR: 77/GA 52: 88)

In the festival both thinker and poet find a crisscrossing of the mortal and divine that grants balance, equilibrium, *Ausgleich*, in a way that harkens back to "a supreme, inceptual equalization." Whatever can and does emerge within the world can emerge only as belonging to this inceptual force of the beginning. All remembrance happens only by attuning itself to the power of the *arche* that rules over and grants a space for whatever is to come forth from it. Here the poet no longer speaks of past and future but of a Dionysian binding and releasing of remembrance and awaiting. The festival instantiates just such a kairological understanding of time as a crisscrossing of that which has been and that which is to come at the celebratory event of the festival. But this balance between the two can never be made permanent. As Heidegger puts it, "Fate is equalized (*ausgeglichen*) *only for a while*" (HHR: 81/GA 52: 93). And this "while" (*Weile*) names the space opened up in habitual life by the coming of the festival and by the festival's celebration of coming as intrinsic to festal time and to the god Dionysus. This is why Heidegger can repeat several times that "the festival is the ground and essence of history" (GA 52: 68, 70, 77, 84, 92, 186). Because the essence of history remains concealed to us in its oppositional forces, we remain unable to uncover its mystery. Yet for Heidegger "the mystery of . . . history (*Geschichte*) essentially prevails (*west*) in fate (*Schicksal*)" (HHR: 160, 81/GA 52: 188, 93). In the "while of the festival" we stand before what Heidegger calls our "distant vocation . . . of experiencing the essence of being from out of inceptual 'time' and its while."

Since the festival *displaces* us from our usual place in the world by releasing us from the habitual, it offers a way of attuning to the time "of" the festival—that is, a time that both belongs to the festival itself as a time of transition and that inaugurates this transition by granting an opening, a *kairos* moment, that lets festive time appear. We can find traces of this double belonging to time in the Anthesteria festival that celebrates the transition of time in the life of young children whose passage into adulthood begins with the consumption of wine in the March time.[64] But this festival itself is first grounded in the child Dionysus Zagreus's death that, by way of a self-initiated divine rejuvenation, in turn makes springtime possible. These crisscrossings between death and life, mortals and gods, emergence and decline, concealment and revelation get balanced (*ausgeglichen*) in a Dionysian merging of opposites in/as equilibrium (*Ausgleich*). At the pivot of these turnings we find no center but, rather, ever more transitions, pivots, torques, and chiastic interlacings. The god of changes, Dionysus, comes to presence through his absence. The god who manifests all things wears a mask that conceals his presence in all things as well. Perhaps the exemplary case of such simultaneous pres-ab-sence lies in Euripides's portrait of Dionysus in the *Bacchae*. There Dionysus appears on stage as the one who, though native to Thebes, is defined by Pentheus as "the Stranger." As the "native stranger," Dionysus thus collapses and confuses the distinction between native and foreign that will lie at the heart of Heidegger's own reading of Hölderlin. And though Heidegger does not take up the threads of this Dionysian configuration of native and foreign in his "Remembrance" lectures, he does pursue his own chiastic reading of this theme in a discussion about "homeland" and "colony" from Hölderlin's elegy "Bread and Wine."

In order to follow Heidegger's idiosyncratic and transgressive reading of Hölderlin here, some background on Hölderlin's own nuanced reading of Dionysus might prove helpful. To begin, we should recognize just how powerfully the image of Dionysus pervades the poem "Remembrance." From the very first line of the poem that alludes to the Northeast wind as the initiatory gesture of greeting, we find an allusion to Dionysian breath, the breath that the god of wind instruments grants to mortals to initiate their praise of the god. It is as if the poet were "frenzied by the god's breath," as Euripides describes it in *The Bacchae* (v. 1094).[65] It is this breath that literally in-spires or in-spirits the poem, functioning as a kind of poetic breath, the "fiery spirit" that grants to poets/mariners the promise of a "good voyage" (v. 3) and of a creative "journey" (*Fahrt*) of poetic exploration.[66] In this image of the mariners (v. 4) we can also find a reference to Dionysus who, when captured by Tyrrhenian pirates, turned them into dolphins and let vines grow up the mast and brought wine to flow forth from the ship into the sea.[67] A famous sixth-century BCE vase-painting by Exekias depicts the god on a ship, a scene of flowing vines and ripened grapes that would be reenacted in the Anthesteria festival of March time. In the second stanza of "Remembrance" we also find a reference to a fig tree that Heidegger identifies with "the fire of the Southern sky" that echoes the Böhlendorff letter's juxtaposition of northern Hesperian sobriety and southern Greek sacred fire (EHP: 125/ GA 4: 101). For Heidegger, this fig tree belongs to a series of references— holidays, brown women, silken soil—that all conjure images of poetic remembrance and longing for the departed gods of ancient Greece. But Heidegger misses a deeper bond to the fig tree here that contributes to his broader misunderstanding of Hölderlin's poetic relation to Dionysus throughout the poem. As he offers his reading of the second stanza's opening, Heidegger writes, "It speaks commemoratively (*andenkend*) and thinks back on the foreign that has been (*gewesenes Fremdes*) in its originary belonging-together with the homely that is coming(*kommendes Heimisches*)" (EHP: 124/GA 4: 101). Yet the reference to figs in Hölderlin's poem "Remembrance" will conjure a different set of images than those alluded to by Heidegger. As Hölderlin put it in his opening of the second stanza:

Still it thinks its way to me, and how	Noch denket das mir wohl und wie
The spread of tree tops, the elm forest	Die breiten Gipfel neiget
Bows over the mill,	Der Ulmwald, über die Muhl',
But in the courtyard grows a fig tree.	Im Hofe aber wächset ein Feigenbaum.

(vv. 13–16)

Before his journey to Bordeaux, Hölderlin had begun a translation of Euripides's *Bacchae* that offers some help in following his reference to a fig tree in verse 16. As he translates the original text from *Bacchae*, he misreads the Greek word *sekos* ("sacred enclosure" or "precinct") as *syke* ("fig tree"). Hence, instead of Dionysus praising Cadmus for declaring the tomb of Semele a "sacred precinct," Hölderlin renders it

> I praise holy Cadmus, who planted here in the
> field a fig tree for his daughter Semele (vv. 10–11)

(DKV II: 690, 1286)

As a tree sacred to Dionysus for its moistness and fecund properties, within Greek cultic ritual the fig tree became a "symbol for sexual intercourse" and an integral element in festive celebrations in remembrance of the god.[68] In this way the fig tree stands for Dionysian erotic fire as well as for the union between entities that are separated and sequestered. By aligning the fig tree with the courtyard in verse 16 and by juxtaposing this with the elm tree in verse 14, Hölderlin manages to fuse into one image two oppositional relations. Here at the chiastic crisscrossing of *native* dwelling (the courtyard) and *foreign* implantation (the fig tree associated with Dionysus and Greece planted in a strange/foreign enclosure), we find another crisscrossing between a native Hesperian tree (the elm) and a foreign fig tree from Hellas. We can also detect here an opposition between two distinct realms: the courtyard (culture) and the fig tree (nature) that are joined chiastically much as are night/day (v. 21) at the crisscross of the vernal equinox. In all of these images and in the ones to follow—brown women, native dancing, journeys to the Indians, the Gironde estuary that opens to the sea from two rivers—we can locate a Hölderlinian poetics of *kairos*, chiasm, contradiction, and a Heraclitean unity-in-difference that suffuses virtually every verse within the poem. We might even go so far as to say that Hölderlin's poetics dwells at the chiastic intercrossing of the native and the foreign that for him constitutes the very heart of his poetic vision of remembrance. To render this as simply as possible: the very inauguration of poetic breath or in-spiration depends upon a receptive greeting to that which comes upon the poet from a foreign sphere (the northeasterly). And while Heidegger's reading of "Remembrance" also draws deeply from this Hölderlinian dyad of the native and the foreign, it fundamentally misreads the source and direction of Hölderlin's poetic geography of the other. Moreover, through his own tendentious and exclusionary form of reading, Heidegger transforms/transmogrifies Hölderlin's poetry and its celebration of the native and the national into his own destinal politics of an elected *Volk*. We can find the outlines of such a politics of exclusion in the way Heidegger elucidates the March festival's celebration of the brown women and in his understanding of the journey to the Indians.

VIII. Heidegger's Destinal Politics of a German National Mission

Several scholars have pointed to Heidegger's "reductive," "arbitrary," "questionable," and even "violent" interpretations of Hölderlin.[69] Jean-Pierre Lefebvre goes so far as to claim that Heidegger's approach to "Andenken"—especially in his contention that "the path" (*Stege*) (v. 9) becomes for Heidegger a "woodpath" or *Holzweg*—results in the "Black Foresting" (*Verschwarzwaldung*) of the poem. Lefebvre argues that Heidegger's provincial emphasis on his own Swabian landscape prevents him from seeing how "*Andenken* is a poem about France, a French poem, the only French poem of Hölderlin's, a poem that is a *retour de France*."[70] Heidegger, of course, suppresses all of the singularly "French" references to the Garonne, the Gironde, and the Dordogne, as well as to the festivals of the March time, the brown women, and the native dancing. Hölderlin's inspiration for the kairotic time of the spring festival was clearly Dionysian; but it was also connected to the French revolutionary festivals that awakened in him the revolutionary impulse to restructure time itself through the celebration of new festivals. German scholars Karlheinz Stierle and Alexander Honold both contend that Hölderlin's emphasis on festival "stands on the ground of French revolutionary and post-revolutionary festivals and celebration hymns and especially on that of the Napoleonic peace festivals with their innumerable peace hymns."[71] Indeed, both read Hölderlin's "Celebration of Peace" as well as his drama *Death of Empedocles* as attempts to found a new German festival that would affirm the democratic impulses of the French Revolution while simultaneously celebrating a properly German communal identity. In the first version of *Death of Empedocles*, the tyrannical archon Critias mocks Empedocles's followers and their efforts to institute "a feast to outdo all the feasts" (DE: 44/DKV II: 286). But Hölderlin finds this cynical attitude wanting and in Empedocles's last words he affirms "the holy spirit of life" and "the grape's full force" (DE: 102/DKV II: 353). As ever, Hölderlin offers a forceful challenge to Critias's authoritarian politics even as he provides an energized politics of republican participation that draws on French revolutionary ideals. But Heidegger will respond to all these hints and pointers by ignoring, denying, suppressing, and eliding any positive references to either France or French revolutionary thinking in the way he interprets "Remembrance."

Instead Heidegger will resolutely underline the inextinguishable bond between Hesperia and Hellas that he finds outlined in the Böhlendorff letter. On this basis Heidegger will interpret all references to the "brown women" (v. 18), to "native dancing" (v. 48), and to the sea-faring journey "to the Indians" (v. 49) as indications for Hölderlin's commitment to an exclusively Graeco-German axis of affinity that runs throughout "Remembrance." Hence, Heidegger will read "the brown woman" not as displaced African or West Indian migrants/former slaves but as "Greek":

> When Hölderlin names "the brown women thereat," those of Southern France, therefore, then they and everything in which they share, that is, everything that is greeted together with them, stand for the Greek world. (HHR: 71/GA 52: 80)

Here Heidegger repeats his familiar refrain that anything connected to the south, the sun, fire is a coded Hölderlinian reference to ancient Greece. Any incursion into the interpretive boundaries of the poem from Africa or Asia must be rigorously staved off so that the axis of Graeco-German exclusivity can be maintained. Here the Remembrance lectures serve as another fundamental expression of Heidegger's longstanding task of "saving the West" through a relentless preservation of the originary kinship between the ancient Greeks and the modern Germans. This bond is essential to "saving the West," a task that constitutes the essence of the German vocation (EdP: 40; GA 80: 693). As Heidegger framed it in his 1936 lecture "Europe and German Philosophy":

> This possibility of salvation demands two things of us:
>
> 1. The *preservation* of the European peoples against the Asiatic.
>
> 2. The *overcoming* of our own deracination and fragmentation. (EdP: 31; GA 80: 681)

It is through this conflict with the forces of dispersion that a *Volk* comes into the nearness of its origin; from out of this nearness there emerges the soil/ground (*Boden*) upon which a standing and persisting is possible: *genuine autochthony*.

Hölderlin writes:

. . . With difficulty
That which dwells near the origin, abandons the locale."

. . . Schwer verlässt
Was nahe dem Ursprung wohnet, den Ort.

("DieWanderung" vv. 18–19) (EdP: 32)

Here again we see how Heidegger recruits Hölderlin for his program of Graeco-German autochthony as the only hope left to the West. On the basis of this presumed German connection to the Greek *arche*, Heidegger insulates Hölderlin from any non-Western topoi that might threaten the Greek-sanctioned inheritance of the German *Volk*. In so doing, Heidegger will extend his reading of the Greek origin to include the foreign—but now only as the binary other of the native German homeland of autochthonous dwelling. Hence, he will write, "For Hölderlin, Greece is the Other of the Western World" (HHR: 70/ GA 52: 78). Yet even as he acknowledges a dimension of alterity within his circumscribed reading of "Remembrance," he immediately marks the boundaries of such alterity by stressing that here, "The one and the other belong within a singular history." It is precisely this emphasis on exclusivity and singularity that characterizes Heidegger's interpretation of India within the poem. In several ways Heidegger will appropriate the otherness of India to his Germanocentric vision of the proper and the proprietary. Heidegger argues here that though India appears as farther away from the poet's homeland when measured cartographically, it is, he claims, "nonetheless nearer, if we ponder the essential, the passage to the source, the arrival in Germania" (HHR: 156/GA 52: 184). Read through the encoding of the Böhlendorff letter and "The Ister" hymn (v. 7), "India" now becomes synonymous with "the Indus"—the river of origin for all things Greek and Dionysian. In this sense, India serves as the name for the Greek "other" of Germania, the designation of an archaic source whose power animates the homeland through a difficult, chiastic gambit of re-appropriation. Only in and through a poetic *Andenken*—commemoration/thinking toward what is coming—can this originary source be properly encountered. Hence, India comes to function within Heidegger's festive celebration of the Graeco-German bond as a name for the (forgotten) inceptual origin that holds the mystery for Germania's destiny. And although Hölderlin did unquestionably embrace the mystery of the Graeco-German bond, he was also deeply fascinated by the call of what he termed the "Oriental." As Eva Kocziszky argues in her book *Hölderlins Orient*, "Hölderlin's unremitting interest for the cultures of the Orient shows itself throughout all his work."[72] Kocziszky claims that even as Hölderlin's poetics turned on the axis of Athens-Jerusalem, he was also preoccupied with "the Egyptian, the Ionian (Asia Minor), the Asiatic (the Caucasus) and the Arabic-Hebraic" so that he does not fit neatly into the framework of either a neoclassical or romantic approach to the Orient. As she emphasizes, Hölderlin's poetry needs to be understood as profoundly "untimely" insofar as "it looks back to the cultural prototype of Athens-Jerusalem even as, at the same time, it points ahead to the future through its vigorous accenting of the interpretation and cultivation of this endowment."

Even as we can grant to Heidegger his emphasis on the Dionysian roots of Hölderlin's "India" and on the Indus River as the originary homeland of the Hesperian-Hellenic *Volk*, we also need to recognize the inevitable Heideggerian distortions of what the Orient means within Hölderlin's poetic geography. Hölderlin does, of course, link the young Bacchus/Dionysus to the rivers of India in both "The Ister" (vv. 7–8) and "The Only One" (v. 56). But there are other references as well: Hölderlin refers to the youthful Bacchus's journey from the Indus in "The Poet's Vocation" (vv. 2–3); in "Germania," he writes of the eagle's journey from the Indus (v. 42), and in "The Eagle" (v. 10) there is another reference to the Indus as the land of origin (SPF: 78–79; 190–191; 294–295). And yet Hölderlin's preoccupation with both India and Asia Minor always turns on the problem of mediation, or *Vermittlung*. How is the poet, as demi-god who mediates the distance between mortals and gods, to mediate the *historical* distance between modernity and antiquity as well as the *cultural-geographical* distance between Hesperia and the primordial homeland(s) of Asia Minor and India? Heidegger wildly oversimplifies this relation by ignoring/suppressing the Asiatic and concentrating purely on Graeco-German mediation. There are deep and abiding problems here that penetrate to the core of Heidegger's racialized history of being and its influence upon his interpretation of Hölderlin. The well-known Hölderlin scholar Bernhard Böschenstein, who worked closely with Heidegger on the poem "Greece," found his approach to the Oriental, to India, and to Asia nothing less than "racist":

> I find it inexcusable that Heidegger totally effaces the brown women from the middle of "Remembrance" and replaces it with an ode that thanks German women at that place where he should have spoken of the brown women. That is, Heidegger was a raging racist. "Remembrance" is a poem that describes a journey across the ocean to America. There "Indians" are mentioned and Heidegger says they are the primordial Germanic tribe. He turns everything around. He says that the colony signifies the return to the mother. This is exactly the opposite of what Hölderlin says. For Hölderlin the colony is the movement away from the mother and for Heidegger there is always only the return to the mother. In "Homecoming" there is this wonderful bacchantic burst at the beginning of the poem, yet for Heidegger this is merely the return to what is his own. . . . In "The Journey" we have this marvelous verse: "But I am bound for the Caucasus!" (v. 25). Heidegger passes over this verse. For Heidegger it must always be only Germany, always only the return to one's own, always only the fatherland and in his reading of "Remembrance" this is absolutely grotesque.[73]

Nowhere in Heidegger's Hölderlin lectures is this systematic exclusion of other races and cultures on display as powerfully as in "Remembrance." There, in his discussion of "the brown women" and the journey "to Indians," we find perhaps his most egregious form of German exceptionalism and its consequences for non-German peoples. In the first case, Heidegger transforms Hölderlin's allusion to the brown women of North Africa or the West Indies into "the German women" who heroically "save the advent of the gods," an advent that "remains the primal event of history" (EHP: 131/GA 4: 107). Theodor Adorno castigates Heidegger here for "dragging the German women in by the hair" since they clearly do not belong in a poem about Bordeaux. Adorno then goes on to claim that Heidegger "already fears the appearance of

French women as subversive" and hence hastens to turn them into good "German" women through his philosophical-philological sleight of hand.[74] But Heidegger's unwillingness or inability to grant Hölderlin his own interpretive space for a proper "remembrance" of his experiences in Southern France proves deeply troubling—not merely because of the philological violence it exercises over Hölderlin's poems, but more so because it betrays a more fundamental form of racial exclusion that permeates Heidegger's work. Hence, if "the brown women" appear to Heidegger as "subversive" and threatening, so too do "the Indians" and any genuine encounter with the Asiatic or with the foreign Other. This kind of marginalization and exclusion appears all too forcefully in Heidegger's treatment of India and Indians in the poem. That Heidegger reads all references to India within Hölderlin's work as encoded ciphers for ancient Greece merely contributes to this overall pattern of suppression, elision, and systematic eradication. But Hölderlin's work proceeds in a fundamentally different manner by moving away from the homeland and the native and engaging the foreign as something worthy of understanding on its own terms. In thus exposing the native to the philosopheme of the Other, Hölderlin likewise exposes the native to its own deep ambiguity and questionability.

In the published version of the poem, the beginning of the fifth stanza reads:

> But now to Indians   Nun aber sind zu Indiern
> The men have gone,   Die Männer gegangen,

(SPF: 252–253)

Yet in an earlier draft Hölderlin had written it this way:

> To India   Nach Indien sind
> The friends have been drawn. Die Freunde gezogen.[75]

A comparison of these two drafts brings to notice that the earlier one is direct and unequivocal: the friends have gone abroad to India, the nation in East Asia through which both the Ganges and the Indus flow. But in the revised version Hölderlin deliberately introduces a note of ambiguity. Now the men have gone "to Indians"—in German the difference is indicated by one letter: *Indien* (India) and *Indiern* (Indians). With this one barely perceptible pen stroke Hölderlin opens up the whole *topos* of the poem in multiple and contrastive ways. Here the very enthymeme of the Orient becomes in a literal sense dis-orienting in that it crisscrosses the people of India from the East with the project of European colonization and subjugation in the West—specifically with French dominion in the West Indies, which had been threatened by slave revolt in the colonies. Here the bi-directional movement of the poem from East to West, indicated by the breath of memory brought on by the Northeast wind, shifts the focus from ancient India to modern French colonies in the West Indies. Hence the allusions to mariners and to a sea voyage need to be read through this other axis that turns from the Orient to colonies in the Americas. Hölderlin's poem "Columbus," that heroicizes the sea voyages of Vasco da Gama, the Knights Templar, and Admiral George Anson as

voyages of discovery	Entdeckungsreisen
as attempts to distinguish	als Versuche, den hesperischen
the Hesperian orbis from	orbis gegen den
the orbis of the ancients	orbis den Alten zu bestimmen

(SPF: 304–305)

indicates something of this attempt to situate the Greek-German conversation within a context that extends beyond the borders of Europe.

Again, we should remember that, for Hölderlin, Bordeaux is a city at the threshold between two distinct domains: land and water, communal dwelling in the city versus the isolation of mariners. As the place that mediates two oppositional realms, this topos organizes the movement and structure of the poem in two directions at once and indeed in such a way that appears ambiguous, if not contradictory. And though Heidegger's reading acknowledges and affirms this ambiguity and contradiction as one of the poem's distinct features, he limits its range to the Graeco-German sphere of autochthonous affinity. Hence, Dionysus can function as the god of the chiastic crisscross here, but his genuine identity as the Asiatic Other will be suppressed and elided in terms of what Heidegger will later call "The Western Conversation" (GA 75: 57–196). But Hölderlin's poem *performs* this crisscross in the way it maps the northeast wind's blowing in two different directions: from the Northeast to the Southwest (Swabia to France, France to the West Indies) and from the Southwest to the Northeast (France to Swabia, the West Indies to France). When we then recalibrate the wind's bi-directional force as a way of centering the energies of the poem we are left with a very different kind of poetic geography from that of Heidegger. During the time of Hölderlin's stay in Bordeaux he was exposed to the influx of migrants, foreigners, and slaves who populated the harbor district. As Michael Franz has argued, it was from this harbor that Napoleon Bonaparte sent 25,000 troops to Santo Domingo in December 1801 to reassert French authority over the Island of Hispaniola (today Haiti and the Dominican Republic).[76] Whereas slavery had been abolished in France in 1793 as part of the revolution's affirmation of the Rights of Man, in the colonies slavery persisted. In response to this, there emerged a slave rebellion led by Toussaint L'Ouverture, himself an ex-slave. Clearly, this topic of French imperial suppression of a colonial uprising became a daily topic of conversation in Bordeaux in the early months of 1802 just as Hölderlin arrived there. Moreover, Hölderlin's employer in Bordeaux, Daniel Christoph Meyer, was a wine merchant, and he is sure to have heard tales about the commercial trade of wine to the West Indies during his stay in Bordeaux.

Against this background, Hölderlin's allusion to men going to "the Indians" can now be read in a very different register than that of Heidegger. For it was Napoleon's own imperial reaction against the revolutionary impulses within the West Indies that led to Toussaint's capture and imprisonment back in France. For Hölderlin, this betrayal of French revolutionary ideals and the suppression of colonial freedom in favor of French bourgeois commercial interests must have proven difficult to accept.[77] Within Hölderlin's poetic geography, the West Indies, the land "discovered" by Columbus, can now be read as a topos of freedom from the traditional power structures of Europe, a place where the hopes of a new beginning might appear in an intimate relation to the first beginning that had appeared in Eastern India. From this optic of a West Indian relation to Bordeaux and the northeast trade winds that blow the spirit/wind of repression and reaction from Europe to the colonies, we can now see how Bordeaux might function as a kind of middle point between ancient and modern, reaction and revolution, East and West, India and the West Indies, the settlement of the homeland and the journeying to the colony. Within this other configuration, the problem of the native and the foreign, as with the relation of homeland and colony, can now be read as a revolutionary call to challenge the settlements of the homeland in a way that is profoundly unsettling.

IX. The Passage to the Foreign and the Journey Homeward

If throughout the "Remembrance" lectures we can trace the outlines of Heidegger's monocular understanding of the Greek-German vocation to save the West, then in the conclusion to these lectures we can also catch sight of Heidegger's own refusal to grant a space of tolerance or recognition of other peoples' right to engage in the Western Conversation about the future of the Greek bequest. As Heidegger brings these lectures to their close, he once again returns to the question of the Indians who, he insists, come from the Indus River in Asia. There at the Indus River lies "the distant provenance of Germania," Heidegger tells his listeners. Moreover, "Within the realm of Hölderlin's hymnal poetry, 'Indus' is the poetic name for the primordial homeland (*Urheimat*) that, however, nonetheless remains remote" (GA 52: 185). Here Heidegger will connect the Indus River in India to the Danube River in Germany by way of a poetic geography of reversal whereby the source of the native river has its authentic origin in the foreign homeland that preserves "the secret of history" as a mystery about inceptual remembrance. To follow the mysterious threads of such a history, Heidegger once again alludes to the chiastic logic of Hölderlin's famous Böhlendorff letter of December 4, 1801, that declares: "Yet one's own must be learned just as much as the foreign" (DKV III: 460). It proves difficult to understand the mystery of this logic, Heidegger claims, since it "is spoken seldom, and when it is, then for the most part only in passing, in an interim remark or in a rough draft that is then not at all taken up into what is explicitly said or crafted" (HHR: 161/GA 52: 189). Hence to offer some help with coming to terms with this mystery, Heidegger turns to a fragment from Hölderlin's elegy "Brod und Wein" that the poet composed years after his initial draft. It is in this crucial fragment that Heidegger finds "the essence of history" (HHR: 161–162/GA 52: 189–190):

> namely at home is spirit
> Not at the commencement, not at the source. The home
>   consumes it.
> Colony and bold forgetting spirit loves.
> Our flowers and the shades of our woods gladden
> The one who languishes. The besouler would almost be
>   scorched.

> nemlich zu Hauss ist der Geist
> Nicht im Anfang, nicht an der Quell. Ihn zehret die Heimat.
> Kolonie liebt und tapfer vergessen der Geist.
> Unsere Blumen erfreun und die Schatten unserer Wälder
> Den Verschmachteten. Fast wär der Beseeler verbrandt.
>
> (DKV I: 747; HHR: 161–162/GA 52: 189).[78]

Heidegger's placement of these lines at the end of his lecture course serves a double function within the lectures themselves. On the one hand, they serve the structural function of reenacting the very arc of Hölderlin's poetic thinking as Heidegger understands it. That is, they trace the archetypal movement of Hölderlin's poetry as a journeying away from the homeland into the foreign and then back again as a "Return to the Homeland" (DKV I: 252). In this way, at the very end of Heidegger's own journey of exploring the sense of Hölderlin's "Remembrance," the lectures return to the source of that journey as a recollective remembrance of the source of poetry itself in the homeland. On the other hand, however, Heidegger's larger concern involves an understanding of the essence of history as itself a movement of foreign exploration and native return. This signifies for Heidegger thinking the proper of the homeland in relation to the commencement of thinking in the early Greeks. On this reading, the movement of the German spirit begins as a journey outward from its home in Germania into the foreign (the Greek commencement) in order to return home to the proper by way of a poetic *Andenken* (both a "remembrance of" the first commencement and a "thinking toward" the other beginning). As Heidegger will continue to emphasize, the authentic German homecoming involves an essential encounter with the early Greeks, a logic of journey and return that he finds expressed in the Böhlendorff letter. Several times in his essays and lectures on Hölderlin, Heidegger will cite these lines from "Brod und Wein" as the key to an understanding of the Greek–German relation (GA 4: 89–94; GA 52: 188–193; GA 53: 155–166, 176–178; GA 75: 140–151, 190–191). What this fragment attempts, Heidegger claims, is no mere revision of a first draft; rather, it constitutes an attempt "to think it in a more originary way" by thinking of "the coming dispensation" (*das kommende Geschick*) that awaits the Germans (GA 75: 140).

If the fragment speaks of spirits not being at home, then this needs to be understood not as some general proclamation about human spirituality but as an indices for grasping "what stands before us as the dispensation of the historical world."[79] What concerns Heidegger here is a coming to terms with Germany's native endowment in the epoch of the world wars as it attempts to carry out its singular vocation of saving the West from its own self-annihilation—which would mean the triumph of either American capitalism or Soviet communism. In order for the Germans to take on the burden of this "Western responsibility," however, they need to freely embrace what is authentically their own (GA 16: 378, 398, 414, 452). This can only happen, Heidegger believes, when they first journey outward from the homeland and come to know themselves in and through the foreign. Again and again, Heidegger will define the situation as being able "to see the great threat that Bolshevism and Americanism unite themselves in a single essential form that thrusts German culture from out of its unity and destroys its place as the center of the West itself."[80] This vision of Germany as the very center (*Mitte*) of the West, caught "in the great pincers between Russia on the one side and America on the other," hearkens back to Heidegger's 1935 lectures "Introduction to Metaphysics" (IM: 40–41/GA 40: 40–41). There he defines this German "standing in the center" as the authentic German "vocation." He writes:

> But this *Volk* will gain a fate from its vocation only when it creates *in itself* a resonance, a possibility of resonance for this vocation, and grasps its tradition creatively. All this implies that this *Volk*, as a historical *Volk*, must transpose itself—and with it the history of the West—from the center of its future happening into the originary realm of the powers of being. Precisely if the great decision regarding Europe is not to go down the path of annihilation—precisely then can this decision come about only through the development of new, historically *spiritual* forces from the center. (IM: 41/GA 40: 41–42)

Throughout the period of National Socialist hegemony—and that means throughout the years when Heidegger carries out his most extended conversation with Hölderlin (GA 4, GA 39, GA 52, GA 53)—this discourse about "the German vocation" with its "Western responsibility" gets framed as a meditation on the native and the foreign. This conversation takes place, in turn, as a thinking of the first Greek beginning in the West. Still, this reflection on the first beginning is no mere historical reflection. On the contrary, it bespeaks an understanding of history as an other history than the traditional narrative of states, peoples, economies, and social movements. What Heidegger attempts to think here is a history of beyng that opens up the possibility of a transition to an other beginning, a possibility whose preparation lies in listening to the poetic voice of Hölderlin. As Heidegger writes in "Concerning the Beginning":

> Beyng-historical thinking takes upon itself the preparation of the inceptuality of the Other beginning; it is the leap into this. Such thinking prepares a poetizing that has already happened in Hölderlin's hymns, that is, essentially unfolds in an authentically inceptual way. . . .
> But from where does the interpretation of Hölderlin's poetic vocation come? And from where the knowledge of its historical inceptuality?
> From knowledge of the history of beyng! (GA 70: 156)

Yet Heidegger also recognizes that Hölderlin's poetic word has remained unheard in the age of the world's night. And he asks:

> But why has Hölderlin's word still not been experienced and still yet not been known as the voice of beyng itself? (GA 70: 167)

For Heidegger the answer to this question lies less in any specific human failing than in the destinal-epochal sendings of beyng itself. That Hölderlin has not yet been heard belongs to the history of that epoch that understands itself superficially as a decline (*Untergang*) in Spengler's sense. This contemporary epoch has, however, not yet grasped Hölderlin's own understanding of decline (*Untergang*) as but a transition or *Übergang* that prepares the possibility of another beginning for the West, one whose own coming to be rests upon an originary connection to the first beginning of Western thinking in the Greeks.

What the "Brod und Wein" fragment thus signifies for Heidegger is twofold. First, it involves a way of connecting Hölderlin's poetic vocation—not only to the German vocation of saving the West—but as a way of transitioning out of the epochal decline of the first Greek beginning. Second, it offers a way to open up Western thinking to the concealed possibilities within that beginning that were foreclosed in and through the metaphysical determination of Western philosophy. What Heidegger understands here is that the very possibility of beginning can begin only when the beginning itself withdraws: "to the inceptuality of the beginning there belongs withdrawal" (GA 70: 60). Since Hölderlin thinks of the West as "Hesperia" (from the Greek *hespera*—"evening"/Latin: *vesper*) or *Abendland* (land of evening) and of the East as the Orient (Latin *oriens* from the verb *oriri*, "to arise"), he will offer a poetic geography of history that turns on the place of Greece as the axis between West and East.[81] Yet the way Hölderlin configures these relations and the way Heidegger takes them up again in his reflections on Germany's European mission remain ever at odds. For what Hölderlin means by "the Orient" is "the country of origin of the dionysiac," that ever elusive element of the foreign that refuses to become domesticated in the native.[82] Hölderlin expresses something of this impulse in a letter to Friedrich Wilmans, the publisher of his Sophocles translations:

> Greek art is foreign to us because of the national convenience and shortcoming it has always relied upon, and I hope to present it to the public in a more lively manner than usual by accentuating more forcefully the oriental element (*das Orientalische*) that [the German] public has denied and correcting its artistic failing wherever it crops up. (E&L: 215/ DKV III: 468)

Here we find Hölderlin coming up against the limits of what constitutes Greek art at the crossing of the Greek and Oriental. Precisely at this crossing, however, we find the dionysiac performance of transition, traversal, and transformation, a performance of negotiating limits that both separate and unite the spheres of contention and opposition that obtain between them. For Hölderlin, poetic art happens at the border/ limit between the Greek and German language that takes place in translation; it happens in the border-crossing journey from the homeland out into the foreign and it comes about in the historical transition from the gods' withdrawal from the earth and their return. In each of these three exemplary experiences of the limit we come upon the decisive role of Greece as the bearer of "impossible conjunctions" between what belongs to the native and what calls to us from the foreign.[83] In "Remembrance" we can find the topoi of these limits between wind and sun (vv. 1–4), night and day (v. 21), shadow and light (vv. 26–29), silence and speech

(vv. 30–36), the leaves of the fig tree in the courtyard and the leafless mast of the ship upon the sea (vv. 16 and 46), and between the amnesiac slumber of dreams and the remembrance of poetic abiding that ordains an *anamnesis* that endures (vv. 28–29 and vv. 57–59). Here at the borders, boundaries, and limits of human experience, Hölderlin demarcates the task of authentic German identity: to achieve a poetic measure of dwelling that would honor the passageway between divided realms such that each would find its proper balance only in the crossing itself. For this task of dwelling at the limit, the poet chooses Dionysus as his guide—Dionysus the demi-god who is *both* Oriental and Greek, human and divine, foreign and native, libidinous disciple of joy and tragic bearer of suffering, the one whose very name expresses the principle of harmonious opposition that gives birth to all *physis*.

There are moments in Heidegger where the full force of this Hölderlinian insight comes to expression. In his postwar essay "Building Dwelling Thinking," Heidegger writes of the limit as that site that allows for a kind of originary jointure, a *topos* of gathering that grants its own countervailing force of oppositional disjunction. There Heidegger writes:

> A limit is not that at which something ceases but, as the Greeks recognized, a limit is that from which something *begins its essential unfolding* (*sein Wesen beginnt*). That is why the concept is that of *horismos*, i.e., the limit or horizon. (PLT: 154/GA 7: 156)

In this phenomenological expression of the limit as the horizon that brings together opposing realms without letting their contentious relation collapse into mere agreement, Heidegger finds the chiastic *Mitte* or center of Hölderlin's thinking. And for the later Heidegger this Hölderlinian understanding of the *limit* as the site where the poet abides in the conflictual intimacy (*Innigkeit*) of Heraclitean *polemos* becomes the very way of understanding what it means to dwell poetically upon the earth. We might even go so far as to say that this chiastic crossing at that site that the young Hölderlin termed "the middle of life" (*die Mitte des Lebens*) enables the transition, transformation, and migration from one's own into the foreign, understood as a nomadology of the self into the strange and alien realm of all that is other (DKV II: 42).[84] But Heidegger will parse this transition very differently from Hölderlin by abandoning the poet's emphasis on nomadology and exile and reading every journey outward into the foreign as a turn that always enacts and demands a re-turn. We can find the contours of just such a reading in the way Heidegger situates the "Brod und Wein" fragment in the laying out of his "Remembrance" lectures.

There Heidegger stresses the journey of "spirit," a journey that he designates as a *"passage* to the source" since at the beginning spirit is not at the source and "has not yet come to itself" (GA 52: 190). Before we come to a fuller sense of this fragment's meaning, however, we need to confront what Heidegger means by "spirit" and by "beginning." In his 1946 lecture "Poverty" Heidegger opens his essay by citing a line from Hölderlin's fragment on European historical periods from the Hellingrath edition:

> For us, everything is concentrated upon the spiritual (*auf's Geistige*); we have become poor in order to become rich.[85]

In his remarks Heidegger makes it clear that he rejects the long-standing metaphysical definition of spirit as "the opposite of matter" or as a Christian "essence."[86] Rather, like Hölderlin, Heidegger seeks to understand it as "a concentration, i.e., a gathering (*Versammlung*) upon the relationship of beyng to our essential unfolding, a relationship that is the center, the middle, that is everywhere as the middle of a circle whose periphery is nowhere." Spirit, in other words, occurs as an appropriating event (*Ereignis*) rather than as a possession of the human being. What properly occurs (*sich ereignet*) here is "a thinking-poetizing naming of an appropriating event that is concealed in beyng itself," one that from the realm of the proper "reaches out far beyond into what is coming." Yet, for Heidegger, spirit's reaching out far beyond itself into the foreign happens so that it might come back to itself in the proper.

This return home brings forth a renewed appropriation of what spirit left behind in its passage to the foreign, a passage from the beginning outward, back to the beginning as a beginning again. But what is this beginning? Throughout the Hölderlin lectures Heidegger thinks it in terms of Greece. In his first Hölderlin lecture, Heidegger writes: "the beginning is that from which something arises or springs forth . . . the beginning—the origin—first appears and comes to light in a happening and is fully there only at its end" (HGR: 3/GA 39: 3). And in the Parmenides lectures, Heidegger adds: "We call what precedes and determines all history the beginning. Because it does not reside back in a past but lies in advance of what is to come, the inceptual again and again turns out to be precisely a gift to an epoch. In essential history the beginning comes last" (P: 1/ GA 54: 1–2). For Heidegger this *essential* history begins in Greece since it was there that "the primordial essence of truth [as] *aletheia*" originates (P: 147/GA 54: 218). This, Heidegger claims, "is the event (*das Ereignis*) of the history of the West." Moreover, as Heidegger puts it in "The Western Conversation," it was there in Greece that "the transition of the Oriental to the Occidental properly occurred (*sich ereignet*)" (GA 75: 141). Such a reading reinforces Heidegger's claim that the Occidental spirit can only come to itself in and through its relation to the first Greek beginning—even if this beginning had been closed off and concealed virtually at the outset of its appearance. What stands before us as the task of our vocation, then, is to heed the promise of a commencement whose inceptual force had been both forgotten and foreclosed at its very inception. The long history of Occidental thinking has been one of incipient disclosure and subsequent foreclosure of what remains concealed in the beginning.

Confronting this sense of the Greek beginning, Heidegger can write at the end of the "Remembrance" lectures: "The beginning does not begin with the beginning" (GA 52: 189). It is this "mystery of history and of the commencement" that Heidegger holds as the way of approaching the spirit's journey from the homeland poetized in Hölderlin's "Brod und Wein" fragment. But it is precisely Heidegger's insistence on reading both the "foreign" and the "beginning" as belonging to the *event* of Greece that will so overdetermine his understanding of Hölderlinian *remembrance* as to make him blind to its dionysiac relation to the foreign. We can find the traces of this reading in the way he understands the spirit's relation to the colony.

In his lectures Heidegger explains it as follows:

> In the beginning, the homeland is still closed off within itself, uncleared and unfree, and thus has not yet come to itself. This coming to "itself" demands a coming from something other. Going away to an other is the initial, as yet unappropriated distancing of the ability in relation to that for which it is an ability and within which it is to become free usage. Because the homeland demands a becoming homely, yet the latter, as a coming to oneself, must be a coming home, for this reason the spirit of the homeland itself demands the foreign from which a homecoming can only ever proceed:

Colony, and bold forgetting spirit loves. (HHR: 161–162/
GA 52: 190)

On this reading, Heidegger understands "colony" as a way station of spirit on its journey to the homeland and, more than that, sees the "foreign" as that which stands in service to the homeland as a way for it to "come to itself." This Heideggerian emphasis on one's own (*das Eigene*), the native, and the homely winds up reducing the other, the foreign, and the unhomely to what helps the homeland come to its "free use" of them, following Heidegger's understanding of the Böhlendorff letter. But Heidegger adds a caveat: the journey of return to one's own is not a self-centered assimilation of the foreign, but an essential unfolding of what spirit signifies—and that is a waiting for that which is coming, the return of the gods to the earth. Hence Heidegger can write: "The sojourn (*Aufenthalt*) in the foreign and the learning of the foreign, not for the sake of the foreign, but for the sake of one's own, demands that enduring waiting that no longer thinks of one's own" (HHR: 162/ GA 52: 190). At least two problems emerge here as we try to follow Heidegger's own contorted, transgressive reading of Hölderlin's "Brod und Wein" fragment. First, we cannot help but notice that in his attempt to relate spirit to the foreign "colony," Heidegger invariably privileges the ownmost over the alien even as he defines the foreign only in relation to the native homeland. Hence, he can think of the foreign as "the still unappropriated homeland," the other whose alterity is thought only and ever in terms of the proper, the native, the homely, and the selfsame. Within such a configuration, remembrance will be thought of as "a thinking ahead (*Vordenken*) to the other of the foreign. That is, one's own" (HHR: 164/GA 52: 193). Heidegger reinforces this privileging of the proper in his 1943 essay "Remembrance" when, in his discussion of the northeast wind, he claims that "this wind 'calls' the poets to find themselves in the destiny of their historical essence" (EHP: 111-112/GA 4: 87). He then goes on to write:

> In this preference for the northeast there prevails the love for the experience of the *fiery spirit* in the foreign land. The love for the unhomely, purely for the sake of becoming homely in what is one's own, is the essential law of destiny (*Geschick*) by which the poet is sent (*geschickt*) into the grounding of the history of "the Fatherland."

For Heidegger, of course, the outlines of this "essential law of destiny" can be found in the Böhlendorff letter, a text that serves as his Rosetta Stone for understanding the poetic movement of spirit both in "Remembrance" and in the "Brod und Wein" fragment. That law is governed by a logic of return and homecoming that guides spirit forth from out of its native dwelling into the foreign colony—there only "for the sake of" the native return—and then back again to the homeland as a passageway from the colony back to native soil. But there are hints and allusions within the "Brod und Wein" fragment that point in a very different direction than the one laid out by Heidegger. This leads us to the second problem with Heidegger's reading—the fact that he misses (or suppresses) the striking references to Dionysus in the fragment, especially the relation of the god to the "colony."

As Heidegger parses the fragment—read always through his own interpretation of the Böhlendorff letter—"colony" is understood primarily as a way station on the journey of return to the homeland. As Heidegger puts it in his "Remembrance" essay (1943):

> *The spirit . . . loves the colony.* The colony is the daughterland which points back to the motherland. Insofar as the spirit loves the land of such a nature, its mediate and concealed love is only for the mother. That is the native earth that is . . . however, *difficult to secure, that which is closed off.* Because the spirit does not merely flee into the foreign, but rather *loves the colony,* it is thus in an essential sense lovingly *not at home.* (EHP: 117/GA 4: 93)

By his very gesture of conceiving colony as "daughterland" and the homeland as "motherland," Heidegger betrays his own axiomatics of journey *as* return that prevails throughout his "Remembrance" lectures. In this way he repeats the selfsame logic of German exceptionalism that he finds in the work of the Hölderlin scholar and editor, Friedrich Beissner. Taking the Böhlendorff letter as "the best commentary to interpreting these difficult verses," Beissner reads the homeland:colony relation as that between Hesperia:Hellas where Germany becomes the homeland and Greece the colony.[87] Yet such an interpretation proves problematic at best and fails to account for the Dionysian relation to "colony" in the poem. By identifying "spirit" in the fragment as "the German spirit" or "the spirit of the *Volk*" according to a logic of exile and return, Beissner announces a German exceptionalism that will find its echo in Heidegger's work. But this whole figuration of Greece as a kind of "spiritual colony" for German spirit's journey homeward misconstrues deeply the meaning of Hölderlin's verse.

In the Ister hymn (which we will look at more closely in the next chapter), Hölderlin alludes to the myth of Herakles who travels northward from Greece to Hesperia to secure the leaves of the olive branch so as to offer shade and coolness against the fiery sun of Olympia (SPF: 254–255). Drawing upon a Herakles myth told by Pindar in his Third Olympian Ode, Hölderlin positions Hesperia as a Greek colony and the wandering Heracles as the colonizer.[88] This return is then reversed in Heidegger's parsing of the "Brod und Wein" fragment so that ancient Greece becomes the "colony" for a modern German form of journey and return. But the details of the language in Hölderlin's hymn invite a different reading.

Jochen Schmidt, like Adolf Beck and Johann Kreuzer, makes a strong case for reading this fragment as a variation on the underlying Dionysian emphasis within the poem. On this reading, Dionysus appears as the one who "loves colony" since he is "that god who does not remain in one place, but always is in quest of new soil upon which to plant his seed" (DKV I: 747).[89] For Schmidt, Dionysus's journey from out of the homeland to the northern forests of Hesperia is undertaken to receive cooling shade, since at his birth he was "midwifed by the thunderstorm's fire" as Hölderlin expressed it in his own translation of Euripides' *Bacchae* (DKV II: 690). Here Hesperia/Germania—land of the evening sky, the Occident—will be thought of as Dionysus' colony. In an emendation of v. 54 of "Brod und Wein," Hölderlin writes again of Dionysus. In the published version the text reads:

Thence has come and back there points the god who's to come.

Dorther kommt und zurük deutet der kommende Gott.

(SPF: 152–153)

And in the Homburger Folio edition, Hölderlin alters it:

Thence has come and there laughs transplanted, the god.

Dorther kommt und da lachet verpflanzet, der Gott.[90]

With the help of these additional lines, the allusion to colony in the other draft now begins to take focus. The colony functions as a kind of

"Pflanzniederlassung" (the planting of seeds in a new colony), a new site for the god of wine to plant seeds for the vine to grow.[91] In the spirit of laughter and mirth, the god breaks free from the limits of the homeland and joyfully wanders afield planting and sowing his seed in all senses of the term. If we can say that Dionysus "loves colony," then now "the foreign" colony is to be understood not as a medial way station on the path of return to the homeland, but as a foreign excursion that leads the way to other distant and unknown destinations. Here the suggestion is that the god plants a colony in the foreign land that will stand apart from the homeland and will not seek to return to it. Within this context it is helpful to remember that the Latin noun *colonia* (denoting a "farm" or "estate") derives from the verb *colere*, "to cultivate" and has to do with agri-culture (cultivating a field or acre, *agra*).[92] The Greek term for colony, *apoikia*, indicates a being apart from (*ap*) the home (*oikos*), from the Greek verb *apoikizein* "to plant in other fields," where the new growth becomes a transplantation different from the source, never to return thereto.[93] *Apoikizein* thus designates a "sending away from home" or "emigration" without the thought of homecoming.

Heidegger will, however, ignore or suppress any trace of Dionysus as colonizer and will insist on reading Germany as the homeland and Greece as the colony. As Bernhard Böschenstein will plainly put it: "Here Heidegger gets everything backwards. He claims that the colony signifies the return to the mother. But this is exactly the opposite of what Hölderlin says. For Hölderlin, colony is the passage away from the mother, whereas for Heidegger there is always only a return to the mother."[94] As Böschenstein sees it, Heidegger's "cult of Greece"—and his need to thematize it as a way station on the path to authentic German homecoming—forestalls and occludes any attempt to understand the foreign *as* foreign on its own terms. Instead, Heidegger configures the foreign as the other of the native and in so doing reappropriates the foreign's own proper to the proper of the homeland, thereby suppressing/forgetting its very alterity. This kind of willed oblivion pervades Heidegger's reading of *Andenken*. The very assumptions that Heidegger makes anterior to his engagement with Hölderlin's poem—namely, that Germany is the privileged, singular homeland; that because of its consanguineous relation with the ancient Greeks it alone among modern nations can save the West; that every confrontation with the foreign is always already undertaken for the sake of the homeland—all of these absolutely non-philosophical presumptions foreclose from the outset any authentic "experience of the foreign" in its very foreignness (GA 4: 115, 126). Always Swabia will be privileged as the place of return; everywhere the foreign will function as a prop for the proper so that its impropriety and strangeness can be appropriated to the nativist project of self-disclosure. Heidegger's inability to think the colony *as* colony, however, is hardly an exception. His monocular focus on Germany and Greece prevents him from noticing several distinctive aspects of Hölderlin's "Remembrance."

Hölderlin proved himself to be an avid reader of travel literature (Richard Chandler, Robert Wood, Baron Anson, Choiseul-Gouffier) about seafaring to South Sea islands, expeditions to Greece, Asia Minor, and the Americas. In *Hyperion,* "Tinian," "Kolomb," "Die Wanderung," among other works, we see Hölderlin expressing his love of travel and for adventures in wandering. Moreover, in poems such as "The Traveller" he alludes to the "African desert" (v. 1), the "north pole" (v. 20), to "pilgrims" (v. 85) to "prescient mariners" (v. 80), to "the good camel" (v. 14), and to "the ice of the Arctic" (v. 43) (SPF: 136–143). These notions of wandering, migrating, traveling, wayfaring, journeying, and setting sail do not appear as mere appendages to Hölderlin's poetizing, but as fundamental philosophemes that shape his very sense of the native and the proper. This deep and abiding preoccupation with travel was combined with Hölderlin's interest in geology, cartography, topography, astronomy, climatology, and geopolitics so much so that the Hölderlin scholar Helmut Mottel has come to speak of "Hölderlin's Nomadology."[95] And yet Heidegger will remain inattentive to these nomadological motifs that persist in Hölderlin's poetry and instead will continue to accentuate "the law of becoming homely for the Germans" (HHI: 137/GA 53: 170). The journey into the foreign will continue to be glossed over except as it relates to the homeland. Hence, Heidegger can write near the end of the "Remembrance" lectures: "The sojourn in the foreign and the estrangement in the foreign have to be, so that in its contact with the foreign, the proper begins to shine. This distant shining awakens a remote inclining toward what is one's one" (HHR: 147/GA 52: 175–176). Journeying stands in service to the proper: "the voyage across the ocean thus stands under the concealed law of the return home to one's own." In his eagerness to carry out this law of repatriation, Heidegger overlooks even the most basic human features of Hölderlin's poetic wandering. For example, in his focus on the law of return in the Böhlendorff letter, Heidegger skips over Hölderlin's anticipation about his forthcoming journey and his confession to his friend: "I am happy about the prospect of seeing the sea and the sun of Provence" (E&L: 208/DKV III: 461).

If we can make sense of Heidegger's design in the "Remembrance" lectures, then perhaps we might say that poetic *Andenken* serves the function of retrieving the origin of the proper in and through a commemoration that simultaneously thinks ahead toward that which is coming. This kind of commemorative thinking always takes place, however, as a kind of homecoming, a coming (home) whose ownmost possibility lies in a retrieval of the foreign other (Greece) for the sake of the properly native (German, Swabian). That Heidegger will conjoin this interpretation of "remembrance" to the celebration of fallen German soldiers in the Russian campaign of winter 1942, should help us to situate its theme of homecoming in a more critical light. This "return to one's own," as Heidegger understood it, would always be marked by a metaphysics of national supremacy that celebrated the selfsame, the kindred, the native, and the proper. In conjunction with the historical circumstances of his time and his own commitment to a narrative of German historical destiny, the revelations of the *Black Notebooks* hardly come as a jarring surprise. The logic of national exclusion and of a beyng-historical conspiracy of "world Jewry" find their confirmation in the "Remembrance" lectures. From our own historical perspective we can now see how misbegotten these lectures would have appeared to a young Paul Celan, were he to have been present in the Freiburg lecture hall in WS 1941–42. But Celan was, of course, "absent"—given his forced labor in Czernowitz.

After the war Celan would compose a poem with the same title as Hölderlin's (and as Heidegger's 1943 essay)—"Andenken." Celan's labyrinthine poetic style draws upon several of Hölderlin's striking images: "the fig tree," "the sea wind's breath," "shipwreck," and a remembrance of a beloved woman who has died—but now not Susette Gontard, but Celan's mother, murdered in a concentration camp in Transnistria in 1942. For Celan, remembrance conjures images of exile rather than of return, images of a caesura so total and irrecoverable that they offer no hint of a possible homecoming from out of the foreign. Death's sting does not help to initiate a journey homeward but, rather, impels the poet to an exile so formidable that he cannot help but imagine the shipwreck of his dead father's hopes of a "return" to the Holy Land where figs and almonds grow.[96] Celan's fractured hopes of a Zionist homecoming for his dead father offer a stark contrast to Heidegger's own hopes of a German homecoming borne on the northeast wind of Hölderlin's "Andenken."

In *Writing the Disaster*, Maurice Blanchot reflects on the *topos* of memory and of remembrance and of the way disaster "disestablishes itself" in such a way that "the disaster is related to forgetfulness—forgetfulness without memory, the motionless retreat/retracing (*retrait*) of what has not been traced (*tracé*)."[97] In this retreat of the trace that obliterates memory, we find an "un-story . . . that cannot be forgotten because it has always already fallen outside memory." The disaster cannot be appropriated; it resists every gesture or movement of return in the sense of re-appropriation. If there ever were a possibility of "remembrance" then it could only be one of "remembering forgetfully" from "the outside." What remains after Heidegger's remembrance is an absence so profoundly forgetful that the traces of its memory recede into oblivion, an oblivion that dis-establishes the axiomatics of German national self-determination that spurs Heidegger's hope of a "remembrance on the first beginning in Greece that remains outside of Judaism . . ." (GA 97: 20). Against this oblivion of memory, Celan's "Andenken" raises the spectre of a commemoration that has always already foreclosed the possibility of a coming—especially that of a "homecoming" of spirit in Heidegger's sense. What "remains" here rather is a poetic memory where "spirit" (*Geist*) has confronted the ghostly possibility of its own impossibility. There, in what Derrida has called an "exile without return," we are left to ponder the devastating effect of a Heideggerian homecoming that leaves no space for the exiled other except as the colonized stranger who bends to the will of the colonizer.[98] In Hölderlin's poem "The Ister" we find, however, a different relation to the stranger: the gesture of hospitality. In the course of the Ister's flowing, as Hölderlin has it, the river "invited Heracles as guest" to come to its shore to find shade from the fiery Hellenic sun and to return home with the gift bequeathed to it in a Pindaric welcome of hospitality (SPF: 254–255).[99] On Heidegger's reading of "Andenken" and of the "Brod und Wein" fragment we find no hospitality, only an adamant refusal to greet the foreign as anything but another version of the native, now made proper through the colonial imperative. In Heidegger's reading of the Ister hymn we find this gesture reconfirmed and taken into possession.

3

Heidegger's "Ister" Lectures
Ethical Dwelling in the (Foreign) Homeland

> The Ister whiles by the source and is reluctant to abandon its locale because it dwells near the origin.
>   And it dwells near the origin because it has returned home to its locality from its journeying to foreign parts.
>
> —Martin Heidegger, *Hölderlin's Hymn "The Ister"*[1]

> There is no origin, if origin presupposes an original presence. . . . every beginning is a beginning over.
>
> —Maurice Blanchot, *The Writing of the Disaster*[2]

I. "Hölderlin" as the Name for an Other Beginning of Thinking

The question about the place of Hölderlin within Heidegger's long and twisting thoughtpath confronts us with nothing less than the very question about the meaning and direction of Heidegger's thought itself. "Hölderlin" is less the name of a poet for Heidegger than it is the name for a way of rethinking in a deeply originary way the meaning and sense of the whole Western tradition of thinking. Hölderlin—in this sense—is the name that grants the possibility of an "other" beginning for thinking, a commencement that takes up again, in a language that is something wholly other than "metaphysical," the first beginning of Western thinking in Anaximander, Parmenides, and Heraclitus. Heidegger countenances such an interpretation in his notebook of the late 1930s, *Besinnung*, by claiming that Hölderlin is "the poet of the other beginning of our future history" (GA 66: 426). What this means for Heidegger is that Hölderlin's poetry—through its deeply thoughtful dialogue with the thinkers/poets of the first beginning—is able to enter into conversation with the provenance of that history in all its questionability. Through a daring—and at times violent—translation of Greek idioms and forms, Heidegger puts forward a breathtaking vision of a German future that emerges from the power of that initial commencement, even as this possibility depends ever more forcefully on the way the poet traces its decomposition and loss in and through that very history. What emerges here is a vision of history read through Hölderlin's poetic myth of an auroral consummation of the marriage between gods and mortals, a *hieros gamos* that celebrates the shared bond between divinity and humanity. Yet Hölderlin's work is also marked by an all too self-conscious awareness of the loss of this unity within human history, one where the gods have fled ("Brot und Wein," v. 147) and left a distraught humanity in a state of confounding bereavement. In this condition of "sacred mourning" ("Germania," v. 6), the poet seeks a fitting word that might attune his fellow mourners to the gravity of their plight in a "time of destitution" ("Brot und Wein," v. 122). Only then, in bringing the word to the *Volk* and gathering their grief into a welcoming call for the return of the gods to the earth, can the poet begin his proper task: to vouchsafe a proper dwelling for human beings upon the earth.

For Heidegger, the very question of historical humanity is most powerfully expressed in this Hölderlinian configuration of history as a tripartite process of unity-loss-return. In Hölderlin's myth, this takes the form of an originary unity between divinities and humanity (*hieros gamos*) that is punctuated by a long epoch of human heedlessness and indifference to the divine sanctuary provided by the earth. In this age of confusion and dislocation, the gods take flight and leave a destitute humanity to confront the nihilism of "the world's night" (DKV I: 243). Like Hölderlin, Heidegger too believes that no form of human calculation, planning, or contrivance can engineer the return of the gods to the earth. At best, our only hope is that if we attend to the abyssal absence of divine radiance and solicitously prepare a site for their "coming," then perhaps we might one day be blessed with the return of the gods upon the earth. Heidegger expressed the full power of this tripartite historical narrative of unity–loss–return in lapidary form in the famous "Spiegel Interview" of 1966: "Only a god can still save us" (GA 16: 671). Yet at the heart of this Hölderlinian judgment about the path and trajectory of human history is the poet's own preoccupation with "homecoming" ("Heimkehr"), with both the possibility and necessity of finding our authentic home upon this earth, of dwelling in proximity to the gods, in abiding in the promise of the gods' return. I want to suggest here that this Hölderlinian preoccupation with *Heimkehr*, homecoming, poetic dwelling, and finding one's proper or authentic (*eigen-tlich*) abode upon the earth, will come to constitute one of the essential themes in the late Heidegger's philosophical corpus. Indeed perhaps no other question will shape this later thoughtpath as powerfully as this one about "poetic dwelling" or what Heidegger will alternately designate as our *Weltaufenthalt* (our sojourn/stay/abode within the world) (GA 8: 229; GA 14: 75; GA 16: 748).

This question about poetic dwelling—so poignantly addressed in his 1953 essay ". . . dichterisch wohnet der Mensch auf dieser Erde"—will, however, be rethought by Heidegger precisely in terms of Hölderlin's own formulation in the Böhlendorff letter of 1801 (DKV III: 459–462) of the relation between one's own/the proper/*das Eigene* and the foreign/the strange/*das Fremde*. On Hölderlin's telling, the poet can properly come into what is his "own," or *Eigene*, only when he undergoes a journey to and through the foreign or *Fremde*. The foreign stands in an enigmatic and perplexing relation to the proper; yet it is not merely something "alien" or "strange." Rather, the foreign has an inmost and essential relation to the proper—precisely in its character as what is improper or strange. Hence, Hölderlin can speak of the path to one's ownmost as "the most difficult" since it lies in too great a proximity to our native haunts.[3] To come into our own demands of us that we first "veritably appropriate what is foreign" so that the way into one's own (*das Eigene*) involves an appropriation (*Aneignung*) of that which is not our own. For the German poet, this demands an intimative confrontation with the ancient Greeks that resides less in imitation or mimesis of Greek art on the model of Winckelmann or Weimar classicism than it does in a chiastic reversal of the Greeks' own innate propensity to seek out their opposites as a path to embracing what is fitting for them.

Heidegger will take up this understanding of "the experience of the foreign" that he finds articulated in the Böhlendorff letter and grasp it as essential not only to understanding Hölderlin's poetry but as a guiding thread for thinking through the proper task of the Germans in an epoch of the world's night (GA 4: 115).⁴ For Heidegger, the question of finding a pathway through the foreign as a way of coming into one's own will come to shape not only his interpretation of Hölderlin and his role in the historical fate of the Germans but will serve as decisive for an understanding of the fate of humanity in the technological epoch of homelessness and nihilistic devastation during and after the Second World War. Yet there is a deeply political element in Heidegger's reading of Hölderlin that we will need to address. Amidst all of Heidegger's insightful remarks on poetic dwelling, commemorative thinking, the saving power, the holy, the return of the gods to the earth, and the possibility of another beginning, we can also find a resolutely *political* understanding of Hölderlin's hymnal poetizing that at times violently reshapes the tenor and spirit of Hölderlin's own work and language. In this chapter I want to expand my reading of Heidegger's "Hölderlin" by looking more carefully at the relation between the native and the foreign. Heidegger's reading here comes to warrant a singularly Germanocentric vision of national triumph and ascendancy rooted in a historico-destinal mission to save the West based on the Germans' consanguineous relation to the ancient Greeks. This Germanocentric vision of history will become the focus of Heidegger's Summer Semester 1942 lectures on *Hölderlin's Hymn "The Ister."* What marks these lectures, written during the time of Germany's struggles in the Soviet Union, is a certain anxiety about the mission and futural task of the German *Volk* to take up the originary Greek insight into what he elsewhere calls "the Western vocation of the essence of the human" (GA 77: 221).

Though written during the second year of the German campaign in Russia during World War II, the roots of these lectures go back to the Great War and the failure of Germany to secure its place in the Western pantheon of nation-states. What authorizes this peculiarly nationalistic reading of Hölderlin is the work of Norbert von Hellingrath, the editor of a five-volume collection of poems, essays, letters, translations, and drafts that includes the first publication of "The Ister" (whose title Hellingrath provided).⁵ As a young aesthete under the sway of Stefan George's vision of a new "Germania," Hellingrath conceived of Hölderlin as the poet who might lead Germany to its proper spiritual mission to save the West from the vulgarities of the Western democracies committed to materialism, mass culture, and the triumph of mechanism and efficient bureaucracy. Hellingrath, like George, turned Hölderlin into the prophet of what he designated as "a secret Germany," one whose inner essence could never be understood in mere social, economic, or political terms. Such a vision of the poet suppressed all of Hölderlin's own political hopes for a Swiss-Alemannic-Swabian republic founded upon Rousseauistic ideals against the old monarchistic order of reactionary repression. In his *Black Notebooks*, Heidegger acknowledges his bond to this Hellingrathian interpretation of Hölderlin, writing that Hölderlin is the name for "the invisible front" of a "secret spiritual Germany" (GA 94: 155), one whose ultimate task lies in "the saving of the West" (GA 13: 16; GA 55: 69, 108; EdP: 40).

In his very first lecture course on Hölderlin from the winter semester of 1934–1935, Heidegger indicates that the only way to grasp the poem "Germania," which poetizes the fate of the Fatherland, is to cultivate a fundamental attunement of "sacred mourning," that experiences the departure and flight of the gods (GA 39: 87). Given the devastating losses of the Great War, it is hardly surprising to find Heidegger thematizing such mourning as a way into "belonging to the homeland": "It is in such a homeland that the human being first experiences itself as belonging to the earth" (GA 34: 88). It is within and through this same connection to the homeland that Heidegger will read Hölderlin's river hymn "The Ister." What emerges in these lectures is a poetic-thinkerly reflection on what it means to be "at home" (*zuhause*) in "one's own" (*Eigenes*). But given the logic of Hölderlin's Böhlendorff letter, this possibility of appropriating the native and the proper crucially depends on a passageway through the foreign, strange, alien, and other. Hence, in the middle of this lecture course, in a reflection that constitutes the very core of Heidegger's reading of Hölderlin, we find a long discussion of "The Greek Interpretation of Human Beings in Sophocles' *Antigone*" (HHI: VI/GA 53: V). Here in Heidegger's reading of the figure of Antigone we will find a way to understand the mission and task of the Germans in a world marked by violent struggle (World War II/Thebes) and internecine division and self-destruction. As Heidegger takes up the question of the essence of the human being poetized in the first choral hymn of *Antigone*, we come to confront the singular power of the homeland as the force that animates Heidegger's vision of modernity in the age of the world's night.

II. Dwelling in the Intimacy of Truth: Oppostional Harmony and the Böhlendorff Logic

In his very first set of Hölderlin lectures from 1934–1935, Heidegger focused on the problem facing the German *Volk* which, through his reading of the Böhlendorff letter, he defined as "the free use of what is one's own (*das Eigenen*)" (HGR: 264/GA 39: 291). This, as Hölderlin taught him, "is the most difficult." Near the end of these lectures, he remarks that although in the popular imagination "difficulty" connotes misfortune, distress, and adversity, thought within the language of poetic measure, bearing difficulty is the highest kind of good fortune since it attunes us to the conflictual intimacy or "Innigkeit" of harmonious discord that expresses the deepest unity "in the middle of beyng" (HGR: 259/GA 39: 285). This Hölderlinian notion of *Innigkeit* pervades both the 1934–1935 course on "Germania and the Rhine" as well as the 1942 course on the Ister. In fact, in both courses Heidegger associates *Innigkeit* with the mysterious power of rivers and with Hölderlin's reading of Sophocles (HGR: 130/GA 39: 148). Here, *Innigkeit* is to be understood less as a psychological mood, insight, or feeling than as "the supreme force of *Dasein* . . . This force evinces itself in withstanding the most extreme conflicts of beyng from the ground up" (HGR: 106/GA 39: 117). It is an "attuned, knowing standing within that sustains the essential conflicts of that which, in being opposed, possesses an original unity—the harmoniously opposed'" (HGR: 106/GA 39: 117). In other words, *Innigkeit* is that which "holds things apart in conflict and at the same time joins them together" (EHP: 54/GA 4: 36). In the primordial conflict that reigns throughout all beings there runs a deeper sense of unity and harmonious wholeness that lies concealed to humans. It is the poet's task to express the mystery of such conflict, but precisely in a way that shelters its mysterious character without reducing it to a mere "solution" in the manner of an unmasking.

What remains most mysterious to Heidegger throughout his Hölderlin lectures, however, is Dasein itself, since for him "Dasein has become foreign to its historical essence, its mission (*Sendung*) and its mandate (*Auftrag*)" (HGR: 114/GA 39: 135). It is in grappling with the mysterious character of "bearing witness to its own Dasein" that the human being is able to bear witness to "its belonging to the earth" (EHP: 54/ GA 4: 36). Since the earth itself emerges only in contentious strife, the human task is to become intimate with such oppositional conflict in and through its poetic capacity for "withstanding the most extreme conflicts of being from the ground up" by becoming conflictually intimate (*innig*) with what is harmoniously opposed (*das Harmonischentgegengesetzte*) (GA 39: 117, 119, 249). In the mystery of such conflictual intimacy (*Innigkeit*) lies "the highest form of truth," one that holds sway in relations between gods and mortals and manifests itself in both the flight and arrival of the gods. "There is mystery only there where *Innigkeit* reigns," Heidegger maintains. Moreover, "the mystery is not just any riddle/enigma; the mystery is conflictual intimacy—yet this is beyng itself" (HGR: 227/GA 39: 250–251). As a poet whose poetry has as its task the poetizing of this mystery as *Innigkeit*, Hölderlin is able to hold things together in a poetic idiom that simultaneously honors their separation and contention. Such a vision of variance as congruity emerges both in his *mythos* of the flight and return of the gods *and* in his river hymns that poetize both the estrangement and conjunction of gods and mortals as well as the mediating role of both the river and the poet who, as demi-gods, are able to manifest the enigmatic unity of opposing realms without losing their mysterious character. Whether in "The Rhine" or "The Ister" hymn, Hölderlin takes up the theme that lies at the heart of Heidegger's reflections—namely, the sense of the way each river—in its position "between human beings and gods"—poetizes "the poetic dwelling of human beings upon this earth" (HHI: 142/GA 53: 178).

The question for Heidegger in the Ister lectures of SS 1942 (as it was in WS 1934–1935 in the Rhine hymn lectures) is whether we are ready "to receive that which is coming (*das Kommende*) as the truth of the earth and of the homeland" (GA 39: 223). To do so requires of us that we stand in the grounding attunement of sacred mourning and stand within the conflict between hiddenness and unhiddenness, concealment and revelation that reigns throughout all being and manifests the *Innigkeit* of authentic *aletheia*. What marks these lectures is a poetic-thinkerly reflection on the simplest yet deepest question of human existence: how are we to dwell? What does it mean to authentically dwell upon the earth so that, in doing so, we become intimate (*innig*) with the truth of being? Only later in the "Letter on Humanism" will Heidegger take up this question explicitly as a question about an "originary ethics" rooted in an *ethos* of authentic dwelling that sets apart the familiar abode of humans (*ethos*) from the open region of the unfamiliar that enables divine presence (*daimon*) (PM: 271/GA 9: 356). But the traces of a profoundly Hölderlinian ethics of dwelling properly upon the earth and beneath the sky begins to show itself in the way Heidegger engages Hölderlin's poetizing of the river hymns. Here in raising the question of one's own and the foreign in terms of the relation between the first beginning and the other beginning, Heidegger thinks the chiastic relation between the ancient Greeks and modern Germans through the very course of the Danube River as it leaves its source on a journey homeward.

Here in these lectures I believe that we find a Heidegger who (despite all his German exceptionalism with its fear of other nations, cultures, languages, and lines of descent) takes up a fundamentally *ethical* reflection on the meaning of the homeland as our proper place of dwelling upon the earth. Moreover, in these same reflections we find crucial hints, pointers, and indications of an ethics that, abjuring the metaphysical "ethics" of right and wrong, offers insights into a fitting relation between the proper and the strange, the native and the foreign, one's self and the Other. In this thinking that ponders the proper abode of the human being upon the earth, we are enjoined to take up our responsibility for letting being come into our care—and of responding (as well as co(r)-responding) to the claim it makes upon us (GA 12: 70, 166, 169f.). This *ethical* dimension of responding to the claim of being has profound consequences for our own possibilities of dwelling since in dwelling we take care of/shelter the openness of being in the historical "da" into which we are thrown. If the question of ethics has to do with the authentic possibility of dwelling—and if dwelling in its most essential form is "the fundamental character of being, in keeping with which mortals exist" (GA 7: 163)—then the question of the Ister lectures is fundamentally *ethical*, since it is in poetizing (and especially in the hymnal poetizing of rivers found in Hölderlin's "Der Ister") that we genuinely confront "the fundamental event of beyng as such" (HGR: 233/GA 39: 257), "the full essence of being human" that occurs in and as dwelling (HHI: 43/GA 53: 52). For what these lectures take up is the question of "the essence of Western humankind" in all its relations to world, to earth, and to the gods, and it is to this question of human essence—who are we?—that Heidegger turns in these lectures, especially in his discussion of Sophocles's choral ode from the tragedy *Antigone*.

III. Translation and the Uncanny Essence of Human Being

Heidegger's Ister lectures are divided into three parts: the first section deals with the poetizing of the essence of rivers; the second with the Greek interpretation of the essence of human being; and the third with the poetizing of the essence of the poet as demigod. What Heidegger thinks here as "Wesen" or "essence" is neither an empty universal nor an externally timeless presence but, rather, the verbal sense of the way something is, how it unfolds historically.

In *Contributions to Philosophy* Heidegger writes, "the coming to pass of the truth of beyng—that is essential occurrence (*Wesung*)" (CP: 226/GA 65: 288). Moreover, he thinks this essential occurrence as historical—namely, as involving an appropriative relation to that which has been whereby our projecting of the future depends upon the way we appropriate that which has been even as we often do not attend to the ways in which we have always already been appropriated precisely by that which has been. Hence Heidegger can write: "Beyng essentially occurs (*west*) as the appropriating event (*Ereignis*)" whereby "the appropriation (*Er-eignung*) destines the human being to be the property of being (*Eigentum des Seyns*)" (CP: 204, 207/GA 65: 260, 263). In our belonging to beyng as what is proper to it, however, we need to confront its otherness, alterity, or impropriety—but not merely as that which is "other" to the proper. On the contrary, what is essential to this essential unfolding of essence is that its otherness lies at the very heart of the proper, confronting us there in what is our own (*Eigenes*) as what we need most of all to appropriate (*ereignen*). That is, in the very place where we dwell, at the center of our being at home within being, we are thrust out from the home, left homeless and exposed to the impropriety of all that we cling to as "proper." The poet Georg Trakl captures something of this essential estrangement from the proper in his poem "Frühling der Seele," where he writes: "Es ist die Seele ein Fremdes auf Erden" ("The soul is a stranger upon the earth") (v. 22). Hölderlin's tragic hero Empedocles expresses something of this same Heideggerian question when, in his dialogue with Pausanias, he reveals: "Ich bin nicht, der ich bin" ("I am not who I am"; DE: 179/DKV II: 406). This revelation is, however, less an admission about psychological anomie or socio-cultural estrangement than it is a profoundly ontological insight into the otherness that lies at the heart of human identity.

The very staging of the Ister lectures enacts something of this essential movement of spirit as it ventures outward from its belonging to the home (section 1) carrying out its journey into the foreign (section 2) and then, finally, turning back toward the home in its reflections on the poetizing of the essence of the poet (section 3). What I would like to focus upon, however, is the way Heidegger moves his focus from "The Poetizing the Essence of the Rivers in the Ister Hymn" to "The Greek Interpretation of Human Beings in Sophocles' *Antigone*" as a way of addressing the problem of human homelessness precisely as that which calls for a journey outward into the foreign. Such a journey requires a crossing of national borders and a traversal of linguistic boundaries such that in the encounter with that which is foreign, we engage its alien character as what properly belongs to us as our property. In order to appropriate this property, however, we first need to "shatter the blind obstinacy of habitual (*gewöhnlichen*) opinion" that serves to block our passage into the "truth" of what stands alien and opposite to us (GA 53: 76). This movement from the national to the foreign will come to shape the whole movement and direction of Heidegger's Ister lectures as they take up the German encounter with the ancient Greeks by way of an "interpretation"—"translation" of Hölderlin's *own* interpretation/ translation of Sophocles' first choral song from *Antigone*. What Heidegger designates as most worthy of translation is the very first line of this choral ode that announces the essence of the human being as *to deinon*—which Heidegger translates into German with three different terms: *das Furchtbare* (the frightful), *das Gewaltige* (the violent), and *das Ungewöhnliche* (the inhabitual). Before we turn to a discussion of this translation, however, we need to pause and reflect on Heidegger's own understanding of translation as well as his decision to focus on the *deinon*.

Deinon is a Greek term that remains ambiguous. In Liddell-Scott's Greek dictionary it signifies both "wonderful" and "terrible" at the same time.[6] Its range of meanings extend from "marvelous," "skillful," "clever," and "awesome" to "fearful," "violent," "fierce," "excessive," and "awful."[7] Within this cluster of definitions, no single one emerges as the most appropriate for rendering its multivalent significations. On the contrary, in grappling with the recalcitrance of this enigmatic term, we enter into the very enigma of translation itself as a *transposition* or *Übersetzung* (translation) literally, in the German—*über* (trans)-*setzen* (placing, posing, setting). *Übersetzen* in German also means a "ferrying across," as in a river crossing—and hence the discussion of translation as a practice and movement of carrying, conveying, or shuttling across and back between the banks of a river appears as much more than a mere "meta-phor" in the usual sense—*meta* + *pherein* in Greek also signifying the act of "ferrying" (*pherein*) over or across (*meta*).[8] *Übersetzung* or "translation" also involves us in an experience of *Versetzung* ("displacement") whereby we are dislodged and unsettled in ways we cannot anticipate.[9] In the case of Hölderlin's own translations of Sophocles this extends to the poetic experience of the essence of the human being as what is "terrible," "dreadful," or "shocking" (*entsetzlich*). Only when the human is exposed to (*ausgesetzt*) its limits in the foreign or other can it come into its own as the proper. As Heidegger sees it, the way that the human being "dwells upon the earth" is essentially "poetic"—which he grasps as nothing other than "exposure to beyng" (*Ausgesetztheit dem Seyn*) (GA 39: 36). For him the very core of this exposure to beyng happens in the first line of the choral song where the human being is described as *to deinotaton*—"the uncanniest" ("Unheimlichste"). And yet, Heidegger contends: "Uncanniness does not first arise as a consequence of humankind; rather, humankind emerges from uncanniness and remains within it" (HHI: 72/GA 53: 88–89). In a fundamental way Sophocles's choral song *enacts* within the action of the play, the very displacement or *Versetzung* of the human being that it takes as its central theme. In other words, precisely as the political drama unfolds, it is interrupted or displaced by a choral hymn that sings such displacement as belonging to the essence of the human being as "the displaced one." In an uncanny way, then, the burial of Antigone's brother—(*Bei-setzung*) confronts the edict or law (*Ge-setz*) promulgated by Creon to assert his own (*sich durchsetzen*) political hegemony after the familial strife between Antigone's two brothers spills out into a civil war that threatens the very existence of the *polis*.[10] As Heidegger attempts to "translate" the poetic meaning of Sophocles's ode on displacement into its own German idiom, he decides to reenact Sophocles's dramatic interruption in *Antigone* by interrupting his own lecture course on Hölderlin's river hymn "The Ister" with a strange reflection on tragedy, translation, and the sense of the uncanny. By focusing on the meaning of the choral ode in Antigone as a poetological displacement akin to Hölderlin's own displacements in his strange and idiomatic translations that rupture the limits of language, Heidegger enacts a double movement of interruption.[11] In this doubling gesture of rupture as inter-ruption both Sophocles and Heidegger attempt to manifest within language the very site of the rupture that is human existence or Da-sein. Yet Heidegger's gesture seeks not only to manifest such a rupture but to "translate" it by showing how translation itself emerges in the rupture between the original word (*das Eigene*) and its trans-lation into a foreign idiom.

The problem of translation here is not to be understood in any literary or philological sense. For Heidegger, translation is less a question about faithfully rendering an original meaning in a foreign tongue than it is a philosophical question about the meaning of language within human existence. Keeping with the sense of translation as *Über-setzung*, Heidegger stresses that "genuine translation is always an encounter or *Aus-einander-setzung* (a setting-apart-from-one-another)" (GA 53: 79–80). Moreover, it is not to be thought of as a "passing over into a foreign language with the help of one's own. Rather translation is more an awakening, clarification, and unfolding of one language with the help of an encounter with the foreign language. Reckoned technically, translation means substituting (*Ersetzen*) one's own language for the foreign language or vice-versa." In authentic translation, however, one's own language becomes foreign to one. Here one's "encounter with a foreign language [is] for the sake of appropriating one's own language" (HHI: 65–66/GA 53: 80–81). Once again Heidegger stresses that it is "for the sake of" the proper that the foreign is appropriated at all and not out of either a curiosity about or a need for the Other. Hence, it cannot surprise us when he claims that "we are allowed to learn the Greek language only when we must learn it out of an essential historical necessity *for the sake of* our own German language" (my emphasis). What preoccupies Heidegger here is less an interlingual translation between Greek and German than it is the intralingual "translating within one and the same language." In this sense, we need to understand Heidegger's translation of the choral ode from *Antigone* as part of his overall strategy in the Ister lectures that involves a journey into the foreign for the sake of the native and proper. Here the act of translation serves as a kind of fulfillment of Hölderlin's vision in the Böhlendorff letter of a becoming homely in and through the experience of the foreign—or of becoming properly German only through the encounter with the ancient Greek. But again, even this movement outward is thought by Heidegger as an undertaking for the sake of the native.

Understood structurally, then, the first section of the Ister lectures offers an account of Hölderlin's poetic language that sees it as difficult, recalcitrant to easy appropriation, standing opposite us as a strange and alien discourse. In its strangeness within the German language it appears as "the foreign of one's own" (*das Fremde des Eigenen*) and as "what is most difficult" to appropriate (HHI: 49/GA 53: 61). And yet if the Germans are to come into their own and carry out Hölderlin's mandate of coming to dwell poetically upon the earth, then they must be able to appropriate what is foreign within the native. That is, they must be able to carry out a translation of Hölderlin's German poetic language within native German idioms. But if section one stands as "the interpretation of Hölderlin's hymns [as] a translating within our German language"—then how are we to understand the turn to Sophocles's *Antigone* in section two (HHI: 62/ GA 53: 75)? How does the translation of Sophocles's ancient Greek song into modern German by way of a reflection on the poetic language of Hölderlin fulfill "the law of the encounter between the foreign and one's own [as] the fundamental truth of history" (HHI: 49/61)? For Heidegger, this structural issue that shapes the focus of section one and section two (as well as their interconnection) reprises the larger issue of the role that translation has played within the history of Western thinking. As Heidegger sees it, the Latin translation of Greek philosophical terms (*hypokeimenon* as "subjectum," *hypostasis* as "substans," *symbebekos* as "categoria") proved disastrous since it took over these rich philosophical word clusters and rendered them merely as "technical terms" without undergoing the originary Greek experience of that which lay hidden in this strange and forbidding language. Foremost among all these thoughtless renderings was the Latin translation of *aletheia* as *veritas* (truth), which understood it in terms of *adequatio* or correctness by way of comparison with what is "false" (*falsum*) (P: 39–49/GA 54: 57–71).[12] In the process of such a translation the whole ontological play between hiddenness (*lethe*) and un-hiddenness (*a-letheia*) fell back into oblivion. For as Heidegger put it in "The Origin of the Work of Art," "the rootlessness of Western thought begins with this translation" (BW: 149/GA 5: 8).

As Heidegger attempts to reclaim some of the originary power of these lost Greek terms, he turns to the poetic language of Sophocles—mediated by Hölderlin—as a pathway into the originary Greek experience of being as *aletheia*. Specifically, he turns to both an interlingual translation of Sophocles's essential word *deinon*, which he then renders as "unheimlich" (uncanny) and an intralingual translation of *Unheimlichkeit* in three different ways as *das Fürchterliche, das Gewaltige, das Ungewöhnliche*. His translations here not only offer a way into the complexities and ambiguities of these originary Greek words, however; more essentially, they stage a Hölderlinian history of Western thinking as a movement from originary unity to dispersion and loss as a possible pathway for preparing an "other" beginning for thinking. In so doing, these lectures attempt to find in the ambiguities, enigmas, paradoxes, and chiastic crossings of Sophoclean language a positive indication for turning the Western tradition away from its metaphysical dependence on fixity, certitude, and the logic of universal reason. This Heidegger will find in Sophocles's interpretation of the human being as *deinon*.

IV. Tragedy and the Definition of the Human Being as a "Katastrophe"

The uncanny thing about Heidegger's interpretation of the human being as the most uncanny is that its uncanniness is not something that stands opposed to the human being as the alien, strange, or foreign. Rather, it is precisely this uncanniness that belongs to its origin as the provenance of all its diverse possibilities. Already in his first Hölderlin lectures Heidegger had indicated "that the historical being of the human being is shot through (*durchsetzt*) by ambiguity and indeed essentially so" (HGR: 34/GA 39: 36). In his Parmenides lectures of WS 1942–1943 Heidegger again speaks of an "essential ambiguity" that pervades Greek tragedy and that does so not out of any "dramatic 'effect' but spoken to them from out of the essence of being" (P: 79/GA 54: 117). It is this *essential* ambiguity of the human being—the fact that what is strange and uncanny about it is not merely its violence, power, skill, or cunning. Rather, what marks the human being as the uncanniest of all those other creatures on the earth who crawl, swim, canter, burrow, meander, and take flight is that it is *essentially* so as part of how it comes to dwell upon the earth. For Heidegger, this means that human dwelling is marked by a profound and tragic opposition between the yearning to be at home in one's essence and the counterturning pull of a movement that drives the human being out of its home in a fundamental way. In the very ambiguity of the Greek word *to deinon* ("the uncanny")—which connotes both the wonderful and the terrible at the same time, both the awesome and the aw(e)ful—Heidegger finds "the fundamental word of [*Antigone*], indeed of Greek tragedy in general, and thereby the fundamental word of Greek antiquity" (HHI: 67/GA 53: 82). Yet we must be clear: not only is the language of tragedy ambiguous, contradictory, and counterturning in its essence, but so too is the human being. Moreover, the uncanniness of the chorus' language, as well as the uncanniness of Antigone herself, bespeak an even deeper and more profound uncanniness which is that of beyng itself. And yet within all the uncanniest of being's manifestations—thunderstorms, tornadoes, tsunamis, earthquakes—"the most powerful 'catastrophes' we can think of in nature and in the cosmos are nothing in terms of their uncanniness compared to that uncanniness that the human essence in itself is" (HHI: 77/GA 53: 94).

What matters here for Heidegger in his dialogue with both Sophocles and Hölderlin is to take up this question about the uncanniness of the human being precisely as a question about how human beings can dwell authentically upon the earth. In other words, this is a question about our *Aufenthalt*, *ethos*, sojourn, stay, or abode upon the earth that understands it neither as a question about residence, settlement, domestic habitat nor as one concerning our "wandering around" or venturing outward in ever newer adventures. Rather, what is at stake here is a question of "originary ethics," a question about the proper way to dwell for the human being that involves both tarrying/abiding in a native abode as well as journeying outward into the foreign. It involves an awareness that in order to be able to dwell in the proper, native, and homely, we first need to abide in the abode of the unhomely, the uncanny, the improper. This is what distinguishes us as the exception among beings: that we both inhabit and are inhabited by an inescapable uncanniness that pervades our *ethos*:

> This kind of uncanniness (*Unheimlichkeit*), namely *unhomeliness* (*Unheimischkeit*), is possible for human beings alone, because they comport themselves toward beings as such, and thereby understand being. And because they understand being, human beings alone can forget being. (HHI: 76/GA 53: 94)

This sense of the uncanniness of the unhomely—namely, that we are not at home even in our home—finds its expression in the Greek word "katastrophe"—literally, a "turning" (*strophe*), "down," "against," "away from," (*kata*), that is a "reversal" or an "overturning." As Heidegger succinctly puts it: "human beings are in their essence a *katastrophe*—a reversal that turns them away from their own essence. Among beings, the human being is the sole catastrophe" (HHI: 77/GA 53: 94). Moreover, the exemplary instance of such catastrophe manifests itself for Heidegger in the figure of Antigone, who risks everything to attain her proper task of becoming homely—even as she everywhere encounters "the fact that the homely refuses itself to [her]" (HHI: 90/GA 53: 111). In this she proves exemplary since her fate manifests the very counterturning strife that is at the heart of the human venture to attain a home within being, to enter into its proper *ethos* or abode.

What Heidegger suggests here is that this abode shows itself as the open site for the unconcealment of beings, an unconcealment that happens only in its continuous struggle with that which remains concealed. In other words, it is not on account of the human being's role as a "subject" that being opens up at this site; rather, it is due to being's own appropriation of the human being as the site of its disclosure that we can be at home at all. But even here we either fail to recognize this open site as open or we "forget" that it essentially prevails (*west*) within and as the very essence (*Wesen*) of the human being. This being shows itself as the one who stands in the truth of being as *aletheia*, the one who ultimately emerges in and through the counterturning hiddenness/disclosure of its historical abode/*ethos*. Again, Antigone is exemplary in this way since it is she who takes upon herself "the 'drama' of becoming homely." More to the point, "Antigone's becoming homely first brings to light the essence of being unhomely. Becoming homely makes manifest the essential ambiguity of being unhomely" (HHI: 115, 102/GA 53: 144, 126). She does this by pursuing the impossible. That is, she decides "to pursue that against which nothing can avail" and takes this sense of the impossible as her point of departure for all of her undertakings in the play. In so doing, she decides (as she tells Ismene) "to take up into my own essence (*ins eigne Wesen*) the uncanny that here and now appears."[13] Here Heidegger makes clear that what is uncanny—namely, the unhomely—"is nothing that human beings themselves make but rather the converse: something that makes them into what they are and who they can be" (HHI: 103/GA 53: 127–128).

On Heidegger's reading, Antigone (far more than Creon) steps out of the site of the unhomely of her own power. And unlike her father Oedipus, she *knowingly* "takes it upon herself to be unhomely" (HHI: 109–110/GA 53: 136–137). Yet such a decision, if it is to be authentic, "must spring from a belonging to the hearth and thus stem from a kind of being homely." What matters here above all is Antigone's authentic resolve to embrace her fate as the one who embodies "the supreme uncanny"

(HHI: 104/GA 53: 129). If, like Creon, her uncanny expulsion from the hearth of being (*Hestia*) were occasioned by a mere presumptuousness or *Vermessenheit* that measured all beings from the horizon of subjective volition and self-assertion, then such a movement would merely result in the forgetting of being. But because her unhomeliness emerges out of "a 'thoughtful remembrance' (*Andenken*) of being" that thinks of this unhomeliness as but a preparatory passageway to a homecoming at the hearth of being, Antigone succeeds in fulfilling the fundamental law of human history as "becoming homely in being unhomely. Antigone *is* the poem of being unhomely in the proper and supreme sense" (HHI: 121/GA 53: 151).

With this interpretation of Antigone as the one who knowingly takes upon herself, that is, "suffers" the uncanny and "fittingly accommodates herself" (*sich schickt*) "as her all-determinative point of departure that against which nothing can avail," Heidegger moves beyond Hölderlin's own grasp of Antigone. If Hölderlin sees her as acting lawlessly against Creon's law of the *polis*, Heidegger goes farther and argues that Antigone also acts against the gods—since Zeus protects the law of the polis as well as that of funerary custom.[14] For Heidegger, Antigone does not fulfill the law of the gods; rather, she becomes intimate (*innig*) with the Holy in such a way that she fulfills the law of becoming homely out of her being unhomely. This destiny (*Geschick*) is fitting (*schicklich*) since it is self-sent (*sich schickt*); it accommodates itself to the enigmatic contradictions and ambiguities of the human being that manifests itself as a "katastrophe" (HHI: 109/136). Within the framework of the choral ode this will be expressed in the contradictory language of the oxymoron.

V. The Language of Contradiction: Oxymoron and Tragic Manifestation

One of the uncanny paradoxes of Greek tragic language is its ability to reveal the hidden in such a way that this very hiddenness becomes manifest even as it shelters its concealment in the very act of showing itself *as* concealed. Here hiddenness does not suddenly appear as revelation in the sense of an unmasking or laying bare; on the contrary, what is revealed is less a "secret" than the very manifestation of secretiveness as that which remains impenetrable or aporous. If phenomenology lets itself be understood as an attending to the ways that being manifests itself, and if in Sophocles's *Antigone* the primordial way that human being manifests itself lies in language, then we can properly call the first choral song of this play a phenomenology of language since what manifests itself here is the hidden unity of tragic being that appears in the contradictory form of an oxymoron. The language of the ode expresses these contradictions in "the fundamental word" of *Antigone*—namely, *deinon*—but also in two other word pairs from the middle of the second strophe—*pantoporos/aporos*—and the middle of the second antistrophe: *hypsipolis/apolis*.

In all of these various designations, Heidegger attempts to relate each one of them back to his central question about the proper dwelling or home of the human being upon the earth. What he sees above all here is the very counterturning character of the *deinon* set within the counterturning language of the poet. As *pantoporos* ("everywhere venturing forth"), the human being ventures everywhere, pressing beyond all limits, traversing boundaries, reaching in far flung directions to arrive in places where none has ever gone. Yet, at the same time, in all such undertakings and in every place it ventures, the human being everywhere comes to nothing—that is, remains *aporos* ("without any way out"). As it seeks to impose its Cartesian mastery over all beings and to contest every assault against its dominion, the human being confronts the aporia at the heart of human being—that in our attempts to be at home everywhere upon the earth, we have become profoundly unable to abide within any home at all. It is in terms of this paradoxical doubling that our essence as human beings unfolds. Antigone comprehends just such a countermovement as the essence of her own being. In so doing, she reverses the very terms that Creon imposes upon her as the outcast one, the one expelled from the *polis*, forced to leave the home and forfeit her abode among the living. In an uncanny way, through her intimacy with the uncanniness of being, she manages to reverse her status as that one dispossessed of the city (*apolis*) and achieve the highest place in the city (*hypsipolis*). In so doing she thereby displaces the standing of Creon as the one who stands for the highest sense of the city.

Like her father (brother) Oedipus, whose fate is marked by a double reversal from being *apolis* (exposed on Mt. Cithaeron) to becoming *hypsipolis* (solving the riddle of the Sphinx and becoming king) and then losing his kingship (*hypsipolis*) and being expelled (*apolis*) as the *miasmos*, Antigone enacts the double movement of "counterturning within the essence of human being" (HHI: 85/GA 53: 105).[15] In "forfeiting the site" (*apolis*) of her home above the earth, she risks becoming unhomely. And yet precisely on account of this uncanny risk, Heidegger claims, she embraces "what is fitting" (*das Schickliche*) as "that which is destined to her" (*zugeschickt*) from a realm beyond the gods, a realm that Sophocles leaves "without a name" and about which, as Antigone confirms, "no one knows" (1.457) (HHI: 117–118/GA 53: 147). Still, Heidegger himself does dare to name this realm beyond the gods, beyond the cult of funerary ritual and consanguineous blood lines. He names this "being itself," and he identifies it as "the ground of being homely, the hearth." Here Heidegger breaks with Hölderlin, Hegel, Karl Reinhardt, Heinrich Weinstock, and other prominent German classicists by rejecting any claim that *Antigone* presents the struggle between "religion" and the "state," "family" and the "city," chthonic justice and enlightened law. Rather, Heidegger emphasizes that "the counterplay is played out between being unhomely in the sense of being driven about amid beings without any way out and being unhomely as becoming homely from out of a belonging to being."[16] Against Nietzsche's own interpretation of the Greek tragic chorus as a development out of Archilochus and the dithyrambic music cults, and against any philological account that sees the chorus in terms of its "developmental history," Heidegger understands the chorus as "the essential middle of the tragedy in terms of the history of its essence" (HHI: 119–120/GA 53: 148–150).[17] What the chorus sings is being itself and not any individual being or entity. Here "what essentially prevails as being (*was west als das Sein*) . . . can be said only in poetizing or thought in thinking." Insofar as the last lines of the Antigone ode speak of the hearth as *Hestia* and address the human being's exclusion/expulsion from the hearth, Heidegger takes this as an indication that the hearth is "the site of everything homely." Even more, it is *as* the homely that it comes to manifest "the being of all beings" (HHI: 107, 110, 114/GA 53: 133, 137, 143). In plain terms, "the hearth, the homestead of the homely, is being itself."

Yet the chorus sings of banishing the one who is uncanny (*to deinon*) from the precinct of the hearth, rendering it *parestios*, that is, *para* (outside, away from, far—but also alongside, near, next to) + *Hestia* (house, hearth, home). Nonetheless, Heidegger offers an unconventional if not uncanny reading of this stanza within the overall context of the drama. Most commentators have understood these final words to mean that that figure who has dared to venture upon every path (*pantoporos*) and has sought to attain the height of the city (*hypsipolis*) is not welcome at the hearth of the *polis* and is condemned to a pathless (*aporos*), citi-less (*apolis*) fate.[18] Yet Heidegger does not think of Antigone as the one thrown out of the hearth. On his reading, Antigone readily takes upon herself the loss of the hearth in order to gain a more originary path of entry into the hearth itself. In Heidegger's words, by Antigone "taking such being unhomely into her own (*eigenes*) essence, she is 'properly' (*eigentlich*) unhomely" (HHI: 117/GA 53: 146). In their rejection of the unhomely one, the words of the chorus bespeak "an uncanny ambiguity that concerns being unhomely itself." But, at the same time, these words also attest to "a knowledge of the hearth." As the one figure in the play who, according to Heidegger, has risked this belonging to the hearth by becoming unhomely, Antigone not only embodies the *ethos* of Sophoclean tragedy, but more importantly for Heidegger, she embodies the *ethos* of Hölderlinian poetizing as the possible pathway for a futural German homecoming.

Here in this reading of Antigone as "the purest poem itself," as "the telling of the singular *deinon* and its essential ground," we find the core of the Ister lectures as they both intersect with and diverge from the poetizing of Sophocles and Hölderlin. On Heidegger's telling, what is essential lies in Antigone's putting herself at risk knowingly, in confronting that which remains undecided and indeterminate with a decision about "becoming homely in being unhomely" (HHI: 119/GA 53: 149). The chorus enigmatically announces its reluctance to admit anyone to its hearth who forfeits her belonging to the city "for the sake of risk." And yet Antigone responds in a wholly uncanny way. She decides knowingly *for* her belonging to the hearth, but not in a simple, unproblematic sense. Rather, she determines that the conventional definition of the hearth as a congenial space of Biedermeier comfort and domesticity is inauthentic and undermines the genuine meaning of the hearth as what is of the home. As she sees it, only by risking the home *as* home by becoming unhomely in relation to the hearth can one genuinely come into the essence of the hearth as the homely. Hence, in Heidegger's telling, the last words of the choral ode need to be read as showing us "the risk of distinguishing and deciding between that being unhomely proper (*eigentlich*) to human beings and a being unhomely that is improper and inappropriate (*uneigentlich*)" (HHI: 117/GA 53: 146). Simply expressed, Antigone's decision here between an *authentic* and an *inauthentic* sense of dwelling, proper to the home and hearth, will distinguish Heidegger's reading from Hölderlin.

As Hölderlin reads the drama, Antigone's decision to challenge Creon's edict is less a decision for belonging to the homeland than it is one against the order of the gods and indeed one executed with a violent disregard for the boundaries of the singular. Instead, Hölderlin claims, Antigone exceeds these boundaries in a willful way as she seeks an unmediated union with the gods through death.[19] Heidegger disregards this religious dimension of the play and focuses on the question of dwelling authentically. What preoccupies him throughout these lectures is the German task of appropriating what is properly theirs, that is, what the Böhlendorff letter terms "the national." But again, as Hölderlin made all too clear to his friend, "the *free* use of *one's own* is most difficult."[20] Because what is one's own lies all too near, properly dwelling in such nearness (*Nähe*) is the most difficult precisely because its proximity unthinkingly inures us to what is genuinely our own within it. For this reason we first need to journey into the foreign in order to come into what is our own since this very movement away from the proper brings with it a "remembrance" or *Andenken* of the proper. According to Heidegger, the dramatic action within the play *Antigone* by the character Antigone brings about just such a movement since it confronts us with the decision of dwelling authentically within the uncanny, and indeed doubly so, since the uncanny here appears as what is foreign to the Germans—namely, as the *Greek* form of being unhomely precisely as a way of (authentically) becoming homely.

What Heidegger takes up, then, in his attempt to educate the Germans in the proper way of appropriating the national is Hölderlin's claim that "the Greeks are indispensable for us." This means that they cannot serve as a model to be imitated since what is great in them involves a reversal of their own national endowments. Authentic German homecoming must involve an encounter with the Greeks, but understood in its properly German sense as an "Aus-ein-ander-setzung": a confrontational setting-asunder of the one (the proper) from the other (the foreign or the improper) with the aim of returning back to the proper or national by way of, and in contradistinction to, the improper or foreign. For Hölderlin, this sense of finding one's own home amidst the experience of expulsion from the home occurs most powerfully in hymnal song. It is there in the poetic articulation of the pain of severance and being set asunder that "song becomes a sanctuary or asylum for the homeless ones, those who have lost their place—the authentic refuge from the vacuity and bleakness of a loveless world."[21] The hymn, as Hölderlin envisions it, seeks to find a home for human beings, to secure shelter from the desolation of the world's night that has descended upon humankind since the departure and flight of the gods. Conceived in their larger sense, all of Hölderlin's hymns point to a pathway out of such nihilistic desolation by pointing ahead to the futural coming of the gods, a coming that at the same time foretokens a genuine "homecoming" for humankind. As Heidegger, puts it, "this homecoming is the future of the historical essence of the Germans" (GA 4: 30/EHP: 48). In the river hymn "The Ister" this movement of the self from out of the homeland into the foreign occurs by way of a reversal of the river's own course so that "it appears almost to go backwards" (HHI: 142–143/GA 53: 178). In this reversal, Heidegger finds a pathway out of the nihilism of the world's night, one that identifies the poetizing of the poet with the very movement of the Ister as a river in its journeying. That is, Heidegger understands Hölderlin's poetizing of the river in this hymn as bound up with the selfsame riverine movement of the Ister from its source to its mouth. Both "say" the Holy; each in its own way "brings the dwelling of historical human beings into its essence" (HHI: 139/GA 53: 173). In "Part Three" of the lecture course Heidegger seeks to show how what Hölderlin poetizes in his river hymn is "the Same" as what Sophocles dramatizes in his play *Antigone*: the historical becoming homely of the Germans and Greeks in all their difference. To do so, he reads "The Ister" in and through both the late fragment from "Bread and Wine" and the Böhlendorff letter.

VI. Poet and River as Demi-Gods

Already in his very first Hölderlin lectures on "The Rhine," Heidegger had understood the poet to be the founder of the possibility of historical dwelling upon the earth, one that lay in the poet's standing as a demigod (GA 39: 216). Poetry founds dwelling—and it does so by having the poet stand out into the middle of being and risk being exposed to the strange and alien power of the gods, standing in the middle between humankind and the divinities. As Heidegger puts it, "The unsuspected transition to thinking the demigods is in itself the turning back and turning in toward the homeland and toward the historical *Volk* (*die Rückkehr und Einkehr in die Heimat und das geschichtliche Volk*) in connection to whom (*in Rückbindung zu*) there is a telling of the gods" (HGR: 165/GA 39:

181–182).[22] In his Pindaric hymn, "As on a holiday . . . ," Hölderlin writes of the poet "standing bareheaded beneath the god's thunderstorms" (SPF: 175), leaving him exposed to the destructive force of Zeus's lightning bolts. Standing in the middle between earth and sky, mortals and divinities, the poet risks his very existence in an effort to shelter the homeland and, like the farmer who returns to his fields after a storm-filled night, prepare a historical homecoming for the German *Volk*. In "The Ister" lectures Heidegger will identify the poet as a demigod, one whose essence is to mediate between two different and at times opposing realms, much as a river mediates its two opposite banks and brings them together in and through such opposition (GA 53: 173–174). Standing in the middle between gods and mortals, the foreign and the native, the Greeks and the Germans, antiquity and modernity, *pantoporos* and *aporos*, Hölderlin—like Antigone—belongs in an intimative (*innig*) way to the strife and opposition of these dualities. In this way he is able to penetrate to the heart of this opposition by letting himself be appropriated by its strange and alien character. Standing in the middle as the exposed one (*der Ausgesetzter*), Hölderlin achieves an intimacy (*Innigkeit*) with the discord of opposition that manifests to him as a higher form of harmony, a discordant or conflictual harmony that bespeaks the mystery of authentic dwelling. This intimacy so pervades the poem "The Ister" that Heidegger can say: "The poet is the river. And the river is the poet" (HHI: 165/ GA 53: 203). Each in its own way grounds the historical dwelling of human beings upon the earth, doing so in ways that are fitting to each. In poetizing this intimacy Hölderlin draws upon what Heidegger will call "the law of being unhomely as a becoming homely," a law whose meaning is laid out in both the Böhlendorff letter of 1801 and a late fragment of "Bread and Wine" (HHI: 125/GA 53: 155).

VII. "At home is spirit not at the beginning"

If we can say that the essence of both the river and the poem "The Ister" lies in their shared grounding of the poetic dwelling of the human being—namely, its *ethos*—and if further we understand *ethos* not in terms of traditional ethics but as an originary calling of the human being to its proper home within being, then perhaps we can come to a sense of what the Ister lectures attempt. There Heidegger strives to think *ethos* not only in its historical commencement, but as that which is always to come, precisely in and as this coming itself. More than perhaps anything, Hölderlin is, for Heidegger, the Poet of this Coming. It is he alone among all other poets and thinkers, this "poet of poets," "poet of the Germans," "*the* poet of the other beginning of our futural history," "founder of German beyng," he alone as "the most German of the Germans" who calls his *Volk* to its authentic task. This task stands before the Germans as their becoming homely in the unhomely as a way of grounding their proper dwelling upon the earth (GA 39: 214, 220; GA 66: 426; GA 16: 333). Hölderlin is able to do this, Heidegger claims, because as his poetic task he has taken upon himself the ordeal of suffering the flight and departure of the gods from the earth. In experiencing this destitution, the poet is able to attend to the traces that the gods have left behind, traces that bespeak the intimate belonging together of gods and humans. What binds these two together is what the poet calls "the Holy." "The Holy is the essence of nature," Heidegger writes; it serves as another name for *physis*, that which the poet claims, "is older than time, and stands over the gods of Occident and Orient, . . . the All-creative" (GA 4: 59; "As on a holiday," vv. 21–22, 27, 55–58). But here we must first grasp *physis* as the power uniting chaos and order in their conflictual harmony. Moreover, it is only by virtue of the holy's mediating power that the poet can stand in the middle as the demigod, "drinking heavenly fire and standing bareheaded beneath the god's thunderstorms." In this desolate place, standing in the middle, the poet undergoes the experience of dis-placement, of being unsettled and cast out away from the familiar and the homely (cf. Antigone's expulsion from the hearth, *Antigone*, vv. 370–375). As Heidegger avows, "the holy places all experiencing outside of what is customary for it and thus withdraws from it the place where it stands. Thus, un-settling in this way, the holy is itself the awesomely unsettling (*das Entsetzliche*) (EHP: 85/GA 4: 63–64).[23] Still, even in this experience of displacement, or rather on account of it, the poet, in his essence, "belongs to the holy." What the poet must experience, then, is what the Ister accomplishes in its flowing away from its source: a way to stand in nearness to that which withdraws from it—its holy origin—precisely in and through its own departure from the origin itself.

As a kind of field guide to the twists and turns of this journey outward from the source while remaining intimate to it in nearness, Heidegger offers a reading of a Hölderlin fragment from "Bread and Wine"

namely at home is spirit
not at the beginning, not at the source. The home consumes it.
Colony, and bold forgetting spirit loves.

nemlich zu Hauss ist der Geist
Nicht im Anfang, nicht an der Quell. Ihn zehret die Heimat.
Kolonie liebt und tapfer vergessen der Geist.

(HHI: 126/GA 53: 157; DKV I: 747)

As Heidegger develops his reading of this fragment, he attempts to show an inner relation among "beginning"—"source"—"the home" that does not merely equate all three as signifying the same; rather, he tries to show a hidden and difficult relationship between these terms that governs not only this fragment of "Bread and Wine" but indeed all of Hölderlin's work. This extends to that very relationship between ancient Greece and modern Germany that Heidegger deems essential to the futural destiny of the Germans. It is the selfsame relation between one's own and the foreign that he finds in the Böhlendorff letter; between the *hypsipolis* and *apolis* that characterizes the destiny of Antigone; between locality and journeying in the Ister's movement from its source in Donaueschingen (as it moves reluctantly) to its mouth in the Black Sea. By situating the problem of homecoming in this way, Heidegger attempts to mobilize the myth of a secret Germany as a way to overcome the devastation and loss suffered by the Germans in the Great War. Out of this mythic form of a Hölderlinian national self-determination, Heidegger positions Germany as the only *Volk* able to properly recover the Greek legacy bequeathed to the West, a legacy whose originary power has been concealed and covered over by centuries of oblivion and forgetfulness. The saving of this legacy—and indeed of the Western tradition as a whole—has been handed over to the Germans as their proper task, but what stands at issue for Heidegger (especially during the difficult years of the Second World War) is whether the German *Volk* will be commensurate with the challenge that awaits them. Only Hölderlin can sketch the pathway for this futural German vocation; only Hölderlin's works hold the secret for becoming equal to the task of saving the West from the devastation of "the Anglo-Saxon world of Americanism" and the barbarism of the Soviet Union.[24] To counteract what Heidegger calls "the spiritual decline of the earth," the Germans stand in need of what Nietzsche had called an "educator."[25] In this powerful sense, the Ister lectures stand as Heidegger's own bold initiative of offering to the Germans "Hölderlin as Educator"—the poet who would help initiate an authentic German homecoming by way of a commemorative thinking (*Andenken*) of the beginning as that which is still to come. In its most essential sense this is what the poet heralds in his late fragment from "Bread and Wine."

Heidegger would return to this fragment in a number of his lectures and essays (GA 4: 89–94; GA 52: 188–193; GA 53: 155–166, 176–178; GA 75: 140–151, 190).[26] It would serve him as a kind of shorthand to present what he took as the essential logic of all authentic homecoming, a logic that he saw clearly indicated in the Böhlendorff letter and poems such as "Andenken," "At the Source of the Danube," "The Journey," "The Rhine," and "The Ister," among many others. The basic premise of this logic appeared to Heidegger as something all too direct: "At the beginning spirit is not at home in its own home" (GA 4: 91). The home (*Haus*)—as homeland (*Heimat*)—is "the origin and the originary ground of spirit." Yet at the beginning (*Anfang*) when it is "at home," spirit is not yet in the element of its own (*das Eigene*). As the Böhlendorff letter had made all too clear, the free appropriation "of one's own is the most difficult" (E&L: 208/DKV III: 460). Whiling in the home, residing in the nearness of the home, spirit nonetheless is not yet "at home" in its whiling; that is, it does not yet *dwell* in nearness to its home since the very propinquity of home, its all-too-easy accessibility, occasions a forgetting of its originary force. In the midst of such oblivion, as a way of upending the complacency of its settled patterns of residence, spirit needs to venture out away from the home. It needs to do so in order to find itself and reclaim the concealed power that abides within the home but which, because of spirit's self-contentment and the curious force of beyng's withdrawal and concealment, has remained foreign to it. This logic of reversal, a logic of "the turn" as it were, serves as an essential figure within Heidegger's thinking, one that pervades so much of the Ister lectures and their staging of a Greek-German *Auseinandersetzung* by way of Sophocles's tragic reversal in *Antigone* (*hypsi-(a)polis*) and Hölderlin's poetic reversal of the course of a river in his Ister hymn. In this way Heidegger will relate the "Bread and Wine" fragment to the tension between locality (*Ortschaft*) and journeying (*Wanderschaft*) on the Ister's path "homeward" to the Black Sea.

As Heidegger reads the fragment, it says that spirit "is not immediately homely in its 'at home' . . . These words do not at all mean that spirit 'is' not at the source in the beginning. Spirit is presumably indeed and constantly 'at the source,' but in the beginning (*Beginn*) it is not 'at home' 'at the source.' This is why it must first become homely 'at the source,' and to do so, 'spirit' must first specifically go 'to the source'" (HHI: 129–130/GA 53: 161–162). To grasp what Heidegger attempts to say here, we must distinguish between two senses of the English word "beginning." For Heidegger, the German word *Beginn* refers to the temporal start of something, its simple chronological precedence to that which follows it. The German word *Anfang*, however, refers to the inception of something that commences at the source, from out of an origin (*Ursprung*) that is never past as what lies simply behind us but, rather, always takes the form of what is still to come. It is as if we were caught (Latin *ceptare*, German *fangen*) in (*in-ception*) and at (*an-fangen*) something that held sway through everything and essentially pervaded all that emerged forth from it.[27] Within human history, Heidegger tells us, humankind has "in a certain manner [been] excluded from the origin of its own essence . . . [and] is not yet intimately familiar with the unfolded and essential fullness of its destiny, is not 'at home' in it" (HHI: 130/GA 53: 163). Here spirit pursues its own aims, yet without this intimate affinity for, and remembrance of, its proper origin. Still, however, spirit can never free itself from what is essentially "of" the home—that is, what is "one's own." In the words of the fragment, "the home consumes it" ("Ihn zehret die Heimat"), literally, "preys upon it," "draws all its strength out of it," and yet it remains, as what is still to come, "veiled and ambiguous." To speak in the language of the Ister lectures, spirit is essentially unhomely precisely in its home. For that very reason, spirit "wills the unhomely, the foreign" from "out of the will for its essence" in order to become homely in a proper sense.

The logic here follows Heidegger's earlier reading of Antigone, who knowingly chooses expulsion from the homeland in order to become at home in her unhomeliness. So too does spirit go out from its home, as it "loves colony and bold forgetting"—which is, according to Heidegger, nothing other than "the knowing and mindful courage to experience the foreign, and experiencing that, in the foreign, steadfastly gives thought to one's own" (HHI: 132/GA 53: 165). Throughout this whole journey outward from the home, however, the primary thought of the poet—according to Heidegger—"is the readiness, while in the foreign, to learn from the foreign *for the sake of what is one's own*, so as to defer what is one's own until its time" (my emphasis). We too shall defer a discussion of Heidegger's privileging of the homeland at the expense of the foreign until the end of this chapter. Before moving on to a fuller engagement with Heidegger's fundamental espousal of "the experience of the foreign" only "for the sake of what is one's own," however, we should notice how he appropriates the poetry of Hölderlin to "authorize" just such a gesture, even where Hölderlin's own language provides hints for a radically different path of entry into these texts, one that challenges what we might call Heidegger's "violent" reading of them.[28]

On Heidegger's reading, spirit pursues its journey into the foreign, "loves colony," and takes up the path of the unhomely all "for the sake of what is one's own." In just such a venture the encounter with the foreign is *not* an attempt to appropriate the foreign—but always and everywhere an attempt to appropriate one's own, the proper, and the native. Hence, Heidegger can claim that "the relation to the foreign is never a mere taking over of the Other" (HHI: 143/GA 53: 179). It is, rather, a matter of coming back to the source, the homeland, the beginning via the encounter with the Other—a logic that Heidegger finds in the very course of the Ister itself and in Hölderlin's verses about the river where he writes:

> Yet almost this river appears
> To travel backwards and
> I think it must come from
> The East. (SPF: 256–257)

VIII. Of Time and the River: Naming, Reversal, and Historical Dwelling

If in the "Bread and Wine" fragment we find that spirit cannot remain at home if it seeks to dwell essentially "at the source," then in the Ister hymn we can also apprehend a reflection of that selfsame vision. There the poet shows how a river can only enter into communion with its source by leaving it behind and flowing outward into its appointed destiny. This destiny is provided by the banks that give it form and limitation and against which it must struggle to retain its intimacy with its source. This narrative of the river's course is, by all means, poetized by the poet in the telling of the poem—but now as a description of the Ister's slow and reticent passage from out of its source. What Heidegger chooses to emphasize in Hölderlin's admittedly "enigmatic" language is its reference in verses 1 and 15 respectively to a "Now" and a "Here." These designations not only refer to time and space but more so to what Heidegger calls "locality" (*Ortschaft*) and "wandering" (*Wanderschaft*). As Heidegger puts it, "Insofar as the river itself dwells in the locale in its essence; it *is* its locality" (HHI: 35/GA 53: 42). Yet, at the same time, while providing humans with a locale for dwelling—in enabling settlement, agriculture, trade, and transport—the Ister also moves past such settlements in that it journeys far beyond the locale, moving away from the homeland and, in doing so, becoming "unhomely" as it were. In this movement away from the home, however, it does not simply leave the home behind it; rather, it moves *toward* it in an enigmatic, if not contradictory sense.

The very first words of the poem—"Now come, fire!"—speak to this sense of tarrying in the present and speaking from the present into an anticipated future—the futural coming of the gods—whose very coming emerges from a remembrance or *An-denken* of a founding origin, the source or *arche* out of which all coming emerges and to which it returns. Part of this difficult and enigmatic logic of journeying from and dwelling in the locale goes back to two decisive thematic *topoi* that reign throughout the poem. The first involves the very name of the river itself: "Ister." Originally, the Greeks knew only the lower course of the river, which they named "Istros." Following their settlements of both the upper and lower parts of the river, the Romans named the former "Danubius" and the latter "Ister."

> Yet Hölderlin . . . names precisely the upper course of the Donau with the Greco-Roman name for the lower course of the river, just as if the lower Donau had returned to the upper, and thus turned back to its source. (HHI: 10/GA 53: 10)

This reversal of the river's flow is underscored in the poem itself by Hölderlin's cryptic utterance that the river appears "to go backwards" (vv. 41–42). Two quite distinct narrative topoi intersect here at the source of the Danube. The name of the river in its poetic telling at the commencement of a historical "now" comes into play with the "here" of the river's flow and origin.

In the first stanza of the poem, the poet attests that "we" (presumably the German *Volk* that awaits the arrival of the gods) "sing from the Indus / Arrived from afar and / From Alpheus" (vv. 7–9). And with this gesture to the two ancient rivers that allude to Germany's "origin" in both Asia (Indus) and Greece (Alpheus), Hölderlin again takes up the theme of "heavenly fire" from the Böhlendorff letter that was native to the Greeks but remains foreign to the Germans.[29] Yet Heidegger will suppress this Asiatic "origin" of the Greek bequest to Germany and ignore what Hölderlin took to be essential to the encounter with the Other *as* Foreign.[30] Instead, he will proceed with his narrative about the "special inner bond" between Germany and Greece that willfully disregard's Hölderlin's affinity for what he terms "the Oriental."[31] (Such a gesture will, of course, fatefully determine the way Heidegger takes up the question of the Asian "other" precisely in SS 1942 when the Germans are involved in a brutal conflict with the Soviet Union about the future destiny of Europe.) But as Heidegger attempts to "think more clearly the essence of the river" (HHI: 39/GA 53: 46), he comes back to the theme of reversal.

In the Ister's backward-turning movement, Heidegger finds a confirmation of the law of becoming homely in and through its being unhomely. That is, in the Ister's movement away from its source in Donaueschingen (its home, its arche, and its origin) toward the Black Sea (i.e., in Hölderlin's shorthand "Greece," "Asia," "the foreign," or "unhomely"), we find the same movement as Antigone choosing expulsion from the *polis* (i.e., becoming *apolis*) in order to come into a more originary kinship with the *polis* of the homeland (i.e., becoming esteemed of the *polis*, becoming *hypsipolis*). The Ister "appears" to go backward since "the true flow of the river" is *toward* its provenance, even as the actual flow moves away from it (HHI: 36/GA 53: 43). This is why, at its inception, the river "flows hesitantly" where it encounters "a mysterious counterflow that pushes counter to its originary springing forth."[32] This geophysical description of the Ister's hesitancy intimates "the mysterious concealment of the intertwining relations toward the foreign and one's own" (HHI: 143/GA 53: 178). But it also offers a hint of the way humans come to dwell. Part of this mysterious and enigmatic design appears in one of Hölderlin's allusions to Heracles in the second stanza of the poem. The poet writes that the Ister:

Invited Hercules as guest
Gleaming from afar, down there by Olympus,
When he in search of shade
From the sultry Isthmus came,
For full of courage were
They even there, yet there was need, for spirit's sake
Of cooling too./

Den Herkules zu Gaste geladen,
Fernglänzend am Olympos drunten,
Da der, sich Schatten zu suchen
Vom heissen Isthmos kam,
Denn voll des Muthes waren
Daselbst sie, es bedarf aber, der Geister wegen,
Der Kühling auch.

(HHI: 140/GA 53: 175)

Before composing "The Ister" hymn, Hölderlin had worked diligently at translating some of the victory odes of Pindar in an effort to carry through poetically the law of encounter between foreign and native described in a December 1801 letter to Böhlendorff. Part of that encounter goes back to a claim about the Greeks' need to cultivate what was unnatural and foreign to them: namely, "Western Junonian sobriety," that gift innate to the non-Greek Hesperians. For the Greeks to excel in their art, Hölderlin claimed, they needed to overcome and indeed reverse their own natural inclination toward "sacred pathos" as "fire from heaven" (i.e., their nearness to the gods). That is, to speak in the language of the Ister lectures, in order to come into their own, the Greeks needed to "pass through something foreign." Only by such an inversion or reversal of their own innate tendencies could what was properly their own first become their own property (HHI: 135–137/GA 53: 168–170). Similarly, the Germans could only come into their own by encountering the Greeks' "fire from heaven" as the unhomely, the non-native, that which, precisely because of its foreignness drives them on toward "grasping themselves in the face of what is ungraspable." In this way, the foreign becomes "serviceable" to the task of freely using what is one's own. This, for Heidegger, constitutes "the essential law of Western and German humankind," a law that needs to be grasped at exactly "this decisive historical time of the Germans." The details of this law can be read in the way the poem describes the journey of Heracles northward from Olympus—site of the Olympian games founded by Heracles—by way of the Ister to the shady groves of Hesperia where he is invited to be a guest. There he takes the olive branch from the river's bank and, upon his return, plants it on the treeless plain of Olympia to offer protection and shelter from the blazing sun ("fire from heaven") for the Greek athletes who compete there. This journey northward from the fire of the Greek sun to "appropriate" the shade of an olive branch and then return homeward to plant it on Greek soil—and indeed at the very spot where the Alpheus River flows—indicates a profound resonance with Pindar's own description of Heracles's journey to Hesperia in his third Olympian ode.[33] Hölderlin had long worked on a translation of this ode (which remained unfinished). And yet in the surviving manuscript we can find all the details of "The Ister's" description of this Heraclean itinerary. In his translation from Pindar's Greek, the word Hölderlin chooses to translate *mnama* (v. 27) is "Angedenken"—that recollective thinking of what has been fraught with profound implications for what is coming.[34]

We find in two other Hölderlin poems from this same period, "At the Source of the Danube" and "The Journey" (both from 1801), similar narratives about "the journey to the East"—in the form of both a river's push to its origin in Asia and the migration of colonists eastward to seek their origins. "The Journey" describes the peregrinations of Swabian wanderers who leave the Neckar to travel eastward "to the source"—the shores of the Black Sea—where they encounter Greek settlers who invite them to tarry a while with them (DKV I: 324–327, 850–857). The poetic allusions here are dense. The settlement on the shores of the Black Sea is one founded by Greek colonists who moved north from the Ionian coast. Hence, the Swabian settlers meet Greek settlers in a gesture of mutual exchange and guest-friendship. These Hyperborean wanderers commingle with these Greek "children of the sun" (v. 36) and produce a cross-cultural fertilization that bespeaks Hölderlin's poetic dream of a future Swabian republic nourished on its bonds to ancient Hellas. What Hölderlin draws upon here is an old Pindaric myth about the *hospitality* of this region to Hesperian settlers.[35] Hence, it changes its name from the sea inhospitable to strangers/foreigners (*pontos axeinos*) to that sea friendly/hospitable to strangers/foreigners (*pontos euxeinos*). Here too we see how for Hölderlin a changing of names—much as that from "Donau" to "Ister"—comes to signify not only a cross-cultural interchange and fertilization, but the very *ethos* of a poetic possibility of dwelling that affirms the necessity of journeying to the foreign (here, specifically, the Greeks) in an effort to appropriate what is one's own.

Moreover, in "The Journey," Hölderlin also poetizes the extreme difficulty of leaving the homeland and initiating the movement of departure.

> Schwer verlässt,
> Was nahe dem Ursprung wohnet, den Ort./
>
> For whatever dwells
> Close to its origin is loathe to leave the place.
>
> "The Journey," v. 36 (SPF: 182–185)

As in "The Ister," the difficulty/hesitancy of departing from the origin will characterize so much of the German attempt to appropriate the Greek. But beyond this gesturing back to the Greek origin of the German *Volk*—in the flow of the river backwards and in the re-naming of the Donau with its originary Greek name—"The Ister" also announces the coming of a new epoch and the possibility of a return of the gods to the earth. And indeed it does so in its very first line—at its origin, as it were.

> Now come, fire!
>
> (v. 1)

The annunciation of the Now in its imperative form speaks to the power of its language as itself what Heidegger will call an "Ereignis" or "appropriating event" (HHI: 9/GA 53: 9). This "Now come," Heidegger tells us, "has already 'occurred'"—*sich ereignet*—in a way that like the river itself draws on that which has been (*das Gewesene*) as the very source or *Quelle* of an ongoing event—like the flow of a river. Time here is not pigeonholed into distinct temporal boxes of past-present-future but lets itself be thought of as a river-like flow from a source whose counterpull encounters all that which has been in its *Gewesenheit*, in its having-beenness. Such an encounter is less a preteritive burden of what can never be changed than it is the wellspring and *arche* of a coming event that appropriates us to its originary power by way of its annunciating call in the kairotic present. It is this call that issues forth from the poet at the *arche* of the poem. Such a call announces neither a proclamation nor a command; instead, it instantiates the very time of a coming, the awaited *parousia* of the god(s). The poet does not bring about this coming of his own power. Rather, his words serve as a hymnal invocation and song of praise to the gods to prepare humankind for their return.

But this "Now-time" of the opening verse brings together "in a concealed, unitary relation [both] what has been and what is of the future" in an enigmatic way. It does not simply name this time, as if the river were a metaphor of some extrinsic movement; rather, it is of this time and *is* time itself (HHI: 12/GA 53: 12). In such a movement, Hölderlin brings the temporality of this Now-time (v. 1) into relation with the spatiality of dwelling by calling upon the river as the source of their unity. Within this first stanza the poet then presents this originary emergence of time from out of the river's source as a temporal journey from out of Asia—the source of human history. In his allusions to the Indus and Alpheus rivers, Hölderlin traces the course of human civilization, much as his friend Hegel, from the East toward the West as the movement of the sun and its worshippers, who greet the anticipated break of day with a hymnal song. These celebrants are eager "to see the day" and follow the sun's journey westward from India through Greece and then onward to Hesperia, land of the Ister. Nonetheless, the poet warns us that reaching this destination and finding "what is fitting" (*das Schickliche*) offers impediments. "Not without pinions may / Someone grasp at what is nearest / Directly / And reach the other side" (vv. 11–14), the poet writes. In this arcane and enigmatic diction Hölderlin speaks of the difficulty of "being-in" what is near (*die Nähe*), of being able to abide in one's abode *properly*, precisely because it is so near and thus appears as far and distant to us. One is reminded of the opening passage of "Patmos" (written in the same year as "The Ister"), a poem that likewise speaks of the long-awaited *Einkehr* ("coming/arrival") of the gods:

Nah ist
Und schwer zu fassen der Gott./

(Near is
And difficult to grasp, the god.)

(SPF: 230–231)

and of the need for "wings . . . to go across (*hinübergehen*) and return (*wiederkehren*)" (vv. 15–16) over the chasms of Alpine mountains that stand at "the summits of time" (v. 10). In Heideggerian terms, we can read this to mean that owing to the ingrained indifference written into our everyday existence, we are unable to heed the very nearness of a god's presence in the simplest ways of our being. But the poet's call may serve as a kind of rousing summons that, through our commemorative thinking (*Andenken*), might bring us into a temporal unity with the river's course and mindfully allow us to enter into its kairotic manner of appearance.

In times past it was exactly this kind of ability to become at one with the time of the river that enabled humans to build at the Ister's banks and, with their "wings," make the journey across its broad expanse. In this gesture of building "Here" (v.15) by the river, we also find the initiatory spur toward "dwelling." But for Heidegger it is not simply these settlers, come from afar, who dwell near the river; "the river itself dwells" in becoming homely in a locale even—and precisely—as it journeys away from this locale. Through this enigmatic movement out of its source, the river—like the locale—"is both there and here, not by chance, but under the concealed law of a journey" (HHI: 35/GA 53: 42). We need also to remember how both the river and the poet take on their respective roles as demi-gods, those beings who dwell *between* the gods and the *Volk*. In his essay "Hölderlin and the Essence of Poetry," Heidegger writes of the poet: "He is the one who has been cast out—out into this *between*, between gods and humans. But above all and only in this between is it decided who the human is and where its existence is settled" (EHP: 64/ GA 4: 47). As the "between," the river teaches humans how to dwell; it provides a home and an asylum for these homeless beings who lack a "Here" and are unable to dwell in nearness to what is their own. This foundering on the part of humanity to secure an authentic dwelling can be traced back to its failure to recognize the "law of becoming homely" as first requiring the journey into the foreign.

In his translation of Pindar's fragment "Die Asyle" (Asylum), Hölderlin writes about how the human being remains homeless, without a *Halt* (footing/support) or an *Aufenthalt* (dwelling place, abode) upon the earth, until it recognizes its fate in an originary need for an encounter with the gods—in and through its intimation of the gods' presence in nature or *physis* (DKV II: 771–772). It is Themis, goddess of justice, whom Hölderlin (channeling Pindar) calls upon to help provide asylum or refuge for a fugitive humanity cut off from its primordial dwelling place in concert with the gods. Seeking the justice of the homeland, pursuing a site, a stead, a haunt "where he can abide" (*sich halten*), the human being takes upon itself its most fundamental task upon the earth: finding a home. Like Oedipus in his threefold struggle with the (concealed) truth of the oracle, like his daughter (sister) Antigone's contentious journey from being the outcast (*apolis*) to finding her proper home within the earth, Hölderlin's vision of human dwelling is fraught with the tragic potential of coming undone as we recklessly seek to master the unmasterable labyrinth that fashions our own destiny. As we have seen, tragedy lies at the heart of the Ister lectures. We can see this not only in the way that these lectures concentrate upon Antigone as their center, or in the way that they juxtapose the struggles of Greek drama with those of German historical experience. Beyond this we find it in the way that Heidegger understands conflict as the quintessential expression of a concealed harmony whose lineaments remain disguised and indiscernible for those who lack the proper attunement of "intimacy."

In his *Parmenides* lectures of WS 1942–1943 composed just months after the Ister lectures, Heidegger writes that "tragedy has as its single source in the conflictual essence of *aletheia*" (P: 90/GA 54: 134). As an example of just such a conflict, Heidegger refers to "the rise and fall of the human being in its historical abode of essence—*hypsipolis/apolis* (far exceeding abodes/homeless)—as Sophocles (*Antigone*) calls the human being." At the center of the Ister lectures we see this selfsame conflict between exceeding one's abode and being without any abode that marks the fates of Antigone and her father. Above all, we see that for Heidegger tragedy has to do with "the abode of the essence of this humanity." It trades in the indistinct and ambiguous currency of human self-understanding and deception, that realm of appearance marked by "distortion and oblivion" that characterizes the counterturning essence of the human being. With the story of Oedipus we come to the heart of just such a conflict. As the native born "stranger" to the city of Thebes, we find Oedipus caught within the nets of a language that, for all his oracle-busting canniness, he cannot unravel. This filial son of Laius will be expelled from the *polis* only to return as its "savior"—the *basileus* become *tyrannos*.[36] But because he cannot decipher the concealed meaning of *his own* (*eigener*) "name" (*Oedipus*: etymologically, *oidein*: "to swell up/be swollen" + *pous*: foot)), he remains trapped within the veils of cover-up and dissembling that pervade his and his family's history. This cycle of self-deception (in and through self-denial masked as self-assertion) continues throughout the family saga. Moreover, as we see in Antigone's all too canny attempts to defy Creon's "law" and persist in attending to her family duty of proper burial rites for her brother, the criminal is shown to be a family member in a double sense. Both Polyneices's defiance of his brother Eteocles and Antigone's of her uncle Creon confuse and conflate family quarrels with political conflict and do so in ways that evade their own aims and intentions. For in the world of tragedy we see how the canniest of human actors are undone by the uncanny logic of the tragic situation. In all these ways we see how tragedy reveals that the foreign is really the native—although hidden to us upon our first viewing. Only that individual who is canny enough to grasp the essential uncanniness of being will succeed in navigating the treacherous waters of the human sojourn that forms the river of/as time. Only they who are able to become "intimate" or *innig* to the truth of tragedy as that which reveals the irreconcilability of inward contradiction will be able to abide both the permanence of this journey (the "Here" of settlement) as well as its utter permutability (the shifting twists and turns that the river takes as it leaves its "home").

In this tragic phenomenology of time as the showing/concealing of the human being as *the* uncanniest, as the one who, in Tierisias's words, cannot evade time since "Time has found [us] out" (OT, v. 1213), we stand at the very center of Greek tragedy—and its uncanny relation to German homecoming. Heidegger would indicate that the conflicts at the heart of tragedy reveal the back and forth, mutually determinative counterturning that characterizes the human sojourn upon the earth. As beings whose very existence is marked by homelessness, exile, and banishment from the hearth at the center of being, we humans stand at the crossroads of a conflict that is not of our own making but, rather, expresses the very truth of being as *a-letheia*, as a hiddenness at odds with revelation. The Greek tragedians knew this conflict and were able to express it so powerfully that their very language opened a site for human dwelling, a place where the deepest conflicts of/in the *polis* could show themselves in and as this hiddenness through the mask of tragic presentation. These tragedians were able to become "intimate," or *innig*, with this conflict in such a way that they experienced it as another form of what Heraclitus termed *harmonia* (GA 39: 124, 249–251, 258–260). In this way they came into intimacy (*Innigkeit*) with "the mystery of beyng." Few thinkers and poets, Heidegger believed, were able to draw upon this experience in an authentic and historically decisive way until Hölderlin. In Hölderlin's river hymns this same intimacy will be revealed in the way the poet experiences the river as the site for "the dwelling and *Dasein* of the Volk." In an originary way, Hölderlin was able to poetize in "the most intimate intimacy . . . the telling opening up (*Eröffnung*) of intimacy" (HGR: 235/GA 39: 260). In "The Ister" this takes the form of a poetic saying of the uncanniness of being as that which we can never control or dominate, but to which we must remain open. This uncanniness perseveres in the most enigmatic ways possible and it is our task to abide this uncanniness as the very law of being *as* time, as the temporal conflict between the forward-moving journey outward from the *arche* and the backward-turning return to the source from out of this originary departure. This journey—not merely "described" in the poem but "in-scribed" as the living word of the poet's journey in/as time—shows itself as the pathway for any possibility of authentic dwelling. In "The Ister," as in *Antigone*, what comes to presence is "the potential of human beings for being homely" by confronting what is unhomely within their own home. This "law of becoming homely as the law of being unhomely . . . grounds the poetic dwelling of human beings" (HHI: 164–166/GA 53: 202–203). And, for Heidegger, it offers the possibility of a historical homecoming of the Germans, a way for them to "open in the direction of the holy that essentially prevails (*west*) over gods and humans."

If in Sophoclean tragedy it is the chorus who offers the most uncanny and ambiguous utterances about human dwelling as the site of an at times insuperable homelessness, then within the German language it is Hölderlin's river hymns that express this irreconcilable conflict. All of Heidegger's efforts here are aimed at opening this relation to our notice, of attempting to make us ever more mindful of our need to address the uncanny essence of our own canny attempts to evade that which cannot be evaded: the abyss at the heart of being This *Abgrund*, the abyssal non-ground of all that is, pervades every human venture to ground its own home. As Heidegger brings his lectures to a close, he confronts his listeners with their underlying meaning, which he finds above all in the language of the poet's words.

> This poetry demands of us a transformation in our ways of thinking and experiencing, one that concerns being in its entirety. (HHI: 166–167/GA 53: 205)

As part of this transformation, he enjoins us to "let go of . . . our presumptive measure of truth, so as to enter that free realm in which the poetic is." He then raises a question which Hölderlin famously posed in one of his late poems, "In lovely blueness":

Is there a measure on earth?

and he reminds us that Hölderlin answered this question by avowing "There is none." "This sounds like a token of hopelessness and despair," Heidegger tells us; "And yet it names something else and points to something else"—something that exceeds our own ability to measure with the *gnomon* of human will and volition. Neither through our own self-assertion nor through our thoughtless inattention to the manifestations of being that everywhere surround us in their nearness, will we ever be able "to set or seize upon the measure." Yet there does lie the possibility of intimating such a measure, if we can but "bear and suffer it." This can happen if, by attending to the poetic word, we can become intimate with the conflictual strife of *aletheia* that pervades the phenomenality of being. If, through such intimation, we can let ourselves be "suddenly struck" (*plötzlich betroffen*) by "the truth of this poetry," then—in our attunement—we open for the appropriating event of a poetic measure that would enable us to genuinely dwell upon the earth.

We find something of this same difficult and intimative manifestation of poetic truth in another letter that Hölderlin wrote to his friend Böhlendorff in 1802 after he returned from his journey to Bordeaux. In his experience of traveling on foot from Nürtingen over the mountains of Auvergne to Bordeaux, Hölderlin shed the quotidian habits of his domestic existence so forcefully that he began to perceive the world in a wholly strange and foreign way. Exposed to the dangers of isolation and dispossessed of his conventional strategies of defense, Hölderlin remained so raw to the manifestations that surrounded him that he remarks: "As it is said of heroes, so may I say of myself—Apollo has struck me" (E&L: 213/DKV III: 466). Here once more we find another reference to the enigmatic law of homecoming from out of the foreign that emerged in the first Böhlendorff letter of 1801—namely, the need for reversing one's "national" gifts in order to "properly" grasp them in and through the appropriation of the foreign.

Again, within the Böhlendorff logic of Hölderlin's law of homecoming, the Greeks were naturally gifted with "fire from the heavens"—namely, "the still radiance of pure lucidity" granted to them by "the god of light," Apollo (HHI: 135–136/GA 53: 168–170). Yet this native endowment became a burden to them since they all too casually embraced their national gifts and were thereby overcome by "an excess of destiny" that cut them off from what was properly theirs. Only when they learned to provide a measured balance (*Mass*) to this excess (*Übermass*) by "passing through something foreign, namely through the 'clarity of presentation'" did "what was properly their own first become their property." In the same way, the Germans' task stands before them as a counterturning reversal of their inborn endowments so as to be able to become who they properly are by appropriating Greek "sacred fire," the light of Apollo, much as Hölderlin was able to do. In SS 1942 this Hölderlinian process takes the form of what Heidegger calls "the law of historicality." That is, what is "natural" for human beings can only truly become "natural" when it is appropriated by them in and through their history. What emerges from the "source" of a *Volk*—much as that which emerges from the source of a river—must flow outward from its home and endure the journey into the foreign as a way of coming to be what it is. Only by leaving the home and risking the journey into the foreign or unhomely can a *Volk* truly come into its own or "proper" sense of itself. Tragedy shows us that this journey may be undermined by difficulties beyond our ken and may reveal that what we thought was foreign actually belongs to us as the native and proper. Reversal, inversion, ambiguity, contradiction, chiasm, and catastrophe all mark the pathway of this venture into what awaits us. Uncanny is the law of our journeying. Hence, it should little surprise us that the very opening of "The Ister" hymn begins on a note of contrariety and incongruity: a poem about a river and the flow of its water commences with "fire"—and indeed the fire of Apollo.

From its very inception, the language of Hölderlin's poem presents the impossible coeval encounter of fire and water, those two primordial elements that both bring together and set asunder the earth and the heavens (air). By beginning in contradiction, as it were, Hölderlin sets in motion the path of a reversal to come: the impossible, backward-turning movement of the Ister itself that sets into place the contradictory, inverted relation of antiquity and modernity, Greek and German, past and future, what has been (*das Gewesene*) and what is coming (*das Kommende*) as proceeding from the selfsame source. It is as if at the inception of the poem that serves as an *arche* of the path of Western history and its movement(s), Hölderlin has confused the singularity of the beginning through a strange kind of doubling that serves to invert its meaning. No *arche* may be "stable" and "secure"; like the river itself, it flows away from its origin into the multiplicity of time's registers. What the river poetizes is the path of a dwelling or *ethos* that does not cling to *one* identity, but that opens itself to the risk of exposure to unseen possibilities that may threaten its sheltered sense of who and what it is.

Heidegger seems to grasp the power of Hölderlin's assault here upon the fortress of metaphysics and its monomaniacal insistence upon oneness, unity, tautology, identity, and selfsameness. Often throughout the Ister lectures Heidegger appears to heed Hölderlin's judgement about the danger of an all too fervid embrace of the identical, the separate, the exclusive, and the single expressed in one of Hölderlin's epigrams, "Root of All Evil":

> To be at one is divine and good; but whence then this sickness among humans that there be only One and only this One?
>
> Einzig zu sein ist göttlich und gut; woher ist die Sucht denn Unter den Menschen, dass nur Einer und Eines nur sei?
>
> (SPF: 19/DKV I: 222)

Heidegger's own rendering of the law of becoming homely indicates the need for an other who is foreign, alien, strange, different, multiple, and unfamiliar. In his attunement to the river hymn as the poetizing of an authentic *ethos* of human dwelling, he offers a deeply thoughtful account of a proper form of abiding in the abode of the foreign as one's own. Moreover, as he reflects on "the mysterious concealment of the intertwining relations toward the foreign and one's own," he offers something like an ethical insight into the heart of human dwelling. In a remark from the Ister lectures that appears as if it were written by Levinas, Heidegger claims:

> The relation to the foreign is never a mere taking over of the Other.
>
> (HHI: 143/GA 53: 179)

But Heidegger's concern here is less with an ethics of the Other than a tragic account of the blindness of the human being in the face of the conflicted essence of *aletheia*, of its hiddenness and revelation, of its concealment and self-showing. If metaphysics begins with the thetic self-positing of the subject as the center of any possible philosophical inquiry, then Heidegger's own thinking begins with the fact of human thrownness and the experience of displacement that emerges therefrom. As a homeless being, unsettled and thrown into an historical "there" that is not of its own making, *Dasein* confronts the essential conflict at the center of its being—and it does so first of all by evading such conflict and running ahead precipitously to the specious certainties provided by the world of the "they." This is all too often Dasein's initial reaction to its experience as an unsettled being in the world. To fight off this profoundly unsettling experience, Dasein all too often embraces an inauthentic version of who it might become, so that it might avoid having to confront the nullity at the core of its existence.

Coming into one's own, then, appears not as a "natural" impulse of self-affirmation, but as a difficult task that eludes most human beings. To "dwell" authentically upon the earth—to experience one's belonging to a place, a land, a language, a *Volk*, as one's proper site for unfolding one's ownmost possibilities and, as Pindar put it, "becoming that one who one is (meant) to be"—reveals itself as the most difficult task facing the human being. This insight, that the human being is a being whose essence runs counter to itself and that, moreover, it is precisely that being that "forgets" its own essence, stands at the center of Heidegger's Ister lectures. We see this in Heidegger's privileging of Sophocles's tragedy and Hölderlin's poetry as the supreme exemplars for showing us that "everything that is, is essentially pervaded by its counter-essence" (*durchwest vom Gegenwesen*) (HHI: 52/GA 53: 64). It is in laying emphasis on this counterturning movement of the human sojourn upon the earth that Heidegger comes to focus upon Hölderlin's river hymns as the very manifestation of this counter-essence in their movement away from the source and in their counterturning backflow to the source.

For our purposes here, what matters is that we recognize Heidegger's presentation of Hölderlin's river hymns in the summer semester of 1942 as a way for him—exactly in the crisis moment of Germany's foreign excursion into the Russian hinterlands of Stalingrad—to address the question of what "das Eigene" signifies for the German *Volk*. The choice of this theme is hardly arbitrary. In the summer of 1942 the German Reichswehr was embarked upon one of its greatest and most perilous missions: the venture to conquer the Russian threat and secure German hegemony at the center of Europe and beyond. This bold and audacious "journey into the foreign" was understood by Heidegger not only as a military campaign for German victory but, far more, as a struggle over the very essence of the West, of its self-definition and self-preservation, of its defense of Western culture against the Asiatic hordes threatening at Germany's eastern borders and impeding the spread of German *Lebensraum*. Heidegger interpreted this bold venture in terms of "the history of being" as the German defense of its Greek endowment.[37] As the only nation capable of both preserving and transforming this Greek endowment—due to its shared linguistic and philosophical tradition—Germany was charged with the task of saying "being" originarily, much as the early Greeks did in the epoch before the onset of its metaphysical oblivion began in Plato and Aristotle. What was at stake, then, for Heidegger was nothing less than Germany's own struggle for self-identity, for coming into its own, for establishing (*einsetzen*) its own self-assertion through its foreign mission (*Einsatz*) in Russia. Within this geopolitical ontology of the homeland, the Ister lectures come to us as Heidegger's attempt to effect a readiness for engagement on the homefront by facing up to the task of Germany's journey into the foreign. Here Sophocles and Hölderlin will both be conscripted into service as a way of helping the Germans come to understand their special mission and destiny with the history of the West.

But even apart from these narrowly "political" impulses that help shape Heidegger's concerns here, we also find an understanding of the native and foreign that threatens to undermine the very relation between *das Eigene* and *das Fremde* that stands at the center of the Ister lectures. The difficulty for us, reading them through the history of the last century and its relentless violence, lies in attempting to draw upon Heidegger's own powerful insights into the tragic nature of human dwelling on the one hand *and* in then reading them through the tragic blindness of Heidegger's own provincial assertion of German exceptionalism and its attendant metaphysics of racial exclusion and excision. The revelations in the recently published *Black Notebooks* about Heidegger's reaction to the force of "world Jewry" within the history of being offer strong evidence of his inveterate opposition to—and indeed fear of—the Other.[38] This extends to Heidegger's anxiety/apprehension about the Jew, the American, the Russian, the Asiatic, the non-autochthonous, non-German "urban dweller" who threatens the very possibility of "authentic dwelling" in the age of the departed gods. Heidegger's opposition to these forces of dispersion and world-darkening cannot merely be dismissed as the cultural prejudices of a provincial German nativist threatened by the de-centering forces of a modernity marked by the forgetfulness of being. As if in this way we could then neatly separate these "unfortunate prejudices" from the profundity of Heidegger's own philosophical thoughtpath. These observations about the role of world Jewry strike at the very core of Heidegger's philosophical project and the way it situates modernity within the whole history of being. The Hölderlin lectures steer clear of any overt mention of the Jews or of their role in the devastation of the earth and of world-darkening. Nonetheless, it is their omission from this conversation and in the way Heidegger suppresses Hölderlin's own frequent allusion to Jewish (and Christian) themes that we find an entrenched and rebarbative hostility to "letting" the Other "be."[39] In his myopic and xenophobic suppression of the Jewish spirit within the West and especially within German thinking, Heidegger manages to complete his own Oedipal turn to a realm of tragic blindness.

Heidegger's insistence on the singularity of an inner, "essential" Greek–German bond that remains inaccessible to other nations and languages blinds him to the complexity of Hölderlin's own polychromatic understanding of the Greek "event." If for Hölderlin the very name and topos of "Greece" represents a contested space of appropriative engagement (and arrogation) of Near Eastern, Jewish, Christian, Asiatic, and "Oriental" influences, for Heidegger this will appear otherwise. "Greece" and its Ionian legacy will be cleaved off from Asia minor and will stand as the self-generated, autochthonous flowering of pure Hellenic genius, the inception of a Western history in which "Jerusalem" will stand as the Other to "Athens." It is this kind of monocular focus on the Hellas–Hesperia axis that will lead Heidegger to claim, "There is only *Greek* tragedy and no other beside it" (P: 90/GA 54: 134). Likewise, Hölderlin's allusions to the "Indus" River in "The Ister," to "brown women" and the sailors' voyage to "the Indies" in "Remembrance," as well as to the wisdom tradition of Judaism in essays and poems will be suppressed in favor of the pure and singular Graeco-Germanic Hölderlin of Heidegger's own *Inszenierung* or self-staging. As this self-identical topos of Graeco-German "difference," Heidegger's masterful presentation in the Ister lectures needs to be grasped both as a narrative about Germany's path toward poetic dwelling *and* as an assault upon those who threaten such dwelling in the form of Americans, Russians, Jews, Asians, and other non-Germans.

In the Ister lectures Heidegger stages the Native encounter with the Foreign by pointing to the singular bond between Greeks and

Germans that shapes his whole presentation. What matters most to Heidegger in his figuration of this binary structure is the question of poetic dwelling, which he defines as the way of "being properly homely" (*das eigentliche Heimischsein*) (HHI: 137/170–171). Drawing on the originary dialogue of Hölderlin with Sophocles, Heidegger finds in *Antigone* a way of enunciating "the law of becoming homely for the Germans" that will guide his understanding of poetic dwelling: "Dwelling itself, being homely, is the becoming homely of a being unhomely." What is truly unhomely, Heidegger tells us, is "the uncanny," which points to the most fundamental sense of human being—namely, that the human being is a being whose essence runs counter to itself. Both Sophocles and Hölderlin show the counterturning essence of the human being with exemplary care. Moreover, both show this counterturning essence of human being as the struggle to "be" in this place where we find ourselves, the place where we dwell. Drawing on these poetic ways of showing the counterturning essence of human dwelling, Heidegger lays bare how dwelling is nothing we can ever achieve of our own volition, nothing accomplished or effectuated by human planning but, rather, essentially prevails as an *Ereignis* or "appropriating event" that brings us into our own by grappling with the uncanniest of our historical displacement and its various forms of withdrawal, concealment, expropriation (*Enteignis*), and mystery. Only by confronting this uncanniness as that which belongs to being and as that which "looms forth in the essence of human beings" can we confront the genuine homelessness of the human being as the beginning of a path into authentic dwelling. For Heidegger, then, poetic dwelling depends on entering into the nullity of our own existence, the abyss or *Abgrund* that grounds the ground (*Grund*) of our sojourn upon the earth. It involves recognizing the human being as—in its essence—a *katastrophe*, a being that turns (*strophe*) against (*kata*), away from, its own essence in a backward-turning reversal that moves it away from its own home into the uncanny realm of the unhomely. It is this vision of the conflicted, counterturning essence of the human being as that being—solely and incomparably among all other beings—who is not "at home" in being, above all not in its own being, that marks the human being as "tragic." To tragedy, as we know from Sophocles, belongs irony, that linguistic form by which appearance and truth, one's own/native and the other/foreign, fall back upon one another in a movement of dramatic reversal and inversion. The stranger is revealed as a native (*Oedipus*), the accuser as the accused, the highest in the city as cityless, and the person of many means and ways as that being who can find no way out.

Preeminent among these tragic figures of irony stands Oedipus, that in-sightful riddle-solver who is blind to his own tragic fate. Within the play's tragic action, Oedipus stands at the middle of three crossroads when he murders Laius. These three crossroads will be configured by Sophocles as three roads of time that, in the present moment, bring together three oracles from the past: Laius's charge that his offspring will kill him (OT: ll. 711–714); Apollo's revelation that Oedipus will kill his father and sleep with his mother (OT: ll. 787–793); Creon's inquiry about the cause of the plague in Thebes (OT: ll. 95–98). In this maze of intersecting roads, Oedipus is blind to how time configures his own fateful present, the *topos* of the now, which he resists and cannot acknowledge. Perhaps, drawing on this Sophoclean image, we might imagine Heidegger as the most insightful thinker of his epoch, blind to the fateful destiny of his own historical situation. In one of the late lectures of the Ister course from the summer of 1942, Heidegger writes of the "catastrophe" as that which has no grasp of history, that which is unable to enter into what the essence of history might mean.[40] Thinking of tragedy in terms of the catastrophic, we cannot help but be exposed to its monstrous contradictions, to the playing of the uncanniest kind of difference(s) precisely in that attempt to stabilize and secure what is singular. Heidegger's own Germanocentric staging of the "poetics" of dwelling in terms of the native and foreign bespeaks its own monstrous form of irony since it is precisely during the months of these philosophical performances in 1942 that the Third Reich will perform its own monstrous execution of over three million Jews.[41] Attempting to offer a "Final Solution" to the Jewish "problem" in Europe, Reinhard Heydrich will engineer a masterplan for the master race to implement so as to render the Jewish people "ahistorical." Yet precisely at this historical moment of this monstrous catastrophe, Heidegger will think of the "catastrophic" as that which refuses to think of the homeland in terms of a poetics of historical dwelling. This question of catastrophe and the tragic strikes at the core of the Ister lectures, whose own figuration of the native/foreign relation authorizes—precisely under the name and imprimatur of Hölderlin—the exclusion and expropriation of *Judentum* ("Jewry") from the very thinking of the Occident and its history. Some may console themselves that in his published writings Heidegger does not resort to standard National Socialist clichés of Anti-Semitism that proliferate in the writing of Baeumler, Krieck, Rosenberg, Hildebrandt, and others.[42] But in this gesture of exclusion, suppression, denial, and disinheritance, Heidegger both instantiates and carries out his own uncanny form of the monstrous.

In his *Black Notebooks* Heidegger will more properly (improperly?) address his reasons for eliminating the Jew from his own narrative of the history of being. As "rootless," deracinated, calculative, reckoning, the Jew lacks any authentic sense for the originary. In his unremitting pursuit of new strategies for planning, control, mastery, and effectuation, the Jew embodies the spirit of machination that defines European and Occidental modernity. Heidegger himself will, however, vehemently reject the introduction of "race" into this way of situating the problem of world Jewry. As he puts it in a *Black Notebook* entry from 1941:

> The question concerning the role of *world Jewry* is not a racial one; it is, rather, the metaphysical question concerning the type of humanity which, *without any restraints whatsoever*, can take charge of the uprooting of all beings from being as its world-historical "task."
>
> Die Frage nach der Rolle des *Weltjudentums* ist keine rassische, sondern die metaphysische Frage nach der Art von Menschentümlichkeit, die *schlecthin ungebunden* die Entwurzelung alles Seienden aus dem Sein als weltgeschichtliche 'Aufgabe' übernehmen kann.
>
> (GA 96: 243)

In its world-historical task of uprooting all beings from being, world Jewry comes to embody the technological *ethos* of modernity. In so doing it reveals its utter inability to grasp *ethos* as the originary poetic sojourn of human beings upon the earth, a way of coming to dwell in intimacy with the conflictual strife of *aletheia*. All of this will be thought by Heidegger in terms other than "race." Rejecting the construal of race as something belonging to biology, sociology, psychology, or any form of *Weltanschauungs-philosophie*, Heidegger will conceive of "world Jewry" as the fulfillment of a *seynsgeschichtliches Geschick* assigned to Jews in their office as the agents of machination. As the brokers of a new form of technological-financial-industrial will to power, the Jews help to complete modernity's unrestricted dominance of the world's resources and thereby consummate the centuries-long process of the oblivion of being begun in the metaphysics of antiquity. In their machinational push at mastery of beings, however, the Jews will have unleashed an essential form of *Seinsvergessenheit* that will result in their *Selbstvernichtung*, or "self-extinction"—as if by instrumentally engineering the reduction of beings to "resources" available for conscription, transport, delivery, and consumption, they will have been responsible for their own demise.[43]

Heidegger's analysis of world Jewry here, as monstrous and as frightful as it may be, is marked, however, by yet another form of uncanniness whose historical incarnation may appear to us as ironic, if not paradoxical. At the same time of the Ister lectures in 1942, just as he formulates his analysis of world Jewry in the *Black Notebooks*, Heidegger will have come to see his earlier support of National Socialism as flawed and misconceived. By 1942 Heidegger will have understood the National Socialist push toward world conquest as another instantiation of the selfsame forces of unbridled dominion and machination as in the Allied enemies, especially America and Russia. That is, precisely as Hitler's regime makes its push toward realizing the "final solution" to its Jewish problem, Heidegger will have come to see its policies of technological dominion over the earth as the completion of an epoch of oblivion that earlier he had believed they had sought to challenge.[44] And here we can speak of the paradoxes that shape both Heidegger's own thinking and our interpretation of it—for precisely at that very moment that Heidegger rejects the National Socialist dream as belonging to the selfsame metaphysics of machination as in America and Russia, his own interpretation of world Jewry within the history of being undergirds its politics of destruction and extermination. And even though the Ister lectures themselves do not boldly and forthrightly proclaim a vision of racial exclusion and removal, their way of configuring the question of the native and foreign reveals a dangerously nativistic privileging of what is one's own that philosophically supports the ontological racism evident in the *Black Notebooks*.

IX. German Hospitality?

In his own configuring of Hölderlin's experience of the foreign within his "Ister" poem, Heidegger remarks, "The Ister *is* that river in which the foreign is already present as a guest at its source" (HHI: 146/ GA 53: 182). And, as we have seen, Heidegger reads the presence of guest-friendship, *xenia*, and hospitality—especially in the way Heracles is welcomed as guest—as essential to the whole *topos* of dwelling, residing, sojourning, and abiding that forms the middle of these lectures. Yet despite this recognition of hospitality as indispensable both to Hölderlin's way of poetizing and to the problem of the native/foreign, Heidegger fundamentally misses what is essential about the guest/host relation.[45] For him, the guest serves the function of helping the host to come into his own by way of an encounter with the stranger who is always alien and other. But the otherness or alterity of the Other is never addressed in its otherness for the Other. That is, the Other's own experience of this alien encounter for the sake of the Other as Other is suppressed in favor of the self's own native identity. Here the foreign Other serves the purpose of helping to bring the native dweller into closer relation to its home by offering such a stark contrast to its own sense of homeliness. In this way, it enters into the *territorium* of the native, on the native's terms, and solely for the sake of the native's own sense of its native and national identity. In this way, Heidegger never comes to genuinely experience the "foreign" in the sense of Hölderlin's own poetic ideal of hospitality.

In his poem "The Journey," Hölderlin weaves a tale of his Swabian ancestors who ventured to the foreign shores of the Black Sea and were welcomed there in guest-friendship by their Greek hosts. On these foreign shores, as the poet relates, they sat curiously under an olive tree where they remained bewildered at "die eigene Rede des andern"—"the other's own speech" / "the native speech of the other" (SPF: 184–185). That is, these German-speaking guests were struck with wonder at the foreign sounds emitted from their hosts' mouths. In this allusion to "the ownmost speech of the other" that is the other's *own*, and not "mine," Hölderlin comes to the recognition of a hospitality that honors not only the human stranger, but beyond even that, the presence of a divine strangeness that takes the form of the human.[46] This incomprehensible "dialogue" between two groups of different racial and linguistic stock will be transformed by Heidegger into a monologic affirmation of the German nation and its own native consanguinity. In the Ister lectures this takes the form of Heidegger's willful insistence that what matters above all is "to learn from the foreign for the sake of what is one's own" (HHI: 132/GA 53: 165). This same ideal will also be expressed in the

"Remembrance" lectures of WS 1941–1942 where Heidegger remarks: "The sojourn into the foreign and the learning of the foreign [happens] not for the sake of the foreign, but for the sake of what is one's own" (GA 52: 190). By reaffirming his monologic understanding of "dialogue" between the native and the foreign, Heidegger succeeds in completing his catastrophic understanding of the human being as the one caught up in denying its own essence. As blindly as Oedipus, Heidegger forges ahead with his singular and exceptionalist reading of "the secret Germany" and its *Sonderweg* not only within European history but within the history of being. Vouchsafed and authorized with the signature of Hölderlin, whose poetics of naming will be appropriated in the name of German exceptionalism, Heidegger will affirm his own Germanocentric history of being as the only viable path for preparing the other beginning for thinking. It is only to the Germans that the path of this other beginning will open. Hence, in the *Black Notebooks* he will write: "Only the German can say and poetize being in a new, originary way" (GA 94: 27).

If the question of authentic dwelling is, as I believe, at the heart not only of the Ister lectures but of all Heidegger's late work, then perhaps we need to read these lectures in at least two counterturning ways. That is, on the one hand, we need to read them as offering genuinely profound philosophical insights about dwelling and homecoming in the face of the uncanny homelessness that threatens the human being at its very core. On the other hand, we also need to read them as advancing a racialist ontology of national self-identity that problematizes Heidegger's whole relation to the history of Western thought. This is Heidegger's legacy to us. I believe we need to confront this uncanny paradox that lies at the heart of Heidegger's thinking. Such an insight renders our relation to him and his work ever more difficult, ever more precarious. Here the very fact of our relation to Heidegger is suffused with ever greater risk and danger, perhaps even a "danger" that does not let itself be rescued or overcome by any "saving power"—not even that of Hölderlin or his gods.

4

Historical Interlude

Heidegger in 1945–1946

> Do we have any idea that Hölderlin's poetizing is a destiny in our history, the epoch of complete neglect as an unguarding (*Verwahrlosung*)?
>
> —Martin Heidegger, *Zu Hölderlin-Griechenlandreisen*[1]

> The West as a whole is now homeless.
>
> —Martin Heidegger, *Zum Ereignis-Denken*[2]

I. Heidegger's "Kahlschlag": The Poverty of Thinking

The Second World War in Europe ends on May 8, 1945. While the effects of this change were enormous across Germany, Europe, and the entire Western world, for Heidegger, the war's end yielded nothing extraordinary. At least at first. In his private notes he writes:

> Hausen Castle in the Danube Valley, on May 8, 1945. On the day that the world celebrates its victory and does not yet recognize that for centuries already it is the victim of its own rebellious insurrection. . . .
>
> The war at its end; nothing's changed, nothing new, on the contrary.
>
> What has already long endured must now emerge in an evident way. (CPC: 157, 160/GA 77: 240–241, 244)

Heidegger goes on to claim that "the war decides nothing. The decision is only now beginning to prepare itself—even and especially, before everything, the decision of whether the *Germans* as the heart-center of the West fail in their historical vocation and *become* the victim of *foreign ideas*." Over the next several years, Heidegger would attempt to confront the paradoxes of the war's termination in the aftermath of German defeat and subjugation. What would emerge in so many of the essays that Heidegger wrote in this period from "Poverty" (1945) to "Hölderlin's Poetry: A Destiny" (1945), to "The Letter on Humanism," "What are Poets For?," and "The Verdict of Anaximander" (all from Fall 1946) was his own deeply personal response to the "tragedy" of German history as thought through Heidegger's own *Denkweg*. In a world scarred by the violent destruction of all social, political, economic, and institutional order, Heidegger would come to rethink the meaning of "poverty" (*Armut*), "devastation" (*Verwüstung*), "desolation" (*Verödung*), "abandonment" (*Verlassenheit*), and "homelessness" (*Heimatlosigkeit*) that beset the German *Volk* in "the destitute time of the world's night."[3] But, as ever with Heidegger, the proliferation of the violence and carnage brought on by the war only masked a more essential form of abandonment and upheaval than that produced by tanks, airplanes, bombs, or military operations.

To address this plight of modern technological humanity, Heidegger writes a short essay that has its inspiration in the words of Hölderlin, an essay that addresses the question of the West's spiritual impoverishment in the epoch of the world wars. It is as "a world-event that beleaguers the earth" that Heidegger grasps the "devastation" of the Second World War (CPC: 139/GA 77: 215). In late November of 1944, Freiburg was besieged by Allied air strikes that killed 3,000 people. The inner part of the old city was seriously damaged, and in the face of the oncoming winter the lack of heat and plumbing would prove difficult for those who remained. Just before the bombing occurred, the fifty-five-year-old Heidegger was drafted into the *Volkssturm* where he was commissioned to dig defensive ramparts along the Rhine. During the weeks that followed, Heidegger was spared having to face active battle by the intervention of the *Reichsdozentenbund* and its director, Eugen Fischer, who explained to authorities that Heidegger's work as a world-famous philosopher required that he attend to his own manuscripts.[4] During this difficult time, Heidegger writes to his brother Fritz: "If I hadn't been called up by the *Volkssturm*, then I would probably be dead" (HAS: 113–114). As he attempts to justify his retreat from having to do actual military service in December 1944, Heidegger writes to the Rector of Freiburg University and explains how it is imperative that he rescue his manuscripts from the Allied onslaught and bring them to safety in his hometown of Messkirch. As he puts it: "In truth, my works do not belong to me personally; rather, they serve the German future and belong to it."[5] Again, Heidegger will construct a narrative that his writings belong to the German future, a theme he cultivates in the Black Notebooks (GA 94: 523).

To secure protection, the philosophical faculty moved to the isolation of Burg Wildenstein in the upper Danube Valley near the cloister of Beuron. There Heidegger remained for several months after first securing his manuscripts in the underground vault of his brother Fritz's bank in Messkirch. While the rest of Germany lay in chaos from the Allied assault upon the Fatherland that left cities in ruins, farms destroyed, and populations decimated and on the run, Heidegger took refuge in the castle of his lover, Princess Margot von Sachsen-Meiningen, and in this atmosphere of peaceful isolation and erotic fulfillment he found a moment of reflection that helped him to place the frenzy of the war in what he believed was a broader and more essential context. On June 27, 1945, among a small group of colleagues and students, Heidegger delivered a short lecture that would crystallize his thoughts on the just-completed war. Heidegger began with a citation from Hölderlin's fragment "Concerning Periods of History" that divided all of Western history into three eras: "the ancient world, the middle ages, and modern times."[6] Hölderlin began his reflections by claiming, "For us, everything is concentrated upon the spiritual (das Geistige); we have become poor (arm) so as to become rich." In his essay "Poverty," Heidegger would draw upon this Hölderlinian conceit of spiritual impoverishment as a way to situate his own historical era within the schema of a history of the West. In the Hellingrath edition that Heidegger used, this fragment was preceded by another piece titled "Communismus der Geister," written by the young Hölderlin. This editorial arrangement proved significant in at least two ways. First, it helped Heidegger to situate his own comments on "communism" at the end of the "Poverty" essay in relation to the Hölderlinian citation on spirit. Second, I believe it had a deeper significance for Heidegger as a model for his own dialogue "Das abendländische Gespräch" ("The Westen Conversation"), which will be the focus of the next chapter.[7] In the fragment, Hölderlin paints the scene of a dialogue that occurs at sundown near a river—the same setting that

Heidegger chooses for his "Western Conversation." As he reflects on the staggering material poverty that has spread throughout his homeland in 1945, Heidegger positions it in dialogue with the theme of "dwelling" (*Wohnen*) (GA 73: 1200).

"The West as a whole is now homeless," Heidegger writes in his notebooks; "it is the fundamental situation of the world" (GA 73: 763). And yet, Heidegger contends, "when considered from the whole and from what properly belongs to Western destiny (*abendländischen Geschickes*), the danger of the famine, for example, and of the lean years in no way consists in the fact that perhaps many people die—rather, it lies in the way that those who do survive wind up living only to eat—so that they may live" (GA 73: 880). This kind of meaningless life falls victim to a deep and profound kind of boredom, where "in this emptiness the human being goes to ruin." Despite this, the path of material ruin and physical hunger harbors a clue to "the essence of poverty." Essential poverty lies, for Heidegger, in a spiritual poverty where "beyng (*seyn*)" so poor means "being deprived of nothing but that which is unnecessary." Only by giving up that which is (spiritually) unnecessary, Heidegger seems to say, can we "become poor in the authentic sense." Heidegger then turns to the political question that dominates German public consciousness in the days after the war, during the time of what the Germans called the *Kahlschlag*.[8] *Kahlschlag* denotes the felling of forest trees that leaves in its wake a bleak and barren landscape. Hence, in reference to Germany's physical state of collapse of 1945 it refers to the laying waste of cities and towns as well as to spiritual ruins within German culture. Many Germans are fearful that their country will be wholly overturned by the Allied postwar world order and that this might usher in the practices of communist economic dominance. Heidegger responds by insisting that it is not "communism" that threatens to make the Germans poor; nor is the essential form of poverty anything to be fearful of. As he mentions several times in his essay, "everything for us concentrates itself upon the spiritual." Moreover, Heidegger takes this form of con-centration literally. That is, he understands it as a "gathering that takes place (*sich ereignet*) as the relation of being to our essence, a relation that is the center, the middle, that is everywhere as the middle of a circle without a periphery" (GA 73: 877). And again Heidegger emphasizes that Hölderlin's insight is not to be marginalized by framing it within the historical conditions of his own time. On the contrary, it comes to us as "a thinking-poetizing naming of an appropriative event that is hidden in beyng itself, one that extends far beyond its own time into that which is coming."

In this chapter, I want to look a bit more carefully at the historical situation facing Heidegger in 1945 at the war's end and also at the ensuing sixteen months from May 8, 1945, to the end of the Nuremberg trials in October 1946. During this time, Heidegger undergoes profound changes in his personal life: he loses his teaching position; his marriage is threatened with dissolution; he faces the wrath of the Freiburg denazification committee for his activities as rector in 1933–1934, and, he suffers a nervous breakdown. As Germany's existence confronts dramatic changes stemming from the loss of the war, so too does Heidegger's. It is there in this time of uncertainty and suffering that Heidegger writes some of his most important work: "Letter on Humanism," "The Verdict of Anaximander," "Why Poets?," and "The Western Conversation." Before addressing the unique circumstances of "The Western Conversation," and its relation to Hölderlin, I think it important to situate this dialogue within Heidegger's own factical life situation since this critical piece is written as a response to some of the deepest issues facing Heidegger personally as he confronts his dream of a Hölderlinian future for Germany.

Authorized by Hölderlin, then, to interpret his own historical epoch in terms of that which is coming, Heidegger turns to his own beyng-historical intimation of the epoch of the world wars. In a bold, magisterial voice Heidegger proclaims:

> It is not through "communism" that we will become poor—this poorly chosen name for the destiny of the historical world that stands before us. We *are* poor only when everything is for us concentrated upon the spiritual.
>
> Only when the European nations attune themselves to the foundational tone of poverty, will they become rich peoples of the West, a West that is not in decline and cannot perish since it has still not yet begun to rise.

Heidegger continues:

> Wars are not able to decide historical destinies, since they already rest upon spiritual decisions and stick obstinately to them. Even world wars are unable to decide this. But these

wars themselves—and their result—could provide the European peoples with the inducement to bring about mindful reflection (*Besinnung*). This reflection itself, however, arises from other sources. It must begin to flow from out of the peoples' own essence. That is why self-reflection is needed in the reciprocal conversation of the peoples with one another. (GA 73: 881)

At the end of the war, as Germany is collapsing all around him, Heidegger turns once again to Hölderlin as a way of thinking through the essence of German identity. During this whole era—the *Machtergreifung* of 1933, the German victories at the outset of World War II, the devastation and losses of 1944–1945, and the *Kahlschlag* of 1945–1947—Hölderlin accompanies Heidegger through each turn and loss. Above everything, it is in Hölderlin's understanding of "spiritual 'concentration' as the foundational tone" that Heidegger locates the poverty of modern Europe. Amidst the devastation and homelessness of the war's nihilation, Heidegger grasps poverty not as dearth, lack, or shortage but as being free of the compulsion for what one needs. In this way "poor" and "rich" no longer constitute forms of "having" but concern the beyng of Da-seyn as steadfast perseverance (*Inständigkeit*) in the foundational tone of stillness (GA 73: 708–711). This sense of "indigence as beyng is a 'having' that has everything, because it can do without nothing," a way of being that Heidegger terms *Gelassenheit*, or "letting be." In his notebooks Heidegger writes: "Poverty is the overflow (the letting flow-over) of what is unnecessary. The flooding-over and the river. The rivers (Ister and Rhine) and poverty" (GA 73: 711). And in this juxtaposition of poverty and the overflow of rivers, Heidegger finds a way to reflect on the transformed relation to home and homelessness that pervades the postwar European world. In his dialogue "The Western Conversation," Heidegger will offer his own wide-ranging thoughts on the meaning of such homelessness for the status of postwar German culture and will again link the "the spirit of the river" to the meaning of *Gelassenheit* as that which sets its essence free (GA 75: 64).

And yet during this time of postwar tumult and disruption, the tranquility and calm of such *Gelassenheit* would elude Heidegger, especially in the rhythms and attunements of his own existence. Only weeks after his "Poverty" lecture at Burg Wildenstein, Heidegger's Hölderlin-idyll on the Danube would be rudely interrupted by charges of the Freiburg de-Nazification committee for his actions as rector of the university and for his avid support of Adolf Hitler. Within a very short period the stakes would rise. Now Heidegger's private library lay under the threat of confiscation; his Freiburg house was requisitioned and he was forced to allow a French sergeant and his family to occupy part of his living quarters. Beyond this, not only was his teaching position in jeopardy, his very economic livelihood came under threat. To address this dire situation, Heidegger rallied quickly. He made contact with French philosophers; he wrote to old friends from earlier days (Bishop Conrad Grober and professor Romano Guardini, among others) and made plans to set up a study group devoted to the work of the French philosopher Blaise Pascal. Yet none of these initiatives spared Heidegger from the final decision of the French *l'epuration* commission that submitted his case to the cold formalism of a military-political tribunal.[9] In January of 1946, Heidegger's life lay in ruins all around him. His academic career appeared to be an end; his affair with Princess Margot von Sachsen-Meiningen had pushed Elfride to consider a break in their marriage; his two sons were incarcerated in Russian prisoner of war camps; and the final blow came with a damaging letter from his old friend Karl Jaspers that had tilted the university committee's judgment against Heidegger's reinstatement to his former teaching post. In the bitter cold of a January winter, with poor heat and little hope for his future as a philosopher, Heidegger suffered a nervous breakdown. He was sent to a psychiatric clinic in Badenweiler, some twenty-five kilometers from Freiburg. Heidegger remained under the care of Dr. Viktor Gebsattel for several months.[10] Although Heidegger later maintained that his collapse was a minor episode, lasting only three weeks and "overcome" by hikes in the woods and Gebsattel's friendly conversation, the facts of the matter reveal a much more complicated situation. The Freiburg historian Hugo Ott speculated that in the face of all these grim life crises, Heidegger considered suicide, a conjecture unconfirmed in any documentary evidence that I know of.[11] And yet the seriousness of the situation speaks to Heidegger's own fragile psychological state in the winter of 1945–1946. In his letters to Elfride we have clear evidence that the recovery period from the breakdown was not three weeks but several months, into the late spring of 1946.

In letters that he wrote from Badenweiler to his wife Elfride and his brother Fritz, we can see how painful this public censure of his academic career proved to be and how deeply it scarred Heidegger's vision of himself and his role as a German thinker. His bile against the Freiburg academic Senate emerges in a letter to Fritz: "Without mention—or the slightest recognition—of my thirty-year academic teaching career, I am sent packing. . . . That is now the end of my Freiburg existence. In this way, from all sides, they have banished 'the danger' of my thinking from the university" (HAS: 133). But this private rancor against the university would not remain solely in the private sphere. Rather, Heidegger quickly came to identify the bitter campaign against him at the university with a larger Allied plan of retributive justice against Germany. What emerges in his notebooks and correspondence during this time is a stark catalog of bitter resentment against the university, against the French military tribunal, and, above all, against Allied efforts to "re-educate" the German *Volk* by imposing harsh penalties upon the defeated German nation. Heidegger directs his most resolute critique at America's efforts to reshape German culture by imposing its "moral-political" understanding of "justice" on the defeated nation. What invites notice here is how, at the very moment that he comes under assault for his political ties to National Socialism, Heidegger redirects blame to the Allied powers that have come to impose a new postwar order of justice and responsibility upon the defeated German *Volk*. Heidegger's private writings abound with the rhetoric of revenge, *ressentiment*, and self-justification. And were this merely a question about Heidegger's personal motivations or psychological failures, this issue would not command our attention.[12] But in the years 1945 and 1946, these issues would come together in a perfect storm around "the question of German guilt" and responsibility for the war, the mass exterminations, and the passive acceptance of a regime characterized by terror, violence, and monstrous criminality.

II. Heidegger's Revenge: War Guilt, Retribution, and the Politics of *Ressentiment*

In 1946, Karl Jaspers published *The Guilt-Question: A Contribution to the German Question*, a book that took an uncompromising stance on the issue of German culpability in the crimes of the Nazi state. For Jaspers, the issue was clear: in terms of *political* guilt the Germans were collectively liable and were "co-responsible" for "actions committed by the state."[13] Yet on the issue of *moral* guilt, Jaspers claimed that it was something that each individual needed to ask of himself. As he saw it, "the morally guilty are those who are capable of atonement, the ones who knew or could have known better," but who persisted in their shame and "let themselves be anesthetized and seduced or let themselves be bought with personal gain." But it is on the question of what he terms "metaphysical guilt"—"the absence of absolute solidarity with the human being as a being who is human"—that Jaspers hits upon his most pressing point. This solidarity is violated, Jaspers argues, when I witness an injustice or a crime and I do nothing—"If I survive where the other is killed, this I know from a voice within me: that I am still alive is my guilt." Two years later, Herbert Marcuse, a former student, will write to Heidegger and lay at his feet the charge of guilt and responsibility for "never publicly denouncing any of the deeds or ideologies of the Nazi regime . . . a regime that in each and every way was the deadly caricature of the Western tradition that you yourself so urgently set forth and legitimated" (HCW: 161–163).[14] Heidegger responds in defensive fashion and tells Marcuse: "After 1945 . . . the Nazi partisans carried out their *volte face* in the most revolting way, but I had nothing in common with them." And to Marcuse's accusation that he had supported "a regime that murdered millions of Jews, that made terror something normal and that turned everything tied to the concepts of spirit and freedom and truth into its opposite," Heidegger replies:

> I can only add that if instead of writing "Jews" we put "East Germans" (*Ostdeutsche*), then the same holds true for one of the Allied powers—with the difference that everything that happened after 1945 was made known to the world at large, whereas the bloody terror of the Nazis had in fact been concealed from the German Volk.

He then adds:

> In conclusion, I would like you to consider that even today false propaganda persists—for example, that rumors are spread that contradict the truth. I have learned about downright crazy calumnies against me and my work.

To Marcuse's charge of guilt for his actions and responsibility for his support of Hitler's coalition of terror, Heidegger responds by citing a famous line from Jaspers's *The Question of Guilt*: "that we are still alive is our guilt."[15] And yet Heidegger's reference to Jaspers here cannot be taken as positive. On the contrary, Heidegger was furious at Jaspers for his damning letter to the de-Nazification committee. In the *Black Notebooks* he writes with contempt about the judgment in Jaspers's "secret report" to the Dean of the Freiburg faculty that when the academic conditions in Germany improve, Heidegger may be allowed to return to the university. Again, Heidegger is livid. He wonders whether "Jaspers has ever had a philosophical thought—or whether, rather, he has only plied a 'psychology' of philosophy which, in its psychological relativizing of everything" winds up as "an instrument of existentiell self-justification," one that is nothing but a "half-understood psychological metaphysics of the West" (GA 97: 62). Heidegger then adds: "Does anyone seriously believe that this is 'philosophy'? Or even *thinking*?"

Once more here we find Heidegger parrying all charges against him by defending his actions and by shifting guilt away from the Germans themselves and onto the shoulders of the Allied conquerors whose imposition of military "justice" he finds repulsive. Again, in the *Black Notebooks* he writes about the dangers of the Allies' unbridled technological conquest rooted in the planning and reorganization of European life:

> One notices the perplexed floundering of the "Western powers" in their political plans for Europe. Some of them suppose we are still living in the 17th century. The responsibility for such thoughtlessness—or is it already something more: an inability to think?—exceeds by many thousand degrees the irresponsible, dreadful trade with which Hitler raged around Europe. . . . The Christian-liberal relation to communism that pervades the world today is just as foolish and ignorant and—smug as the conduct of the all too clever and genteel members of the bourgeoisie in Germany against National Socialism. (GA 97: 250)

And Heidegger adds:

> The German Volk is politically, militarily, and economically ruined; ruined as well is the strength of the *Volk*—as much by the criminal insanity of Hitler as through the foreign will to exterminate that has finally made its move. . . . This calculating is still not at its end. There still remains the task: *to extinguish the Germans spiritually and historically*. Let us have

no illusions. An ancient spirit of revenge is making its rounds upon the earth. The intellectual history of this revenge will never be written since it hinders the spread of such revenge; this history does not appear even once in public presentations: the public sphere is itself already a form of revenge. (GA 97: 444–445)

If Heidegger had reasons to believe that he had been publicly persecuted during the years of National Socialist rule (his failed rectorate, the supposed ban on his publications, the refusal of his 1937 trip to the Descartes Congress in Paris, the alleged SA surveillance of his seminars, etc.), during the postwar era such suspicions were given full rein.[16] Jaspers's disloyalty only reinforced what he had been experiencing amongst his former colleagues in Freiburg—a sense that both in his person and in his work he was castigated as a pariah. And in the *Black Notebooks* we find a running series of comments expressing outrage over the Allies' co-optation of "justice"—in their administration of the universities and of the courts, especially in the widely publicized "show trials" at Nuremberg. Heidegger's response, channeling Nietzsche, is clear and uncompromising: "morality thinks that justice consists in revenge" (GA 97: 50). And in response to the Allies' attempts to impose their own humanistic standards of moral judgment upon the German *Volk*, Heidegger offers this rebuttal: "Where does the greater presumptive arrogance lie? In criminal offenses or in judicial judgment thereon?" (GA 97: 64). At a time when other prominent German intellectuals such as Jaspers, Thomas Mann, and Friedrich Meinecke were calling for the reintroduction of humanist values back into German culture as a way to confront the catastrophe, Heidegger will respond by offering a brutal critique of such clichés in his "Letter on Humanism" (PM: 239–276/ GA 9: 313–364).[17] Moreover, he will subtly offer a critique of Nuremberg justice by writing "The Verdict (*Spruch*) of Anaximander" in fall of 1946 as the trials come to a close.[18] Both of these essays, however, are measured and restrained. In his *Black Notebooks*, Heidegger removes his gloves as it were, and goes on the offensive. Again, in response to Allied nostrums and sanctimony, he admonishes the Germans not to let themselves be provoked by the Allies' impulses to act and judge. He reflects on how, "within the neglect of the world of the will to will that is supposed to be 'healed' by 'moralism' and 'humanism'—through moral preachers who, [the Allies] out of their own mania for revenge at the same time allow the greatest, most insane abominations that contribute to the devastation of a *Volk*" (GA 97: 122).

Yet, Heidegger warns, if the Germans are to come into their proper *Geschick* or destinal dispensation, then they can never achieve this "through social and moral rules" (GA 97: 201). Nor will they be able to turn to the traditional panaceas provided by morality or politics since "war's disaster can never be explained in a moral or political way" (GA 97: 44). For Heidegger, the dangers to self-reflection and the path to national identity not only come from foreign intervention. As Heidegger notes, even within German philosophy itself, the danger of self-forgetfulness persists in the work of those who, like Jaspers, wished to build upon the foundations of Judeo-Christian moral thinking and a Christianized understanding of Greek tradition. As Jaspers noted in an essay from 1945:

> We need to win back our Western footing in the Bible and in antiquity for our entire population. Here lies the origin and measure for our whole lives; here too lies the starting point for a transformed appropriation of this legacy.
>
> What matters most in all of this is the awakening of self-responsibility in the individual.[19]

Of course, Heidegger would adamantly reject Jaspers's path of German self-reflection in the wake of the war's disaster. For him, the Christian element of "humanist" responsibility was more the problem than the solution. It was precisely in this Christian form of morality that Heidegger identified the source of the devastation that lay everywhere around Germany, the one imposed by Allied justice. In his dialogue "An Evening Conversation," Heidegger addressed "the devastation (*Verwüstung*) that covers the earth of our homeland" and came to understand it as belonging less to morality, than to the centuries-long development within the history of beyng that he called *Seinsverlassenheit* ("the abandonment of being") (GA 77: 213). For Heidegger, this is something that belongs to the very uncanniness of being rather than to the merely subjective incursions of human rapacity. Hence, no mere moral reflection could suffice "to become familiar with devastation as an appropriating event that prevails outside of guilt and atonement" (CPC: 140/GA 77: 216). Much as with his notorious comments about Jews in the postwar *Black*

Notebooks, Heidegger will underline the metaphysical devastation of Christianity as that which, like the Jewish tradition from which it sprang, signifies "the principle of destruction" (GA 97: 20). Precisely in the context of the French postwar *épuration* of universities, courts, government, and other administrative structures, Heidegger unmasks the Allied push for justice as a crudely disguised form of lust for revenge. In the wake of so much destruction and chaos, Heidegger writes in his private notebooks:

> What is surprising is that the greatest shocks and the enormity of suffering and sorrow call forth nothing essential; they merely augment the flight into going along with what is left over in the midst of that which remains. . . . Or one saves oneself through moralizing and contents oneself with petty longing for revenge. (GA 97: 418)

But there was also a backlash to the Allied victory among the German people. In the wake of all the destruction and the moral outrage directed against them by foreign critics, many Germans started to consider that *they* were the genuine victims of the just-completed war. Karl Jaspers too demanded that Germans "Never Forget," and yet he realized that the task of re-educating the German people would take time. For Jaspers, the Germans must not, as some crude form of "payback," be themselves exterminated for their crimes. On the contrary, they should be re-educated to "recognize human rights" and go through a process of "historical self-reflection."[20] As Jasper puts it, "In historical self reflection we must make present the ground of the millennium from which we live." This means recovering the world tradition of Judeo-Christian morality so that "the four million Germans . . . and four million [sic] Jews" will not have died in vain.

Jaspers responds that any attempt to blame "the Germans" as a collective group suffers from the same kind of typological characterization that the Nazis applied to Jews. As he writes: "This is a form of thought that, as a medium of hatred, is directed at other peoples and groups."[21] For Jaspers, the right direction for Germany was to acknowledge the reprehensible actions of the Third Reich, give voice to the dangers of the German "nation-state" and "to awaken the self-responsibility of the individual." The task of the German future remained clear: to embrace the values of the West's rational-ethical tradition of democratic freedom and individual responsibility. Part of this re-education involved affirming that the path toward German purification (*Reinigung*) lay in resuscitation of Christian-humanist values in the service of freedom and scientific progress. But Heidegger was repulsed by this vision of Germany and the West.

While many of his contemporaries spoke of 1945 as the "Hour Zero" (*Stunde Null*) that would offer a clean break with Germany's Nazi past, Heidegger went a different direction. Unlike those who seized the opportunity of postwar chaos and destruction as a way to completely clear the landscape of Germany's past so as to have a new starting point, Heidegger wished to offer something vastly different—a form of Hölderlinian *Andenken* on the genuine meaning of *Heimat* as journey into the foreign. And yet, as ever for Heidegger, the situation is decidedly complex. For him, the opposition that Jaspers draws between morally corrupt violence and morally committed humanism seems deeply suspect. As Heidegger had observed already in 1940, "The imperialistic-warlike and the humanist-pacifistic ways of thinking are only 'convictions' that belong to each other . . . because the ways of thinking merely represent off-shoots of 'metaphysics'" (GA 96: 133). Where the Allies seek to draw moral distinctions within war and assign guilt to Germans by forcing them to fill out the administrative "Questionnaire" about Nazi activities, Heidegger rejects such thinking as yet another "off-shoot" of the revenge motif he finds in Judeo-Christian morality.[22] We find the same deeply problematic logic in Heidegger's response to the Germans' own situation in 1945–1946.

Confronted with the competing moral-economic-political-institutional demands of their situation that affected every aspect of German factical existence, many Germans opted to enact a *Kahlschlag* mentality in regard to the Nazi past by making a clean break. As we saw, the term *Kahlschlag* comes from the forestry practice of "clear-cutting trees" and leaving behind a spare, barren landscape that, while impoverished, removes any traces of encumbrance that could prevent new growth. During this postwar era the German author Wolfgang Weyrauch coined the term to denote an attempt to clear the rubble (*Trümmer*) from the bombings and get on with the work of purgation and removal.[23] And yet despite these German efforts to put the past behind them, the Allied trials at Nuremberg and the daily broadcasts on German radio that lasted from October 1945 through October 1946 prevented that from happening.[24] Heidegger's reaction was deeply ambivalent. On the one hand, he too wished to draw a line between his Nazi past and his postwar future. His responses to the Freiburg de-Nazification commission make that clear (GA 16: 367–369, 372–394, 397–404, 409–415, 421–422). After confronting these public accusations against him, he retreated into silence—at least publicly. In the *Black Notebooks* we see him challenging the Allies' imposition of a victor's justice: "The fate of wars can never be explained in moral-political terms; all perspectives of blame and exculpation don't fit the situation" (GA 97: 44). Heidegger goes on to claim, "We should also know that the confrontation between 'democracy' and its counterpart, fascism, is never an essential one because it remains within the political and fails to recognize that metaphysics and its essential dominion is still to be decided." Heidegger's insights here cannot simply be reduced to political expediency or more self-justification of his own behavior during the Third Reich. They reflect, rather, his longstanding critique of Western metaphysics from the perspective of the history of beyng, within which both the Allies and the Nazis are complicit in the unfolding of a pervasive machination that he will later address in a more neutral way in the Bremen lectures. Nonetheless, Heidegger's stance does serve to absolve him of any responsibility for his support of the Hitler regime. He writes to Jaspers in 1948 that he "simply felt ashamed" and felt "painful" about his relations with Jaspers from 1935 to 1945 (HJB: 196–197). At the same time he also offers the weakest of excuses, claiming that he was so caught up in his charge as rector, that he "did not look beyond the university and did not notice what was actually happening" (HJB: 200).

In the *Black Notebooks* Heidegger removes his gloves, as it were, and attacks the Allies relentlessly. The bile, rancor, and bitterness of having to endure a "foreign" occupation of his homeland and to be subject to "foreign" administrative justice can be found in his private remarks (e.g., GA 97: 20, 50, 64, 82–85, 117, 134–135, 146, 250, 258). Heidegger's fear is that the Allied efforts of "reconstruction" are motivated by the "old spirit of revenge" whose task remains "the spiritual-historical extinguishing of the Germans" (GA 97: 444). By pointing so determinedly at the scandal of German guilt, the Allies attempt to deflect attention away from their own acts of atomic destruction. With deep hyperbole Heidegger notes, "more harrowing than the heat-wave of the atomic bomb is the 'spirit' in the form of world-journalism" (GA 97: 154). "The atomic bomb destroys through extinguishment . . . world-journalism by constructing the mere appearance of being (*Schein von Sein*) on the spurious ground of unconditioned rootlessness." He goes so far as to compare the Allied use of the Atom bomb on Japan with their administrative efforts in a postwar German reconstruction:

> Today with curiosity one clutches at the analytic and journalistic reduction of the atom bomb phenomenon to pulp . . . one overlooks that from the same origin that this instrumentality springs there is, to be sure, a more widely unseen machinery of death launched on the Germans—with this difference. Instead of being eradicated in an instant, the poverty and pain are given in doses that are inconspicuous and furtive, veiled over with Christian clichés and democratic tirades. The contrivance of this killing-machinery, whose functionaries remain anonymous, is not one degree less than the technical reason that was expanded on the construction of the atom bomb. (GA 97: 15)

Throughout this difficult period Heidegger refrains from a genuine *Auseinandersetzung* either with his own political commitments or with recent German history. Instead what predominates is a posture of denial, avoidance, and shifting blame to others without accepting any real responsibility in either a personal or national sense. The time is long past when we can simply ignore this wholescale refusal to enter into a genuinely philosophical confrontation with his own and his nation's National Socialist past. Reading the bitter entries in the *Black Notebooks* we can see how Heidegger's public stance of "silence" on the Shoah was a self-conscious, strategic decision to avoid having to endure the brutal professional criticism he knew would undoubtedly follow.

But again, it would be a mistake to simply read Heidegger's works from this period as truculent rejoinders to the Allied takeover of German life. To be sure, Heidegger was bitter about the need to confront his accusers—both from the Freiburg faculty and the French military authorities. And yet Heidegger's impulse to situate the events of 1945–1946 within the history of beyng and not simply European "political" history was undoubtedly sincere. It is against this background that we need to understand Heidegger's remarks on Europe—"'Europe' (what is that? Now that America and Russia, in the same way as Japan, are 'European')" (GA 97: 150). Heidegger understands the events of the war and of the peace as tied up in what he terms a "world-destiny" (*Weltgeschick*) whereby the various national powers "do not make this destiny, they only fulfill it." What will be necessary is a kind of thinking (*Denken*) that nourishes itself through commemoration and/as remembrance (*Andenken*). As Heidegger puts it: "In thinking there waits the dwelling in destiny. Thinking founds, commemoratively, the light of what once was" (GA 97: 153). It is through *Andenken* that the oblivion of being brought on by the war can be confronted. It is in Germany, Heidegger contends, that "the long time of commemorative thinking" can come to pass since it is in this "evening of time" that the Germans' vocation is "to be the shepherds of the West" (GA 97: 51).

At the crossroads of his own personal Gethsemane and the historical-ontological collapse of the West, Heidegger will respond by turning to Hölderlin as the poet capable of saving the West by helping the Germans to reclaim their identity at the center of Western self-reflection. The dialogue that Heidegger begins to compose in 1946—"Das abendländische Gespräch"—will be written as a response to this double crisis of personal and national persecution. As the Nuremberg verdicts are announced in October, condemning thirteen German defendants for "crimes against humanity," Heidegger will challenge the very logic of Christian moral judgment and legal accountability based on "personal responsibility." He will do this by offering his own "metapolitical" account of nonjudicial justice, thought through the Greek notion of *dike* and will put forward a notion of "Western responsibility" that emerges in conversation with Hölderlin's vision of a "vaterländische Umkehr," or "national reversal."[25] In both his public and private writings, Heidegger will propose a forceful reading of *Geschick*—though not as predetermined "destiny" but as the sending of beyng—that will invert the moral categories of *Täter* and *Opfer* (perpetrators and victims) that defined the proceedings at Nuremberg. Moreover, in "The Western Conversation" he will rethink the destiny of *Geschick* in terms of a renewal of German identity that revitalizes his own notion of "a secret Germany" bequeathed to the Germans by Hölderlin (via Hellingrath). It is in terms of this singular and exceptional German vocation to save the West that Heidegger will position all the quotidian happenings of Allied triumph and dominion. In an exemplary sense, it is this condition that animates Heidegger's own understanding of the *Kahlschlag* as harboring a deeper and richer meaning, one whereby Germany's palpable economic poverty is grasped in an essential way as a "poverty" of richness that releases poverty to its ownmost need of overcoming material need and rendering Germany rich enough to embrace the historical destiny assigned to it. Here, in a historical configuration where the perpetrators become the victims and the defeated become the victors, the Germans come into their "Western responsibility" through their reflection on the concealed power of the first Greek beginning (GA 16: 378, 398, 414, 452). But what is this Western responsibility in Heidegger's sense? And how might it play into a new form of German renewal? For Heidegger, this question brings forth a reflection on the first Greek beginning, the originary force that has been forgotten and concealed through the European project of securing dominion over the earth through technological will to will. Rethought according to genuine accountability for the sense of Western destiny, the vocation of the Germans becomes clear. Now, the German defeat signals less a military or political disaster than an opportunity for the German *Volk* to come into its proper vocation. Such a vocation means that the Germans understand themselves as the *Volk* chosen to save the West—which means fighting off the noxious influence of foreign ideas and foreign domination. As Heidegger puts it in his notes:

> We are the *Volk* of poets and thinkers. Yet we are this *Volk* first of all in the vocation of a destinal dispensation that remains concealed. (GA 73: 862)

Yet Heidegger steadfastly maintains that non-Germans cannot grasp this essential identity of the German *Volk* as the *Volk* of poets and thinkers:

> Not knowing what they are saying, foreigners have only skimmed over the surface of the historical-Western (*abendländisch*) essence of the Germans.
> This slavish submission to the foreign—i.e., the modern industrial-economic-national-cultural state [leads the German to] an exclusion of the possibility of seeking and finding their essence. (GA 73: 862)

Indeed, Heidegger claims, as they confront the epochal devastation of the modern world, the Germans experience "a falling away from their essence." They remain "un-free—alienated from what is their own (*das*

Eigene)" and in this "falling away they are not able to remember their Western vocation (*abendländische Bestimmung*)" (GA 73: 863). What the Germans will need to counter this forgetfulness consists in a form of Hölderlinian *Andenken*.

Coming to terms with German national identity at a time when the very future of the German nation lay in Allied hands proved to be one of the most essential themes in Heidegger's work of the postwar epoch. And, as ever, when he reflected on what it meant to be German, Heidegger turned to the work of Hölderlin, who he continued to identify as the poet "of" the Germans—namely, that poet who not only sprung from German stock, but whose poetic vocation was to poetize the vocation of Germanity. In the *Black Notebooks*, Heidegger lays out in forceful terms just what such a vocation entails:

> Now one talks incessantly only of the Americans and the French, of the English and the Russians and of how we are faring with all of this and their efforts at educating us. No one thinks about how the Germans are doing, whether they still and for once are at home in themselves, whether they know at all who they truly are, whether they are able to think and . . . to flourish in the truth of their essence, whose truth is: to be shepherds in the West (*Abendland*)—because evening (*Abend*) is the time and its land is the space in whose time-space the abode of truth grounds itself, from which one day historical humanity and the destiny of the gods—both re-turning into beyng (appropriating event) [*beide rück-kehrend ins Seyn* (*Ereignis*)]—find their essence: the festival of beyng itself, singular and simple: to be pliant and to rest in the peace of the festival. (GA 97: 51)

It is this Hölderlinian vision of the gods' return to earth after the long world's night of nihilistic devastation and homelessness that animates Heidegger's postwar hopes of helping the Germans (despite themselves and their Allied overlords) to come into their sense of the proper (*das Eigene*). But as ever with Heidegger's "Hölderlin," the relation to the proper and one's own involves a kind of journeying fraught with difficulty and impediments. The Allied occupation offers only the proximate occlusion to a German homecoming. Even if the Allies were suddenly gone, the work of German self-reflection would still need to proceed in earnest. Hence, in a curious and inverted sense, Heidegger comes to experience his own persecution, as well as the persecution of the German *Volk* at Nuremberg, as a positive provocation to spur the *Volk* to self-reflection. As Heidegger put it: "Becoming poor does not mean losing one's possessions and falling victim to privatization; becoming poor is the essence of learning what is authentic poverty" (GA 73: 710–711). For the Germans to experience an authentic homecoming means for them to enter into the positive sense of absence—of detaching themselves from the metaphysics of subjective possession and attuning themselves to the freeing momentum of need, lack, poverty, and deprivation.[26] Going back to his earlier Hölderlin lecture courses from World War II (GA 52: 112–113, 188–193; GA 53: 155–166, 176–178), Heidegger had offered a reading of *Geist* as not being at home in the beginning. In the pivotal years of German collapse—with cities in ruin, railways disjointed, supply networks destroyed, storehouses empty, imports cut off, families separated, wholescale populations on the move and in disarray, famine spreading, the brutal cold of winter upending domestic security—the very figure of homelessness became a synecdoche for the brutal effects of the war. For Heidegger, "homelessness," like poverty, was something whose authentic sense lay in "das Geistige"—understood as a relation to beyng that was neither initiated nor directed by the human being. It is precisely in this sense that Heidegger speaks of what he had earlier termed the "gift of impoverishment" since without it the human being remains unmindful of its essential relation to being (GA 69: 111). In such a relation, beyng is not something that stands "over against" the human being; nor is the human being "encompassed by" beyng (GA 97: 292). Rather, "the human being 'is' beyng, the one who properly occurs (*ereignet*) in its guardianship (*Wahrnis*) of beyng." Within Heidegger's thinking, then, poverty, like homelessness, becomes a trope for understanding the Second World War as part of a planetary-technical process of history in which beyng remains unthought and can only emerge in nihilistic form as a metaphysical representation as a being. That is, beyng withdraws into absence as the self-evident effects of this withdrawal take the form of destruction, devastation, homelessness, and poverty. That such homelessness prevails is evident to everyone in Europe. And yet the authentic sense of such homelessness remains concealed to all but a few, Heidegger maintains. In a draft titled "Homelessness-Homeland-Dwelling," Heidegger explains:

Homelessness

We think of it first of all, or even exclusively, in its relation to human beings. . . . The destruction of residences, the devastation of lands, expulsion and resettlement give rise to a homelessness that is above all a rootlessness. The mass of homeless humans are, however, the given "material" for new kinds of arrangements designed by the will. Everything that merely issues forth from this kind of arrangement can never form a homeland because arranging—and everything having to do with the will is arranging—can never think anything at all like a homeland. Homeland is not something that is made by human beings. Homeland is nothing that first comes from humans, nor is it only related to humans as the site of lodging, settlement, and subsistence.

The homeland is the opening of ap-propriation (*Er-eignung*) of the earth as the locale of the preparation of dwelling, a preparation that guards the arrival of beyng (*die Ankunft des Seyns wahrt*), from whose true-ness (*Wahr-heit*) gods and humans first receive the region of their encounter.

Homeland is, as this happening of appropriation, the destinal dispensation of beyng (*als diese Ereignung das Geschick des Seyns*).

Homeland is the historical locale of the truth of beyng, summoned and received by the earth, rooted in it and in it concealed.

The essence of the homeland springs forth from the true-ness of beyng that needs the human being (*das den Menschen braucht*) and for this reason, enregioning (*vergegnend*) homeland and earth, brings the essence of the human into ownership (*vereignet*) of its long, steadfast inabidingness (*Inständigkeit*).

Out of this essence of the homeland, that needs to be thought from beyng, we can first experience homelessness as the destinal dispensation of beyng that belongs to the West (*als Seynsgeschick des Abendlandes*). (GA 73: 755–756)

For Heidegger, such homelessness comes forth as something assigned by beyng, and it is "out of this beyng-historical homelessness that the will to will draws its forces, impulses, and domains, as well as its schemes and arrangements and regulations." Moreover, as Heidegger puts it, "the place of this homelessness is the modern city," supplied with its technical contrivances that render its inhabitants unmindful of all its various kinds of machination—including the Allied plan of re-education. Caught in this urban wasteland, "at home in this homelessness," the Germans remain prisoners of the Allied apparatus of postwar reforms, modeled on American urban culture, that "now urge the Germans forward even against themselves" (GA 97: 84).[27] As Heidegger stresses in the *Black Notebooks*: "The Germans now stand in the shadow of a treachery urged on them to betray their own essence." In these notebooks Heidegger writes often of what he terms "the betrayal of thinking" that threatens German Dasein, one that amounts to what he calls "self-extinction" (*Selbstvernichtung*) (GA 97: 83).[28] What appears on the surface as homelessness, however, masks a yet deeper homelessness of ontological provenance. What attracts notice here is how deeply Heidegger confronts this thematic of a betrayal of thinking in the notebooks from 1945–1946. Among the Germans, Heidegger will single out Jaspers as the philosopher whose work on "Philosophische Logik" carries out its own version of such a betrayal even as it undermines any effort at genuine thinking (GA 97: 353, 61). Heidegger will also make a reference to Ernst Krieck, the former NS rector, as a "pseudo-philosopher," whose work represents a "betrayal of thinking" (GA 97: 61). Nonetheless, the real betrayal of thinking for Heidegger goes beyond the miscarriages of individual thinkers to focus on the Germans' own failure to address their most urgent needs. Again, beyond the assault on his academic career by university officials or the French authorities, "the betrayal of thinking has to do much more with the historical vocation of the *Volk*" (GA 97: 83). This involves nothing less than "the surrender of everything that is originary." To counter this betrayal of thinking, Heidegger offers a biting critique of the usual "public" forms of publishing a book with the expectation of making it a public forum for influence and usefulness. Against such "clueless babble," Heidegger strives to cultivate a "stillness of thinking" attuned to "concealed beyng" (GA 97: 66).[29] This kind of thinking seeks "to prepare for beyng the opening of an arrival marked by an appropriative event"—one characterized by "neither moral appeal nor staged by a psychological paroxysm" (GA 97: 85). Rejecting both "science" and "culture," this kind of thinking could never merely take the form of contemplative introspection. Rather, as Heidegger put it, "it must occur (*sich ereignen*) as a destinal homecoming to the persistently prevailing rootedness (*Bodenständigkeit*) of the most proper homeland, one that safeguards the origin" (GA 97: 67).

Ultimately, Heidegger's postwar energies were riven by his own personal and professional crises. After recovering at Badenweiler during the spring of 1946, Heidegger vigorously turned his focus to the looming situation of Germany's future destiny apart from Allied dominion. As he considered all the havoc wrought by Allied tanks, airstrikes, and administrative despotism, Heidegger offered this brutal assessment: "the German Volk and Germany itself is a single KZ (concentration camp)" (GA 97: 100). Attributing this mode of subjugation to America's "killing machinery" forged by a "technical reason" that led to the construction of the atom bomb (GA 97: 151), such an organized, machinational imperative to conquer and subdue was not "merely the monstrous creation of the yearning for revenge;" it was, rather, part of "the destiny of beyng itself" (GA 97: 148–149). This destiny did not emerge solely out of American imperial-technological power. Its arc and trajectory lay deep in the metaphysical roots of the history of beyng. Hence, Heidegger's philosophical force would get directed to situating Germany's postwar devastation not only within the brutal politics of American "re-education" and "rehabilitation," but within the beyng-historical narrative of the West within which Europe's own destinal politics of self-extinction needed to be situated. It is this long, 2500-year history of Western thinking, with its turn away from the first Greek beginning in Plato and Aristotle through the world's night of post-Cartesian instrumental rationality, that comes to occupy Heidegger's philosophical attention here. It is within this context that Heidegger in 1946 can write: "The destruction of Europe, no matter how it may proceed, whether with or without Russia, is the work of the Americans. 'Hitler' is merely the pretext. Yet, taken as a whole, the Americans are Europeans. In this way Europe destroys itself. This corresponds to the subjectivity that in the consummation of modernity exists metaphysically" (GA 97: 230). Left to this metaphysical impasse, Heidegger pursues "an other kind of questioning, one that awakens an other kind of mindful paying heed to beyng."

Confronted with this long history of metaphysical forgetfulness, Heidegger offers a beyng-historical narrative of the West that situates the American occupation of Germany within a deep-rooted historical trajectory that emerges in antiquity and whose traces can be discerned in the political events of 1946. From within this narrative, the Allied revenge exacted at Nuremberg follows the centuries-long history of *Seinsvergessenheit* that pervades the Western tradition. This long history will have been marked by tensions that Heidegger identifies as shaping the very core of Western identity, tensions between early Greek philosophy and Judeo-Christian monotheism, between East and West, between Europe and the Occident, between American-Russian technics and German poetic thinking, between the devastation and homelessness wrought by Allied administrators and the promise of homecoming held forth by "the poet *of* the Germans" (GA 39: 214, 220). For Heidegger, both the Jewish and Christian forms of monotheism serve to construct an occlusion of the West's essence, one that cuts it off from its originary commencement in pre-Socratic Greek thinking. In so doing, monotheism produces for itself, a creator-god (Jehovah) who makes himself to be the chosen God that tolerates no other gods besides himself. This God becomes the avatar of Europe's later, machinational history of dominion over *physis*, the ideal form of the new subjectivity modeled on the metaphysics of production. Following this beyng-historical understanding, Heidegger interprets this god as the forerunner of the later functionaries of machination—namely, the despotic leaders of Russian and German socialism. Hence Heidegger can write, "The modern systems of total dictatorship spring forth from Judeo-Christian monotheism" (GA 97: 438).

Within the climate of postwar guilt, recrimination, punishment, and revenge, Heidegger's analysis shifts the focus away from the immediate causes of Germany's Year Zero to the fundamental metaphysical tradition within which such collapse is even possible. Hence, Heidegger will underscore that though *destruction* (*Zerstörung*) is everywhere visible across the German landscape, what underlies this historical condition is the beyng-historical *devastation* (*Verwüstung*) that was set into place by Judeo-Christian monotheism. On this reading, destruction is understood as the material havoc produced by the technical instruments of war, while devastation will be thought as the product of modern rationality that reduces thinking to its calculable instrumental aims and applications. In this form of human intelligence, "thinking" is never allowed to flourish, since it will be harnessed to the task of utility and implementation where machinational power gets directed at planetary dominion. For Heidegger this devastation characterizes not merely recent European history in a strictly historiological sense. On the contrary, it becomes an essential part of his beyng-historical narrative of Western history going back to the turn away from the first Greek beginning. This history of beyng extends over more than two millennia and its relevance for Heidegger is to show the deep roots of instrumental thinking that go far back beyond the seventeenth-century revolution in science and technology.

Within this history of machinational destiny, Heidegger sees Judaism as playing a defining role. For Heidegger, "the question of the role of world Jewry is not a racial question, but the metaphysical one about the kind of humanity that, in an *utterly unrestrained* way, can take over the uprooting of all beings from being as its world-historical 'task'" (GA 96: 243). As part of their historical development, Jews settled in urban areas where capital, finance, trade, and commerce led them to the fluid, impermanent structures of existence that inevitably shaped their racial imperative toward machinational dominion over beings. What emerged out of this Jewish penchant for dominion was a metaphysical deracination born from the Jewish gift of instrumental control and calculative rationality. Heidegger defines this within the metaphysical tradition of the West as "the principle of destruction," one that makes the Jews unable to even begin to think an originary bond to the first Greek beginning (GA 97: 20). This kind of metaphysical or "beyng-historical" anti-Semitism gets written into Heidegger's postwar account of Germany's vocation to save the West.[30] Moreover, though it does not make its appearance in his 1946–1947 dialogue, "Das abendländische Gespräch," this beyng-historical reading of anti-Semitism looms as a defining trope for Heidegger's overall thematic of "saving the West." Given the Allied crusade at Nuremberg against German racial atrocities, Heidegger knew that he needed to adopt a kind of public/private strategy for writing about Jewish themes. In his published essays from the postwar era, he restrains from engaging the question of Jewish "self-extermination" even as he writes about it in his private notebooks (GA 97: 159, 357, 369, 409, 438). And yet despite this kind of self-censure, Heidegger's whole discussion about "Europe" and "the Occident" is defined by fiercely anti-Semitic prejudices whose origins go back to his provincial Messkirch milieu and have absolutely no *philosophical* justification. And yet they so overdetermine his understanding of European history as the instrumental march toward calculative rationality and machination that they come to play a crucial role in his beyng–historical narrative of the West.

What defines this narrative is its essential movement away from—as well as its forgetfulness of—the first Greek beginning. As Heidegger views it, the Jews represent in their essence, the very principles that undermine this early Greek beginning. These include their monotheistic theology, their commercial bond to capital, their mobile form of existence that marks them as rootless and deracinated. On this basis, Heidegger makes it all too clear that "the concealed inceptual essence of the history of the West that signifies the first Greek beginning remained outside Judaism and that means outside Christianity" (GA 97: 20). We might also add that, for Heidegger, the possibility of saving the West that dominates his thought in the 1940s lies wholly outside Judaism in its essence. This remains in part due to the Jews' own calculative relation to language as something instrumental and fluid, adaptable to the changing commercial milieu in which language is spoken. Hence, on this reading, Jews lack the deep connection between "Sprache and Heimat" (language and homeland) that animates Heidegger's whole approach to language—especially his relation to the poetry of Hölderlin, his Swabian kinsman.

III. Hölderlin, the West, and Destiny

In Heidegger's vision of Europe and of the West it is this close relation between language and homeland that shapes the very question of Western destiny. Within this 2500-year history only two languages emerge as destinally consanguineous—ancient Greek and modern German. It is this "special, inner affinity between the German language with that of the Greeks and their thought" that Heidegger singles out as essential to the recovery from modernity's nihilism (GA 16: 679). And again the Jews stand outside this "special, inner bond" precisely because of their non-autochthonous relation both to their own culture and to the deep and abiding bond that links Germans and Greeks. For Heidegger, the central figure in this whole mythic beyng-historical narrative is, of course, Hölderlin. Already in his very first lecture on the poet, Heidegger had taken up a reading marked by the essential claim that "Hölderlin is in an exceptional sense the poet—that is, the founder of German beyng" (HGR: 201/GA 39: 220). Moreover, he is this founder because of "the singular, essential point that his work . . . has grounded the beginning of an other history: that history starts with the struggle (*Kampf*) over the decision concerning the arrival or flight of the god" (HGR: 1/GA 39: 1). For Heidegger, this "god" is neither of Christian nor Hebrew origin but springs forth out of the concealed and privileged bond to the ancient Greeks, a bond he sees as essentially foreign to Jews. In his reading of Heidegger's own relationship to Jews, Philippe Lacoue-Labarthe comes to understand Heidegger's break with "the foreign" other as part of what he terms "the German schism."³¹

> Hölderlin was one of the first centers of this division, of this internal schism: the concern with the proper, the experience of the foreign, the tearing, and the return home: this is the German schism! Hölderlin was a victim of it. It is the whole of German history since the echo or the shock that was provoked by the French revolution.

Given Heidegger's dramatic cleavage of Hölderlin from the Judaic tradition, it is hardly surprising that Emmanuel Levinas would stake out a hostile position to this most German of poets. In an interview Levinas replies:

> Hölderlin lacks gravity. Perhaps this is an antipathy that arises from the fact that Heidegger makes Hölderlin more important than the Bible. For Heidegger, Hölderlin is more important than anything else. All this Germanic world that is magnified there, the gods that have fled, that is absolutely foreign to me . . . In any case, I do not look for wisdom in Hölderlin, who is foreign to me."³²

Yet Heidegger will insist on the singularly German bond to the Greeks that obtains in Hölderlin's poetic language. In the most fundamental sense, what matters for Heidegger is for the Germans to ultimately recognize "Hölderlin as the 'transition,'" and as "the poet of an other beginning" (GA 94: 248). It is in Hölderlin's work alone that Heidegger uncovers hints for a renewal of the German vocation to save the West from the depredations of Jewish mercantile planning, American technological hegemony, and Russian-Asiatic Bolshevism. Accordingly, Heidegger can announce in the crucial period of 1945–1946 that "Hölderlin's poetry is a destiny for us" (GA75: 350). In a draft, Heidegger writes:

> This is not a choice for us; *Hölderlin* is a *destiny* in our history (*ein 'Geschick' in unserer Geschichte*).
> Destiny: sent to us (*uns zugeschickt*),—as we are to it. (Essential history). We do not have a choice; we can evade

> destiny—through neglect, forgetting. Hölderlin is to-come, futural. (GA 75: 350–351)

As Heidegger grasps it, Hölderlin is in this "world-historical moment of the present epoch" ever and again, the poet "of" the Germans since it is he alone who offers them the path of/toward self-reflection. In the epoch of Year Zero and the *Kahlschlag*, Hölderlin holds out to the Germans the possibility of an authentic "homecoming,—a 'Journey Homeward' . . . To find that which is fitting (*das Schickliche*)—but how?" (GA 75: 357). For Heidegger, this can happen only if the Germans tend to their own homeland, now oppressively threatened by foreign occupation, and the brutal realities of devastation, poverty, and defeat. Here the homeland endures as an absence within the presence of Allied administrative interdiction. Yet precisely in its power as the absential, the homeland remains wedded to the origin. When Heidegger thinks the origin he thinks, of course, of Greece, following the lead of Hölderlin and Nietzsche. To connect the German *Volk* to this Greek beginning and to identify the German vocation of the saving of the West through a destinal reclaiming of that beginning's force and power becomes the preoccupation of this thinker in a destitute time. If this great Greek beginning still lives, then it is primarily in the poetic language of Hölderlin, poet of beginnings. The question for Heidegger is this: "Can the great beginning still come?" (GA 4: 176). It can, he believes, if the Germans can join together in celebrating the festival of the gods' return—but the celebration can never be a return to the Greek beginning. On the contrary, the great beginning can only come as what awaits the Germans. Heidegger then asks: "Does the West still abide?" And he answers: "It has become Europe." The question that Heidegger raises here—"to what extent *is* the West?"—comes to define the thematic structure of "The Western Conversation" (GA 73: 857–858). In his notebooks on *Event* from this same period, Heidegger writes, "The destinal dispensation of the Germans is sent in advance on the path to the West." Here "Europe" means "the essential self-forgetting of the West—the not yet once being able to think of the Land of Evening." All of this comes to signify for Heidegger "the self-extermination of Europe out of the will to will." Ultimately, what emerges here is the question about Germany's place in the West and in Europe, a question that defined Heidegger's postwar discussion about the history of beyng and of Hölderlin's relation to it and to the German vocation to save the West.

In 1946 Heidegger attempts to address the German situation of crisis by crafting a *Gespräch* between a Younger Man and an Older Man on the banks of the Ister, the site for him of Germany's hoped-for renewal. Heidegger had already lectured on "The Ister" in the summer semester of 1942, a course already discussed in chapter 3. But this postwar dialogue takes up the question of Hölderlin's river hymn within the new landscape of Allied dominion in Germany and focuses on the meaning of the Ister for such a reflection. In Heidegger's geophilosophical reading, the Ister (Danube) functions as a river that connects southern Germany to the Black Sea as it traverses the new political landscape of an American-Soviet dominated Europe. But it also harkens back to the historical sense of the river that links Hölderlin's hymnal poetizing with Pindar's epinician odes, especially the third Olympian ode (vv. 10–18) that recounts the story of Heracles's journey northward to Hesperia.[33] Here Heracles's journey north to the land of evening (*hesperas*, *Abendland*, Occident) is undertaken to secure the olive branch "brought/from the shady springs of Ister/to be the fairest memorial (*mnama*, *Andenken*) of the athletic games at Olympia," as Pindar recounts it.[34] On this reading, the Ister functions as the geographical axis of ancient Europe, uniting North and South, West and East by both bringing together its distant limits (Donaueschingen in Southwestern Germany and the Black Sea, the boundary of the Asiatic) and dividing them into regional oppositions. What comes to be at stake in this dramatic-poetic staging of the Ister as the site of an originary kinship between ancient and modern, Greek and German, Oriental and Hesperian is nothing less than a philosophical dialogue about the very meaning of the West and of Germany's place within it.

Heidegger takes up this project in his dialogue "The Western Conversation" (*Das abendländische Gespräch*) by framing it as a *Gespräch*—namely, as an originary gathering (*Ge-*) of language (*Sprache*) whereby the participants in the conversation become gathered in the event of language itself. In one of his dialogues from the winter of 1944–1945, "Agchibasin," the "Guide" (*Der Weise*—the wise one whose words "show, point, indicate" [*weisen*]) explains that "in an authentic conversation an event properly takes place wherein something comes to language" (CPC: 36–37/GA 77: 57). Understood in this way, an "authentic conversation first brings the word to language" so that here "a conversation first waits upon reaching that of which it speaks. And the speakers of a conversation can speak in this sense only if they are prepared for something to befall them in the conversation which transforms their own essence." In this way, "The Western Conversation" is less a *Gespräch* "about" the West than a conversation or dialogue that emerges "vom Abendland"—of/from the West (GA 75: 158). Here the West is not the "object" of a third-hand discussion but that which presences to us (*uns an-west*) through our *Gespräche*; it remains as "a coming whose coming remains sheltered in itself." For Heidegger, what comes to language here is the possibility of a turning within the history of the West as a movement that might bring with it a saving turn toward that which is coming. This whole discourse itself turns on the thematics of Hölderlin's figuration of a "turning of time" (*die Wende der Zeit*) that comes in *kairos* fashion. Human beings, "weak vessels that we are, can endure the gods' fullness"—as the poet tells us, but "only at times" (SPF: 102–103, 156–157). This turning of time can only come, however, of its own power. No human initiative can bring it to bear or hasten its coming. Still, the return of the gods in Hölderlin's poetic eschatology can happen only in a time of danger, for as Heidegger often noted, "where danger is, there also grows that which saves" (SPF: 230–231; GA 7: 29; GA 79: 72). The time of postwar German occupation by the Allies presents just such a time of danger; however, as Heidegger notes:

> Yet first the human being must experience the default of the god in a pure way without saving itself through evasion or temporary assistance, but also without making this god-lessness into an opinion or point of view instead of recognizing in it a destiny . . . that belongs to beyng under whose pre-and ab-sencing, the gods still stand and that essentially prevails over them (*das 'über' ihnen west*). (GA 75: 39)

In his pentecostal elegy "Bread and Wine," Hölderlin had prefigured this time of the gods' coming in terms of a day-night-day configuration of human history. Within this poetic theology, the originary "day" signifies the unity of gods and mortals in the festive time of the *hieros gamos*, the marriage ceremony that brings them together. Following the departure of the god(s) from the earth—*deus absconditus*—there reigns the dark night of godlessness and destitution. Yet within this "world night," amidst the time of mourning the gods' absence, there nonetheless appears a pentecostal flame of hope and salvation that announces a later coming of the god(s). "Bread and Wine"—written in 1800, precisely at the turn of a century, the very "turning of time" prefigured in the Christian *parousia*—announces just such a hope for the new day to dawn. This time awaits the day of the gods' coming, the day for mortals to reclaim the earth as their proper dwelling place. Such a coming day can come for the poet, however, only if he has "fully experienced, that old, steadfast word of fate that a new bliss rises in the heart, when it endures and suffers through the midnight of grief, and that, like the nightingale's song in the darkness, the world's song of life first divinely sounds for us in profound suffering" (H: 211/DKV II: 172). Hence, for Hölderlin,

> . . . the gods, who once were
> Here and shall come again when the time is right . . . (DKV
> I: 290)

stand at a turning point in history: the Hesperian night of godlessness through which mortals must come if they are to greet the new day. The opening verse of "The Ister"—"Now come, fire!"—alludes to this new day, the "right time" or *kairos* moment of the gods' return.

In "The Western Conversation," Heidegger will draw heavily upon this Hölderlinian configuration of history as a salvific scheme of day-night-day transformation, seizing upon the image of "das Abendland"—the land of evening, the West, the Occident—as the name for an axial turning within history. In rethinking the meaning of the West—precisely at the moment of one of the greatest upheavals within Western history (World War II)—Heidegger again turns to Hölderlin, whose own vision of the Hellas–Hesperia relation was expressed in his river hymn, "The Ister." For Hölderlin, Western history can best be understood as a "shift from the Greek to the Hesperian" where Hesperia refers to the time of vespers, the time of evening (L. *vespera*, Gk. *hesperos*) (E&L: 327/DKV II: 915). The Indo-European root *wespero* likewise hints at this etymological link to "West" and "Western," the site of "the evening star." If, for Hölderlin, Greek culture represented the dawn or ascent of Western history, then the modern epoch of godlessness can best be expressed in the Hesperian realm of evening, dusk, and recession. In 1945, Heidegger plays on both the sidereal and the eschatological meaning of the German term *Abendland* to refer to the historical condition of the West as "going under" (*Untergang*) or "declining" at evening. To grasp his own historical situation of decline, Heidegger configures it in terms borrowed from two of Hölderlin's most well-known hymns, "Patmos" and "Bread and

Wine." Each of these poems speaks of the sacred mourning of mortals when "the Father" turned his face away from them (DKV I: 290) and when in "Patmos" the poet poignantly notes:

> Yet they were mourning, now that
> Evening had come (*Es Abend worden*). (SPF: 234–235)

Confronting this loss, entering into its most profound sense of abandonment, destitution, default, and poverty, Heidegger reframes Hölderlin's poetics of sacred mourning in terms of a possible homecoming that needs to take place if the Germans are to find their proper vocation within the history of the West, the land of evening.

It is this situation of default that spurs Heidegger's 1946 essay "What Are Poets For?," where he writes:

> The appearance and sacrificial death of Christ, for the historical experience of Hölderlin, mean that the end of the days of the gods is drawing near. Evening is upon us . . . The evening of the world's time draws itself close to its night. The world's night extends its darkness. The world-epoch is defined by the remaining away of God, by "the default of God" . . . Not only have the gods and God fled, but the gleam of godhood within world history has been extinguished. The time of the world's night is the destitute time, because it is becoming ever more destitute. The time has already become so destitute that it is no longer able to mark the default of God as default. (PLT: 91/GA 5: 269)

In this time of evening marked by the default and departure of the gods, Heidegger performs a dialogue on the very sense and meaning of the West, a dialogue between two figures—"the Younger Man" and "the Older Man"—that, drawing on the poet's conviction of a special role within that history for the Germans, exhumes Norbert von Hellingrath's vision of "a secret Germany" from out of the wreckage and ruins of the Second World War. If the time of evening has descended upon the Fatherland, threatening it with the dark night of nihilism, Heidegger holds forth a different prospect for the Germans.

Writing after the war to his old NS colleague Rudolf Stadelmann, Heidegger tells him that the receipt of his letter from Tübingen reminds him of "the voice of the poet from his tower on the native river of the homeland," the Neckar (GA 16: 370–371).³⁵ Referencing the postwar chaos, Heidegger tells Stadelmann, "everyone is now thinking of decline (*Untergang*). But we Germans cannot go under (*untergehen*) because we still have not yet arisen (*aufgegangen*) and must first endure through the night." In two other texts from the same period, Heidegger takes up the whole metaphysics of the sun's decline and ascent as a way of situating "the peoples of the Occident" and the West itself (GA 73: 81; GA 97: 143). In the *Black Notebooks* he draws on this field of metaphor to situate Europe in its relation to the West:

> Europe *is* already in decline (*ist schon untergegangen*)—i.e., it has already passed over to (*übergegangen*) America and Russia. In these "new" worlds, however, the old one is, in the course of the coming centuries, being brought to its end. Here there is no beginning, but only the broadest and flattest outflow. But "Europe" is not the West. The West recedes into twilight and for a long time fades away in the world's night. But it does not go under (*es geht nicht unter*) because it cannot decline (*untergehen*), since it has still not yet arisen (*aufgegangen*). (GA 97: 143)

In a second letter to Stadelmann that discusses the possibility of Heidegger's changing universities from Freiburg to Tübingen, the philosopher tells his fellow Swabian:

> I am convinced that the Western spirit will awaken from out of our Swabian land. (GA 16: 396)

In several private entries written in his notebooks during the same period, Heidegger positions his own homeland Swabia at the center of the longed-for turn away from metaphysics. And in the letter to Stadelmann he confesses that:

> For the last half-year I spent time in the land of my birth [Swabia], at times in the closest proximity to the ancestral house of my forefathers in the upper Danube Valley, downstream from Burg Wildenstein. Such nearness (*Nähe*) has proven stimulating. My thinking has become far more than

mere interpretation [of Hölderlin]. It has become a genuine conversation with the poet, whose bodily proximity is now an element of my thinking. (GA 16: 370)

The effect of this "bodily proximity" to Hölderlin in 1945–1946 was to lead Heidegger to a monumental form of self-mythologizing that positions the thinker in a direct line of crucial dates within German intellectual-cultural history, a relation that he characterizes as "uncanny":

The play and uncanniness of historiological dates in the foreground of abyssal German history:

1806 Hölderlin departs and a German Confederation begins.

1813 The swell of the Germans reaches its height and Richard Wagner is born.

1843 Hölderlin departs the "world" and a year later Nietzsche comes into it.

1870/76 The founding years of the Second German Reich and the appearance of Nietzsche's *Untimely Meditations*.

1883 Zarathustra, Part One is published and Richard Wagner dies.

1888 (Late December): Nietzsche's "euphoria" before his breakdown and——

September 26, 1889 [Heidegger's birth] (GA 94: 523)

It would be all too easy to characterize Heidegger's preoccupation with such abyssal history as flagrantly self-serving and vainglorious. Indeed, his comments about "the long path of the Messkirch child of a sexton" or the etymology he provides of his own name, "Heid-egger" from the *Black Notebooks* do display the swagger of a self-preoccupied strutter (GA 97: 33, 62). And yet there is something much deeper here for Heidegger, something that he finds essential for understanding the possibility of renewing Hellingrath's promise of a "secret Germany."

In several letters to his brother Fritz, Heidegger explains his deep commitment to Swabia and to his belief that the rebirth of Germany—and of the West—is intimately bound up with a return to the hidden spirit of Swabian creativity. Yet this love of the homeland comes at a price for Heidegger. Inevitably, this homeland reverie finds little place for Germany's rich, urban culture or the world of the Berlin salon. Moreover, what lies concealed in this coded language is a hostility to Jews, whose rootlessness could never find a home on Swabian soil. Hence, it is hardly surprising to find Heidegger railing against the postwar crusade to rename the streets of Messkirch in accordance with the new Allied campaign of "re-education." He comments to Fritz: "I find the changing of street signs . . . and a 'Heinrich Heine Street' wholly uncalled for, because it is senseless in Messkirch" (HAS: 127–128).[36] But his mood improves markedly in a letter to Elfride where he writes that amidst all the postwar "chaos it is nice to think that my Hölderlin manuscripts may rest together near the rocky cliffs of the Danube River" (MLS: 237). Preserving these manuscripts in the last days of war was only part of Heidegger's project. He tells his brother, "the encounter with Hölderlin has become an event for me so that I now first dare, with all modesty, to speak with him in conversation (*Gespräch*). This encounter, that has become a homeland for me, is the most priceless and it includes all love, fraternity, and friendship. The homeland remains, of course, Fritz; it is through us first newly grounded. What was for a long time left unguarded is only now coming into its own daylight" (HAS: 125). He then ends his letter by citing the famous line from Hölderlin's hymn "Mnemosyne":

. . . Long is
The time, but what is true
Comes to pass.

Lang ist
Die Zeit, es ereignet sich aber
Das Wahre. (DKV I: 1032)

Anyone who reads the letters of Heidegger to his brother Fritz cannot help but notice this persistent, unfaltering emphasis on the meaning of homeland and native ground for the salvation of Germany—and for the West. Bound up with this abiding reflection on homeland, of course, is the enduring conversation with Hölderlin. Amidst all the furor of the postwar changes—from Allied propaganda and administrative dominion to Germany's own self-flagellation about "the war's events"—Heidegger poses a dramatic question: "amidst such world-catastrophes that are now coming to pass (*sich ereignen*), what do we know of the mystery of history (*das Geheimnis der Geschichte*)?" (HAS: 128). During this chaotic period of national disruption, Heidegger counsels his brother to avoid getting seduced by rumor, idle chatter, propaganda, or the all too frequent "daily news bulletins" that besiege German public consciousness without surcease. What preoccupies Heidegger most through all of this disorder is "the historical confrontation" between Europe and the West. As he views it, this is tied to "the concealed destiny" that awaits the Germans as a pathway out of the current time of destitution. This pathway cannot emerge if the Germans wallow in the present and occupy themselves with the workaday situation of postwar rehabilitation and reconstruction. What is needed is, rather, a leap or "Sprung" out of the present historiologically calculated time of the Western nations into "the unique possibilities of Western history." This leap cannot succeed as a simple leap out of the present and "into" the future, however. It must, rather, be "silently unfolded toward its transitionality and possible force of preparing a transition" (GA 95: 141). In an age of machinational calculation where essential beyng has been forgotten and rendered palpable only by way of beings, this preparation can happen only by attuning ourselves to the concealed power of the first beginning. As Heidegger put it in one of his earliest lecture courses from the war, "Only that which begins and is of inceptual force is futural; what is of the present is always already past" (GA 51: 93). And it is to this conversation with the first Greek beginning—via a meditation on the poetry of Hölderlin—that Heidegger turns in the years 1946–1948 in his dialogue "The Western Conversation."

5

Heidegger in Dialogue with Hölderlin

"The Western Conversation"

> We know only this much: when Hölderlin speaks of history, he always has the history of the West in mind.
>
> —Martin Heidegger, *Zum Ereignis-Denken*[1]

> The destiny of the Germans is the West.
>
> —Martin Heidegger, *Zum Ereignis-Denken*[2]

I. Heidegger's "Conversation" with Hölderlin

In his very first lecture course on Hölderlin from WS 1934–1935, Heidegger describes his relationship to the poet as a form of *Gespräch*—a "conversation," one that goes far beyond mere chatter, prattle, or exchange of views to extend to the very heart of language as what Heidegger calls an "essential event" (*wesentliches Ereignis*) (EHD: 57/GA 4: 39). In the *Gespräch* what properly occurs is not a mere "dia-logue" (understood as an interlocution where ideas are discussed), but an attuning to language's claim upon us—a listening to the claim exerted upon us by the gods. Such listening happens not merely as a "hearing" (*hören*) that enables the possibility of acoustic comprehension. Rather, it properly occurs as a "hearkening" (*horchen*) to a *Grundton* that lays emphasis upon that which sounds in the essential event of language.

It is within language, Heidegger tells us, that the human being comes to itself in its most original relation to beyng. "Our beyng occurs in conversation," Heidegger declares; "in the conversation, language occurs, and this occurrence is properly its beyng" (HGR: 63–64/GA 39: 69–70). Moreover, "the event of language is the commencement and ground of the properly historical time of human beings," a commencement that begins in conversation. In what follows, I want to trace some of these possible pathways of conversation in Heidegger's postwar piece "The Western Conversation" which, I believe, offers a new and different way of approaching the question of *Gespräch*—but now in a different style and register than in Heidegger's earlier treatises, lecture courses, essays, notebook entries, and academic writings. By looking at how *Gespräch* functions within "The Western Conversation," I hope to offer a reading of Heidegger's conversation with Hölderlin, one that endures throughout his life. But I also want to look at how the historical-cultural circumstances of "The Western Conversation's" composition powerfully shape the way the conversation unfolds. In the summer of 1945, just months after the Nazi surrender to Allied forces on the Western front, Heidegger writes to his brother Fritz about the future of what he terms "Western spirit" (HAS: 129): "It is becoming ever clearer to me that our homeland—the core of this Southwestern part of Germany—will be the historical birthplace of Western spirit (*des abendländischen Geistes*)" (HAS: 129–130). It is in this "spiritually-fulfilled and, at the same time, earthbound land of beauty," Heidegger insists, that the future of the West lies. Yet Heidegger is no fool. He sees wreckage everywhere around him and knows that the military defeat will weigh heavily upon the German people for a very long time. Still, amidst all of the devastation and ruin, Heidegger sees a possible path of hope and redemption. What invites notice here is how Heidegger approaches the theme that has preoccupied him since the early 1930s—"the salvation or decline of Europe and of Western culture [*abendländischen Kultur*]" (HAS: 22). In a letter to Fritz composed two days after the start of World War II, Heidegger writes that "the future of Western history is so dark as never before" (HAS: 54). By January 1943, as the battle of Stalingrad rages and the fate of a German victory hangs in the balance, Heidegger warns that what is decisive is "to see the great threat that Bolshevism and Americanism are uniting themselves into a single essential form so as to destroy Germanity itself and remove it from its place as the center of the West" (HAS: 86). As the war ends, and the prospects for a German future darken, Heidegger seizes upon the present historical situation to rethink his whole approach to the question of Germany's future role as "the center of the West." If earlier, during the time of Stalingrad, Heidegger believed that a German victory was essential to the saving of the West, now, after experiencing the bitterness of defeat, he seizes upon a new trope—the thematics of loss, destitution, and poverty. Only those who can experience the authentic affliction of poverty, Heidegger contends, can hope to enter into "die Nähe des Seyns" (GA 97: 116).

In the experience of "conversation" Heidegger hopes to open up a relation to language's hidden poetic depth that helps human beings to work through the quotidian prattle of everyday chatter to find a way into the very mystery and *play* of language. Attuned to such play, the philosopher hopes to come into dialogue with the poet who, on his own terms, sets human beings into an *encounter* with the gods so as to release them from the bonds of their homelessness and hold out hope for renewing their relations with the gods who have fled. In this way, Heidegger's new style of writing dialogic, conversational discourses shies away from the rhetorics of an assertoric writing by letting language's own free play unfold in conversation. What emerges from such a conversation is what Heidegger will term "das wesentliche Ereignis der Sprache" (the essential unfolding of language's proper occurring) (GA 4: 39). Heidegger insists that "we *are* a *Gespräch*/conversation" (GA 4: 41). This means that conversation is not a mere exchange of words that can occur because we have the faculty of speech. On the contrary, our speaking always already rests upon our being a conversation—that means *being* in a festal relation to the gods.

In an attuned conversation, the interlocutors let the matter under discussion unfold and come to light. In such a *Gespräch* it is we who are gathered to the philosophical topos by the play of language itself. In this sense, what the intimate conversations between the Younger Man and Older Man on the banks of the Ister enact and bring about in their "Western Conversation" are less conversations *about* the West than they are conversations *from* the West, from out of its very center. Here "the West" is not something we can represent as an object or *Gegenstand* for our discussion; it emerges as a question that exceeds preconceived and established meanings, a question whose very possibilities need to be constantly interrogated and brought into doubt. Our thinking about the West, then, can properly unfold, Heidegger argues, only if we approach its essence as still unfolding, much like a river on a path to its source.

This thinking *from* the West and not merely *of* it truly thinks "when it delivers us over to its claim" upon us (BL: 96/GA 79: 101). Again, these conversations take place from out of the West's very center, from its fateful position as what stands ahead of us in its coming; as participants in the conversation, we must be prepared to wait for its coming (*ein Warten, aber nicht ein Erwarten*) (GA 77: 116). As Heidegger writes in one of his *Feldweggespräche*, "In waiting we leave open that upon which we wait" (GA 77: 116). This is the meaning of the *Gegen*-wart des *Gespräches*, which takes place as a waiting for the coming of the West. What the West is does not take the form of something fixed or secure; it is not something that we can represent to ourselves or something which we can bring to a stand.

On the contrary, the essence of the West unfolds as an appropriating event, that is, its *Wesen west als Ereignis an*. Moreover, this *Gespräch* takes place as the musical, rhythmic play of language, one where the players are themselves attuned to the foundational tone of language's possibilities. Such a *Gespräch* takes place at the banks of a river, the Ister, and since rivers themselves enact the essential unfolding of their destinies as they move from mouth to source, Heidegger situates his Western conversation at the site of a river marked by historical destiny. It is at this river that links East and West, antiquity and modernity, the Hesperian future and the Hellenic origin, that Heidegger offers a meditation on what the West can mean precisely in a time of destitution and decline.

II. The *Schwung* from the First to the Other Beginning

"The Western Conversation" opens on a muted but telling note. A Younger Man begins by telling his older companion about the potential of poetry to manifest the hidden unity of language and landscape:

> As if the word were to soar with momentum above the hesitant river, in the gleaming valley between the waiting woodlands, on the evening (*Abend*) of a gracious day in the approaching summer—so eventful (*ereignishaft*) is the saying of Hölderlin that now resonates for me ever more abidingly in the Ister-hymn.

It is as if the first words of the Younger Man wish to sound an opening note that might announce the most abiding themes of what is to follow: the resonance of Hölderlin's poetic word in the beauteous natural landscape of Southwestern Germany at eventide, a time of turning, in a season of turning (from spring to summer). As the Younger Man describes it, the poetic word oscillates in a valley above the river where the vaulting momentum (*Schwung*) of the word's "birth" acts as a countervailing force that both complements and contrasts with the singing of the river itself. As the dialogue between the Older Man and the Younger Man continues, it is "as if the conversation swings (*schwingt*) into a counter-swing (*Gegenschwung*) with the saying of the singer, who sings to us the essence of the river on whose mysterious banks the path of our conversation leads us along" (GA 75: 59). Here the Younger Man responds: "How may I be admitted to such a counter-swing if the beginning of the momentum's swing does not take place (*ereignet*) and carry me to the favor (*Huld*) of the word?" In these opening pages of the dialogue the two interlocutors speak of attuning themselves to "the spirit of the river" by letting the river's momentum prevail. Such attunement requires of them a releasement to the river's "lyre swing" (*Leierschwung*), the way it unfolds in its play with the surrounding landscape and the stillness that pervades its path of coming. To properly attend to this resonating power of the river requires of the listeners, however, to "steadfastly stand within (*Innestehen*) . . . the open of its river path" (GA 75: 60). Only then—in their stance of *Innestehen*—are they able to hear the sounding of the river's song that finds its consonant expression in Hölderlin's own poetic song of the river—"The Ister" poem. What remains essential to grasp here is how this momentum-propelled swaying (*Schwung*) of the poet-singer's saying acts as a counter-swing (*Gegenschwung*) to the river's own singing. In this way the momentum-driven swinging of the river, its back-and-forth undulations against the banks of the streaming water, opens the way for the conversation to properly occur as the coming into play of *Ereignis*. This poetic reverie on the banks of the Ister brings to mind the opening scene of Plato's *Phaedrus* on the banks of the Ilissus where the young Phaedrus carries out a dialogue with the "older man" (Socrates) about the sense of philosophy's proper task.

Heidegger shapes this conversation as a festival of poetic language, one attuned to the discourse of the *arche*—the ruling origin of all that is—that he names "beyng." As the Older Man remarks: "Only there, where it joins in wedlock with the human being, does beyng prevail." And the Younger Man responds: "And the festival of this marriage ceremony is the beginning" (GA 75: 60). There the Younger Man comments that "the beginning is more inceptual than the inception," serving as the *arche* for what can emerge forth from it. In this way, the conversation between these two serves to weave together four intersecting themes that will prevail throughout "The Western Conversation": the *arche* of Heidegger's biographical-familial origin; the *arche* of the Ister as river; the *arche* of the Occident as the origin of German dwelling, and the *arche* of language as poetry. All of these various discourses of/from/toward the *arche* come together here to help initiate a turning, or *Kehre*, that remains wedded to the sense of dwelling in the homeland. It is this *Heimkehr*, or "homecoming," that matters most to Heidegger in the dramatic years 1946–1948 when the very sense and possibility of German national identity is threatened at its core: from the Allies' victor's justice from without and from the Germans' own guilt and perplexity from within. In this environment of apprehension and mistrust, Heidegger finds in this conversation with Hölderlin the pathway back home to his ownmost vocation as a thinker in a time of destitution. Such a conversation helps Heidegger to rehabilitate his academic career And, beyond this, to reinforce his sense of purpose as a philosopher. He now begins an unusual journey homeward by confecting his own provincial myth of "homecoming" in the very region of the Ister's *arche*—the confluence of the Breg and Brigach rivers near Donaueschingen in the southern Black Forest.

Heidegger's focus on the Ister and its origins goes back to Hölderlin's hymn "Der Ister" written, as Hellingrath tells us, in 1803.[3] For Hölderlin, this poem finds its complement in two earlier hymns from 1801: "The Journey" (*Die Wanderung*) and "At the Source of the Danube" (*Am Quell der Donau*) (DKV I: 321–327). Like Hölderlin, Heidegger becomes fascinated by the historical ties that bind Swabia to ancient Greece. In "The Journey," Hölderlin relates the story of an eastward journey of early Swabians from the Black Forest to the region around the Black Sea, that is, from the source of the Danube to its mouth. To provide a dramatic dimension to this myth of autochthonous kinship between modern Germans and ancient Greeks, Heidegger adds a personal note. In a self-styled mythological account of his own ancestry, Heidegger relates that his grandfather "was born at the same time" as Hölderlin wrote "The Ister," thus linking the poet and the thinker in a destinal bond that confirms Heidegger's own place within the history of beyng.

Armed with this *mythos* of his grandfather's nearness to Hölderlin's understanding of German destiny, Heidegger takes up "The Western Conversation" as a task bequeathed to him from the hidden history of beyng. But there were more pressing historical forces at work in Heidegger's choice of the upper Danube Valley as the site for this philosophical conversation about German destiny. In the years that Heidegger was writing "The Western Conversation," European archaeologists had once again begun to excavate sites from the seventh century BCE near the estuary of the Danube where it flows into the Black Sea.[4] The city of Istros was once an ancient Greek colony of Miletus, the Ionian polis where Thales and Anaximander first introduced the practice of philosophy. For Heidegger, then, the course of the Ister as it flowed eastward from Swabia to Istros on the Black Sea, colony of Miletus, provided a spatial conjuncture of historical destinies. It is this archaic force linking West and East, Hölderlin and Anaximander, the refulgence of the first Greek beginning with the hopeful German preparation of an other beginning that animates the Western Conversation on the banks of the Ister/Danube. The two men walk as they converse, patterning their verbal exchanges on the changes in the movement of the river itself. Each of the interlocutors comes to signify a specific relation within the beyng-history of the Occident. The Younger Man alludes to the Germans' status as newcomers within this history as compared to the ancient Greeks (the Older Man). And as for the significance of these anonymous names of the interlocutors, Heidegger did not choose them arbitrarily. They echo the names of "the Young and the Old" from Hölderlin's 1801 elegy "Homecoming." The crucial lines read:

> But the best thing of all, the find (*Fund*) that lies beneath
>   the rainbow
> Of holy peace, is preserved for the young and the old.

> Aber das Beste, der Fund, der unter des heiligen Friedens
> Bogen lieget, er ist Jungen und Alten gespart.

(DKV I: 294)

Already, during the later years of the war, Heidegger had cited these lines from "Homecoming" and had interpreted them in light of Hölderlin's revisions from the Homburger Folioheft. There, in place of the first draft's "the best thing of all, the find," Hölderlin had written, "but the treasure (*Schatz*), the German, that beneath the rainbow of peace is preserved for the young and the old."[5]

Heidegger cites these lines often in his 1943 essay "Homecoming" and cites Hölderlin's word "Fund" thirteen times in his discussion. His point there is that "the treasure, the German . . . has not yet been transferred into the ownership (*übereignet*)" of the Germans themselves but remains "still withheld" from them (GA 4: 14). It is this "still withheld essence of the homeland," the one "preserved for the young and old," that echoes Heidegger's abiding call to reanimate Hellingrath's Hölderlinian dream of "a secret Germany," the one that (drawing on the language of Hölderlin's hymn "Germania"), Heidegger had called "the forbidden fruit . . . the Fatherland, our Fatherland Germania" (HGR: 4, 108/GA 39: 4, 120). During his early enthusiasm for a National Socialist revolution in Germany, Heidegger had insisted that "the Fatherland—the historical beyng of the *Volk*—is sealed in secrecy and indeed essentially and forever." And even after the war when this early dream of national revolution had been shattered on the power-political initiatives of the Nazi hierarchy, the dream of a secret Germany endured—even (and perhaps especially) after the Allied destruction of the German land.

In the postwar era when German national consciousness was besieged by calls of "Finis Germaniae," Heidegger went on the offensive to counteract Jaspers's plea for the recognition of collective German guilt (GA 97: 44).[6] For Heidegger, "The Western Conversation" continued a private, underground protest against such public demands by keeping alive a persistent faith in the secret Germany. This treasure—"the German"—would preserve the possibility of a homecoming whereby "the people who dwell in the land first become at home in the still withheld essence of the homeland" (GA 4: 14, 22–23). Even the depredations of the war could not eviscerate this dream; it continued to live for Heidegger in the belief that "the Swabian homeland, is precisely the site of nearness to the origin." Here, "Suevia"—the ancient name for the region of the upper Danube Valley—comes to signify "the hearth," "the origin," and "the place of nearness," a name that for Heidegger designates the hope of "an awakening of Western spirit" (GA 16: 396). This is, on my reading, what is at stake for Heidegger in his dialogue "The Western Conversation"—the very hope of an awakening of the secret Germany out of the ashes of the Second World War. In Hölderlin's poetic celebration of the Swabian landscape and the native streams and rivers of Suevia, there emerges for Heidegger a powerful *mythos* for a futural German homecoming that seeks to heal both his own personal ordeal at the hands of the de-Nazification committee in Freiburg, as well as Germany's national humiliation by the Allied tribunal at Nuremberg. "The Western Conversation," I would argue, can hardly be understood without situating it within this overall vision of German national self-scrutiny that Heidegger attempts as a way to situate himself within a project of national self-renewal after the Second World War.

In 1801, at the ending of another "German" war, Hölderlin wrote the elegy "Homecoming" as a way to celebrate the end of the Coalition Wars between French and German-Austrian-Russian armies. The resulting "Peace of Lunéville" (1801) provided Hölderlin with the hope of a fundamental turning (*Umkehr*) in/of time, one that would transform the splintered German *Volk* into a true nation by preparing it for an event of coming, a *parousia* of the gods who had fled. In an emendation of his poem "The Nearest (the) Best" (1804–1805), Hölderlin writes of a hope that "God sustains us . . ." in that he would provide "a turn of/in my Fatherland."[7] As Hölderlin had indicated, this was indeed "the best thing of all," "the treasure"—namely, the hope of the German nation to experience a revolution in/of time so as to welcome back the gods to the earth. In his poem "Kolomb," Hölderlin speaks to the same hope, but now understands it as being intimately bound up with

>   voyages of discovery
>   as attempts at determining
>   the Hesperian orbis against
>   the orbis of the ancient Greeks. (SPF: 305)

This attempt to characterize the coming age as one of a great confrontation between modern Hesperian (German) culture and the ancient Greek world reinscribes the logic of the famous Böhlendorff letter as a revolutionary turning (*Kehre*) that needs to be experienced and worked through as both a reversal (*Umkehr*) and a return (*Rückkehr*).[8] In determining the relation between Hesperia and Hellas, as that between antiquity and modernity, Hölderlin offers a poetic geography and a poetic history for thinking through the turning at the limit, border, and boundary between East and West, Orient and Occident. Such a possibility for a radical turn Hölderlin finds in Greek tragedy with its logic of reversal, a logic that the poet adopts in his river poems—especially "The Ister"—that present a "national reversal (*vaterländische Umkehr*) [as] the reversal of every mode of understanding and form" (E&L: 331/DKV II: 919–920). But Hölderlin also notes that such a reversal can be occasioned by "a spiritual violence of the time"—something that Heidegger knew all too well.

III. The Opening of "The Western Conversation"

In the midst of all this postwar distress, Heidegger has lost his teaching position, has suffered a nervous breakdown, and has retreated to a psychiatric clinic in Badenweiler to undergo a "cure" from the renowned psychiatrist Viktor Gebsattel. There, in late February 1946, Heidegger again writes to his brother Fritz in a mood of sweeping change and transformation that he "must remove himself from all public life" and turn himself "purely to the openness of beyng" (HAS: 136). What matters most to Heidegger here is that both brothers, in each of their different work spheres, "shelter the spirit of the homeland." As Heidegger formulates it:

> In a world-epoch where the human being has become altogether homeless and our own Volk, on its own soil, has everywhere lost its homeland so that it has become marked by rootless confusion, it must become clear that the homeland is something wholly other than random dwelling in a habitable region. The unsettling effects of the loss of the homeland, or of being free from it, can turn out in opposing or contrary ways. (HAS: 136)

He then concludes:

> I often have the feeling that the elemental atmosphere of the homeland that has been tainted in the last decades must once again swing back (*zurückschwingen*) into its elemental simplicity. (HAS: 136)

It is in terms of this reflection on homelessness and the threat now posed to the enduring power of the homeland that Heidegger's "Western Conversation" emerges. With no direct authorial declaration about the site of the conversation, the details of the topos within which it takes place emerge in piecemeal fashion. By paying close attention to the almost casual references of the opening pages, we learn that the two interlocutors find themselves on the banks of the upper Danube River near its source, or "Quelle." It is evening on a glorious day in late spring as the Younger Man and Older Man converse. It is the time of a rhythmic, seasonal turning. And in the very first words of their conversation we find a nodule point for several intersecting themes. The Younger Man begins:

The saying (*Sagen*) of Hölderlin is said so forcefully in terms of the event that it is as if the poetic word were soaring in the brightly gleaming valley above the hesitant stream between the waiting woodlands (*als schwinge das Wort im glänzenden Tal über den zögernden Strom*) that look out over it on the evening of a glorious day in the season of an ever-nearing summer. It is this saying of Hölderlin's in the Ister hymn that resonates ever more abidingly with me now. (GA 75: 59)

The Older Man responds that perhaps the force of this poetic word resonates so powerfully in the Younger Man owing to his own familial history. As he puts it, the Younger Man's nearness to the word is perhaps tied to "the nearness of the ancestral home that stands in the midst of the quiet meadow at the edge of the forest, there where it stands beneath the cliffs in close proximity to the river." The Older Man's words here present nothing other than the self-mythologizing account of Heidegger who persists in coupling Hölderlin's composition of the Ister hymn in 1803 with the birth of his grandfather in a sheep stall near the source of the Donau at "the same time as the Ister hymn was written."[9] As Heidegger styled it:

> Perhaps the poet Hölderlin had to become a determining destiny in the confrontation with a thinker whose grandfather was born at the same time as the genesis of "The Ister" hymn and the poem "Remembrance"—according to ancestral records in ovili, in the sheepfold of a dairy farm that lies near the banks of the river in the upper Danube Valley beneath the cliffs. The hidden history of saying (*Sagen*) knows no accidents. Everything is destinal sending (*Schickung*).[10]

The Younger Man then replies that perhaps his own response to the power of his ancestral home springs forth from an attunement to what he calls "the birth of the word, the poetic word, at the inception, one which rests in freedom" (GA 75: 59). The Older Man, in turn, remarks that these words are deeply veiled from easy apprehension. And yet, he claims, they "resonate in a counterpoised way to the saying of the poet, who sings to us the essence of a river on whose mysterious banks the path of our conversation is carried along." The Younger Man concedes that if he has indeed entered into a counterpoised resonance with the river—and with Hölderlin's river hymn—then it is the favor of the poetic word that has brought him to such a point of intersection. Listening to the word, attuning himself to its rhythms, modulations, timbre, and tonality, helps bring him into a relation of conflictual intimacy with the word's inceptual force, a power that the poet terms "Innigkeit." We become conflictually intimate with the river in and through the poetic word's power to simultaneously shelter the mystery of the river, even as it opens us to its very character. Here, in an attuned relation to the resonating themes of river, poetic word, ancestral home, and the meaning of Hölderlin as the Swabian poet nominated as the voice of these intersecting forces, we find the concealed saying of the whole dialogue.

Yes, the two interlocutors will go back and forth on parsing the unusual language of Hölderlin's Ister hymn, turning over in their conversation its reverse bends and turns so that the river's topography will get read poetologically and the poetry, in turn, will come to instantiate the very topos of a German homecoming. In this sense, what transpires in the dialogue is less something that might be called "interpretation" than it is a way of entering into the resonance of the word as it sounds in the very dwelling of the Ister. Here the poetic word comes to sound as an appropriating event "that lets the human being belong (*gehören*) to beyng in a togetherness" that can only come through an attuned hearing (*hören*) whereby the human being is "brought into ownership (*vereignet*), delivered into ownership (*zugeeignet*)" of its own essence (GA 79: 126). As Heidegger later expresses it in his Freiburg lectures of 1957: "the appropriating event is the realm, resonating in itself (*der in sich schwingende Bereich*), through which the human being and being reach one another in their essence and achieve their essencing by losing those determinations that have been given to them by metaphysics" (GA 79: 126). Moreover, it is language—especially the language of the poet—that grants to humans "the most tender resonance, one that holds everything together in this relation, suspended in the structure of the appropriating event."

Poetry reveals itself as "the fundamental configuration of historical Dasein . . . that first lets the question of who we are become a question in our Dasein" (GA 39: 59). In this sense it is not to be understood as a form of personal expression or as a genre of literary style but, rather, as "that distinctive occurrence within the event of language in whose power the human being stands as historical" (GA 39: 67). Here poetry comes to us as a *Gespräch*, or conversation. Moreover, language happens in and as this conversation in such a way that in entering into conversation we enter into the event of language. Yet we must also grasp here that conversation involves an ability to keep silent as well, wherein we come to understand silence as a fundamental poetic attunement that lets us enter into the essential occurrence of the word. In this sense, what transpires in the conversation between the Younger Man and Older Man is an attempt to think through the meaning of Hölderlin's Ister hymn at the geographical site of the Danube, a thinking that aspires to move away from "interpretation" into the very movement and oscillation of Hölderlin's poetic word as it converges with the river itself. At this point of poetological-topographic intersection, the Younger Man vouchsafes that the fundamental meaning of their conversation constitutes nothing less than the "endeavor to bring poetry into an essentially transformed relation to human beings" (GA 75: 81–82). This means above all recognizing that no effort of human enterprise can bring about such a transformation; its possibility "can only happen out of beyng itself." Moreover, as the Older Man expresses it, "the resounding of poetic song in our epoch and for the coming epoch is itself a faith that does not depend on the ability and intention of the human being, but is held open and sheltered in the destinal dispensation (*Geschick*) of beyng."

What emerges in the conversation of the two men at, of, by, from, through, and beside the Ister is the profound sense that "in the poetry of Hölderlin the possibility waits for us of another way for beyng to appear" (GA 75: 81). This is what poetic song promises—even in the wake of devastation and the darkening of the world's night: the poetic possibility of another way of beyng's resonating through the word. But again, hearing this word and belonging to its oscillations and reverberations can only happen with the help and sustenance of the mediating power whose force helps us to move across and between two separate realms. Within "The Western Conversation," the Younger Man names this force "the eagle." As we know from references to Hölderlin's hymns "Germanien" and "Der Adler," the eagle stands as Zeus's emissary to human beings, the one who comes from the Indus river, flies over Mount Parnassus and traverses the Alps in order to deliver this message to the Germans: it is your time now. You have been chosen to take up the mission of Western responsibility bequeathed to you from father Zeus. For Hölderlin, the eagle's errand is to make the Germans aware of their ancestral kinship to the ancient Greeks and thereby secure their place in the transmission of the Western bequest. For Heidegger, this bequest is one that moves from Asia westward over Ionia—from East to West along the lines carved out by that ancient river, the Istros. In the concealed and mysterious language of the poet, this river "seems to travel backwards" from its source—where the Breg and the Brigach streams cross—pressing onward for almost 3,000 kilometers to its mouth on the edge of the Black Sea. To grasp the meaning of this poem for their evening conversation about the West, the Younger Man then cites verses 11–14 from Hölderlin's Ister hymn:

> Nicht ohne Schwingen mag   Not without wings may someone
> Zum Nächsten einer greifen   Grasp for what is near
> Geradezu   Directly
> Und kommen auf die andere   And reach for the other side.[11]
>   Seite.

The Younger Man then explains that the journey across the continents requires the wings of the eagle; but so too does the journey from the one side of the Ister to the other. The leap across the stream requires èlan, momentum, or gusto—what the poet calls "Schwung." Here the interlocutors pursue this connexus between the wings of the eagle—*die Schwingen*—and the oscillating momentum of the *Schwung* necessary "to come to the other side." The Older Man then goes on to say that hearing Hölderlin's poetic word likewise requires *Schwingen*—both wings and the soaring vault of poetic attunement to the power of the word as such. Much as in Plato's *Phaedrus*—that dialogue between the younger man and older man on the banks of a river where the souls of the interlocutors grow wings to bear themselves upward to the homeland from which they have been exiled—so too Heidegger's interlocutors require an *Umschwung* or reversal/revolution for them to begin their poetic journey homeward. In this way, as the Younger Man puts it, "the oscillating momentum of the eagle's wings (*der Schwung der Adlerschwingen*) deeply pervades our being so that we can hear the melodies of poetic song" (GA 75: 87).

But there are questions that remain fundamental for thinking about the meaning of "The Western Conversation." Hence, I think we need to ask: How is the dialogue form as *Gespräch* important to the kind of work that Heidegger attempts in the postwar era? That is, is it a kind of *Holzweg* for Heidegger that he takes up in the mid-1940s and abandons? Or does it presage something more fundamental? What does this dialogue form tell us about language—especially poetic language—as a way of attuning ourselves to the relation of conflictual intimacy that is not simply a human relationship, but one that involves the sway and counter-sway between being and language?

At the same time, given the political context of the dialogue, we also need to read it critically. For what Heidegger hopes for in the dialogue is that the Germans will claim what he terms their "Western responsibility" to the word of Hölderlin, and in so doing will take upon themselves "the founding vocation of the Germans." And here we are left with troubling indications about Heidegger's own political initiatives as a thinker. Hence, despite all of the devastation addressed in this dialogue, it seems as if Heidegger has learned little—if anything at all—about the deadly metaphysics of national self-assertion that characterizes his work of the middle to late 1940s. In the end, as ever with Heidegger, we confront a thinker whose philosophical vision cannot be detached from those political ideas that threaten to occlude its most inceptual insights through an errancy that imperils the very thinking that it sets out to unfold.

IV. The Ister as Fateful Site of an Ordeal

In one of the determining passages of "The Western Conversation" (and indeed about midway through the text) as the participants continue to parse out the contemporary meaning of Hölderlin's "Ister" song, the Older Man raises a prescient question about the destiny and ordeal of German history. As they reflect on the meaning of the *Prüfung* for Germany's historical situation, he asks: "Is it time to prepare the bridal feast on the other side [of the river] and thereby to prepare the people of this land to be able to dwell poetically on the other side?" (GA 75: 136). The Younger Man then responds by questioning whether it is indeed time for such a transformation and beyond that asks what *time* as such truly is. For him, both of these questions are determined from out of the *Schickung* that comes upon both humans and gods. Moreover, he asks whether the song of Hölderlin's poem "The Ister" is called to the preparation of the feast. He then makes a telling point that will shape the remainder of the dialogue. This *Prüfung* that "goes through the knees" is not something that the poet undertakes on his own; rather, poets—in their very office as poets—are placed in a *Prüfung* (trial/test/

ordeal). That is, they are challenged by the *Prüfung* in such a way that their very identity as poets consists in their being claimed by the demands that the *Prüfung* places upon them. For this test to "pass through the knees" ("Der Ister," v. 5) means for the conversation partners that it concerns their very being—which, in turn, signifies that it takes the form of a decision about whether they are able to stand in the face of their *Geschick*—and to pass the test that this *Geschick* places them under. Or whether they will break down.

But what is this *Geschick*? And how might poets be able to pass through the trial under which the *Geschick* places them? As the older man formulates it, the test consists in whether such poets will be able to stand (*stehen*) in the presence of the arrival of "the angel of the fatherland" ("Stutgard" v. 91) or whether their knees break and they are not able to pass this test because they fall under its burden (SPF: 148–149).

The Older Man then expresses something that gets to the very heart of "The Western Conversation":

> The test concerns *das Geschickliche*; the test itself is *geschicklich* insofar as it enjoins the bard and those near to him to enter a realm where it is decided whether they find *das Schickliche* [what is fitting] or fall victim to *das Unschickliche* [what is unfitting]." (GA 75: 136–137)

What emerges in this conversation between the two men is, then, a reflection upon *das Geschickliche* and Hölderlin's identification of the trial itself *as* the *Geschickliche*. What the two men attempt to reflect upon at a crucial turning point within German history is whether the Germans are ready to confront the dispensation (*Schickung*) sent to them from out of beyng—that is, whether they are fatefully attuned enough to respond to the call that emerges from Hölderlin's Ister hymn, the one calling them to the festal table to celebrate the return of the gods.

Are these two capable of entering into the nearness (*Nähe*) of the dispensation that has been sent to them? Are they able to carry out and perform their fateful-historical (*geschicklich- geschichtlich*) task of receiving what they have been given—namely, what is their very own (*das Eigene*)? Can they pass through the difficult trials that confront them in their own historical moment and, by doing so, prepare the bridal feast for the gods' return? These are the questions that stand before them.

On this basis stands the fateful decision about whether they will be able to properly differentiate between their own and the foreign (*das Eigene und das Fremde*) as well as between what has fatefully been sent to them, that is, what is fitting (*das Schickliche*) and what is improper and unfitting (*das Unschickliche*). As the conversation sways in attunement with the curves and bends of the Danube itself, the interlocutors find themselves confronting the difficult and perplexing implications of Hölderlin's poetic song for their own historical situation. Was Hölderlin able to find this nearness to his own *Geschick*? Was he thereby able to carry out (*austragen*) the task set to him by his poetic vocation and destinal dispensation (*Geschick*)? In Heidegger's own sense, was Hölderlin able to found a history oriented to the poetic dwelling of human beings upon the earth (GA 75: 137)? And can Hölderlin's historical encounter with destiny help contemporary Germans attune themselves to their own fateful-historical vocation?

V. Hölderlin, Destiny, and the German Bequest

In his "Notes on the *Antigone*," Hölderlin writes about the contours of Greek tragic presentation and connects it to the needs and aims of a German "national" literature. As he reads it, German national ideas differ from the Greeks:

> . . . insofar as the Greeks' main aim is to grasp themselves (*sich fassen*) since this was their weakness, whereas the main aim in the modes of understanding for our own age is to hit upon something successfully (*etwas treffen zu können*), to have destiny (*Geschick zu haben*) since having no destiny, being *dysmoron*, is our weakness. (E&L: 330/DKV II: 918)

It is this logic of inverting a weakness and turning it into a strength that Hölderlin calls a national reversal, one that he believes crucial to the flourishing of both Greek and German art: "for national reversal (*vaterländische Umkehr*) is the reversal of every mode of understanding and form" (E&L: 331/DKV II: 919). Yet Hölderlin makes a distinction between two aspects of *Geschick*—the first is having a destiny, a *Geschick*, that ties one to an epoch and its unfolding. The second sense of *Geschick* lies in its adjective form *geschicklich*, which denotes skill, dexterity, adroitness, and virtuosity. For Hölderlin, the poet is blessed with this sense of attuning himself to the unity of organic being, losing himself within its balanced measures and being able to translate this unity into poetic song. When the poet is able to do this he becomes *geschicklich*. What Hölderlin's diagnosis of his own epoch relates is a simple yet profound truth: our age, the age of Hesperian night, is without destiny. We are, as he relates in his "Notes on the *Antigone*," "fateless" (*das Schicksalslose*) (E&L: 330/DKV II: 918). Our age lacks a sense of its proper destiny and it is only by journeying outward from our native ground into foreign lands that we can begin to undertake the necessary task of recovery that will occasion our rescue and salvation.

For the German *Volk* to enter into its own identity requires that it come to terms with the legacy of the West, which means the ancient Greeks. But a *Volk* cannot come to itself simply through an act of appropriating the foreign and making it one's own. The foreign must be entered into in such a way that it remains *foreign*—which means other, strange, alien. Hölderlin's famous "Scheltrede an die Deutschen" ("Invective against the Germans") from his epistolary novel *Hyperion* made it clear that he did not think the Germans were ready for the task of taking up their own destiny. They were too sundered from their native identity, torn and splintered (*zerrissen*) by their profligacy and pettiness. These Germans, the poet declared, excelled in their talent for "exaggeration and deficiency;" they were "dull and inharmonious, like the shards of a discarded vessel" (DKV II: 168). In a word, they lacked the sense of their own destiny and even conspired to escape it by throwing themselves into the busyness and business of everyday life—what Heidegger would later term the world of "das Man" (GA 2: 168–173). In his essay "On Religion" and in the first Böhlendorff letter, Hölderlin lamented the condition of his age as one which lacked an organic connection between the human being and the gods of nature that prevented him from sharing in a "higher fate" (E&L: 235/DKV II: 562). What the Germans needed to learn in their encounter with the Greek "foreign" element was that they "cannot have anything in common with them . . . apart from a living relation and destiny (*Geschick*)" (DKV III: 460). The Greeks had a destiny—but they perished because they lost the measure (*Mass*) of their living relation between art and nature. Instead, they succumbed to the excess (*Übermass*) of form that destroyed their own sense of balance and proportion. As Hölderlin had indicated in his alcaic ode "Nature and Art or Saturn and Jupiter," our destiny or lot depends upon a balance in the scales (*Waage*) of justice and judgment (SPF: 74). In his later fragment ". . . meinest du, Es solle gehen . . . ," the poet raises the fateful question about the destiny of Germans in relation to the Greeks:

> . . . do you think
> Things should go
> As they once did? They wanted to ordain
> A kingdom of art. But in the process
> Neglected what was native (*das Vaterländische*)
> To them, and Greece, the most beautiful,
> Perished in a wretched way.

> . . . meinest du
> Es solle gehen,
> Wie damals? Nämlich sie wollten stiften
> Ein Reich der Kunst. Dabei ward aber
> Das Vaterländische von ihnen
> Versäumet und erbärmlich ging
> Das Griechenland, das schönste, zu Grunde.

(DKV I: 399)

Hölderlin's analysis of the decline and exhaustion of Greek art proffers a lesson to the Hesperian world: the Greeks were unable to keep alive the living relation to their gods due to their excessive formalism and one-sided dedication to the technical rules of art. In the process they lost their vital connection to the national—the source of their aesthetic creativity. This neglect of the *living relation* was one of the essential conditions for the departure and flight of the gods. The Greeks became alienated from their native endowments and were thereby unable to fulfill their destiny. The same dangerous path stands at the center of the Germans' failure to embrace their native destiny.

The Germans have not properly learned how to avoid the lessons provided by the ancient Greeks. Instead, through their otiose dedication to both classicism and historicism they have likewise destroyed the living relation to the gods. Grasping such a failure, Hölderlin writes to his friend Neuffer about the character of the modern world and "the impoverished, spiritless century that has no order at all" (E&L: 85/DKV III: 258).

It is this Hölderlinian analysis of German failure that presents to Heidegger a way of approaching Germany's situation in 1945–1946. Hölderlin's diagnosis of the modern Hesperian age as one of supreme oblivion about the withdrawal and hoped-for return of the gods, thus stands for Heidegger as an insight into the future destiny of the Germans. Through all of his readings of Hölderlin, Heidegger remains committed to the possibility of a fulfilled time, the time of a futural coming of the gods. Such a possibility can happen, he maintains, only in a renewed poetic relation to the Greeks that rejects the classicism of academic tradition and opens itself for receiving the destinal dispensation to which Hölderlin calls his fellow Germans. The gods are near, but difficult to grasp, as Hölderlin writes in "Patmos," vv. 1–3 (SPF: 230). Still, there remains the possibility of a timely *Einkehr* or "entry into the nearness of the gods that have fled" (GA 4:195). Such an *Einkehr* requires, however, a patient practice of waiting, for as the poet writes in "Mnemosyne" (second version):

Lang ist	Long is
Die Zeit, es ereignet sich aber	The time, yet what is true
Das Wahre.	Comes to pass. (DKV I: 1032–1033)

The gods may not come with the rapidity demanded by a modern age accustomed to speed and instantaneity. On the contrary, the preparation for their coming requires a comportment of waiting and releasement. Despite the poet's call for our attunement to the gods' absence, we remain oblivious to the deep and abiding sense of homelessness that pervades our epoch. We remain out of tune with the sounding of our historical destiny.

"The Western Conversation" opens on this theme of attunement (or lack thereof) and immediately addresses the need for a certain *Schwung*—a push, a vault, a soaring flight of imagination that might help us to enter into the *Übergang* or transition between the epochs. Heidegger situates this conversation on the banks of the upper Danube since it sounds the resonance of several intersecting themes: his Swabian Heimat, the Ister poem of Hölderlin, and the oscillations of a Heraclitean river that situates modern Hesperians in an intimate conversation with ancient Hellas. Perhaps above all what "The Western Conversation" ventures is an experiment with the theme of language that might, if it succeeded, flow like a river on its journey homeward. Part of language's destinal force lies within the realm of its power to name. Hölderlin's "The Ister" renames the Donau (Danube) with its Latin name by way of a translation from the original Greek name "Istros." In doing so, Hölderlin attempts a complex retrieval of the river's ancient unity between the upper half of the stream (Danuvius) with its source in Hesperian Swabia and the lower half (Ister) with its mouth at the very edge of ancient Hellas (Black Sea). In this spatial counterpoint between north/south, as between west/east, the poet finds a temporal resonance that bonds antiquity and modernity all along the axis of a horizontal/vertical intersection. Such a movement is, however, profoundly marked by reversal and inversion. In the poet's words,

> Yet almost this river seems   Der scheinet aber fast
> To travel backwards and   Rükwärts zu gehen und
> I think it must come from   Ich meine, er müsse kommen
> The East.   Von Osten.

(SPF: 256–257)

The poet then adds: "Much could/Be said about this." We can read Heidegger's "The Western Conversation" as the commentary that has much to say about this reversal and the need to connect such reversal with the course of German destiny. Like the Ister itself, German destiny will be marked by turnings, reversals, and journeys into the foreign that will define this destiny as one of an alien homecoming. In so situating the German homeland in an intimate bond with the Greeks, Hölderlin breaks with Winckelmann's model of mimesis that has the Germans slavishly imitating the Greek canons of art. Instead, Hölderlin gives voice to a new sense of German destiny, one rooted in language rather than merely "aesthetic," "political," or "historical" recuperation. For Hölderlin, the possibility of the Germans finding themselves constitutes nothing less than an *Ereignis*—which Heidegger takes to mean a way of entering into a destinal event of appropriation. But what is this *Geschick*? And how does Heidegger come to place such emphasis on *Geschick* as the defining vocation of the Germans in search of their Hölderlinian identity?

Part of what Heidegger outlines in his writing of the postwar era from 1945 to 1950 is an account of Western metaphysics as the destiny or *Geschick* of the West. His inspiration for the shape of this destinal arc of Western thinking closely follows Hölderlin's own scheme of Hesperian destiny as tracing the path of the sun's ascent, reign, decline as a pattern of a day-night-day.[12] Here the sun's movement begins as the fiery rising in the Orient (Greek dawn), followed by the onset of evening and world night in the sun's descent (*hesperos*, Gk. evening) and finally, the recursion to daylight that culminates in the coming dawn that brings with it the return of the gods to the earth.

Heidegger's destinal history of being was powerfully shaped by this Hölderlinian understanding of Orient and Occident as the determining axes of human history. And like Hölderlin, Heidegger did not grasp this overarching design of Western history as something that had merely sprung forth from the poet's subjective conception of poetry—or in Heidegger's case, philosophy. The voice of the late hymns was no longer the personal voice of Hölderlin but the prophetic voice of *the* poet of the Western vocation. In much the same way, the voices of "The Western Conversation" abandon any traditional purchase on the notion of "authorship" and open themselves to being appropriated by the Western destiny about which they converse. These voices perform their own dramatic pageant of a new German vocation on the banks of the upper Danube in the seasonal time of turning in spring/summer 1946.[13] The voices of "The Western Conversation" speak as those who, during the awful era of defeat, death, and decimation, welcome the promise of a fulfilled time that awaits a patient people still preparing the pathway of a renewed German destiny. The logic of this destinal dispensation (*Geschick*) follows the structure of the "Armut" essay (Poverty) whereby the German land (as the savior of the Evening-Land) "has become poor in order to become rich" (GA 73: 711). The Germans' *Geschick* is to endure famine, starvation, and defeat so as to attune themselves to the grounding tone of poverty that brings on "a mourning that proves joyful." As Heidegger puts it: "In this tranquil tumult rests its releasement (*Gelassenheit*), which is accustomed to recovering from everything filled with need" (GA 73: 706).[14]

Heidegger will embrace the contemporary plight of devastation in 1945–1946 as an occasion for a profound *Umkehr*—not of military victory or political transformation but of a more profound poetic turning:

> Everything is for now reversed, as the reversal is thought more deeply . . . Poverty is the fundamental tone of the language of

poetic conversation. It is the conversation in which the West comes to its language. From out of this fundamental tone the nations of Europe will first be attuned. In no other way is it possible for the nations of Europe to become the peoples of the West (*Völkern des Abendlandes*)—which are historical in that they dwell poetically in the truth of the appropriating event. (GA 73: 708)

This is poverty's defining role—to attune the Germans to their conflictually intimate destiny as the only *Volk* capable of rescuing the West from its collapse. Within this being-historical narrative, the Germans' experience of loss and devastation in the Second World War prepares them for authentically entering into the ontological homelessness that pervades modernity. Hence Heidegger can write in his *Ereignis* notebooks that "the danger of hunger, affliction, and the lean years is not that many people die, but that those who survive only live so that they might eat" (GA 73: 707). He then adds, "In this emptiness the human being goes to ruin." Here, as in his later remarks from the Bremen lectures about the technicity of death in the gas chambers, Heidegger deflects attention away from the historical consequences of destitution to their destinal meaning (GA 79: 27). *Authentic* poverty is "an abundance (*Überfluss*) of being," not a lack; it is like a river that overflows and in its overflowing points to a sense of poverty (GA 73: 711). Entering into the event of genuine poverty, attuning ourselves to its authentic force, prepares a kind of homecoming that "gathers and preserves temporality in its ekstatic-aletheic sense" (GA 73: 763). Such "homecoming is to be thoughtfully anticipated being-historically in the appropriative event of the truth of being."

In order to grasp this being-historical sense of poverty as bound to "the appropriative event of the truth of being," we need to think about it in terms of destinal dispensation. For Heidegger, such an understanding of *Geschick* lies in a thoughtful differentiation between what is "European" and what is "Western," part of the Land of Evening—*das Abendland*. On Heidegger's reading, the term "Europe" does not signify something geographic or regional. In other words, Europe is not primarily a spatial configuration defined by land, water, mountains, or seas. It is, rather, a destinal site for Heidegger, one marked by the *Geschick* of modern technology that is characterized by a way of responding to the sending of being in the various forms of possession, production, representation, and the drive toward planetary dominion over beings' way of manifesting. This destiny cannot be simply thrown off and abandoned as if it were a historical option or ideological choice. Being European in the epoch of modernity means remaining inattentive to the fallout from this planetary will to will that defines the contemporary condition. As Heidegger puts it in *The Event*:

> . . . we have still forgotten that a destiny has been sent and that the event has been appropriated over to us (*übereignet*). On account of this forgetting, we persist in the technology and historiology of the actual, and we know and feel history (*Geschichte*) only as a happening (*Geschehen*). We do not know the evening of historiality (*das Abend des Geschichts*) and we do not surmise our assignment (*Zugewiesenheit*) to the land of evening. We are still European and still possess the European aspiration to the planetary . . . We haul that which is of an other origin into the contrived technics that pervade the world and the human being's assigned role within it. (E: 288/GA 71: 332–333)

For Heidegger, Europe is synonymous with the planetary program of *Gestell*—the destiny of the modern epoch—whereby the essence of all beings will be understood as "orderable." Human beings carry out the work of requisitioning (*Bestellen*) beings for their own purposes, even as they are themselves conscripted by this requisitioning in an ever-expanding cycle of instrumental implementation. As Heidegger puts it in his Bremen lectures of 1949:

> Positionality positions (*Das Ge-Stell stellt*). It wrests everything together into orderability (*Bestellbarkeit*) . . . Positionality essences as the plundering drive that orders the constant orderability of the complete standing reserve. What we thereby think as *positionality* is the *essence of technology*. (BFL: 31/GA 79: 32 33)

This "technology"—in all its planetary distension—eliminates the distinction between "one's own" and "the foreign." In this form the "planetary" becomes what Heidegger terms *idiotisch*—that is, that which belongs to the *idion*, which in Greek means "one's own, the proper, in which the contemporary human being finds itself within the order of the masses" (GA 96: 264).[15] Nothing planetary can be understood apart from the *idiotisch*. The example Heidegger provides is the radio (from the 1940s).

> Only the planetary human being can be *idiotisch* and the *idiotischer* human being must be planetary. The *idiotisch* essence of the radio is still completely undeveloped. It is not enough that a radio is playing in every house and on every floor. Every "family" member, the servants, the children must have their *own* radio so that everyone can "be" what every other one is in the same way. (GA 96: 265)

Within this vision of planetary sameness the radio becomes the emblem of technological-historiological Americanism which, for Heidegger, denotes the failed machinational extension of European will to will. Europe, then, serves as the name of a historical imperative toward a specific form of forgetfulness and oblivion that imperils the very bond to the originary Greek *arche*. In this way, the name "Europe" stands for a historical decision about the "self-destruction of its own essence" (HAS: 122). The Second World War connotes for Heidegger a kind of flood from America that has returned to Europe out of its own modern will to will. America and Americanism thus are, in their essence, European.[16] In every sphere, from technological innovation to the new forms of political organization, including the instrumentally driven management of carrying out war plans, Europe has failed to recognize itself. Heidegger admits as much in his letters to Fritz where he remonstrates against the Allied administration of postwar Germany:

> Certainly the still "European" man—who has still not experienced the Land of Evening—can not suddenly construct an "other" history and establish itself within a "new order." Even this is thought "technically" and not historically—that is, from out of a concealed destiny. (HAS: 128)

From his postwar experiences he comes to see that Europe is on the path of self-destruction and that only through a retrieval of the Greek beginning can the Land of Evening properly experience its decline so that it might rise again. Heidegger had indicated the outlines of such a destinal arc at the end of his Parmenides lectures (WS 1942–1943) where he understood the destiny of the West as a form of homecoming to its concealed Greek beginning. What is at stake here, Heidegger claims, "is not simply the being and the non-being of our historical *Volk*, nor the being and non-being of a 'European' 'culture,' for there what matters is merely beings" (P: 162/ GA 54: 241). What matters, rather, is the journey to the home of the goddess Aletheia; this is the genuine vocation of the thinker whereby "the journey to the home of the goddess is a thinking towards the beginning."

The West, *das Abendland*, as the Land of Evening, the land of going-under (*Untergang*) and of the sun's descent, stands as the destiny sent out to Western humanity, one that offers the promise of a new dawn, a new ascent or *Aufgang*. But this promise of the dawn can be fulfilled only if we can properly bear the destiny of the West's *Geschick* that remained unthought in the first Greek beginning. The metaphysical thinking that emerges as a departure from the originary Greek beginning is not something that can be thrown off like a jacket. It belongs to the destinal dispensation of that beginning. Hence, as Heidegger puts it, metaphysics is not something that can be overcome (*überwinden*) but remains as a "necessary fate of the West and the presupposition of its planetary dominion" (GA 7: 75). The structures of metaphysical thinking belong to this history and until we recognize and acknowledge their power there can be no recovery (*Verwindung*) possible from their persistent way of manifesting. The West's metaphysical destiny is homelessness. Simply preparing a homecoming does not serve as a cure for such homelessness, Heidegger maintains, unless we enter into the destinal history that has brought it about. That is precisely why, as Hölderlin wrote to Böhlendorff, "the Greeks are indispensable to us" (E&L: 208/DKV III: 460). The *Geschick* of the West not only has its provenance with the Greek dawn, but its own history of decline and opening to another beginning depend on a commemorative thinking (*Andenken*) of the beginning—and of its own errancy. What Heidegger thinks as "Europe" develops out of the errant path forged by metaphysics away from the Greek dawn. Europe is the name for the destiny of the *Abendland* that shows itself as ensnared within the composite scaffolding of technological thinking. But the relation here is crucial. Even as Europe shows itself as the historical destiny of the *Abendland*, the Land of Evening cannot be reduced to its European form. Concealed within the great beginning there remained unacknowledged possibilities for a very different kind of destinal outcome, possibilities that remained veiled in the obscurity of their poetic formulation. In his 1946 essay, "Letter on Humanism," as he tried to confront the new order of an Allied-dominated Europe that had brought it under the instrumentality of *das Gestell*, Heidegger summoned Hölderlin's word as a way to rethink the world-historical destiny that everyone around him had mistakenly identified with political-military-technological dominion. Distancing himself from his earlier *völkisch* reading of the poet, Heidegger now sees Hölderlin "not patriotically, not nationalistically, but being-historically." Now, Heidegger argues,

> When Hölderlin composes "Homecoming," he is concerned that his "countrymen" (*Landsleute*) find their essence. He does not at all seek that essence in an egoism of his Volk. He sees it rather, in the context of a belongingness to the destiny of the West (*das Geschick des Abendlandes*). But even the West is not thought regionally as the Occident in contrast to the Orient, not merely as Europe, but rather world-historically out of nearness to the origin. (PM: 257/GA 9: 338)

Now Heidegger stresses a homecoming to the West as origin rather than to a narrowly drawn "German" homeland. As the whole planet is becoming ever more unremittingly "European" in terms of colonialism, technological progress, the uniformity of cultural lifestyles, Heidegger points to the great danger of Europeanization that threatens the rescue of the West. For him, "Europe" brings to completion the metaphysical epoch of planetary dominion begun in the age of colonial expansion and technological hegemony:

> *The West and Europe.*—"Europe" is a planetary concept which includes evening and morning, Occident and Orient, indeed even transfers the weight to the land of the morning, the East. *The "West"* is a historical concept which determines the essential history of the Germans out of confrontation with what is Eastern; but this confrontation does not devolve upon what is Western.
>
> "Europe" is the actualization of the decline of the West. There is no longer the least inducement to take the field against the "pen pusher" Oswald Spengler. (BN III: 217/GA 96: 274)

Again, in the *Ereignis* notebooks he writes of " 'Europe' and the essential self-forgetfulness of the West" (GA 73: 857). It is precisely this *Europe* "that still not even once can think of the Land of Evening."[17]

Still, through it all—the defeat, the devastation, the war, his own personal crisis of mental health and professional viability—Heidegger clings to his Hölderlinian faith in the elected status of the Germans. He realizes that Europe is collapsing all around him and that "devastation and self-annihilation" threaten on all sides. Yet it is precisely this dire situation that leads him to write that "an essential transformation must be imminent and imperceptibly preparing something Other for the Germans so that, themselves transformed, they can be brought to their hour" (GA 73: 857). All through the capitulation and the Allies' takeover, he clings to his faith in the Germans:

> We are the Volk of poets and thinkers. Yet we are this first of all in the vocation of a concealed destiny. For this very reason we will first become this Volk. (GA 73: 862)

The Germans' designated vocation is to save the West in the face of European nihilism. For Heidegger, "The German is on the way to the West and has its essence in furnishing counsel for, and addressing the enigma of, the Land of Evening" (GA 73: 862). As he recovers from the shock of the German defeat, he sees that

> The Germans
> The Fall-Away from Essence
> Without Commemorative Thinking
> With this Fall-Away, no recollection of their Western vocation.
> Without recollection, no encouragement.
> Without hearkening to this they are un-free—
> alienated from what is their own (*im Eigenen dem entfremdet*).
> (GA 73: 863)

It is in terms of this alienation from their essence that Heidegger, in his 1946 essay "Letter on Humanism," presents an account of "the homelessness of the modern human being from the essence of the history of being" (PM: 257/GA 9: 738). In this "public" account Heidegger steers clear of any narrowly provincial privileging of the Germans within this overarching history, given the victor's justice of Nuremberg and his *epuration* by French authorities in Freiburg. But in his private manuscripts from this same period he assigns the Germans a special task: to confront the nihilistic history of European machination by way of an encounter with the first Greek beginning. This alone will offer the possibility of an authentic homecoming. In his notes he writes:

> The historical human being has a homeland.
> The destiny of the Germans is the West.
> The West—as the Land of Evening—destines the homeland
>   of the Germans.
> What is the Land of Evening? (GA 73: 750)

Only by confronting the provenance (*Herkunft*) of modern nihilism does the possibility of a futural coming emerge. As Heidegger writes, "To have an origin means: to belong to a coming that is sent (*geschickt*) from an appropriating event" (GA 73: 751). But to attune ourselves to such a coming requires what Heidegger terms *Edelmut*, or "noble-mindedness." This is a difficult term that Heidegger employs in a variety of ways, playing off the root meaning of the German term *Mut*, which ordinarily signifies "courage." This term also has resonances from the long philosophical tradition going back to Plato's understanding of the *psyche* (soul) as *nous-thymos-epithymia* (*Vernunft-Edelmut-Begierde*) and to the medieval notion of soul in Meister Eckhart. For Eckhart, *Gemüt* (MHD: *gemüete*) denotes a unitary balance within the soul of spiritual-sensual forces. As Reiner Schürmann has explained, *gemüete* designates "the common root" of intellect and will that come together to broach the divisions of psychological-moral-metaphysical activities of humans.[18] It abandons the subjectivist possession of things through "re-presentation" letting spirit detach itself from the world of beings as "external." This allows for a relation to God (being) that "is more intimate to the mind than the mind is to itself." Here there is no scission between being and acting, but rather a unity of all things without division. In this way, instead of accepting a split between *Grund* and *Abgrund* as ground versus abyss, they are experienced as belonging together. Heidegger draws upon this whole medieval German tradition of *Mut* and *Gemüt* in his use of several cognates such as *Langmut* (forbearance), *Anmut* (grace), *Grossmut* (magnanimity), as well as in the forms of *Zumutung* (impudence) and *Vermutung* (presumption) (GA 97: 86, 93, 109, 123, 143, 183, 196, 208; GA 73: 751, 758–759, 792, 835, 840, 847, 853, 863–866).

In one of his "Country Path Conversations," Heidegger ties these various strands of *Mut* to a way of comporting ourselves that patiently attends to an "other thinking"—one that requires courage (*Mut*) and forbearance (*Langmut*) (GA 77: 186–187). The possibility of such a transformation in thinking remains intimately tied to the *Edelmütige* (the noble minded); this comes to expression in the conversation:

> **Scholar:** The human is he who is required in the essential occurrence of truth. Abiding in this fashion in his provenance, the human would be touched (*angemutet*) by what is noble (*vom Edlen*) of his essence. He would surmise (*vermutete*) noble-mindedness (*das Edelmütige*)
>
> **Scientist:** This surmising could hardly be anything other than waiting, which we think of as the indwelling of releasement.
>
> **Scholar:** And if the open-region were the abiding expanse, forbearance (*Langmut*) could surmise the furthest, surmising even the expanse of the abiding-while itself, because it can wait the longest.
>
> **Guide:** And forbearing noble-mindedness (*der langmütige Edelmut*) would be a pure resting-in-itself of that willing which, renouncing willing, has let itself engage in what is not a will.
>
> **Scholar:** Noble-mindedness would be the essence of thinking and thus of thanking. (CPC: 96-97/GA 77: 148)

In "The Western Conversation" Heidegger draws on the nobility of mind (*das Edle*), as a way to reflect on what thinking is and to attempt, by way of conversation rather than assertoric argument, a new kind of thinking attuned to site, place, locality, and habitat. This new attempt at thinking breaks with the metaphysics of rationality, *nous*, reason, and logic even as it essays a recovery of the tradition of logic in conversation with the poetics of *Edelmut*, *Langmut*, and what Hölderlin termed "Dichtermut" (poetic heart/spirit) (SPF: 98). Thinking belongs to place; it is literally a situated relation to the landscape within which we find ourselves. That is why "The Western Conversation," a conversation about the destiny of the West, takes place on the banks of a river (the Danube) that divides

Europe in half. As the destiny of the West moves from Asia to Europe, the river flows in reverse. Following the spatial course of the river's flow, Heidegger crosses it with the temporal movement of spirit from Greece to Hesperia as a way to upend the linear logic of Hegelian World-spirit's journey from the Orient to Occident. In a deeply Heideggerian sense, the West's authentic destiny can be followed only through a comportment of *Edelmut*, not one of sober rationality.

For the dialogue partners, their attempts to unfold the inscrutable meanings of Hölderlin's "Ister" hymn help to raise the very question of German identity in the postwar epoch. Their genuine concern here is less the philological task of grasping Hölderlin's Ister song within the literary-historical tradition from which it sprang. On the contrary, their singular and unique focus is to understand Hölderlin's hymn as itself an essential "trial" or "Prüfung" that tests the Germans' own spiritual courage and readiness to confront their historical legacy and vocation precisely at this moment of extreme historical crisis that has shaken the European world to its very foundations. What does the future hold? Will the Germans be able to summon the reserves of their own historical faith in their appointed mission (*Sendung*) of "saving the West," the task assigned to them from out of the history of beyng, as Heidegger understands it (EdP: 40; GA 13: 16; GA 55: 108)? In the early years of National Socialism, Rector Heidegger posed this pressing question: "Will we once again venture the gods and along with them the truth of the Volk?" (GA 94: 187). By 1946 this historical task had been challenged and threatened, Heidegger believed, by Anglo-American aggression and the machinational drive for political-economic dominance. The war and its aftermath had shaken the Germans to their core—and yet for Heidegger, the essential question still remained: would the Germans be able to draw upon a historical faith in their singular role in Occidental history and come to terms with their appointed task as saviors of the Western tradition? For Heidegger, the answer to this question could come only from Hölderlin and his poetic bequest to the German *Volk*. Yes, the language and political form of this message would need to change, given the dominance of Allied bureaucracy over central Europe. But Heidegger's underlying faith in the Hölderlinian task of the Germans to provide an alternative path to Anglo-American/Soviet machination never faltered. The *fundamental* problem facing the Germans was the same in 1946 as it had been in 1934: "*Dasein* has become a stranger to its historical essence, its mission (*Sendung*), and its mandate (*Auftrag*)"

(GA 39:135). How to bring Dasein (namely, German Dasein) into nearness to what is its own (*Eigenes*) and thereby to bring it into intimate relation with its proper mission and mandate? This becomes the task of "The Western Conversation" as Heidegger understands it. Can the Germans pass the test sent to them from out of the history of Beyng and come to embrace their destinal dispensation (*Geschick*)? However they decide this question, the path must be hewn in close proximity to the poetic language of Hölderlin.

VI. Poetic Geography and Destinal History: The *German* Danube

The very nature of this poetic task that Hölderlin assigns to the Germans can be traced along the path carved out by the Ister's own path of journeying. That is, as Heidegger had emphasized in his lecture course of SS 1942, rivers *are* time itself (HHI: 12/GA 53: 12). When the two interlocutors attempt to follow this law of German destiny, they find the ciphers for its decoding in the very verses of Hölderlin's Ister song. There they parse the meaning of verse 15, where the poet writes: "But here we wish to build." What this double call announces is the inception of a new historical age of building (*bauen*) where the "here" and "now" come together in a decision that signals that the historical trial/test has been passed *and* that the *Schickliche* has been found. But what does this mean?—first, for the interlocutors in their attempts to understand the Ister hymn and, second, for Heidegger as he attempts to situate Hölderlin as the poet who stands as the voice of German futurity?

To address these questions, I believe we need to situate them against the very topos of "The Western Conversation" as a philosophical conversation about the future of Western destiny, thought from out of the historical situation of Western Europe in 1946–1948. But such a task also requires that we understand it topographically as a conversation about the Ister's own geographical-historical unfolding. What the river achieves in its movement from west to east, from source to mouth, from the southern Black Forest to the Black Sea will be grasped by Hölderlin as a *Geschichtsphilosophie* that reveals a hidden German destiny. Heidegger too would understand the Ister—as river *and* as poem—as unfolding a philosophical history of the West that connects the west and east, north and south, Germany and Greece, modernity and antiquity. Heidegger will take over the poetic terms of Hölderlin's own conversation with Greek antiquity and transform it here in "The Western Conversation" into a meditation on the future of the Occident. Hence, he will refer to Deutschland as "Germania" and to the *Geschick* of Germania as "Hesperia." The logic here is fractured and difficult to follow. "Hesperia" refers to the land of "evening" (Gk. *hesperos*, Lt. *vesper*, the evening star). Hölderlin takes the term from Lucan's *Pharsalia* and transforms it into a concept that stands in contrast to "Hellas," the ancient Greek word for Greece itself.[19] As Heidegger reads it, however, these very terms need to be rethought and re-situated within a larger conversation, a "Western" conversation about the very meaning and direction of Greece within Western history. Hence, the Older Man remarks: "We may not simply bring Hesperia into contrast with Hellas, because Hölderlin thinks Hellas in an Oriental way as a land of the rising of heavenly fire" (GA 75: 141). And the Younger Man replies:

> You say "a" land and not the land, for Greece is the world epoch not of the first arising (*Aufgang*) and beginning (*Anfang*) but, rather, of the proper occurrence (*sich ereignen*) of the transition (*Übergang*) of the first arising of fire from heaven—that is, the transition from the Land of Morning (*das Morgenländische*) to the Land of Evening (*das Abendländische*).

Several things come into play here both for the interlocutors in "The Western Conversation" and also for Heidegger. To repeat, when a conversation is authentic or proper, an event takes place wherein something hidden comes to language. For Heidegger, what comes to language within such a conversation is the *Geschick* or destinal dispensation of the Germans. Where do the Germans fit within the transmission of the Greek legacy within Europe? How has the "spirit" or *Geist* of the West been able to endure? And what role have the Germans played within such a history?

To trace the lineaments of such a history and to properly grasp the direction of Heidegger's Hölderlin conversation, precisely in the years after the devastation of the Second World War, means to understand it as part of a larger conversation that dominated German cultural life in the years right after the loss of the First World War. There, in an era of despair, collapse, trauma, and decline, Hölderlin took on a decisive role as the prophet of futural renewal. Out of the ashes of the Great War and of Hellingrath's buried myth of a "secret Germany," the George

Circle member Max Kommerell wrote that the task of a new beginning was bequeathed to the Germans in the wake of the lost war. In his 1928 study, *The Poet as Führer*, Kommerell counseled the Germans that Hölderlin's role was "in the midst of aging and disintegration to once again begin anew."[20] What Heidegger takes from this mythic construction of a Hölderlinian future for the Germans is the powerful sense that to "be" German means to be in in conversation with the destinal dispensation bequeathed to them by the West—a bequest begun in ancient Greece. Here, the question of destinal dispensation or *Geschick* concerns the interwoven connexus between Germania and the West. Following Hölderlin's "Brod und Wein," if to be German means to embrace one's proper identity as "the fruit of Hesperia" (v. 150), then the very unfolding of Western history needs to be understood as a process of maturation where the Germans prepare themselves for receiving the bequest provided them—namely, their *Geschick*. To be *geschicklich* means to belong to *das Geschick*; it signifies a ripeness and readiness for receiving the trial/test of Western experience itself and posing the question of destinal identity anew: "Who are we?" "We" are the fruit of Hesperia, the people whose own identity has been tested in the struggles of two world wars and by a machinational history of technological-industrial dominion such that its very survival has become an essential question. But this very trial proves to be an "essential moment" in the thinking of *das Geschick* and that which belongs to it, *das Geschickliche*. As the Younger Man grasps it, this *Geschick* sounds most powerfully as song, so it makes sense to him to connect it with Hölderlin's Ister hymn where such a song sounds throughout. As he puts it, "*das Geschickliche* is that *Geschick* that rests in the Western tradition, understood as 'Abendland'—the land of evening—and has become ripe for the task of grasping what this destinal dispensation entails." And yet problems arise since this *Geschick* is in no way present to the Germans but must first be "found" (GA 75: 138–139).

The Germans' task, then, consists in finding what has been dispensed to them, but this dispensation is, in turn, nothing other than what is their own, their *Eigenes*. In direct terms, the task of the Germans consists in making what is proper to them (their *Eigenes*) their own property (*Eigentum*). But to appropriate in a proper way what is proper to one as one's property becomes something difficult. A trial or test is needed to see whether one is up to the task of coming into one's own. Moreover, the Younger Man also understands that such a process takes time. It undergoes delays and holdups. It does not transpire directly or without interruptions. The essence of a historical *Geschick* unfolds in a way similar to that of a river: it moves from source to mouth in a journey that unfolds its hidden potentialities. Such a journey moves from the native ground of the source to the foreign opening at the mouth in an excursus of self-discovery that happens as an encounter with the foreign. (Such a process mirrors the course of the Ister itself that at its very source is hesitant and marked by both delay and restraint, the famous "Donauversickerung"—where the Danube sinks into the riverbed and conceals itself as it were.)[21]

As the Older Man attempts to make sense of this whole process, especially as it shapes the journey of the Ister, he returns to a discussion of stanza nine from Hölderlin's "Brod und Wein" hymn. There, in the movement of spirit away from the homeland, the two interlocutors find a model not only for the unfolding of rivers but for the very process of historical-destinal dispensation as both *Geschichte* and *Geschick*. The text, which Heidegger interprets in several works, appears yet again in "The Western Conversation":

> Believe, those who it has tested! Namely at home is spirit
> Not at the beginning, not at the source. The homeland consumes it.
> The spirit loves the colony, and brave forgetting.
> Our flowers and the shades of our forests give joy
> To those who languish. It is as if the besouler were almost consumed by fire.
>
> (DKV I: 747)

What this fragment signifies—and how it gets interpreted as a Rosetta stone for understanding Hölderlin's relationship to Western history— was already discussed in Heidegger's WS 1941–1942 lecture course on "Andenken." There, Heidegger explained, this crucial fragment from "Bread and Wine" "pervades all the relations of the essence of history that Hölderlin knows" (GA 52: 190). It provides the basis not only for Heidegger's reading of the Ister hymn, but for his understanding of "The Western Conversation" itself. Yet Heidegger's approach here is hardly to be understood as a purely philological contribution to a scholarly debate about the emendations to stanza nine of "Bread and Wine." On the contrary, it belongs to a much larger discussion about the whole of

Hölderlin's poetic corpus in its relation to the Greek bequest. Drawing on Friedrich Beissner's editorial labors in his 1933 book, *Hölderlins Übersetzungen aus dem Griechischen*, Heidegger comes to see this fragment as decisive for the whole of Hölderlin's poetic corpus, and not merely as a poetic notation to a particular poem. This fragment had not been included in Norbert von Hellingrath's four-volume edition of Hölderlin's work and thus Beissner comes to define it as a "new fragment" and gives it a central position in the debate begun by Wilhelm Michel about Hölderlin's purported "abendländische Wendung" or "turn to the Occident."[22] Following Beissner's overall design, Heidegger takes this fragment, along with the famous Böhlendorff letter, as one of the two pillars for Hölderlin's understanding of the relation between Germany and ancient Greece, Hesperia and Hellas, antiquity and modernity, Occident and Orient. But the manner in which Heidegger proceeds and the structural coherence of his reading will be defined by his Hellingrathian faith in the select role of the Germans in for unfolding a "secret Germany" within Western history. To understand what is at stake for Heidegger in "The Western Conversation," then, is to grasp the specific sense that Heidegger assigns to this particular fragment as the axial center of his reading of the Western *Geschick*.

VII. The Bread and Wine Fragment and German Destiny

In the first stanza of the "Ister" hymn, the poet writes of those who "have come from afar" from the Indus and the Alpheus, have experienced the trial "through the knees" and who, on account of that, have been able to perceive the forest's song that accompanies them upon their journey. Here, in this opening gesture, the poet also notes that these poetic singers "have long sought *das Schickliche*" (the fateful, that which is fitting, that which is sent them) (SPF: 254–255). Heidegger then interprets this to mean that the understanding of what is fatefully assigned to us as our own, what is proper to us, takes a very long time. Perhaps over 2,500 years—or longer. In other words, one needs to work long at readying oneself for receiving the bequest of a tradition, since it neither lies there "present" to us, waiting to be appropriated, nor does it come to us of its own accord without the work of preparation. To say, as the poet does, that "long we have sought *das Schickliche*" is to say that the history of the West is a long process of seeking what is our own. The topic of "The Western Conversation" thus unfolds as a way to address this work of appropriation and to ready ourselves for taking up the task of "carrying out" (*Austrag*) the destinal assignment that has been sent to us (*das Geschickte*). That is, to accept and come to understand our *Geschick*. But the roots of such understanding are deeply concealed within the narrative history of our tradition since that which is sent to us is also withheld. Hence, the process is long and delayed.

We see the outlines of such a process in the very design and performance of Hölderlin's Ister hymn that speaks of the deferred flow of the river at its source, its hesitation in beginning, its long and expansive journey to its mouth. It is this movement and tension between provenance and destination that pervades Hölderlin's Ister hymn even as it shapes the very dynamics of "The Western Conversation" as a way of thinking through the task of German history and its futurity. The Younger Man and Older Man emphasize this dilatory pace, speaking of these hesitations of the river as a model for the slow and thoughtful process of interpretation that attends to the difficulties of the poet's verses. The Younger Man goes so far as to claim that this hermeneutic slowness "springs forth from the inceptively hesitant nearness to what once singularly reigned" (GA 75: 66). Indeed, the very first sentence of "The Western Conversation" alludes to both *waiting* and *hesitation* as belonging to the resonant possibilities of the poetic word. For both the interlocutors and for Heidegger, these esoteric references find their cipher in the "new fragment" discovered by Beissner about Hölderlin's relation to the singular source of the Greek bequest that reigns over the very movement of the Ister hymn. Again, to cite this compelling verse:

> Nemlich zu Hauss ist der Geist
> Nicht im Anfang, nicht an der Quelle (DKV I: 747).

Much as Beissner, Heidegger views these verses not as a commentary on the last stanza of "Bread and Wine" but as an insight into Hölderlin's own philosophical-poetic interpretation of Western history, a *Geschichtsphilosophie* that presents itself in the form of a poetic *Geschichtstheologie* organized around the event of the gods' departure. At the beginning of its journey, the *Geist* (spirit/mind) of the West does not "know" itself. Rather, it requires two millennia or more to come to understand what is proper to it, to come to understand that spirit is not mere presence, but that absence and withdrawal reign within it as well. At its inception, spirit is not at home with itself and cannot carry out the promise of its fulfillment. It requires the experience of a kind of self-estrangement and self-forgetting that propels it outward from its home into an encounter with the foreign. In this text, Hölderlin names this process of journeying outward "the love of the colony" (v. 154)—an odd characterization to be sure, but one whose poetic-historical sense emerges when we remember the ancient Greek word for colony—*apoikia*.[23] The Latin term for colony, *colonia*, derives from the verb *colere*, "to cultivate," and has ties to the language of gardening, husbandry, and the transplantation of roots to new environs or seed beds. The Greek word roots stress yet a different set of relations. *Oikos* in Greek has to do with the home or *Heimat*—the realm of the familiar, the proper, one's own; the prefix *ap-* denotes "away from," "apart," not of the *oikos*. In this sense, the spirit's love of colony refers to a gesture away from the home, in excess of the home but, on Heidegger's reading, a deeper drive to find the essence of the home—even if it lies within the foreign.

As Heidegger had already put it in his *Andenken* lectures: "The inception does not begin with the beginning" (GA 52: 189). This is the secret mystery of all historical movement. The *Geschick* of a *Volk* does not appear at its beginning, but must be *übereignet*, transferred into ownership through and by its journey into what is foreign—namely, what is not its own. But Heidegger never properly acknowledges the full otherness of the foreign. Rather, for him, the foreign presents a way station on the path of spirit's journey to self-recognition. It stands opposite spirit awaiting its appropriation in spirit's journey homeward. Hence, Heidegger will read the passage on "colony" from "Bread and Wine" as an indication for the homeland's coming-to-itself by a journey into what is strange and alien to it. Moreover, he will designate this very movement from out of the homeland into the colony as defining the very essence of *das Geschickliche*. As he reads it, spirit moves from out of its origin in the homeland and despite "forgetting" this, "by all its forgetting, it still safeguards the origin from out of the homeland" (GA 75: 146). Accordingly, Heidegger will write that "*das Geschickliche* is the journeying out of the homeland into the colony." This journey defines spirit's *Geschick* in terms of its emigration—first in the colony, which Heidegger defines as the "daughter of the motherland," wherein spirit "finds the homeland through building and dwelling and in preparing the feast"—and then, through this, finally learns "true poverty, which consists in no longer having any needs." Spirit's *Geschick* here "remains concealed in the hidden history of its journey from the homeland into the colony, where it should ripen into the fruit of the West, the highest bridal feast of the reconciliation between day and night" (GA 75: 147). Through all of its journeying into the colony, spirit never truly comes to recognize the Other in its alterity. Rather, "the love of the colony," sent to spirit from out of its *own* need for authentic homecoming, emerges out of the recognition that while spirit resides in the homeland presently, it does not yet *dwell* there. To achieve an authentic dwelling, spirit needs to "forget" its own home by departing forth from it into a colony where it experiences a new measure for dwelling that sends it back to its homeland with renewed understanding of what the home is comprised of. This narrative of leaving the homeland, founding a colony, forgetting the homeland, and then, after a trial/test of authentic learning, returning home, constitutes the *Geschick* of the poet as the exemplar of Western homecoming. In Heidegger's reading, then, the love of the colony expressed by spirit is nothing other than a forgotten (and repressed) form of love for the motherland (GA 4: 93). This "law of history," as Heidegger puts it, "has its essence in the return to what is proper to one, a return that can only be made as a journey out into what is foreign" (GA 4: 95). But such a reading presents its own problems since it defines the very movement of Western spirit's self-recognition as a return to the self via the foreign whereby the foreign (colony) gains recognition only as a means to come to fuller self-recognition. But again, as we saw in our reading of Heidegger's "Andenken" lecture course in chapter 2, Heidegger has overdetermined Hölderlin's understanding of Western spirit's journey in order to present his own forceful interpretation of the West in the years following Germany's defeat in yet another world war.

Perhaps we can read spirit's love of the colony here as the affirmation of Hölderlin's claim in the Böhlendorff letter that "in the process of civilization what we are actually born with, the national, will always become less and less of an advantage" (E&L: 207/DKV III: 460). Here, of course, Heidegger would agree. And yet what proves less certain is whether this deep and abiding impulse to flee the homeland in search of the foreign is truly an impulse that opens the pathway back *toward* the homeland. Perhaps we need to understand Hölderlin's many references to "sailing," "voyages of discovery," the open sea, and the adventures of Lord Anson and Captain James Cook in "Tinian" and "Kolomb" as indications of a new ethos of Western discovery and expansion of the older European horizons. On this reading, Hölderlin appears less as the poet of *Heimkehr* and return and much more as the nomadic poet of wayfaring and exploration, of a nomadology of wandering that looks to the open sea and to the life of mariners ("Andenken, vv. 4, 40–50) as a future-directed journeying that does not grasp the foreign merely as a useful excursus on the way back to the homeland and primarily for the homeland's sake (GA 52: 190). Perhaps Heidegger's reading of Hölderlin has it backward. Perhaps "Greece" is less the "colony" of the Germans than the Germans are the colony of Greece. And, moreover, perhaps the famous "Bread and Wine" fragment speaks not of the relation between Greece and Hesperia, but instead, as Beda Allemann, Jochen Schmidt, and Hans-Joachim Kreutzer have emphasized it, concerns the relation of heaven to earth, gods to mortals, and above to below.[24] Taken as a whole, we might say that Heidegger gets it half right. On the one hand, in his reading of Hölderlin's "Ister," Heidegger unfolds one of the most powerful ethical insights in his entire corpus. That is, as he puts it in his SS 1942 lecture course *Hölderlin's Hymn "The Ister"*: "The essence of one's own is so mysterious (*geheimnisvoll*) that it unfolds its ownmost essential wealth only from out of the supremely thoughtful acknowledgment of the foreign" (GA 53: 69). Such an insight serves as Hölderlin's own poetic care in the river hymns: the mystery of the coming-to-be-at-home of human beings. Yet, at the same time, Heidegger seems to forget his own earlier insight from WS 1934–1935 that for Hölderlin the earth will become a homeland only when it opens itself to "the power of the gods" (GA 39: 53–54). That is, he seems to forget the *ethical* insight of Hölderlin's own poetic theophany—namely, that there is genuine risk in opening oneself to the wholly "other" (cf. Semele, "Wie wenn am Feiertage," vv. 45–60) since it could result in the annihilation of the self. Heidegger's emphasis on colonization and return, whereby the journey outward is undertaken in the service of the journey homeward, seems to forget this crucial ethical insight of risk, danger, and the possibility of self-destruction. Perhaps *das Geschick des Geistes* demands more than mere appropriation of the foreign; perhaps it requires, above all, the exposure to its foreignness as something wholly other and not appropriable by an alien colonizer. Moreover, perhaps Hölderlin's journey outward unfolds not in the service of a *Heimkehr* but as a nomadological push ever westward to the Indies, to America, and to the unknown regions of a world from which one might never return.

Several times in their conversations, the Younger Man and Older Man refer to human beings as "dwelling in the abyss" whereby they explain that "rivers . . . carry the abyss *to* humans, so that they can dwell there, where their essence is rooted" (GA 75: 75, 154). Heidegger plays out this connection to the abyssal by linking it to mother Earth that, as Hölderlin puts it in "Germania," "is the mother of everything, and bears the abyss" (v. 76). If, as Heidegger continues to emphasize, the preoccupation of the poet in the river hymns is to prepare the feast of celebration between mortals and gods and thereby be able to establish/institute/found/endow (*stiften*) a poetic dwelling for humans upon the earth, then recognizing the need to genuinely encounter the gods in their unsettling alterity seems to be a crucial part in founding a settlement for dwelling. By not properly recognizing this experience of profound alterity as part of the spirit's journey homeward, I think, Heidegger risks missing the kernel of Hölderlin's ethopoetic insights into the possibility of human dwelling. In terms of the poetic *Austrag* of the river hymns, this means that spirit's journey of self-unfolding must venture out in the foreign lands and cut furrows into the earth, tearing it apart and opening up new paths for passage and transport. It must move from source to mouth—and, as the etymological play of its language shows, when the river arrives at its mouth from its source, it will have done so only by virtue of having riven the earth through its tears, rends, and incisions. The **river's arrival derives** from its having **riven** the earth.[25] As Hölderlin puts it in "The Ister":

> It is however meet that the rock be broached
> And the earth furrowed,
> Without welcome would it be else, unabiding
>
> Es brauchet aber Stiche der Fels
> Und Furchen die Erd,'
> Unwirthbar wär es, ohne Weile (vv. 68–72)

And then the poet remarks:

> But what that one does, the stream,
> No one knows.
>
> Was aber jener thuet der Strom,
> Weis niemand. (vv. 71–72).[26] (SPF: 256–257)

Hence, after the poet's portrayal of the various cuts, tears, rends, and furrows that the river excavates upon the earth's surface, he leaves us with a gnomic closing verse. The river remains foreign to us despite our native dwelling upon its banks. What the river does, no one knows, since it founds a wholly different way of being than that available to human beings. *Physis* remains mysterious, ever sheltering its own secrets, steadfast in its recalcitrance to human calculability.

What emerges from the source cannot be accounted for solely in terms of the river's flow; the source exceeds its point of origination and, in this excess, the river find its path. Such a poetic ontology of the riverine bespeaks the power of arrival and of what is to come. And here Heidegger hits upon something that characterizes all of his various Hölderlin writings—that the beginning is something that persists only as long as its coming. "Anfang bleibt als Ankunft"/ "Beginning remains as arrival" (EHP: 195/GA 4: 171). Again we return to the enduring theme of "The Western Conversation." After a long discussion about the intimate connection between the opening verse's reference to the "Now," and verse 15's allusion to the "Here," the two interlocutors take up the underlying theme of the river's poetic course of journeying—namely, its emblematic status as the instantiation of the West's destiny. Each of the speakers grasps the river's various bends and turns as indications of the larger themes addressed by the "Brod und Wein" fragment, whose "verses offer a saga of the destinal dispensation of spirit," "the Western destiny of spirit in contrast to another named kind of destiny," for example, "the Eastern" or "the Oriental" (GA 75: 140–141). Here the West will be understood as "the land of evening" (*Abend- land*) in contrast to the East, thought of as "the land of morning" (*Morgen-land*). Much depends upon following Heidegger's contorted logic here. Heidegger sees Western history as a move from East to West, much as Hegel, Herder, and Hölderlin before him. And like them he grasps the West as the epoch of "the coming destiny" (*das kommende Geschick*). But, as he reads the treatment of colony and journeying in the "Brod und Wein" fragment, Germany becomes the homeland and Greece the "colony" of German spirit. Here one would have to consider such an interpretation in terms of the long German preoccupation with ancient Greece and the cultural-racial uses of such Philhellenic *Geschichtsphilosophie* that privileges Germany's elected status as the savior of the Western tradition.[27] Heidegger formulates the basic outlines for such a reading in a passage from the *Black Notebooks* written around the time he composed "The Western Conversation":

> "The saving of the West!"—can only mean—radical thinking from out of the beginning of the destinal dispensation

of beyng—the Greeks—a West that since then has become planetary.

Radical thinking from out of the beginning in its still forgotten truth—of beyng—forgetfulness. The land of evening (*Abend-land*) must be saved in order first of all that it be exposed to its still concealed essence. . . .

"The saving of the West"—i.e., the step into the Open, from out of which the beyng—historical destiny of the human being in its humanness is decided, that wherein the destiny of the planet is decided in terms of the world's appropriative event. (GA 98: 285–286)

What "The Western Conversation" attempts is a reflection about Hölderlin's "Ister" hymn that, in turn, takes it as a song that sings the destinal dispensation of spirit that becomes historical *in* the West. The conversations that take place are thus always again to be understood as conversations "vom" Abendland—that is, "from," "out of," "in terms of" the West, recognizing all the while that "the West" is nothing objectively present but, rather, exists as what is coming, what is still to come, and will be decided upon depending on how "we" respond to the poetic word of Hölderlin. Hence, the Younger Man can characterize their conversations as a kind of "remaining in coming" (*Bleiben als Kommen*), an abiding in and attuning to that which is still to come: the West (GA 75: 158). But this reading finds its sense only in the reconciliation between East and West, claims the Younger Man: "It ripens in the West (the land of evening) that is itself, however, only *im Geschicklichen des Geschickes* (in the destinal sending of destiny) that belongs to the East (the land of morning)" (GA 75: 146–147). Here the Older Man then responds that the land of evening, whose sun sets and goes down at night, rises up again on that morning when the day springs forth, a day wholly reconciled with the night and in this way always again calls and retrieves this night "as the abyss." This reconciliation takes place as "the highest wedding festival of the reconciliation between day and night." Through the homeland's building and dwelling, which serves as preparation for the feast, the homeland comes to experience "true poverty" that frees the Germans from any necessities and allows them to enter into *das Geschickliche* that has been sent to them. This movement into embracing *das Geschickliche* would then constitute "homecoming," a homecoming of spirit that could emerge only from the love of the colony.

All of this wandering has as its impetus the *Einkehr* or "turning into . . . the other side" of the Ister (GA 75: 162). The destinal sending of spirit on a journey of self-discovery to "the other side" ("The Ister" v. 14) happens as a centuries-long process of "searching for what is fitting" (*das Schickliche*) (v. 10). "Here" is where "we" wish to build; "now" is the time of the coming of fire from the bright sun that still burns in the sky from the land of Homer and the ancient Greeks. Translated into the language of "The Western Conversation," what the two interlocutors seek to express is the story of the Western migration of spirit from Hellas to Hesperia, from the fiery southern lands of ancient Greece to the sober northern lands of Germania that lie "on the other side" of Europe's great divide, the Alps. The Ister's journey eastward from Donaueschingen in the Black Forest to the shores of the Black Sea constitutes the poetic-philosophical journey of spirit as it moves *geographically* from west to east, even as its *historical* journey transpires from East to West. The poetic community of participants sing from the Indus; they come from afar, and from the Alpheus (vv. 7–9); that is, they sing the song calling the gods to the wedding feast of reconciliation between day and night, east and west, antiquity and modernity, fire and shade. The possibility of poetic dwelling here emerges as the successful transition between these oppositions and the acceptance of the destinal dispensation granted to the Germans as "the fruit of Hesperia" ("Brod und Wein" v. 150). "The Ister" hymn sings the song of "the great destiny" granted to the Germans (GA 75: 162). Moreover, the interlocutors in "The Western Conversation" acknowledge this determining role of Hölderlin's song in shaping the trajectory and scope of this poetic-historical journey.

Yet what does this trajectory look like in the years just following the crushing German defeat in the Second World War? How does the understanding of Germany's role in this Western Conversation appear differently than in the lecture course of SS 1942 that understood World War II as a holy campaign in defense of the West against the incursion of Anglo-American machination and ahistoricality?

Heidegger offers no real details about the changes from his earlier reading of "the Ister" in SS 1942 to the postwar dialogue about the Ister. And, in some sense, there is no change. In both readings, Heidegger privileges the Germans as "the fruit of Hesperia," that is, the true inheritors of the Greek bequest, the people chosen to carry on the Western conversation and, in so doing, to save the West. The reception of this task, however, requires patience, time, and preparation. What sends itself to the Germans as their *Geschick*, their destinal dispensation, is at the same time withheld from them. This is why the German spirit "loves colony" as the not yet grasped essence of the homeland. The work of journeying attends itself to the appropriation of the foreign, but the foreign, in turn, reveals itself for Heidegger as the not yet grasped essence of the homeland. What this means is that the essence of the homeland is still to come, still outstanding as the task that awaits the Germans. For Heidegger, what Hölderlin names as "das Vaterländische" (what is of the fatherland) is to be thought as "the veiled destiny (*Geschick*) and mystery (*Geheimnis*) of the West (*des Abendländischen*)" (GA 75: 167, 169). If those who have come from afar (*die Fernangekommenen*) to find their proper/own *Geschick* have not first built and prepared a dwelling, whereby "what is their own as proper becomes their property (*des Eigenen zum Eigentum werden*)," then they will not be able to become those who dwell "on the other side" of the Ister. The capacity for such dwelling lies in grasping what is of the fatherland as the destiny that has been sent to the native inhabitants of the homeland. This is the "Fund" (the discovery/the find) of which the Younger Man and Older Man had spoken in the early part of "The Western Conversation," the *Fund* that the poet first thought as the heart-center of the Ister hymn—the German homeland (GA 75: 82, 139; GA 77: 244).

Given the political realities of his de-Nazification proceedings in the presence of Allied administrative "justice" throughout the devastated land, Heidegger will proceed gently here and take up the thread that he mentioned in "The Letter on Humanism" about understanding Hölderlin as the poet of the international rather than the "national."[28] Here the Younger Man cautions that it would be "an erroneous judgment" to conceive of Hölderlin's Ister hymn as offering something *völkisch* or "nationalistic" (GA 75: 160). And later the Older Man confirms that to read Hölderlin's vision of the fatherland as nationalistic would be to "misinterpret" it (GA 75:167). Heidegger will insist throughout this long dialogue that we conceive of Hölderlin's "Ister" hymn as offering nothing less than a vision of the West as the proper home and destiny of the Germans as they continue to strive to build "on the other side" of the river. And yet despite Heidegger's emphasis on the Western destiny of the Germans—one that does not, he claims, draw upon either the tradition of *völkisch* ideology or political nationalism—he continues to assign a special and chosen role to the Germans as "the fruit of Hesperia" within this redemption narrative of the history of the West in terms of the history of beyng. If in the early years of his National Socialist enthusiasm, Heidegger could wax lyrical about "the historical greatness of the German Volk" (GA 36/37: 3), by 1946 he understands that this egregious form of German cultural-racial supremacy must take another form. Hence, what we find in "The Western Conversation" is a Hölderlinian vision of German nationalism that presents the George Circle's suppressed dream of a secret Germany to fit the new postwar realities of an emasculated German *Volk* forced to accept the new victor's justice imposed by the occupying Allied powers.

Clearly, "The Western Conversation" offers far more than a philosophical justification of German exceptionalism within the history of the West. What the two interlocutors attempt to articulate with their discussion of *Geschick* is, rather, a way to conceive of the gathered sending of beyng's historical epochs in such a way that they present a path of wandering and transformation that follows the hesitations, propulsions, bends, and turns of the Ister itself. Such a vision grasps Western history as a struggle for self-identity via a passage into the foreign out of the origin into a journey that needs to confront what is not of the home. All the while, however, this journey will be thought of as fundamentally constituting a *journey homeward*. Heidegger does not merely understand this German journey through Western history as a triumphal narrative of self-recognition and self-overcoming, however. He acknowledges that there is something deeply abyssal (*abgründig*) in Hölderlin's notion of *Geschick* that is essential to its way and manner of sending. Perhaps here in the Germans' own historical experience of the tragic we can find something of a corrective to the overdetermined historical exceptionalism and superiority that Heidegger all too often assumes. To be able to build again after the destruction of the war will be understood, then, not as mere "postwar reconstruction" but rather as preparation for a more poetically attuned form of "building" (*Bauen*) "on the other side" (vv. 14–15), as Hölderlin puts it. In this sense, being able to build goes beyond the work of the carpenter, stonemason, or engineer; it entails the poetic craft of grasping history (*Geschichte*) in terms of a destinal dispensation (*Geschick*) whose lineaments are difficult to trace and even more difficult to understand. Such work involves a long, thoughtful path of reflection that the two interlocutors attempt on the banks of the Ister at a time and season of turning when a whole people hesitantly confronts the bends and turns in its own history and waits upon a time of coming. This perhaps helps to explain the tempo and rhythm of the

Western Conversation, its stops and starts, its curious way of taking up a theme and then leaving it behind as it moves away to an end that recedes from view and never really "ends."

Ultimately, what Heidegger confronts in his long and hesitant conversation on Hölderlin near the banks of the Ister is a test/trial (*Prüfung*) about the readiness of the Germans to reconstitute themselves in the face of the new historical situation—but also in terms of the old natural (and cultural) landscape. What matters most to him in this long meditative reflection is the proper understanding of the German language—and of how Hölderlin's own poetic word holds the key to the German future. If for Hellingrath and the George Circle, Hölderlin became the prophetic voice of German self-understanding both during and after the First World War, then for Heidegger such a role becomes even more pressing after the end of the Second World War. On Heidegger's reading, the future of the West would not, then, depend on the nation with the most soldiers, tanks, fighter planes, or atomic bombs. Such a history marked by machinational-instrumental control and dominion would lead only to the devastation and decline of the West. But the promise of a new beginning always attracted Heidegger. We might even say that Heidegger's entire philosophical *Denkweg* is marked by such a promise. Even Heidegger's constant preoccupation with homecoming, return, remembrance, and commemoration needs to be understood as part of his lifelong preoccupation with beginning anew and its attendant hope for what is coming. As the poet of *das Kommende*, Hölderlin offers Heidegger the poetic resources for framing this language of what is coming in terms that resist easy appropriation and abuse. Or so Heidegger believed. But Heidegger's own manner of appropriating Hölderlin's poetic word appears to us now, after the many revelations of the *Black Notebooks* and the recently published letters to Fritz Heidegger, as Icarus-like. Heidegger's own hubris carried him too far away from the temperate path and led to his own fall—both in 1945–1946 with the de-Nazification commission/Badenweiler stay and in the contemporary reception of his work in the past decade. Whatever position one takes on Heidegger's own tragic path of German national salvation, we are left with an unclean history of arrogance, resistance, self-justification, cover-up, and the refusal to accept responsibility for his ownmost egregious "errors." Here there is no room for grand gestures of dismissive self-aggrandizement that might be couched in the language of "philosophical" tendentiousness—"He who thinks greatly, must err greatly" (GA: 13: 81). Heidegger's postwar strategy of abandoning *völkisch* appeals to Hölderlin—"Hölderlin is poet of the Germans"—for a more Western-centric reading of the poet—can be attributed to the shifts within German history (GA 39: 214; GA 9: 337–341). After his grueling proceedings with the de-Nazification commission in 1945–1946, Heidegger understood that he had to abandon the language of national supremacy with its appeal to nationalist saviors such as Schlageter and the Heroes of Langemarck for a more tempered and balanced approach. Despite all of the private grief and the public humiliation, however, the promise of a future German homecoming remains even as it assumes a new form. Now Heidegger will speak of "the coming destiny of the West," a destiny whose fullness is not yet come but that will unfold only as a form of coming (GA 75: 139). The destiny of the West has been overwritten with the metaphysical signatures of Plato, Aristotle, Descartes, and Kant. But in the poetic word of Hölderlin, Heidegger hears the tones of a nonmetaphysical kind of language whose deep resonances still need to be heard and engaged. This is the work that the Older Man and Younger Man set out upon in their conversations—the work of a new Hölderlin reception that draws on his prophetic status as "the poet of the other beginning."

What Heidegger sets out to do in "The Western Conversation" is to resituate Hölderlin in terms of the failures and caesurae of German history. He does so by engaging him anew to imagine a transformed German future that clings to the destinal dispensation of "the secret spiritual Germany" of old, but now in terms of a new turning in the history of the West (GA 94: 155). What remains constant through all of these "revolutionary" turnings from 1933 to 1946 is Heidegger's complete faith in Hölderlin as "*the* poet of the other beginning of our history" (GA 66: 406). If in 1938 the plural adjective "our" will be read as "we" Germans, by 1946 the political exigencies of the moment persuade Heidegger to read it as "we" Westerners. But the mission and the mandate remain remarkably the same. In an epoch of machinational devastation, where human beings remain foreign to their own home, how are we to enter into the withheld promise of dwelling poetically upon the earth? How are we to "come to dwell in what is our own" (HHI: 21/GA 53: 24)? How are we to meet the promise of Hölderlin's "Ister" hymn of fulfilling "the human potential for being, in relation to being, [as] poetic" (HHI: 120/GA 53: 150)? These are the questions of authentic dwelling that haunt "The Western Conversation" as it plays out in a Southwestern Germany beset by homelessness, foreign conquest, and devastation.

It is in Heidegger's work of the postwar era that he raises the question of profound displacement and authentic homelessness. Heidegger urges us to take up this question as perhaps the most pressing one facing us in our epoch of technological mastery and colonial expansion. But does Heidegger's question-frame get the basic form of this question right? That is, does his way and manner of questioning offer a genuine path into the question of poetic dwelling and homelessness for our own age? In his book *Dis-enclosure*, Jean-Luc Nancy writes:

> It is urgent that the West—or what remains of it—analyze its own becoming, turn back to examine its provenance and its trajectory, and question itself concerning the process of decomposition of sense to which it has given rise.[29]

Heidegger's task in "The Western Conversation" is to carry out just such an examination of the West as both origin and possibility, source and mouth of a great river that cuts through the heart of Europe and divides it into north and south, even as it does so by imagining a different kind of unity between past and future. The history of Europe as experienced by Heidegger is one long development of technological-instrumental dominion and control over the natural world with the aim of raising the human being into its new status as master and possessor of nature. This machinational history of European colonialism and imperial self-assertion fits into the later Heidegger's interpretation of modern technicity in the epoch of the *Gestell*. But the late Heidegger also offers a powerful critique of such a history and of "Europe's technological-industrial domination that has already covered the entire earth" (EHP: 200–201/GA 4: 176). For him, what European civilization has wrought has proved to be both a displacement and a denial of the destiny (*Geschick*) of the West. Heidegger puts the question bluntly: "Does the West still exist?" And he answers: "It has become Europe." Through its machinational history, European technicity has covered over and concealed the potential of the first great Greek beginning of the West that was never allowed to unfold its full possibilities. In its present form as "the planetary-interstellar world condition," Europe remains cut off from this great beginning. Hölderlin's poetry offers an alternative, however—an alternative that recognizes that "the voices of destiny have never yet become present, never yet been founded as a whole within what is highest in art."

"The Western Conversation" was never completed by Heidegger. He left it in its fragmentary form—either as a tribute to Hölderlin's own poetic tendency to leave open the possibility of further revision and palimpsestic alteration or because he lacked the will to complete a project whose very ethos was marked by incompletion and fragmentation. The manuscript cuts off just at that point in the discussion between the Younger Man and Older Man where they are about to follow the question of poetic dwelling by returning to a consideration of Pindar's Third Olympian Ode that speaks of Heracles's journey to the Hesperian North. Perhaps Heidegger would have continued this discussion by placing it against his earlier treatment of the homeland/colony fragment from "Brod und Wein" and gone on to explore the meaning of Greece for the modern German project of "saving the West." No matter which direction he might have pursued, it is clear that he wished to stake out new territory. As the Younger Man acknowledged, "we know the sojourn (*Aufenthalt*) and yet we do not know it" (GA 75: 194). As with Hölderlin's own poem "The Ister," "The Western Conversation" does not "end" with an ending; it simply breaks off and leaves in its wake the mystery of both ending and beginning. As the conversation between the Younger Man and the Older Man puts it:

The Younger Man: What that one does, the river
No one knows.

The Older Man: So ends the Ister-hymn. No, so it breaks off.

The Younger Man: Because no one knows—not even the poet.

The Older Man: It is, then, no coincidence that the hymn remains unfinished.

The Younger Man: Or is it precisely brought to completion in this way of breaking off?

Heidegger ends the manuscript with a brief notation: "Nicht abgeschlossen"/("Not completed") (GA 75: 196).

Postscript

Wieviel Heimat braucht der Mensch?

—Jean Amery, *Jenseits von Schuld und Sühne*

Any attempt to render some final judgment concerning Heidegger's "Hölderlin" must ever be held in tension with the shifting and always elusive task of coming to terms with Heidegger himself. Heidegger did not render this task any easier with his inability and unwillingness to come to terms with his own work and its implications for our time. Such a truth proves disappointing since Heidegger's work on Hölderlin covers the critical years 1934 to 1948 that shaped modern Germany. Heidegger began this period with an unerring faith in the German national mission and its right to self-assertion. By the end he had certainly undergone profound changes, both in his thinking and his life, changes that moved him from his faith in Hitler and National Socialism. Still, in a fundamental sense, Heidegger's experience of triumph, hope, glory, defeat, and humiliation never succeeded in altering this enduring faith—both in Germany's singular ability to save the West and in the role of Hölderlin for bringing this about. And yet the bitter defeat in 1945 and the harrowing events that followed in 1945–1946 did come as a profound wound. Heidegger was stripped of his right to teach and brought to account for his support of Hitler's regime and for his own profoundly flawed attempt to lead the forces of revolution in Germany. When the war ended on May 8, 1945, Heidegger wrote in his notebook: "The War at an end, nothing's changed, nothing new, on the contrary . . . the devastation (*Verwüstung*) continues" (GA 77: 291). Six years later in his WS 1951–1952 lectures, "What Calls for(th) Thinking?," Heidegger offers a refrain on this motif, claiming: "The wasteland grows. This signifies that the devastation spreads. Devastation is more than destruction . . . Devastation is more uncanny than destruction (*unheimlicher als Zerstörung*)" (GA 8: 31). He then adds, "Devastation is more uncanny than mere extermination" (*als blosse Vernichtung*). What can one possibly say here? We find a profound deafness to the plight of Jewish victims of the Third Reich in such claims, comparing the camp prisoners' horror with the philosophical landscape of the postwar world and finding it inessential. What lingers in this response to devastation and destruction is Heidegger's own sense of wanting to refrain from any possible confrontation with the monstrous criminality of National Socialism and its deeds. The path of Heidegger's postwar response to all this is simple: avoidance, denial, and silence.

In a note from his manuscript *The History of Beyng*, Heidegger had offered a hint of how he had understood the logic of the war and the devastation that would inevitably follow. In a sentence left out of the published manuscript, Heidegger opined: "The question would need to be raised: in what is the strange predetermination of Jewry for planetary criminality grounded?"[1] In his *Black Notebooks*, Heidegger defines criminality as "the devastation of everything into what is broken" (GA 96: 266). There he makes the pointed claim that "Judaism is the principle of the destruction" (GA 97: 20). Once the war is over, Heidegger remains "silent" on the question of the Jews except for his letter to Marcuse in 1947, where he compares what happened to Jews in Nazi Germany to *Ostdeutsche* under Stalin.[2] And in this postwar period something uncanny or *unheimlich* comes to structure Heidegger's approach to the question of Germany's fate under Allied occupation. The whole discourse of German exceptionalism—with Hölderlin as its prophet—goes underground, as it were. We find an exemplary case in "Letter on Humanism," where, retreating from the nationalism of his "Germania" lectures, Heidegger now maintains "when Hölderlin composes 'Homecoming' he is concerned that his countrymen (*Landesleute*) find their essence. In no way does he seek this in an egoism of his Volk. Rather, he sees this essence in the Volk's belonging to the destiny of the West" (GA 9: 338). He then adds: "What is German is not told to the world so that through the German essence the world might recover; rather it is spoken to the Germans so that they, through a destinal belongingness to other Völker, might become world-historical with them (cf. Hölderlin's poem 'Remembrance,' *Tübingen Gedenkschrift 1943*, 322)."[3] And yet the vision of Hölderlinian national renewal, so clearly expressed in the 1943 essay, is extinguished in 1946. Now we find on offer a Hölderlin who is no longer simply "the poet of the Germans" but the figure who leads Germany into "a destinal belongingness to other peoples" (GA 39: 214, 220; GA 9: 338). The historical context of the 1943 essay shows a Heidegger who is clinging to an ideal of German greatness whose day is past. On January 6, 1943, the German Sixth Army capitulates at Stalingrad; in February, Hans and Sophie Scholl are executed; in April, Dietrich Bonhoeffer is arrested, followed by the uprising in the Warsaw ghetto. In May, Rommel's Afrika Korps is defeated, and in June a festival is held in Tübingen to celebrate the 100th anniversary of Hölderlin's death. Several of the speeches held at this event celebrate "the German mission," "German self-assertion," and declare that "whether German youths finds their way to Hölderlin and his spirit is the fateful question that decides whether they are strong and worthy enough to bear this great future."[4] During this campaign of German military struggle, Hölderlin is put forward as "the poet of the ultimate readiness to sacrifice."

In his own contribution to the 1943 Hölderlin celebration, Heidegger writes: "'Remembrance' is the poetic abiding in the essence of the fateful poetic vocation that, in the festive destiny (*Geschick*) of the Germans' coming history, shows the ground of its endowment in a festive way."[5] Here we find a significantly different tone from that expressed in 1946. For in this later piece Heidegger insists that his earlier usage was "not patriotic, not nationalistic, but beyng-historical" (GA 9: 338). And yet during the war years there are too many cases where Heidegger offers a reading of Hölderlin that is deeply tied to his political vision of German national supremacy.[6] In the Ister lectures Heidegger clearly asserts that "Hölderlin poetizes from out of poetic care for the becoming homely of the Germans's Western-historical humanity" (GA 53: 84). And in a letter during the Battle of Stalingrad, Heidegger writes that "Now, slowly, the world-historical trial is coming closer for the Germans" (HKB: 84–85). And then he adds: "We have still not learned that he who thinks from out of the national does not need to think the 'international';" on the contrary, he claims that this distinction has become "untenable." It is "in the realm beyond such a contrast that the founding vocation of the Germans lies concealed." Through all this, Heidegger remains attached to the singular vocation of the Germans, as he expressed it in the *Black Notebooks*: "To be German: to cast forth the innermost burden of the history of the West and to bear it upon one's shoulders" (GA 95: 2).

We have already seen how deeply tied to Hölderlin's understanding of "das Nationelle" Heidegger was and how this would have profound consequences for his understanding of language, *Volk*, and *Vaterland*. And while "das Nationelle" need not be reduced to a nationalist-patriotic creed, for the Germans of the Hitler era, it came to define just such a possibility. Moreover, the whole topos of home, homecoming, *Heimat*, and *Heimkehr* would become a fateful part of this discussion about "the National" in the era of German National Socialism. In the "Letter on Humanism" Heidegger attempts to suppress these nationalist resonances from the Hitler era in an effort to salvage his academic existence. As Heidegger thinks it in 1946, "Heimat" is not something "regional," "geographical," or "national" but instead thought in terms of "nearness to being" (*Nähe zum Sein*) (GA 9: 338). Moreover, as he puts it there, "even the West (*Abendland*) is not thought regionally as the Occident (*Okzident*) in contrast to the Orient, not merely as Europe, but rather world-historically out of nearness to the origin (*Nähe zum Ursprung*)." But has there been a significant shift in Heidegger's thinking from 1942 to 1946 on this question of the National? In his seminar *Geschlecht III*, Jacques Derrida offers this comment:

> Attentive to the fact that this discourse, especially in 1946, resonates from its proximity to the question of German nationalism, Heidegger inverts things, or believes he is inverting things and eliminating the suspicion of German nationalism, whereas, I believe, he does nothing but reproduce the ambiguity or equivocality of every nationalist discourse.[7]

One might have imagined a different kind of education for Heidegger—both philosophical and personal, one that perhaps would have rethought the very topos of *Geschlecht* not as "race," "stock," "lineage," "descent," or any of the other speciesisms performed by National Socialism and its adherents. One might have imagined a Heidegger who would have learned the hard lessons of the war years and reconceived the philosopheme of homecoming in a way that acknowledged its genuinely *alien* character. But Heidegger showed himself unable to take up this difficult work, never properly understanding how malignant such a discourse was in its essential sense. Instead, he cleaved to his *Heimat* discourse long after it had proven itself complicit in the German catastrophe that had led Heidegger before the *epuration* committee. In the postwar writings,

Heidegger does offer poignant insights about releasement, letting-be, *Gelassenheit*, and the wisdom of the Country Path. But the *Feldweg* that opens itself to Heidegger remains closed off to those who do not share the wise serenity of the provincial *Heimat*. As Heidegger explains it, "no one can secure it who does not already have it" (GA 13:90). Only those whose *Geschlecht* has been tied to the paths hewn by their ancestral stock may hear the summons of the *Feldweg*. Heidegger was hardly the first to confect this provincial mix of homeland, dialect, landscape, region, *Volk*, and national lineage. Nor was he alone in yoking Hölderlin to a dream of national renewal that took the form of a destinal community of those born to a singular German endowment. Some others, like Hellingrath, shunned the provincialism of the *Feldweg* for a different kind of German national community, finding it in the language of Hölderlin, poet of the Secret Germany. Only in this "Secret Germany," Hellingrath insisted, could such a dream take form, in a Germany "whose secret is always entrusted only to the very few and is to be sure never accessible to non-Germans" (HV: 121). Writing in SS 1934 on the "mandate of our Volk . . . the secret of the mandate, and the history of the Volk of the earth," Heidegger juxtaposes "*the* false contemporaneity" against "the *secret Germany*" (GA 84: 337–338). After the war this whole lexicon of "das geheime Deutschland" goes underground, as it were, securing its power in the silence of its destinal endowment.

What does emerge, however, is a Heidegger who has undergone a painful experience of exile and disappropriation, a thinker who styles himself a victim of the war years.[8] Writing to Jaspers in 1950, he explains how "we never believed in victory and, if it had come to it, *we* would have been the first to fall" (HJB: 201). He goes on to say, "In spite of everything, dear Jaspers, in spite of death and tears, in spite of afflictions and abominations, in spite of rootlessness and banishment, in this homelessness there properly occurs not nothing; there an advent (*Advent*) conceals itself whose most distant hints we may perhaps experience in a faint flurry." But Jaspers, whose own wartime experience in Heidelberg with a Jewish spouse included the need to secure cyanide capsules in case of Gestapo arrest, would have none of it. He writes back to Heidegger:

> You write further: "In this homelessness . . . an advent conceals itself." My horror grew as I read that. As far as I am able to grasp it, this is pure fantasy which, in line with so many other fantasies—all pretending to be just what we need

in this moment—have made fools of us for the last half-century. Are you on the point of appearing as a prophet who, based on secret tidings, reveals something supernatural? As a philosopher who seduces us away from reality? Who, through fictions, allows what is possible to be neglected? With such things as these one is left to ask . . . What of probation and restoration of one's authority [to teach]? (HJB: 210–211)

For Jaspers, Heidegger's complicity in "that which happened" seems self-evident to all but Heidegger himself. As he sees it, Heidegger's letter offers little hope for reconciliation or acknowledgment of past errors. Jaspers writes: "As I read your letters just now the same entanglement [as 1933] immediately re-established itself. It is as if you had not responded to me in an essential way, in what to me is absolutely necessary" (HJB: 208–210). Heidegger writes that he believes "the business of evil is not at an end" and gripes about Stalin's treaties in Eastern Europe, resuscitating thereby the old NS orthodoxies. Again Jaspers responds: "To read something like this is horrifying for me." He challenges Heidegger by speaking to "the appearance of grandeur in such visions" and worries that Heidegger does not realize that "the power of evil in Germany" lies not in Stalin's threats from outside but within Germany itself due to "the concealing and forgetting of the past, this new so-called 'Nationalism' and the return of the old beaten tracks of thinking and of all the old ghosts which, even though they are vain and invalid, still destroy us." As Jaspers's letter made all too clear, Heidegger had not genuinely grasped what had taken place in Germany over the last twenty years. Still in denial about Germany's role in carrying out the machinations of *das Gestell*, Heidegger shifts the blame outward toward Stalin and the other Allied powers. In doing so, Heidegger proves himself as someone unable to grasp "the question of German guilt" that Jaspers had thrust into the center of postwar thinking.[9]

The very topos of homecoming or *Heimkunft* reaffirms just such a discourse. As Derrida reminds us, the loss of *Heimat* here is not simply the loss of something thought of as "land" or "home-land" but is configured in terms beyond the mere "place" or *Ort* of one's habitat. *Heimat* is thought here as a nearness to being rooted in language that belongs to a way of being open to the *Da* as *das Freie*—the free, open relation to being. Here we do not possess the land as owners of what is proper to us. Rather, we become the opening for the event that appropriates us to its way of unfolding. And while Heidegger does hold open such a space for thinking *Heimat* in this deeply phenomenological way, he nonetheless manages to close it off by securing its boundaries in terms that fall all too uncomfortably within the space of the native and national. It is in terms of such a discourse of *Heimat* that Heidegger will think of *Heimkunft*, or homecoming, as a return home. Such a homecoming is not simply a return (back) home. It involves, rather, an understanding of Hölderlinian temporality such that homecoming happens as an opening to the future and not simply as an atavistic/nostalgic turn to something past. And while for Heidegger the essence of homecoming is this opening to what is coming, we can hardly forget the dangerous, frightful, and *unheimlich* resonances that pervade Heidegger's discourse of an alien homecoming. We see this when Heidegger writes to his brother Fritz in August 1945, "It is becoming ever clearer to me that our homeland—the core of this Southwestern part of Germany—will be the historical birthplace of Western spirit (*des abendländischen Geistes*)" (HAS: 129–130).

Ultimately, we are left with a deep chiasm in Heidegger's understanding of *Heimat* and *Heimkehr*—it is always *unterwegs*, always "to come," always something futural that can never be delimited by the geographical or national boundaries of one nation, one people, one *Volk*. These, as Heidegger well understood, are all the residue of a metaphysics of place that continues to reaffirm subjectivity and "the egoism of the Volk" that are thought ontically, rather than beyng-historically. And yet at crucial moments, Heidegger clings to his own ontic predispositions as a native Swabian at odds with the machinations of modern technology and Jewish calculation. Are these ontic predispositions mere oversights or incidental forejudgments that can be dismissed or overlooked as we come to consider the beyng-historical significance of Heidegger's "Hölderlin"? Or do they remain as undeniable, inalienable prejudices that undermine the very beyng-historical way of thinking that Heidegger opens up to us? This is a question that divides so much of Heidegger scholarship and has been rekindled in the wake of the *Black Notebooks* and palpable evidence of Heidegger's own "regional" prejudices.

Again, in *Geschlecht III*, Derrida offers one response that situates Heidegger's discourse of *Heimat* and *Heimkehr* within the thematics of the German national vocation. For Derrida, Heidegger's "schema of return is the theme on the basis of which is typically determined, I will not say nationalism, every nationalism, all of nationalism, but it is a word—the word *Heimkunft*—without which it is difficult to imagine a nationalism."[10]

And yet, thinking through the implications of Heidegger and *Heimkunft*, Derrida points to a different kind of "journey, the path open toward adventure, path-breaking, what strikes open a new *via rupta*, a new route for a new dwelling, and there, in the dependency or movement of this other line, we have, instead of nostalgic withdrawal toward the original dwelling, colonial expansion, the future as the adventure of culture or of colonization, of the dwelling that is cultivated and colonized starting from new routes." This is Heidegger in nuce: the tension between the nomadological journey that opens new routes *and* the path of the well-worn *Feldweg* that takes us back to our old provincial roots.

In his 1934 radio speech "Creative Landscape: Why Do We Stay in the Provinces?," Heidegger relates the story of how he came to reject the prestigious call to the Humboldt University in Berlin. As he ruminates on the silent power of the Schwarzwald firs and the solitude of the rising elevation granted by the landscape, he relates how he knew that he needed to stay in Freiburg and decline the call. He knows this by attending to the silent gestures offered by his peasant neighbor, who does not utter a word. In this simple gesture of "keeping his mouth tightly shut," we find the self-same provincial silence that Heidegger, like so many others of his generation, clung to as a way to avoid having to answer for the horror of National Socialism. In *Race and Erudition*, Maurice Olender thoughtfully addresses the question of German silence by examining the generational "mutism" that befell the academic community in the postwar era. But Olender was hardly alone in pointing toward this gesture of silence. As W.G. Sebald so powerfully notes in his essay "Air War and Literature," the process of postwar reconstruction "prohibited any look backward," pointing this generation "exclusively toward the future and enjoining on it silence about the past."[11] Like Sebald, Reinhart Koselleck recalled that the generational repression of the NS years was entangled in its own peculiar form of denial. For historical memory to perform its work, Koselleck attests, there needs to be "an awareness of a *before* and of an *after*."[12] But as "Koselleck (b. 1927) recalls, this was not the case: people remained the same 'after and before 1945.' There was no new beginning." This "taciturn generation" confected for itself a useful mythos of a "Stunde Null" that "prevented any raising of consciousness about what had preceded it." Heidegger's case was singular, to be sure. Yet he too joined this generation in refusing to confront the damage wrought in the NS years. In his public discourse there is virtually no trace of anything remaining from the war years. When Heidegger does address issues from this era, he speaks not of the victims of Germany's violence, but of the violence done to Germans themselves by Stalin and the Allies.

In the immediate postwar era as the Nuremberg trials come to dominate German public life, Heidegger writes in the *Black Notebooks* of how, amidst the idle chatter concerning Allied re-education, "no one thinks about how the Germans are doing" (GA 97: 51). Against this public unmindfulness, Heidegger exhorts his fellow Germans to embrace their authentic vocation "to be shepherds in the West." Moreover, he writes of *Heimat* and *Heimkehr* in spite of—or rather owing to—the widespread homelessness that afflicts the homeland. And as the geographic boundaries of this homeland are reconfigured by the machinations of Allied power politics, Heidegger clings ever more fiercely to his Hellingrathian dream of a secret, spiritual Germania. Here again we find the traces of homeland and homecoming not as a dwelling in the familiar and domestic but as a journey in, through, and in tension with the foreign, alien, *unheimlich*. "Homeland" (*Heimat*) here is thought of less as a geographical space than as a region for opening up freely to/ for the future. As the time-space between the first and other beginning, *Heimat* offers the possibility of a transition out of the metaphysics of national-political seizures of "land." All the while through this devastating turmoil of historico-political takeover of "German" lands in the East, Heidegger draws upon Hellingrath's "Hölderlin" as the avatar of a new homecoming for the Germans. This arrogation of Hölderlin in the name of Germany's renewal, so prevalent in the period of National Socialism, now takes a different form in the postwar years. Whereas from 1934 to 1944 Heidegger wrote three sets of lectures and a book on Hölderlin, after the war there are a few short essays—". . . poetically dwells the human being" (1951), "Hölderlin's Earth and Heaven" (1959), and several other occasional pieces, but there are really no sustained public manuscripts dedicated to Hölderlin.[13] It is as if exposing Hölderlin to this public realm in a direct and substantial way would be to short-circuit his poetic power. Hölderlin's name continues to appear in virtually all of Heidegger's most important books and essays after 1945, but he is seldom the focus of these writings. The one exception, of course, is his 1946–1948 piece "The Western Conversation," which remained unpublished until a quarter century after Heidegger's death and has yet to receive the attention it deserves. How are we to make sense of this peculiar silence on Heidegger's part? Does Hölderlin's significance wane during these postwar years as Heidegger opens his thinking to extensive work on language, technology, the history of philosophy, and the Greeks? What also brings notice here is how, when Heidegger does attempt to think anew the relation between thinking and poetizing in these years, he turns to poets such as George, Trakl, Rilke, and Hebel. Yet why does Heidegger not write another major book-length study on Hölderlin after the Second World War? Clearly there are several possible ways to respond to this question, and many fall victim to conjecture or worse. But my sense is that the reasons for this lie less in Heidegger's philosophical thinking than in his own public trials during the years of his *Lehrverbot*. The public discourse of the Federal Republic proves an inhospitable space for the kind of engagement with the poet "of" the Germans that Heidegger wished for. Nonetheless, Hölderlin remains essential to his thinking during these years as the poet of transition between the first and the other beginning. His poetizing preserves the mystery of beyng's withdrawal by "withstanding the most extreme conflicts of beyng from the ground up" (HGR: 106/GA 39: 117).

In this age of the world's night, Heidegger turns to Hölderlin as the one figure in the German pantheon capable of cultivating the fundamental attunement necessary for the time in which the gods have fled. This attunement to the conflictual essence of beyng—understood as the tension/play between concealment and revelation, hiddenness and unhiddenness—Hölderlin names "Innigkeit" (conflictual intimacy) (GA 39: 117). For Heidegger, in an era where rebuilding, re-education, and renewal predominate in a public space where this Hölderlinian attunement is forgotten or occluded, the most appropriate comportment (*Haltung*) becomes one of restraint and reserve (*Verhaltenheit*). Only by attuning themselves to the way beyng unfolds at the same time as a withdrawal that manifests and as a manifesting that conceals can the Germans come into their own. This attunement to the simultaneous showing/hiding of beyng Heidegger names "the mystery" (*Geheimnis*) and, as its etymological roots indicate, such mystery is intimately connected to the homeland (*Heimat*) as the realm within which mystery (*Ge-heim-nis*) finds a home. But dwelling in the homeland is always marked by the exile of the wanderer who is ever in mourning over the absence of the gods. Drawing upon this Hölderlinian mythos, Heidegger thinks the mystery of being in terms of the abyssal grounding of that which never shows itself as presence. Here we find Heidegger's profound insight into the dwelling of human beings upon the earth as one of a ceaseless sojourn that never rests in a "land," but is ever underway as spirit's journey homeward to (itself as) the foreign. No figure within German history understood this as deeply as Hölderlin, Heidegger believed, especially in the way he grasped the question of homecoming. For Heidegger, "the poet's vocation is homecoming (*Heimkehr*), by which the homeland (*Heimat*) is first prepared as the land of nearness to the origin. To safeguard the mystery (*Geheimnis*) of the sparing nearness to the most joyful, and to unfold it so as to safeguard it, that is the care of homecoming" (GA 4: 28). The return home requires that we abide in nearness to the origin—and that we safeguard the mystery by keeping it *as* mystery, as what is foreign to us, rather than reducing it to native familiarity. What is proper to us must remain improper, just as what is native must be ever something foreign. This is the law of "alien homecoming" that Heidegger thinks through as he returns again and again to his reading of Hölderlin's poetry.

There remains much that is thought worthy in this essential confrontation between the native and the foreign in Heidegger's account of homecoming. Every exposure to what is alien and uncanny, everything not of the home, as well as every appearance not of the native ground, remains a crucial part of the native son's return homeward. This basic law of an alien homecoming, so carefully articulated in Hölderlin's Bohlendorff letter, offers the outlines for a measured engagement with the foreign that understands it as essential to what is of the home and the native. But the exile experienced by the native sojourner must also be able to account for the radical foreignness of the stranger whose presence is there not simply for the sake of my own journey. The stranger's own journey, thought on its own terms as native, must likewise be considered as essential to any thinking of an alien homecoming. To dwell poetically upon the earth, to find within it one's native home, means recognizing the other as essential to one's own identity. But it also signifies recognizing the stranger's own native identity in its radical alterity to mine—and not for my own sake. This dimension of the "law" of alien homecoming, so poignantly expressed in Hölderlin's hymn "Die Wanderung" (1801), seems to have escaped Heidegger.[14] When Hölderlin writes in this hymn of "die eigene Rede des andern" ("the other's own speech") (v. 45), he poetizes an ethos of hospitality and guest-friendship, what the Greeks termed *xenia*, that Heidegger either overlooks or denies (DKV I: 325). Heidegger's *Vereinnahmung* (arrogation, expropriation, takeover) of Hölderlin as his mouthpiece for transmitting the hidden truths of the secret Germany stands at odds not only with the poet's ethos, but with Heidegger's own thinking. What Heidegger manages to bring about with this political *Vereinnahmung* of Hölderlin is a nativist-nationalist affirmation of the German *Sonderweg* that reduces the power of futural transformation to that of a single *Volk* and a single nation. Such a vision narrows the path of authentic homecoming and reduces the powerfully open and free dimension within Hölderlin's work to a closed national discourse. Heidegger's own way of grasping the vocation of the West is to think it in terms of being ever *unterwegs*, ever underway towards future sojourning, rather than thinking in terms of a stable land or a final destination. And yet all too often in Heidegger's reading of the poet we find him privileging "die Ansässigen" (permanently settled native residents) over those who journey, which assuredly goes against the most dynamic part of Heidegger's thinking (GA 4: 29). We see such a gesture in the 1943 essay "Homecoming" where Heidegger writes of German soldiers fighting for the *Vaterland* in Stalingrad and asks:

> Are not these sons of the homeland, though far from the soil of the homeland . . . who unsparingly sacrifice themselves for it, are not these sons of the homeland the nearest kindred ones of the poet? (GA 4: 30)

This same kind of narrowly patriotic discourse extends to other areas in Heidegger as well, including the provincial privileging of Swabia in the Black Notebooks and Heidegger's insular sense that "the 'island' of Freiburg could become a site of origin" (GA 97: 54; HKB: 93). Nowhere is there room for non-Germans, German Jews, or non-German speaking peoples. Journeying and being *unterwegs*—the hallmarks of Heideggerian thinking—are reserved for the German elect. What comes of this is the monstrous appropriation of the tropes of exile and victimization from those who suffered most under the trauma of the German Final Solution. In Heidegger's rendering, the positions of perpetrator and victim (*Täter und Opfer*) are thereby inverted such that it is he who becomes the victim of the violence perpetrated by an alliance of Jews, Russians, Americans, French among other enemies of the Reich.

As Heidegger comes to define himself as an exile in the devastated wasteland of postwar German existence, he gives voice to the destiny of his generation or *Geschlecht*, a generation that he always defined in terms of nation, nativity, natality, and species. Here Derrida's insights into Heidegger's German exceptionalism bear reflection. For what is at stake in this whole discourse of *Heimkehr*, homecoming, and return is not some reversionary atavism, but the promise of a futural dwelling. Heidegger's Hölderlin writings abound with this promise of a futural homecoming that understands itself not as a return to some earlier version of Germanity, but as an unfolding of the essence of a homeland whose time has not yet come. Here Heidegger's thought opens itself to the deepest insight of Hölderlin's poetic word as an openness to futurity and possibility. But at the same time Heidegger closes off such possibilities when he assails and libels "the Jews" as not the victims, but the perpetrators, of extermination as machination (GA 97: 20). By inverting the position of perpetrators and exiles and arrogating to himself the position of the exiled thinker in the wasteland of modernity, Heidegger not only violates the authentic victims and their suffering. Much more than this, he betrays the philosophical work that he undertakes in the name of healing, *Heile*, and salvation.

We are left to ponder the deep and abiding contradictions in Heidegger's writings, especially their commitment to a racial politics of German national supremacy at the expense of all other peoples, *Völker*, traditions. In the name of a debased version of an elected German nation, Heidegger winds up betraying in some essential ways the very core of his own work. In so doing, Heidegger remains in derogation of the philosophical "thinking" that he elsewhere so prizes. Such an experiment involves thinking the possibility of what is to come in terms of a releasement to the sending of beyng. This means understanding our task as a kind of dwelling amidst beings—human and otherwise—that exposes us to the coming of that which is to come. As we open ourselves to the call of this event, we attune ourselves to beyng's claim upon us whereby we become conflictually intimate to beyng's own way of revealing and concealing. To close off this kind of dwelling amidst beings by arbitrarily designating one nation, one race, one species, one gender as having a privileged relation to beyng's way of unfolding is to miss profoundly what the event entails. At root, Heidegger understood this or he would not have been able to think the open relation to beyng in the way he did. And yet, at crucial moments, Heidegger remains in default of the very thinking that animates his work. This same default remains operative in important ways in Heidegger's whole approach to Hölderlin. The Hölderlin writings offer some of the most poignant insights within Heidegger's corpus and yet within them we find as well some of the most troubling turns of language.

At the same time that we find an unwearied hope for the coming of the gods, we also cannot help but detect an irremediable temper of tragic loss and forfeiture. Heidegger's entire cycle of Hölderlin lectures comes to us marked by this chiastic tension between the promise of a futural homecoming and the uncanny loss of something irrecoverable—and sacred. From the first set of lectures on "Germania" (1934) to the last public lecture on "Hölderlin's Earth and Heaven" (1959), Heidegger situates the poet between "the *Aufgang* of the great beginning" in the early Greeks and "the *Untergang* of the West" prefigured in Nietzsche and Spengler (GA 4: 179; GA 5: 326). Yet Heidegger could not embrace the romantic trope of a return home as a kind of nostalgic homecoming. He well understood the depredations of a modernity that had destroyed all possibilities of a simple *Heimkehr*. As Hannah Arendt well knew, we are all exiles confronting an uncertain future.[15] Heidegger too, even in his Black Forest idyll, knew of the loss and irretrievability of *Heimat*. It is from this place of exile that the Hölderlin writings come forth. In many ways, Heidegger was a tragic figure who, unlike Odysseus, could never properly return home. There was always an alien element to homecoming for him, a strange and singularly unsettling destitution in the very project of return. In a recent Colm Tóibín novel that deals with Agamemnon's miscarried homecoming to Argos, the figure of Clytemnestra utters these poignant words: "I live alone in the shivering, solitary knowledge that the time of the gods has passed."[16] So it must have appeared to Heidegger as well, as he contemplated the barren landscape of a Western history echoing the madman's proclamation about the death of god.

Some of Heidegger's most significant work on Hölderlin—the course lectures and "The Western Conversation"—was never published during Heidegger's lifetime. The time never seemed right for Heidegger to share this intimate work with a public that he believed was not yet ripe enough for its enigmatic and esoteric truths. Perceiving that following its curious paths and turns required the patience of a poet, Heidegger must have consoled himself with the knowledge that the work belonged to a future for which his contemporaries were not yet ready. In a sense, this work poses to us questions that we need to ask ourselves, whether we are ready for their difficulties or not. The deferral of hope is a curious and delicate enterprise. As Walter Benjamin knew all too well, hope is a precious commodity available perhaps only to those who lack it.[17] But despite this tragic note that accompanies Heidegger's Hölderlin writings, there is always the deferred promise of a future coming. Yes, Heidegger knew all too well that "the West in its entirety is now homeless" (GA

73: 763). But he also knew about the intimations of the gods' return that held forth the promise of a new homecoming for those who had been bitterly defeated by a century of world wars and global gambits. We live in the shadow of Heidegger's failed hopes and can, in retrospect, see most of the failures of his all too narrowly drawn metaphysical attachment to the *Volk*, the nation-state, and the provincial community with all its racial-political prejudices that meant the death and destruction of so many. This we can never overlook. This must remain a permanent part of Heidegger's philosophical legacy which, as a historical phenomenon, constituted the very betrayal of philosophy itself. It is imperative that we never pass over these impossibly provincial and chauvinistic moments within Heidegger's corpus, moments that connect to the most harrowing memories within German history. Certainly Paul Celan could never forget them. Not even as he enjoined "the heart" to:

Cry out the shibboleth, into the alienness of the homeland.	*Ruf's, das Schibboleth, hinaus in die Fremde der Heimat.*[18]

In the teeth of such strangeness, Celan understood that the community of those who had suffered under the nationalistic fantasies of fascistic oppression would need its own form of "remembrance":

Fly your flag at half-mast, memory. At half-mast today and for ever.	*Setz deine Fahne auf Halbmast, Erinnrung. Auf Halbmast für heute und immer.*

In a certain sense we can understand Heidegger's embrace of homecoming, *Heimat*, and Hölderlin as the expression of a desperate, abortive effort to stave off the dispersive, disjunctive effects of a modernity whose logic, in the century of technology's unrivaled escalation, proved implacable and unremitting. In his travel book *Sojourns*, written in 1962 during his first trip to "Greece," the seventy-three-year-old Heidegger expresses his profound ambivalence about journeying to these ancient sites within the packaged *Gestell* of the tourist industry. If his initial impulse was to sojourn to the Greek islands on the trail of *aletheia*, then his journeying confronts a hard truth:

Through their incessant work, modern technology and the scientific industrialization of the world set about (*sich anschicken*) to extinguish every possibility of a sojourn (*Aufenthalt*). (GA 75: 244)

Yet given this desolate vision, Heidegger does not forsake the Hölderlinian promise of poetic dwelling. He keeps it alive in dialogue with the poet, his last link to the languishing of the Greek gods who have fled. And yet the suspicion persists that if Heidegger's "Hölderlin" were ever to become the prophet of an alien homecoming, his words would remain forever foreign and strange. Such words could only bespeak the madness of the poet in the tower and,

if he spoke of this time, he could only babble and babble, all-all, way-ways agagain. ("Pallaksch. Pallaksch.")	*spräch er von dieser Zeit, er dürfte nur lallen und lallen, immer-, immer- zuzu.* ("*Pallaksch. Pallaksch.*")[19]

Notes

Introduction

1. Heidegger, *Gesamtausgabe* 95: 387
2. Derrida, *Geschlecht III* (Chicago: University of Chicago Press, 2020), 153.
3. Friedrich Nietzsche, KSA VI: 313.
4. Socrates's *katabasis* opens with a thwarted return to Athens even as the whole book unfolds as an enactment of *nostos* itself.
5. Michael Theunissen, *Pindar: Menschenlos und Wende der Zeit* (Munich: Beck, 2000), 921.
6. For a history of the Hölderlin reception within Germany see Jürgen Scharfschwerdt, *Friedrich Hölderlin: Der Dichter des deutschen Sonderwegs* (Stuttgart: Kohlhammer, 1994); Henning Bothe, *Ein Zeichen sind wir deutungslos: Die Rezeption Hölderlins von ihren Anfängen bis zu Stefan George* (Stuttgart: Metzler, 1992); Claudia Albert, *Deutsche Klassiker im National Sozialismus* (Stuttgart: Metzler, 1994); Max Kommerell, "Der Heros" in: *Der Dichter als Führer* (Berlin: Bondi, 1928), 427–460. See also Andrew Mitchell, "Die Politik des geheimen Deutschland: Martin Heidegger und der George Kreis," *Existentia*, XXIII (2013): 41–64 and Peter Trawny, "Und nie mein land den schatz gewann": Bemerkungen zu Heideggers George Lektüre im 'Geheimen Deutschland' in: Bruno Pieger, ed., *Stefan George: Dichtung Ethos Staat* (Berlin: Verlag für Berlin-Brandenburg, 2010), 189–205.
7. Here is a list of the books that proved most helpful to my reading of the Heidegger–Hölderlin relation: Jennifer Gosetti-Ferencei, *Heidegger, Hölderlin, and the Subject of Poetic Language* (New York: Fordham University Press, 2004); Véronique Fóti, *Heidegger and the Poets* (New Jersey: Humanities Press, 1992); William McNeill, *The Time of Life: Heidegger and Ethos* (Albany, NY: SUNY Press, 2006); Dennis Schmidt, *On Germans and Other Greeks* (Bloomington: Indiana University Press, 2001); Kathleen Wright, "Heidegger and the Authorization of Hölderlin's Poetry "in Karsten Harries and Christoph Jamme, eds.,

Martin Heidegger: Politics, Art, Technology (New York: Holmes & Meier, 1994), 164–174; William Allen, *Ellipsis: Of Poetry and the Experience of Language after Heidegger, Hölderlin, and Blanchot* (Albany, NY: SUNY Press, 2007); Babette Babich, *Words in Blood Like Flowers: Philosophy and Poetry, Music and Eros in Hölderlin: Nietzsche and Heidegger* (Albany, NY: SUNY Press, 2006) and Robert Bernasconi, "Poets as Prophets and as Painters," *Heidegger and Language*, ed. Jeffrey Powell (Bloomington: Indiana University Press, 2001), 146–162. For German scholarship cf. Peter Trawny, *Heidegger und Hölderlin: oder Der Europäische Morgen* (Würzburg: Königshausen & Neumann, 2004); Susanne Ziegler, *Heidegger, Hölderlin und die alētheia: Martin Heideggers Geschichtsdenken in seinen Vorlesungen 1934/35 bis 1944* (Berlin: Duncker & Humblot, 1991); Stephanie Bohlen, *Die Übermacht des Seins: Heideggers Auslegung des Bezuges von Mensch und Natur und Hölderlins Dichtung des Heiligen* (Berlin: Duncker & Humblot, 1993); Holger Helting, *Heideggers Auslegung von Hölderlins Dichtung des Heiligen* (Berlin: Duncker & Humblot, 1999); Beda Allemann, *Hölderlin und Heidegger* (Zürich: Atlantis, 1954); Anja Solbach, *Seinsverstehen und Mythos* (Freiburg: Alber, 2008); Iris Buchheim, *Wegbereitung in die Kunstlosigkeit: Zu Heideggers Auseinandersetzung mit Hölderlin* (Würzburg: Königshausen & Neumann,1994), and especially, Diana Aurenque, *Ethosdenken: Auf der Spur einer ethischen Fragestellung in der Philosophie Martin Heideggers* (Freiburg, Alber, 2011).

8. Hölderlin GA 4–39–52–53–75; Nietzsche (9 vols.!) GA 6.1, 6.2, 43, 44, 46, 47, 48, 50, 87.

9. For example, in the notion of "the other beginning," *Seyn, Bewahrung* as preservation—among many others. What is deeply Hölderlinian is the political reception of Germany's special mission within the West and especially the Greek-German relation. Cf. also GA 65: "the last God;" "Letter on Humanism" offers remarks on Hölderlin (PM: 257–259/GA 9: 337–339); the analysis of Antigone's Chorus in GA 40 and GA 53; as well as GA 8's "poetic" thinking vs. calculative reasoning.

10. For some help in navigating this difficult and contentious period see Brett Davis's fine study, *Heidegger and the Will* (Northwestern University Press, 2007) and Richard Polt's engaging *Time and Trauma* (Rowman & Littlefield, 2018) that interprets Heidegger's thought in the 1930s. See also my reviews of each: "Situating Heidegger" *American Catholic Philosophical Quarterly* 83, no. 4 (2009): 599–613 and "Thinking Through the Politics of Black and Brown: Heidegger in the Thirties" in *Research in Phenomenology* 50 (2020): 122–131.

11. I use the term "confects" in a Nietzschean sense whereby Heidegger invents such a fiction and one might even say, with hubris, exceeds Hegel's own philosophical design of world history.

12. GA 75 includes a variety of essays, notebook entries, and other writings on Hölderlin. The one exception is Heidegger's travel narrative about his journey to Greece in the 1960s, *Aufenthalte*, which stands heavily under the influence of Hölderlin.

13. Jochen Schmidt, "Hölderlin im 20. Jahrhundert" in Gerhard Kurz, ed., *Hölderlin und die Moderne* (Tübingen: Attempto, 1995), 112.

14. On colony, colonization, and its relation to homecoming, see chapter 2.

15. With the failure of his Rectorate and its miscast political hopes, evident in his political speeches from this time in his program of academic camp gatherings near Todtnauberg in summer/autumn 1933, Heidegger writes: "the success of the camp depends upon new courage, upon the clarity and wakefulness for the futural, on unburdening ourselves from what is past as much as possible, and on the decisive resolve of our will to loyalty, sacrifice, and service"—an unpublished letter cited in Hugo Ott, *Martin Heidegger: Unterwegs zu seiner Biographie* (Frankfurt: Campus Verlag, 1988), 218.

16. Questions about "pain," "suffering," and "sacrifice" will predominate throughout these lectures.

17. Max Kommerell, *Briefe und Aufzeichnungen* (Freiburg: Walter Verlag, 1967), 396, 400.

18. Alfred Baeumler, "Hellas and Germania" in *Studien zur deutschen Geistesgeschichte* (Berlin: Junker & Dünnhaupt, 1937), 305–306. Baeumler writes: "The Greek world has not perished; it stands in a mysterious relation to that which we Germans are and what we seek."

19. Robert Minder, *Dichter in der Gesellschaft* (Frankfurt: Suhrkamp, 1977), 96, 83.

20. Theodor Adorno letter of January 3, 1963, in *Musikalische Schriften*, VI (Frankfurt: Suhrkamp: 1984), 637–638.

21. Thomas Rentsch, *Martin Heidegger: Das Sein und Der Tod* (Munich: Piper, 1989), 181. Rico Gutschmidt, *Sein ohne Grund: Die posttheistische Religiosität im Spätwerk Heideggers* (Freiburg: Alber, 2016), 332–364.

22. Jochen Schmidt, "Hölderlin im 20. Jahrhundert," 112.

23. Jürgen Habermas, *Der philosophische Diskurs der Moderne* (Frankfurt: Suhrkamp, 1988), 168.

24. Peter Trawny, *Martin Heidegger: Eine kritische Einführung* (Frankfurt, Klostermann, 2016), 92.

25. These unpublished letters are cited in Theodor Pfizer, "Die Ausnahme," *Erinnerungen an Martin Heidegger* (Pfullingen: Neske, 1977), 194–195.

26. Heidegger asked that verses from Hölderlin's hymns be read at his grave from Norbert von Hellingrath's Fourth Volume. GA 16: 749–751 and HIB: 208.

27. Jacques Derrida, "Interpreting Signatures," *Dialogue and Deconstruction: The Gadamer-Derrida Encounter*, eds., Diane Michelfelder and Richard Palmer (Albany, NY: SUNY Press, 1989), 60.

28. Jacques Derrida, *Dissemination* (Chicago: University of Chicago Press, 1981), 4, 194.

29. Arno Barnert, *Mit dem fremden Wort: Poetisches Zitieren bei Paul Celan* (Frankfurt: Stromfeld Verlag, 2007), 13, 81.

30. Paul Celan, *Mikrolithen sinds, Steinchen* (Frankfurt: Suhrkamp, 2005), 58.

31. Jacques Derrida, *Of Spirit* (Chicago: University of Chicago Press, 1989), 31, 66.

32. Paul de Man, "Heidegger's Exegeses of Hölderlin," *Blindness and Insight* (Minneapolis: University of Minnesota Press, 1983), 264–265.

33. Hans-Georg Gadamer, *Gesammelte Werke*, III (Tübingen: Mohr Siebeck, 1992), 328, 191.

34. Martin Heidegger, GA 95: 378.

35. In the *Black Notebooks* Heidegger writes that "Hölderlin's poetry is the first overcoming of all metaphysics" BN I: 311/GA 94:428. "Innig" designates for Hölderlin the unity that Heraclitus discerns in/as difference such that unity consists not in the overcoming or removal of difference, but in finding within difference itself a unity of opposites.

36. Hölderlin alludes to the image of "die reissende Zeit"/"the time that tears" in "Der Archipelagus" v. 293 (SPF: 126–127). See also the illuminating remarks in William McNeill, "Remains: Heidegger and Hölderlin Amid the Ruins of Time" in Charles Bambach and Theodore George, eds., *Philosophers and Their Poets* (Albany, NY: SUNY Press, 2019), 159–184.

37. For a sense of the National Socialist *Hölderlinbild* see Bernhard Zeller, ed., *Klassiker in finsteren Zeiten, 1933–1945*, two volumes (Marbach: Deutsche Schiller Gesellschaft, 1983), 325. See also vol. I: 161–164; 319–366; vol. II: 76–135; 300–386 and especially Adolf Hösel, "Der Vermächtnis Hölderlins," *Völkischer Beobachter* 1937, 28 cited in I:324–325.

38. Max Kommerell, *Briefe und Aufzeichnungen: 1919–1944*, ed., Inge Jens (Freiburg: Walter Verlag, 1967), 400.

39. On Heidegger's mastery of the art of self-staging cf. Reinhard Mehring's *Heideggers Überlieferungsgeschick: Eine dionysische Selbstinszenierung* and *Heideggers 'Grosse Politik'* (Tübingen: Mohr Siebeck, 2016).

40. On *Verwindung* see the helpful commmentary in Daniel Dahlstrom, *Heidegger Dictionary* (London: Bloomsbury, 2013), 96, 152, 227, 247 and GA 70: 19–23; GA 73: 752, 787–788.

41. Mehring, *Heideggers Überlieferungsgeschick*, 51.

42. Heidegger himself was of course highly attuned to the resonance of voice in any reading of Hölderlin's poetry. In his directives to his family about which Hölderlin verses should be read at his burial ceremony: "Words of Hölderlin: taken from vol. IV of his *Werke* edited by Norbert von Hellingrath—to be spoken slowly and simply as a leave-taking at my grave," GA 16: 749. For a striking description of Heidegger's voices, cf. Max Kommerell, *Briefe und Aufzeichnungen 1919–1944* (Freiburg: Walter, 1967), 380–383.

43. Willi Fr. Könitzer "Hölderlin und das Wesen der Dichtung: Eine Entgegnung." *Wille und Macht* 5 (1937), 28–30.

44. For typical NS-style appropriation of Hölderlin, cf. Claudia Albert, ed., *Deutsche Klassiker im Nationalsozialismus* (Stuttgart: Metzler, 1994), 189–253.

45. Max Kommerell, *Briefe und Aufzeichnungen 1919–1944*, 400–401, 396–397.
46. See also Gadamer's remarks in *Gesammelte Werke*, III (Tübingen: Mohr, 1987), 328.
47. Cf. Friedrich Nietzsche *Also Sprach Zarathustra* (Leipzig: Kröner, 1930), 146–150.
48. Max Kommerell, *Briefe und Aufzeichnungen 1919–1944*, 397.
49. Cf. Daniel Dahlstrom, *Heidegger Dictionary* (London: Bloomsbury, 2013), 170, for his translation of *Gestell* as "positionality."
50. Dennis Schmidt has offered some of the most penetrating insights on a Heideggerian "ethics" in these essays: "The Later Heidegger," in *History of Continental Philosophy*, ed. Alan Schrift, vol. 4 (Chicago: University of Chicago Press, 2010), 157–175; "On the Sources of Ethical Life," *Research in Phenomenology* 42 (2012): 35–48; "Ethics after Heidegger" in G. Fried and R. Polt, eds., *After Heidegger* (New York: Rowman & Littlefield, 2018), 133–139, and "Where Ethics Begins," *Epochè* 22 (2017): 159–175.
51. Jean-Luc Nancy, *A Finite Thinking* (Stanford, CA: Stanford University Press, 2003), 174.
52. Nancy, *A Finite Thinking*, 175.
53. René Descartes, *Discourse on Method* (Indianapolis: Hackett, 1993), 35.
54. I think this process of *Gleichschaltung* or "bringing into line" goes both ways: at first, Heidegger tries to accommodate himself as Rector to the NS Revolution via his Rectorial Address (RA) and political speeches—yet he seeks to shape or form the message of NS Revolution for his own philosophical program. It is only after failure of his rectorate that he turns to Hölderlin as the new form of/for revolution. Cf. Otto Pöggeler, "Den Führer führen? Heidegger und kein Ende," *Philosophische Rundschau* 32 (1985): 26–67.
55. Cf. Claimed in Adolf Beck, "Das Hölderlinbild in der Forschung: 1939–1944" *Iduna (Hölderlin Jahrbuch)*, I (1944): 203–224. Bernhard Zeller, ed. *Klassiker in finsterer Zeiten, 1933–1945*, 2 vols. (Marbach: Deutsche Schillergesellschaft, 1983).
56. For example, Kathleen Wright's criticism: "Heidegger authorizes his own voice to speak in place of the poet Hölderlin." "Heidegger and the Authorization of Hölderlin's Poetry" in Karsten Harries and Christoph Jamme, eds., *Martin Heidegger: Politics, Art, Technology* (New York: Holmes & Meier, 1994), 167.
57. Max Kommerell, *Briefe und Aufzeichnungen 1919–1944*, 401. Cf. notes 12 and 15.
58. As Heidegger puts it, "The danger is the epoch of beyng, essencing as positionality"/"*Die Gefahr ist die Epoche des Seyns wesend als das Ge-stell*" GA 79: 72.
59. In his letter to Karl Löwith from August 19, 1921, Heidegger uses the term *unum necessarium*, which has its roots in Nietzsche's *Zarathustra* and Rilke's verse. Cf. *Martin Heidegger/Karl Löwith Briefwechsel, 1919–1973* ed. Alfred Denker (Freiburg: Alber, 2017), 55.

60. Maurice Blanchot, "Notre campagne clandestine," *Textes pour Emmanuel Lévinas* (Paris: Place, 1980), 79–87; "Our Clandestine Companion" in *Political Writings, 1952–1993* (New York: Fordham University Press, 2010), 144–152.

Chapter 1

1. Heidegger, CP 421/GA 65: 422.
2. Hölderlin, DE 43/DKV II: 285.
3. John Llewelyn, *The Middle Voice of Ecological Conscience* (New York: St. Martin's, 1991), 96.
4. Norbert von Hellingrath, *Hölderlin Vermächtnis* (Munich: Bruckmann, 1944), 124–125.
5. Georg Simmel, *Der Krieg und die geistigen Entscheidungen* (Munich: Duncker and Humblot, 1917), 9. Manfred Riedel, *Die Idee vom anderen Deutschland* (Kassel: Jenior and Pressler, 1994), 33–38.
6. For a fuller treatment of Heidegger's "politics of the unpolitical" see my *Heidegger's Roots* (Ithaca, NY: Cornell University Press, 2003), especially 180–189 and 232–246.
7. Cf. Claudia Albert, ed. *Deutsche Klassiker im Nationalsozialismus* (Stuttgart: Metzler, 1994); Joachim Storck, "Zwiesprache von Dichten und Denken: Hölderlin bei Martin Heidegger und Max Kommerell," in Bernhard Zeller, ed. *Klassiker in finsteren Zeiten* (Marbach: Deutsche Schillergesellschaft, 1983), II, 345–365; Bernhard Lypp, "Mein ist die Rede vom Vaterland," *Merkur* (41) 1987: 120–135; Phillipe Lacoue-Labarthe, *Heidegger and the Politics of Poetry* (Urbana: University of Illinois Press, 2007); Frank Edler, "Alfred Baeumler on Hölderlin and the Greeks, *Janus Head* 1, no. 3 (Spring) 1999.
8. Hölderlin was conscripted by National Socialism in many ways. One of them lay in the production of small patriotic editions of Hölderlin's verses, suitable for placing in the soldiers' Rücksack. Some of the editions that were popular include: Ernst Müller's *Hölderlins vaterländische Gesänge* (Stuttgart: Kohlhammer, 1942), a collection of Hölderlin's patriotic hymns distributed to soldiers at the Eastern front in a tiny edition of forty-eight pages to fit in a uniform pocket. Other small *Bändchen* of this patriotic sort include: *Hölderlin: Feldauswahl*, ed. Friedrich Beissner (Stuttgart: Cotta, 1943), which states: "im Auftrag der Hölderlin Gesellschaft und des Hauptkulturamtes des NSDAP"; *Hölderlin: Vom heiligen Reich der Deutschen*, ed. Erich Wolf (Jena: Eugen Diederichs, 1935); *Friedrich Hölderlin: Feldpostausgabe* (Weimar: Böhlau, 1943); *Hölderlin in unserer Zeit: Für die Hitlerjugend*, ed. Otto Zander (Leipzig; Skacel, 1944); *Hölderlin: Heldentum; Auswahl für Soldaten*, ed., Amadeus Grohmann (Leipzig: Walter, 1941).
9. Bernhard Zeller, ed. *Klassiker in finsteren Zeiten* (Marbach: Deutsche Schillergesellschaft, 1983), II, 12–15.

10. Kurt Hildebrandt, *Hölderlin: Philosophie und Dichtung* (Stuttgart: Kohlhammer, 1939), 238, 245. He also writes about Hölderlin's "mission which is the awakening of the German Volk," 247.

11. Cf. *Thinking the Poetic Measure of Justice*, 22, 23, 213–230.

12. Heidegger would often disagree with Hellingrath's "philology" but not with the overall "myth" about Hölderlin and his role in German destiny. This myth persisited until Heidegger's last days, so much so that at his funeral service he had used poems read from Hellingrath's edition. Elfride writes to Hellingrath's fiancé Imma von Bodmershof: "N. v H. was also present then" HIB: 153. See also *Norbert von Hellingrath und die Ästhetik der europaischen Moderne* ed., Jürgen Brokoff (Göttingen: Wallstein, 2014).

13. For a fuller discussion of these editions see Werner Volke, Bruno Pieger, Nils Kahlefendt, and Dieter Burdorf, eds., *Hölderlin Entdecken: Lesarten, 1826–1993* (Tübingen: Hölderlin Gesellschaft, 1993) and *Hölderlin Handbuch*, ed. Johann Kreuzer (Stuttgart: Metzler, 2002), 421–438. Ute Oelmann, ed., *Hölderlin-Entdeckungen Studien zur Rezeption* (Stuttgart: Württembergische Landesbibliothek, 2008). See also Wilhelm Böhm, ed. *Gesammelte Werke (Leipzig: Eugen Diederichs, 1905)*. Only Böhm's aspired to be a *Gesamtausgabe*. The other editors collected various poems, letters, prose writings, and *Hyperion*.

14. For a helpful account of the significance of hard jointure for Hellingrath's interpretation of Hölderlin see Albrecht Seifert, *Hölderlin und Pindar* (Eggingen: Isele, 1998) and Frank Edler's dissertation, *The Significance of Hölderlin for Heidegger's Political Involvement with Nazism* (University of Toronto, 1992).

15. StA II: 182, 186. For a more extensive treatment of the Hölderlin-Pindar relationship, see my *Thinking the Poetic Measure of Justice*, 72–82 and 95–108.

16. Friedrich Gundolf, "Archipelagos" in Alfred Kelletat, ed., *Hölderlin: Beiträge zu seinem Verständnis* (Tübingen: Mohr, 1961), 15 and Stefan George, *Werke* II (Munich: dtv, 1983), 301.

17. Wilhelm Lange, *Hölderlin: Eine Pathographie* (Stuttgart: Enke, 1909), 120–121. See also the helpful study by Silke-Maria Weineck, *The Abyss Above: Philosophy and Poetic Madness in Plato, Hölderlin, and Nietzsche* (Albany, NY: SUNY Press, 2002) and Wilhelm Lange, *Der kalkulierte Wahnsinn* (Frankfurt: Fischer, 1992).

18. Clemens Pornschlegel, "Versgehüpfe, Reimgeklingel, Singsang: Heideggers Auseinandersetzung mit Goethe" in K. Eibl & B. Scheffer, eds. *Goethes Kritiker* (Paderborn: Mentis, 2008), 117–134 and Ulrich Raulff, *Kreis ohne Meister* (Munich: Beck, 2010), 253.

19. Friedrich Wolters, *Stefan George und die Blätter für die Kunst* (Berlin: Bondi, 1930), 420–421.

20. Stefan George, *Werke*, II: 299

21. Karl Wolfskehl, "Die Blätter für die Kunst und die neueste Literatur" in *Jahrbuch für die geistige Bewegung*, I (1910): 1–18, 14–15. See also Wolfgang

Martynkewicz, *Salon Deutschland: Geist und Macht, 1900–1945* (Berlin: Aufbau, 2009), 258–304; and Reinhard Mehring, *Heideggers 'Grosse Politik'* (Tübingen: Mohr Siebeck, 2016), 20–29.

22. Carl Schmitt, *Glossarium* (Berlin: Duncker & Humblot, 1991), 152.

23. Stefan George, *Werke*, II, 205–208.

24. Stefan George, *Werke*, II, 301.

25. Max Kommerell, *Der Dichter als Führer* (Berlin: Bondi, 1928) and Stefan Wackwitz, *Hölderlin* (Stuttgart: Metzler, 1985), 143. Hölderlin was popular with the German Youth Movement and expressionism at the same time fulfilling a cultural function within postwar Germany. See also Andrew Mitchell, "Die Politik des geheimen Deutschlands," *Existentia* (2013) vol. 23 (1–2): 41–64 and Peter Trawny, "Politik und Dichtung bei Heidegger: Stefan George und 'das geheime Deutschland," *Existentia* 16, no. 1–2 (2006): 11–22.

26. See Heidegger's 1936 address "Hölderlin and the Essence of Poetry" with its dedication to "Norbert" as a fallen hero; the 1959 address," Hölderlin's Earth and Heaven" with its opening tribute to Hellingrath (GA 4: 32, 175); HIB: , and my *Heidegger's Roots*, 57–63; 310–319 on themes of death and sacrifice of soldierly existence (Schlageter).

27. Max Kommerell, *Briefe und Aufzeichnungen 1919–1944*, 405.

28. I have also drawn on the graceful translation by Dennis Schmidt in *On Germans and Other Greeks* (Bloomington: Indiana University Press, 2001), 167.

29. Bernhard Zeller, ed., *Klassiker in finsteren Zeit*, I, 332.

30. Ernst Müller, ed., *Hölderlins Vaterländische Gesänge* (Stuttgart: Kohlhammer, 1942), 14, 34–35, 25.

31. Willi Könitzer, *Hölderlin: Ein Schicksal in Deutschland* (Berlin: Stalling, 1934), 5–6.

32. Bernhard Zeller, ed., *Klassiker in finsteren Zeit*, I, 324, 341.

33. For a good summary of this Hölderlin industry in Germany see Claudia Albert "Dient Kulturarbeit dem Sieg?—Hölderlin-Rezeption von 1933–1945" in G. Kurz, V. Lawitschka, and J. Wertheimer, eds., *Hölderlin und die Moderne* (Tübingen: Attempto, 1995), 153–173.

34. See for example the wildly fantastical conclusion of Walther Allgöwer's study, *Gemeinschaft, Vaterland, und Staat im Werk Hölderlins*, Universität Basel dissertation, 1939, 143: "The state serves to protect the faithful workers who find themselves together in a community in order to establish the coming kingdom of God."

35. Gerhard Schumann, "Ansprache des Präsidenten," *Iduna*, I (1944): 16. This first issue, of what would later be called the *Hölderlin Jahrbuch* after the war, is a model of NS influence. Schumann was a Nazi-poet. The opening section includes a "Heil Hitler" greeting and speaks of "the German battle for destiny" taking place in Russia. There are also two articles on Hölderlin—his

relevance to soldiers in the war, as well as an article by the editor of the Grosse Stuttgarter Ausgabe, Friedrich Beissner, on "Hölderlin und das Vaterland," 20–34.

36. Stefan George, *Werke*, II, 127.

37. Peter Trawny, *Adyton: Heideggers esoterische Philosophie* (Berlin: Matthes & Seitz, 2010), 8–9, 39–41. Daniel Morat, *Von der Tat zur Gelassenheit* (Göttingen: Wallstein, 2007), 191–204.

38. For a study on the political relation of German poetry to ideals of nationhood see Jürgen Schröder, *Deutschland als Gedicht* (Freiburg: Rombach, 2000), especially 135–152.

39. Gerhard Kaiser, *Pietismus und Patriotismus im Literarischen Deutschland* (Wiesbaden: Steiner, 1961), 40–57.

40. Bernhard Zeller, ed., *Klassiker in finsteren Zeiten*, I, 302–303. Willi Kunz, "Kampfgefährter Hyperion," *Das Innere Reich*, 9 (Dec. 1940): 476–485.

41. Max Kommerell, *Briefe und Aufzeichnungen 1919–1944*, 401. In one of his letters Kommerell asks whether Heidegger's "Auseinandersetzung" with Hölderlin oversteps the accepted limits of balanced interpretation and becomes merely Heidegger's own projection. Even Heidegger himself asks Kommerell: "Is this caprice or the highest freedom?"

42. Jochen Schmidt, "Deutschland und Frankreich als Gegenmodelle in Hölderlins Geschichtsdenken" in H. Scheuer, ed., *Dichter und ihre Nation* (Frankfurt: Suhrkamp, 1993), 176–199, 181.

43. Jean-Luc Nancy, *The Creation of the World* or *Globalization* (New York: SUNY Press, 2007), 50–51, 10.

44. William McNeill, *Time of Life* (Albany, NY: SUNY Press, 2006), xvii, 138.

45. Jean-Luc Nancy, *A Finite Thinking* (Stanford, CA: Stanford University Press, 2003), 174–175.

46. François Raffoul, *The Origins of Responsibility* (Bloomington: Indiana University Press, 2010), 260.

47. François Raffoul, *The Origins of Responsibility*, 223, 241.

48. Jean-Luc Nancy, *A Finite Thinking*, 182.

49. For another reading of "the infinite alterity of the other" see Jacques Derrida, *Spectres of Marx* (New York: Routledge, 1994), 65.

50. See Lévinas's critique of Heidegger in *Totality and Infinity* (Pittsburgh: Duquesne University Press, 1969), especially 45–48 and 77–78. Cf. GA 52: 190 for Heidegger's privileging of the *Eigenes* over *Fremdes*.

51. For a fuller discussion of Hölderlin's Böhlendorff letter see Charles Bambach, *Thinking the Poetic Measure of Justice*, 46–53, and Dennis Schmidt, "The Ordeal of the Foreign and the Enigma of One's Own" *Philosophy Today* 40:1 (1996): 182–196; Peter Trawny, *Heidegger und Hölderlin oder Der Europäische Morgen* (Würzburg: Königshausen & Neumann, 2010), 85–90 and 125–135.

52. In EdP: 31, Heidegger speaks of "saving Europe"—as "the protection of the European *Völker* from the Asiatic." We will see this worked out in a different way in Heidegger's postwar "The Western Conversation" of 1946–1948.

53. See for example the thin paperback editions by Ernst Müller, *Hölderlins Vaterländishe Gesänge* published in the series *Die bunten Hefte für unsere Soldaten* by Kohlhammer in Stuttgart, 1942 or the "Feldpost" edition Friedrich Hölderlin, *Gedichte* (Böhlau: Weimar, 1943) or the Reclams Reihenbändchen Nr. 1, Friedrich Hölderlin, *An die Deutschen* (Leipzig: Reclam, 1943), as well as the collection *O, Heilig Herz der Völker*, ed. Hermann Claudius (Königstein: Langewiesche, 1943), 169.

54. Bernhard Zeller, ed. *Klassiker in finsteren Zeiten*, II, 79.

55. Bernhard Zeller, ed. *Klassiker in finsteren Zeiten*, II, 81–82, 96–97.

Chapter 2

1. Martin Heidegger, GA 73: 717.

2. Cf. Karl George, *Lateinisch-Deutsches Schulwörterbuch* (Hannover: Harnsche Buchhandlung, 1935), 583 and Alois Walde, *Lateinisches Etymologisches Wörterbuch* (Heidelberg: Carl Winter, 1910), 508.

3. Dennis Schmidt, *On Germans and Other Greeks* (Bloomington: Indiana University Press, 2001), 139. Cf. also, Jacques Derrida, *Geschlecht III: Sex, Race, Nation, Humanity* (Chicago: University of Chicago Press, 2020), as well as Herman Rapaport, *Derrida on Exile and the Nation* (London: Bloomsbury, 2021).

4. Nietzsche of course offered the model for such an approach in his "Schopenhauer as Educator" essay, *Untimely Meditations*, Trans. R.J. Hollingdale (Cambridge: Cambridge University Press, 1983). One can find a wide range of works detailing the political reception of Hölderlin—especially Jürgen Scharfschwerdt, *Friedrich Hölderlin: Der Dichter des Deutschen Sonderwegs* (Stuttgart: Kohlhammer, 1994); Jürgen Schröder, *Deutschland als Gedicht* (Freiburg im Breisgau: Rombach, 2000); Claudia Albert, *Deutsche Klassiker im National Sozialismus* (Stuttgart: J.B. Metzler, 1994), Rüdiger Görner, *Hölderlin und die Folgen* (Suttgart: Metzler, 2016), and Eva Kocziszky, ed., *Wozu Dichter?: Hundert Jahre Poetologien nach Hölderlin* (Berlin: Frank & Timme, 2016).

5. J.J. Winckelmann, "Thoughts on the Imitation of the Painting and Sculpture of the Greeks" in H.B. Nisbet, ed. *German Aesthetic and Literary Criticism* (Cambridge: Cambridge University Press, 1985), 33; "Gedanken über die Nachahmung der griechischen Werke in der Malerei und Bildhauerkunst," *Ausgewählten Schrifte und Briefe*, ed. Walter Rehm (Wiesbaden: Dieterich, 1948), 3.

6. Françoise Dastur, "Hölderlin and the Orientalisation of the Greeks," *Pli* 10: (2000): 156–173, (169) and Rainer Schäfer, *Aus der Erstarrung: Hellas und Hesperien im 'freien Gebrauch des Eigenen' beim späten Hölderlin* (Hamburg: Meiner, 2020).

7. Jay Baird, *To Die for Germany* (Bloomington: Indiana University Press, 1990), 1–12. Cf. also Heidegger's speech of November 25, 1933 "Der deutsche Student als Arbeiter," GA 16: 199, that compares the sacrifice of young Germans in 1933 to that of the heroes of Langemarck.

8. Cf. Heidegger's letters to Imma von Bodmershof commemorating the 50th anniversary of Norbert's death: HIB: 84–85, 89, 104, 134. Paul Celan would make much of singular "dates" as anniversaries and uncannily so would Heidegger.

9. Hannah Arendt, "We Refugees," *The Jewish Writings* (New York: Schocken, 2007), 264–274, here 271–274.

10. Giorgio Agamben, "We Refugees," *Symposium* (1995), 49 (2): 114–119.

11. Hannah Arendt, "We Refugees," 273.

12. G. Agamben, "We Refugees," 118–119.

13. Cf. Julia Ireland, "Naming Physis and 'The Inner Truth of National Socialism': A New Archival Discovery," *Research In Phenomenology* 44 (2014): 315–346 and Jürgen Habermas's article 1953 in *Frankfurter Allgemeine Zeitung*, July 25, 1953, "Mit Heidegger gegen Heidegger Denken." Cf. also Daniel Morat, *Von der Tat zur Gelassenheit* (Göttingen : Wallstein, 2007), 310–313.

14. For a more detailed analysis of Heidegger's Freiburg National Socialism cf. Charles Bambach, *Heidegger's Roots: Nietzsche, National Socialism, and the Greeks* (Ithaca, NY: Cornell University Press, 2003). Cf. also Otto Pöggeler, "Den Führer führen? Heidegger und kein Ende" *Philosophische Rundschau* 32(1985): 26–67.

15. Cf. Günter Figal's observations in *Martin Heidegger: zur Einführung* (Hamburg: Junius, 2016), 129–146.

16. Peter Trawny, *Martin Heidegger: Eine kritische Einführung* (Frankfurt: Klostermann, 2016), 79–80, 88.

17. Emmanuel Lévinas, "Interview with Emmanuel Levinas" in Edith Wyschogrod, *Crossover Queries* (New York: Fordham University Press, 2006), 294.

18. Emmanuel Lévinas, "The Trace of the Other," in *Deconstruction in Context*, ed. Mark Taylor (Chicago: University of Chicago Press, 1986), 345.

19. Cf. also an early letter to Elfride where Heidegger unleashes anti-Semitic prejudice: *Mein liebes Seelchen* (Munich: Deutsche Verlags-Anstalt, 2005), 112, 116.

20. Max Kommerell, *Der Dichter als Führer in der deutschen Klassik* (Berlin: Bondi, 1928). Cf. also Christian Weber, *Max Kommerell: Eine intellektuelle Biographie* (Berlin: Walter de Gruyter, 2011), 105–114.

21. Joachim Storck, "Hermeneutischer Disput: Max Kommerells Auseinandersetzung mit Heideggers Hölderlin-Interpretation," *Literaturgeschichte als Profession*, ed. H. Laufhütte (Tübingen: Narr, 1993), 319–343. Cf. Martin Heidegger, "Max Kommerell," GA 16: 364.

22. Christian Weber, *Max Kommerell*, 445.

23. Max Kommerell, *Briefe und Aufzeichnungen*, 396–401.

24. Max Kommerell, *Briefe und Aufzeichnungen*, 403–404, 399.

25. Max Kommerell, *Briefe und Aufzeichnungen*, 399–400.

26. On this use of Hölderlin by Heidegger, cf. Reinhard Mehring, *Heidegger's 'grosse Politik'*, 13–36.

27. Cf. Charles Bambach, "Hölderlin in the Black Notebooks," *Heidegger Jahrbuch* 12 (2020): 153–170 as well as Charles Bambach, "Heidegger's Hölderlin After *Sein und Zeit*" Marion Heinz &Tobias Bender, eds., *Sein und Zeit neu verhandelt* (Hamburg: Meiner, 2019), 437–464.

28. All of the citations from GA 52 in this chapter are taken from William McNeill and Julia Ireland's translation with Indiana University Press, *Hölderlin's Hymn "Remembrance."* I want to thank Prof. McNeill for his timely help in providing me with a working translation.

29. A vestibule or *Vorhof* conjures thoughts of the Latin goddess Vesta, goddess of the hearth etymologically tied to the Greek goddess Hestia, which Heidegger will allude to in GA 53: 134–143.

30. Norbert von Hellingrath, ed., *Hölderlin: Sämtliche Werke* (Berlin: Propyläen, 1943), IV, 301.

31. Friedrich Hölderlin, *Gedichte* (Stuttgart: Cotta, 1826) Ludwig Uhland & Gustav Schwab, eds. and *Sämtliche Werke*, 2 vols. (Stuttgart: Cotta, 1846) Christoph Schwab, ed.

32. Norbert von Hellingrath, "Vorrede,"*Hölderlin: Sämtliche Werke*, IV: xii-xiii.

33. For a reading of this poem different from Heidegger's, cf. Charles Bambach, "The Hermeneutics of Remembrance: A Reading of Hölderlin's 'Andenken'" *International Yearbook for Hermeneutics*, 18 (2019): 58–76. There are several excellent analyses of this poem available: Michael Franz, "Hölderlins Gedicht 'Andenken'" in H.L. Arnold, ed. (Munich: Text + Kritik, 1996): 195–212; Cyrus Hamlin, *Hermeneutics of Form* (New Haven, CT: Schwab, 1998), 82–92; Hannah Eldridge, *Lyrical Orientations* (Ithaca: Cornell University Press, 2016), 79–83, 107–117 and Wolfgang Binder, "Hölderlins 'Andenken'," *Turm Vorträge 1985/86* (Tübingen, Hölderlin-Gesellschaft, 1986): 5–30, among others.

34. Plato, *Republic*, trans. Richard W. Sterling and William C. Scott (New York: W.W. Norton & Co., 1996), 92.

35. In GA 52:1 Heidegger claims he originally wanted to offer analyses of five different poems, among which was "The Ister."

36. Daniel Dahlstrom, *The Heidegger Dictionary* (London: Bloomsbury, 2013), 100.

37. Theodore Kisiel "Situating Rhetorical Politics in Heidegger's Protopolitical Ontology," *International Journal of Philosophy* 8 (2000): 185–208.

38. Charles Bambach, *Heidegger's Roots*, 57–63.

39. Norbert von Hellingrath, ed., *Hölderlin: Sämtliche Werke* IV, xi, xiii.

40. Hellingrath, *Hölderlin-Vermächtnis*, 132–135, 145, 147.

41. Hellingrath, *Hölderlin-Vermächtnis*, 120–121, 139, 144. One could easily say that it was Hellingrath who authorized an "unhistorical" Hölderlin freed from his own context HV: 236.

42. In Wolfgang Martynkewicz's *Salon Deutschland: Geist und Macht, 1900–1945* (Berlin: Aufbau, 2009), 259–260, the claim is made that Hellingrath delivered this lecture as part of a cultural program of "Kriegshilfe." He appeared before the public in his full military "uniform and severe pose" in a room lit by candlelight. This dramatic "self-staging" of Hellingrath helped forge a sense of a martial-poetic bond between elect German initiates and the work of the poet that resounds in Heidegger's own work.

43. R.M. *Rilke / Norbert von Hellingrath: Briefe und Dokumente*, ed. Klaus Bohnenkamp (Göttingen: Wallstein, 2008), 143. Cf. also Friedrich Nietzsche, "Schopenhauer as Educator" in *Untimely Meditations* (Cambridge: Cambridge University Press, 1983), 125–194.

44. Ernst Müller, ed. *Hölderlins vaterländische Gesänge: Die bunten Hefte für unsere Soldaten* (Stuttgart: Kohlhammer, 1942), 3, 6,13,15.

45. Paul Kluckhohn, "Hölderlin im Bilde der Nachwelt," *Iduna: Jahrbuch der Hölderlin Gesellschaft*, I: 15. The letter's closing salutation reads: "Heil Hitler! Alois Nastoll, Feldwebel (sergeant)."

46. Paul Kluckhohn, "Hölderlin bei den Soldaten des Zweiten Weltkrieges," *Iduna: Jahrbuch der Hölderlin-Gesellschaft*, I: 193.

47. *Völkischer Beobachter*, Berlin, February 28, 1937, cited in Bernhard Zeller, ed. *Klassiker in finsteren Zeiten* (Marbach: Deutsche Schillergesellschaft, 1983), 325.

48. F.W. Wentzlaff-Eggebert, *Opfer und Schicksal in Hölderlins "Hyperion" und "Empedokles"* (Strassburg: Hünenberg, 1943), 9.

49. Max Kommerell, *Briefe und Aufzeichnungen, 1919–1944*, ed. Inge Jens (Freiburg: Walter, 1967), 396–399, 405.

50. Heidegger offers similar thoughts on "sacrifice" in his "Postscript" to "What is Metaphysics?" written in 1943 which, I would argue, also needs to be read against the war in Russia. Cf. PM: 236–237/GA 9: 105–106.

51. In a 1966 speech delivered to "Todtnauberger," and "Einheimische" (indigenous natives), Heidegger styled himself as "a man from the Rütte" the cluster of old farmhouses that made up the center of Todtnauberg. This peasant ideal of roots and indigenous soil belongs to the selfsame racialized metaphysics as we find in the *Black Notebooks*. For an interpretation of Heidegger's beynghistorical racism, cf. Peter Trawny, *Heidegger und der Mythos der jüdischen Weltverschwörung* (Frankfurt: Klostermann, 2014), 57–67.

52. Pindar, Olympian II: 54 "fit occasion"—for Pindar's notion of *kairos* cf. Michael Theunissen, *Pindar: Menschenlos und Wende der Zeit* (Munich: Beck, 2000), 800–829 and 882–910.

53. For some background on Greek notions of *kairos*, cf. R.B. Onian's *The Origins of European Thought* (Cambridge: Cambridge University Press, 1951), 343–348.

54. Debra Hawhee, *Bodily Arts: Rhetoric and Athletics in Ancient Greece* (Austin: University of Texas Press, 2004), 65–80. Cf. also Thomas Rickert,

Ambient Rhetoric: The Attunements of Rhetorical Being (Pittsburgh: University of Pittsburgh Press, 2013), 74–98.

55. Alois Vanicek, *Griechisch-Lateinisch Etymologisches Wörterbuch* (Leipzig: Teubner, 1877), 487.

56. Phillip Sipiora, "Introduction: The Ancient Concept of *Kairos*" in *Rhetoric and Kairos*, ed. P. Sipiora and J. Baumlin (Albany, NY: SUNY Press, 2002), 1–22.

57. Liddell-Scott, *A Greek-English Lexicon* (Oxford: Clarendon Press, 1940), 940–941.

58. Franz Passow, *Handwörterbuch der griechischen Sprache* (Leipzig: Vogel, 847), 170.

59. For study of chiasm in Hölderlin, cf. Arnaud Villani, "Figures of Duality: Greek Tragedy in Hölderlin" in A. Fioretos, ed. *The Solid Letter: Readings of Friedrich Hölderlin* (Stanford, CA: Stanford University Press, 1999), 175–200, here 186.

60. Walter Burkert, *Homo Necans: The Anthropology of Ancient Greek Sacrificial Ritual and Myth* (Berkeley: University of California Press, 1983), 214, 225, 221.

61. In his article "Hölderlins Gedicht 'Andenken'" in H.L. Arnold, ed. *Hölderlin: Text und Kritik* (Munich: Edition Text + Kritik, 1996), 195–212, Michael Franz traces the many hidden references to Susette Gontard in Hölderlin's use of "S" and "g" in various configurations, e.g. "Nicht ist es gut, / Seelos von sterblichen / Gedanken zu seyn. / Doch gut / ist ein Gespräch und zu sagen . . ." vv. 30–33. I want to extend this series of references to mourning to reflect the role of the Anthesteria Festival in the poem.

62. On the influence of Heraclitean thinking on Hölderlin cf. Dieter Bremer, "'Versöhnung ist mitten im Streit': Hölderlins Entdeckung Heraklits" *Hölderlin Jahrbuch* 30 (1996–97), 173–199.

63. Daniel E. Anderson, *The Masks of Dionysus: A Commentary on Plato's 'Symposium'* (Albany, NY: SUNY Press, 1993), 8.

64. Walter Burkert, *Homo Necans*, 216–221.

65. Euripides, *The Bacchae*, trans. Stephen Esposito (Newburyport: Focus Library, 1998), 77.

66. On this image of poetic breath in "Remembrance" cf. Lucas Murrey, *Hölderlin's Dionysiac Poetry* (Heidelberg: Springer, 2015), 207-08. Murrey's book follows upon the work of Bernard Böschenstein, *Frucht des Gewitters: Zu Hölderlins Dionysos als Gott der Revolution* (Frankfurt: Insel, 1989). Both works make a strong case for the presence of Dionysian elements within Hölderlin's poetry.

67. Walter F. Otto, *Dionysus* (Bloomington: Indiana University Press, 1965), 93–96; Karl Kerenyi, *Dionysos* (Princeton, NJ: Princeton University Press, 1976), 152, 167 and Richard Seaford, *Dionysos* (London: Routledge, 2006), 17–21. The

image of Dionysus in his boat is portrayed by Exekias in his famous kylix or drinking cup at the Staatliche Antikensammlung in Munich.

68. Walter F. Otto, *Dionysus*, 158, and Johann Kreuzer, ed. *Hölderlin Handbuch* (Stuttgart: Metzler, 2002), 274.

69. William McNeill "The Hölderlin Lectures" in *The Bloomsbury Companion to Heidegger*, ed. F. Raffoul and E. Nelson (London: Bloomsbury, 2013), 230–231; Reinhard Schmuck "Monologisches Gespräch: Heidegger's Vorlesung über Hölderlins Hymne 'Andenken,'" *PMLA* 102, no. 1 (2005): 16–32, and Christopher Fynsk, *Heidegger: Thought and Historicity* (Ithaca, NY: Cornell University Press, 1986), 175.

70. Jean-Pierre Lefebvre, "Auch die Stege sind Holzwege," *Hölderlin Jahrbuch* 26 (1988/89), 209–223.

71. Karlheinz Stierle, "Die Friedensfeier. Sprache und Fest im revolutionären und nachrevolutionären Frankreich und bei Hölderlin" in *Das Fest*, eds. W. Haug and R. Warning (Munich: Fink, 1989), 481–525, here 497. Alexander Honold, "The Celebration of Time in the Revolutionary Community" in *Humanismus und Antikerezeption im 18. Jahrhundert* eds. Uwe Steiner and Christian Emden (Heidelberg: Winter, 2015), 159–177, here 160, 166. Pierre Bertaux, *Hölderlin und die französische Revolution* (Frankfurt: Suhrkamp, 1969), 110. Cf. Also Alexander Honold, *Hölderlins Kalender: Astronomie und Revolution um 1800* (Berlin: Vorwerk 8, 2005).

72. Eva Kocziszky, *Hölderlins Orient* (Würzburg: Königshausen und Neumann, 2009), 119–121.

73. "Hellingrath-Hölderlin-George: Bernhard Böschenstein im Gespräch mit Ulrich Raulff und Jürgen Brokoff," *Norbert von Hellingrath und die Asthetik der europäischen Moderne*, eds. J. Brokoff et al. (Göttingen: Wallstein, 2014), 15–29, here 23–24.

74. Theodor Adorno, *Noten zur Literatur* III (Frankfurt: Suhrkamp, 1981), 447–491.

75. Friedrich Hölderlin, *Sämtliche Werke und Briefe, III*, ed. Michael Knaupp (Munich: Hanser, 1993), 288. See also Dietrich Uffhausen, ed., *Friedrich Hölderlin: Bevestigter Gesang (Die neu zu entdeckende hymnische Spätdichtung bis 1806)* (Stuttgart: Metzler, 1989), 165, and FHA VII: 454.

76. On this whole issue of Bordeaux as harbor city for the wine trade and for the military excursion to the West Indies, I rely on the excellent work of Michael Franz, "Die braunen Frauen, die Indier und die Quelle des Reichtums," *Sprache-Dichtung-Philosophie*, ed. Bärbel Frischmann (Freiburg: Alber, 2010), 17–35.

77. Cf. Günter Mieth, *Friedrich Hölderlin: Dichter der bürgerlich-demokratischen Revolution* (Berlin: Rütten und Loenig, 1978), 139–140.

78. For a different editorial approach to this fragment see also the "Homburger Folioheft" facsimile edition, ed. D.E. Sattler and Emery George, *Friedrich*

Hölderlin: Sämtliche Werke (Frankfurter Ausgabe) Supplement III (Frankfurt: Stroemfeld, 1986), 36.

79. Martin Heidegger, "Die Armut," *Heidegger Studies*, 10 (1994): 10.

80. Martin Heidegger letter to Fritz Heidegger of January 29, 1943, cited in *Heidegger und der Antisemitismus*, eds. W. Homolka and A. Heidegger (Freiburg: Herder, 2016), 86. (*Die Zeit*, Oct. 13, 2016, no. 43), 46.

81. Cf. Charles Bambach, *Thinking the Poetic Measure of Justice* (Albany, NY: SUNY Press, 2013), 36, 51, 63–64, 68–70.

82. Françoise Dastur "Hölderlin and the Orientalisation of Greece," *Pli*, 10 (2000): 156–173.

83. On this understanding of limits for Hölderlin, Dennis Schmidt's article "The Ordeal of the Foreign and the Enigma of One's Own" *Philosophy Today* 21 (1996): 188–196 offers important insights, 191.

84. Helmut Mottel, *"Apoll envers terre": Hölderlins mythopoetische Weltentwürfe* (Würzburg: Ergon, 1998), 115–135.

85. Friedrich Hölderlin *Sämtliche Werke*, III, ed. Norbert von Hellingrath (Berlin: Propylaen, 1943), 621.

86. Martin Heidegger "Die Armut," 6–7.

87. Friedrich Beissner, *Hölderlins Übersetzungen aus dem Griechischen* (Stuttgart: Metzler, 1933), 147–184 and Friedrich Beissner, ed., Friedrich Hölderlin, *Sämtliche Werke*, II (Stuttgart: Kohlhammer, 1951), 608, 620–621.

88. Pindar, *Olympian Odes, Pythian Odes*, ed. William H. Race (Cambridge, MA: Harvard University Press, 1997), 80–81.

89. Adolf Beck, *Hölderlins Weg zu Deutschland* (Stuttgart: Metzler, 1982), 180–183 and Johann Kreuzer, " 'Heimat/ Und Niemand weiss.' Hölderlins Heimat und Exil," *Hölderlin Jahrbuch* 38 (2012–2013): 60–87.

90. Friedrich Hölderlin, *Odes and Elegies*, trans. Nick Hoff (Middletown, CT: Wesleyan University Press, 2008), 154–155.

91. Cf. the notes of explanation in Friedrich Hölderlin, *Sämtliche Werke*, ed. Michael Knaupp, 215 and Luigi Reitani ed., Friedrich Hölderlin, *Tutte le Lirichi:* (Milan: Arnoldo Mondadori, 2001), 1782–1785.

92. Alois Vanicek, *Griechisch-Lateinisch Etymologisches Wörterbuch* (Leipzig: Teubner, 1877), 124.

93. *Papes Handwörterbuch der Griechischen Sprache*, I (Braunschweig: Vieweg, 1871), 266 and Franz Passow, *Handwörterbuch der Griechischen Sprache*, I (Leipzig: Vogel, 1841), 332. Pindar employs the term *apoikia* in both Olympian I, v. 24 and Isthmian VII, 12 to designate colonies as places of settlement for the motherland.

94. "Bernhard Böschenstein im Gespräch mit Ulrich Raulff und Jürgen Brokoff," *Norbert von Hellingrath und die Ästhetik der europaischen Moderne*, 23–24.

95. For the range of Hölderlin's interest in these various scientific disciplines related to travel and wandering cf. Alexander Honold, *Hölderlins*

Kalender: Astronomie und Revolution um 1800 (Berlin: Vorwerk 8, 2005); David Constantine, *The Significance of Locality in the Poetry of Friedrich Hölderlin* (London: Modern Humanities Research Association, 1979); Helmut Mottel, "*Apoll envers Terre*": *Hölderlins mythopoetische Weltentwürfe* (Würzburg: Ergon, 1998), 115–179. See also Martin Anderle, *Die Landschaft in den Gedichten Hölderlins* (Bonn: Bouvier, 1986).

96. In one striking image Celan writes of "the deadman's almond eye / nourished by figs," where he thinks of Leo Antschel's shipwrecked hopes of leaving Europe to "return" to a Jewish homeland in Israel, a hope spurred on by Theodore Herzl's Zionist dream. Paul Celan, *Selected Poems and Prose*, trans. John Felstiner (New York: Norton, 2001), 66–67.

97. Maurice Blanchot, *The Writing of the Disaster* (Lincoln: University of Nebraska Press, 1995), 3, 6, 28 / *L'écriture du désastre* (Paris: Gallimard, 1980), 10, 16, 49.

98. Jacques Derrida, "The Night Watch," in *Derrida and Joyce*, ed. Andrew Mitchell (Albany, NY: SUNY Press, 2013), 95.

99. Hölderlin draws here upon the myth of Herakles's visit to the Ister in Pindar's third "Olympian Ode," vv. 12–17, a poem he had translated himself, DKV II: 701–702, vv. 23–28. In the very gesture of "trans-lation" we find hints of Hölderlin's own notion of hospitality between the Greek and German language.

Chapter 3

1. Martin Heidegger, HHI: 164/GA 53: 202.

2. Maurice Blanchot, *The Writing of the Disaster* (Lincoln: University of Nebraska Press, 1995), 117.

3. Dennis J. Schmidt, *On Germans and Other Greeks: Tragedy and Ethical Life* (Bloomington: Indiana University Press, 2000) and E&L: 207/DKV III: 459–460.

4. Cf. Antoine Berman, *The Experience of the Foreign* (Albany, NY: SUNY Press, 1992); Dennis Schmidt, "The Ordeal of the Foreign and the Enigma of One's Own" *Philosophy Today* 40, no. 1 (1996): 182–196.

5. In 1946, after World War II, in the "Letter on Humanism" (PM: 257/ GA 9:338), Heidegger will insist—contra his lectures in GA 52 and GA 53— that Hölderlin is an "*inter*-national" figure and not to be read as a "nationalist" poet; cf. Norbert von Hellingrath's edition of Friedrich Hölderlin, *Sämtliche Werke*, 6 vols. (Munich: Müller, 1913–1923), with the last two vols. completed by Friedrich Seebass and Ludwig Pigenot.

6. Liddell-Scott, *Greek-English Lexicon* (Oxford: Clarendon, 1940), 374.

7. Franco Montanari, *The Brill Dictionary of Ancient Greek* (Leiden: Brill, 2018), 460–461.

8. Robert Beekes, *Etymological Dictionary of Ancient Greek* (Leiden: Brill, 2016), 936, 1562–1563.

9. Sophocles's play *Antigone*, when read in its Hölderlinian translation, can be understood as a drama about the way the human being is placed, and places itself, within the uncanny and *entsetzliche Setzungen, Auseinandersetzungen, Versetzungen,* and *Übersetzungen des Lebens*.

10. Cf. Miguel de Beistegui, "Translating Essentially," *Thinking with Heidegger* (Bloomington: Indiana University Press, 2003), 169–182.

11. On the problem of interruption in Sophocles's *Antigone* in Heidegger cf. Dennis Schmidt, "The Monstrous, Catastrophe, and Ethical Life: Hegel, Heidegger, and Antigone," *Philosophy Today* 59, no. 1 (Winter 2015): 61–72.

12. Cf. also IM: 203–204/EM:145.

13. Here Heidegger's translation is quite different from Hölderlin, Karl Reinhardt, and Bernhard Zimmerman who stress the "Torheit" and "irren Rat" and "Ungeheure," which misses the ontological play of *deinos*. Cf. Karl Reinhardt, ed., *Sophokles: Antigone* (Göttingen: Vandenhoeckh & Ruprecht, 1961), 22–23; Hölderlin, DKV II: 864; Bernhard Zimmermann, ed. Sophokles, *Antigone* (Düsseldorf: Artemis & Winkler, 1999).

14. For Hölderlin's translation, cf. DKV II: 877. See also Hölderlin, "Notes to Antigone" E&L: 325–332/ DKV II: 913–922 and Anja Solbach, *Seinsverstehen und Mythos: Untersuchungen zur späten Dichtungen Hölderlins und zu Heideggers Deutung* (Freiburg: Alber, 2008), 235–237.

15. The same interpretation of *hypsipolis/apolis* can also be read through *Oedipus Tyrannus*.

16. For a history of Antigone interpretation in terms of "religion" vs. "state"—family vs. polis—psychological issues and gender studies, cf. Bonnie Honig, *Antigone Interrupted* (Cambridge: Cambridge University Press, 2013); Jacques Lacan, *The Ethics of Psychoanalysis* (New York: Norton: 1992), 243–290; Judith Butler, *Antigone's Claim* (New York: Columbia University Press, 2002); Tina Chanter and Sean Kirkland, eds. *The Returns of Antigone* (Albany, New York: SUNY Press, 2014); Karl Reinhardt, *Sophokles* (Frankfurt: Klostermann, 1933); Heinrich Weinstock, *Sophokles* (Leipzig: Teubner, 1937); Bernhard Zimmermann, *Die griechische Tragödie* (Stuttgart: Kröner, 2018); Scott M. Campbell, "The Tragic Sense of Life in Heidegger's Readings of *Antigone*," in *The Science, Politics and Ontology of Life Philosophy* (London: Bloomsbury, 2013), 185–196; Jean Greisch, "Who Stands Fast? Do Philosophers Make Good Resistants?" in B. Gregor and J. Zimmermann, eds., *Bonhoeffer and Continental Thought* (Bloomington: Indiana University Press, 2006), and Norman Swazo, "'Preserving the *Ethos*': Heidegger and Sophocles' *Antigone*," *Symposium* 10 (2006): 441–471.

17. Cf. Nietzsche, *The Birth of Tragedy* (Cambridge: Cambridge University Press, 1999), 29–34.

18. Whether they focus either on Creon or Antigone does not matter; Heidegger focuses almost exclusively on Antigone because she is for the figure of risk and daring for being's sake.

19. Friedrich Hölderlin, E&L: 328–329/DKV II: 916–917; Anja Solbach, *Seinsverstehen und Mythos*, 234–235 and Rainer Schäfer, *Aus der Erstarrung: Hellas und Hesperien im 'freien Gebrauch des Eigenen' beim späten Hölderlin* (Hamburg: Meiner, 2020).

20. Friedrich Hölderlin, E&L: 207/DKV III: 460.

21. Hans-Georg Gadamer, "Hölderlin und George" in *Gesammelte Werke* IX (Tübingen: Mohr-Siebeck, 1993), 234.

22. The German word "Rückbindung" hints back to the Latin etymology of religion as *re + ligare*, a "binding" + "back."

23. Daniel Dahlstrom, *The Heidegger Dictionary* (London: Bloomsbury, 2013), 101–102.

24. HHI: 54–55/68 and IM: 31. We need to remember these lectures are delivered while Germany is at war with Soviet Russia and the United States.

25. "Schopenhauer as Educator" from *Untimely Meditations*, Trans. R.J. Hollingdale (Cambridge: Cambridge University Press, 1983).

26. Cf. also Peter Trawny's analysis in *Heidegger und Hölderlin oder der europäische Morgen* (Würzburg: Königshausen & Neumann, 2004), 85–169.

27. In GA 39: 3, Heidegger explains the difference between them: "A beginning is the onset of something; a commencement is that from which something arises or springs forth."

28. On the topic of "authorizing" a violent reading of Hölderlin, cf. GA 39: 222, 269 and two insightful articles from Kathleen Wright: "Heidegger's Authorization of Hölderlin's Poetry" in Karsten Harries and Christof Jamme, eds., *Martin Heidegger: Politics, Art, Technology* (New York: Holmes & Meier, 1994), 164–174, and "Die Heroisierung Hölderlins um 1933," *Heidegger Handbuch* (Stuttgart: Metzler, 2013), 188–200.

29. For an account of river names with attention to etymology and historical description, cf. my analysis of the Ister in *Thinking the Poetic Measure of Justice*, 56–61.

30. See Heidegger's rejection of the Asiatic origin of Greek thinking in GA 75: 228; EdP: 31–41. Cf. also Spiegel Interview allusion to Greek–German "bond," GA 16: 678–680.

31. Cf. *The Poetic Measure of Justice*; we need to consider that perhaps Heidegger's animus against "the Asiatic" here can be traced to the fact that Soviet troops also had "Asian" groups within them.

32. In the low-lying regions of Swabia near Sigmaringen, Donaueschingen, and Mengen, the Danube flows quite slowly as if it were a brook with nowhere

to go. This is what both Hölderlin and Heidegger refer to in these passages. Heidegger's own family history has a connection to this region, cf. Otto Pöggeler, *Heidegger und die praktische Philosophie* (Frankfurt: Suhrkamp, 1988), 41.

33. The allusion to Olympia as the site of the games (*Kämpfe*)—esp. in 1942—and to Alpheus as a river holy to the gods finds resonance with the Ister as another river with links to this Greek "special" relation to gods and to Nazi Germany's role in Greece during World War II.

34. *Mnama* derives from the Greek verb *mnaomai*, "to remember, think of, ponder," cf. Robert Beekes, *Etymological Dictionary of Greek*, 960. Hölderlin uses the German edition of C.G. Heyne, *Pindari carmina cum Lectionis varietate et adnotationibus* (Göttingen: Dieterich, 1798), revised from the 1770 edition. This edition relied on the error-riddled 1560 Stephanus edition so that Hölderlin's translations proved less reliable philologically, even if they were quite important for Hölderlin's poetological vision of Greek-German transmission.

35. For background to the Heraclean myth of the olive branch and to the theme of "hospitality"/*Gastfreundschaft*, Hölderlin drew upon Benjamin Hederich's *Gründliches mythologisches Lexikon* published in Leipzig in 1770 (Darmstadt: Wissenschaftliche Buchgesellschaft, 1996), 1236–1258. For a closer analysis of the Heracles strain in "The Ister," cf. the fascinating book by Alexander Honold, *Nach Olympia: Hölderlin und die Erfindung der Antike* (Berlin: Vorwerk 8, 2002), 192–230, as well as Norina Procopan, *Hölderlins Donauhymnen* (Eggingen: Edition Isele, 2004), 136–153.

36. Cf. Charles Segal, *Tragedy and Civilization: An Interpretation of Sophocles* (Cambridge, MA: Harvard University Press, 1981), 207–248. Oedipus's swollen feet stem from his parents' decision to banish him on Mt. Cithaeron. His ability to solve the riddle of sphinx cleverly plays off the double sense of "know where," Gk. *oida pous* (OT: 924–928) and "I know feet" etymologies.

37. Cf. Heidegger's comments in *Introduction to Metaphysics* concerning Russia and American, IM: 41, 50/GA 40: 40, 48. See also Heidegger's comments on "Amerika" in GA 97: 51, 143, 150, 161, 181, 220–221, 230, 249, 309, 390, 405, 445. We also find examples of Heidegger's sense of German exceptionalism in his letters to Kurt Bauch. In October of 1942, for example, Heidegger writes, "Why do we prevent ourselves from awakening and unfolding the forces of the present?" He goes on to write, "For now, slowly, the world-historical trial of the Germans is coming nearer" and that "the founding vocation of the Germans remains concealed" HKB: 84–85. Heidegger also claims: "For along with German the Greek language is . . . at once the most powerful and most spiritual of all languages" IM: 62/GA 40: 61. Moreover, in GA 16: 678–680, he speaks of "the inner bond" between Greeks and Germans. It also helps to remember that Heidegger has two sons serving in Russia during World War II.

38. Cf. several important collections of essays deal with Heidegger and the *Black Notebooks*: Walter Homolka & Arnulf Heidegger, eds. *Heidegger und der Antisemitismus: Positionen im Widerstreit* (Freiburg: Herder, 2016); Andrew Mitchell

and Peter Trawny, eds. *Heidegger's Black Notebooks: Responses to Anti-Semitism* (New York: Columbia University Press, 2017); and my review in *Notre Dame Philosophical Reviews*: https://ndpr.nd.edu/news/heideggers-black-notebooks-responses-to-anti-semitism, as well as Ingo Farin & Jeff Malpas, eds. *Reading Heidegger's Black Notebooks, 1931–1941* (Cambridge, MA: MIT Press, 2016) and *Heidegger Jahrbuch: Zur Hermeneutik der Schwarzen Hefte* (2017–2020), 11–12.

39. Cf. Otto Pöggeler, *Schicksal und Geschichte: Antigone im Spiegel der Deutungen und Gestaltungen seit Hegel und Heidegger* (Munich: Fink, 2004), 160–168; Peter Trawny, *Heidegger, Hölderlin oder Der Europäische Morgen* (Königshausen & Neumann, 2010), 85–169; Iris Buchheim, *Wegbereitung in de Kunstlosigkeit* (Würzburg: Königshausen & Neumann, 1994), 249–252. Cf. *The Poetic Measure of Justice*, the chapters on Celan and Heidegger.

40. Within this context Heidegger cites "Americanism" as the example of the "catastrophic" (HHI: 143/179).

41. Cf. Yitzhak Arad, *The Operation Reinhard Death Camps* (Bloomington: Indiana University Press, 2016). In a plan termed "Operation Reinhard"—to counter the assassination of Reinhard Heydrich—NS offered a brutal counter-reaction. It is estimated that about 1.5 million Jews were exterminated in a three-month period from 1942, more than 25 percent of the Jews killed during the whole of World War II.

42. Donatella Di Cesare, *Heidegger and the Jews: The Black Notebooks* (Cambridge: Polity Press, 2018) provides a broader view of Heidegger's racial animus against Jews; cf. my *Heidegger's Roots* for a consideration of Baeumler, Krieck, Hildebrandt.

43. GA 97: 20/Peter Trawny, *Heidegger und der Mythos der jüdischen Weltverschwörung* (Frankfurt: Klostermann, 2013).

44. On Heidegger's notorious remark about "the inner truth and greatness of National Socialism," cf. IM: 222/GA 40: 208); see also Julia Ireland's helpful essay, "Naming *Physis* and the 'Inner Truth of National Socialism': An Archival Discovery," *Research in Phenomenology* 44 (2014): 315–346.

45. On this topic of "hospitality" from a very different perspective, cf. Jacques Derrida, *Of Hospitality* (Stanford, CA: Stanford University Press, 20) and "Hostipitality," *Acts of Religion* (New York: Routledge, 2002), 356–420. See also Emmanuel Levinas, *Totality and Infinity* (Pittsburgh: Duquesne University Press, 1969), 42–48.

46. Hölderlin girds his reading of hospitality in Pindar's odes, but also in Greek *xenia* and the worship of *Zeus xenios*.

Chapter 4

1. Martin Heidegger, GA 75: 360.
2. Martin Heidegger, GA 73: 763.

3. One finds these terms frequently deployed by Heidegger in 1945–1946, for example, *Heimatlosigkeit*: GA 9: 338–341; GA 75: 234; *Verwahrlosung*: GA 9: 341; GA 75: 354–355, 360, 364–365; GA 77: 213; *Armut*: GA 9: 342, 352, 264; GA 75: 142, 147, 156–157; GA 77: 226; GA 78: 245, 247; *Verlassenheit*: GA 75: 8; GA 77: 213–215; GA 9: 339; *Verwüstung*: GA 77: 206–207.

4. Hugo Ott, *Martin Heidegger: Unterwegs zu seiner Biographie* (Frankfurt: Campus, 1988), 155–158.

5. Hugo Ott, *Martin Heidegger: Unterwegs zu seiner Biographie*, 157.

6. Friedrich Hölderlin, "Aufsatz-Entwurf über die Geschichtsperioden," *Hölderlin: Sämtliche Werke*, III, ed. Norbert von Hellingrath (Berlin: Propylaen, 1943), 621–622.

7. "Das abendländische Gespräch" has not yet been translated into English. Nonetheless, I believe it to be one of Heidegger's most important "dialogues" and it will be the focus of chapter 5.

8. In this context we should perhaps remember the deep irony surrounding Heidegger's 1945 essay "Poverty"—delivered at the castle Wildenstein in a bucolic setting near the source of the Danube in early summer while millions were dealing with genuine poverty and devastation.

9. For the biographical facts of Heidegger's plight, cf. Hugo Ott, *Martin Heidegger: Unterwegs zu seiner Biographie* (Frankfurt: Campus, 1988), 19–42, 291–327.

10. For a penetrating treatment of Heidegger's psychiatric state during this period, cf. Andrew Mitchell, "Heidegger's Breakdown: Health and Healing under the Care of Dr. V.E. von Gebsattel," *Research in Phenomenology* 46 (2016): 70–97.

11. Again, see the really helpful account in Mitchell "Heidegger's Breakdown" and in MLS: 239–249, where Heidegger downplays the seriousness of his mental breakdown. Hugo Ott makes this claim about a suicide attempt in an interview from a BBC film *Human, All Too Human* from 2000.

12. See, for example, the reductive psychoanalytic approach of Anton Fisher, *Martin Heidegger: Der gottlose Priester (Psychogramm eines Denkers)* (Zürich: rüffer & rub, 2013), esp. 468–527.

13. Karl Jaspers, *Die Schuldfrage: Ein Beitrag zur deutschen Frage* (Zürich: Artemis, 1946), 39, 41, 48–49.

14. For the German original text, cf. www.marcuse.org/Herbert/pubs/40S-PUBS/47MarcuseHeidegger.htm.

15. Karl Jaspers, *Die Schuldfrage*, 49.

16. See, for example, Heidegger's comments in 1946 in the *Black Notebooks*, where he writes, "the contemptible bustle of thoughtless polemics against my thinking is the kind of grudging recognition that, from its ignorance of the matter at hand, likewise has no knowledge of itself" (GA 97: 180). For Heidegger's reaction to NS persecution, cf. Hugo Ott, *Martin Heidegger: Unterwegs zu seiner*

Biographie, 291–346, and Stephanie Born, *"Die Weltgeschichte aus den Fügen": Paul Celans kritische Poetik und Martin Heideggers Seins-Philosophie nach den Schwarzen Heften* (Würzburg: Königshausen & Neumann, 2019), 123–140.

17. On the response of German intellectuals to the "catastrophe" cf. Friedrich Meinecke, *Die deutsche Katastrophe* (Wiesbaden: Brockhaus, 1946) and Mark Clark, *Beyond Catastrophe: German Intellectuals and Cultural Renewal after World War II, 1945–1955* (Lanham, MD: Lexington, 2006).

18. Charles Bambach, *Thinking the Poetic Measure of Justice* (Albany, NY: SUNY Press, 2013), 131–135, 151–172.

19. Karl Jaspers, *Lebensfragen der deutschen Politik* (Munich: dtv, 1963), 120. Cf. also the poignant essay by Hannah Arendt, "Organized Guilt and Universal Responsibility," *Essays in Understanding* (New York: Schocken, 1994), 121–135 [originally published as "German Guilt" in *Jewish Frontier* 12 (January 1945)]. Arendt's remarks capture Heidegger's plight quite well: "The number of those who are responsible *and* guilty will be relatively small. There are many who share responsibility without any visible proof of guilt," 125.

20. Karl Jaspers, "Antwort," *Lebensfragen der deutschen Politik*, 115–119.

21. Karl Jaspers, *Lebensfragen der deutschen Politik*, 117, 120.

22. Ernst von Salomon, *Der Fragebogen* (Hamburg: Rowohlt, 1988) offers a critical view of the Allies' "questionnaires" and the denazification process within Germany.

23. Wolfgang Weyrauth, "Nachwort," *Tausend Gramm* (Hamburg: Rowohlt, 1949), 207–219.

24. Renè Wolf, *The Undivided Sky: The Holocaust on East and West German Radio During the 1960s* (New York: Palgrave-Macmillan, 2010), 46–68. The daily broadcasts of the Nuremberg trials on German radio during 1945–1946 made this a daily concern, making it hard to "forget." Later trials were also broadcast during the 1960s.

25. Friedrich Hölderlin, E&L: 331/DKV II: 919; Wilhelm Michel, *Hölderlins Abendländische Wendung* (Jena: Eugen Diederichs, 1923), 5–53; Peter Trawny, *Heidegger, Hölderlin oder Der Europäische Morgen* (Königshausen & Neumann, 2010), 85–169; Rainer Schäfer, *Aus der Erstarrung: Hellas und Hesperien im 'freien Gebrauch des Eigenen' beim späten Hölderlin* (Hamburg: Meiner, 2020), 59–84, 255–260.

26. Martin Heidegger, GA 73: 703–712 and the insightful commentary of Krzysztof Ziarek, *Language after Heidegger* (Bloomington: Indiana University Press, 2013), 205–219.

27. We can find a clear example of this in Heidegger's vexation at the Allied powers for distributing photographs of German barbarity in the camps and appending to them the caption: "These Atrocities—Your Fault!" Heidegger cites this in GA 97: 84, 129.

28. On this issue of self-extinction within Heidegger, cf. GA 96: 243; GA 97: 20. See also Donatella Di Cesare, *Heidegger and the Jews* (Cambridge: Polity, 2018), 197–206.

29. It is fairly clear that Jaspers's public acclaim in the postwar era spurs Heidegger's remarks concerning "the betrayal of thinking."

30. See Peter Trawny, *Heidegger und der Mythos der jüdischen Weltverschwörung* (Frankfurt: Klostermann, 2014).

31. Philippe Lacoue-Labarthe, "Interview of June 22, 2000," in Dominique Janicaud, *Heidegger in France* (Bloomington: Indiana University Press, 2015), 388–389.

32. "Interview with Emmanuel Levinas" in Edith Wyschograd, ed., *Crossover Queries: Dwelling with Negatives, Embodying Philosophy's Others* (New York: Fordham University Press, 2006), 292–294.

33. For a fuller discussion of the Hesperian in Hölderlin cf. my *Thinking the Poetic Measure of Justice* (Albany, NY: SUNY, 2013), 36–66, and Rainer Schäfer, *Aus der Erstarrung*.

34. Pindar, *Olympian and Pythian Odes*, ed. William Race (Cambridge, MA: Harvard University Press, 1997), 80–81.

35. Heidegger is of course referring here to Hölderlin, who lived thirty-six years in the tower above the Neckar River.

36. Heine, of course, was a Jew. Heidegger found it wholly out of character to have a street in his Catholic hometown named for a non-autochthonous Jew.

Chapter 5

1. Martin Heidegger, GA 73: 871.
2. Martin Heidegger, GA 73: 750.
3. Norbert von Hellingrath's was the first edition in German to publish this text. Friedrich Hölderlin, *Sämtliche Werke*, IV, ed., Norbert von Hellingrath (Berlin: Propylaen, 1943), 220–222, 413–414. The river's rhythms play off Hölderlin's own poetic rhythms; cf. Wilhelm Böhm, *Hölderlin*, II (Halle: Niemeyer, 1930), 482–484.
4. "Istros" in *Der Kleine Pauly: Lexikon der Antike*, II (Stuttgart: Müller, 1967), 1478.
5. Friedrich Hölderlin, *Sämtliche Werke, Frankfurter Ausgabe*, eds., D.E. Sattler and Emery George (Frankfurt: Stroemfeld, 1986), 29, and Friedrich Hölderlin, *Sämtliche Werke*, IV, ed., Norbert von Hellingrath (Berlin: Propylaen, 1943), 313.
6. Cf. the portrait of modern Germany drawn by the historian Rolf Seferle in his bestselling book *Finis Germaniae* (Leipzig: Antaios, 2017). For a description of the literary background surrounding Heidegger's "Western Conversation," cf.

Robert Savage, *Hölderlin After the Catastrophe: Heidegger-Adorno-Brecht* (New York: Camden House, 2008), 32–95.

    7. Friedrich Hölderlin, *Sämtliche Werke und Briefe*, I, ed. Michael Knaupp (Munich: Hanser, 1992), 421.

    8. See chapter 3 for a for discussion of the Böhlendorff letter.

    9. Otto Pöggeler, *Heidegger und die praktische Philosophie* (Frankfurt: Suhrkamp, 1988), 41; *Martin Heidegger und seine Heimat*, eds., Elisabeth Büchin and Alfred Denker (Stuttgart: Klett-Cotta, 2005), 175–179.

    10. This piece of writing comes from a note card included in the folder of Heidegger's "Ister" lectures from SS 1942 but not published in GA 53. Otto Pöggeler cited it in his essay "Heideggers politisches Selbstverstandnis," in *Heidegger und die politische Philosophie*, ed., Anne Gethmann-Siefert (Frankfurt: Suhrkamp, 1988), 41.

    11. Heidegger cites the Norbert von Hellingrath edition, *Hölderlin: Sämtliche Werke*, IV, ed. Norbert von Hellingrath (Berlin: Propylaen, 1943), 220, which includes an orthographic error. "Nächsten" should be in uppercase; cf. Michael Knaupp, *Hölderlin: Sämtliche Werke und Briefe* (Darmstadt: Wissenschaftliche Buchgesellschaft, 1998), I: 475. On *Schwung* as "momentum" cf. Krzysztof Ziarek, "The Poietic Momentum of Thought: Heidegger and Poetry," in Charles Bambach and Theodore George, eds. *Philosophers and Their Poets* (Albany, NY: SUNY Press, 2019), 185–200.

    12. Cf. the helpful account of Peter Nickel, *Die Bedeutung von Herders Verjüngungsgedanken und Geschichtsphilosophie für die Werke Hölderlins* (Dissertation Universität Kiel 1963) and Jochen Schmidt, *Hölderlins geschichtsphilosophische Hymnen* (Darmstadt: Wissenschaftliche Buchgesellschaft, 1990).

    13. Reinhard Mehring, "Heideggers 'Norbert,' " *Heideggers 'grosse Politik'* (Tübingen: Mohr Siebeck, 2016), 20–25.

    14. Friedrich Hölderlin "Aufsatzentwurf über die Geschichtsperioden" *Sämtliche Werke*, III, ed., Norbert von Hellingrath (Berlin: Propylaen, 1943), 621; Martin Heidegger, "Die Armut," *Heidegger Studies* 10 (1994): 9.

    15. *Brill Dictionary of Ancient Greek*, ed. Franco Montanari (Leiden: Brill, 2015), 965. The reference to the "masses" here speaks to Jose Ortega y Gasset's popular book *The Revolt of the Masses* (New York: Norton, 1932), Spanish original 1930.

    16. GA 97: 230 where Heidegger writes that "The destruction of Europe is . . . the work of the Americans. Hitler is only the pretext. And yet the Americans are, when seen broadly, Europeans. Europe destroys itself."

    17. Cf. the insightful essay by Françoise Dastur, "Europa und der anderer Anfang," Hans-Helmut Gander, ed. *Europa und die Philosophie* (Frankfurt: Klostermann, 1993), 185–196. See also Jacques Derrida, *The Other Heading* (Bloomington: Indiana University Press, 1992), 27. Derrida calls Europe this "Western appendage to Asia" (21) even as he speaks of the "spiritual mission

of Europe" (23) and the archeo-teleological program of all European discourse about Europe, xxvii.

18. Reiner Schürmann, *Meister Eckhart: Mystic and Philosopher* (Bloomington: Indiana University Press, 1978), 144–151. See also the remarkably helpful book by Ian Alexander Moore, *Eckhart, Heidegger, and the Imperative of Releasement* (Albany, NY: SUNY Press, 2019).

19. As a young student in Tübingen, Hölderlin translated the first book of Lucan's *Pharsalia* in 1790. In Lucan's Latin text, Hesperia stands for Italy, in Hölderlin's vision, for "das Abendland." Cf. Dieter Burdorf, *Friedrich Hölderlin* (Munich: Beck, 2011), 65. Drawing on this background, we might well rename Heidegger's "Das abendländische Gespräch" "The Hesperian Conversation." DKV II: 653–654; for the Latin term *Hesperios*, cf. Lucan, *The Civil War* (Cambridge, MA: Harvard University Press, 1928), 30–32.

20. Max Kommerell, *Der Dichter als Führer*, 468.

21. Claudio Magris, *The Danube* (New York: Farrar, Straus, Giroux, 1989), 15–54.

22. Friedrich Beissner, *Hölderlins Übersetzungen aus dem Griechischen* (Stuttgart: Poeschl, 1933), a book Heidegger valued. Cf. also Peter Trawny, *Heidegger und Hölderlin oder Der Europäische Morgen* (Würzburg: Königshausen & Neumann, 2004), 87–89; Felix Christen, *Das Jetzt der Lektüre: Zur Edition und Deutung von Friedrich Hölderlins Ister-Entwürfen* (Frankfurt: Stroemfeld, 2013); Wolfram Groddeck, *Hölderlins Elegie 'Brod und Wein' oder 'Die Nacht'* (Frankfurt: Stroemfeld, 2012).

23. Cf. Franco Montanari, *The Brill Dictionary of Ancient Greek*, 250.

24. Beda Allemann, *Hölderlin und Heidegger* (Zürich: Atlantis, 1954), 168–179; Jochen Schmidt, *Hölderlins Elegie 'Brod und Wein'* (Berlin: de Gruyter, 1968), 200–208; Hans-Joachim Kreutzer, "Kolonie und Vaterland in Hölderlins später Lyrik," in *Hölderlin Jahrbuch* 22 (1980–1981): 18–46. Cf. also the remarks by Adolf Beck in *Hölderlins Weg zu Deutschland* (Stuttgart: Metzler, 1982), 180–190.

25. Cf. Hölderlin's commentary on Pindar's fragment "Das Belebende": "In such regions the river originally had to meander before it could tear/rip (*riss*) a course/path for itself" (P&F: 720–721).

26. I follow here the elegant translation of John Llewelyn, *The Middle Voice of Ecological Conscience* (New York: St. Martin's Press, 1991), 126.

27. Susanne Marchand, *Down from Olympus: Archaeology and Philhellenism in Germany, 1750–1970* (Princeton, NJ: Princeton University Press, 1996); Bernd Witte, *Moses und Homer: Griechen, Juden, Deutschen—eine andere Geschichte der deutschen Kultur* (Berlin: de Gruyter, 2018).

28. Martin Heidegger, PM: 257–259/GA 9: 337–339; GA 98: 285–286, 344–345.

29. Jean-Luc Nancy, *Dis-enclosure* (New York: Fordham University Press, 2008), 30.

Postscript

1. This sentence was left out of the GA 69 volume by its editors. Cf. the back story in Peter Trawny, *Heidegger und de Mythos der jüdischen Weltverschwörung* (Frankfurt: Klostermann, 2014), 51.

2. See chapter 4 for my discussion of this letter and its significance.

3. Heidegger's reference to his 1943 essay as "proof" of his earlier devotion to a non-nationalist "Hölderlin-interpretation" does not stand up to critical scrutiny. The 1943 essay shows a devotion to the self-same vision of German exceptionalism that we have traced throughout the Hölderlin lectures in GA 39, GA 52, and GA 53. The GA 4: 150 passage cited here is identical to the one in the National Socialist version. On the political background of the 1943 Hölderlin *Gedenkschrift*, cf. Gerhard Kurz, "Hölderlin 1943" in *Hölderlin und Nürtingen* (Stuttgart: Metzler, 2000), 103–128.

4. Bernhard Zeller, ed., *Klassiker in finsteren Zeiten, 1933–1945*, vol. 2 (Marbach: Deutsche Schillergesellschaft, 1983), 88, 91, 98.

5. Martin Heidegger, "Andenken." Paul Kluckhohn, ed., *Hölderlin: Gedenkschrift zu seinem 100. Todestag, 7 Juni 1943* (Tübingen: Mohr Siebeck, 1944), 322.

6. See for example his comments on American ahistoricality and Bolshevism's measurelessness in GA 53: 67.

7. Jacques Derrida, *Geschlecht III: Sex, Race, Nation, Humanity* (Chicago: University of Chicago Press, 2020), 99.

8. Dieter Thoma, "Das gestohlene Exil," *Deutsche Zeitschrift für Philosophie* 40, no. 6 (1992): 622–626.

9. Karl Jaspers, *Die Schuldfrage* (Heidelberg: Lambert Schneider, 1946).

10. Jacques Derrida, *Geschlecht III*, 132.

11. W.G. Sebald, *On the Natural History of Destruction* (New York: Random House, 2003), 7.

12. Maurice Olender, *Race and Erudition* (Cambridge, MA: Harvard University Press, 2009), 147–148.

13. This topic demands a chapter-length essay that is beyond the scope of the present book's focus but that addresses the reasons for Heidegger's relation to Hölderlin during the 1950s and 1960s.

14. Cf. Charles Bambach, *Thinking the Poetic Measure of Justice: Hölderlin-Heidegger-Celan* (Albany, NY: SUNY Press, 2013), 53–56, for a discussion of this poem on journeying, hospitality, and *xenia*.

15. Hannah Arendt, "We Refugees," in *The Jewish Writings* (New York: Schocken, 2007), 264–274, here 271–274.

16. Colm Tóibín, *The House of Names* (New York: Scribner's, 2018), 6

17. Walter Benjamin, "It is only for those without hope that hope is given," *Goethes Wahlverwandtschaften* (Frankfurt: Fischer, 1964), 106.

18. Paul Celan, "Shibboleth," *Die Gedichte: Neu kommentierte Gesamtausgabe*, ed. Barbara Wiedemann (Frankfurt: Suhrkamp, 2018), 87.

19. Paul Celan, "Tübingen, Jänner," *Die Gedichte: Neu kommentierte Gesamtausgabe*, 137 *Memory Rose into Threshold Speech*, Pierre Joris, ed. (New York: Farrar Straus Giroux, 2020), 266.

Bibliography

Hölderlin

Adorno, Theodor. "Parataxis." In *Noten zur Literatur* III. Frankfurt: Suhrkamp, 1965. 156–209.

Allemann, Beda. *Hölderlin und Heidegger*. Freiburg: Atlantis, 1954.

André, Robert. *Gespräche von Text zu Text. Celan-Heidegger-Hölderlin*. Hamburg: Meiner, 2003.

Albert, Claudia, ed. *Deutsche Klassiker im Nationalsozialismus*. Stuttgart: Metzler, 1994.

Bajorek, Jennifer. "The Offices of Homeland Security, or, Hölderlin and Terrorism." *Critical Inquiry* 31 (2005): 874–902.

Bambach, Charles. "Heidegger's Hölderlin after Sein und Zeit." In *"Sein und Zeit" neu verhandelt*, eds. Marion Heinz and Tobias Bender Hamburg: Meiner, 2019. 437–464.

———. "Hölderlin in the Black Notebooks." In *Heidegger-Jahrbuch*, 12. Freiburg: Alber, 2020. 153–170.

———. "The Hermeneutics of Remembrance. A Reading of Hölderlin's 'Andenken.'" *International Yearbook for Hermeneutics* 18 (2019): 58–76.

———. "Poetry at the Threshold: Reflections on a New Hölderlin Translation." *Athenaeum Review* 2 (2019): 128–138.

———. "Hölderlin and Celan: A Fragmented Poetics of Remembrance." *Modern Language Notes (MLN) German Issue* 135, no. 3 (2020): 635–657.

Bartel, Heike. "'Aber das Eigene muss so gut gelernt seyn, wie das Fremde': Zur dichterschen Verfahrensweise Friedrich Hölderlin." In *Der fremde Blick*, eds. I. Breuer and A. Sölter. Bozen: Studien Verlag, 1997. 153–168.

Bay, Hansjörg. *Ohne Rückkehr: Utopische Intention und poetischer Prozess in Hölderlins 'Hyperion.'* Munich: Fink, 2003.

———. "'Die eigene Rede des andern': Hölderlins Poetik des Fremden." In *Die Ordnung der Kulturen*, eds. H. Bay and K. Merten. Würzburg: Königshausen & Neumann, 2006. 333–356.

Beck, Adolf. *Hölderlins Weg zu Deutschland*. Stuttgart: Metzler, 1982.
———. "Das Hölderlinbild in der Forschung: 1939–1944." *Iduna (Hölderlin Jahrbuch)*, I (1944): 203–224.
Beissner, Friedrich. *Hölderlins Übersetzung aus dem Griechischen*. Stuttgart: Metzler, 1961.
Beissner, Friedrich, ed. *Hölderlin: Feldauswahl*. Stuttgart: Cotta, 1943.
Bertaux, Pierre. *Hölderlin und die französische Revolution*. Frankfurt: Suhrkamp, 1969.
———. *Friedrich Hölderlin*. Frankfurt: Suhrkamp, 1981.
———. *Hölderlin-Variationen*. Frankfurt: Suhrkamp, 1984.
———. "Hölderlin in und nach Bordeaux." *Hölderlin Jahrbuch* 19/20 (1975–1977): 94–111.
Beyer, Uwe, ed. *Neue Wege zu Hölderlin*. Würzburg: Königshausen & Neumann, 1994.
Binder, Wolfgang. *Hölderlin Aufsätze*. Frankfurt: Insel, 1970.
———. *Friedrich Hölderlin Studien*. Frankfurt: Suhrkamp, 1987.
———. *Hölderlin und Sophokles*. Turm-Vorträge. Tübingen: Hölderlin Gesellschaft, 1992.
Böckmann, Paul. *Hölderlin: Drei Reden. (Die bunten Hefte für unsere Soldaten)*. Stuttgart: Kohlhammer, 1943.
———. *Hölderlin und seine Götter*. Munich: Beck, 1935.
Böhm, Wilhelm. *Hölderlin*, 2 vols. Halle-Saale: Max Niemeyer, 1928.
Böschenstein, Bernhard. *Von Morgen nach Abend: Filiationen der Dichtung von Hölderlin zu Celan*. Munich: Fink, 2006.
———. *Leuchttürme: Von Hölderlin zu Celan*. Frankfurt: Insel, 1982.
———. *"Frucht des Gewitters." Zu Hölderlins Dionysos als Gott der Revolution*. Frankfurt: Insel, 1989.
Böschenstein-Schäfer, Renate. "Hölderlins Gespräch mit Boehlendorff." *Hölderlin Jahrbuch* 14 (1965): 110–124.
Bothe, Henning. *'Ein Zeichen sind wir, deutungslos': Die Rezeption Hölderlins von ihren Anfängen bis zu Stefan George*. Stuttgart: Metzler, 1992.
———. *Hölderlin: Zur Einführung*. Hamburg: Junius, 1994.
Brokoff, Jürgen, ed. *Norbert von Hellingrath und die Ästhetik der europäischen Moderne*. Göttingen: Wallstein, 2014.
Busch, Walter. "Kommerells Hölderlin: Von der Erbschaft Georges zur Kritik an Heidegger." In *Max Kommerell: Leben-Werk-Aktualität*, eds. W. Busch and G. Pickerodt. Göttingen: Wallstein, 2003. 278–299.
Christen, Felix. *Das Jetzt der Lektüre: Zur Edition und Deutung von Friedrich Hölderlins Ister-Entwürfen*. Frankfurt: Stroemfeld, 2013.
Constantine, David, J. *Hölderlin*. Oxford: Clarendon Press, 1988.
———. *The Significance of Locality in the Poetry of Friedrich Hölderlin*. London: Modern Humanities Research Association, 1979.

———. *Friedrich Hölderlin: Selected Poetry*. Translated by David J. Constantine. Eastburn, Northumberland: Bloodaxe Books, 2018.
Dastur, Françoise. *Hölderlin: le retournement natal*. Paris: encre marine, 2013.
———. "Hölderlin and the Orientalisation of Greece." *Pli* 10 (2000): 156–173.
de Beistegui, Miguel. *Aesthetics After Metaphysics*. New York: Routledge, 2014.
Doering, Sabine, and Johann Kreuzer, eds. *Unterwegs zu Hölderlin*. Oldenburg: Bis, 2015.
Doering, Sabine, and K. Dörner, G. Fichtner, eds. *Aus der Klinik ins Haus am Neckar: Der 'Fall' Hölderlin*. Tübingen: Klöpfer & Meyer, 2013.
Eldrige, Hannah Vandergrift. *Lyric Orientations: Hölderlin, Rilke, and the Poetics of Community*. Ithaca, NY: Cornell University Press, 2015.
———. "Gespräch, Gesang: Music, Dialog, and the Human in Celan and Hölderlin." *Modern Language Notes (MLN) German Issue* 135, no. 3 (2020): 658–678.
Fink, Markus. *Pindarfragmente: Neun Hölderlin-deutungen*. Berlin: de Gruyter, 1982.
Fioretos, Aris, ed. *The Solid Letter: Readings of Friedrich Hölderlin*. Stanford, CA: Stanford University Press, 1999.
———. "Hölderlin and the Caesura." *Compar(a)ison* 1 (1995): 109–130.
Foti, Veronique. *Epochal Discordance: Hölderlins Philosophy of Tragedy*. Albany, NY: SUNY Press, 2006.
Franz, Michael. "Die braunen Frauen, die Indier und die Quelle des Reichtums" In *Sprache—Dichtung—Philosophie: Heidegger und der Deutsche Idealismus*, ed. Bärbel Frischmann, 17–35. Freiburg: Alber, 2010.
———. "Hölderlin—Dichter der Dichter." *Studia theodisca—Hölderliniana* 1 (2014): 1–18.
———. "Hölderlins Gedicht 'Andenken.'" *Sonderband Friedrich Hölderlin*, ed. H.L. Arnold. Munich: Text & Kritik, 1996. 195–212.
———. "Poetische Ansicht der Geschichte": Eine Einführung in das Homburger Folioheft. *Hölderlin-Jahrbuch* 40 (2016/17): 9–37.
———. ". . . und anderes denk in anderer Zeit . . .": Hölderlins letzte Gedanken zu Recht und Politik in den 'Pindarfragmenten.' Stuttgart: Metzler, 2020.
Gaier, Ulrich. *Hölderlin: Eine Einführung*. Tübingen: Francke, 1993.
Görner, Rüdiger. *Hölderlin und die Folgen*. Stuttgart: Metzler, 2016.
———. *Hölderlins Mitte: Zur Ästhetik eines Ideals*. Munich: iudicium, 1993.
———. "Im Widerspruch zu Hause: Zu Hölderlins Heimat-Bild," in *Heimat im Wort*. Munich: iudicium, 1992. 50–61.
Hamilton, John. *Soliciting Darkness: Pindar, Obscurity and the Classical Tradition*. Cambridge, MA: Harvard University Press, 2003.
———. "Revolting Translation: Sophocles and Hölderlin." *Metamorphoses* 9 (2001): 113–134.
Harrison, R.B. *Hölderlin and Greek Literature*. Oxford: Clarendon Press, 1975.

Hellingrath, Norbert von. *Pindarübertragungen von Hölderlin*. Jena, 1911.
———. *Hölderlin: Zwei Vorträge* Munich: Bruckmann, 1921.
———. *Hölderlin-Vermächtnis*. Munich: Bruckmann, 1944.
Hellingrath, Norbert von, and Friedrich Seebass, eds. *Hölderlin: Sämtliche Werke*, 4 vols. 3rd edition. Berlin: Propyläen-Verlag, 1943.
Henrich, Dieter. *Der Gang des Andenkens*. Stuttgart: Klett-Cotta, 1986.
Honold, Alexander. "The Celebration of Time in the Revolutionary Community." In *Humanismus und Antikerezeption im 18. Jahrhundert*, eds. Uwe Steiner and Christian Emden. Heidelberg (Winter 2015): 159–177.
———. *Hölderlins Kalender: Astronomie und Revolution um 1800*. Berlin: Vorwerk 8, 2005.
———. *Nach Olympia: Hölderlin und die Erfindung der Antike*. Berlin: Vorwerk 8, 2002.
———. "Hölderlins Orientierung. Poetische Markierungen eines kulturgeographischen Richtungssinns." In *"Die andere Stimme." Das Fremde in der Kultur der Moderne. Festschrift für Klaus R. Scherpe zum 60. Geburtstag*. Köln: Böhlau, 1999. 99–121.
Jamme, Christoph, and Frank Völkel, eds. *Hölderlin und der deutsche Idealismus : Dokumente und Kommentare zu Hölderlins philosophischer Entwicklung und den philosophisch-kulturellen Kontexten seiner Zeit*, 4 vols. Stuttgart: Frommann-Holzboog, 2003.
Jünger, Hans-Dieter. *Mnemosyne und die Musen: Vom Sein des Erinnerns bei Hölderlin*. Würzburg: Königshausen & Neumann, 1993.
Kaiser, Gerhard. *Literaturwissenschaft im Nationalsozialismus*. Berlin: Akademie Verlag, 2008.
Kocziszky, Eva. *Hölderlins Orient*. Würzburg: Königshausen & Neumann, 2009.
Kocziszky, Eva, ed. *Wozu Dichter?: Hundert Jahre Poetologien nach Hölderlin*. Berlin: Frank & Timme, 2016.
Könitzer, Willi Fr. "Hölderlin und das Wesen der Dichtung: Eine Entgegnung." *Wille und Macht* 5 (1937): 28–30.
———. *Hölderlin: Ein Schicksal in Deutschland*. Berlin: Stalling, 1934.
Krell, David Farrell. *The Tragic Absolute*. Bloomington: Indiana University Press, 2005.
Kreuzer, Johan, ed. *Hölderlin Handbuch*. Stuttgart: Metzler, 2020.
Kurz, Gerhard, "Wortkunst: Zum ästhetischen und poetologischen Horizont von Hellingraths Hölderlin Ausgabe." In *Norbert von Hellingrath und die Ästhetik der europäischen Moderne*, ed., Jürgen Brokoff. Göttingen: Wallstein, 2014. 209–229.
Kurz, Gerhard, ed. *Friedrich Hölderlin: Gedichte*. Stuttgart: Reclam, 2000.
———, ed. *Interpretationen: Gedichte von Friedrich Hölderlin*. Stuttgart: Reclam, 1996.
Kurz, Gerhard, Valerie Lawitschka, and Jürgen Wertheimer, eds. *Hölderlin und die Moderne*. Tübingen: Attempto, 1995.

Kommerell, Max. *Der Dichter als Führer in der deutschen Klassik*. Berlin: Bondi, 1928.
Lacoue-Labarthe, Philippe. *Heidegger and the Politics of Poetry*. Urbana: University of Illinois Press, 2007.
———. *Poetry As Experience*. Stanford, CA: Stanford University Press, 1999.
Lawitschka, Valerie, ed. *Hölderlin: Philosophie und Dichtung*. Tübingen: Hölderlin Gesellschaft, 2001.
Lawitschka, Valerie, ed. *Hölderlin und die Griechen: Turm-Vorträge 2*, Tübingen: Hölderlin Gesellschaft, 1988.
Lefebvre, Jean-Pierre. *Hölderlin, Journal de Bordeaux*. Bordeaux: Bibliothek Virgin, 1990.
———. "Auch die Stege sind Holzwege." *Hölderlin Jahrbuch* 26 (1988/89): 209–223.
———. "Von Hölderlins Reisen und zu seinem Aufenthalt in Frankreich." In *Hölderlin und die Griechen: Turm-Vorträge 2*. Tübingen: Hölderlin Gesellschaft, 1988. 129–141.
Link, Jürgen. *Anteil der Kultur an der Versenkung Griechenlands: Von Hölderlins Deutschenschelte zu Schäubles Griechenschelte*. Würzburg: Königshausen & Neumann, 2016.
———. *Hölderlins Fluchtlinie Griechenland*. Göttingen: Vandenhoeckh & Ruprecht, 2020.
———. *Hölderlin-Rousseau: Inventive Rückkehr*. Wiesbaden: Westdeutscher Verlag, 1999.
———. "Rousseaus 'Naturgeschichte der menschlichen Gattung' und Hölderlins Dichtung nach 1800." *Hölderlin Jahrbuch* 30 (1996/97): 125–145.
———. "Hölderlins erstaunlicher Mythos über eine deutsch-griechische Urszene." *KulturRevolution: Zeitschrift für angewandte Diskurstheorie* 64 (2013): 74–81.
Louth, Charlie. *Hölderlin and the Dynamics of Translation*. Oxford: Legenda, 1998.
Martynkewicz, Wolfgang. *Salon Deutschland: Geist und Macht, 1900–1945*. Berlin: Aufbau, 2009.
Michel, Wilhelm. *Hölderlins Abendländische Wendung*. Jena: Eugen Diederichs, 1923.
———. *Hölderlin und der deutscher Geist*. Stuttgart: Klett, 1948.
———. *Hölderlins Wiederkunft*. Vienna: Gallus, 1943.
Mitchell, Andrew. "Die Politik des geheimen Deutschland: Martin Heidegger und der George Kreis." *Existentia* 23 (2013): 41–64.
Mottel, Helmut. *'Apollo envers terre': Hölderlins mythopoetische Weltentwürfe*. Würzburg: ERGON, 1998.
Müller, Ernst. *Hölderlin: Studien zur Geschichte seines Geistes*. Stuttgart: Kohlhammer, 1944.
———. *Hölderlins vaterländische Gesänge (Erläutert)*. (*Die bunten Hefte für unsere Soldaten*). Stuttgart: Kohlhammer, 1942.
Müller-Fink, Wolfgang. "Heideggers Heimat: Hölderlin." In *Die Dichter der Philosophen*. Munich: Fink, 2013. 13–32.

Nikolopoulou, Kalliopi. *Tragically Speaking: On the Use and Abuse of Theory for Life*. Lincoln: University of Nebraska Press, 2012.
Otto, Walter F. *Die Götter Griechenlands*. Bonn: Friedrich Cohen,1929.
———. *Dionysos: Mythos und Kultus*. Frankfurt: Klostermann, 1933.
Pieger, Bruno, "Norbert von Hellingraths Hölderlin." In *Wissenschaftler im George-Kreis: Die Welt des Dichters und der Beruf der Wissenschaft*, eds. Bernhard Böschenstein et al. Berlin: de Gruyter, 2005. 115–136.
Pieger, Bruno, ed. *Stefan George: Dichtung Ethos Staat*. Berlin: Verlag für Berlin-Brandenburg, 2010.
———. "Norbert von Hellingrath und die Entdeckung des späten Hölderlin." In *Hölderlin: Philosophie und Dichtung*, ed. Valerie Lawitschka. Tübingen: Hölderlin Gesellschaft, 2001. 131–156.
Pieger, Bruno, Werner Volke, Dieter Burdorf, eds. *Hölderlin Entdecken: Lesarten, 1826–1993*. Tübingen: Hölderlin Gesellschaft, 1993.
Pigenot, Ludwig. "Briefe aus Norbert von Hellingraths Nachlass." *Hölderlin Jahrbuch* 13 (1963/64): 104–146.
Polledri, Elena. ". . . immer bestehet ein Maas": *Der Begriff des Masses in Hölderlins Werk*. Würzburg: Königshausen & Neumann, 2002.
Procopan, Nina. *Hölderlins Donauhymnen*. Egglingen: Isele, 2004.
Raulff, Ulrich, and Brokoff, Jürgen. "Hellingrath-Hölderlin-George: Im Gespräch mit Bernhard Böschenstein" In *Norbert von Hellingrath und die Ästhetik der europäischen Moderne*, ed., Jürgen Brokoff. Göttingen: Wallstein, 2014. 15–29.
Reinhardt, Karl. *Sophokles*. Frankfurt: Klostermann, 1933.
Riedel, Manfred. *Geheimes Deutschland*. Köln: Böhlau, 2006.
Reitani, Luigi, ed. *Friedrich Hölderlin, Tutte le Lirichi*. Milan: Arnoldo Mondadori, 2001.
———. "Die Entdeckung der Poesie. Norbert von Hellingraths bahnbrechende Edition der Werke Hölderlins." In *Neugermanistische Editoren im Wissenschaftskontext*, eds. R. Kamzelak, R. Nutt-Kofoth, and B. Plachta. Berlin: De Gruyter, 2011. 153–165.
Reuss, Roland. ". . . *Die eigene Rede des andern*": *Hölderlins 'Andenken' und 'Mnemosyne.'* Frankfurt: Stroemfeld, 1990.
Roeske, Kurt. *Antigones tödlicher Ungehorsam: Text, Deutung, Rezeption der 'Antigone' des Sophokles*. Würzburg: Königshausen & Neumann, 2009.
Rosenfield, Catherine. *Antigone: Sophocles's Art, Hölderlin's Insight*. Aurora, CO: Davies, 2010.
Ryan, Lawrence. "Hölderlins Antigone." In *Jenseits des Idealismus*, eds. C. Jamme and O. Pöggeler. Bonn: Bouvier, 1988. 103–122.
Sattler, D.E. *Friedrich Hölderlin: 144 fliegende Briefe*. 2 vols. Bremen: Luchterhand, 1981.
Savage, Robert. *Hölderlin After the Catastrophe: Heidegger-Adorno-Brecht*. New York: Camden, 2008.

Scharfschwerdt, Jürgen. *Friedrich Hölderlin: Dichter des "deutschen Sonderweges."* Stuttgart: Kohlhammer,1994.
Schmidt, Jochen. *Hölderlins geschichtsphilosophische Hymnen.* Darmstadt: Wissenschaftliche Buchgesellschaft, 1990.
———. *Hölderlins letzte Hymnen.* Tübingen: Niemeyer, 1970.
———. "Der Nachlass Norbert von Hellingraths." *Hölderlin Jahrbuch* 13 (1963/64): 147–150.
———. "Tragödie und Tragödientheorie: Hölderlins Sophokles-Deutung." *Hölderlin-Jahrbuch* 29 (1994/95): 64–82.
Schroeder, Jürgen. *Deutschland als Gedicht.* Freiburg: Rombach, 2000.
Sikes, Elizabeth. "Dionysian *Dankbarkeit*: Friedrich Hölderlin's Poetics of Sacrifice." *Södertörn Philosophical Studies* 10 (2004): 33–60.
———. "The Decline (and Fall?) of the Fatherland: The Problem of Historical Memory in Hölderlin's Theory of Tragedy." *International Studies in Philosophy* 40, no. 1 (2008): 101–111.
Stampoulou, Symeon. *Der heilige Tyrann: Die Auseinandersetzung Hölderlins mit Sophokles.* Baden-Baden: Deutscher Wissenschafts Verlag, 2011.
Sommer, Christian. *Mythologie de l'évènment: Heidegger avec Hölderlin.* Paris: Presses Universitaires de France, 2017.
Steiner, George. *Antigones.* New York: Oxford University Press, 1984.
Stierle, Karlheinz. "Die Friedensfeier. Sprache und Fest im revolutionären und nachrevolutionären Frankreich und bei Hölderlin." In *Das Fest*, eds. W. Haug and R. Warning. Munich: Fink, 1989. 481–525.
Stone, Alison. "Hölderlin on Nature." In *Nature, Ethics and Gender in German Romanticism and Idealism.* London: Rowman and Littlefield, 2018. 101–120.
Tambling, Jeremy. *Hölderlin and the Poetry of Tragedy.* Brighton: Sussex Academic Press, 2014.
Theunissen, Michael. *Pindar: Menschenlos und Wende der Zeit.* Munich: Beck, 2000.
Trawny, Peter. "Und nie mein land den schatz gewann": Bemerkungen zu Heideggers George Lektüre im 'Geheimen Deutschland.' In *Stefan George: Dichtung Ethos Staat,* ed. Bruno Pieger. Berlin: Verlag für Berlin-Brandenburg, 2010. 189–205.
Varwig, Freyr. "Still hingleitende Gesänge lehrtest du mich . . . : Natur und Natürlichkeit in Redefluss Hölderlins." *Hölderlin Jahrbuch* 13 (1963/64): 147–150.
Wackwitz, Stefan. *Friedrich Hölderlin: Sammlung Metzler.* Stuttgart: Metzler, 1997.
Weichelt, Matthias. *Gewaltsame Horizontbildungen: Max Kommerells lyrischer Ansatz und die Krisen der Moderne.* Heidelberg (Winter, 2006).
Weineck, Silke-Maria. *The Abyss Above: Philosophy and Poetic Madness in Plato, Hölderlin and Nietzsche.* Albany, NY: SUNY Press, 2002.
Weinstock, Heinrich. *Sophokles.* Berlin: Die Runde, 1937.
Zeller, Bernhard, ed. *Klassiker in finsteren Zeiten, 1933–1945,* 2 vols. Marbach: Deutsche Schillergesellschaft, 1983.
Zuberbühler, Rolf. *Hölderlins Erneuerung der Sprache aus ihren etymologischen Ursprüngen.* Berlin: Schmidt, 1969.

Heidegger

Allen, William S. *Ellipsis: Of Poetry and the Experience of Language after Heidegger, Hölderlin, and Blanchot.* Albany, NY: SUNY Press, 2007.
Appelhans, Jörg. *Martin Heideggers ungeschriebene Poetologie.* Tübingen: Niemeyer, 2002.
Arendt, Hannah. *The Jewish Writings.* New York: Schocken, 2007.
Aurenque, Diana. *Ethosdenken: Auf der Spur einer ethischen Fragestellung in der Philosophie Martin Heideggers.* Freiburg: Alber, 2011.
Babich, Babette. *Words in Blood Like Flowers: Philosophy and Poetry, Music and Eros in Hölderlin, Nietzsche, and Heidegger.* Albany, NY: SUNY Press, 2006.
———. "The New Heidegger." In *Heidegger in the Twenty-First Century*, eds. T. Georgakis and P. Ennis. Dordrecht: Springer, 2015. 167–188
Baeumler, Alfred. "Hellas und Germanien." In *Studien zur deutschen Geistesgeschichte.* Berlin: Junker & Dünnhaupt, 1937. 295–311.
———. "Der Kampf um den Humanismus." In *Politik und Erziehung.* Berlin: Junker & Dünnhaupt, 1937. 57–66.
Bambach, Charles. "The *Ethos* of Dwelling in Heidegger's *Letter on Humanism*: A Reading of Heraclitus Fragment B119." *International Yearbook for Hermeneutics* 15 (2016): 90–107.
———. *Heidegger's Roots: Nietzsche, National Socialism and the Greeks.* Ithaca, NY: Cornell University Press, 2003.
———. *Thinking the Poetic Measure of Justice: Hölderlin-Heidegger-Celan.* Albany, NY: SUNY Press, 2013.
———. "Thinking through the Politics of Black and Brown: Heidegger in the Thirties." *Research in Phenomenology* 50, no. 1 (2020): 122–131.
———. "Ethos—Aufenthalt: Heideggers Kritik an der metaphysischen Ethik." *Heidegger und der Humanismus. Heidegger Jahrbuch* 10 (2017): 62–78.
Benjamin, Andrew. *Place, Commonality, and Judgment: Continental Philosophy in the Ancient Greeks.* London: Bloomsbury, 2012.
Bernasconi, Robert. "Poets as Prophets and as Painters." In *Heidegger and Language*, ed. Jeffrey Powell. Bloomington: Indiana University Press, 2001. 146–162.
———, ed. *Race and Racism in Continental Philosophy.* Bloomington: Indiana University Press, 2003.
———. "'We Philosophers': *Barbaros medeis eisito.*" In *Endings: Questions of Memory in Hegel and Heidegger*, eds. R. Comay and J. McCumber. Evanston, IL: Northwestern University Press, 1999. 77–96.
Biella, Burkhard. *Eine Spur ins Wohnen legen: Entwurf einer Philosophie des Wohnens mit Heidegger und über Heidegger hinaus.* Düsseldorf: ParErga, 1998.
Biemel, Walter. "Zu Heideggers Deutung der Ister-Hymne." *Heidegger Studies* 3/4 (1987/88): 41–60.
Blok, Vincent. *Ernst Jünger's Philosophy of Technology: Heidegger and the Poetics of the Anthropocene.* London: Routledge, 2017.

Bohlen, Stephanie. *Die Übermacht des Seins: Heideggers Auslegung des Bezuges von Mensch und Natur und Hölderlins Dichtung des Heiligen*. Berlin: Duncker & Humblot, 1993.

Bruns, Gerald. *Heidegger's Estrangements: Language, Truth, and Poetry in the Later Writings*. New Haven, CT: Yale University Press, 1989.

Buchheim, Iris. *Wegbereitung in die Kunstlosigkeit: Zu Heideggers Auseinandersetzung mit Hölderlin*. Würzburg: Königshausen & Neumann, 1994.

Campbell, Scott. "The Tragic Sense of Life in Heidegger's Readings of *Antigone*." In *The Science, Politics and Ontology of Life Philosophy*. London: Bloomsbury, 2013. 185–196.

Cassin, Barbara. *Nostalgia: When Are We Ever at Home?* New York: Fordham University Press, 2016.

Crowell, Steven. "Reading Heidegger's 'Black Notebooks.'" In *Reading Heidegger's 'Black Notebooks' 1931–1941*, eds. Ingo Farin and Jeff Malpas. Cambridge, MA: MIT Press, 2015. 29–45.

Dahlstrom, Daniel. *The Heidegger Dictionary*. London: Bloomsbury, 2013.

Davies, Katherine. *Heidegger's Conversation: Towards a Poetic Pedagogy* (Forthcoming).

Davis, Bret. *Heidegger and the Will: On the Way to 'Gelassenheit.'* Evanston, IL: Northwestern University Press, 2007.

———, ed. *Heidegger: Key Concepts*. Durham, NC: Acumen, 2010.

de Beistegui, Miguel. *Heidegger & the Political*. New York: Routledge, 1998.

———. *The New Heidegger*. New York: Continuum, 2005.

———. *Thinking with Heidegger: Displacements*. Bloomington: Indiana University Press, 2003.

Denker, Alfred, and Holger Zaborowski, eds. *Heidegger und der Nationalsozialismus: Interpretationen*. Heidegger-Jahrbuch, 5. Freiburg: Alber, 2009.

Derrida, Jacques. *The Monolingualism of the Other*. Stanford, CA: Stanford University Press, 1998.

———*On Cosmopolitanism and Forgiveness*. London: Routledge, 2017.

———*Of Hospitality*. Stanford, CA: Stanford University Press, 2000.

Di Cesare, Donatella. *Heidegger, die Juden, die Shoah*. Frankfurt: Klostermann, 2016

———. *Resident Foreigners: A Philosophy of Migration*. Medford: Polity, 2020.

Drewniak, Tomas. "Polis-Hypsipolis-Apolis. Die Heimatlosigkeit und der semantische Überschuss des Seins im Lichte der Heideggerschen Auslegung des Antigone Chorlieds." In *Denkerische und dichterische Heimatsuche*, eds. T. Drewniak and A. Dittmann. Görlitz: Viadukt Verlag, 2012.

Düsing, Klaus. "Die Mythologie des späten Hölderlin und Heideggers Seinsgeschichte." In *Die Gottesfrage im Denken Martin Heideggers*, eds. N. Fischer and F.W. von Herrmann. Hamburg: Felix Meiner, 2011. 129–148.

Edler, Frank. *The Significance of Hölderlin for Heidegger's Political Involvement with Nazism*. Unpublished doctoral dissertation, University of Toronto, 1992.

Farin, Ingo, and Jeff Malpas, eds. *Reading Heidegger's 'Black Notebooks' 1931–1941*. Cambridge, MA: MIT Press, 2015.

Figal, Günter. *Martin Heidegger: Zur Einführung.* Hamburg: Junius, 2016.
———. *Zu Heidegger: Antworten und Fragen.* Frankfurt: Klostermann, 2009.
Foti, Veronique. *Heidegger and the Poets.* New Jersey: Humanities Press, 1992.
Fried, Gregory. *Heidegger's 'Polemos.'* New Haven, CT: Yale University Press, 2003.
Fried, Gregory, and Richard Polt, eds. *After Heidegger?* London: Rowman and Littlefield 2018.
Freydberg, Bernard. "On Hölderlin's *Andenken*: Heidegger, Gadamer and Henrich—A Decision?" *Research in Phenomenology* 34 (2004): 181–197.
Froment-Meurice, Marc. *That is to Say: Heidegger's Poetics.* Stanford, CA: Stanford University Press, 1998.
Fynsk, Christopher. *Heidegger: Thought and Historicity.* Ithaca, NY: Cornell University Press, 1986.
Gadamer, Hans-Georg. *Gesammelte Werke,* 10 vols. Tübingen: Mohr Siebeck, 1985–1992.
Gasché, Rodolfe. *Europe, Or the Infinite Task.* Stanford, CA: Stanford University Press, 2009.
Geiman, Claire. "Heidegger's *Antigones.*" In *A Companion to Heidegger's "Introduction to Metaphysics,"* eds. Richard Polt and Gregory Fried. New Haven, CT: Yale University Press, 2000. 161–182.
Gethmann-Siefert, Annemarie. "Heidegger und Hölderlin. Die Überforderung des 'Dichters in dürftiger Zeit.'" In *Heidegger und die praktische Philoosphie,* eds. A. Gethmann-Siefert and Otto Pöggeler. Frankfurt: Suhrkamp, 1988. 191–227.
Gordon, Peter. "*Heidegger* in Black." *New York Review of Books* 61, no. 15 (October 2014): 28–39.
———. "Prolegomena to any Future Destruction of Metaphysics: Heidegger and the Black Notebooks." In *Heidegger's Black Notebooks: Responses to anti-Semitism,* eds. A. Mitchell and P. Trawny. New York: Columbia University Press, 2017. 136–151.
Gosetti-Ferencei, Jennifer. *Heidegger, Hölderlin, and the Subject of Poetic Language.* New York: Fordham University Press, 2004.
Greisch, Jean. "Who Stands Fast? Do Philosophers Make Good Resistants?" In *Bonhoeffer and Continental Thought,* eds. B. Gregor and J. Zimmermann. Bloomington: Indiana University Press, 2006. 84–101.
Grosser, Florian. *Revolution Denken: Heidegger und das Politische, 1919 bis 1969.* Munich: Beck, 2016
Grossmann, Andreas. *Heidegger Lektüren.* Würzburg: Königshausen & Neumann, 2005.
Gutschmidt, Rico. *Sein ohne Grund: Die post-theistische Religiosität im Spätwerk Heideggers.* Freiburg: Alber, 2016.
Haar, Michel. *The Song of the Earth: Heidegger and the Grounds of the History of Being.* Bloomington: Indiana University Press, 1993.

Han, Byung-Chul. *Martin Heidegger: Eine Einführung.* Stuttgart: UTB, 1999.
———. *Abwesen.* Berlin: Merve, 2007.
Harries, Karsten. *Art Matters: A Critical Commentary on Heidegger's "The Origin of the Work of Art."* Dordrecht: Springer, 2009.
———. *Martin Heidegger: Politics, Art, and Technology,* eds. Karsten Harries and Christoph Jamme. New York: Holmes & Meier, 1994.
———. "Dem Dichten vor-denken: Aspekte von Heideggers 'Zweisprache' mit Hölderlin im Kontext seiner Kunstphilosophie." *Zeitschrift für philosophische Forschung* 38 (1984): 191–218.
Heidegger, Arnulf. "Zur Entstehungsgeschichte der Gesamtausgabe von Martin Heidegger." In *Seefahrten des Denkens. Dietmar Koch zum 60. Geburtstag,* eds. A. Noveanu, Julia Pfefferkorn, A. Spinelli. Tübingen: Narr/Francke/Attempto, 2017. 147–153.
Heinz, Marion, and Tobias Bender, eds. *"Sein und Zeit" neu verhandelt.* Hamburg: Meiner, 2019.
Heinz, Marion, and Sidonie Keller, eds. *Martin Heideggers 'Schwarze Hefte.'* Frankfurt: Suhrkamp, 2016.
Held, Klaus. *Marbach Bericht über eine neue Sichtung des Heidegger-Nachlasses.* Frankfurt: Klostermann, 2019.
———. "Heideggers eigenartiger Antisemitismus." *Zeitgemässe Betrachtungen.* Frankfurt: Klostermann, 2017. 195–205.
Hyland, Drew, and John Manoussakis, eds. *Heidegger and the Greeks.* Bloomington: Indiana University Press, 2006.
Ireland, Julia. "Heidegger, Hölderlin, and Eccentric Translation." In *Heidegger, Translation, and the Task of Thinking,* ed. Frank Schalow. Dordrecht: Springer, 2015. 253–267.
Jacobs, David C. *The Presocratics after Heidegger.* Albany, NY: SUNY Press, 2007.
Jamme, Christoph. "Dem Dichten vor-denken: Aspekte von Heideggers 'Zweisprache' mit Hölderlin im Kontext seiner Kunstphilosophie." *Zeitschrift für philosophische Forschung* 38 (1984): 191–218.
Janicaud, Dominique. *Heidegger in France.* Bloomington: Indiana University Press, 2015.
———. *The Shadow of That Thought: Heidegger and the Question of Politics.* Evanston, IL: Northwestern University Press, 1996.
Kisiel, Theodore. "The Siting of Hölderlin's 'Geheimes Deutschland' in Heidegger's Poetizing of the Political." In *Heidegger und der Nationalsozialismus II: Interpretationen,* ed. Alfred Denker and Holger Zaborowski. Freiburg: Alber, 2009. 145–154.
Kleinberg-Levin, David. *Gestures of Ethical Life: Reading Hölderlin's Question of Measure After Heidegger.* Stanford, CA: Stanford University Press, 2005.
Knowles, Adam. *Heidegger's Fascist Affinities.* Stanford, CA: Stanford University Press, 2019.

Kommerell, Max. *Briefe und Aufzeichnungen, 1919–1944*. Freiburg: Walter-Verlag, 1967.
Krell, David Farrell. *Lunar Voices: Of Tragedy, Poetry, Fiction, and Thought*. Bloomington: Indiana University Press, 1995.
Kühn, Walter. *Vermischte Zustände: Heidegger im literarisch-philosophischen Leben der fünfziger Jahre des zwangzigsten Jahrhunderts*. Würzburg: Königshausen & Neumann, 2015.
Lacoue-Labarthe, Philippe. *Heidegger, Art and Politics*. Oxford: Blackwell, 1990.
Lambropoulos, Vassilis. *The Rise of Eurocentrism*. Princeton, NJ: Princeton University Press, 1993.
Loscerbo, John. *Being and Technology: A Study in the Philosophy of Martin Heidegger*. The Hague: Martinus Nijhoff, 1980.
Lyotard, Jean-François. *Heidegger and "the jews."* Minneapolis: University of Minnesota Press, 1990.
Lypp, Bernhard. "Mein ist die Rede vom Vaterland." *Merkur* 41 (1987): 120–135.
Maten, Rainer. *Heidegger Lesen*. Munich: Fink, 1991.
McNeill, William. "The Hölderlin Lectures." In *The Bloomsbury Companion to Heidegger*, eds. Francois Raffoul and Eric Nelson. London: Bloomsbury, 2013. 223–236.
———. *The Time of Life: Heidegger and "Ethos."* Albany, NY: SUNY Press, 2007.
———. "Remains: Heidegger and Hölderlin Amid the Ruins of Time." In *Poets and Their Philosophers: Reflections on the Poetic Turn in Philosophy Since Kant*, eds. Charles Bambach and Theodore George. Albany, NY: SUNY Press, 2019. 159–184.
———. "'A Scarcely Pondered Word': The Place of Tragedy. Heidegger, Aristotle, Sophocles." In *Philosophy and Tragedy*, ed. M. de Beistegui and S. Sparks. London: Routledge, 2000. 169–189.
———. "Uncanny Belonging: The Enigma of Solitude in Heidegger's Work." *Proceedings of the 47th Annual Meeting of the Heidegger Circle*, 2013. 147–165.
Mehring, Reinhard. *Heideggers 'grosse Politik': Die semantische Revolution der Gesamtausgabe*. Tübingen: Mohr Siebeck, 2016.
———. *Martin Heidegger und die 'konservative Revolution.'* Freiburg: Alber, 2018.
Mitchell, Andrew. *The Fourfold: Reading the Late Heidegger*. Evanston, IL: Northwestern University Press, 2015.
———. "Heidegger's Breakdown: Health and Healing Under the Care of Dr. V.E. von Gebsattel." *Research in Phenomenology* 46, no. 1 (2016): 70–97.
Mitchell, Andrew, and Peter Trawny, eds. *Heidegger's Black Notebooks: Responses to Anti-Semitism*. New York: Columbia University Press, 2017.
Moore, Ian Alexander. *Eckhart, Heidegger, and the Imperative of Releasement*. Albany, NY: SUNY Press, 2019.
———. *Dialogue on the Threshold: Heidegger and Trakl*. Albany, NY: SUNY Press, 2022.

Morat, Daniel. *Von der Tat zur Gelassenheit: Konservatives Denken bei Martin Heidegger, Ernst Jünger, und Friedrich-Georg Jünger.* Göttingen: Wallstein, 2007.
Moskopp, Werner. "Meta-, Post-, und Neo-Ethik—Die Aufgabe des Denkens." In *Heidegger und der Humanismus. Heidegger Jahrbuch* 10 (2017): 134–147.
Mugerauer, Robert. *Heidegger and Homecoming: The Leitmotif in the Later Writings.* Toronto: University of Toronto Press, 2008.
Nancy, Jean-Luc. *The Banality of Heidegger.* New York: Fordham University Press, 2017.
Ott, Hugo. *Martin Heidegger: Unterwegs zu seiner Biographie.* Frankfurt: Campus, 1988
Oudemans, Th. C.W. *Tragic Ambiguity: Anthropology, Philosophy and Sophocles' 'Antigone'* Leiden: Brill, 1987.
Peters, Werner. "Mitte und Mass." In *Die Mitte: Vermessungen in Politik und Kultur*, eds. B. Guggenberger and K. Hansen. Opladen: Westdeutscher Verlag, 1992. 31–37.
Pöggeler, Otto. *Schicksal und Geschichte: Antigone im Spiegel der Deutungen und Gestaltungen seit Hegel und Heidegger.* Munich: Fink, 2004.
Polt, Richard. *Time and Trauma: Thinking through Heidegger in the Thirties.* London: Rowman & Littlefield, 2019.
———. "The Black Notebooks as Thought Journals." In Alfred Denker and Holger Zaborowski, eds. *Zur Hermeneutik der Schwarzen Hefte, Heidegger Jahrbuch* 11 (2017): 45–60.
Pornschlegel, Clemens. *Der literarische Souverän: Zur politischen Funktion der deutschen Dichtung bei Goethe, Heidegger, Kafka und im George-Kreis.* Freiburg: Rombach, 1994.
Powell, Jeffrey, ed. *Heidegger and Language.* Bloomington: Indiana University Press, 2013.
Prins, Albert. "Heideggers Andenken: Zwiesprache und Gewalt." In *Poesie und Philosophie in einer tragischen*, ed. *Kultur* H. Kimmerle. Würzburg: Königshausen & Neumann, 2004. 72–86.
Raffoul, François. *The Origins of Responsibility.* Bloomington: Indiana University Press, 2010.
Risser, James, ed. *Heidegger toward the Turn: Essays on the Work of the 1930s.* Albany, NY: SUNY Press, 1999.
Rockmore, Tom. *On Heidegger's Nazism and Philosophy.* Berkeley: University of California Press, 1992.
Rohkrämer, Thomas. *Martin Heidegger: Eine politische Biographie.* Paderborn: Ferdinand Schöningh, 2020.
Rojcewicz, Richard. *The Gods and Technology: A Reading of Heidegger.* Bloomington: Indiana University Press, 2006.
Roland-Jensen, Flemming. "Die hesperische Landschaft der Mitte: Ein Beitrag zu Hölderlins vaterländischem Denken." *Text & Kontext* 4, no. 1 (1979): 31–40.

Sallis, John. *The Return of Nature*. Bloomington: Indiana University Press, 2016.
———. *Echoes: After Heidegger*. Bloomington: Indiana University Press, 1990.
Schmidt, Dennis, "Ethics after Heidegger." In *After Heidegger?*, eds. Gregory Fried and Richard Polt. London: Rowman and Littlefield, 2018. 133–140.
———. "Heidegger and the Call for an Original Ethics." *Kronos* 6 (2017): 112–119.
———. "Hermeneutics and Ethical Life: On the Return to Factical Life." In *The Blackwell Companion to Hermeneutics*, eds. F. Raffoul and E. Nelson. Oxford: Wiley-Blackwell, 2016. 65–71.
———. "Where Ethics Begins . . . ," *Epoche* 22, no. 1 (2017): 159–175.
———. "The Monstrous, Catastrophe, and Ethical Life: Hegel, Heidegger and Antigone." *Philosophy Today*, 59, no. 1 (2017): 61–72.
———. "The Idiom of the Ethical." *Epoche* 17, no. 1 (2012): 15–24.
———. "The Later Heidegger." In *The History of Continental Philosophy. Volume 4, Phenomenology: Responses and Developments*, ed. Alan Schrift. Chicago: University of Chicago Press, 2010. 157–176.
———. "The Ordeal of the Foreign and the Enigma of One's Own." *Philosophy Today* 40, no. 1 (1996): 188–196.
———. *Lyrical and Ethical Subjects*. Albany, NY: SUNY Press, 2005.
———. *On Germans and Other Greeks: Tragedy and Ethical Life*. Bloomington: Indiana University Press, 2000.
Schürmann, Reiner. *Broken Hegemonies*. Bloomington: Indiana University Press, 2003.
Seubert, Harald. *Heidegger-Lexikon*. Stuttgart: UTB, 2020.
Sikka, Sonja. *Heidegger, Morality and Politics: Questioning the Shepherd of Being*. Cambridge: Cambridge University Press, 2018.
Solbach, Anja. *Seinsverstehen und Mythos: Untersuchungen zur Dichtung des späten Hölderlin und zu Heideggers Deutung*. Freiburg: Alber, 2008.
Sommer, Chrstian. "Abendländische Dichtung und europäischen Literatur." In *Schreiben Dichten Denken: Zu Heideggers Sprachbegriff*, ed. David Espinet. Frankfurt: Klostermann, 2011. 29–40.
———. "Das harte *Geschlecht*: Derrida Reading Heidegger in *Geschlecht* III." *Philosophy Today* 64, no. 2 (2020): 441–449.
Storck, Joachim. "Hermeneutischer Disput: Max Kommerells Auseinandersetzung mit Martin Heideggers Hölderlin-Interpetation." In *Literaturgeschichte als Profession: Festschrift für Dietrich Jöns*. Tübingen: Narr, 1993.
———. "Zwiesprache von Dichten und Denken: Hölderlin bei Martin Heidegger und Max Kommerell." In *Klassiker in finsteren Zeiten*, II, ed. B. Zeller. Marbach: Deutsche Schillergesellschaft, 1983. 345–365.
Swazo, Norman. "Preserving the *Ethos*: Heidegger and Sophocles' *Antigone*." *Symposium* 10 (2006): 441–471.
Taminiaux, Jacques. "Plato's Legacy in Heidegger's Two Readings of *Antigone*." In *Heidegger and Plato*, eds. C. Partenie and T. Rockmore. Evanston, IL: Northwestern University Press, 2005. 22–41.

———. "Das Heimweh nach Griechenland in der deutschen Frühklassik." In *Hölderlin und die Griechen*, ed.Valerie Lawitschka, ed.,. Tübingen: Hölderlin-Gesellschaft, 1987/88. 22–41.
Thomä, Dieter. "Das gestohlene Exil." *Deutsche Zeitschrift für Philosophie* 40, no. 6 (1992): 622–626.
Thomä, Dieter, ed. *Heidegger Handbuch*. Stuttgart: Metzler, 2013.
Thomson, Ian. "Heidegger's Nazism in View of his early Black Notebooks: A View From America." In Alfred Denker and Holger Zaborowski, eds. *Zur Hermeneutik der Schwarzen Hefte*, Heidegger Jahrbuch 11 (2017): 184–209.
Trawny, Peter. *Heidegger und Hölderlin oder Der Europäische Morgen*. Würzburg: Königshausen & Neumann, 2004.
———. *Heidegger und der Mythos der jüdischen Weltverschwörung*. Frankfurt: Klostermann, 2014.
———. *Heidegger: Eine kritische Einführung*. Frankfurt: Klostermann, 2016.
Trawny, Peter, ed. *"Voll Verdienst, doch dichterisch wohnet/Der Mensch auf dieser Erde."* Frankfurt: Klostermann, 2000.
Trawny, Peter, and Andrew Mitchell, eds. *Heidegger, die Juden, noch einmal*. Frankfurt: Klostermann, 2015.
van der Heiden, Gert-Jan. *The Voice of Misery: A Continental Philosophy of Testimony*. Albany, NY: SUNY Press, 2019.
Van Reijen, Willem. *Martin Heidegger*. Paderborn: Fink, 2009.
Vedder, Ben. *Heidegger and the Gods*. Pittsburgh: Duquesne University Press, 2006.
Vetter, Helmuth. *Grundriss Heidegger: Ein Handbuch zu Leben und Werk*. Hamburg: Meiner, 2014.
Warminski, Andrzej. *Readings in Interpretation: Hölderlin, Hegel, Heidegger*. Minneapolis: University of Minnesota Press, 1987.
Weber, Christian. "Die Hölderlin-Rezeption im Dialog mit Martin Hedegger und Hans-Georg Gadamer (1941–1943)." In *Max Kommerell: Eine intellektuelle Biographie*. Berlin: Walter de Gruyter, 2011. 437–477.
Wenz, Gunther. *Der Ister: Heidegger deutet Hölderlin*. Munich: Bayerische Akademie der Wissenschaften, 2019.
Weston, Nancy. "Poetic Justice: Heidegger on Poetry as the Saying of Law." *Heidegger Jahrbuch* 8 (2014): 29–40.
Withy, Katherine. *Heidegger on Being Uncanny*. Cambridge, MA: Harvard University Press, 2015.
Witte, Bernd. *Moses und Homer. Griechen, Juden, Deutsche: Eine andere Geschichte der deutschen Kultur*. Berlin: de Gruyter, 2018.
Wolfe, Judith. *Heidegger and Theology*. London: Bloomsbury, 2014.
Wolfson, Eliot. *The Duplicity of Philosophy's Shadow: Heidegger, Nazism, and the Jewish Other*. New York: Columbia University Press, 2018.
Wrathall, Mark. *Heidegger and Unconcealment: Truth, Language, History*. Cambridge: Cambridge University Press, 2011.

Wrathall, Mark, ed. *The Cambridge Heidegger Lexicon*. Cambridge: Cambridge University Press, 2021.
Wright, Kathleen. "Heidegger and the Authorization of Hölderlin's Poetry "In *Martin Heidegger: Politics, Art, Technology*, eds. Karsten Harries and Christoph Jamme. New York: Holmes & Meier, 1994. 164–174.
———. "Gespräch mit Hölderlin II: Die Heroisierung Hölderlins um 1933." In *Heidegger Handbuch*. Stuttgart: Metzler, 2013. 188–199.
———. "Gewaltsame Lektüre deutungsloser Zeichen. Heidegger liest Hölderlins 'Andenken.'" In *Texte und Lektüren: Perspektiven in der Literaturwissenschaft*, ed., Aleida Assmann. Frankfurt: Fischer, 1996. 229–246.
———. "Heidegger's Hölderlin and the Mo(u)rning of History." *Philosophy Today* 37, no. 4 (1993): 423–435.
Zaborowski, Holger. *Eine Frage von Irre und Schuld?: Martin Heidegger und der Nationalsozialismus*. Frankfurt: Fischer, 2010.
Zaborowski, Holger, and Alfred Denker, eds. *Zur Hermeneutik der Schwarzen Hefte, Heidegger Jahrbuch* 11–12 (2017–2020).
Ziarek, Krzysztof. *Language after Heidegger*. Bloomington: Indiana University Press, 2013.
———. "The Poietic Momentum of Thought: Heidegger and Poetry. In *Poets and Their Philosophers: Reflections on the Poetic Turn in Philosophy Since Kant*, eds. Charles Bambach and Theodore George. Albany, NY: State University of New York Press, 2019. 185–200.
———. "Poietic Justice." In *Law and Art: Justice, Ethics, and Aesthetics*, ed. Oren Ben-Dor. London: Routledge, 2011. 33–44.
Ziegler, Susanne. *Heidegger, Hölderlin und die alētheia: Martin Heideggers Geschichtsdenken in seinen Vorlesungen 1934/35 bis 1944*. Berlin: Duncker & Humblot, 1991.

Index

Abendland (land of evening), 165, 245, 255–57, 285, 288, 296, 316
"Das abendländische Gespräch" (Heidegger), 18, 243–44
Abgrund, 7, 214, 221, 291
Abwechselung (alternation/change), 143
Adyton: Heideggers esoterische Philosophie (Trawny), 59–60
Agamben, Giorgio, 100–101
aletheia, 102–3, 168, 183, 189, 192, 213, 215, 217–18, 233, 288, 327
alien homecoming, 4–5, 13
 journey of, 6
Anaximander, 6, 22, 66, 178, 228, 231, 237, 269
Andenken, 117, 129, 162, 174, 202, 205, 211, 240, 243, 255
 philosophical form of, 9–13
"Andenken" (Celan), 174–75
"Andenken" (Hölderlin)
 and "Black Foresting," 153
 as commemorative thinking, 125–36
Anfang (beginning), 202–3, 295, 304
Anmut (grace), 291
anomie, 71–72, 185
Antigone (Sophocles), 188–89, 194, 206
 authentic dwelling, 214, 221
 characterizing destiny in, 201–3
 and Greek tragic presentation, 279–80
 language of contradiction in, 193–98
apoikia, 172, 300
apolis, 102, 194–96, 206, 212
aporos, 6, 194, 196, 199
appropriating event (*Ereignis*), 3, 18, 22–23, 69, 77, 123–24, 139, 141, 185, 209, 221, 267, 283
appropriation (*Aneignung*), 179
Arendt, Hannah, 25, 99–101
Aristotle, 9, 19, 38, 56, 67, 219, 249, 310
Aufenthalt (dwelling place), 10, 20–23, 26, 36, 70, 72–73, 92, 169, 199, 211–12, 312, 321
Augenblicksstätte, 111
Auseinandersetzung, 10, 31, 51, 88, 106–7, 202, 242
Ausgleich, 143, 148–50
authentic (*eigentlich*), 95–96, 102, 196

Bacchae (Euripides), 150–53, 171
Baeumler, Alfred, 41, 223
Balkanization, 100
Battle of Stalingrad, 89, 264, 315
Bauch, Kurt, 57, 127

373

Bauen (building), 294, 308
Beck, Adolf, 171
Being and Time (Heidegger), 17, 21, 131, 172
Beissner, Friedrich, 41, 170, 298–99
Benjamin, Walter, 326
Besinnung (Heidegger), 178
beyng
  concealed, 248
  of demigods, 80–92
  founder of, 3, 53, 54, 106
  German, 3, 34, 40, 51, 54, 98, 200, 252
  middle of, 88, 182
  as poetic event, 69–75
  understanding, 54–55
  voice of, 12–13, 15, 28, 113, 135, 164
beyng-historical, 2–3, 10, 15, 99, 133–36, 164, 174, 231, 247, 249–52, 305, 315, 319
Black Notebooks (Heidegger), 3–4, 6, 57–58, 103, 105, 109, 133, 134–35, 174, 181, 219, 223
  attacking Allies, 241–42
  betrayal of thinking, 248
  and embracing vocation, 321–22
  Europe in relation to West, 259
  laying out vocation in, 244–46
Blanchot, Maurice, 41, 175
Blochmann, Elisabeth, 58
Böckmann, Paul, 41
Bodmershof, Imma von, 63
Böhlendorff, Casimir, 52–53, 77, 95–96
  letter, 74, 77, 84, 86, 88, 122, 162, 170, 182, 179–80, 201–2, 301
  logic of, 97, 182–84, 215–16
Bordeaux, 5, 52, 82, 95, 115, 120, 146, 151, 157, 159–60, 215
Böschenstein, Bernhard, 157, 172

"Bread and Wine" ("Brod und Wein") (Hölderlin), 126, 147–48, 150, 161–65, 256–57
  journey of "spirit," 167–69
  problems with transgressive reading of, 169–71
  reading re-turns in, 166–67
"Building Dwelling Thinking" (Heidegger), 166–67
Bürger, Heinz Otto, 56
Burkert, Walter, 146

Celan, Paul, 42, 174–75, 327
celebrating *(feiern)*, 138
chiasmus, 145
chiazein, 145
chiazo, 145
Coalition Wars, 61, 271
colony, 126, 145, 150, 157, 161, 204
  love of, 171–72, 203–4, 300–301, 305, 307
  spirit's relation to, 168–70
  as way station, 170–73
"Columbus" (Hölderlin), 119, 159
"Communismus der Geister" (Hölderlin), 229
"Concerning the Beginning" (Heidegger), 164
conflictual intimacy *(Innigkeit)*, 54, 78–79, 84, 86, 91, 166, 182–83, 274, 277
Contributions to Philosophy (Heidegger), 14–15, 34, 59–60, 111–12, 185
"Country Path Conversations" (Heidegger), 292
"Creative Landscape: Why Do We Stay in the Provinces?" (Heidegger), 320–21

Dasein, 21–23
  force of, 78, 182

German, 8, 27, 87–88, 92, 248, 294
historical, 25, 35, 39, 52, 67–68, 88, 274
and mystery of "das Reinentsprungene," 75–80
and *polis*, 102–3
Dastur, Françoise, 97
"Death for the Fatherland" (Hölderlin), 90, 98, 129
Death of Empedocles, 153
"Death of Empedocles, The" (Hölderlin), 78
Declaration of the Rights of Man and of the Citizen," 100
decline *(Untergang)*, 7, 34, 145, 164, 257, 288, 326
deinon, 186–90, 194–96
deinotaton, 187
demi-gods, 80–92
  finding traces of presence of, 83–84
  heavenly fire, 83–84
  poet and river as, 198–99
Denken, 117, 135, 243
Denkweg, 10, 228, 309
des Eigenen, 118, 307
destiny *(Geschick)*, 45, 128, 131, 137, 169, 193, 307, 311, 315
  authentic destiny, 137
  destinal sending of, 305
  excess of, 216
  German, 12, 35, 41, 50, 82, 92, 109, 137, 268–69, 283–84, 294, 298
  historical, 3, 15, 19, 174, 244, 266, 282, 288–89, 305
  metaphysical, 288
  of the *Volk*, 79, 86
  Western, 230, 244, 252, 284, 294, 304, 307
destruction *(Zerstörung)*, 250

devastation *(Verwüstung)*, 250
". . . dichterisch wohnet der Mensch auf dieser Erde," 179–80
Dichtermut, 292
"Die Asyle" (Asylum), translation of, 211–12
Dionysus, 75, 121, 146–47
  as god who is coming, 147–48
  and reading of "colony," 171–72
  recognizing as colonizer, 172–73
  in "Remembrance," 150–51
dismemberment *(sparagmos)*, 146
displacement *(Versetzung)*, 144, 187

Edelmut (noble-mindedness), 291–93
Edelmütige (the noble minded), 292
das Eigene, 77, 82, 88, 140, 169, 179, 188, 202, 218, 245, 278
das Eigenste der Heimat, 126
das eigentliche Heimischsein, 220–21
Eigentum, 126
das Eigne, 219
Einkehr, 210–11, 282, 306
Einsatzgruppen, 99
emergence *(Aufgang)*, 145, 288, 295, 326
Empedocles, 78, 81, 108, 153, 185
  as "founder of beyng," 53–54
das Entsetzliche, 200
èpuration, 239, 291, 316
Ereignis, 3, 18, 22, 123, 141, 167, 185, 209, 245
  and festival as gesture, 139
ethos, 191, 217
  co-respondence, 26–27
  ethicality of being and, 18–31
  ethos of *Gelassenheit*, 73
  ethos-physis-logos, 2
  historical belongingness, 21
  Hölderlinian *ethos*, 74–75
  and poetic dwelling, 25, 72–73

ethics, 13, 19, 21, 24, 26, 29, 74, 183–84, 191, 199, 217
"Europe and German Philosophy" (Heidegger), 154–55
Europe, saving, 286–90
"Evening Conversation, An" (Heidegger), 238–39

Fahrt, 151
festival *(Fest)*, 138
  Anthesteria festival honoring gods, 146–47
  and balance of equlibrium, 145–53
  Bordeaux festival, 146–47
  as coming-together, 138–39
  displacement from usual place, 150
  expressing rleation to history, 137–38
  and Graeco-German beginning, 136–44
  holy as festivity grounding, 141
  and kairos, 141–44
  as not taking place "in" history, 139–40
Fischer, Eugen, 228–29
Franz, Michael, 160
das Fremde, 82, 88, 179, 219
French Revolution, 64, 153, 253
"Friedrich Hölderlin: Prophet of the German Volk" (Petersen), 56
das Furchtbare (the frightful), 186, 189
future *(Zukunft)*, 144

Gadamer, Hans-Georg, xxxii, 108
Gebsattel, Viktor, 233, 272
Gedächtnis, 117
Gegenstand, 265–66
Gelassenheit, 18, 232
George Circle, 29, 98, 108
George, Stefan, 44, 46, 59, 132
Germania, 180–81

"Germania" (Hölderlin), 48–49
  addressing failure of French Revolution, 64–65
  Heidegger reading of, 49–60
  last lines of, 89–90
  lectures on, 36, 38–39, 52, 64, 69, 74, 144, 314
Germany
  de-Nazification committee of, 30, 232, 236, 241, 270, 307, 309–10
  and decline of Greek art, 280–82
  destinal politics of, 153–60
  dream of German greatness, 9
  "Finis Germaniae," 270
  forging own form of tragedy, 96–97
  granting "poetic bequest" to, 39–40
  homecoming as futural task, 127–28
  Hour Zero *(Stunde Null)*, 240
  inner fatherland vision, 61–62
  national reversal, 279–80
  need for national literature for, 279–94
  proper *Geschick*, 237–38
  Prüfung of, 277–79
  recognizing inner affinity with language of Greeks, 122–23
  role in Western Coversation, 306–8
  searching for *Eigenes* of, 296–97
  secret character of Fatherland, 54–55
  secret Germany, 46–49
  secret Germany mythos, 61–65
  "standing in the center," 163–64
  taking on burden of "Western responbility," 163–64
  testing readiness of, 309–12
  Western responsibility, 122, 277
  Year Zero of, 250–51
Geschichte, 112, 131, 137–38, 149, 253, 262, 286, 297

Geschichtsphilosophie, 294, 299–300, 304
Geschick, 117, 193, 243, 277–79, 279–80, 296
  as defining vocation of Germany, 283–84
  poverty and, 285–86
das Geschickliche, 277–79, 296, 300–301, 305
Geschlecht, 324–25
Gespräch ("conversation"), 255, 263–66
Gestell, 19, 25, 30, 71, 286, 289, 311, 318, 327
das Gewaltige (the violent), 186, 189
Gewesenheit, 144, 209
das Gewesene, 117, 216
Glaucon, 117
Gleichschaltung, 27
gnomon, 215
Goebbels, Joseph, 58
Gontard, Susette, 146, 174
Great War. See World War I
Greece, 8–9
  as bearer of "impossible conjunctions," 165–66
  as colony, 170–73
  crossing of Oriental and, 165–66
  essential history beginning in, 167–68
  poem and approach to Oriental, 157–60
  tragic language, 193–98
"Greece" (poem), 157–60
"Greek Interpretation of Human Beings in Sophocles' Antigone, The," 181, 186
Grohmann, Amadeus, 130
Grossmut (magnanimity), 291
"Ground of Empedocles, The" (Hölderlin), 78–79
Grund, 291

Guilt-Question, The (Jaspers), 234–35

Habsburg Empire, 100
harmonia, 213–14
harmonious discord, 182–84
hearkening, 112–13
Heidegger, Martin
  analyzing hospitality, 224–26
  approach to Hölderlin, xix–xxxii
  and attunement, 322–23
  on "Being-with," 73–74
  and "brown women" threat, 154
  beyng as poetic event, 69–75
  channeling spirit of Greeks, 109–10
  characterizing alien homecoming, 4–5
  commitment to Swabia, 261–62
  communication with Jaspers, 234–38
  conversation with Hölderlin, 263–66
  crafting Gespräch, 255
  critiquing world Jewry, 133–35
  cult of Greece, 172
  and Danube, 294–98
  and decline of Greek art, 281–82
  defining Hölderlin of, 13–18
  destinal history of, 283–85
  destinal politics of, 153–60
  in dialogue with Hölderlin, 263–312
  emphasizing homecoming as futural task, 127–28
  as figure at end of tradition, 51–52
  final judgment of Hölderlin of, 313–28
  Freiburg National Socialism, 105
  German bequest, 279–94
  on Geschick of Volk, 300–301
  historical interlude of, 227–62
  Hölderlin as transition, 1–9

Heidegger, Martin *(continued)*
  on human beings as "dwelling in the abyss," 302–4
  ignoring Hölderlin nomadological motifs, 173–74
  inability to grant space of tolerance, 161–75
  insights into German exceptionalism of, 324–28
  interpreting "Holidays and Festivals," 123–24
  interpretation of Antigone, 190–93
  interpreting human being, 21–22, 190–93
  interpreting opening "Remembrance" stanza, 118–22
  Ister as fateful site of ordeal, 277–79
  "Ister" lectures, 177–226
  Kahlschlag of, 227–34
  and mystery of "das Reinentsprungene," 75–80
  navigating Hölderlin of, 29–31
  opening of "Western Conversation," 272–77
  and originary springing forth, 65–69
  Parmenides lectures, 212–13
  philosophical "Andenken," 9–13
  points of intersection, 40–42
  postwar energies, 249
  private National Socialism, 91
  question of historical humanity, 178–79
  question of Western destiny, 252–62
  on reading Hölderlin, 35–36
  reading of "Germania," 49–60
  regarding Hölderlin grandiose, 7–8
  "Remembrance" lectures, 93–175
  revenge of, 234–52
  Schwung, 266–71
  secret Germany as mythos, 61–65
  self-identification, 51
  spiritualizing Great War, 37–38
  in "Spiegel Interview," 26
  staging "Remembrance" lectures, 110–16
  styling as victim, 316–18
  and technological modernity, 12–13
  understanding of "colony," 169–71
  understanding personal delusions, 103–5
  winter semester lectures, 33–34, 37–38
  writing to Bodmershof, 63–64
Heimat, 1
Heimkehr (homecoming), 1, 179, 266–71
Heimkunft, 318–20
Hellingrath, Norbert von, 5, 42–49, 98–99, 115–16, 128, 132, 180–81
  educator of Germans, 129
  myth of secret Germany, 47–48
  questioning selflessness of, 108–9
  referring to death of, 99
Heraclitus, 6
Herakles, allusion of, 171
Heydrich, Reinhard, 222
hiddenness *(lethe)*, 189
hieros gamos, 126, 178
Hildebrandt, Kurt, 6, 41, 223
historical interlude
  Heidegger *Kahlschlag*, 227–34
  question of Western destiny, 252–62
  revenge of Heidegger, 234–52
Historie, 112
history
  of beyng, 2, 8, 10–13, 33–35, 103, 112–14, 131, 238, 241, 249–50, 268, 293–94

discussing, 112
"of our *Volk*," 3, 40, 106
rethinking, 94–95
of West, 26, 50, 94, 125, 134, 136, 163, 168, 229, 252, 256, 258, 299, 307, 310, 315
history (*Geschichte*), 138, 324–25
History of Beyng, The (Heidegger), 314–15
Hitler, Adolf, 233
"Hölderlin and the Essence of Poetry" (Heidegger), 15–16, 112, 211
"Hölderlin and the Germans" (Hellingrath), 94, 128–29
"Hölderlin and the Orientalisation of the Greeks" (Dastur, Françoise), 97–98
Hölderlin Jahrbuch, 129
Hölderlin, Friedrich
 addressing failure of French Revolution, 64–65
 allusion to men going to "the Indians," 159–60
 analyzing decline of Greek art, 281–82
 bodily proximity to, 259–60
 Bordeaux as journey into foreign, 95–99
 characterizing, 4
 conceiving myth of, 98–99
 as creation of Great War, 37–38
 dreams of Hellas, 115–16
 Empedocles as "founder of beyng," 53–54
 on fate of language, 10–11
 as figure at end of tradition, 51–52
 final judgment of Heideggerian, 313–28
 as founder of beyng, 3
 as founder of German beyng, 34
 German bequest, 279–94
 and German destinal politics, 153–60
 Germans as *Volk* of, 128
 and Germans coming together, 44–45
 "Graeco-Germanic" antidote, 62
 and Great War, 33–42
 of Heidegger, 13–18
 Heidegger in dialogue with, 263–312
 heroicization of, 108–9
 Hölderlin violence, 12–13
 Hölderlin-mythos, 38–39
 interpreting das Nationelle, 93–102
 interpreting turn to, 5–6
 "interpretative violence" regarding, 16–17
 Ister lecture poetic language, 188–89
 Langemarck Hall for, 98–99
 lectures announcing "what is coming," 65–67
 misinterpretation of, 43–44, 57–59
 myth as deciphered by Hellingrath, 42–49
 as name for other beginning of thinking, 177–81
 as name of myth, 2–3
 name significance, 114–15
 name synonym, 12
 100th anniversary of death of, 315
 opening of "Western Conversation," 272–77
 originary relation to language, 36
 originary springing forth, 65–69
 perspectives of hemispheres, 165
 physis as *poiesis*, 69–75
 Pindar translations, 43–44
 poet as Führer, 51
 poetic geography of, 160
 poetic language of contradictions, 147

Hölderlin, Friedrich (continued)
    poetry as priestly office, 44–46
    (Political) Educator ideal, 94–95
    and poverty of thinking, 227–34
    as prophet, 27–28
    publishing works of, 90–91
    question of historical humanity, 178–79
    and question of Western destiny, 252–62
    radically rethinking ethics, 24–25
    reading travel literature, 173–74
    Schwung, 266–71
    as seer poet, 43
    and significance of demigods, 80–92
    skepticism of, 26
    spiritual-cultural ideal of, 61
    tensions in appropriating, 18–31
    as transition, 1–9, 253–54
    translating *Bacchae*, 151–53
    translating own interpretation, 186
    as "voice of beyng," 15–16
    as voice of other beginning, 8–13
    without history, 61–65
    work as important German literature contribution, 42–43
Hölderlin: Heroism (A Selection for Soldiers), 130
"Hölderlin's Earth and Heaven," lecture, 321, 326
"Hölderlin's Hymn "The Ister" (Heidegger), 19
"Hölderlin's Hymn: As on a Holiday" (Heidegger), 16
"Hölderlin's Hymn: Remembrance" (Heidegger), 94–95
Hölderlin's Vaterländische Gesänge, 56
Hölderlinbild (Heidegger), 28, 34, 37, 40, 56–57, 60, 62, 94, 109
Hölderlins Vaterländische Gesänge ("Hölderlin's Songs of the Fatherland"), 90

holiday (*Feiertag*), 138
holy (*das Heilige*), 138
holy wedding (*hieros gamos*), 138
Homburger Folioheft, 269
homecoming, 323–28
    alien, 4–5, 13, 283, 319, 323, 328
    authentic, 2, 126, 202, 246, 291, 301, 324
    German, 122, 162, 172, 174, 196–97, 202, 213, 245, 270, 274, 310
    law of, 215–16
    topos of, 318
"Homecoming" (Heidegger), 130, 270
"Homecoming" (Hölderlin), 271
homelessness, 246–49
"Homelessness-Homeland-Dwelling" (Heidegger), 246–49
Honold, Alexander, 153
human being
    defining as "katastrophe," 190–93
    essence of, 8, 181, 186, 212, 221
    exodus of, 99–102
    interpreting, 21–23
    possibility of, 3, 67, 75
    within language, 264–66
    uncanny essence of, 185–90
"Hymns of the Fatherland" (Hölderlin), 129
Hyperion, 64
hypokeimenon, 189
hypostasis, 189
hypsipolis, 194–96

idiotisch, 286–87
Iduna: Jahrbuch der Hölderlin-Gesellschaft, 58
Iliad (Homer), 142–43
India
    ignoring/suppressing Asiatic from, 156–59
    linking Indus River to Bacchus, 156

as originary homeland of *Volk*,
  256–57
reading "brown woman" as Greek,
  154–56
Indus River, 156, 161, 220, 275
Innigkeit (conflictual intimacy), 54,
  78–79, 84, 86, 91, 166, 182–83,
  274, 277
Inständigkeit, 232, 247
Inszenierung, 109, 220
Introduction to Metaphysics
  (Heidegger), 19
Irre, 114
"Ister, The" (Hölderlin)
  annunciation of Now in, 209–11
  coeval encounter of fire and water,
    216–17
  ethics of Other, 217–18
  first stanza, 206, 298–99
  hospitality in, 224–26
  interpreting backward-turning
    moment, 206–8
  intimacy in, 213–14
  Ister as fateful site of ordeal,
    277–79
  narratives similar to, 208–9
  power to name, 282–83
  river arrival, 303–5
"Ister," lectures
  deciphering home of spirit, 199–204
  German hospitality, 224–26
  Greek tragic language, 193–98
  harmonious discord, 182–84
  Hölderlin as name for other
    beginning of thinking, 177–81
  human being as "katastrophe,"
    190–93
  narrative of course of river, 204–24
  poet and river as demi-gods,
    198–99
  uncanny essence of human being,
    185–90

Jaspers, Karl, 233, 234–36, 239–40
Jews, 101, 220, 238–39, 261, 314,
  324
  and occlusion of first beginning,
    125–36
  assigning *seynsgeschichtliches
    Geschick* to, 223–24
  historical development of, 251–52
  relationship with Heidegger,
    252–53
  during Third Reich, 222–23, 235
  as *topos*, 136–37
"Journey, The" (Hölderlin), 225–26
journeying *(Wanderschaft)*, 202, 205

Kahlschlag, 227–34, 240–41, 254
kairos
  moments, 124–26, 141, 143–44,
    144, 150, 257
  and festive times, 150
  following etymological traces of,
    142
  and *opportunitas*, 143
  and weaving, 143
Kampf, 82, 84–90
Kampfgemeinschaft, 14
katastrophe, 71
  human being as, 190–93, 221
Kehre, 3, 34, 94, 271
kerannymi, 143
Kluckhohn, Paul, 129–30
Kocziszky, Eva, 156
"Kolomb" (Hölderlin), 173, 271
das Kommende, 65, 68, 117, 162,
  183, 216, 309
das kommende Geschick, 162, 304
Kommerell, Max, 16–17, 29, 51, 52,
  296
  Hölderlin encounter, 108
  questioning Heidegger, 132
Königliche Landesbibliothek, 43
Königzer, Willi, 6, 15–16, 56

Kreuzer, Johann, 171
Krieck, Ernst, 41

Lacoue-Labarthe, Philippe, 252–53
land of evening (*Abendland*), 165,
 245, 255–57, 285, 288, 296, 316
Langmut (forbearance), 291–92
language
 engaging with, 19–20
 essence of, 35
 German language, 43–44, 165,
  188–89, 214, 252, 309
 play of, 265–66
 poetic language, 22, 39, 46, 52–54,
  100, 131, 147, 188, 253
 proper essence of, 20
 quotidian exchanges with, 20–21
law of historicality, 216
Lebensraum, 219
Lefebvre, Jean-Pierre, 153
"Letter on Humanism" (Heidegger),
 22, 183, 228, 231, 237–38,
 289–91, 314, 316
Lévinas, Emmanuel, 74, 106–7, 217,
 253
Llewelyn, John, 35
locality (*Ortschaft*), 202, 205
"Logic as the Question Concerning
 the Essence of Language"
 (Heidegger), 103–4

Machtergreifung, 232
Marcuse, Herbert, 235
McNeill, William, 70
Mehring, Reinhard, 14
Menorah Journal, The, 99–100
metapolitics
 of *Volk*, 102–16
middle of life (*die Mitte des Lebens*),
 166
Mindfulness (Heidegger), 59
monotheism, 250–51

Mottel, Helmut, 173
Mount Aetna, 53
Müller, Ernst, 41, 56, 129

Nancy, Jean-Luc, 21, 72, 74, 311
National Socialism, 6, 8–9, 27, 41,
 55, 60, 222–24, 293
 challenging, 103–5
 confrontation with, 106–7
 and sacred mourning, 91
das Nationelle, 92, 103, 316
 Hölderlin interpretation of, 93–
  102
 parsing out meaning of, 93–95
Nationalsozialistische Monatshefte, 6
Nazis, 235, 239, 241
 journals of, 56
Nicomachean Ethics, 67
Nietzsche, Friedrich, 17, 42, 56, 86,
 105, 129, 133, 237, 254, 260,
 326
"Notes on the *Antigone*" (Hölderlin),
 279–80
nous-thymos-epithymia (*Vernunft-
 Edelmut-Begierde*), 291

Occident, 11, 26, 87, 96, 128, 135,
 171, 222, 250–51, 257, 268–69,
 271, 284, 293, 295, 299
Oedipus, 142, 192, 212, 221–22, 226
Oikos, 300
Older Man, "The Western
 Conversation," 266–71, 312
 and *Geschick*, 296–98
 human beings as "dwelling in the
  abyss," 302–4
 Ister as fateful site of ordeal,
  277–79
 opening of "The Western
  Conversation," 272–77
Olender, Maurice, 320
Opfer (victims), 243

Index

opportunitas, 143
Orient, 22, 126, 156, 159, 200, 271, 284, 289, 293, 298, 316
 crossing of Greeks and, 165–66
origin (Ursprung), 65, 203, 316
"Origin of the Work of Art, The" (Heidegger), 70 189
Ortschaft (locality), 202, 205
Ott, Hugo, 233
our ownmost (eigenste), 95

pantoporos, 6, 194–95, 199
Parmenides, 6, 66, 167, 178
parousia, 210, 257, 271
"Patmos" (Hölderlin), 210, 257–58, 282
patriotic reversal (vaterländische Umkehr), 57, 97
Peace of Lunéville, 61
Petersen, Carl, 56
Pflanzniederlassung, 172
physis, 67, 211–12
 and equinotical time, 145–53
 as poesis, 69–75
Pindar, 6, 47, 76, 81, 142, 255
Plato, 9, 267
Poet as Leader (Führer) in Classical German Literature (Kommerell), 107
poetic dwelling, 66–68
 and Mystery of "das Reinentsprungene," 75–80
 and other thinking, 179–80
 physis as poiesis, 69–75
poetic truth, 21, 215
poetry
 beyng as poetic event, 69–75
 fundamental attunement, 78–79
 as historical dasein, 274–75
 poetic geography, 294–98
 poetic suffering, 80–92
 vocation of poet, 75–80

poiesis, 25, 27, 29, 66–67
 physis as, 69–75
polis, 102–3, 187, 193–94, 196, 202, 212–13, 269
possession (Eigentum), 95, 126, 185, 296, 307
poverty, 230
 authentic, 246, 285
 being-historical sense of, 285–86
 defining role of, 284–85
 and overflowing rivers, 232
 sense of, 285
 true poverty, 300–301, 305
"Poverty" (Heidegger), 167
Priesterdichtung, 44
Prüfung (test/trial/ordeal), 277–79, 293, 309

Quelle, 121, 209, 272, 299
"Question Concerning Technology, The" (Heidegger), 70–71

Reign of Terror, 64
Reinigung (German purification), 240
"Remembrance," lectures
 balance of equilibrium, 145–53
 commemoriatve thinking, 125–36
 destinal politics, 153–60
 greeting of wind, 116–24
 Hölderlin and "The National," 93–102
 passage to foreign, 161–75
 staging of, 110–16
 time of festival, 136–44
 Volk metapolitics, 102–16
"Remembrance" (Heidegger)
 celebrating kairos moment, 124
 as enacting remembrance, 125–36
 figure of sacrificial victim in, 131
 gift of inspiration bestowed by winds, 121–22
 hearkening, 113–14

"Remembrance" (Heidegger)
(*continued*)
highest form of suffering, 132–33
placement of "Brod und Wein," 161–65
racism in, 157–58
reading opening stanza, 118–20
usage of wind in, 110–11
"Return to the Homeland," 162
Rezeptionsgeschichte, 28
rhetoric, 19, 89–90, 92, 143, 234
"Rhine, The," lectures, 76–77, 92
"Rhine, The" (Hölderlin), 65–69
    and demigods, 80–92
    enacting destiny of Volk, 79–80
    mystery of "das Reinentsprungene," 75–80
    opening verse significance, 85–86
    reading as movement of opposition, 79
Rilke, Rainer Maria, 129
rootedness (*Bodenständigkeit*), 249

Sachsen-Meiningen, Margot von, 229, 233
sacred mourning, 7–8, 11, 64, 85, 91, 144, 178, 181, 183, 258
sacrifice (*Opfer*), 131–32, 243, 324
Sämtliche Werke (Hölderlin), 128
das Schickliche, 195, 277–79
Schirach, Baldur von, 15
Schmidt, Jochen, xxv, xxvii, 64, 171, 302
Schmitt, Carl, 47–48
Schwab, Christoph, 115
Schwung ("The Western Conversation"), 266–71
secret Germany, 46–49, 52–55
    Hölderlin without History, 61–65
"Secret Germany, The" (George), 49
Seinsvergessenheit, 224, 250
Seinsverlassenheit, 238

self-absorption, avoiding, 98
self-extinction (*Selbstvernichtung*), 224, 248
seynsgeschichtliches Geschick, 223
sich aufhalten, 22–23
sich ereignen, 11, 96, 249, 262, 295
Simmel, Georg, 39
Socrates, 80–81, 117, 267
sojourn, 5, 10, 20–24, 26, 72, 169, 173, 179, 221, 226
    human sojourn, 6, 92, 213, 218
Sonderweg, 13, 37–38, 99, 109, 226, 324
"Song of the Germans" (Hölderlin), 137–38
Sophocles, 6, 47, 187–88, 221
    apolis, 102, 194–96, 206, 212
    aporos, 6, 194, 196, 199
    hypsipolis, 194–96
    pantoporos, 6, 194–95, 199
"Spiegel Interview" (Heidegger), 1, 26, 71, 179
spirit, 167
    colony as way station for, 169–70
    deciphering home of, 199–204
    dispensation of, 304–5
    German spirit, 162, 170, 304, 307
    Homecoming of, 175, 305
    love of colony, 301–2
    metaphysical definition of, 167
    movement of, 170, 186, 293, 297
    passage into foreign, 167–68
    Western spirit, 259, 264, 270, 319
Stadelmann, Rudolf, 258–60
Stierle, Karlheinz, 153
strangers/foreigners (*pontos axeinos/euxeinos*), 208–9
Swabia, 5, 159–60, 173, 259–61, 268–69, 283, 324
symbebekos, 189

Täter (perpetrators), 243

thinking, poverty of, 227–34
Thus Spoke Zarathustra (Nietzsche), 17–18
time of transition *(Übergangszeit).*, 148
time-space *(Zeit-Raum)*, 111
"Titans, The" (Hölderlin), 63
topos, 54, 60, 136, 159–60, 166, 175, 220, 222, 225, 265, 272, 274, 294, 316, 318
tragedy, 190–93, 213, 222
 forming, 96–97
 German, 93
 god of, 147
 Greek, 190, 213, 220, 271
Trakl, George, 185
transition *(Übergang)*, 34, 113, 145–49, 164, 282, 295
translation, problem of, 188
Trawny, Peter, 59–60
Treaty of Versailles, 6, 100
Tübingen Stift, 62, 90

Übersetzung (translation), 186–87
Uhland, Ludwig, 115
Umkehr (reversal), 61, 97, 122, 243, 271, 279, 284–85
das Ungewöhnliche (the inhabitual), 186, 189
un-hiddenness *(a-letheia)*, 189
unheimlich, 71
Unheimlichkeit, 71, 189, 191
das Unschickliche, 277–79
Untergang (decline), 7, 34, 145, 164, 257, 288–89, 326
Urania, fatherland association wth, 61

"Verdict *(Spruch)* of Anaximander, The," 237
Vermessenheit, 193
Vermittlung, 84, 156

Vermutung (presumption), 291
verstellt, 71
"Voice of the Volk" (Hölderlin), 54, 90
Volk, 1, 106, 178, 218
 as community formed through language, 39
 connecting to Greek beginning, 254
 das Nationelle and, 93–95
 and demigods, 80–92
 educating, 82–83
 emphasis on chosen status, 135–36
 entering own identity, 280–81
 follwing German defeat, 244–45
 guardians of, 105
 metapolitics emerging out of, 3–4
 metapolitics of, 102–16
 poet and river as demi-gods, 198–99
 poet as priestly office, 44–45
 rehearsing, 111–12
 sacrificial death for, 52
 self-awareness regarding, 11–12
 start of World War II, 57–58
 teaching about own history, 139–40
 and understanding of "colony," 169–71
Völkischer Beobachter, 6, 56
Vorenthalt, 22
Vor-stellen (human representation), 71

"Wahrsein und Dasein in Aristoteles," 127–28
Wanderschaft (journeying), 202, 205
Weltanschauungs-philosophie, 223
Wentzlaff-Eggebert, F. W., 131–32
Wesen, 192
wespero, 257

West
- beyng-historical narrative of, 249–50
- destiny of, 11, 34, 110, 288–89, 292–93, 310
- *Geschick* of, 284, 288, 311
- going under, 257–59
- historical narrative of, 249–51
- history of, 26, 50, 94, 125, 134, 163, 168, 219, 229, 252, 258, 294. 307–10
- as journey from daylight, 26
- and "principle of destruction," 251
- salvation/decline of, 264–65
- saving of, 181, 254, 265, 304–5
- stressing homecoming for, 288–90
- *Wesen west als Ereignis an*, 266
"Western Conversation, The" (Heidegger), 159–60, 168, 232, 255–56, 262
- acknowledging role of Hölderlin in, 306
- Bread and Wine fragment and German destiny, 298–312
- German bequest, 279–94
- Heidegger's "conversation" with Hölderlin, 263–66
- Ister as fateful site of ordeal, 277–79
- journey homeward, 308–12
- nobility of mind, 292–94
- opening of, 272–77
- poetic geography, 294–98
- remaining in coming in, 305
- resituating Hölderlin in, 310
- *Schwung* from first to other beginning, 266–71
- testing German readiness, 309–12
Western destiny (*abendländischen Geschickes*), 230, 244, 252, 284, 294, 304, 307

Western vocation (*abendländische Bestimmung*), 245
Weyrauch, Wolfgang, 240
"What are Poets For?" (Heidegger), 258
what is coming (*das Kommende*), 65–69
Wildenstein, Burg, 229, 232
Wilhelm, Lange, 44
Wilmans, Friedrich, 165
Winckelmann, J. J., 82, 95–96
wind
- greeting of, 116–24
- imagery, 110–11
Wolfskehl, Karl, 46
Wolters, Friedrich, 44–45
world Jewry, 219
- critique of, 133–34
- embodying *ethos* of modernity, 223–24
- observations of role of, 219–20
- question of world of, 107
- role of, 251
- and *Volk*, 135–36
World War I, 98, 128–29
- out of spiritual desolation of, 36–37
- remembrance, 36–37
World War II, 1, 94–95, 127, 180–81, 264, 287–88
- Heidegger *Kahlschlag* following end of, 227–34
- Wester Conversation following, 308–12
world-destiny (*Weltgeschick*), 242–43

Younger Man, "The Western Conversation," 266–71, 312
- and *Geschick*, 296–98
- human beings as "dwelling in the abyss," 302–4
- Ister as fateful site of ordeal, 277–79

opening of "The Western
   Conversation," 272–77

Zinkernagel, Franz, 42
Zumutung (impudence), 291

www.ingramcontent.com/pod-product-compliance
Lightning Source LLC
Chambersburg PA
CBHW020119240426
43673CB00038B/534